ISBN 978-1-330-81470-3
PIBN 10108930

1 MONTH OF
FREE
READING

at
www.ForgottenBooks.com

By purchasing this book you are eligible for one month membership to ForgottenBooks.com, giving you unlimited access to our entire collection of over 700,000 titles via our web site and mobile apps.

To claim your free month visit:

www.forgottenbooks.com/free108930

Similar Books Are Available from
www.forgottenbooks.com

AMERICANS IN EASTERN ASIA

*A Critical Study of the Policy of the United
States with reference to China, Japan
and Korea in the 19th Century*

BY

TYLER DENNETT

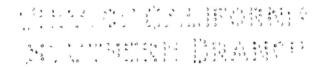

46931

New York
THE MACMILLAN COMPANY
1922

Press of
J. J. Little & Ives Company
New York, U S. A.

PREFACE

THE reader is entitled to some intimation as to what he may find in the following pages.

This is a study of the origin and development of American policy in Asia—in China, Japan, Korea, with passing attention to Siam, and the regions of the Indian and Pacific Oceans—in the 19th Century. It is an entirely fresh study, based on original records and documentary sources, the first book ever attempting to cover the entire field. In large measure the human interest and the peculiarly personal qualities of the record of Americans in Asia have been retained. The actors are permitted to speak for themselves in their own words.

The viewpoint is from Washington, not from Tokio, or Peking. American relations with the separate nations of the East, with the Japanese, the Chinese, the Koreans, have developed not separately but as a unity which the student disregards at his peril. There has not been one policy for one country and another policy for another. The policy has, in principle, been the same; the results of the policy were different because the peoples were different.

The tap-root of American policy has been not philanthropy but the demand for most-favored-nation treatment. One frequently meets the assumption that the Open Door Policy was invented by John Hay and first applied in 1899. The Open Door Policy is as old as our relations with Asia. It was pronounced in China as early as 1842, and the spirit of the policy is as old as the Declaration of Independence. The policy was not limited to China. It was enunciated on the coast of Africa in 1832, and was repeated in Japan and Korea many times before 1899. The policy had been so fully developed before 1869 when William H. Seward

v

retired from the Department of State, that no new principle
has ever been introduced since that time. Neither Mr. Hay
nor Mr. Hughes appears to have considered that they were
creating anything new.

How can most-favored-nation treatment be secured?
This was the persistent question in the 19th as it will be
throughout the 20th Century. In pre-treaty days at old
Canton the American merchants obtained it by conciliation
of the Chinese. Caleb Cushing sought to make it secure by
treaty and by elaboration of the principle of extraterritoriality. Commodore Perry strongly advised the acquisition of
territory. Anson Burlingame set out to secure it by agreements between China and the powers. Seward was willing
to join in an almost unlimited cooperative policy with the
powers against the Asiatic States. He even proposed a joint
armed expedition with the French into Korea. His successors in office steadily withdrew from cooperation with
the European Powers and turned to cooperation with and
support of Japan. At the time of the Sino-Japanese War
it was the United States alone which stood between Japan
and the intervention of the European powers before the
conflict was over. The United States not only desired the
open door, but it also sought the development of Asiatic
States strong enough to be their own door-keepers. It
wanted a strong East; the other powers did not. On this
difference of policy cooperation between the United States
and the other Western powers was wrecked. At the beginning of the McKinley Administration the American Government was in a dangerous position of isolation. The open
door was gravely threatened. McKinley returned to the
policy of territorial acquisition advocated by Perry. Then
John Hay set out to restore the cooperative policy and
found his model in Burlingame's method of agreement between the powers. Hay would have preferred an alliance
with Great Britain, Japan and as many more powers as
could have been brought to agree upon the open door and a
strong East. Hay was a statesman fifty years, perhaps,

ahead of his time, but there are many now living who will some day witness the realization of Hay's dream. Indeed, in a measure it is already realized in the treaties of Washington in 1922.

In the 19th Century the issue in American policy in Asia was not the open door. That was never a question. The real issue was whether the United States should follow an isolated or a cooperative policy to make sure of the open door. An isolated policy was essentially belligerent. It inevitably led to a pitting of the United States against not one but all of the powers and against the Asiatic states as well. It was the isolation of 1897 following the wreck of the cooperative policy which forced the United States to retain the Philippines, just as the distrust of British and French designs in the fifties had led to the attempt of some loyal but misguided Americans to seek the appropriation by the United States of Formosa. As a matter of fact the American flag did fly over the principal port of the island for a year. Likewise today a wreck of the newly established cooperative policy would in the end lead to belligerency, and very likely to still further acquisitions of territory by the United States. Those who scoff at such a speculation will do well to study the past records.

The maintenance of a cooperative policy is, therefore, so utterly important for the peace of the East and of the world, that it is well to turn one's attention to the records and study well why and where the cooperative policy failed. Such a study is quite as important for the Japanese, the French, the British and for the other peoples of the West as it is for Americans. Cooperation failed partly because Americans were poor cooperators, but not wholly for that reason. It also failed because other cooperating powers sought to wrest the power of that cooperation to serve their separate purposes. The present policy may easily be wrecked upon a similar reef.

This study of the past is approached in no partisan spirit. The writer does not regard himself as an apostle of

peace, or of any other doctrine. He is mindful of the fact
that there is something in the atmosphere of Asia which
makes it very difficult for most people to see the half-tones.
All has a tendency to appear very black or very white. The
writer does not regard Great Britain as the benevolent
source from which all blessings flow, nor does he find the
Englishman the arch mischief-maker of world politics. He
regards the Japanese neither as innocent lambs nor ravening
wolves. Least of all has he any desire to see created any
alliance of powers for the exploitation of China which must
remain for so many years the great unknown quantity in
the world equation. But whether we like or trust each other
or not we all have to live together in a world which is becoming smaller every day—and we must either fight each
other or cooperate. The basis of cooperation must be understanding. In the following pages, therefore, the Englishman, Continental, Chinese and Japanese as well as the
American are invited to view the pictures of themselves as
they appear in the American records.

At the risk of incurring the dislike which attaches to all
iconoclasts, the writer has aimed to record the facts as they
are, mindful that they do not lead to verdicts which have
long been accepted. The exultant, complacent boaster of
his nation's virtue, whatever the nation, will not find this a
satisfying source-book, not if he reads it through to the
end. No nation, either of the East or of the West, has
escaped the valid charge of bad faith. The guilt of all
parties being clearly proven it has seemed profitless to continue the discussion of guilt with a view to determining the
relative degrees of wickedness. Each nation, the United
States not excepted, has made its contribution to the welter
of evil which now comprises the Far Eastern Question. We
shall all do well to drop for all time the pose of self-righteousness and injured innocence and penitently face the
facts.

Cordial relations between the United States, Japan and
Great Britain are now constantly being rendered unstable

by the perpetuation of historical fictions which were created
at some time in the past to justify a position not otherwise
defensible, and then reiterated with such frequency as to
give them the currency of inspired truth. It is hoped that
the following pages, carrying as they do the documentary
evidence for the statements made, will contribute towards
the retirement of some of these fictions and also clear a
path for honest dealing and franker understanding in the
future.

The proportions assigned to the various phases of this
study would have been different had it been the purpose
to survey the international relations of China, Japan and
Korea with the Western powers. In the international
relations of the East with the West the last thirty years of
the century bulks larger than the preceding seventy years.
In a review of American policy the reverse is true, and this
fact has determined the proportions of this study. The
creative period in the relations of the United States to
Eastern Asia practically came to an end in 1868. The
following thirty years were relatively barren in both American enterprise and statesmanship. While the three very full
closing years of the century may be claimed as the vestibule
to a contemporaneous period which is not yet concluded,
these years are equally the conclusion of an epoch and bring
the cycle of policy back to a point of cooperation similar
to that when William H. Seward retired from the Department of State and Anson Burlingame was launched upon his
mission to the Western Powers. To follow the policies of
the McKinley administration down through the recent years
to the Treaty of Versailles and the Treaties of Washington
would be to enter upon a discussion where speculation and
hearsay evidence would have to be substituted at important points for documentary facts. This period has already
been traversed by many excellent writers and it has therefore seemed wiser to bring this study to a close with a statement of the initial policies of the McKinley administration

and a comparison of them with the precedents of the preceding century.

Some of the material which appears in the following chapters has already been published in different and more elaborate form in the Journal of International Law (Jan. 1922), and in the American Historical Review (Oct. 1922), while several of the chapters, now much revised, were originally printed for the use of the American Commissioners in the Conference on the Limitation of Armaments and the Problems of the Pacific, but never released for general circulation.

Bibliographical footnotes in a most abbreviated form have been inserted wherever the subject matter appears of sufficient importance to require them, or where the statements in the text are at variance with those which have appeared in other works on the subject. The student who cares primarily for the sources of history is recommended to read first of all Chapter XXXV, Notes on Bibliography, where the source material for the entire field is reviewed.

Acknowledgments to writers of books and pamphlets which have proved of value in the preparation of this work appear in Notes on Bibliography (Chapter XXXV) and in the bibliographical index. In addition to these the author is under such obligation as only those who have been placed under a similar debt can fully appreciate to the following: to the officials and attendants of the Library, the Bureaus of Appointment and of Rolls and Indexes of the Department of State, and of the Libraries of Congress, of the Carnegie Endowment for International Peace, of Columbia University, of the New York, Wisconsin, and Minnesota Historical Societies, the Manuscripts Division of the New York Public Library, and the Missionary Research Library; to James Rankin Young for information about his distinguished brother, John Russell Young; to Murray Olyphant for data and literature concerning his famous grandfather, D. W. C. Olyphant; to Hon. Charles Denby for helpful suggestions about the period in China when he served in the American Legation at Peking under his honored father; to Hon. Henry White for information drawn from the rich stores of his memory as Secretary of the American Embassy at the Court of St. James; to Dr. J. Franklin Jameson, Editor of the American Historical Review, for encouragement and suggestions, and especially for securing from His Excellency, J. Jules Jusserand, copies of important dispatches contained in the archives of the French Embassy at Washington, and to Waldo G. Leland for securing the copy of a document from the Ministry of Foreign Affairs in Paris; to Drs. Stanley K. Hornbeck, A. L. P. Dennis, Henry W. Wriston, and to Gaillard Hunt for many such helpful suggestions and counsel as comes from frequent conversations with those who have given their lives to a study of phases of the subject embraced in this volume; to many friends scattered over Eastern Asia and Eastern Africa from Tokio to Bombay and Cape Town who have offered a ready and never-failing hospitality to a tired traveler; and, finally, to Nelson Trusler Johnson, Edwin Lowe Neville and Baron Serge A. Korff who have been patient and kind enough to read the manuscript critically.

CONTENTS

xiii

PART III. A PERIOD OF CONFUSION

PART IV. THE COOPERATIVE POLICY

PART I

THE EAST INDIA TRADE

CHAPTER I

THE BEGINNINGS OF AMERICAN COMMERCE

AMERICAN policy in Asia has been a development of the policy of early Americans—those pioneers who crossed the seas and sometimes set up their habitations on what were to the western world the frontiers of the East. To understand the policy in its later amplifications and applications it is very important to know something of the early trade and the conditions under which it was accomplished.

The term 'East India Trade' itself belongs to the generation which immediately followed the close of the American Revolution. One finds it in the literature of the day and in the speeches in Congress. The use of the term is important. The Americans viewed Asia as a whole and called it the East Indies. The trade so described included all the commerce the destination or origin of which lay in either the Indian or western Pacific oceans.) There was not, for example, at the time Adam Seybert wrote (1818) any one section of the trade so conspicuous as to overshadow other parts; the Calcutta, Sumatra, Northwest Coast and Canton trade stood side by side. They were all more or less related to each other and interdependent and, in turn, were all so much a part of the South American, West Indian and European commerce that the separate trade reports can never be untangled. The East India trade was merely a part of the fabric of the foreign commerce of the United States, and yet it was conducted under certain distinctive and unique conditions, political and economic, which gave rise to separate policies. Even the earliest American traders had to have a policy in Asia and the policy which necessity as well as wisdom dictated became the foundation of subsequent policies adopted by their government. Mod-

3

ern American policy in Asia is largely a body of precedents which have accumulated from decade to decade since the close of the war of the American Revolution. These precedents have a remarkable consistency due in large measure to the unchanging geographical and slowly changing economic and political conditions under which American trade with Asia has been conducted.

This trade may best be understood when one visualizes the scenes of the activities—the economic condition of the colonies at the close of the Revolution, the ships, their owners, officers and crews, the departure from the Atlantic seaboard, the barter for goods, the return cargoes, and the life of those who tarried for a few years in the Eastern ports.

Previous to the Revolution the American colonists knew of Asia only through the tea which found its way to such ports as Boston harbour, or was smuggled in from Holland; [1] through the small amount of expensive silks and the larger amount of Chinese and Indian cottons which wore well; and through the tales of the pirates who seventy-five years earlier had stalked through the streets of their ports. [2] At the close of the war we cannot call by name more than one or two native born Americans who had ever been on the coasts of Asia, and in 1784 probably there were not a half dozen people on all the Atlantic seaboard who had any first hand knowledge whatever of the other side of the world. Where the first charts came from by which the American vessels sailed to the East is a mystery.

In the last Captain Cook expedition to the Pacific, which left England in July, 1776, and returned in 1781, were two Americans, John Gore of Virginia and John Ledyard of Connecticut. [3] They were the first lieutenant and corporal of the marines, respectively, on the *Resolution*. Of Gore nothing else is known, but Ledyard's service to his country was considered in later years of sufficient importance to merit the attention of Jared Sparks, the biographer of Washington. Ledyard had entered Dartmouth College in

[1] Small numerals in text and notes refer to bibliographical references at ends of chapters.

1772 to prepare himself to be a missionary to the Indians, but had retired after a few months to go to sea. Working his way back to America in the British navy, he deserted in 1782 and made his way home to Connecticut for a brief period, and then ordained himself a missionary to American merchants to convert them to trade with Asia, the limitless possibilities of which had been impressed upon him when he had seen fur skins, purchased on the Northwest coast of America for a sixpence, and sold in Canton for $100.

Ledyard urged the advantages of the trade upon merchants in New York, Philadelphia and Boston. At least twice he was within sight of success, once at New London, where the frigate *Trumbell* was actually engaged for the purpose and then diverted elsewhere, and also in New York where Daniel Parker was employed, presumably by Robert Morris of Philadelphia, to purchase a ship for a trial voyage. The ship was purchased, named the *Empress of China*,[4] and sent to Canton in February, 1784, but Ledyard, whose zeal and enthusiasm did not qualify him, perhaps, for great responsibilities, was never permitted to carry out the great plans of which he was the author.

Within the next four or five years we hear of certain Englishmen [5] who drifted to America after some years of experience in the East, but none of them appear to have been recognized as important assets in teaching the Americans the arts of the new trade. American trade with Asia . was begun without the direct assistance of any others than Americans and made its way, needless to say, in the face of no inconsiderable opposition from British competitors, notably the East India Company, as well as with the blessing of a few Englishmen who welcomed any undermining of the East India Company monopoly.

Of general causes leading to the initiation and develop ment of the East India trade little need be said. This branch of the commerce of the new nation was merely a part of a lively expansive movement which burst the bounds at every possible point and spread over the face of the earth in search of produce, trade, capital and wealth. At the close

of the Revolution there were idle ships just in from their
privateering; there were sailors; there was a market
in America for the produce of Asia, which had formerly
come in British vessels; [6] and there was a market in China,
as the Americans already knew from the pre-revolutionary
trade, for at least one American product—ginseng, a root
utilized by the Chinese in medicines.[7] Furthermore, there
was the potent urge of poverty. As a non-manufacturing
people, shut up in a limited area which was not producing
many essential articles of diet, and impoverished by a costly
war, the United States was as far as possible removed from
economic self-sufficiency. The first Americans went to Asia
because they had to go—they had to go everywhere. In
later years, when this necessity was removed, they showed
their preferences by electing to remain at home.

THE AMERICAN PORTS

The American ports especially concerned in the East
India trade were Salem and Boston, Providence, a few of
the ports of Connecticut, New York, Philadelphia, Baltimore, and to a slight extent Norfolk. It is difficult to assign
to each of these ports its exact relative place in the growing
trade, for the relative positions were constantly changing,
and each city, from Philadelphia north, possessed at some
time or other its own peculiar eminence. To regard the
trade as having in any way been limited to any single state
is misleading. New York could claim the distinction of the
first completed voyage; Philadelphia, as was in accord with
its wealth and population, had for a while the largest
tonnage; Salem and Boston were distinguished for their
ship owners; and eventually the trade showed a tendency
to concentrate in the Port of New York, whither Massachusetts, Rhode Island, Connecticut, Pennsylvania and Maryland sent their agents to buy and sell, irrespective of what
state claimed ownership of the capital invested, or of the
ships employed.

The *Empress of China* was owned and fitted out jointly
by Robert Morris of Philadelphia and a group of New York

merchants represented by the firm of Daniel Parker which went bankrupt in 1785. The captain was John Green, who had probably commanded a privateer in the Revolution. The supercargo was Major Samuel Shaw of Boston, who had served with distinction in the war and who, but for his untimely death in 1794 en route from China, would probably have risen to eminence in the life of the young nation. The *Empress of China* left New York February 22, 1784, sailed directly to Canton and returned directly, arriving home May 12, 1785. She was furnished with the customary sea-letter with the rather inclusive introduction to the "most Serene, most Puissant, High, Illustrious, Noble, Honorable, Venerable, Wise and Prudent, Lords, Emperors, Kings, Republicks, Princes, Dukes, Earls, Barons, Lords, Burgomasters, Councillors, as also Judges, Officers, Justiciaries and Regents of all the good cities and places, whether ecclesiastical or secular, who shall see these patents or hear them read." [8] The cost of vessel (360 tons), the outfit, and the expenses of the voyage are reported to have been $120,000.[9] The cargo, what there was of it, consisted of something over forty tons of ginseng. The profits of the voyage were reported as $37,727—in Major Shaw's estimation hardly enough to go around, and certainly very modest when compared with the reported profits of the expedition which followed.

The return of the *Empress of China* created, nevertheless, something of a sensation. To James Madison a correspondent [10] wrote:

"I imagine you have heard of the arrival of an American vessel at this place in four months from Canton in China, laden with the commodities of that country.

"It seems our countrymen were treated with as much respect as the subjects of any nation, i. e., the whole are looked upon, by the Chinese as Barbarians, and they have too much Asiatic hauteur to descend to any discrimination. Most of the American merchants here are of the opinion that this commerce can be carried on, on better terms from America than Europe, and that we may be able not only to supply our own wants but to smuggle a very considerable quantity to the West Indies. I could heartily wish to see the merchants of our state engage in the business.

"Don't you think that an exemption from duty on all goods imported immediately from India in (American) bottoms to our state might have a good effect?"

This agitation so soon begun for protection legislation for the China trade did not lapse. Both Pennsylvania and New York [11] adopted protective duties, and by 1791 the federal government had extended to the China trade such favors as now seem almost incredible when one comes to consider their value. The China traders not only enjoyed the protection of the navigation act of 1789 which imposed a discriminating tonnage tax of forty-six cents per ton on foreign bottoms, and the protection of the tariff act of the same year which gave to the American importer a 12½ per cent. protection in duties on East India imports other than tea, and on tea a protection which absolutely excluded importation in any but American bottoms; but they also enjoyed the special favor of a warehousing system with drawbacks for reexportation and, most important of all, a two years' delay in the payment of tea duties.[12] Tea duties equalled or exceeded the prime cost of the tea at Canton.[13] When one adds to these favors the liberal credits extended to the Americans in India and China it is not difficult to see why the trade prospered.

The arrival of the *Empress of China* was followed shortly by that of the *Pallas,* with a cargo of $50,000 worth of teas taken by Thomas Randall, Shaw's partner and former companion in arms. The *Pallas* had been chartered at Canton and was commanded by Captain John O'Donnell, an Englishman and former Indian merchant who immediately became an American citizen and embarked upon the East India trade from Baltimore. Robert Morris took the cargo of the *Pallas* and became so enthused by the prospects of the China trade that he made a proposition to Shaw and Randall to return to Canton as his agents. The terms, however, were not considered satisfactory. Morris followed up the trade from Philadelphia and the partners almost immediately accepted an offer from a company of New York merchants. Shaw sailed again for Canton in 1786, planning on this voyage to stop at Batavia. "The terms on which I go," wrote Shaw to his brother, "promise something clever."

At least nine voyages to the Far East, some of them to India but not to China, were initiated from New York before the end of 1787.

Two months before the *Empress of China* had sailed from New York the sloop *Harriet* (55 tons) had cleared from Boston, bound for Canton with ginseng. Nine months after the departure of the first New York venture the *Grand Turk,* belonging to Elias Haskett Derby, sailed from Salem for the Cape on a similar errand but with a more diversified cargo. Neither the *Harriet* nor the *Grand Turk* went far beyond Cape Town; the sloop secured her small return cargo out of the private ventures of the officers of the re turning British Indiamen, but the *Grand Turk* with its larger cargo space did not succeed so well.

"Captain Ingersoll's object," wrote Shaw, who found the *Grand Turk* at the Cape on his return from Canton, "was to sell rum, cheese, salt provisions, chocolate, loaf-sugar, butter, etc., the proceeds of which in money, with a quantity of ginseng, and some cash brought with him, he intended to invest in Bohea tea. But as the ships bound to Europe were not allowed to break bulk by the way, he was disappointed in his expectation of purchasing that article, and sold his ginseng for two thirds of a Spanish dollar a pound. .   He intended remaining a short time to purchase fine teas in the private trade allowed to officers on board the India ships, and then to sail to the coast of Guinea to dispose of his rum, etc., for ivory and gold dust; thence, without taking a single slave, to proceed to the West Indies and purchase sugar and cotton with which he would return to Salem."

Captain Ingersoll assured Shaw that Derby would rather sink the whole capital employed than be directly or indirectly concerned in the 'infamous' slave traffic.

Boston was relatively slow in following up the voyage of the *Harriet,* but Salem, especially through Derby who acted on information secured at the Cape by Captain Ingersoll, plunged boldly into the trade and soon had several ships in the Indian Ocean, many of which reached Canton. In 1789 there were no less than ten Salem ships in and out of the Isle de France (Mauritius). Meanwhile Boston had sent out the *Columbia* and the *Lady Washington* to the

Northwest coast (1788), and the Massachusetts trade with the Far East was well launched. The Bay State developed a good deal of individuality in the East India trade. It specialized to a greater degree than did the other ports, in certain branches, trading much with Mauritius, Calcutta, Madras, the pepper coast of Sumatra, and the Northwest coast of America. While the Massachusetts shipowners were also merchants, supplying their own markets, they were primarily interested in the carrying trade. Their vessels were, to use a modern term, 'tramp freighters.' The points at which they turned homeward were usually either Canton or an Indian Ocean port, but the voyage in either direction might include visits to half a dozen European ports, or several cities of South America. Freight rates ranged from $2.25 to more than $4 per ton per month.[14] Needless to say, the Massachusetts traders prospered.

Philadelphia entered the trade directly in 1787, sending out at least five vessels, a total of over 1600 tons, or more than could be claimed in that year for all of the other ports together. The Philadelphia ship owners, Robert Morris excepted, were little given to explorations or experiments; rather, they set to work to build up a fleet to supply their needs along established and proven routes, chiefly to Calcutta, Madras and Canton. The East India trade of the city quickly passed into the hands of a few substantial merchants of wealth like Stephen Girard and Samuel Archer who managed the trade in close conjunction with their wholesale or retail merchandising. In this class of trade Philadelphia retained its leadership more than twenty years, after which it was forced to yield gradually to New York.

The trade of Providence was very similar to that of Philadelphia. It appears to have been better supplied with capital at the outset than either New York or Massachusetts, but the growth of the trade was foredoomed to limitation because Providence was a poor distributing point. Before the war of 1812 Providence had already begun to withdraw its capital from the trade to devote it to the spinning industry.[15]

The Vessels Employed

The fleets of the East India traders make a peculiar appeal to the imagination. One reads in their tonnage and in the records of their builders something of the economic history of the struggling young nation; in their adventures, trials, failures and successes, something of the hardihood of the youthful American spirit.

One cannot see without a thrill the departure of the 55 ton sloop *Harriet,* or of the not much larger sloop *Experiment* from Albany just two years later. The *Harriet* went only to the Cape, but the *Experiment,* carrying a crew of seven men and two boys, pushed on to China and returned in eighteen months with a cargo of tea, China-ware and other goods. In 1790 Captain Joseph Ingraham, formerly mate on the *Columbia,* who had already circumnavigated the globe, took a parting look at his native shore and then launched the *Hope,*[16] "being only 70 tons & slightly built" into the bosom of the ocean for a voyage around the Horn to the Northwest coast. Thirteen months later Ingraham reached Macao with his cargo of pelts. And while he was there, in came the 90-ton *Lady Washington* with Captain John Kendrick from Nookta Sound, four years out of Boston harbor.

Such voyages as these were by no means exceptional. The *Pilgrim,* 62 tons, sailed from Boston on a sealing voyage in the South Pacific in September, 1803, and four years later arrived at Canton with between twelve and thirteen thousand seal-skins. The schooner *Rajah,* built for the Sumatra pepper trade was only 130 tons, and carried a crew of only ten men. The voyage of the *Betsey* (93 tons) of New York in 1797-8 is notable. She went to the South Seas by way of Cape Horn, thence to Canton, and then back to New York by way of Good Hope, a voyage of twenty-three months. There was a crew of thirty, not one of whom was over twenty-eight years old. The net proceeds of the trip were in excess of $120,000, on an initial outlay for the cost of the vessel, outfit, insurance and interest of $7,867.

After deducting the duties, the shares of the captain, the officers and the crew, and the capital invested, there was asserted to be a clear profit to the owners of $53,118—on a twenty-three months trip of a 90-ton vessel! [17]

We are not to believe that these tiny sloops, snows, brigantines, brigs and schooners were selected for the Pacific and China trade in preference to larger craft. Their use bears witness to the poverty of the traders and their lack of capital. As rapidly as wealth permitted the Americans built larger craft—from 250- to 300-ton vessels for the Pacific and circuituous routes, and slightly larger for the direct trade with India and Canton. With few exceptions there were no American vessels anywhere near 1000 tons in the East India trade until after 1840. Meanwhile the American ship owner came to see that although the British ships of the day were ranging in size from 600 up to 1400 tons, American vessels of half their size and a third their crews were both safer and more economical for the East Indies. The largest American vessel at Whampoa in 1813 was 493 tons; the smallest was 86 tons. The thirty-nine vessels which touched at Honolulu between February and May, 1826, were of from 200 to 400 tons; ten years later at the same port the vesels averaged about 320 tons, and in 1842 they ranged around 350 tons. The largest vessel at Batavia in the summer of 1834 was 465 tons.[18]

The experience of Major Shaw with the *Massachusetts* built especially for him and launched at Quincy, September, 1789, illustrates the experimental character of much of the early trade, and also throws some light on the spirit of the men engaged in it.

Shaw, after a thorough investigation of the methods of trade used by the British and European companies in the East Indies inclined to the opinion that large ships were advantageous. "The experience of nearly a century," he wrote in his journal after his return to China from India in 1786, "has convinced the Europeans of the utility of managing their commerce with this country by national companies and with large ships." Shortly after this Shaw and his partner, Thomas Randall, drew up a contract with Eli Hayden "American merchant and supercargo of the brigantine *Columbia,* whereof is master Solomon Bunker, now riding at anchor at the port of Whampoa and bound for New York," by which Hayden was to place an order in Massachusetts for a ship which would meet the needs of the case as Shaw understood them. The length of the keel was to be one hundred and sixteen feet, and the ship was to have "three decks, and a round house with a stern gallery from the round house, and a quarter gallery above and below, with thirty-two ports on her second deck and a forecastle on her upper deck." [19]

"With respect to the other dimensions and disposition of the ship," continued the contract, "those of the *Worcester* (an English ship now at Whampoa) are annexed to these presents, but it is understood by the parties to this contract and engaged by the said Eli Hayden that he will build the aforesaid ship agreeably to the models to be formed and given by the same (at the expense of Shaw and Randall) by the person who shall hereafter be appointed for that purpose . . . it being further engaged that all the aforesaid and every other article which shall enter into the construction of the said ship previous to her being launched and delivered to said Shaw and Randall, or their assigns, in the water and after at the risque of said Eli Hayden, shall be well and truly the best, the very best quality, it being the true intent, spirit and meaning of the present contract that the said ship shall be built as well and as strong as wood and iron can make her."

To William Hackett, of Salisbury, Massachusetts, who had built the *Alliance,* were entrusted the responsibilities of making the models and superintending the building of the ship. The instructions to him contained the following paragraph indicative of the national pride which characterized very many of the China traders:

"This ship is designed for the India trade, where ships from all nations meet and where probably the best ships the world can produce may be seen. It is the expectation of Messrs. Shaw and Randall that they can produce from America such a ship as will bear the inspection of the most critical eye, both as to construction and workmanship.

The *Massachusetts* appears to have met the qualifications. Both British and French naval commanders who were visiting in Boston in their national ships at the time of the launching expressed their admiration of the model of the vessel, and the *Massachusetts* was afterwards pronounced at both Batavia and Canton to be "as perfect as the then state of the art would permit." The vessel sailed from Boston in March, 1790, and her commander, Job Prince, afterwards reported to Hackett, her builder:

> "The ship *Massachusetts* surpassed our most sanguine expectations so that she met the approbation of all the Europeans at Canton. And though their eyes were open to spy defects and their tongues ready to find fault, they confessed that they could not."

The report of Amasa Delano, second officer of the *Massachusetts,* sheds another light on the obstacles of ignorance and inexperience which the early Canton traders had to overcome before substantial success crowned their efforts. Delano stated:

> "The ship was as well built as any ship could be under the circumstances. The timbers were cut and used immediately while perfectly green. It was white oak, and would have been very durable had it been docked and properly seasoned. . . . She was, however, rotten when we first arrived in China. She was loaded principally with green masts and spars taken on board in winter directly out of the water with ice and mud on them. The lower hold was thus filled, and the lower deck hatches caulked down in Boston and never opened until we were in Canton. The air was then found to be so corrupt that a lighted candle was put out by it nearly as soon as by water. . . . We had taken four or five hundred barrels of beef in the lower hold, placed in the broken stowage. When fresh air was admitted so that men could live under the hatches the beef was found almost boiled, the hoops were rotted and fallen off, and the inside of the ship was covered with a blue mould more than half an inch thick."

And yet four or five decades later the Americans had learned how to carry even cargoes of ice over the same route and dispose of them from Calcutta to Canton at a profit.

Major Shaw seized an opportunity to sell the *Massachusetts* and invested his funds in a cargo which he was able to freight to Bombay. At the latter port he transferred part of the cargo to an American ship and took the balance in a Danish vessel to Ostend to be disposed of in the European market. He is reported to have received $65,000 for his ship. If such were the truth his venture had by no means ended in disaster for it is unlikely that the *Massachusetts* cost more than $40,000—$50 a ton. The sale of American built vessels in the ports of Asia was common in those days.

CREWS, CAPTAINS AND OWNERS

Of great interest to the student of the American policy in Asia is the character of the men who sailed these ships and represented the new nation in the ports of the East. They were good, average American-born citizens, recruited either from the sea-faring population or from the farms. As late as 1834, judging from various consular reports, the number of foreign born did not exceed twenty-five per cent., and in the first six months of that year, out of the 276 sailors in 19 vessels which entered Manila, all but 25 were native born. Sailors on the sealing and fur-trading voyages had a share in the profits, and in the direct trade with Asia they often made small ventures of their own, buying cargo space in the ship in which they sailed. They had before them the possibility of either working up through the grades until they became masters of their own ships, as many of them did, or of accumulating enough capital to buy a farm or enter trade at home. The American sailors were therefore quite unlike the crews of the British Indiamen, recruited from the dregs of English cities, which at Canton spread terror in their path, creating no end of trouble for the British authorities and even imperilling the continuance of the trade itself.[20] The early American sailor, be it admitted, was also quite unlike his successor who appeared on the China coast after the opening of California. The American sailor of the early fifties in China had all the vices of the earlier English sailor, plus initiative and a liberty. The character of the American sailor who appeared in the East in the early days was a distinct asset to American trade at a time when good will counted for much. He merited better treatment than he sometimes received.

The American consul at Canton, shortly after the close of the War of 1812, reported [21] that the American sailors adrift in Canton preferred service under almost any flag rather than their own.

"It has often occurred," he wrote, "that the commanders of vessels which have been on long, tedious and laborious voyages, sometimes two or three years, particularly on the Northwest coast of America and the Pacific Ocean, illtreat and unnecessarily punish their seamen for the sole purpose of driving them to desert from their vessels, that they may forfeit their consular claim for wages, through which means they are driven to the necessity of entering into foreign service .
this takes place particularly about the time of the arrival at this port, from which period as many seamen are not wanted to navigate the vessel to the United States or Europe, as were necessarily employed in the previous and more lucrative part of the voyage."

The hazards of a sailor's life in those days were also formidable. Out of a crew of sixty-one which had sailed the *Massachusetts* to Canton in 1790, fifteen had in the course of years died either at Canton or en route, four were murdered at or near Macao, one contracted leprosy and one became a slave in Algiers.

Of the ship masters it may be said that while some of them were hard drivers and merciless, they were on the whole an exceedingly able set of men, the type of the American pioneer. Many of them were sons of ship-owning families, and many more were graduated into the ranks of the merchants and bankers of the next generation, while not a few owned their vessels and added to their holdings until they had a fleet of their own. One reads the tale of a Boston banker in the fifties who was reported, half a century before, to have commanded a ship from Calcutta to Boston [22] "with nothing in the shape of a chart on board but a small map of the world in Guthrie's geography." One may well question the accuracy of the details of this story and yet find in it a measure of truth.

We may clearly distinguish three classes of owners. Many of the smaller vessels were owned and fitted out on shares. The six share-holders in the *Columbia* and the *Lady Washington* in their memorable voyage to the Northwest

coast and Canton were three Boston merchants, Charles
Bulfinch the architect, a son of Elias Haskett Derby, and a
New York merchant. There were many such expeditions.
2 Another class was the large retail and wholesale merchants,
particularly of Philadelphia and New York. They appear
to have managed their voyages for their exclusive and
individual interests; one does not find evidence that the
small adventurer had any part in these enterprises. There
were also the shipping companies, owned by individuals, by
families, or by a group of individuals. The Derbys of Salem
were of this class. They admitted a large number of small
ventures which were managed by the supercargoes on a
commission of $2\frac{1}{2}$ per cent and for which the owners paid
either the regular freight charges or divided the profits with
Derby. In the voyage of the *Astrea* in 1789, there were
twenty-four of these private consignments.[23] One man
would send a few casks of ginseng, another a few boxes of
"dollars," a third some snuff, and many sent wine or beer.
In other instances the stock in these trading companies was
rather widely distributed. In 1814 the firm of Oliver Wolcott and Company of New York reported sixteen individuals
as having a total stock of $405,000 in the China trade.
Among the share-holders were William Rhinelander, Rufus
King, Archibald Gracie and Eli Whitney.[24]

The early trade had in it a large element of speculation.
The price of tea fluctuated greatly and the market was frequently glutted. The trade in Indian fabrics and in silks
was steadier but even under the best of market conditions
the trade was hazardous. A full cargo in a four or five
hundred ton ship was valued at from three to five hundred
thousand dollars. Wrecks were not uncommon, insurance
was high, and there were few men in the United States at
the beginning of the last century who could lose any large
amount of money and remain solvent. Following the War
of 1812 there was a period of intense speculation ending in
very extensive failures. In 1825 one Philadelphia house
failed [25] owing the government nearly $900,000 in unpaid
duties. This failure carried others with it and not long

afterwards a New York house failed for $3,000,000. During
the third decade of the century one of the wealthiest of the
Boston firms claimed hardly to have made the interest on
the money invested.

After the War of 1812 the trade showed a marked tendency toward concentration in the hands of a few firms. It
was stated that in 1825 seven eighths of the China trade
was conducted by four firms: Messrs. Perkins and Company
of Boston; Archer who was connected with the Browns of
Liverpool, Jones, Oakford and Company of Philadelphia;
and Thomas H. Smith of New York. In 1829 one half of
the entire trade was said to be in the hands of the house of
Perkins. The day of the small trader had not entirely
passed but a few merchants had a very great advantage.
The pioneer days were over but they had served a most
useful purpose in American industrial and commercial development. The "merchant prince" had appeared at Canton but at the same time many an American at home had
withdrawn from the China trade with sufficient capital to
serve his needs as he entered into the new industrial life
of the nation. The importance of the early China trade is
to be gauged not so much by the net trade returns for each
year as by the fact that it offered a means for the accumula-
tion in a few years of a large amount of capital of which
the rapidly growing states were in urgent need.

CARGOES

The outward cargoes of the East India traders present
an interesting study.

The first American merchants went to the East not so
much to sell as to buy. The East Indian trade arose out of
no notable demand in the United States for a market for
surplus produce, but rather out of a desire to secure for the
United States certain commodities such as Indian muslins,
spices, Chinese teas and silks for which there was a demand.
The East was economically self-sustaining; it required
nothing from the West. The problem of exchange thus

created was the most serious obstacle which the American merchant had to meet. What could he take to Asia to give in exchange for the produce which he required?

Fortunately for the American the acceptable articles of exchange in the various ports from Mauritius to Canton were varied. There were, scattered across Asia, considerable settlements of white men who were dependent in part for the satisfaction of their needs, both personal and industrial, upon commodities which had to be carried to Asia from the West. The Americans seized upon this trade with avidity. The native markets in each country would absorb certain articles which the United States produced, or which the American merchant could collect en route to the East. Hence the advantage of the circuitous trading. A vessel might start for Canton with farm produce or with flour. At some European or Mediterranean port this cargo would be exchanged for a cargo for Mauritius, or India or else where. Sometimes there would be three or four exchanges of commodities before the ship reached Canton.

The way in which the Americans attempted to solve this formidable problem of exchange may best be seen in some of the old manifests. The *Grand Turk* of Salem carried as outward cargo in 1785: pitch, tar, flour, rice, tobacco, butter, wine, bar-iron, sugar, oil, chocolate, prunes, brandy, beef, rum, hams, candles, soap, cheese, fish, beer, porter, port and ginseng, as well as some specie. The *Astrea* in 1789 carried, in addition to many of the articles noted above: snuff, shoes, harness and saddlery. The *Asia,* sailing the same year from Philadelphia, carried rum, specie and British manufactured goods. The *General Washington* from Providence in 1791, in addition to wine, spirits and ginseng, carried tar, iron bars, anchors, shot and cannon. For many of the commodities in the above lists there could be only a limited demand; they were obviously intended to supply the needs of Europeans rather than of Asiatics.

A few years later we find very much simpler manifests. For the voyage of the ship *Triton,*[26] which left New York for Canton in 1804, capital to the extent of $120,000 was advanced by seven New York merchants and firms, and this was invested as follows: 9533 beaver skins at $5 each, $47,665; and 70,372 Spanish dollars, costing $71,882. The ship *Lion*,[27] sailing from New York early in 1816, carried among other items, 60 cases of opium, valued at $30,015, and also 45 kegs, and 2 boxes of Spanish dollars, valued at $110,000. The appearance of furs, opium, and an increasing proportion of specie in the later manifests reveals the condition of the problem of exchange. The Americans had been forced to fall back on Spanish dollars the demand for which had pushed them to a premium, and were supplementing this precious medium of exchange with furs and opium.

This export of specie exerted a very disturbing effect on the condition of American currency, especially after the War of 1812. A committee appointed to consider the subject made a report in the House of Representatives in 1819 [28] that " the whole amount of our current coin is probably not more than double that which has been exported in a single year to India, including China in the general term." The largest China merchant in New York in 1824 admitted that out of his total exports to China of $1,311,057 for that year, nearly $900,000 was specie. His other items of export were British manufactured goods, $356,407, and American produce, chiefly furs and ginseng, to the extent of only $60,000. At that time a Boston merchant, probably Thomas H. Perkins, wrote:

"There has been a strong prejudice existing against the China trade in this country, under the idea that specie was necessarily exported to procure cargoes from China. So far is this from the fact, *in our case,* that, although our importations have averaged more than a million dollars annually for several years, in the products of China, of which silks and nankeens form a considerable portion, that we have not shipped a Spanish dollar for the past *three years* to China. Our funds arise from the export of opium from Turkey, British goods from Great Britain, lead and quick-silver from Gibraltar, and the same articles on a large scale from Trieste."

The same writer asserted that he had already made the experiment of shipping American cotton goods to China, Manila, Java, and to the Mediterranean ports and to

Smyrna, and was satisfied that in the "more gross cotton fabrics" the American manufacturers could already compete successfully with their British rivals. Another merchant predicted a trade with China in raw cotton in competition with the Bengal product "whenever raw cotton can be purchased in this country at ten cents a pound." The next year cotton went down temporarily to eleven cents, but the merchant never lived to see the day of 'ten cent cotton.' The exportation of cotton goods, however, of the coarser grades, steadily increased.

It was asserted in 1852 [29] that the United States had shipped silver to China since 1784 to the extent of $180,000,000. The American port records show nearly $70,000,-000 to have been shipped between 1805 and 1818. As to the total amount which had been received in China from American ships there could only be wild guesses, for no one knows how much specie for the East was collected on the circuitous voyages.

The inward cargoes from the Far East consisted of cotton and silk textiles from India; spices; and from China. tea, nankeens, cassia, China-ware, straw mats and matting, sugar and drugs. Tea and nankeens formed the greater part of the value of the China cargoes. One has but to examine this list of commodities to see how slender was the permanent basis for the American trade with the East. When the United States had become a manufacturing nation and had developed the logical sources of supply nearer home, there remained only tea and spice as articles of constant demand, and the United States did not become a nation of tea drinkers. Tea was a luxury [30] in the early days, costing in 1791 from twenty-eight cents to more than a dollar a pound, according to grade. Coffee became more popular, and it was cheaper. Expanding population and reexportation, rather than increased per capita consumption, accounted for the growing East India trade.

BIBLIOGRAPHICAL NOTES

1. See, for example, Philip Cuyler Letter Book (N. Y. Pub. Lib. Mss. Div.). At the outbreak of the Seven Years' War Cuyler ordered several barrels of tea (July 20, 1756) from John Hokson of Holland through Captain Corne "who sails this day from Rotterdam."

2. Documents Relative to the Colonial History of New York (Albany, 1854). Vol. 4, pp. 307-10, 446, 459, 480.

3. "The Life of John Ledyard," by Jared Sparks, Cambridge, 1828.

4. "The Journals of Major Samuel Shaw, the first American Consul at Canton, with a life of the author," by Josiah Quincy, Boston, 1847.

5. "East India Trade of Providence, 1787-1807," by Gertrude Selwyn Kimball, Brown University Historical Papers, 1-10, 1894-99; 3 Dip. Corres., of U. S., Sept. 19, 1783-March 4, 1789 (Washington, 1837) p. 771.

6. See, for example, America and England (Mss. in Bancroft Collection, N. Y. Pub. Lib.); and, Letters of Phineas Bond, American Historical Association Reports, 1896, Vol. 1.

7. "Oriental Commerce," by William Milburn, London, 1813, 2 vols.; "Statistical View of the Commerce of the United States of America," by Timothy Pitkin, Hartford, 1816.

8. Papers of Continental Congress, Reports of Committees, Vol. 5, p. 11. (Mss. Div., Lib. of Congress); Annex to the Treaty of Amity and Commerce of Oct 8, 1782, between the United States and the Netherlands.

9. "Progress of New York in a Century, 1776-1876," by John Austin Stevens, New York, 1876.

10. Madison Papers (N. Y. Pub. Lib.) Vol. 14; W. Grayson to Madison, May 28, 1785.

11. Laws of Pennsylvania, 1785, p. 669; 1787, p. 241; Laws of New York, 1787, chap. 81, cited in "American Commercial Legislation before 1789," by A. A. Giesecke, New York, 1910.

12. See "History of Early Relations between the United States and China," by K. C. Latourette, Transactions of the Conn. Academy of Arts and Sciences, Vol. 22, 1917, pp. 78-9, footnote, for complete summary of protective legislation and its detailed changes.

13. Report on the China Trade (S. Doc. No. 31:19-1) gives much information as to the cost of teas at Canton.

14. Kimball; "Statistical Annals of the United States," by Adam Seybert, Philadelphia, 1818.

15. President Washington, Jan. 7, 1792, declined to furnish Brown and Francis of Providence a recommendation to be used in Europe in securing a $100,000 loan to build a vessel for the East India trade on the ground that "it would be almost impossible to separate my private from my official capacity in this case." (Misc. Letters, Dept. of State).

16. Journal of the Voyage of the Brigantine *Hope,* by Joseph Ingraham (Mss. Div., Lib. of Congress).

17. Fanning Memorial. H. Doc. No. 57; 26-1
18. Consular Letters from Canton, Honolulu and Batavia. Dept. of State.
19. Hudson Collection; Papers relating to the building of the ship *Massachusetts* at Braintree, Mass., 1787-91 (N. Y. Pub. Lib.).
20. House of Commons, Sessional Papers, 1821, Vol. 7.
21. Canton Letters, Vol. 1, Feb. 3, 1815. See also Misc. Letters, Nov 1, 1816, C. J. Ingersoll to Mr. Monroe; and also see H. Doc. No. 71:26-2, Sept. 22, 1805, Snow to Madison.
22. Edward Everett, in Hunt's "Lives of American Merchants," Vol. 1, p. 139.
23. See Manifest of the *Astrea,* printed at length, p. 58ff., "Hunt's American Merchants," Vol. 2.
24. Account Books of Oliver Wolcott & Co. (N. Y. Hist. Soc.)
25. H. Doc. No. 137:19-1; S. Doc. No. 31:19-1, give an extensive exhibit of the condition of the trade after 1820. See also Worthy P. Sterns, "Foreign Trade of the United States, 1820-40"; *Journal of Political Economy,* Vol. 8, 1899-1900.
26. Wolcott Account Books.
27. *Ibid.*
28. Lowndes Report, Jan. 26, 1819, H. Doc. 111:15-2.
29. S. Ex. Doc. No. 49:32-2.
30. "Old Merchants of New York," by Walter Barrett, Clerk, 5 Vols. New York, 1885. Vol. 4, p. 213. Barrett, although making an enormous number of misstatements, is nevertheless a valuable source of information for all the early trade, particularly for that after 1820.

CHAPTER II

THE PORTS OF ASIA AND THE PACIFIC

As we follow the American vessels to Asia we note that there were two possible routes: around the Cape of Good Hope, or around Cape Horn and westward across the Pacific.

The eastward route was usually selected by the larger Indiamen from Philadelphia, New York, Providence and Massachusetts which engaged in the direct trade with India or with China. This route also offered many advantages to the tramp which depended in part on cargoes offered from port to port. In any case the route lay across the Indian Ocean, past the Malay peninsula, and up the China Sea. Ports along the way invited attention and were, in fact, a necessity for the replenishing of ship's stores, if not for trade.

Isle de France and India

The American trade with Isle de France (Mauritius) opened in April, 1786, when the *Grand Turk* arrived with an assorted cargo evidently intended to meet the needs of the French settlement. The ship was then chartered to the extent of two thirds of the space by a Frenchman to carry freight to Canton, the charterer agreeing to pay all the port charges. The *Grand Turk* returned to Salem in May, 1787, with a cargo of tea, ox-hides, shammy skins, buckskins, wine, muslins and bandanna handkerchiefs. Derby followed up the Mauritius and Indian trade and, finding it more profitable than that with Canton, devoted himself to it during the last eight years of his life. When he died in 1799 he was reported to be possessed of a million dollars, the largest fortune in the United States. Commerce with

24

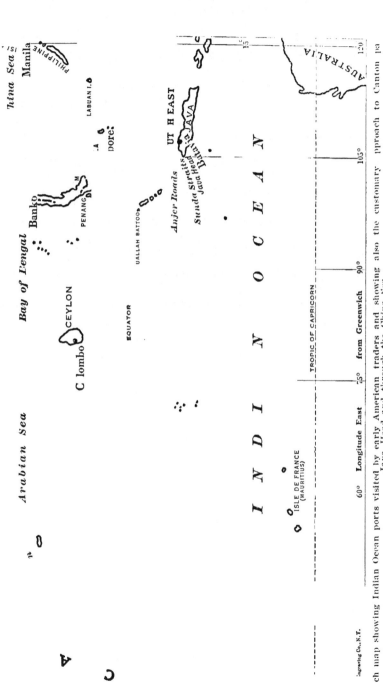

ch map showing Indian Ocean ports visited by early American traders and showing also the customary pproach to Canton by Java Head and through the China Sea.

agneting Co., N.Y.

Mauritius reached its height in 1800; there were seventeen arrivals at Salem alone from Mauritius in the years 1797 and 1798.

The Mauritius trade has an interest aside from its intrinsic value, for it was largely through the action of the French Government in extending the hospitality of the French ports in the Indian Ocean to American ships in 1783, and in formally opening them to American trade the next year, that the ports of British India were thrown open to Americans on especially favorable terms.   Indian produce had become available to American vessels at the French ports.   The Dutch and the Danes also were friendly to the Americans and they also had settlements in India.   There were, besides, the ports of the native princes.   It was the policy of Great Britain with her own nationals to control the trade in such a way that all produce exported from India would either be imported to England or at least pay toll in London, but international competition made it impossible to maintain such a monopoly against American ships.   The Americans would get the cargoes in any case. The East India Company, therefore, notwithstanding the fact that no commercial treaty existed with the United States, and in spite of such rancor and jealousy as remained from the late war, determined not only to admit American vessels to British India but even to offer special inducements to bring them there.[1]

The first American ship to enter an Indian port was the *Chesapeake* of Baltimore.   The vessel had been built especially for the trade and was commanded by her owner, Captain John O'Donnell, who had brought the *Pallas* into New York in 1784.   The *Chesapeake* cleared, probably from Norfolk, in the latter part of 1786 and returned to Perth Amboy in 1789.   She was warmly welcomed in India, the Supreme Council of Bengal exempting her, as a mark of special favor, from all customs duties.   Lord Cornwallis and the Government of India issued an order that American ships at the East India Company's settlements should be treated in all respects as the most favored foreigners.   This policy was confirmed in the commercial treaty with Great Britain in 1794 (Article 13). The privileges secured were even greater, for Americans paid only 6 per cent import duties, the same as those paid by the English, whereas other nations paid 8 per cent. Furthermore, the Americans were exempted from the 2 per cent export duty which was paid by all others, except the British. And then, although the treaty of 1794 limited the trade in American vessels to direct trade with American ports, special licenses were issued permitting Americans to carry Indian produce to other ports of the Indian Ocean and to China, thus linking the peninsula in those circuitous voyages to which American ships were so well adapted.

Derby of Salem had four vessels in the Indian Ocean in 1787. They visited Surat, Bombay and Calcutta. They carried among other commodities, Bombay cotton to Canton, and brought Indian cotton to Salem. Derby's son returned from the East in 1791 after a residence of three years in which he had directed a very lively trade which reached from Bombay to Canton, and was reported to have made $100,000 on his various transactions. The *Betsey* of Baltimore, the *Commerce* of Philadelphia, and the *Leda* of Boston all visited India in the season of 1786-7. While exact evidence is lacking it is probable that before 1790 the total American tonnage in the Indian ports exceeded that at Canton.*

The American tariff of 1816 [2] imposed a protective duty on coarse cottons, setting on them a minimum valuation of twenty-five cents a yard, the effect of which was to place the India trade under a severe handicap. Nevertheless a certain amount of commerce continued. In the season of 1829-30 there were sixteen vessels with a tonnage of 4941

*The major portion of this commerce with India had been claimed for both Salem and Philadelphia, but records sufficient for comparison are lacking. Between 1785 and 1799 Derby made forty-seven voyages to the East Indies. Between 1800 and 1842 the vessels entering the port of Salem were: from Calcutta, 115; Bombay, 20; Bengal, 6; Madras, 6. There were also two from Ceylon and two from Siam. Before 1812 Joseph Peabody of Salem, out of a total of 164 voyages, had 38 from Calcutta alone. During this same period Peabody had only 17 voyages to Canton. The years of the greatest activity for the Salem-India trade were 1802-7 and 1816-22. In 1800 twelve vessels loaded at Calcutta for Boston.

tons clearing from British India ports, and the following
year nineteen vessels. The India trade, which had dwindled
as the Americans learned to manufacture their own cottons,
picked up again in the two decades which preceded the Civil
War. The American tonnage at Calcutta in the second half
of the year 1845 [3] was 8889 tons (19 vessels), almost all
of it being from Boston or elsewhere in New England.
The inward cargoes at Calcutta consisted of lumber, cotton
goods and ice; the outward cargoes being made up chiefly
of hides, salt peter, indigo, and opium. The ice trade with
Calcutta had been initiated in 1835 and came "just in time
to preserve Boston's East India commerce from ruin." [4]
In 1857 one hundred and fifty-two American vessels de
parted from British India ports with cargoes valued at
$11,000,000.

The appointment of an American consul in India was
a subject of consideration very soon after the close of the
Revolution. Captain O'Donnell [5] of the *Chesapeake* had
applied for a position as general commissioner for the
United States for the Far East. He desired authority to
negotiate trade agreements with "the principal independent
powers of Asia" which he described as Tippoo Saib, son of
Hyder Ally, the Marattas on the coast of Malabar, the
King of Acheea in Sumatra, and the Malay King of Ternati.
He also outlined a plan by which British merchants in India
would be able to evade the rules of the Company monopoly
by shipping their fortunes to the United States under the
protection of blank passports issued by O'Donnell. To this
plan John Jay reported to the Continental Congress somewhat testily that if residents of India were to come to the
United States, their coming should be accomplished "by
means perfectly unexceptional, and not by the sovereign
of this country giving false evidence of American property
. . . to vessels, officers and crews entirely foreign to the
United States." The request was denied. As for treaties
with the independent powers of Asia, the Continental
Congress was too much preoccupied even to entertain the
idea. Political connections with Asia, so long as ports were

open and trade reasonably free, was farthest from the thought of the American people.

The necessity for a consul at Calcutta increased, especially to care for American sailors at a time when American vessels were being sold in Indian ports. George Cabot of Boston, November 16, 1792, in a letter to President Washington [6] urged the importance of appointing a consul and mentioned the "very precarious tenure" of American rights in India. He thought that an agent on the spot might be able to accomplish something "by availing ourselves as much as possible of the competition" which existed between the rival French, Dutch, Danish and English interests. Cabot, as well as many other Massachusetts merchants recommended the appointment of Benjamin Joy of Newberryport and Boston. The appointment was made and Mr. Joy reached Calcutta in 1784. He engaged William Abbott, the secretary to the Nabob of Arcot, to act as consular agent and vice consul at Madras, but was unable to find a suitable person to serve in Bombay. Joy was received cordially by the British Government but without orders from London he could not be recognized as consul.

Consul Joy remained in India less than two years and resigned his commission from Boston January 24, 1796. Two successors were appointed in 1796 and in 1801, respectively, one from Philadelphia and the other from Massachusetts, but it does not appear that either of them ever entered upon the duties of the office. The next consul was James B. Higginson of Massachusetts who entered upon his work in 1843.

The India trade of the United States was entirely without political significance. However, the close association of American and British merchants in both the direct India-American and in the India-Canton trade exercised an influence on American policy in China, for it brought the Americans and the English together at Canton and accounted for the disposition of many of these merchants to seek common action in 1839 and later.

ADVENTURES—MOCHA, SUMATRA, SIAM

While the national establishments of Great Britain and the European powers in the Indian Ocean led their merchants to confine their trade chiefly to ports under their respective flags, the Americans were inclined to exploration and the discovery of new markets.

American trade along the coast of Africa, Arabia and Persia in the early decades of the nineteenth century appears to have been greater than that of all the European nations combined. The *Recovery* of Salem (Captain Joseph Ropes) opened the coffee trade with Mocha in 1798 and soon a thriving commerce, by way of the Cape, was established between Mocha and Smyrna. At the latter port the trade was quickly related to China, as well as directly to the United States, by the exchange for Turkey opium.

From Mocha the American trade spread in all directions through the domains of the Sultan of Muscat whose sway extended from the Persian Gulf to Cape Delgado on the coast of Africa. While the trade appears to have decreased after the War of 1812, its importance was considered of sufficient moment to include a treaty with the Sultan as a part of the program of Edmund Roberts in 1832. In the thirty-two months, September, 1832, to May, 1835, out of a total of forty-one vessels with a total of 6559 tons, visiting Zanzibar, thirty-two vessels of 5497 tons were American.[7] Of the American vessels, twenty were from Salem, three from Boston, and three from New York. The exports consisted chiefly of gum copal, aloes, gum arabic, columbo wood, drugs, ivory, tortoise-shell, hides, bees-wax, and cocoanut oil. Shortly after the ratification of the treaty a special effort was made by some New York merchants to develop this trade but the panic of 1837 intervened. However American influence at Zanzibar was predominant, according to an English historian, until at least 1859. During the fifties American vessels at Zanzibar ranged from twenty-four to thirty-five annually, while British vessels never numbered more than six.

The trade with the pepper coast of Sumatra began soon after 1790, when Captain Jonathan Carnes of Salem brought home a cargo which sold for seven hundred per cent profit. Such fabulous profits could not be kept secret and the trade grew rapidly. In the spring of 1803 there were twenty-one American vessels on the northwest coast of Sumatra after pepper. The Americans came to have practically a monopoly. In 1820 it was asserted that the Americans were sending forty vessels, of about two hun dred tons each, to Sumatra annually.[8] It would appear that the trade at this time was nearly equal to that at Canton.

As a result of the attack by the natives of Quallah Battoo on the *Friendship* of Salem in 1830, the U. S. Frigate *Potomac* was ordered to visit the coast and punish the natives—a commission which was executed with great thoroughness.[9] The action of the natives was usually represented as entirely unprovoked by the Americans, but there is reason to doubt such statements. There are hints that some of the Americans overreached themselves in their barter, even to the extent of using scales with hollow beams in which quicksilver had been inserted.

Of the trade with Siam little is known. What little there was appears to have been conducted from Batavia and later from Singapore, and its growth was restricted by excessive port charges, high duties, and the arbitrary rights of preemption exercised by the king and high officials until the treaty of 1833.

BATAVIA AND MANILA

The Batavia trade of the United States was of some importance in itself, and more especially because of the relation of Batavia to China and Japan. Although the American treaty of 1782 with the Netherlands seems not to have contemplated any such trade, the Americans were freely admitted to the port, except for a few months at the beginning of the season of 1790-1 when the Dutch gov-

ernor, prompted perhaps by the Dutch East India Company, was disposed to prohibit it.   Both the *Astrea* and
Three Sisters of Salem had difficulty in that season, but
Blanchard and Thomas H. Perkins, the supercargoes, man
aged to "fix" matters with the authorities.   Shortly after
wards Major Shaw arrived on the *Massachusetts,* and met
with similar opposition.   Clothed in his authority as Ameri
can Consul at Canton, Shaw entered a vigorous protest
which aroused the disgust of the Dutch governor that the
Americans should be inaugurating the custom of Merchant-
consuls, but the restrictions on American trade were not
renewed.

The relations between the Dutch and the Americans
became very friendly, and when the newly created Batavian
Republic hesitated to trust the annual Company ship to
Nagasaki under a flag which the British might not respect,
the *Eliza,* under the American flag, was chartered for the
voyage (1798).   For several years thereafter the American
flag appeared regularly in Japan each season, and when the
Department of State, in 1832, began to assemble information with a view to treaty relations with Japan, it was
mainly through Dutch sources and through Americans who,
in the employ of the Dutch, had been to Nagasaki, that the
information was secured.

Unlike the British in India, the Dutch discouraged
American trade with Java.   The import and export duties
for goods in foreign vessels was double what it was for the
Dutch.[10]   Provisions, however, such as were needed by the
Dutch garrison could be supplied cheaper by America than
by Holland, and this trade became of some value in the
days when it was of so much importance to collect abroad
as many Spanish dollars as possible for Canton.   Nine
tenths of the importation of salt provisions into Java in
1825 were made by the Americans.   Singapore, with its
freer trade regulations, became a rival to Batavia and the
American trade with the latter port declined sharply, being
in 1832 only a small fraction of what it was ten years
earlier.   In 1834 the principal articles taken out of Batavia

in American vessels were rice, sugar, pepper, coffee and quicksilver.

The chief importance of Java to the Americans was that the regular route to Canton was past Java Head and through the straits of Anjier and after the long voyage from the Cape, some place of refreshment as well as of communication was a necessity. John McClallam was United States commercial agent for Batavia in 1807.[11] Just before the establishment of the American embargo he was instructed to keep in touch with the ships passing from Canton and touching at Anjier Point, and to take proper measures for apprising them of the "crisis and for guarding them against the risks to which it might expose them." Similar instructions were sent to the consul at the Isle de France, but whether either of these consuls ever actually discharged any duties in their respective posts is not known. The first American officer to communicate with the State Department from Batavia wrote in 1818, acknowledging the receipt of his commission as "agent for the United States for commerce and seamen." The Nether lands Government did not recognize consular representatives in Java.

Manila, because of its geographical position, was an outpost of Canton for the trader whether he approached China by way of the Cape, the Horn, or the Northwest coast. Independent of the China trade, the Philippines were of slight importance to Americans. The exact date of the beginning of the trade is difficult to fix. The *Enterprise* (Captain Adam Babcock) left Boston in 1788 and was at the Isle de France in 1792. There the *America* was purchased and the two vessels went to Manila and purchased sugar for Ostend. They were captured in the Straits of Sunda by a squadron of British and Dutch ships and taken into Calcutta, though for what reason is not known.[12] This trade in sugar continued, and in 1819 the American consul reported trade also in indigo, coffee and cotton. There were 23 American vessels at Manila in 1819, more than in any two previous years.[13] There was only one

American resident in the city for the greater part of the time until 1825, when the consul could find no American to whom he could turn over the duties of his office while he visited the United States. The rice trade from Manila to Canton sprung up about this time, owing to the new port regulation at Canton which permitted a reduction of duty to "rice ships." [14] The Americans then made increasing use of Manila as an avenue by which the onerous port charges at Whampoa might be lightened. A trade in *beche de mer*, a sea slug much prized by the Chinese as an article of food, appeared about 1830. Four years later the consul reported that unbleached and colored goods of coarse texture, of American manufacture, had begun to come into Manila by way of China. In the last six months of 1835, 13,876 tons of American shipping arrived, the largest amount up to that date ever reported.

The policy of the Spanish Government placed no special obstacles in the way of the growth of American trade though the consul was not recognized. The first consul was appointed in 1817.

The only American firm of importance was that of Russell, Sturgis and Company, founded about 1825, and subsequently incorporated in the famous Russell and Company at Canton.

The Fur Trade

The route around the Horn and across the Pacific to China was selected by fur traders, by circuitous traders at South American ports, and occasionally by "out of season" vessels in the direct trade with Canton. The monsoon changed about the first of November in the China Sea, making difficult the direct approach to Canton from the South. Those vessels therefore which did not fall in with the course of the monsoons and the general tide of trade at Canton, and arrived in the winter, or departed in the summer, often chose to effect their approach to or departure from the coast of China by way of the Pacific route.

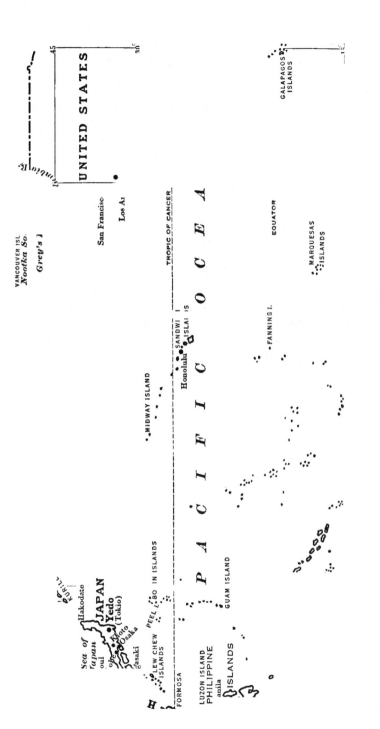

Sketch map showing Pacific Ocean ports visited by early American traders, the approach to the China coast from the Pacific and the geographical relationships which have determined the increasingly complicated political and economic problems of the Far East.

The value of ginseng as an article of exchange at Canton was quickly proven to have been over-estimated. The fur trade sprang up to take its place and to create for itself an even greater importance. As long as the supply of furs held out and the cost of collection was slight, they met ad mirably the pressing need of Americans for an article of barter.

The fur trade falls easily into three classifications: the furs which were brought from the interior—from the region of the Great Lakes and the Mississippi Valley—to the Atlantic ports and then shipped as part of the regular cargoes to Canton; the seal-skin trade with the Falkland Islands and the South Pacific; and the trade with the Northwest coast in both land and sea skins. With the continental trade through the Atlantic ports we are little concerned, for while the trade was extensive for thirty or forty years— until the European market for furs offered better prices—it exerted no important or distinctive influence upon Ameri can relations with the Far East.*

The seal-skin trade appears to have been begun inadvertently. About the time of the departure of the *Empress of China* from New York and the *Grand Turk* from Salem, "Lady" Haley of Boston sent her ship *States* to the Falkland Islands for sea-elephant oil and furs[15]. The *States* is reported to have been of the incredible size of about 1000 tons. This ship brought back 13,000 skins which were supposed to be those of sea-otter. The experimental character of the early trade with Asia is clearly revealed in the transactions which followed. The cargo of the *States* proved to be seal-skins for which there was no known certain market. They were sold for a trifling sum in New York and then placed on board the brig *Eleanora* (Captain Metcalf) which took them to the coast of India. Just why furs should be taken to such a market is not very apparent. Captain Metcalf sailed from New York probably about the same

*The American Fur Trade papers in the New York Historical Society and the University of Wisconsin libraries, as well as the testimony of the Americans in Canton, show clearly that in the thirties of the last century the continental, like the Pacific fur trade with China, had practically ceased.

time Captains Kendrick and Grey departed for the Northwest coast. The *Eleanora* lingered on the coast of India a
while and then brought its cargo to Canton where it found
a ready market in 1788. It was the first cargo of American
furs carried to Canton. The *Eleanora* then entered the
Northwest coast trade and was wrecked a few years later
at Macao.

The seal-skin trade developed rapidly. It was carried
on almost exclusively by the Americans in small vessels
with relatively small crews. The initial capital required
was merely the cost of the vessel and outfit. The crew
slaughtered the seals, skinned them and prepared the pelts
for market. When the cargo was obtained the vessel sailed
immediately for Canton either directly or by way of the
Sandwich Islands. While the trade lasted, that is, until the
seals were nearly extinct, it was probably the most profitable branch of the East India trade. It was, however, both
ruthless and reckless, and within a generation the seals had
become so scarce that it was no longer profitable.[16] This
trade quickly lured the Americans from the Falkland
Islands over into the South Pacific and by 1820 there were
relatively few good harbors in the Pacific south of the
Equator which had remained unvisited by American ships.
Over not a few of the Islands the American flag had been
raised,[17] or American sailors, shipwrecked, deserted or deserting, were playing the rôles of either monarch or adviser
to the natives, after traditional Anglo-Saxon fashion.

THE NORTHWEST COAST

The resources of the Northwest coast for the Canton
trade were first disclosed to the survivors of the last Captain Cook expedition. In 1778 Captain Cook had made
some surveys of the coast and had landed at Nootka Sound
where he acquired some furs from the Indians. Within ten
years after Captain Cook's visit to the Northwest coast no
less than seven states—Russia, England, Portugal, Spain,
France, Austria (Belgium) and the United States—were

represented in that region all, with the exception of the Austrians and Portuguese, setting up some sort of claim to sovereignty over the areas which were found to be so richly productive. In the face of such formidable prospective competition the Americans were especially favored by the handicaps placed upon their competitors. Only the English and Russian efforts to promote trade became earnest. The English efforts were encumbered by the monopoly of the East India Company. English vessels to the Northwest coast were allowed only by special permission of the Company, and were required to bring their cargoes back to China and exchange them, not for Chinese produce which could be taken to England and the Continent, but for specie which must be deposited with the East India Company. For this specie the Company would issue bills on London at twelve months, sight[18] The Americans, on the other hand, by barter at Canton were able to get about twenty per cent more for their pelts and were at the same time free to carry their cargoes wherever they pleased, dispose of their produce quickly, and by taking them to the Continent could make a second turnover before returning to the United States. The restrictions of the Company monopoly, therefore, practically eliminated the British traders from the competition. The Russian trade was under the handicap of being conducted far from its base of supplies, and the Russians were excluded from the Canton market, being confined to the overland trade with China. Thus the Americans were in a favored position which they were well able to utilize.

John Ledyard's missionary work, further enriched by the publication of Captain Cook's journals, and the reports of the trade at Canton, bore fruit in 1787 in the fitting out of the *Columbia* and the *Lady Washington* in Boston. Captain John Kendrick, master of the Columbia, was the commander of this famous expedition. The instructions to Kendrick were to send the sloop *Lady Washington* to Canton as soon as a cargo of furs had been obtained, while the *Columbia* was expected to remain on the coast. Kendrick

was particularly cautioned not to mistreat the Indians. His
wages were five pounds per month and a commission of
five per cent on the net proceeds of the voyage.[19]

The *Columbia* and her tender made a long voyage and
did not reach the coast until too late in 1788 to collect any
furs so they spent the winter at Nootka. The following
summer, provisions running short, Captain Kendrick transferred himself to the *Lady Washington* and sent the *Columbia* under the command of Captain Robert Grey to
China. While Kendrick remained on the coast Grey exchanged his furs at Canton and returned to Boston by way
of the Cape of Good Hope. The *Columbia* was so unfortunate as to arrive in Boston when prices were depressed
and the voyage did not achieve financial success. However,
Captain Grey was sent out the second time and in May,
1792, anchored in the harbor on the coast of Washington
which bears his name, and also discovered the mouth of
the Columbia River, thus making one of the primary claims
which were later urged by the Government of the United
States for the possession of Oregon.

Captain Kendrick appears to have been the man with
the imagination. He was so enamoured of the Northwest
coast that he began the purchase of land at Nootka Sound.
One tract, eighteen miles square, he purchased from
Tarasson, an Indian Chief, for "two muskets, a Boat's sail
and a quantity of Powder"; another tract at the head of
Nootka Sound, nine miles around, was bought for "two
muskets and a quantity of powder"; and still another tract
eighteen miles square cost four muskets, a large sail and
some powder.[20]

To some of Captain Kendrick's heirs who subsequently
sought to realize on these estates, John Howell, who had
been a clerk on the *Columbia,* wrote supplying some inter
esting details of the character of the man:

"I have had an opportunity of seeing most of Capt. Kendrick's
purchases on the N. W. coast of America and cannot flatter you with
any hopes of profit from them even to your great-great-great-grand-
children. They cost but little, it is true; and when the Millennium

shall arrive and all the nations of the earth shall be at peace your posterity may perhaps settle there. That Capt. Kendrick considered his title a good one I have sufficient proof of, when one day he told the Commandant at Nootka Sound that *he bought his* territories while other nations *stole* them; and that if they [the Spanish] were impertinent he would raise the Indians and drive them from their settlements. This, though a *bold,* was nevertheless a moderate project for a mind like his. Two of his favorite plans were to change the prevalence of the Easterly winds in the Atlantic Ocean and turn the Gulf Stream into .the Pacific by cutting a canal through Mexico. But with all his follies he was a wonderful man—and worthy to be remembered beyond the gliding hours of the present generation. He was stunned [*sic*] by his appointment to the *Columbia.* Empires and fortunes broke on his sight. The passing, two-penny objects of his expedition were swallowed up in the magnitude of his Gulliverian views. North East America was on the Lilliputian, but he designed N. W. America to be on the Brobdingnagian scale.''

An interesting illustration of the manner in which the trade with the Indians was conducted is preserved in the journal of Captain Joseph Ingraham of the *Hope* which reached the coast in 1791. To his great disappointment he found that the cloth and trinkets which he had brought out from Boston were not greatly desired by the Indians, previous traders having supplied their needs. Ingraham ingeniously met the situation by having his blacksmith set up his forge on deck and fashion iron collars, rings and bracelets which became extremely popular. For one iron collar he was able to obtain three skins which were worth about $75 at Canton. Ingraham reached Macao in November where several fur ships had already preceded him. Before the end of the year there were at least seven cargoes of furs placed on the market including a consignment from the Spanish Company at Manila and the *Lady Washington's* from Nootka.

Washington Irving, in his "Astoria," asserted that in the summer of 1792 there were twenty-one vessels on the Northwest coast, the greater part of which were American and owned by Boston merchants. Twenty-five years later Thomas H. Perkins of Boston, who had engaged in the trade very extensively, stated: "We formerly calculated that the collection of sea-otters purchased by the American ships annually was about 14,000 furs, the value of them in China may be averaged at twenty-five dollars each—making an aggregate of $350,000; the trade employed from six to ten ships from 200 to 300 tons." [21]   Perkins complained that the trade had already fallen off to less than a quarter of its former value, due to Russian competition. About the same time William Sturgis wrote that he had been on the coast in company with as many as sixteen American vessels. Such figures serve to show how very small this trade was even in its most prosperous days, but they also show, when studied in the light of the American exports from Canton which were paid for in furs that the trade was exceedingly profitable in proportion to the capital invested.

The fur trade was supplemented at an early date by partial cargoes of sandal-wood from the Sandwich Islands and other places in the Pacific, and by the trade in *beche de mer,* only a part of which passed through Manila.

The seal-skins brought to Canton from the South Pacific from 1805 to 1834 were reported as amounting to nearly 1,800,000, the valuation of which may be placed most conservatively at $3,500,000. Sea-otter pelts from the Northwest coast during the same period amounted to about 160,000, or at least $4,000,000. The value of the land skins shipped directly from Atlantic ports was probably less than either of these items. The value of the entire fur trade before 1805 can only be guessed at. The entire fur trade of the United States from all sources with Canton from its beginning until its end soon after 1830 may be placed at between $15,000,000 and $20,000,000.[22] The value of the trade when the bartered China products were transferred to Europe or the United States and sold would, of course, show a very great increase over the value in Canton. The value of the exports from the United States to the Northwest coast in the twenty-eight years from 1789 to 1817 averaged annually about $163,000. No known figures afford a sound basis for exact statements; all that can be said is that the trade was of the utmost value to the young nation at a time when vessels and crews were easily obtained and Spanish dollars were scarce.

Unlike the trade in the South Pacific, that with the Northwest coast left a permanent mark in the establish ment of a claim for Oregon Territory, in the settlement of Astoria in 1811, and also in the development of a port at Honolulu. A glance at the map shows that by 1832 Ameri cans had not only visited most of the Pacific Islands, but had actually established themselves for longer or shorter periods at no less than seven points: Sandwich Islands, 1787; Nootka Sound, 1788; Marquesas, 1791; Fanning, 1797; Fifi, 1800?; Galipagos, 1832; and Peel, 1832. Indeed, this list might be greatly expanded were one to count every point where Americans were known to have been. The significance of the list is, however, not in its length but in its shrinkage in the course of the next few decades, and in its lack of influence on the development of the United States. American interest gravitated into the North Pacific; whale fisheries took the place of the Northwest coast trade and sustained the development of an American settlement at Honolulu.

An American agent for commerce and seamen was appointed at Honolulu in 1820. American missionaries had already arrived. The Sandwich Islands was an object of lively interest to American trade and philanthropy. It was, however, until the American nation had crossed the continent, reached the Pacific Coast, and opened up trade with Japan, a lonely outpost.

BIBLIOGRAPHICAL NOTES

1. Milburn's "Oriental Commerce" (Ed. 1813).
2. Statutes at Large, 2:768
3. Calcutta Consular Letters.
4. "Maritime History of Massachusetts," by S. E. Morison (Boston and New York, 1921), p. 282.
5. 3. Dip. Cor., pp. 773, 766.
6. Misc. Letters (Dept. of State).
7. Edmund Roberts Papers (Dept. of State); Zanzibar, the Island Metropolis of Eastern Africa, by F. B. Pearce, pp. 133-4.
8. House of Commons Sessional Papers, 1821. Vol. 7.
9. "American Naval Vessels in the Orient," by Charles Oscar Paullin. (Proceedings of the U. S. Naval Institute, 1910).

THE PORTS OF ASIA AND THE PACIFIC 43

10. Batavia Consular Letters; Milburn's Oriental Commerce. (Ed. 1813).
11. Despatches to Consuls, Vol. 1, p. 297.
12. Calcutta Consular Letters.
13. Manila Consular Letters.
14. Parliamentary Papers, 1830. Vol. 5:122; the 'Fan Kwae' at Canton, by an Old Resident (W. C. Hunter) London, 1882. p. 100.
15. "Voyage of the *Neptune*," Diary of Mr. Ebenezer Townsend, Jr. (Papers of the New Haven Colony Historical Society, 1888. Vol. 14.)
16. "Voyages Round the World," by Edmund Fanning (New York, 1833) gives many details of this trade.
17. "American Relations in the Pacific and the Far East," by James Morton Callahan, in Johns Hopkins University Studies. Series XIX. Nos. 1-3. (1901.)
18. Sessional Papers, 1821. Vol. 7.
19. Correspondence concerning Captain Kendrick and the Settlement of his Estate. (Dept. of State.)
20. *Ibid.*
21. *Ibid.*
22. Fur trade statistics are to be found in a variety of sources: Pitkin's "Commerce of the United States" (Editions 1816, 1835); "Chinese Repository," April, 1835; Sessional Papers, 1821; *Hunt's Merchants Magazine,* Vol. 3 (1840).

CHAPTER III

EARLY CHINA TRADE

HAVING in mind the American vessels as they begin to converge upon the port of Canton from their various routes and with their varied cargoes, we may visualize the early trade at that port.

The *Empress of China* arrived at Macao August 23, 1784, and "saluted the town." [1] Having spent a few days in this historic Portuguese-Chinese port where the French and Swedish consuls extended to Major Shaw and Captain Green many courtesies, the *Empress* proceeded to Whampoa, twelve miles below Canton and anchored in the river where all the foreign ships were required to discharge and receive their cargoes. The Americans remained four months, setting sail from Whampoa December 28, 1784. A few weeks later the *Pallas*, a chartered ship already referred to, departed for New York with the second cargo under the care of Thomas Randall, Shaw's partner. The two vessels carried 880,100 pounds of tea.

The following table, which can be regarded as only approximately accurate since exactness was never a quality of the early Canton trade reports, is a fair index of the relative growth of the trade before the War of 1812. In comparing American with British ships and cargoes it must be borne in mind that the average tonnage of the American vessels was probably less than half that of the British, and the American cargoes of tea contained a larger proportion of the cheapest grades.

It will be noted from the table that the American trade was characterized by the most astonishing fluctuations both in the number of vessels visiting Canton and in the quantity of their outward cargoes. These fluctuations reveal the

44

AMERICAN, BRITISH, AND CONTINENTAL CLEARANCES AND EXPORTATIONS OF
TEA AT CANTON, SEASONS 1784–5 TO 1810–11 *

Season	Clearances			Export of Tea in lbs.		
	American	British	Continental	American	British	Continental
1784–5	2	14	16	880,100	10,583,628	16,551,000
1785–6	1	18	12	695,000	13,480,691	15,715,900
1786–7	5	27	9	1,181,860	20,610,919	10,165,160
1787–8	2	29	13	750,900	22,096,703	13,578,000
1788–9	4	27	11	1,188,800	20,141,745	9,875,900
1789–90	14	21	7	3,093,200	17,991,032	7,174,200
1790–1	3	25	7	743,100	22,369,620	2,291,560
1791–2	3	11	9	1,863,200	13,185,467	4,431,730
1792–3	6	16	13	1,538,400	16,005,414	7,864,800
1793–4	7	18	5	1,974.130	20,728,705	3,462,800
1794–5	7	21	7	1,438,270	23,733,810	4,138.930
1795–6	10	15	4	2,819,600	19,370,900	2,759,800
1796–7	13	23	3	3,450,400	36,904,200	2,515,460
1797–8	10	17	5	3,100,400	29,934,100	2,714,000
1798–9	13	16	6	5,674,000	16,795,400	4,319,300
1799–0	18	14	4	5,665,067	26,585,337	1,577,066
1800–1	23	19	7	4,762,866	29,772,400	3,968,207
1801–2	31	25	1	5,740,734	38,479,733	185,533
1802–3	20	38	12	2,612,436	35,058,400	5,812,266
1803–4	13	44	2	2,371,600	31,801,333	2,132,666
1804–5	31	38	3	8,546,800	28,506,667	3,318,799
1805–6	37	49	4	11,702,800	22,810,533	1,809,466
1806–7	27	58	2	8,464,133	32,683,066	1,534,267
1807–8	31	51	2	6,408,266	25,347,733	1,144,266
1808–9	6	54	–	1,082,400	26,335,446	none.
1809–10	29	40	–	9,737,066	26,301,066	none.
1810–11	12	34	—	2,884,400	27,163,066	none.

*Table rearranged from Melburn's Oriental Commerce, vol. 2, p. 486 (First
Ed.). These statistics, being based on seasons rather than upon years, and
being taken from Canton reports, cannot be made in every case to correspond
with such departures and returns from American ports as are available. They
are, however, the most complete set of figures known for this period.

experimental and speculative character of the beginnings
of the trade. In the season of 1789-90 fourteen vessels took
away from Canton more than three million pounds of tea.
Such heavy imports into the United States produced a
glutted market and the following year there were only three
vessels and the outward cargoes from Canton amounted to
only about one fourth of those of the previous year. The
recovery of the trade which immediately followed is to be
explained by the reexportations of tea from the United
States to Europe which followed the establishment of a

system of drawbacks in the American customs. During the remainder of the period the American trade at Canton was influenced immediately and directly by the extent to which it was possible for the Americans to engage in the European trade during the Napoleonic wars. Every variation of the political conditions in Europe and the American relation to them was directly registered in the amount of tea, per season, exported from Canton in American vessels. American policy in Canton was therefore primarily concerned with keeping open the supplies of tea and the avenues of trade.

With these facts in mind it is of primary interest to note the conditions under which the trade at Canton was being conducted.

MACAO, WHAMPOA AND CANTON

All foreigners in China were strictly confined to three localities; Macao, the old Portuguese leasehold under the simultaneous government of both the Portuguese and the Chinese; Whampoa, the anchorage in the Canton River, twelve miles below the city where foreign vessels were required to anchor and from which they were not permitted to depart until the issuance of the final 'grand chop' indicating that every requirement of the Chinese authorities had been complied with; and, the 'factories' or 'hongs' outside the city wall at Canton.

Macao had three functions in trade. It was the base from which the Portuguese conducted their commercial operations, and also the base for a large part of the smuggling operations in which all of the foreign merchants joined impartially. The city was an outpost of the Chinese Government where, exclusively, the permits to the foreign ships to go to Whampoa were issued. Every foreign vessel had to approach Canton through Macao. The third function of Macao was to afford a resort to the foreigners from Canton in the summer months, in times of illness, or whenever their conduct at Canton was obnoxious to the Chinese. Macao

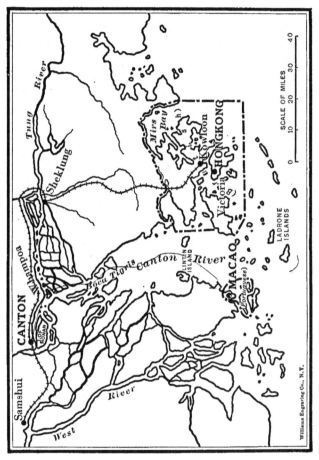

Sketch map showing approach to old Cant n, by way of Macao, the Boca Tiis and Whampoa.

was, for example, the refuge, though by no means the sole
residence, of the foreign missionaries.   Foreign women who
came to China were permitted to reside only at Macao.
The colony was governed by Portugal much in the same
way that Manila was governed by Spain, or as Batavia or
Calcutta, respectively, were governed except as modified
by the tenacious jurisdiction insisted upon by the Chinese
who had never relinquished their sovereignty.   During the
summer the foreigners from Canton sustained at Macao a
highly developed, ceremonious and luxuriant social life
dominated by the British and resembling the social life of
Calcutta and Madras.   In 1832 Edmund Roberts reported
that the city enjoyed the reputation of being [2] "one of the
most immoral places in the world"—a statement not supported by other testimony.   The Americans entered upon
this social life in proportion as their means and manners
allowed.   Until wealth crowned their labors their part in
it was small.

Whampoa was the second barrier to Canton.   The river
was not navigable to large vessels above the anchorage,
and the factories could not have accommodated either all
the foreign population or all the trade.   The sailors, of
whom there were at the height of the season from two to
three thousand, lived on the ships at Whampoa and visited
Canton only in small groups; they were, however, allowed
to go ashore at the anchorage where settlements had grown
up which doubtless merited the reputation which Roberts
assigned to Macao.   Provision was also made at Whampoa
for the repair and refitting of the foreign vessels. The lively
and varied scene at the anchorage never failed to impress
the foreigner on his first visit to China.   It was the subject
of numberless descriptions and not a few paintings.

The first stage of the commercial operations began at
Whampoa.   The vessel paid its port charges—which in the
case of the American vessels was usually about $4000—a
sum which fell heavily upon the smaller craft for the payments were not graduated to vessels below 400 tons.   A
linguist and a comprador, if not already obtained at Macao,

must be taken at Whampoa. The hong merchant who was to transact the business of the vessel at Canton was also secured. He immediately had the cargo transferred to smaller craft and taken to Canton where it was sold or bartered for the return cargo. The hong merchant paid all the inward and outward duties. The master of the vessel was thus relieved of all responsibility except the care of his ship and the control of his crew, and the super-cargo had only to follow his goods to Canton, indicate his choices of commodities for the return voyage and then watch carefully that he did not get cheated. Trading with China thus became the simplest of transactions in which the comfort of the trader was disturbed only by the thought that it was quite impossible for him to know the extent to which his payments for government dues and services rendered were extortions unwarranted by law or evaded by his competitor.

The factories were long narrow buildings of two or three stories in height and extending back towards the city wall. Goods were landed at small docks and carried across a park or parade ground to the front of the factories which were divided into sections perpendicularly with storage rooms, offices on the lower floor and living quarters above for the commission agents, supercargoes and guests. Factory and residence space was rented from the merchants who owned the hong. Every foreigner coming to Canton had to be guaranteed by some one of the hong merchants, usually the one who transacted the business of the voyage. Foreigners were not permitted to enter the city nor were they allowed to leave the factory grounds either by land or water except under very limited conditions. They could not walk in the country; they were, theoretically, denied the use of boats; but on occasion, with a suitable Chinese guide and pro-tector, they might visit the flower-gardens at Fati on the other side of the River. The foreigners were, in fact, vol-untary prisoners.

By the Chinese Government the trade was limited to the hong merchants, usually about a dozen in number, who paid highly for their privilege and in turn became surety for the good conduct of the foreigners. These merchants were organized into a 'co-hong' for concerted action in fixing prices, for mutual protection, and for the management of the trade. Some of the hong merchants became very wealthy; others experienced frequent financial reverses due either to the enmity of the government officials who levied tribute or to their own native instinct for speculation and gambling.

Back of the co-hong stood the provincial officials, the chief of whom was the Viceroy, representing the Emperor. Each official had purchased his way to the position he occupied and then recouped himself from the trade. The Imperial Government had only two concerns: that an ever increasing amount of revenue be forwarded to Peking; and, that the foreigner be so 'soothed' and controlled so that foreign nations would have no opportunity of acquiring any foothold in the Empire, or of advancing a mile further in the direction of the capital. The obligation resting upon the provincial government therefore was to keep Peking satisfied and at the same time to levy from the trade as much tribute as it would bear. The powers of the Viceroy were very broad. His method of governing the foreigner was through the co-hong. He could make or break the Chinese merchant, fining, removing, even banishing him. The foreigner, in turn, as already indicated, was absolutely in the hands of the hong merchant from the day his vessel came to anchor at Whampoa until he had his return cargo on board. From the point of view of the Chinese Government the system was nearly nigh perfect. The Government in no way officially recognized the presence of the foreigner and admitted him to no direct intercourse, and yet the Government controlled the trader as only despots can. The ruination of the hong merchant involved the ruination of the foreigner to whom the hong was always in debt until the return cargo was safely on board at Whampoa. The foreigner had little choice but to submit.

There was, on the other hand, a recognition of the fact

that injustice to the foreigner and encroachments upon such of his rights as he had not voluntarily surrendered, would lead to irritation and trouble. The key-note therefore of the relationship between the Chinese and the foreigners was accommodation. This word occurs with great frequency in the literature of the time. It became of obvious advantage to everyone concerned that all relationships be managed in such a way as to insure harmony, which is another favorite Chinese word.

The last resorts of the Imperial officials for the enforcement of their will upon the foreigners were to stop the trade and then, if necessary, to cut off communications with Whampoa and Macao, thus effecting the complete imprisonment of the traders. Since the government recognized no distinction between nations and might visit the sins of one merchant upon the entire body of traders by stopping the trade, a certain solidarity of public opinion developed which imposed upon each individual trader the obligation to accept the decisions of the majority.

Conditions of American Trade

Solidarity of interest transcending national lines was, however, modified by certain stern facts. When a British vessel came to Whampoa, although compelled to submit to the uniform port and trade regulations, it came under the shadow of the East India Company—a very powerful organization. Until the dissolution of the Company monopoly in 1834 the British merchant came to Canton only by leave of the Company and remained only so long as he acted in conformity with Company discipline. While these regulations and restraints operated greatly to restrict liberties both personal and commercial, and handicapped the British merchants in competition with Americans, they also bound them together with the protection of a mighty commercial organization at their back. And back of the Company was the British Government which was vitally interested in its success. The Company, in a variety of ways, could bring pressure to bear upon the Chinese and if a trial of strength became necessary, the East India Company with its resources and reserves was in a far better position than the individual American merchant, to meet a strike with a boycott. The Chinese Government professed entire indifference as to whether the trade continued or not, but the foreign trade of China, by the time the American arrived, was so much a part of the economic fabric of many parts of the Empire that the Government would have found the expulsion of the foreign trader very difficult. The East India Company dominated the foreign colony at Canton. It could not, however, count upon such support from the Americans as the British residents were compelled to give. The individual American traders, far more than their British competitors, required that the harmonious relations of the trade be continued from day to day. Disturbances meant relatively greater losses to Americans for their reserves were less, and long continued disturbance of the trade would mean ruin.

This condition was somewhat modified as the Americans came to build up strong and well capitalized commission houses and mercantile establishments, and as the trade came into the hands of a few wealthy firms, but it was modified only in degree. The Americans could not afford to be very self-assertive or to meet the arrogance of the Chinese with arrogance of their own. This peculiar situation of the Americans controlled their conduct, and made them, unlike so many of their brother pioneers on the continental frontiers of America, a peculiarly peace-seeking folk.

Furthermore, the Americans immediately upon their entrance into the China trade, became very deeply involved in credit transaction with the hong merchants. The Chinese were easily able to bring to Canton a larger stock of tea than the foreigners, all of whom suffered from the lack of a suitable and adequate medium of exchange, could take away. Notwithstanding the stringent prohibitions of the government the hong merchants disposed of large amounts of their surplus goods to the Americans on credit. True, this surplus was usually what was left after the Company had made its selection, and was inferior, but neither the Americans or the Continentals who consumed the tea were such connoisseurs of tea as were the British, and, besides, the Americans could sell cheaply. These credit accounts which were entirely dependent upon the good will of the Chinese, were an additional incentive to peace.

The Americans came to occupy a middle position in both the trade and politics of Canton. On the one hand were their British brethren with whom their interest in the continuance of the trade with the minimum of exaction and interference was identical, and on the other hand were the Chinese merchants whose good will and prosperity were matters of the utmost concern to the Americans. Throughout the pre-treaty days in China these three groups—English, American and Chinese—constituted the only important elements in the situation. The representatives of other foreign nations, now less, now more in number, counted for little. In every issue between the foreigner and the Chinese the important question was whether the Americans would find it most to their profit to stand with the English or with the Chinese. Indeed, this alignment continued long after the signing of the foreign treaties, and underlay American political as well as trade policy for a century. Sometimes the Americans stood with the British for concerted action, but when the concerted action proposed by the British would have a tendency to weaken the Chinese merchants, or when the British adopted policies directly inimical to the American trade, the Americans were disposed to support the Chinese. In the face of British arrogance and aggression the Chinese and Americans were allies.

THE AMERICANS AND THE BRITISH

As may have already been inferred, the relation of the Americans to the Chinese at Canton was only half the problem. There was also the relation of the Americans to the representatives of the other nations. The international relations of the Chinese Empire were often second in importance to the international relations of the foreigners *in* China.

The *Empress of China* arrived at Canton at a time when the Continental European trade was on the wane. Portugal retained a shadow of her former greatness at Macao, and Spain, dwelling indolently at Manila, carried on some trade with China by way of the Pacific and South America, but neither of these nations was aggressive at Canton. The "Imperialists," i.e., the Germans, still retained a company but it was in charge of a Scotchman who was daily expecting instructions to close out the business. French trade also was in a precarious situation. There was no French company at Canton although a consul remained, and the trade was being carried on by private merchants and the personal assistance of the king. Sweden and Denmark were represented only by a few private traders who derived no small part of their profit by smuggling tea into England.

During the seasons from 1784 to 1790 the total number of foreign vessels at Canton was: Portuguese, about 14; Spanish, 8; Imperialists, 0; Swedish, 9; Danish, 12; French, 10. In the same period the Dutch had 28; the English, 106 Company and 97 'country' ships; and the Americans had 28.

Major Shaw reported that the Netherlands, operating from Batavia as a base through the Dutch East India Company, was, next to England, in the best commercial position at Canton. But the Netherlands trade labored under the handicap of a Company monopoly and was soon to fall foul of the Napoleonic wars. It was never an important factor in China after the Americans appeared and within a few years, until the restoration of peace in Europe, the Americans inherited practically all of it.

To Great Britain the British East India Company establishment at Canton was the outpost of a commercial empire which had been steadily advancing across Asia and into the Pacific since the Seven Years' War when France had been practically eliminated from India. To China England was bringing the accumulated experience of several decades in dealing with Oriental trade and politics, and the advantages of a 'half-way' station in India to which the English in China could appeal thus avoiding the delay incident to communication with London. Major Shaw recorded in his journal the opinion formed on the spot that Great Britain apparently had the intention of monopolizing the trade of China. The Americans feared that the Lord Macartney Embassy to Peking (1793) had for its secret object the securing of some monopolistic or exclusive trade advantages from the Chinese. As early as 1816, when the Lord Amherst Mission to Peking was being projected it was common talk among the Americans at Canton that ultimately the English would "take possession of some place and make an establishment to suit their own purposes in spite of the Chinese" [3]—an expectation which was realized twenty-five years later in the occupation of Hongkong.

The Americans appeared at Canton lacking almost every advantage which had belonged to the nations already established in the trade. Between the Atlantic seaboard and China by way of the Indian Ocean there was hardly a single safe port of refuge or of refreshment where the Americans might let down an anchor without permission of Great Britain or of some European power. Furthermore, while the other traders in case of difficulty might fall back on supplies and support relatively near at hand, at Macao, Manila, Batavia, or India, there was between the Americans at Canton and their sole base of supplies a voyage of at least three and perhaps six months. In addition to these handicaps was the inexperience and the lack of capital which characterized the initial adventures.

The Americans needed friends; they could not afford to have any enemies. At Canton they inherited the friendly interest of those European powers which had looked with favor upon the American War of the Revolution. The *Empress of China* was introduced to Macao and Canton by French traders,[4] some of whom had fought under Ad-

miral Grasse in Chesapeake Bay, and the Dutch were
equally friendly. The officials of the British East India
Company were also personally very cordial to Major Shaw
on his first visit, but subsequently qualified their friendliness upon orders from the Company. "It is true," wrote
Shaw, "that the Court of Directors in their instructions to
the supercargoes the present season, have enjoined it upon
them to use every endeavor to prevent the subjects of
Great Britain from assisting or encouraging in any shape
the American commerce." This was to the Americans a
very serious matter as the Tory, Phineas Bond, fully realized when he wrote to Lord Carmarthen from America in
December, 1787: "A very little matter by way of check
would unhinge the trade and completely damage all the
plans of those engaged in it." [5] So long as the Americans
had reason to fear the English as something more than
commercial competitors in a perfectly free field, that is,
until after the close of the War of 1812, there was little
friendliness between the Americans and the English in
China. However, policy and wisdom required the use of
forbearance. As Ebenezer Townsend wrote, apologetically,
upon his arrival at Macao in 1798, after he had made his
ceremonial call upon the commodore of the English ships
at Typa: [6] "I suppose we were under no obligation to call
on the Englishmen, but it is the practice."

The Americans, notwithstanding the embarrassments
due to the previous political activities of the European
powers in the East and the growing jealousy of the British,
had certain advantages in their youth, their small, less
costly and more easily managed vessels, their freedom from
all suspicion as plotters against the Chinese Empire, and
their position of political neutrals in the European conflicts.
'In the ten years from the season of 1788-9 the amount of
tea exported from Canton in other than British and American vessels declined from eleven to one and one-half million
pounds. The European trader practically disappeared.
Meanwhile the American trade from Canton direct to Europe and indirectly through America mounted apace. In

1803 more than half of the tea imported to America was reexported to Europe.[7]

The character of the American trade in the period just preceding the War of 1812 may be illustrated from the claims submitted by a New York firm against the Danish Government in consequence of the capture of some American vessels by Danish privateers about 1810. The claim for one vessel was listed as follows:[8]

Value of ship in Spanish dollars............		$25,000.00
Goods shipped in Canton belonging to Minturn and Champlin		9,851.07
Cotton shipped at New York for Gothenburg	$4,038.46	
Freight of same: 24,706 @ 6c..............	1,482.36	
Insurance on 4,038 @ 10%.................	403.80	5,924.62
Amount of freight of tea on board belonging to Chinese merchants at Canton, as per freight list and agreement, which would have become due had the ship arrived at Gothenburg		38,309.87
Demurrage $80 per day		33,280.00
Court charges, etc.		5,000.00
		$117,365.56
Capt. Eldridge's Adventure—		
Invoice cost at Canton	$3,270.92	
Insurance @ 6%	196.26	
Insurance—New York to Gothenburg @ 12½%	408.87	
Freight—Canton to N. Y. and Gothenburg	1,050.00	
Interest on same for 2 years @ 6%.	490.50	5,416.55
Trimmage on goods belonging to Chinese @ 5%		1,915.40
		$124,697.61

In the items of the claim by the same company for another ship which had been similarly captured we find:

"Amount of the cost of tea belonging to Houqua as per invoice	$58,005.00
Premium of insurance of same to N. Y. @ 10%	6,455.00
Interest on cost of same in Canton @ 15%	8,700.75
Commission in New York, 5%..............	3,222.50
	$76,373.25

In the same cargo with Houqua's consignment was one from Consequa, another hong merchant, for $32,009.

From the above exhibit, which appears not to have been exceptional, we note the extent to which the Chinese merchants were trading with Europe by way of America, and also have some insight into the relation of the American merchants to both the Oriental and the Continental trade. The cargo of the ship *Nimrod*, landed in 1811 and sold in Copenhagen about September, 1814, consisted of sugar, coffee, almonds, cream of tartar, blue and yellow nankeens, nutmegs, cloves, mace, cassia and nankeens. Out of the same cargo casks of rice and Buenos Aires hides were sold at Kiel. In short the Americans were collecting from China, the Indian and the Pacific Ocean, and from South America, assortments of commodities and then sending them to Europe by transshipment from Atlantic ports, and were levying toll in the form of profit, commissions and freight, at every stage of the journey. These claims also reveal how precarious were the conditions under which the trade was being conducted. The firm submitting the claims had become practically insolvent because of the capture of their vessels by Danish privateers.

The Human Element in the Trade

The human element in the early American relations with China was so very important that it is worth while to seek a clear understanding of it both on the Chinese and on the American side.

The Chinese official was uniformly and habitually dishonest. The first American ship to come to anchor at Whampoa was met with demands for "sing-songs" for the hoppo, that is, for presents to the customs officer; no vessel was ever free from such demands until the inspectorate of maritime customs under foreign supervision was extended to all the ports after the treaties of 1858. Chinese and foreigners alike, therefore, lived in an atmosphere which reeked with bribery, and in which within certain broad

limits, law went to the highest bidder. The American
merchant had merely to charge up these items as a part
of the cost of doing business. These charges were so
manipulated that it was often difficult to divide with certainty what went to the officials and what was retained by
the hong merchant who in graft as well as in trade became
the intermediary. Nor is it easy to assert with confidence
where the fines imposed by the mandarins were merely
exactions and where they were justified. For example, the
owner of the ship *Lion* of New York, was charged $2000
in 1816 for a fine "imposed by the Hoppo for suspicion of
smuggling on board ship" which Kinqua, the hong merchant, advised the agent to pay without complaint.[9] In
general, it would appear that, after all port charges and
regular duties had been settled, the merchants according
to established custom, paid additional charges for the
privileges of smuggling.

It would be surprising to find in an atmosphere of so
much dishonesty that the standard of commercial integrity
was high. Opinions differed widely as to the righteousness
of the commercial codes at Canton. Major Shaw, himself
a man of the highest character, pronounced the commercial
standards of the hong merchants as good as those anywhere,
not overlooking the fact that the hong merchants were the
better for being carefully watched. Shaw's partner, Thomas
Randall, complained bitterly [10] of the dishonesty of the
Chinese and, indeed, complaints were very common. In
the instructions to a supercargo in 1815 we read that
"Consequa is a liberal Chinese, but involved in debt. Bab-
oon you must not have anything to do with." And the
supercargo when making his report the following year remarked: "It is unfortunately the case here that there is
no man to be relied upon but Houqua and he has too much
business." Houqua, it was asserted, charged more but he
was reliable both as to time and as to quality. Indeed,
Houqua's character was so well known in America that
teas bearing his chop sold at superior prices.[11]

As for the character of the Americans, again accounts

differ. Probably no generalization for more than a very
brief number of years could safely be made. In the track
of Shaw and Randall came a few adventurers, some by way
of India, some from the Northwest coast, who were not to
be trusted. As late as 1815 it as asserted that only Perkins
and Company, whose agent was the young John P. Cushing,
and Philip Ammidon were reliable. As typical of the
unique position of confidence which Cushing had already
attained not only among the Americans but also among
the Chinese we may cite a contract between an American
supercargo and a hong merchant in which the latter agreed
to sell "500 chests of new Hyson tea to be put on board
ship *Lion* at Whampoa at my risk and expense within two
months from this time, said Law to pay me the market
price. . . . If the quality and price cannot be agreed between said Law and myself . . . Mr. J. P. Cushing's opin
ion shall be binding." [12]

In the estimation of the British merchants the commer
cial character of the Americans was low [13] but this estimate
comes from men who were feeling acutely the increasing
competition of the American trade. With the establishment of regular commission houses at Canton whose commercial relations were continuous from year to year, the
quality of the Americans appears to have steadily improved
until the adventurer without reputation to maintain or
character to lose was all but eliminated.

The character of the trade, the conditions at once des
potic and yet lawless, demanded the general acceptance of
a conventional code—it would not have passed for scrupulous honesty outside of Asia—which would regulate contacts and prevent conflicts. If it be admitted that neither
foreigner nor hong merchant was more honest than ex
pediency demanded, it must be remembered that at least
a moderate degree of honesty in every community is essen
tial to the maintenance of peace, and peace was of the
utmost importance to Chinese and foreigner alike. A
disturbance of the peace was the cardinal sin for it meant
a diminution of profits.

The personal relations of the Chinese and Americans came to be those of mutual respect and even, in many cases, of affection.[14] The Americans were, for the most part, Yankees who had been reared in the ignorance of a color question, and who came to China directly and not, as the other foreigners, through India and Malaya, where the foreigner had asserted a color supremacy and the native had accepted it. The Chinese are by nature wholly unlike the Malay or the natives of India, in that they demand by their personal dignity and willingness to resort to methods of non-intercourse, the respect of those who deal with them. The Americans were willing from the outset to grant this respect; the other foreigners were not. The Americans were thus again left in a preferred position in the regard of the Chinese and at a time when personal relationship counted for so much. They were able to capitalize this good will and make it yield dividends.

So long as the American merchant in China met his foreign competitor unaccompanied by the strong arm of a European government, the American held the advantageous position. The moment the foreign government intervened the American was placed under a handicap, for while personal relations counted with the Chinese in times of peace, in the face of the threat of force, the Chinese with rare exceptions yielded to his threatener. Perhaps it is not too much to conclude that American interests in China were never again in such good shape as they were between 1825 and 1840 when all the foreign merchants were compelled to compete with each other in seeking peace and good will, while the Chinese Government held the whip hand over them. To be sure the Americans, as the others, were compelled to submit to a certain amount of injustice, but the injustice which the Americans suffered from the Chinese in the days of the early trade was as nothing to the injustice which the Americans suffered later when their competitors brought to China their armies and their navies to support their often arrogant and unjust pretensions. American trade in China owes something of its liberties to the force of British, French, Russian, German and Japanese arms, but when the balance is struck it is found that in the aggressions of other powers upon China the Americans have lost far more than they have received.

MAJOR SAMUEL SHAW

One item only remains to be treated in reviewing the position of the early American trader at Canton—the relation of the American Government to its citizens in China.

The China trade of the United States at the outset was recognized as valuable, was heavily protected and practically subsidized. This system did not disappear until 1832 when duties on tea were removed. But to the East India merchant who lived in the East the Government of the United States could offer no protection or assistance. Upon his return from his first voyage Major Shaw made a report of the conditions at Canton and the prospects for American trade to John Jay, "the Honorable, the Minister of the United States for Foreign Affairs" of the Continental Congress. Acting upon the recommendation of Jay the Congress "elected" Shaw to the position of consul "at Canton in China." The election was, however, more of a tribute to Major Shaw, personally, than an effort to promote the trade. Shaw had a distinguished record in the Revolution. "Although neither salary nor perquisites are annexed to it," [15] wrote Jay to Shaw, "yet so distinguished a mark of confidence and esteem of the United States will naturally give you a degree of weight and respectability which the highest personal merit cannot very soon obtain for a stranger in a foreign land."

Major Shaw regarded the appointment conscientiously as an opportunity to render a public service and made two subsequent extensive reports as consul in which he freely placed his knowledge of the trade at the disposal of any interested fellow citizen.[16] By President Washington Shaw was reappointed and he continued to serve until his death in 1794. Thomas Randall, Shaw's partner and vice-counsel, also made an elaborate report to Alexander Hamilton,[17] with special reference to the use of specie in the trade.

The next consul was Samuel Snow of Providence who, like Shaw, had first gone to Canton as a supercargo [18] and then returned to establish a commission agency. Snow arrived in China toward the end of 1799 [19] and remained about four years, becoming the first really resident consul. He did not interpret his duties so broadly as Shaw had done, confining himself, largely, to the care of distressed seamen and semi-annual reports of the vessels and cargoes that entered and cleared. Snow left Canton at the end of 1804, turning over the duties of his office to Edward Carrington of Providence who succeeded to the position of consul in 1806. Carrington served for about two years after which the office was vacant until 1814. The post was, however, considered of some importance, for in 1811 George E. Coles wrote to Mrs. Dolly Madison: "Dear Cousin: . . . While I was in Philadelphia some of the friends of B. C. Wilcocks, with whom I became slightly acquainted, requested me to recommend him as a fit person to be made consul for Canton in China." [20] Wilcocks received the appointment just before the close of the War of 1812 and served for about seven years. Throughout this period and, indeed, until 1854, the consul was merely a merchant whose only compensation was the fees of the office, the dignity of the position, and such information as to the business transactions of his competitors as would become available to him because of his access to official reports.

No provision whatever was made to obtain for the consulate the services of an interpreter. Indeed, the American trade at Canton was conducted for more than forty-five years before there was even one American citizen there who could read, write, understand or speak Chinese with any certainty. So keenly did Wilcocks feel this deficiency of the Americans at Canton, as well as their need for a resident physician, that in 1818 he offered, at his own expense, to educate a suitable young man to become an interpreter for the consulate.[21] He proposed to pay his expenses at the Anglo-Chinese school at Malacca which the missionary William Milne had established, and suggested that a young physician would be the most useful. Permission thus to make use of this school had been secured through Dr. Robert Morrison, whose missionary career in China had been begun at the American consulate under Edward Carrington.

The American share in the inauguration of Dr. Morrison's famous missionary labors is worthy of note as supplying another indication of the difference between the attitude of the British and the Americans towards the Chinese. Dr. Morrison had been refused permission to take passage from London for China in an East India Company ship and therefore came to the United States in 1807. From New York, May 12, 1807, Morrison sailed for China, carrying a letter from Secretary of State Madison to Consul Carrington "requesting him to do all that he can, consistently with the interests of his country" [22] to assist the missionary. For several months after his arrival in China Morrison lived in the factory of Mr. Carrington and was known as an American because he did not dare to acknowledge his British citizenship. The British had brought from India a policy which involved the withholding from the Chinese such benefits of the western world as would enable them to meet the foreigners on equal terms. The Americans, from the earlier days, never shared in such a policy.

BIBLIOGRAPHICAL NOTES

1. Shaw's Journal is incomparably the best contemporary American source for the beginnings of American trade in China.
2. "Embassy to the Eastern Courts of Cochin-China, Siam, and Muscat," by Edmund Roberts (New York, 1837), p. 165.
3. William Law Papers (New York Pub. Lib. Mss.) Letter written by Law to N. Y. correspondents, Nov. 21, 1816.
4. 3 Dip. Cor. pp. 767-8, Sept. 1, 1785, John Jay to Continental Congress, recommending that Jefferson at Paris be instructed to express the appreciation of the American Government for the courtesies shown to Major Shaw at Canton. For the interesting subsequent correspondence which took place in Paris, see Américanistes et Français à Canton au XVIIIᵉ Siècle, by

Henri Cordier, in *Journal de la Société des Américanistes de Paris* (Paris, 1898). M. de Vergennes, Minister of Foreign Affairs, seized the opportunity thus afforded to protest against the protective measures inimical to French commerce which had been adopted by various American states.

5. Letters of Phineas Bond.
6. Voyage of the *Neptune*.
7. Pitkin's "Commerce of the U. S." (1816).
8. William Law Papers.
9. *Ibid.*
10. Alexander Hamilton Papers, Vol. 12, pp. 1551ff; Aug. 14, 1791, Randall to Hamilton (Lib. of Congress).
11. William Law Papers.
12. *Ibid.*
13. See, for example, Majoribank's testimony, Sessional Papers, 1821, Vol. 7.
14. Hunter's "Fan Kwae" embodies the prevailing spirit of the Americans towards the Chinese.
15. 3 Dip. Cor. p. 769, Jan. 30, 1786, Jay to Shaw.
16. Appendices, Shaw's Journal.
17. Alexander Hamilton Papers (see *supra,* Note 10.).
18. Kimball's East India Trade of Providence.
19. Canton Consular Letters.
20. Madison Papers, June 10, 1811, George E. Coles to Mrs. D. P. Madison (N. Y. Pub. Lib.).
21. Misc. Letters (Dept. of State) July 4, 1818, C. J. Ingersoll to J. Q. Adams.
22. "Memoirs of the Life and Labors of Robert Morrison" (2 vols. London 1849), Vol. 1, p. 106ff.

F.	Lacey	6'6
F	Washington	6'3"
C	Erickson	6'5"
G.	Goodrich	6' "
G	Goss	6'2"

F	Lacey	6'6"
F.	Erickson	6'5"
C	MacIntosh	6'6"
G	Goodrich	6' "
G	Goss	6'2"

PART II

THE FIRST TREATY WITH CHINA

CHAPTER IV

THE FOUNDATION OF AMERICAN POLICY IN ASIA

THE early American policy in Asia, meaning merely the policy of early Americans for there was no other policy, was purely negative in its origins. It appeared only when there was opposition or obstruction to the trade. Where trade was free there was no policy. Where there was a policy its weight was in direct ratio to the desire of the Americans for the trade.

There never was an American political policy in the Indian Ocean. The trade was either free or was open to Americans on equal or on more favorable terms than those enjoyed by their competitors. England took possession of the Isle de France in 1810. The War of 1812 destroyed the trade with British India, and the tariff of 1816 put a curb on its reestablishment. Economic necessity—the general poverty of the States and the need for Indian produce—had forced the Americans into the Indian Ocean trade, and the steady growth of wealth and industry in the United States reduced the necessity for such adventures. The profits which at the beginning had been steadier and more certain than those in the China trade, declined and suffered in the competition with British produce. The United States had little produce to send to India and as for specie, it yielded a better return at Canton. Furthermore, the China trade had the advantage of the protection and assistance of the Government of the United States. The term 'East India trade' came more and more to mean the Canton trade.

Because there had been opposition and obstruction to the American trade in the Pacific Ocean there had been a policy in those regions. However, it was the purely negative one of keeping the trade routes and the markets open. The Americans declined to be excluded from the Northwest coast and would have opposed any curtailment of their rights at Honolulu had any measures of obstruction been adopted. But the fur trade ceased to be a factor in the Far Eastern trade after 1820. The whale fisheries entered the North Pacific but they did not immediately create a new link in the chain of commerce with Asia. By the fur trade Americans had been taught to look upon the Pacific Ocean and the Sandwich Islands in relation to the Asiatic trade [1] but it was not until the settlement of the Pacific Coast of the United States, the development of Shanghai and the opening of Japan, that American policy in Asia came again to include the Pacific Ocean. Meanwhile American policy in the Far East merely meant the policy of the Americans at Canton.

The Americans at Canton had but one desire—to keep the trade open to Americans on terms as favorable as, or more favorable than, those enjoyed by their competitors who were chiefly British. A brief review of the trade from the close of the War of 1812 until the outbreak of hostilities between the British and the Chinese in 1839 is therefore in order.

REVIEW OF TRADE: 1815-1839

The period is characterized by three facts: the consolidation of commerce in the hands of a very few wealthy firms and commission houses; the establishment of a system of exchange by which bills on London were substituted for specie; and the introduction of manufactured goods, first British and then American, which altered the relations of the Americans to the China trade and made them begin to regard China as a limitless market in which to sell rather than as a limited market in which to buy.

The earliest American trade at Canton had been conducted by supercargoes who travelled with the vessels. The next step in commercial organization was the establishment of permanent firms which either dealt on commission or represented directly some mercantile house the headquarters of which was in the United States. Shaw and Randall beginning as supercargoes, established a firm to engage in commission business, as well as in the transaction of their personal ventures. The *Columbia* and the *Lady Washington* when setting out for the Northwest coast were consigned to Shaw and Randall. This firm, however, was soon dissolved because of the death of Shaw, and seems never to have thoroughly established itself. Samuel Snow of Providence who succeded Shaw as consul established himself in Canton about 1800 as a resident commission agent, presumably giving special attention to the requirements of the Providence merchants. He, also, had begun as a supercargo on the *Ann and Hope* of Providence in 1795. Thomas H. Perkins and Company of Boston established a branch in 1803, in charge of John P. Cushing, a youth of sixteen. This firm, while primarily transacting the Perkins business, also engaged in a commission trade. B. C. Wilcocks of Philadelphia became a resident commission agent and in time became the third American consul. Daniel Stansbury of Baltimore became agent for the New York firm of Minturn and Champlin. Nicholas G. Ogden and Cornelius Sowle represented John Jacob Astor. Philip Ammidon with Providence connections, and Samuel Russell of Middletown, Connecticut, who had begun commercial life as a supercargo out of Providence appeared as residents at Canton. Thus the commercial life of the American community developed.

Gradually the supercargo disappeared from the American vessels and his work was done by the resident commission agent. One hears very little of supercargoes after 1815. Following the close of the War of 1812 further organization and differentiation of the trade took place. The firm of Samuel Russell and Company, of which the partners were Russell and Ammidon, Edward Carrington, Cyrus Butler, and B. and T. C. Hoppin of Providence, was formed in December, 1818, the two first named being designated to represent the firm in Canton for five years.[2] At the end of this period the firm was reorganized under the name of Russell and Company, with the approval and help of the house of Perkins, which retired from Canton three years later. The Russell house was further consolidated by the incorporation of some smaller firms and came to occupy a financial position in China comparable with that of the famous British firms. For many years it handled only a commission business although many of the partners acting as individuals, were also merchants. Olyphant and Company at Canton was organized in 1828 out of the ruins of the firm of Thomas H. Smith by D. W. C. Olyphant who had served an apprenticeship in New York, Baltimore, and then in Canton as the supercargo and agent of Smith.[3] This firm came to occupy a position second only to that of Russell and Company, until Augustine Heard, leaving the Russell firm, established the house which long bore his name. The only other important firm was that of W. S. Wetmore. It is' significant that out of the much larger number of American merchants who came to and departed from Canton, only these firms, Russell, Olyphant, Heard and Wetmore, survived the competition of decades. Some, like John C. Cushing, retired with wealth; others failed grandly and. left only pitiful derelicts.

The effect of this consolidation of American interests was to stabilize business, and to increase the influence of the surviving merchants in their dealings with both the Chinese and with the other foreigners.

The establishment of a system of exchange, by which bills on London were substituted for specie, came before 1830 as a result of the increased commercial relationship between the United States and England, and the growth of the opium trade.

A part of the American trade with China was financed from London even before 1800. Shortly after 1815 American merchants began to buy British manufactured goods, chiefly cottons, in the English market, and to take them to China where they were able to sell them cheaper than the East India Company.[4] Agents of the Company complained that the American goods were not only of inferior quality, even those which had been rejected by the Company in London, but that the Americans even went so far as to adopt a 'chop' (trade-mark) so closely representing that of the Company as to deceive the purchaser. These charges could hardly be controverted. The effect of this trade in British manufactured goods was to make London a clearing house for a considerable amount of European and China trade which had formerly been settled either in Canton or Europe by payments of specie. Meanwhile the opium trade from India to China increased to the point where China was consuming more foreign produce than the value of the tea, silks, etc., which the foreigner was taking out of China. China settled the balance against her in silver. The Empire had become, by means of opium, a buying more than a selling nation. More and more the Americans came to Canton not with specie but with bills on London which they disposed of in return for their outward cargoes. In other words, by taking out Chinese produce, and settling the account in London, they helped the Chinese to adjust the balance of trade. Importation of specie from America was reduced 80 per cent in the years 1831-40, over the previous decade.[5]

The influence of this new development of the trade was in the direction of the identification of American and Brit ish interests in China. There was, however, a check on this influence.

The import of foreign merchandise in American vessels into China reached its highest point in 1825 when it was valued at nearly $5,500,000. In that year the value of the domestic produce sent from the United States to China was $160,000 although three years before the sum had approached half a million. In 1826 the invoices show the beginning of the exportation to China of American cottons to the extent of about $15,000.[6] This trade in American domestics increased steadily and in ten years had risen to $170,000. In 1838 it passed the half million dollar mark. Meanwhile the Americans were bringing away from China less and less nankeens and silks, and were also taking less and less British manufactured goods into China.

American domestics, coarse grades of white and printed cottons, grew in popularity and successfully met the British competition. In nine months from October 1, 1842, to July 1, 1843, the United States exported to China domestic produce to the value of more than $1,700,000, and two years later passed the two million dollar mark; meanwhile the Americans had reduced their importations of British and European produce into China to less than $200,000. True the Americans were still taking from China very much more produce than they were bringing to it; in the decade ending with 1840 the imports into China amounted to not quite $13,000,000 and the exports from China were $61,000,000. But the Americans had had a glimpse of Asia as a market for American manufactured goods, and that glimpse influenced the policy of Americans and guided the formation of the policy of their government.[7]

After 1840 American policy in Asia was always directed with an eye to the future—to the day when Americans would supply the seemingly limitless markets of the East. Meanwhile the doors to these markets must be kept open. This was as much the policy of Americans in 1840 as it was American policy eighty years later.

One other fact of the trade development may be mentioned although its importance at the time was greatly overestimated. At the close of the War of 1812 the Americans resumed their China trade with a rush. The volume of trade, exports and imports together, mounted from $7,000,000 to about $19,000,000 in four years. In the season 1817-8 the gross amount of the American imports and exports at Canton actually exceeded those of the British East India Company, while the American tonnage employed was 18,000 as compared with 21,000 for the British. But the Americans were speculating and paid dearly. The tonnage employed in the decade ending with 1840 showed an actual decrease over that in the previous decade. The total British trade in 1830 was $43,000,000 as compared with $3,500,000 for the Americans; in 1840 the American exports to and imports from China were only $7,000,000. It is obvious that American commercial relations with China were valued not so much because of their present returns as for their future possibilities.

With these facts as to the growth of the trade in mind we pass to a consideration of the relation of the American Government to its citizens in China from 1800 until the beginning of the agitation for a treaty, i.e. after the dissolution of the East India Company monopoly in 1834.

RELATION OF UNITED STATES GOVERNMENT TO AMERICAN CITIZENS IN CHINA

The consul was not an imposing functionary. The common affairs of the American community were usually ordered in what was really a 'town meeting' over which the consul, as a courtesy, was asked to preside. The rights of the minority were amply safeguarded in these meetings, for the individual was subject to no law save that of expediency. The consul administered the estate of the dead, disciplined mutinous sailors and cared for such of them as could not care for themselves, but he lacked even the authority to demand accurate trade reports from the captains and supercargoes. "The secret manner of transacting business at Canton," wrote Samuel Snow to Secretary of State Pickering (November 9, 1800) in response to a request for a trade report, "made it almost impossible to obtain any accurate knowledge of the cargoes in the common way. . . . On that account my note to the different captains bordered as closely on a demand as the nature of the thing would admit of, and the reports have come in more full than I had even expected myself." The only emoluments of the consular office were the fees which, up to 1836, had rarely exceeded $500.

The relation of the consul to the Chinese authorities abounded in absurdities. They called the consul the chief 'tai-pan' (supercargo). Theoretically they did not recognize him at all, and yet actually they looked to him to exercise over his countrymen as despotic a control as any Chinese official similarly placed would not hesitate to employ. The chairman of the Select Committee of the East India Company, and the French consul, unlike the American official, did possess very extensive powers both judicial and executive. To complicate matters still more the Chinese, reasoning from the analogy of their own governmental practice, assumed as a matter of course that the American officials, like their own, were corrupt and dependent for advancement and wealth upon methods such as their own officials uniformly employed. Furthermore the consul shared the contempt with which the Chinese authorities looked upon all traders. The Chinese regarded men who would desert their homes and the tombs of their ancestors to reside in a foreign land for the purposes of trade as singularly degraded. A Chinese merchant, similarly placed, would at once be violating the law and forfeiting all privileges of protection from his government.

The insecurity of the Americans during the trying period before 1815 led them to petition Congress for a more efficient consular establishment.*

The petition stated:

"The consul of the United States residing here has not the means of being sufficiently useful to his countrymen with their intercourse with the Chinese Government, and of supporting the dignity of the flag of which he has charge; in consequence of which it frequently happens that impositions are placed upon the memorialists that are avoided by the citizens or subjects of other nations whose representatives have the means to oppose with firmness and effect the first attempts which, if successfully repelled, are seldom renewed; but when once a new imposition has been submitted to, it is considered an established custom, and demanded as a right from the nation that has yielded."

*The date of this petition, which is found in the first volume of Canton Consular Letters, is unknown. From the signatures attached to it, it would appear that it could not have been later than 1815 and it may have been prepared as early as 1806. Dr. Robert Morrison, who embarked for China from New York in the spring of 1807, mentions the movement then under way to secure better protection for the consul at Canton, and two years later President Jefferson received an application from Judge A. B. Woodward who wished a commission to represent the United States diplomatically in China, with power to negotiate a treaty.⁸

The petitioners asked for a consul, unconnected with the trade, at a salary of $3,000 and residence. They also urged the appointment of an experienced physician to care for the sailors, with the liberty to engage in private practice. Allowances were also requested to pay for a linguist or for the cost of translating documents.

To this appeal there appears to have been no response from the Government of the United States.

The nearest to an official opinion on American policy at this time is to be found in the correspondence of Thomas Jefferson, at the time of the Embargo. The incident also throws some light on the conditions under which its China trade in those days was conducted. A Chinese merchant, then in New York, wished to return to China while the embargo was in operation. He appealed to President Jefferson, even going to Washington to see him. The President wrote to Albert Gallatin, Secretary of the Treasury, enclosing a blank passport for the vessel which the Chinese merchant agreed to provide for himself, saying: [9]

"I enclose Mr. Madison's letter which contains everything I know on the subject. I consider it a case of national comity, and coming within the views of the first section of the first embargo act. The departure of this individual with good disposition may be the means of making our nation known advantageously at the source of power in China, to which it is otherwise difficult to convey information."

A few weeks later President Jefferson wrote with reference to the same matter:

"The opportunity hoped from that, of making known through one of its own characters of note, our nation, our circumstances and character, and of letting that government understand at length the difference between us and the English, and separate us in its policy, rendered that measure a diplomatic one, in my view, and likely to bring lasting advantage to our merchants and commerce with that country."

This, the first expression of opinion from so high a source, correctly stated a policy with reference to China which remained fundamental in American dealings with China long into the future, although it showed few results for at least another half century. It was difficult for the

Chinese to differentiate between the two English-speaking nations, and consequently the English and the Americans were accustomed to bear each other's sins.

Unhappily President Jefferson was, in this incident, the innocent victim of a shrewd hoax. When the New York merchants picked up the *Commercial Advertiser* of August 13, 1808, they learned that the distinguished mandarin was none other than a dock loafer who had come to the United States in a recent ship from China. Their displeasure was still further increased by the fact that the vessel on which he had returned to China the day before was the *Beaver,* belonging to their enterprising competitor, John Jacob Astor.

The merchants officially protested to President Jefferson. The *Commercial Advertiser* made it the subject of an acid editorial. In a public letter Astor defied the protestants offering to prove that the President had not been deceived. However, the ship did belong to Astor, and Picqua, the so-called mandarin, probably had no more influence in Peking than did his ambitious patron. Meanwhile the *Beaver* was able to get in an extra voyage to Canton, while other American ships were tied up by the unpopular embargo. Astor was reported to have made no less than $200,000 by the voyage.[10]

After the resignation of B. C. Wilcocks in 1821 the consular office was filled only in a haphazard way until the appointment of Peter W. Snow of Providence, son of the second consul (1835). One consul died shortly after his appointment; his successor served less than two years owing to the failure of the firm with which he was connected, and the third appointee in the interim, although holding the appointment for ten years, never lived during that time at Canton. In fact, during the first fifty years of American trade relations with China, the total terms of service rendered by regularly appointed consuls continuously resident at Canton was only fourteen years. In the intervals the duties of the office were discharged, if at all, by some merchant who was either delegated by the person holding the office or who voluntarily assumed the responsibilities.

That the American Government was not, however, entirely unconscious of the presence of its citizens in China, or regardless of the value of the trade, is evident from the fact that at various times naval protection was proposed. As a result of the depredations of the French privateers and naval vessels, the United States ship *Congress* was sent to the Far East in May, 1800.[11] This vessel reached Batavia and cruised in the Straights of Sunda for two months. She offered homeward convoy to fifteen American merchantmen. In 1815 the United States sloop *Peacock* was sent to the East Indies to protect American shipping and to prey upon the British trade. She also reached Batavia and captured four English merchantmen, all after the declaration of peace, but never reached Canton. Four years later the *Congress,* fitted out to protect the China trade from pirates and to afford a practice cruise, dropped anchor at Lintin (November 3, 1819), some forty miles below the mouth of the Canton, or Pearl River. The Chinese authorities promptly refused to allow the frigate to be supplied with provisions, and through the hong merchants issued a demand to the consul that the *Congress* leave immediately. This was the customary Chinese method for dealing with visits of foreign naval vessels. Only three years before H. M. S. *Alceste,* attached to the Lord Amherst Embassy, had been similarly treated and had defied the Chinese, forcing its way up to Whampoa. Captain Henley of the *Congress* would have liked to do the same, but greatly to the relief of the American merchants he restrained himself. Had he disobeyed the orders of the mandarins the American trade would probably have been stopped. There is no more certain index to the character of the policy of Americans in Canton at that time than the fact that the presence of an American naval vessel was an embarrassment.

Although Captain Henley was hospitably entertained at the factories when he went up to Canton in a merchant vessel he was made to feel that his official services were not desired. In the spring, when he offered to convoy the American vessels down through the Straits the offer was declined by the merchants and captains who feared that such assistance would be offensive to the Chinese.

Subsequently on several occasions American naval vessels visited the mouth of the river. By the Chinese authorities they were always ordered away, and by the Americans they were welcomed only with apprehensions. The American had no desire whatever for a 'gun-boat policy; it could only create ill feeling among the Chinese and it would interfere with the trade.

We may now review the policy of the American merchants in meeting the irritations which arose out of the contacts with other foreign powers at Canton, and out of the impositions of the Chinese authorities.

RELATIONS WITH THE PORTUGUESE AND ENGLISH

The Portuguese Governor of Macao in 1803 was unwilling to admit the American consul to residence at Macao during the summer months, an awkward and discriminating action, in view of the fact that no foreigner was allowed to remain at Canton after the close of the trade.*

The Americans solved the difficulty by violating the rule of the Chinese, making, doubtless, a few presents to the officials, and living at the factories during the summer, until the Macao authorities were persuaded to extend a freer hospitality. Major Shaw, the first American consul, had established the precedent by spending the summer of 1787 at Canton with the supercargo of the *Columbia* and another American. Indeed the Americans seem never, at that time, to have been very careful about such rules. Captain Cleveland reports with reference to this custom of moving to Macao in the summer: "This routine has of late years been broken by the disregard of etiquette and the established seasons on the part of the Americans who, coming and

---

*There was no treaty between the United States and Portugal at that time.

going all the year round, have inverted all the ancient rules of doing business at Canton.[12]

The troubles with the British authorities were much more serious both for the Americans and for the English. As early as the season of 1804-5 the first clash came over the desertion of British seamen to American ships, and the British insistence on the right of search. Desertion in those days was a very serious matter, for there was no ready labor supply at Canton from which to draw to fill the vacant place. An Indiaman required a crew of about 130, and it was not to be expected that the British captains would view with indifference the escape of their men to American ships, sometimes with the active solicitation of the American captain and the promise of higher wages and a bonus. Captain Cleveland states, in describing a voyage he fitted out from Canton to the Northwest coast of North America in 1799: "Most of my men were deserters from the Indiamen; and they were generally the worst of a bad lot." To this practice was added the claims of the British war-ships which came to Canton each year to convoy the returning East India Company fleet, of the right to take from American ships any of the crew who were unable to give indisputable proof of their American citizenship, and in case of necessity, to take them anyway.

Towards the end of the year 1804 H. M. SS. *Caroline* and *Grampus* began to search American ships and when they left Chinese waters carried two American seamen with them, despite the protests of Carrington. The commander of the *Caroline* replied to the consul's protest:

"In reply to your letter of yesterday, requesting the dischage of three men from His Britannic Majesty's ship under my command, calling themselves subjects of the United States of America, to which you sign yourself consular agent:—

"I am to inform you that all such solicitations must be made to the Lords of the Admiralty in England, as without orders from them no man can be discharged by a Captain of the British Navy."

These passages between the Americans and the British, in which the fault was by no means exclusively on one side, continued. In November, 1807, the *Topaz* of Baltimore was boarded by British naval forces at Whampoa, and the captain of the *Topaz* was shot. The ship was seized, her specie confiscated, and the ship was sent to Bombay as a prize, on the ground that the *Topaz* had been engaged in piracy off the coast of South America.

The American brig *Rambler* of Boston, a letter of marque vessel, captured the English *Arabella* of Calcutta, in 1814, and in distress was forced to put in at Macao with her prize. The captain of the *Rambler* directed the prize to be anchored under the guns of the Portuguese fort, whereupon the Governor of Macao ordered her to leave the harbor, although she was without provisions and proper ballast. In the course of the dispute a Portuguese crew took the *Arabella* out and anchored her near the British fleet. The British forthwith took possession of the vessel. Consul Wilcocks complained bitterly to James Monroe, Secretary of State, not merely at the "flagrant outrage" committed by Robert O'Brien, Esq., commander of H. M. S. *Doris,* and of the "pusillanimous conduct of the Governor of Macao" but also of the fact that the Portuguese had been permitting the British officers to live at Macao whence they had gone out to attack many American ships.

The Chinese took a hand in the quarrel between the Americans and the British, demanding that the superintendent of the East India Company send away H. M. S. *Doris,* after she had chased an American ship up to Whampoa and captured her there at the anchorage. The *Doris* had also captured an American ship, the *Hunter,* off the Ladrone Islands and brought her to Chinese waters as a prize. When the superintendent replied that he had no authority over the English men-of-war and could not order them away, the Chinese ordered the servants away from the English factories, and threatened to stop the trade. The English, in turn, withdrew from Canton, and in the end the Chinese gave way. In the agreement between the Chinese and the English in which this controversy was settled, it was stipulated that in the future the Americans should not be permitted to dispose of prize-goods in the Canton market. This provision was inserted because both the *Rambler* and the *Jacob Jones,* another American letter of marque, had brought to Canton no less than $10,000 in specie, forty chests of opium, and some piece goods, all captured from English ships, and with the loot purchased outward cargoes.

While American trade with Canton was all but paralyzed during the War of 1812, nevertheless a system of parole was established in 1814 by which American sailors were returned to the consul by the captain of H. M. S. *Doris,* on condition that they would promise not to take up arms against the English navy. Meanwhile the displeasure of the Chinese at the British disregard of their port regulations operated to the benefit of the Americans.

RELATIONS WITH THE CHINESE GOVERNMENT

From the very beginning of the trouble with the English in 1804 the Americans realized that there were only two possible sources of protection for them; their own government, or the Chinese, and they knew full well that no help was possible from the United States naval forces. Therefore Carrington wrote to Captain Ratsey of H. M. Brig *Harrier,* October 14, 1805:

"Should the demand which I have made to you not be complied with, I shall make a formal representation and appeal to the Chinese Government of this unprecedented and outrageous violence against the rights of nations."

There being no satisfactory response to this demand, Carrington called together the American merchants, super-cargoes and captains, and laid the case before them. As a result of this meeting a formal representation was drawn up and signed by the consul and twenty-seven other Americans. It was addressed to "His Excellency, John Tuck, Governor of the Province of Canton." The acknowledgements of and concessions to Chinese authority which were made in this document were an expression of the fundamental principle

which guided the American merchants in their dealings with
the Chinese for the next fifteen or more years, and which
at least some of the American merchants at Canton, even
after the opening of the five ports in 1844, were slow to
discard. After reciting the facts with reference to the controversy with Captain Ratsey, and stating that if the
English officer carried out his threat to come to Whampoa
and search American ships anchored there, the American
captains had decided to repel his visits with force of arms,
if necessary, the representation further stated:

"The undersigned further respectfully represent to your Excellency that the citizens of the United States have for many years
visited the city of Canton in the pursuit of honest commerce, that
their conduct during the whole period of intercourse has been regulated by a strict regard and respect for the laws and usages of this
Empire, as well as the general law of nations, and that by their
fidelity in trade, and their peaceable demeanor, the most perfect harmony, confidence, and good understanding has ever been maintained
between the subjects of this country and the citizens of the United
States, from which has flowed a very extensive and rapidly increasing
commerce, mutually advantageous and honorable to both parties;
"That by the ancient and well established laws and usages of all
civilized nations, the persons and property of friendly foreigners
within the territory and jurisdiction of a sovereign and independent
Empire, are under the special protection of the government thereof,
and any violence or indignity offered to such persons or to the flag
of the nation to which they belong, is justly considered as done to the
government within whose territory the outrage is committed;
"That by the same law of nations, the civil and military agents
of the government are strictly prohibited from assuming any authority
whatever within the territory of the other nor can they seize the person of the highest state criminal, who may have eluded the justice of
their own!
"How great, then, is the outrage and indignity which has been
committed in the port of Canton, upon the citizens and the national
character of the United States! .   The undersigned, therefore, with
the highest respect and deference, pray your Excellency to exercise
that power and justice with which you are clothed, as well as to cause
the American seamen to be restored, as also to secure them from any
aggression of the kind in the future within the territory of China,
which they presume, unquestionably extends to the seas which bound
its shores."

It is difficult to know whether this memorial, with its
sweeping concessions as to the jurisdiction of Chinese

authority, was ever seen by the Governor of the province. Carrington wrote to James Madison, November 25, 1805:

> "As the Chinese Government does not recognize foreign ministers or consuls, I consider it advisable to join the American merchants residing at Canton, and the supercargoes and the commanders of the American ships, with me in the representation; hoping it would have the desired influence with the several security merchants to encourage them to present the same to their government, and give our complaints their full force."

At any rate, the hong merchants replied that their government would not take cognizance of disputes between foreigners although they arose within Chinese territory, a principle which, however, China did not follow consistently. Nevertheless it is quite likely that the Chinese authorities were entirely familiar with the contents of the memorial, and fifteen years later, in accordance with it as well as with their own desire, they claimed jurisdiction over the American ships at Whampoa in the Terranova case.

It could hardly be expected that this policy of non-intercourse upon which the Chinese Government insisted, would work out exclusively to the disadvantage of the foreigners, and there were not a few occasions when the fictitious arrangements were brushed aside by the Chinese themselves. A Philadelphia merchant sued Houqua, the famous hong merchant, in a Pennsylvania court for failure to keep his engagements in 1818 as to the quality of tea and obtained a judgment for $25,000. How the defendant was represented in this suit or by what means the judgment was collected is not known.[13] The plaintiff, however, was shortly after the trial revealed as a notorious smuggler who became insolvent, owing the government more than three quarters of a million dollars in duties.

Several of the hong merchants were reported to have been in much embarrassment because of the extent to which they had supplied the American traders on credit. Houqua, afterwards so friendly to some American firms, was at that time extensively involved in these transactions and learned to become more discriminating in his extensions of credit.

One merchant, Consequa, who was reported to have lost $1,000,000 in credit transactions with Americans, even went so far as to address a memorial to "His Excellency, James Madison, President of the United States of America, or to the President of the United States for the time being." He stated that he had been led, after years of extensive dealings with the Americans, to give them long credits, although it was against the laws of the Empire. While trade was flourishing he had heard no complaints, and the losses had not been greater than he could well bear, but more recently he had had many unhappy experiences with the American traders. Some of the Americans, he stated, had not only declined to pay, offering frivolous excuses, but had even applied the capital to other branches of their business. Consequa recites: [14]

"When such debtors come, or reside in China, they cannot claim the aid of the laws of the imperial dynasty on their behalf. They [the laws] prohibit such confidence as he [Consequa] has placed in the subjects of the United States, and he would not presume to avow to the chief of a great nation, that he has infringed the laws of his own empire, but in the full consciousness that he has been guilty of no disloyal or injurious act or intention toward it, whilst to honorable minds he thinks his China would be strengthened by this circumstance [business with foreigners].

"He does not presume to solicit your Excellency's protection and consideration, but in so far as may be in accord with justice and the laws of the United States, they being so far and so greatly celebrated for their equal protection of the rich and the poor, and for their dealing equal measure to their citizens and to those of aliens, but he does ask for your protection and countenance in asserting and claiming his rights in conformity to your laws and where an appeal to courts of justice becomes necessary, that the forms and proceedings which have been devised for the security of man, may not be allowed to be wrested to his injury, a perversion to which the best are liable."

Consequa appointed a representative to present his petition, and supplied him with the necesssary proofs and papers to show his losses.

TERRANOVA INCIDENT

This policy of submitting to Chinese authority found its most famous expression in the well known "Terranova case." [15] Francis Terranova, an illiterate Italian seaman from the *Emily,* of Baltimore, was accused at the beginning of the season of 1821 of having caused the death of a boat-woman who had come up to the *Emily* to trade with the sailors. The consul attempted to settle the matter by the offer of a liberal payment to the relatives of the boat-woman but the captain of the *Emily* took matters into his own hands and, backed by the majority of the American community, was disposed to fight the case. The Chinese assumed jurisdiction and although the Americans were persuaded that the sailor was not guilty, and that the Chinese could not be trusted to give a fair trial, yielded. The unfortunate sailor was tried by Chinese authorities on board the *Emily,* found guilty, and the Americans were ordered to surrender him for punishment. The Americans demurred, the trade was stopped, the ship's security merchant, who owed large sums to Americans, was arrested, and the Americans found themselves confronted by a necessity. The holding of the security merchants might mean the financial ruin of his American creditors. Terranova was surrendered, and a few days later he was strangled, notwithstanding promises to the contrary and notwithstanding the provision of Chinese law making manslaughter punishable only by a small fine.[16]

Before the sailor was taken from the *Emily* a group of American merchants drew up a statement of the case and presented it to Houqua to give to the Chinese authorities. In it they said: [17]

"We consider the case prejudiced. We are bound to submit to your laws while we are in your waters, be they ever so unjust. We will not resist them. You have followed your ideas of justice, and have condemned the man unheard. But the flag of our country has never been disgraced. It now waves over you. It is no disgrace to submit to your power, surrounded as you are by overwhelming force, backed up by a great Empire. You have the power to compel us."

This bombastic declaration, amazing as it would seem, issued by any group of Americans, is still more remarkable when one remembers that those who signed it were among the most fearless sea-captains and pioneers that the United

States had ever produced. It shows how completely the
Chinese held the foreigners in their power by means of the
one weapon—stopping the trade. But it shows more than
that. It reflects the opinion of the day in American history
when 'national honor' was far more loosely defined than it
is today. More than twelve years later the *North American
Review*, in commenting on the incident, said:

"But as a question in the law of nations and casuistry, it would
bear an argument whether the United States could rightfully go to
war against the Chinese for administering their own laws on persons
voluntarily coming within their jurisdiction."

And in the treaty concluded with Siam in 1833, and ratified
by the Senate two years later it was agreed: "Merchants
of the United States trading in the Kingdom of Siam shall
respect and follow the laws and customs of the country in
all points." It is hardly to be doubted that the decision of
the Americans in submitting to Chinese jurisdiction in the
Terranova case, represented fairly accurately the state of
American public opinion on the rights of Americans in
China.

A few weeks later the English reversed the Terranova
precedent in the case of some sailors who were accused of
killing some Chinese in a mêlée. The British authorities
declined to surrender the sailors, but previous to 1821, they
had yielded to Chinese jurisdiction in many similar instances.[18]

The next two decades of the history of American relations with China mark a gradual displacement of this policy
of submission by one more in harmony with the rising power
of the young nation. Indeed, as one observes the rising tide
of national consciousness in the American traders after
1822, one is reminded of the conversation recorded by Major
Shaw, the first American consul at Canton, in his journal
during his first visit.[19] After Shaw had concluded a certain
bargain with a Chinese, the haggling having extended over
several days, the merchant asked:

"You are not Englishman?"

"No."

"But you speak English word, and when you first come, I can no tell difference; but now I understand very well. When I speak Englishman his price, he say 'So much,—take it,—let alone.' I tell him, 'No, my friend, I give you so much.' He look at me—'Go to hell, you damned rascal; what! you come here—set price my goods?' Truly, Massa Typan, I see very well you no hap Englishman. All Chinaman very much love your country."

"Thus far," writes Shaw, "it may be supposed the fellow's remarks pleased me. Justice obliges me to add his conclusion: 'All men come first time China very good gentlemen, all same you. I think two three times more you come Canton, you make all same Englishman too.'"

This prophecy was never entirely fulfilled, for the Americans found that their policy, while not always flattering to national vanity and often differing widely from the spirit of those other American pioneers who fought their way across the American continent, was very profitable in China, and a useful means of obtaining special favors.

During the entire period before the treaty of 1844, the Americans in Canton were left entirely without instructions from the Government of the United States. No official comment was ever made on the Terranova case. In 1822 President Monroe gave a letter addressed to the Emperor of China to an American merchant, and John Quincy Adams, as Secretary of State, addressed a letter to the Viceroy of Canton.[20] Neither letter, so far as is known, was ever accepted.

BIBLIOGRAPHICAL NOTES

1. Floyd Report on Oregon, Reports of Committees 45 :16-2; Annals of Congress, 17-2, pp. 398; 418, 423, 588-6.
2. "Personal Reminiscences, with Recollections of China," by Robert Bennett Forbes (3d ed., Boston, 1892). The addenda gives many details of the organization and history of Russell and Company.
3. "Sketch of the Life of D. W. C. Olyphant," by Rev. Thatcher Thayer (New York, 1852); Hunter's "Fan Kwae"; Barrett's "Old Merchants of New York."

4. Sessional Papers (1821) Vol. 7.
5. "Foreign Commerce of the United States," by J. Smith Homans (New York, 1857), table, p. 181.
6. *Hunt's Merchants Magazine,* Vol. 11 (July-Dec., 1844), table, p. 55.
7. Trade statistics for the period before 1840; Pitkin; Seybert's Statistical Annals of the U. S.; an exhaustive analysis in Sessional Papers, 1821, Vol. 7, and in Parliamentary Papers, 1830, Vols. 5 and 6, in which the American trade is somewhat exaggerated for the purpose of making a case against the East India Company monopoly; Report of the Secretary of the Treasury, July 1, 1840, H. Doc. 248, 26-1; see also H. Doc. 35, 27-3; and, *Hunt's Merchants Magazine.*
8. Madison Papers (Lib. of Congress), Vol. XXXV, May 27, 1809, A. B. Woodward to Madison.
9. Jefferson Papers (Lib. of Congress), Jefferson to Gallatin, July 25, and Aug. 15, 1808.
10. Barrett's "Old Merchants of New York," Vol. 3, pp. 6-10.
11. Paullin's "American Naval Vessels in the Orient."
12. Shaw's Journal; and, "Voyages," by Richard J. Cleveland, New York, 1855, p. 72; *China Review,* Vol. 5, p. 152.
13. Niles' Register, April 23, 1825.
14. Canton Consular Letters (approximate date, 1815).
15. H. Doc. 71, 26-2, Nov. 1, 1821, Wilcocks to Adams.
16. Miscellaneous Notices, by Sir Geo. T. Staunton, London, 1822, 1850, pp. 409-10.
17. *North American Review,* Oct., 1834, pp. 58-68.
18. See "International Relations with the Chinese Empire," by H. B. Morse, London, 1910, Vol. 1, pp. 99-107, for a complete list of the cases of homicide in which the foreigners were accused by the Chinese.
19. Shaw's Journal, p. 199.
20. J. Q. Adams Memoirs, Philadelphia, 1875, Vol. 6, p. 491.

CHAPTER V

THE AMERICANS AND THE ANGLO-CHINESE WAR

In the conclusion of the first American treaty with China two series of actions converge: on the one hand the policy of the Americans in China towards both Chinese and British; and, on the other, the slowly awakening interest of the Government of the United States in Chinese affairs. Until very shortly before the decision to negotiate a treaty the one had very little relation to the other.

Before 1840 the American Government assumed towards its citizens resident in China an attitude not very dissimilar to that taken by the Chinese towards their own emigrés: Let them shift for themselves. The merchants in Canton, thus left to themselves, and not at all protesting at the policy of the government, adopted a course in which they had perfected themselves—that of conciliation—and in the main they prospered. From the execution of Terranova to the beginning of 1839 the annals of Chinese-American relations were quite uneventful.

Just as in all frontier communities, so at Canton, men possessed influence or not according to their abilities. Wilcocks, Ammidon, Russell and Cushing were acknowledged leaders. In the third decade of the century Cushing was credited with having been the most influential of all foreigners among the Chinese.

Taking advantage of a rice famine in Canton in 1825, and utilizing his intimate friendship with the hong merchant Houqua, Cushing secured a reduction in the tonnage dues on ships laden with rice coming to Canton. Whereas other ships had to pay the full tonnage tax, ranging from $3000 to $6000, whether full or empty, "rice-ships" were to pay only about $1150. After 1833 these were admitted entirely free. This arrangement was, to the Americans especially, a substantial benefit because they had an even greater difficulty than the English in finding cargoes for import which could be absorbed in the Chinese market, and also because the regular tonnage dues fell heaviest on the smallest ships, and the Americans at that time were still employing relatively small vessels.[1]

The dissolution of the East India Company monopoly caused a ripple in the tide of American affairs, but hardly more. The removal of the overshadowing 'Company' made way for the rise and the increased prestige of independent firms, an advantage which some of the American firms were in a position to seize. In the fresh competition which followed the advent of many new firms and individuals, the Americans fared well, having gone through their period of financial difficulties ten years earlier. The Lord Napier incident caused a brief stopping of the trade, which the Americans accepted with their accustomed complaisance.*

The national antipathies which had separated the Americans and the English during so much of the earlier period were mitigated as American houses dealt in English manufactured goods, and as banking relations became more intimate. From the dissolution of the Company until 1839 the relations between the English and Americans were unusually cordial. Their interests were much the same.

The dissolution of the East India Company monopoly (1834) due in part to the extraordinary success of the independent American merchants was ominous for the continuance of peaceful relations between England and China. The dissolution of the monopoly, the release of individual mer-

*Lord Napier arrived in China in July, 1834, with a royal commission as chief superintendent of British trade. It was expected that he would take the place of the former chairman of the Select Committee of the East India Company, as the representative officer of the British Government, and that he would also exercise some enlarged judicial and executive powers which had not belonged to the agents of the East India Company. The manner of his coming to China was sadly bungled and the Chinese refused to receive him, at length stopping the trade to force his retirement to Macao. Lord Napier died at Macao, October 11, 1834 [2]

Sir George T. Staunton,[3] formerly chairman of the Select Committee of the East India Company, stated: "Lord Napier, owing to the unfortunate omission of our government to apply for and obtain from the Chinese authorities in due time his formal recognition, . . . had no official station or public privilege in China whatsoever."

chants from the thrall of the Company restrictions, and the greatly increased competition for the trade, also increased the points of irritation between the English and the Chinese. Most ominous was the fact that under the new arrangements, affronts offered to the merchants were no longer to be considered merely as difficulties of a trading company. They became national insults. The blunder of the English foreign office in the manner of sending out Lord Napier created a bad situation. The subsequent policy of Captain Charles Elliot, English superintendent of trade, wavering as he did between a desire to keep the trade going and to vindicate national honor, encouraged the Chinese in the opinion that the mastery of the situation lay with China just as it had in the past when she was able so completely to control the merchants by stopping the trade.

Another factor which operated against the continuance of peaceful relations was China's fear of England. The Chinese Government had not been unmindful of British aggression in India, Burmah, the Malay Peninsula, and the archipelago. The Manchu dynasty was conscious of the fact that it was really alien to China, and that it was unpopular with large numbers of people, as was proved by the increasing number of insurrections. The Peking Government feared that the English might effect a coalition with rebellious spirits within the Empire to displace the Manchus. Above these general causes of distrust and irritation lay the immediate facts that each year the exportations of specie to pay for the opium were increasing, and the Chinese economists could see in this only the gradual impoverishment of the Empire, while the demoralizing effect of opium smoking was everywhere apparent. The opium trade received a new impetus in 1836 when, for a few months, it was reported and confidently believed that the trade was to be legalized. After a brief debate the Imperial Government decided against legalization, and instead demanded the expulsion from Canton of nine foreigners, at least one of whom was American; but the foreigners remained. The traders became bolder from month to month, not only increasing the sales along the coast but bringing the drug again to Whampoa, and even to Canton. The government accordingly stiffened its opposition and a conflict became inevitable.[4] In 1838 the Imperial Government determined to destroy the opium trade, seizing the opportunity to effect at one stroke a moral reform, establish an important economic regulation, and, by no means incidentally, to curb the growing power of the foreigners in South China.

While it had always been the fond hope of the Americans, from the beginnings of their relations with the Chinese Government, so to conduct themselves as to win a preferred place in Chinese estimation, as far as the government was concerned, the policy had not been successful. Before the officials all foreigners were alike, and the Americans, because of their close similarity to the English, were often confused or identified with the latter to a point which effectually thwarted the American effort to maintain good will. The fact that the Chinese officials assumed the American share in the opium trade to be very much larger than it was, added to the difficulty and made it certain that whenever the Chinese assumed the aggressive, the English-speaking people would share alike the displeasure of the Chinese.

Foreigners Imprisoned in the Factories

On December 12, 1838, the Chinese attempted to execute a Chinese opium dealer in the public square in front of the factories, almost directly under the American flag. Some American and British residents interfered and the execution took place outside the factory boundaries. After the execution a "large and desperate mob was raised by the imprudence and folly of a small number of English and American young men," to borrow the phrase of the American consul in his official report. The mob, which numbered 7000 or 8000, was dispersed by the Chinese authorities and shortly afterward Captain Elliot appeared with about 120 men hastily collected from the ships at Whampoa.[5]

The Chinese persisted. Late in the afternoon, February

26, 1839, when most of the foreigners were absent from the factories taking their recreation, twenty mandarins and a hundred soldiers brought another native opium dealer into the square and executed him without opposition. The reason given was "that all foreigners who are engaged in the traffic of this prohibited article may witness the dreadful punishment inflicted on the natives for their violation of the laws of the Empire."

"The execution," writes the American consul, "is considered by the foreigners a direct and positive insult." At the suggestion of Captain Elliot, and after consultation with the French and Dutch consuls who agreed on common action, Consul Snow, in protest, hauled down the American flag. "I have," he reported, "on deliberation, concluded not to set mine again until receipt of orders from you (Secretary of State) to that effect, or circumstance should make it proper to do so." [6]

Three weeks later, March 18, Commissioner Lin who had arrived from Peking with the most explicit orders to destroy the opium trade, issued an ultimatum to the foreigners. Charging them with ingratitude, he pointed to the receiving ships at Lintin which had been repeatedly ordered away, asserted that he had the names of the foreign opium merchants, and demanded that every chest on the store-ships be surrendered. He gave three days in which to reply, and promised to stop at no half-way measures. He also demanded that the foreigners give bonds that they would bring no more opium to China and would concede to the Chinese Government the right to punish violations "with the extreme penalty of the law." [7] Consul Shaw reported the request for the opium as a 'just demand.' Commissioner Lin believed that he held in his hand a still invincible weapon—the power to stop the trade. "Let our ports once be closed against you," he declared, "and for what profit can your several nations any longer look? Yet more: our tea and rhubarb, seeing that, should you foreigners be deprived of them, you therein lose the means of preserving life, are without stint granted to you for transportation, year by

year, beyond the seas. Favors never have been greater."
Consequently when the foreigners attempted parleys and
promised compromises he stopped the trade (March 22).
Five days later the compradores and coolies were withdrawn
from the factories and the following day, all the streets, except one, leading to the square, were walled up. The foreigners became prisoners; soldiers surrounded them on land,
and war junks cut off their access to the river.

All the foreigners acting together notified Lin, March
25, that the settlement of the opium question was to be left
entirely with the various consuls and national representa
tives. Consul Snow therefore entered with fear and trem
bling upon duties never delegated to him by his government
and never contemplated in his commission. So far as the
American merchants were concerned, the consul was put
forward for the time as suited their convenience, and as a
matter of equal convenience, later discarded.[8]

Snow's not very simple problem was to disentangle
American from British affairs to the satisfaction of the
Chinese. Fortunately for him, as well as for the American
merchants concerned, Captain Elliot, whose policy was to
keep the foreigners united against the actions of Lin, was
disposed to assume full responsibility for the Indian opium
in the hands of the Americans, and it was surrendered to
him. Two duties remained for Snow: to prove to Lin that
the Americans were not concerned in the trade to an equal
extent with the English; and to settle the disputed question
of the nature of the bond which should be given in the future
as a pledge of total abstinence from opium trading by
American merchants. He positively refused to sign the
bond proposed by Lin, referring the question to Washington, in this matter acting in concert with the Dutch, and
with the approval of the merchants. Eventually the
Americans accepted the bond in a very modified form. The
task of making clear the American share in and attitude
towards the opium trade in general was more difficult, but
two weeks after the imprisonment had begun in earnest, he
was able to report to the State Department: "The Govern-

ment is satisfied, I think, that no opium is grown in our country; that the Americans in the future will not, under any circumstances, engage in the trade." [9]

The next question facing the Americans was whether the concert of action hitherto maintained with the other nations, should be continued. The delivery of the opium was progressing rapidly, and the port was to be opened May 5, to permit passage to Macao for those who desired it. Captain Elliot proposed that the foreigners, acting together, should now turn the tables on the Chinese and withdraw from Canton to Macao, thus stopping the trade on their side, as Lin had stopped it for the Chinese. The English had tried such a policy before and it had been successful. It was argued that this was a suitable time to convince the Chinese that they were quite as dependent on the trade as were the foreigners. [10]

But the American merchants * were of a different mind. From the day when the English withdrew from Canton the foreign nations went their separate ways, and fortunately or unfortunately, according to the point of view, each nation was compelled, individually, to assume for its actions the responsibility which the Americans, at least, had been hitherto more or less disposed to ignore or shift.

"The British residents," wrote Commander George C. Read (May 28) of the U. S. East India Squadron which had arrived at Macao a month earlier, "are evidently displeased with the course our countrymen have adopted." [11].

The displeasure of the English did not continue long for it was soon discovered that the presence of the Americans at Canton was of very great assistance to the English in getting out the cargoes which had been piling up during the winter.

An American merchant, then the manager of Russell and Company, many years afterward stated, in language which no doubt faithfully reflects the policy of the Americans: "When the English left Canton, Elliot himself personally begged Russell and Company to follow his countrymen,

*For the American share in the opium trade see Chapter vi.

saying, 'If your house goes, all will go, and we shall soon bring these rascally Chinese to terms.' I replied that I had not come to China for health or pleasure, and that I should remain at my post as long as I could sell a yard of goods or buy a pound of tea; that we Yankees had no queen to guarantee our losses, etc. Elliot replied that he would soon make Canton too hot for us." [12]

For the next few months the Americans did a land-office business. Freights between Hongkong and Canton were higher than from Hongkong to America, and the Americans carried the goods in and out for the English, sometimes going through the formality of evading the law by loading ships with English goods at Hongkong, taking them over to Manila, and bringing them back to Canton without breaking bulk. Every sort of vessel that could float was pressed into service including not a few, it may be feared of the idle English fleet now transferred to American ownership in very informal ways, and in no way entitled, according to American maritime law, to fly the American flag.[13]

The gentleman above quoted wrote that afterwards Captain Elliot said to him at Macao: "My dear Forbes, the Queen owes you many thanks for not taking my advice as to leaving Canton. We have got in all our goods, and got out a good supply of teas and silk. If the American houses had not remained at their posts, the English would have gone in. I had no power to prevent them from going. Now the trade of the season is over, and a large force at hand, we can bring the Chinese to terms."

The momentous events of the three following years, so far as they concern Anglo-Chinese relations, can be narrated with brevity. The Chinese took the offensive, ordering the English from Macao whither they had retreated from Canton. The latter in turn, moved to Hongkong, living for a time on shipboard, but gradually forming a settlement on the island. A blockade of the river was established by the English the next year (June 28, 1840), after the season's trade had been cared for, and the trade was reopened the the following year for a few weeks to take care of the accumulated produce. So far as Canton was concerned, the war ended May 27, 1841. Fifteen months later, August 29, 1842, the Treaty of Nanking was signed. The following year, October 8, 1843, a supplementary treaty which included important additional items, as well as a tariff, was signed at the Bogue.

THE AMERICANS PETITION CONGRESS

In order to bring the narration of other events important to the Americans in China up to 1844, when the American treaty was negotiated, it is necessary to review the request of the American merchants to Congress for the appointment of a commercial agent; the condition of public sentiment in the United States; and the action of Commodore Kearny in securing the assent of the Chinese to "most-favored-nation" treatment for the Americans.

After the English had left Canton the Americans addressed a memorial to Congress (May 25, 1839) explaining the American share in the opium trade, asking for the appointment of a commercial agent to be sent to China to negotiate a commercial treaty, and asking also for the dispatch to Chinese waters of a suitable naval force for the protection of American lives and property.[14]

The memorial, after summarizing the cause of the aggressive measures adopted by Commissioner Lin, proposed:

"We would, therefore, with all deference and respect express our opinions that the United States Government should take immediate measures; and, if deemed advisable, to act in concert with the governments of Great Britain, France and Holland, or either of them, in their endeavors to establish commercial relations with this empire upon a safe and honorable footing, such as exists between all friendly powers; and by direct appeal to the Imperial Government at Peking, to obtain a compliance with the following among other important demands:"

These demands included: (1) Permission for foreign envoys to reside near the court at Peking with the usual diplomatic privileges. (2) Promulgation of a fixed tariff. (3) A system of bonding warehouses, or some regulations for the transshipment of goods for reexport. (4) Liberty of trading at other port or ports in China. (5) Compensation for losses caused by stoppage of legal trade and guarantees for the future. And the further provision (6) "That until the Chinese laws are distinctly made known and recognized, the punishment for wrongs committed by foreigners upon the Chinese, or others, shall not be greater than is applicable to the like offenses by the laws of the United States, or England; nor shall any punishment be inflicted by the Chinese authorities upon any foreigner, until the guilt of the party shall have been fairly and clearly proved."

When this memorial was prepared the opium had been surrendered to Captain Elliot who had thus become responsible for the payment for it, and the drug had been destroyed. The English had withdrawn from Canton and it was evident that they would soon begin hostilities. It was also assumed, for it had been a matter of discussion for years, that when the peace had once been broken it would not be restored until other ports in China had been opened to trade, and some assurances had been given as a basis for stable diplomatic relations. On other matters as well the time was fast approaching for a general settlement. The memorial pointed out that the recent action of the authorities had been indiscriminate and unjust in that it had made no effort to differentiate between the innocent and the guilty, and had shown scant regard for facts and evidence. The present action of the Chinese Government must be resented or in a short time all foreign trade would be driven out. In conclusion the Americans express the 'candid conviction' that the appearance of a naval force from the United States, England and France upon the coast of China would, without bloodshed, obtain from the government proper acknowledgments and treaties. The significant features of the memorial were: absence of bitterness towards the Chinese; proposals for joint action with England; and the confident expectation that peaceful measures would suffice.

The Americans had taken their imprisonment with good humor. There had been some alarm at the outset of the confinement but the intentions of Lin soon appeared aggressive only in the sense that he was determined to enforce a policy of non-intercourse. He intended no bodily harm to the Americans. Prisoners they certainly were but the supplies, while nominally cut off, were actually smuggled in each night, and one of those confined afterwards reported that the prisoners suffered more during their confinement from over-eating and lack of exercise than from want of any necessity of life.[15] The arrival, late in April, of Commander Read with the *Columbia* and *John Adams* at Macao, had been an assurance to the entire community, and yet the Americans had felt so much better able to handle the situation at Canton, unassisted, that the consul had asked Read to delay coming to Canton until after the affair was settled.[16]

"It would be a fête gratifying, I doubt not," wrote the Chaplain of the Squadron, "to all the officers of our ship from the highest to the lowest to force the Bogue, and to demand without delay the Americans now held within their premises at Canton. But the apprehension is that, as their numbers are comparatively so small and a mob of a numerous populace is ever so ready to do the bidding of the reckless and the abandoned, our approach might be attended with danger from the rabble at Canton. The authorities themselves have said, all that they have to do for the destruction of those now within their power is to allow the mob to do their wishes. And there may be truth in all this, as there is a general impression among the lower classes of the Chinese at Canton that the foreign factories are filled with the precious metals, and that the plunder were well worth the sacrifice of the heads of a few 'foreign devils' that have the custody of it."

Probably the sudden appearance of the American naval vessels had a more important influence in dissuading Commissioner Lin from occupying Macao in such a way as to prevent the English from carrying out their plans to withdraw to that city as soon as the opium was delivered.[17]

It was not so much the action of the Chinese as that of the British which moved the Americans to ask for a com missioner to negotiate a treaty. Left to themselves, the

Americans would have been content with the old arrangements or at least they would not have moved to change them. They were even entirely willing—provided the merchants of other nations would agree to a similar course—to forego the opium trade, as the price of their future safety and comfort. Indeed they would have welcomed the end of the opium traffic, for its suppression would mean better markets for American produce. But now that the house of cards was tumbling, and the benevolent despotism under which they had been living was in the way of being altered, they not unnaturally wished the United States to be represented in the coming settlement.

CONGRESS BECOMES INTERESTED

When Congress took up the discussion of the Anglo-Chinese War in 1840, American public opinion was better prepared than at any time previously to express itself. The commercial interest in China, while still confined to the Atlantic seaboard, had broadened. Whereas twenty-five years before the steady drain of specie caused by the trade had created popular prejudice against it, now the growth of manufacturing in the North which looked to the South for supplies of raw cotton, tended to arouse a general interest in the markets of China. The reports of the American missionaries who had already been at work in China for a decade had stimulated in the United States an ever growing philanthropic interest in the Empire and their reports on the evils of the opium trade were a powerful factor in shaping public opinion. The American people were also alert to find in the conflict merely another phase of world-wide British aggression with which they had been made familiar in the War of 1812, the memory of which was still green. The tumultuous events of 1839 at Canton were followed in the United States with lively interest.

Early in January, 1840, the memorial of the American merchants at Canton asking for naval protection and the appointment of a commissioner to negotiate a treaty was presented to the House by Abbott Lawrence of Massa-chusetts.[18]

A resolution * passed in the House February 7, 1840, asking the President for information "respecting the condition of the citizens of the United States doing business during the past year in China; the state of the American trade with that country; and the interests of the people and commerce of the United States, as affected by the recent measures of the Chinese Government for the suppression of the contraband or forcible introduction of opium into China. Also whether the British Government had given notice to that of the United States of a purpose to blockade the ports of China, or of other hostile intentions towards that Government." [19]

In April a large group of Boston and Salem merchants and ship owners interested in the China trade, apparently fearing that Congress might be spurred to precipitate action, also memorialized Congress, urging caution. They submitted some additional information and expressed the fear that while the attention of the Chinese Government was engaged in the war the usual efforts to suppress the pirates along the coast would be neglected, and that American shipping, which was usually slightly armed and carried on with small crews, would be endangered. They therefore approved the request of their correspondents in China for an American naval force in Chinese waters. But beyond taking this action, they hoped that the government would proceed with great deliberation. They would even deprecate giving to any naval commander any powers to interfere in the conflict between England and China, or to enter into any diplomatic relations with the Chinese. "The result of more than one attempt," they stated, "of our British neighbors to improve their position with the Chinese has been upon each occasion the imposition of further restraint upon all foreigners and such, we believe, would follow any negotiations on the part of the Americans based upon the established usages among other nations." [20] This memorial, signed as it was

*Report submitted February 25, 1840.

by many who had already spent years in China, expressed
the wisdom of age as compared with the wisdom of youth,
and the advice was accepted. The East India Squadron,
under Commodore Kearny, was dispatched to China, but no
further step was taken.

It is interesting to observe in this memorial the inference
that the British aggression in China, so far from being regarded as an opportunity by the Americans, was really
looked upon as an embarrassment.

Public sentiment in the United States at the time was
clearly reflected in the following episode in the House
(March 16, 1840) when Caleb Cushing rose to interrogate
the chairman of the Committee on Foreign Affairs, and to
correct some 'misapprehensions' which appeared to
exist abroad as to the intentions of the United States in
China.[21]

After recalling the fact that he had proposed the resolution calling upon the President for information with reference to China, and that the memorial of the Canton merchants had been referred to the Committee on Foreign
Relations, he said:

"I am somewhat disturbed to learn, through the intelligence
brought by the *Great Western*, that these movements here are construed in England as indicating a disposition on the part of the
American Government 'to join heart and hand with the British Government, and endeavor to obtain commercial treaties from the authorities in China.' Now as for myself, I wish to say that this is a
great misconception, if it be not a wilful perversion, of what is contemplated here. I have, it is true, thought that the present contingency,—when the Americans in Canton, and they almost or quite
alone, have manifested a proper respect for the laws and public
rights of the Chinese Empire, in honorable contrast with the outrageous misconduct of the English there,—and when the Chinese
Government, grateful for the upright deportment of the Americans,
has manifested the best possible feeling toward them,—I have thought
that these circumstances afforded a favorable opportunity to endeavor to put the American trade with China on a just and stable
footing for the future.

"But God forbid that I should entertain the idea of cooperating
with the British Government in the purpose, if purpose it has, of
upholding the base cupidity and violence and high-handed infraction
of all law, human and divine, which have characterized the operation
of the British, individually and collectively, in the seas of China.

. . . I trust that the idea will no longer be entertained in England
that she will receive aid or countenance from the United States in
that nefarious enterprise."

Thus began the myth in the United States, at a time
when the Americans at Canton were riding rough-shod over
Commissioner Lin's embargo on English trade, and smuggling the English cargoes for the season, both in and out
of the port, that the American in China was an angel of
light. This complacency is entirely comparable with the
contemporaneous misrepresentations in England of Chinese
ethics and foreign policy.

Within a year three reports were laid before Congress;
a report of the Secretary of State, February 25, 1840, a report of the Secretary of the Treasury on the China trade,
July 1, 1840,[22] and a supplementary report of the Secretary
of State, January 25, 1841,[23] the last in response to a request
of John Quincy Adams, chairman of the House Committee
on Foreign Relations, for "copies of all documents in the
Department of State or other departments, showing the
origin of any political relations between the United States
and the Empire of China; the first appointment of a consul
to reside at or near Canton; whether such consul, or any
subsequently appointed, has ever been received or recognized in that capacity; and the present relations between
the Government of the United States and that of the Celestial Empire."

These three reports and the two memorials above discussed comprise a documentary history of American relations with China, giving in great detail the Terranova
incident of 1821, and the events of 1839.

Public sentiment ran strongly to disapproval of the Brit
ish action. It is notable that this opinion was by no means
confined to religious and philanthropic circles, but that it
extended to commercial interests. "China has a perfect
right to regulate the character of her imports,"[24] asserted
a writer in *Hunt's Merchants Magazine*. The leading
article in the same magazine for January, 1841, had pointed
out that while the importations of opium from India into

China had created a favorable condition for English commerce, it had not been beneficial to Americans. There was a general feeling that the extinction of the opium trade would help the commercial interests of the United States, as well as the moral and physical welfare of China. American and Chinese interests were in this, as well as in other points, identical.

The attitude of John Quincy Adams on the China question is especially worth noting for several reasons. He had been Secretary of State at the time of the execution of Terranova, and while he had refrained from expressing an opinion on the action of the Americans, he had been made familiar with an aspect of Chinese-American relations little understood or appreciated by those who were discussing the question in 1840-43. He was also the chairman of the Committee of Foreign Affairs, and at the same time he was intimately acquainted with the Boston and Salem merchants. A clue to the way Adams' mind was working is to be noted in his remarks on presenting for a third time (December 16, 1840) his resolution asking for the supplementāry report on the state of American political relations with the Celestial Empire. He recounted an incident [25] which, although not then made public, should be noted here. Snow had reported, after the English had withdrawn from Canton, and while the Americans were enjoying such unbounded prosperity through their almost complete monopoly of the trade, and were in more or less conflict with the Chinese authorities over the signing of the bond, and the importation of British goods:

"Correspondence with this government is exceedingly troublesome, for the replies to the Commissioner's edicts are seen by the Kwang-Chow-foo (Prefect) for the purpose of correcting any error that may be made in the translation, as any unguarded expression would bring him into certain trouble. The reply, of which I now send you a copy, was returned by this officer, requesting that I add an expression of gratitude for all favors bestowed upon me by the great Emperor, and likewise a hope for the continuation of the Celestial dynasty's trade with my nation, placing the *Celestial dynasty* about an inch higher on the paper than *my nation,* thereby admitting their superiority. I declined doing either, and sent it as originally written. These trifles serve to show their determination never to permit a foreign nation to presume to an equality with their own."

This, thought Adams, was the '*true* ground' of the war then raging between Great Britain and China—'this boasted superiority above every nation on earth.' Without going into a discussion of the objects and causes of the English war with China, it must be recognized that whatever may have been the immediate issues, Adams was right as to the fundamental instability of any relationship where English men—or Americans—were called upon to submit their lives and property unreservedly to a despotism, however benevo lent that despotism might ordinarily be in practice.

Adams made a careful study of both the American Gov ernment reports and the English blue books on the situation in China,[26] and in December, 1841, in a lecture before the Massachusetts Historical Society, he said:

"The fundamental principle of the Chinese Empire is anti-commercial. . . . It admits no obligation to hold commercial intercourse with others. It utterly denies the equality of other nations with itself, and even their independence. It holds itself to be the center of the terraqueous globe, equal to the heavenly host, and all other nations with whom it has any relations, political or commercial, as outside tributary barbarians reverently submissive to the will of its despotic chief. It is upon this principle, openly avowed and inflexibly maintained, that the principal maritime nations of Europe for several centuries, and the United States of America from the time of their acknowledged independence, have been content to hold commercial intercourse with the Empire of China.

"It is time that this enormous outrage upon the rights of human nature, and upon the first principle of the rights of nations should cease. .

"This is the truth, and, I apprehend, the only question at issue between the governments and nations of Great Britain and China. It is a general, but I believe altogether mistaken opinion that the quarrel is merely for certain chests of opium imported by British merchants into China, and seized by the Chinese Government for having been imported contrary to law. This is a mere incident to the dispute; but no more the cause of war, than the throwing overboard of the tea in the Boston harbor was the cause of the North American Revolution.

"The cause of war is the *kotow!*—the arrogant and insupportable pretensions of China, that she will hold commercial intercourse with the rest of mankind, not upon terms of equal reciprocity, but upon the insulting and degrading forms of relation between lord and vassal."[27]

"The excitement of public opinion and feeling by the delivery of this lecture," Adams recorded in his journal, "far exceeds any expectation that I had formed." Dr. John Palfry, editor of the *North American Review*, declined to print it as an article in the magazine.

Rev. Peter Parker, M. D., the first American medical missionary to China, visited the United States at this time and was very actively engaged in arousing and educating public opinion on the China question. He laid the matter before President Tyler and was frequently in touch with John Quincy Adams. In March, 1841, he urged that the United States extend its good offices to mediate between England and the Celestial Empire. Subsequently Parker asked Adams if he would consider the position of commissioner to China, to which the latter replied that he might, if the offer came from authorized quarters, but he thought that a formal mission at that time (June 2, 1842) was inexpedient.[28]

COMMODORE KEARNY'S MOST-FAVORED-NATION AGREEMENT

Six weeks after the signing of the Treaty of Nanking, between England and China, Commodore Kearny, being under the impression that the treaty had not yet been concluded, addressed the following letter to the Governor of Canton: [29]

"The undersigned is desirous that the attention of the Imperial Government might be called with respect to the commercial interests of the United States, and he hopes that the importance of their trade will receive consideration, and their citizens, in that matter, be placed upon the same footing as the merchants of the nation most favored."

A week later Kiying replied:

Decidedly it shall not be permitted that American merchants shall come to have merely a dry stick (that is, their interests shall be attended to). I, the Governor, will not be otherwise disposed than to look up to the heart of the great Emperor in his compassionate regard towards those men from afar, that Chinese and foreigners with faith and justice may be mutually united, and forever enjoy reciprocal tranquillity, and that it be granted to each of the resident merchants to obtain profit, and to the people to enjoy life and peace, and universally to participate in the blessings of great prosperity, striving to have the same mind."

Commodore Kearny returned to Macao in January, 1843, after a cruise to Manila, and heard rumors that only English vessels would be allowed to trade in the newly opened ports. In a private conversation Admiral Sir Thomas Cochrane told him that "the other nations must look out for themselves." Kearny therefore took opportunity, while communicating with the Governor about the settlement of some claims, to urge the necessity for most-favored-nation treatment to Americans in China. The Governor, under the misapprehension that Kearny had authority to settle the matter for the United States, replied that it was only necessary for him to await the arrival of the commissioners from the Emperor to make an agreement with reference to the trade "and when some plan is adopted, then a personal interview may be held with your honor, the commodore, and face to face, the relation of the two countries may be arranged, and the same reported to the Emperor."

The American officer thought he detected in the reply of the Governor an assumption of superiority for China as compared with the United States and therefore replied, disclaiming that the United States would come to China in the attitude of begging a favor.

"The commodore also avails of this communication again to say," he went on, "that what His Imperial Majesty grants to the traders from other countries, his own sovereign will demand for his merchants."

Kearny therefore urged the appointment of commissioners to negotiate a treaty. To this the Governor replied, withdrawing a little from his former cordiality, and assuring the commodore that anything so formal as a treaty was quite unnecessary.

On September 20, 1843, the consular agent at Canton notified the Secretary of State [30] that the trade had been thrown open to all foreigners on an equal footing. He stated: "Our countrymen have now all the privileges granted to the British, and the feeling of the Government and people of China continues favorably disposed towards Americans."

Credit for persuading the Chinese to open the ports to all nations on equal terms was claimed by the English Plenipotentiary, Sir Henry Pottinger,[31] but a subsequent discovery at Canton placed the matter in a different light. The Chinese text of Article VIII of the English treaty of 1843, when translated back into English, was found to be some what different from the original English text. It contains the following explanation:

"Formerly the merchants of every foreign nation were permitted to trade at the single port of Canton only, but last year it was agreed at Nanking, that if the Emperor should ratify the treaty, the merchants of the various nations of Europe should be allowed to proceed to the four ports of Foochow, Ningpo, Amoy and Shanghai for the purposes of trade, to which the English were not to make any objections. .   "[32]

From this it seems clear that neither to Sir Henry Pottinger nor to Commodore Kearny, but to the Chinese them selves belongs the credit of having opened their ports freely to other nations.

In the light of subsequent history this fact becomes especially interesting for the most-favored-nation clause, as applied to China became what is really the foundation of the more widely famed "open-door" policy. This policy, while obviously to the advantage of the Americans, was, equally clearly, the deliberate choice of the Chinese themselves. The Chinese have adopted a similar policy repeatedly in more recent times.

This promise of most-favored-nation treatment, the introduction of which into Chinese international affairs in the form of an iron-bound treaty agreement, is due primarily to Commodore Kearny, became in practice something far more than a block by which the door to commercial privileges could be held open. The clause had not been inserted in the Treaty of Nanking but it did appear in the British Supplementary Treaty of 1843, negotiated a few months after Kearny left China, and it has been included in every subsequent treaty engagement with a foreign Power. The open door of equal commercial opportunity, which it guaranteed, was one thing, and entirely desirable for China, but quite different was the fact that it became a device by which every nation thereafter could secure for itself any privilege which had been extorted by some other Power from China by force, or tricked from her by fraud, without having to assume the moral responsibility for the method by which the concession had been obtained.

Usually in after years when China took a hand in the international game she must play alone, against the entire and united company of Powers, a trick taken by her most unscrupulous opponent counted equally for the benefit of all.

The Mission Created

After the news of the signing of the Treaty of Nanking had been received, President Tyler (December 30, 1842) addressed to Congress a special message written by Daniel Webster, Secretary of State, dealing at length with the situation in the Sandwich Islands and in China. The message summarized the reports of the opening of new Chinese ports to British commerce but expressed ignorance as to whether these ports would also be open to the trade of other nations. It noted that the American trade while subject to great fluctuations, had reached as much as $9,000,000 annually, and would doubtless be greatly increased by means of access to the new ports.

"Being of the opinion," said the message, "that the commercial interests of the United States connected with China require at the present time a degree of vigilance such as there is no agent of this government on the spot to bestow, I recommend to Congress to make appropriation for the compensation of a commissioner to reside in China, to exercise a watchful care over the concerns of American citizens, and for the protection of their persons and property, empowered to hold intercourse with the legal authorities and ready, under instructions from his government, should such instructions become necessary and proper hereafter, to address himself to the high functionaries of the Empire, or through them to the Emperor himself." [33]

The President's message proposed a *resident* commissioner, continuously attending to the commercial and diplomatic affairs. The report on the proposed action by the Committee on Foreign Relations, presented January 24, 1843,[34] was much less specific proposing an appropriation of $40,000 to enable the President to accomplish that object, without deeming it necessary to designate the specific rank or character of the agents whom he may employ for that purpose, or more especially to limit the contingent expenses which may occur in the process of its accomplishment." This latter provision aroused the suspicions of many who did not have great confidence in President Tyler, and the report was passed (March 3, 1843), in an amended form providing that no person should be employed in the mission for more than $9,000, exclusive of outfit, and that no agent should be appointed without the advice and consent of the Senate.[35]

Even this arrangement was not satisfactory to every one. Senator Benton strenuously objected to the mission as being "wholly personal and invented for the indemnification to one person, for vacating his place for the benefit of another. I repeat it," cried Benton, "the mission is not created for the country but invented for one man; and he is now waiting to take it, and to go up and bump his head nineteen times against the ground in order to purchase the privilege of standing up before his Celestial Majesty."

Senator Benton's remark referred to the rumor that Edward Everett, then minister at the Court of St. James, was to be appointed to the mission, thus creating a place in London for Daniel Webster who was about to resign as Secretary of State. Whatever may have been the facts at the base of the rumor, and Webster denied in a personal letter to Everett that there was any basis for it, the selection of Edward Everett for the mission was evidence of the extreme importance which was now attached to the establishment of suitable diplomatic relations with China.

"It is not intended," wrote Webster to Everett, March 10, 1843,[36] "to dazzle the Emperor by show, nor soothe him by presents; still the mission should be respectable, and the commissioner should have the means proper and necessary to carry forward the undertaking.
Mr. Adams came to see me yesterday. He feels the greatest anxiety that you should undertake the China mission which he regards as a most important affair."

But Everett declined the nomination, and the post was given to Caleb Cushing of Newburyport, Massachusetts, a member of the Committee on Foreign Affairs, and a warm supporter of President Tyler. Senator Benton, a bitter partisan in the opposition to the President, described Cushing [37] as one who had been three times rejected in one day upon nomination for the position of Secretary of the Treasury, and said of him:

"He had deserted his party to join Mr. Tyler. He worked for him in and out of the House, and even deserted himself to support him—as in the two tariff bills of the current session; for both of which he voted, and then voted against them when vetoed."

A member of the House described him as the man who "had voted for every bill and then justified every veto."

"Cushing at the time of his appointment was forty-four years old, and had served in the House as a Whig since 1834. He was the son of a Newburyport ship owner, an amazingly brilliant lawyer, and probably as familiar with the questions with which he would have to deal in China as any man who could have been selected from public life. The secretary of the mission was Daniel Webster's son, Fletcher.

BIBLIOGRAPHICAL NOTES

1. Forbes' "Personal Reminiscences," p. 338; *Hunt's American Merchants*, Vol. 1, p. 64; Hunter's "Fan Kwae," p. 100; Sessional Papers, 1830, Vol. 6, p. 377.
2. Morse's "International Relations," Vol. 1, pp. 118-44, gives a full account of the Napier incident.
3. Staunton's Miscellaneous Notices, p. 16.
4. Chinese Repository, Vol. 5, July, 1836, pp. 138-144.

5. H. Doc. 119:26-1, Dispatch No. 17, March 5, 1839.
6. *Ibid.*
7. *Op. cit.,* No. 18, Mar. 22.
8. *Op. cit.,* No. 19, Apr. 19.
9. *Ibid.*
10. *Op. cit.* No. 20, May 13.
11. Captains' Letters (Navy Dept.) May 28, 1839, No. 101.
12. Forbes' "Reminiscences," p. 149.
13. *Ibid.,* pp. 151, 155.
14. H. Doc. 40:26-1.
15. "China and the China Trade," by R. B. Forbes (Boston, 1844) p. 49.
16. "The Flag Ship," by Fitch W. Taylor, New York, 1840. (2 vols.) Vol. 2, pp. 110-11.
17. H. Doc. 119:26-1, No. 21, May 22, 1839.
18. H. Jour. (26-1) p. 189; VIII Cong. Globe, p. 109; H. Doc. 40:26-1.
19. H. Jour. 26-1, p. 368; H. Doc. 119:26-1.
20. H. Jour. 26-1, p. 781; H. Doc. 170:26-1.
21. VIII Cong. Globe, 26-1, p. 275.
22. H. Doc. 119:26-1; H. Doc. 248:26-1; H. Doc. 71:26-2; H. Jour. 26-2, p. 46.
23. H. Doc. 71:26-2.
24. *Hunt's Merchants' Magazine,* March, 1843, p. 205.
25. H. Doc. 119:26-1, Dispatch 25, Sept. 25, 1839.
26. John Quincy Adams Memoirs, Vol. 11, p. 30.
27. Chinese Repository, Vol. 9, May, 1842, p. 281.
28. "Life and Letters of the Rev. and Hon. Peter Parker, M. D.," by Stevens and Marwick (Boston and Chicago, 1896) pp. 182-5, 220-1; Adams Memoirs, Vol. 10, pp. 444-5.
29. S. Doc. 139:29-1; The Kearny correspondence at Canton was published with great fullness in this document.
30. Canton Consular Letters, Vol. 3.
31. Littell's *Living Age,* Vol. 4, p. 387, quoting an address made by Sir Henry Pottinger.
32. Chinese Repository, Vol. 12, Mar., 1844, p. 145. (This article, as it appears in the treaties published by the Chinese Maritime Customs, is translated still differently). See also S. Ex. Doc. 67:28-2, Cushing to Calhoun, Aug. 26, 1844.
33. H. Doc. 35:27-3 gives this message in fuller form than Richardson, including the most recent trade statistics.
34. H. Report 93:27-3.
35. V. Statutes at Large, 24-28 Cong. Vol. 15, p. 624; H. Rept. 93:27-3. XII Cong. Globe, pp. 323, 325, 391.
36. Webster Papers (Lib. of Congress).
37. Benton's "Thirty Years' View." Vol. 2, p. 514.

CHAPTER VI

THE AMERICAN SHARE IN THE OPIUM TRADE

As has already been intimated the Americans entered the opium trade at an early day. They carried the drug to China from both Turkey and India. "Among the productions of Turkey, and Egypt," reads an old consular trade report from Smyrna, "there are many that would answer well for the internal consumption of the United States, or for their foreign expeditions." [1] Opium was mentioned as an article which might be shipped to India with profit, but the Americans quickly learned that the growing market for opium was farther East. The American trade in Turkey opium began as early as 1805, perhaps earlier, when three American brigs, two from Philadelphia and one from Baltimore, cleared from Smyrna with the drug. In that year the Americans took out one hundred and twenty-four cases and fifty-one boxes of the drug.

TURKEY AND INDIA OPIUM

The trade with Turkey increased, though not very rapidly, during the first three decades of the century. Vessels from Boston and Salem appeared in 1806,[2] and there had been one from New York the previous year. The American shipping returns for the year 1823 show the clearance of 18 vessels: 12 of Boston; 1 of Salem; 1 of Duxbury; 3 of Baltimore and 1 of Philadelphia. The following year there were 17 vessels, 14 of which were from Boston. They carried 1651 cases of opium. The largest amount of this drug reported as exported from Smyrna in any one year before 1830 was 1741 cases and chests. Complete figures are more difficult to obtain after 1828 for shortly before that

time the Turkey trade was shifted, in part, to Constanti-
nople. That the trade was profitable is shown by the fact
that one of the special agents employed by the United
States at that time to study trade conditions with Turkey
with a view to effecting a treaty with the Empire, reported
that opium would probably prove to be one of the most
profitable items in the trade.

Direct voyages from Turkey to China were not common
after the first few years. The opium was either shipped
directly to American ports and then transshipped to China
after subtracting the amount necessary for the American
market, or else it was transferred to China-bound vessels in
English ports. Sometimes, however, the cargoes were transshipped from one vessel to another at sea near Gibraltar.[3]

In China the Turkey opium was not so highly valued as
that from India. It sold for less and was sometimes used
in the adulteration of the higher priced product. It is
quite impossible to determine with any precision the
amounts of Turkey opium which were delivered in China,
for the smuggling was great. The earliest figures from
Canton show the following importations: Season 1805-6,
102 chests; 1806-7, 180 chests; 1807-8, 150 chests. It is
asserted by one who traded in it extensively that from 1827
to 1830 the Americans disposed of from twelve to fourteen
hundred piculs annually.[4] Whatever the amount, the
Americans were thoroughly identified, in the minds of the
Chinese, with Turkey opium.[5] When the survivors of the
wrecked bark *Sunda* were taken to Canton in 1839 and had
an interview with the commissioner, one of them reported:

"He [the commissioner] asked the names of the places from
whence the different kinds of opium were brought and requested me
[Dr. Hill] to write them down for him, which I did. On mentioning
Turkey, he asked if it did not belong to America, or form a part of
it and seemed a good deal astonished on being told that it was nearly
a month's sail distant."

The Americans' share in the importation of opium from
India is even more difficult to determine. American ships
carried cargoes freely from British India to Canton, and in

these consignments opium eventually appeared. At the time of the surrender of the opium to Commissioner Lin in 1839, out of a total of 20,283 chests, there were in the possession of Americans 1540 chests consigned to English firms. None of this consignment was from Turkey, but the Americans had about fifty cases of Turkey opium which they did not deliver.[6]

At no time did the American importation of opium form a very considerable share either of the total import of the drug or of the total amount of American imports, although it was reported in a Boston newspaper (1839) that the American interest in the "opium affair at Canton" amounted to a million and a quarter dollars. This, however, may have been an exaggeration. In the season 1818-9, the Americans are credited with importing 807 chests of Turkey opium alone, almost twenty per cent of the total import of the drug, but this was exceptional. Before 1840 Americans usually received on consignment in Canton, or carried in American vessels not more than one tenth of the total importations of opium, amounting in value some years to slightly more than one tenth of the total American importations to China.[7]

In the year 1800, in response to an Imperial edict, both the East India Company and the Chinese Co-hong ceased to handle the drug, and after 1809 the hong merchants were required to give bond that each ship secured by them carried no opium when it came up to the Whampoa anchorage. The trade was, however, carried on by the independent merchants openly in disregard of the edicts and with the connivance of the Chinese port authorities, until about 1821 when the Chinese Government again assumed a menacing attitude. From that time on "receiving ships" were anchored at Lintin, forty miles down the bay, and the transactions were for the most part confined to the delivery of the opium to the receiving ships by the inbound vessels. The trade was gradually extended from Lintin by the dispatch of small sailing vessels up and down the coast. The American flag flew over one or more of these receiving ships,

probably without interruption, from 1821 until the readjust-
ment in the trade caused by the beginning of the opium war.
From these receiving ships was transacted other business,
such as the sale of ship's supplies and the sale of enough
rice to empty vessels to enable them to come to Whampoa as
'rice ships' thus entering under the reduced port charges,
but the most lucrative part of the trade was in opium. The
owner of the American receiving ship at Lintin from 1830
to 1832 stated that he had made there a sufficient fortune
to enable him to leave China, as he then thought, for good.
His explanation of his rôle as opium trader was

"I shall not go into any argument to prove that I considered it
right to follow the example of England, the East India Company, the
countries that cleared it (opium) for China, and the merchants to
whom I always have been accustomed to look up to as exponents of
all that was honorable in trade."

He then mentions four firms, two of Boston, one of Salem
and one of New York.[8]

However, the leading American merchant at Canton,
John P. Cushing, discontinued dealing in opium after the
edict of 1821, perhaps influenced to do this by his good
friend Houqua. Cushing left Canton in 1828.

The Americans were far more deeply involved in the
opium trade at that time than appears from any statistics.
The existence of the trade itself conferred on them a direct
commercial benefit, for it reduced the necessity for the importation of specie by the substitution of bills on London.
Opium was sold in ever increasing quantities, and the
Americans, as well as the English and other foreigners, used
the bills thus obtained in place of specie to purchase their
return cargoes. In this phase of the opium trade the
Americans, all of them, benefited as much as, or more than,
the other traders. As the supply of furs began to diminish,
after 1820, and while the American cotton trade was in its
infancy, the increased importation of opium from whatever
country and by whomever transported, was a very important consideration. The system was vicious and short-
sighted economically, as the merchants afterwards came to

see. The consumption of opium demoralized the producing and consuming powers of China, led to greatly increased importation of specie, and the ill-will of the people, but when the capital of the American merchants was still relatively small, and the supply of acceptable specie limited, the opium trade, like slaves and distilleries, entered into the foundation of many American fortunes.

It is, therefore, the more remarkable that when the Chinese Government had clearly made up its mind to destroy the trade, there was so little effort made by the American merchants in China, or by their correspondents at home, to effect its legalization. It is also notable that at least one American firm, that of Talbot, Olyphant and Company of New York (Olyphant and Company of Canton), abstained entirely from the direct opium trade.

Conflicts with Chinese—the Pledge

Probably the most potent check on the growth of the American opium trade was the recognition of the fact that its existence was a constant menace to the maintenance of harmonious relations with the Chinese Government for, as has already been explained, peace was to the Americans the supreme virtue. More than twenty years before the advent of Commissioner Lin at Canton, the Americans had been made to feel the dangers of the opium traffic to peaceful trade.

The ship *Wabash* (Captain C. L. Gantt) of Baltimore, arrived in China May 22, 1817, with $7000 in specie and some opium. The vessel was boarded by pirates, the chief mate and some of the crew murdered or drowned, and the vessel looted. In making a report of the affair to the Governor, Consul Wilcocks wrote to the Secretary of State that "in enumerating the loss I was careful not to mention the opium." But his precautions were in vain for when the pirates were arrested some of the opium was found in their possession. "The latter circumstance," wrote Wilcocks, "occasioned not a little disgust on the part of the

Viceroy." However, the Viceroy sent a communication to the acting Hoppo (Customs officer), who in turn communicated it to the hong merchants, to give to the American consul, who was to report to the President of the United States of America what steps had been taken to apprehend and punish the pirates.

This was followed by the first official notification addressed directly to the Americans on the subject of opium. It was sent by the hong merchants to Wilcocks, and read as follows:[9]

"May He be Highly Promoted:

"We approach to inform you that foreign opium, the dirt used in smoking, has long been prohibited by an order received; it is not allowed to come to Canton; if it is presumptuously brought, the moment it is discovered, it will immediately involve the security merchant; and the cause of the said vessel bringing the dirt for smoking to Canton will also assuredly be examined into; and a prosecution begun which will impede her departure. The consequences are exceedingly important. We, being apprehensive that the foreign merchants of your honorable country who come to Canton to trade, may not all fully know the hindrance arising from bringing it to Canton, do therefore especially prepare a letter to inform you.

"Benevolent Brother, to write a letter immediately back to your country and tell these things to your honorable country's president, that all the ships which come to Canton may be caused to know that Opium, the dirt used in smoking is an article

THE CELESTIAL EMPIRE

prohibits by an order received from the Son of Heaven, and hereafter, most positively, they must not buy it and bring it to Canton.

"If they bring it, the moment we examine into it and find it out, certainly we will not dare to be security for the said ship, and moreover will assuredly report it fully to the Great Officers of the Government who will, according to law, investigate and prosecute. Decidedly you will not dare to conceal the affair for those (who import it) and thereby bring guilt on ourselves. The trade of the said ship will assuredly be impeded by the smoking dirt and when seeking to repeat, it will be a difficult thing (for the persons concerned) to find it availing.

"Do not say that we did not speak soon enough.

"We pray you, Benevolent Brother, to write a letter immediately and tell these things. It will be fortunate if you do not view it as a commonplace affair, and so delay, and cause future impediments.

"To Mr. Wilcocks, Benevolent Brother, for his perusal,

"We, Younger Brothers, commonly called—" (eleven names).

John Quincy Adams, as Secretary of State, replied to Wilcocks:

"The Communication from the Co-hong merchants to yourself has been published (*National Register, 1818*) agreeably to the wishes of those merchants."

In 1821 a quarrel between the various Chinese officials and the Terranova case dragged once more the opium smuggling into the light of day. The practice of the British, American and Portuguese ships was exposed in a proclamation from the Viceroy.[10] The guilt of the Americans was mitigated, observed the Viceroy, "because they had no king to rule them," but all foreigners were warned that the opium smuggling must stop. Wilcocks was ordered by the hong merchants, at the request of the Viceroy, to investigate each American ship personally and put a watch on her, to see that she contained and disposed of no opium. The *Robinson*, an American vessel, was to be forbidden to come to the port again and the *Emily*, of Baltimore, to the crew of which the unfortunate Terranova had belonged, was to have half her cargo confiscated, and she also was to be forbidden the port. At length the Viceroy agreed to remit the confiscation of half of the cargo of the vessels, but remarked in an edict to the hong merchants:

"As to one of the four ships, viz., Cowpland's (the *Emily* of Balti more) it contained merely about a thousand catties of foreign tin, worth scarcely anything—and it paid for port charges upwards of one thousand four hundred taels, from which it appears that the said vessel came for no other purpose but to sell opium—INFINITELY DETESTABLE.

"Rightly did Heaven send down punishment, and cause Francis Terranova to commit a crime for which he was strangled. This ship should be punished more severely. Only as the other ships have had clemency extended to them, and the value of the cargoes given back, I shall remit the sentence on all equally, and shall deal with it as with the others to inflict a light punishment.

"In one word

THE CELESTIAL EMPIRE

permits tea, rhubarb, etc., to be sold to keep alive the people of the said nations. Those persons who are annually kept alive thereby are more than ten thousand times ten thousand. How substantial a favor is this! Yet these foreigners feel no gratitude; nor wish to render a recompense; but smuggle in prohibited opium, which flows and poisons the land.

"When the conduct is referred to the heart, it must be disgusted. When referred to the reason, it is contrary to it.

"In broad day, on earth, there is the Royal Law. In Hades after death are gods and demons. These foreign ships pass an immense ocean, go through gales of wind, boisterous seas of unknown dangers, entirely preserved by the condescending protection of

THE CELESTIAL GODS

and therefore they should hereafter rouse themselves to a zealous reflection—to bitter recompense—to reformations—and alter their inhuman unreasonable conduct—and they will receive forever the gracious bounty of

THE CELESTIAL EMPIRE."

It was as a result of the effective measures taken by the Chinese and the dangers which the hong merchants now incurred by giving a bond for ships, that the opium business was removed from Canton and Whampoa to receiving ships at Lintin.

That the crisis of 1839 had been brought on by the opium trade was clearly and frankly recognized by the American merchants when they addressed to Congress their memorial asking for a commissioner and a treaty. The memorialists made an honest statement of the condition of the traffic, drawing especial attention to the fact that while it had been carried on by smuggling the Chinese officials, from the lowest to the highest, had shared in the accompanying bribery, large amounts of opium having been delivered at Lintin directly to boats carrying the flags of the high officials, the chief customs officer and even the governor. The Americans pointed out that the Chinese Government possessed ample power to control the trade and was now adopting a somewhat inconsistent and unjust method in that it was proceeding first not against its own subjects, but against the foreigners. This was a characteristic method of Chinese procedure.

Before addressing the memorial to Congress most of the Americans at Canton had signed a "voluntary pledge" to abstain from the trade in the future. In this pledge the other foreign merchants had joined, and it is clear from the spirit of the memorial that the Americans, at the time they signed it, supposed that the foreign opium trade of China was definitely finished.

"Whether we view the subject in a moral and philanthropic light," stated the memorialists, "or merely as a commercial proposition, we are extremely desirous to see the importation and consumption of opium in China entirely at an end." [11]

In subsequent years the vision of their signatures to this pledge to the Chinese and this memorial to Congress must have plagued the signers not a little, though it did not prevent them from evading and even openly violating the promises they had made. The British and the Parsee merchants were the first to forget their promises, and the Americans were not long in yielding to the demands of competition in a trade of which opium had become an integral part, but there is little doubt but at the time of signing these documents the Americans were perfectly sincere.

However, three days after signing of the pledge, Commander George C. Read of the U. S. Frigate *Columbia* reported to the Secretary of the Navy from Macao: [12]

"There is yet much opium on board the English vessels now lying in the roads of this place, which will never be returned to the country from whence it came. A sale of it must be made here on the coast, and I shall not be surprised to hear of its being smuggled under American colors. If such illicit commerce should be persisted in, and vessels should be detected in the act, notwithstanding all the difficulties and dangers to which it would expose the foreigners at Canton, I feel that I should be justified in seizing them, but what to do with them afterwards would be a question of serious consideration, and merely to drive them off the coast would be to permit return. But I trust there are none among them so wicked."

The opium trade began again almost immediately after the surrender of the twenty thousand chests, but the Americans for a time kept their pledge. One of the signers of the memorial to Congress, then the superintendent of Russell and Company, writing five years later said: [13]

"The trade was carried on . . . we believe, entirely by the British —the Americans having retired from it as soon as they found it to their interests to do so, fearing that it would embarrass their regular business, and knowing that they would be within the power of the local authorities of Canton, while the British were out of their reach at Macao and at Hongkong."

On two subsequent occasions Consul Snow reported to the State Department[14] that so far as he knew there was not an American in China in any way engaged in the trade.

COMMODORE KEARNY'S ACTION

In response to the request of the Americans in Canton for Naval protection (presented to Congress January 9, 1840), Commodore Lawrence Kearny was dispatched to China in command of the East India Squadron with orders to protect Americans, and also to take action against any Americans who might have entered the opium trade. He found upon his arrival, April, 1842, only two years after the pledge had been given, evidence not to be doubted[15] that Captain Read's fears had been well grounded. The American flag was being used extensively to cover opium smuggling, and American citizens, as individuals, if not as firms, were actively engaged in the trade.

Immediately after his arrival Kearny requested the American vice consul at Canton, who was afterwards shown to be implicated in the smuggling, to have published the following letter:[16]

"SIR:—The Hongkong Gazette of the 24th instant contains a shipping report in which is the name of an American vessel engaged in carrying opium,—therefore I beg you will cause to be made known with equal publicity, and also to the Chinese authorities by the translation of the same, that the Government of the United States does not sanction 'the smuggling of opium' on this coast under the American flag in violation of the laws of China. Difficulties arising therefrom in respect to the seizure of any vessels by the Chinese, the claimants certainly will not under my instructions find support, or any interposition on my part after the publication of this notice."

The publication of this notice was greeted with derision by the English[17] and lost some of its force when the Governor of Canton, a few days later addressed the hong merchants:

"I find, on examination, that the Americans have acted in a manner most highly respectful and obedient. Their vessels hitherto engaged in the commerce of Canton, have always been confined to the legitimate and honorable trade, and never concerned with the carrying of opium."

Kearny set about with earnestness to protect the American flag from the stain of further opium smuggling, but received little cooperation from the consular officer. He remained on the China coast for more than a year, and just before he left actually arrested the *Ariel,* taking away her papers and sending her to Macao. To the Secretary of the Navy (May 19, 1843) he wrote from Amoy:

"The American flag is now the only cover for this illicit trade, Sir Henry Pottinger having issued a proclamation against it; and the English craft having been turned away from the rivers, has placed the Americans in a peculiarly advantageous position, as freighters, under the flag of the United States. . . .

"With regard to the *Ariel,* I have taken her papers and colors from her; and I have obliged her master to discharge the whole of her cargo here, and then he is to return to Macao. Her papers are endorsed by me in a manner which will render them unavailable, and are returned sealed to the consulate. Were it not for the risk, I would send her to the United States; but she capsized once or twice in Boston harbor before she sailed, and is now a dangerous vessel. Should I fall in with any sea-worthy vessels of her character, I shall send them home, that their case may be properly decided by the laws, of which the owners, as well as the consular establishment of the United States, seem to have been clearly regardless in making transfers that are illegal. These sham sales are well known, by which our national character is daily losing ground, and will so continue to do while the public consular duties are confined to merchants whose interests are so deeply involved in the transactions before cited."

But the only ground Kearny could find on which to arrest the *Ariel* was not that she was an opium smuggler, but that her ownership was vested nominally in a man professing American citizenship, yet who had not been in the United States for at least six years. The *Ariel* quickly resumed trade again. She had been built and sent to China expressly for that purpose.

Whatever may have been the legality of the transfer by which the fleet of American opium smugglers appeared in Chinese waters under other than their real ownership, the interested parties had not been inattentive to the status of United States law on the subject of smuggling opium into China, as may be seen from the following incident.

Commodore Foxhall A. Parker, commanding the East India Squadron, was ordered to proceed to Bombay in the latter part of 1843 and there take on board the newly appointed American commissioner and convey him to China. In his orders was the following item, substantially the same as Kearny's instructions three years before: [18]

"You will take all occasions to impress upon the Chinese and their authorities that one great object of your visit is to prevent and punish the smuggling of opium in China either by Americans, or by other nations under cover of the American flag, should it be attempted."

While Parker was lying in the harbor waiting for the arrival of Cushing, Fletcher Webster, Secretary of the Mission, arrived from Boston as a passenger on the brig *Antelope*. The vessel having disembarked her passenger, proceeded, under the nose of the U. S. East India Squadron, to load opium for China. Whereupon Parker looked up his instructions and tried to look up the American law on the subject. He reported (November 27, 1843) to the Secretary of the Navy:

"I cannot find any law which will authorize my interfering to prevent or punish smuggling by Americans or others in foreign countries. The only course that appears proper for me to pursue is not to interfere in their favor, should they be taken by the Chinese authorities.

"The schooner *Zephyr*, of Boston, sailed from this port a few days ago for China, loaded with opium, and the brig *Antelope*, also of Boston, is now up for a freight of opium only, for the same place."

"You will oblige me by sending particular instructions on this subject."

But no instructions ever came. This episode ended any efforts on the part of the American naval officers to prevent opium smuggling.

The American builders of the opium clippers had also not overlooked the fact that these vessels could look to no American authority for protection. In the first place they were built to outsail any other ships afloat, and they did. In the second place they were heavily armed. The *Antelope,* for example, carried two guns on each side, besides a "Long Tom" amidships. Boarding pikes were arranged in great plenty on a rack around the main-mast, and the large arms chest on the quarter deck was well supplied with pistols and cutlasses. "We were fully prepared," wrote one of the officers, "for a brush with the rascally Chinese and determined not to be put out of our course by one or two Mandarin boats."[19]

BIBLIOGRAPHICAL NOTES

1. "Smyrna Consular Letters," Vol. 1, enclosure in, Wm. Steward, April 25, 1803, to Secretary of State.
2. Smyrna Letters.
3. Forbes' "Reminiscences," p. 124; Sessional Papers (1830) Vol. 6, testimony of Joshua Bates, p. 378.
4. Forbes' "China Trade," p. 27.
5. Chinese Repositoy, Vol. 8, Jan. 1840, p. 486.
6. Hunter's "Fan Kwae," p. 146.
7. Niles' *Register,* Oct. 12, 1839, p. 112, quoting Boston *Transcript;* Morse's International Relations, Vol. 1, pp. 206-11.
8. Forbes' "Reminiscences," p. 145.
9. Canton Consular Letters, Vol. 1, Sept. 23, 1817, Wilcocks to Secretary of State.
10. S. Wells Williams' "Middle Kingdom," Vol. 2, pp. 379 ff; H. Doc. 71:26-2.
11. H. Doc. 119:26-1, p. 31; H. Doc. 40:26-1.
12. Captains' Letters (Navy Dept.), May, 1839, No. 101.
13. Forbes' "China Trade," p. 50.
14. Canton Consular Letters, Vol. 3, Sept. 23, 1839, Jan. 11, 1840.
15. S. Doc. 139:29-1. The mere fact that these reports from Kearny were published is an indication of the policy of the Government of the United States.
16. Chinese Repository, Vol. 11, April, 1842, p. 259.
17. Canton *Register,* April 5, 1842.
18. East India Squadron Letters (Navy Dept.), Feb. 27, 1843, Sept. 25, 1845, p. 36.
19. Lubbock's "China Clippers," p. 26; Clark's "Clipper Ship Era," p. 58.

CHAPTER VII

PREPARATION FOR THE CUSHING MISSION

In preparing to negotiate a treaty with China the
United States was at a distinct disadvantage as compared
with Great Britain, the only formidable commercial rival,
for the American Government was without any large store
of accumulated wisdom and precedents for dealing with
Oriental states. Before making the Treaty of Nanking
Great Britain had already concluded trade agreements or
political treaties with nearly every native state of Africa
and Asia with which the Western World was in contact.
England was therefore merely extending her elaborate and
closely integrated commercial system to include one more
outpost. The appropriation of Hongkong for a military,
naval and trade base was, for example, but the newest
application of a policy of commercial expansion the technique for which had been maturing for a century. The
United States, in contrast, had entered into treaty relations
with only two Asiatic states and in these instances the
American efforts had been casual, unrelated to any general
policy, and unproductive of much experience which could
be turned to account in securing a treaty with China.
However, a brief review of the mission of Edmund Roberts
to Cochin China, Siam, and Muscat in 1832-4 is important
not merely to complete a chapter of American history but
also because the Roberts Mission did have some slight
influence on the preparations for the Cushing Mission.

The Edmund Roberts Mission

Edmund Roberts of Portsmouth, New Hampshire, was
a merchant and a supercargo [1] who had risen to the rank of

ship owner only to lose what little he had accumulated by "bare-faced robbery under the Berlin and Milan decrees," to use his own description of the process by which his property had been appropriated and his fortunes ruined. For a number of years he had engaged in fruitless efforts to rehabilitate himself but with little success. In 1823 he was appointed United States Consul at Demarara. Four and a half years later he was a supercargo on an American vessel at Zanzibar where he was subjected to vexatious delays and impositions by the officers of the Sultan of Muscat. To his Highness he addressed a letter complaining that American vessels were not being received upon equal terms with those of England. He invited the Sultan to enter into correspondence with the American Government and suggested that he offer to make a treaty with the United States. Roberts did not fail to point out to the Sultan that the United States "can never come in contact with your Highness as the English Government will, sooner or later, for it is contrary to the constitution of the United States to own colonies out of their proper territory. Acts of this kind have been the cause of more devastating war than any or all the other outrages put together."

The Sultan was so impressed with the representations of Roberts that, although he did not wholly comply with his requests, he did ask the American supercargo to procure for him some bombs and shells with which to drive out the Portuguese, and enjoined Roberts to keep the matter secret from the English.

Roberts on this voyage probably penetrated the Orient no farther than Bombay. Immediately upon his return to the United States he took up with Levi Woodbury, senator from New Hampshire, the suggestion which had evidently been in his mind at Zanzibar, viz., "that considerable benefit would result from effecting treaties with some of the native powers bordering on the Indian Ocean."

Meanwhile the British Governor General of India succeeded in making a treaty with Siam in 1826. While the negotiation of this treaty was in process John Shellaber,

United States Consul at Batavia, sought a commission to negotiate treaties with some of the independent native sovereigns near Java, having particularly in mind a treaty with Siam.[2]

The report of the plundering of the pepper ship *Friendship* of Salem by the natives of Quallah Battoo on the northwest coast of Sumatra in 1830 roused the Government of the United States to action. Meanwhile Edmund Roberts, with the persistence which was his most conspicuous characteristic, had been pressing his suggestion upon Levi Woodbury who became Secretary of the Navy in the Jackson administration. In 1831 Shellaber came home from Batavia on leave and renewed the proposition which he had made six years before. Shellaber returned to his post the next year supposing that he was to be designated to the mission which was then decided upon but Roberts, backed by his influential friend Woodbury, received the appointment January 26, 1832. The government directed the U. S. S. *Potomac*, the sloop *Peacock*, and the schooner *Boxer*, to undertake an expedition against the natives of Quallah Battoo,[3] and at the request of the Navy Department, Roberts was made a special agent of the United States to meet, confer, treat, and negotiate with the kings of Siam and Cochin China. He was assigned to the *Peacock* where he was entered on the rolls as "secretary to the commander." The reason given for the creation of this somewhat equivocal and ignominious rôle was secrecy, but it is difficult to resist the conclusion that it was a fair index of the importance of the mission in the estimation of the government. The salary was fixed at $1200, and only after pleadings by Roberts was it increased to $1500. During part of the outward voyage the special agent was compelled to sleep on the gun deck of the *Peacock*—an indication, perhaps, of the prevailing customary scorn of naval officers for civilians.

From the outset the Department of State appears to have been far more interested in securing a treaty with Japan and set about collecting the necessary information.

Some of this was secured from Shellaber, who as consul at Batavia had been familiar with the Dutch trade at Nagasaki, and some of it came from unknown sources. Before Roberts left the United States in 1832 the State Department was in possession of a large part of the information about Japan on which the Perry expedition twenty years later was based. A commission, similar to those already issued for Cochin China and Siam, to negotiate with Japan was issued to Roberts July 6, 1832.

The subject of diplomatic relations with Oriental despots presented some embarrassments peculiar to a republican government. In submitting an outline program for the proposed negotiations Shellaber wrote to the Secretary of State:

"I beg leave to suggest that there be no expression in the letters (from the President) to these sovereigns (of Siam, Cochin China and Japan), or credentials of the mission, that may lead those people to think that the United States is a republic. Those despots would affect to become alarmed at an intercourse with the United States as free as it is, if they come at the knowledge of its peculiar government through its own official papers."

From the Rev. Robert Morrison, the famous British missionary and sinologue of the East India Company at Canton, to whom Roberts had written soliciting advice as to the proper manner to approach such potentates, Roberts had received some instructions which were valuable and are especially interesting as coming from one who had a real sympathy for the Asiatic, a thorough knowledge of his ways, and had also been the Chinese secretary and interpreter of the unsuccessful Lord Amherst Embassy to Peking in 1816. The advice was to avoid vague pretexts and special excuses, and to approach the kings directly and boldly as the representative of an independent people who would have nothing to do with "kowtowing." The relationship to be established must be reciprocal, not that of lord and vassal. Roberts was warned, however, not to make himself "too cheap" in the negotiations; he was to be kind and courteous, but to insist on "some little formalities." A little display and show of clothing, Morrison thought, would have a certain weight and create a favorable impression.

Roberts advised the Department of State that "in ne gotiations with the Asiatics all *apparent* acknowledgment of inferiority which precedes the signature to letters such as 'your humble servant' would be construed all too literally by the potentates of Asia and ought therefore to be avoided in drafting the letters from President Jackson.

The considerations raised by Shellaber, Morrison and Roberts required careful thought but the Government of the United States decided, while not flaunting its republicanism, nevertheless, not to conceal its true colors. The letters from President Jackson carried by Roberts in 1832 did not obscure the fact that Andrew Jackson was "President of the United States" and the unbending salutation "Great and Good Friend" fairly throbbed with a republicanism such as the despots of Asia had never envisaged in their worst dreams.

Secretary of State Livingston even went so far as to decide not to send any presents with Roberts, but at the latter's earnest solicitation this decision was reversed. The list of the gifts included: 100 rifles, 100 muskets, 100 sets of infantry accouterments, 2 heavily gold-mounted swords, 2 full length mirrors, 10 pairs of lamps, 250 yards of carpeting, 5 pairs of stone statues for the king and officials of Siam; and 2 pairs of glass lamps, a sword, a rifle and a pair of pistols, a silk flag and a map of the United States, and a set of the gold, silver and copper coins of the United States, for the Sultan of Muscat. A steam engine mounted on a "highly polished rail car" and a "railroad 12 feet in diameter which can be screwed to the floor of the room" was also included in the purchases, but owing to a delay in the shipments this unusual present appears never to have reached its intended recipient.

The *Potomac* sailed for Quallah Battoo in advance of the *Peacock* and when the latter reached Anjier Roads the expedition to Sumatra had been completed. Roberts was therefore free to devote himself directly to the gentler methods of diplomacy. After securing the services of J. R. Morrison, as interpreter, the *Peacock* set sail from Macao for the coast of Cochin China. The *Boxer*, which had been intended for the use of the mission in approaching the shallow harbors, had not yet arrived, and the *Peacock* found it impossible to approach closely to Hué. Contact with the local officials was established farther down the coast, but Roberts met with obstacles. The Cochin Chinese immediately raised questions of etiquette and the kowtow, and the American envoy refused to yield. The *Peacock* departed for Siam in disgust. At Bankok the reception was all that could be desired, and a treaty was concluded March 30, 1833. The linguistic difficulties of the negotiations are evident in the fact that the text of the treaty was in four languages—English, Chinese, Portuguese and Siamese.

The Roberts treaty with Siam, when compared with the British treaty of 1826, shows no notable differences. By it American vessels secured a very great reduction in the measurement dues such as the British had already secured. There were to be no import or export duties, and freedom of trade without governmental interference was stipulated. There was no slightest suggestion of extraterritorial concessions. From the American treaty, however, was omitted certain provisions which had been included in the British treaty defining the procedure and penalties in cases of manslaughter.

Roberts attempted to secure the legalization of the opium trade which had been prohibited in the British treaty, but at the last minute this 'valuable and highly profitable' article was placed in the list of contrabands.

At Batavia Roberts received from Secretary of State Livingston a letter again instructing him to proceed to Japan, but Roberts decided that such an expedition at that time would be impractical. The terms of service on the *Peacock* were soon to expire, and Roberts was without funds to provide for the Shogun presents which would stand comparison with those sent annually by the Dutch. The wind was fair for Muscat and the *Peacock* took advantage of it. There is no evidence that the American Government had any real interest in that part of the Mission which was however very near to Roberts' heart because of his previous experience at Zanzibar.

A treaty with the Sultan, the first commercial treaty he had ever signed, was concluded September 21, 1833. It provided for a reduction of duties from seven and one-half per cent on both exports and imports to a single five per cent charge to be levied merely on such goods as were landed. There was to be no export duty and no pilotage charge. The treaty also contained a most-favored-nation clause. Extraterritoriality was stipulated to the extent that the American consul was to be the exclusive judge of all disputes and suits in which American citizens were engaged with each other. Six years later the British Government made a treaty with the Sultan which included the advantages gained under the American treaty and added to them amplified extraterritorial concessions.

The treaties with Siam and Muscat were duly ratified by the Senate and in March, 1835, Roberts was commissioned to exchange their ratifications. He was also directed to resume the negotiations with Cochin China and then to proceed to Japan. His compensation was increased to $4,400 a year but his request for an increase in rank was not granted. He exchanged the ratifications as planned but at Bankok contracted a disease which made his efforts to get into communication with the authorities at Cochin China fruitless, and as his illness increased it became necessary to hurry on to Macao where he died June 12, 1836. The untimely death of Roberts brought to an end the proposed mission to Japan.

WEBSTER CONSULTS THE MERCHANTS

The omission of China from the program of Edmund Roberts on both the first and the second missions is significant. Neither Roberts or Shellaber had urged a treaty with China and there had been no demand for it among the China merchants.

As soon as Congress had approved of the proposed China mission in 1843, and before it was known who would be the commissioner, Daniel Webster sent a circular letter to most of the American merchants resident in Boston, Salem, New York and elsewhere, engaged in the China trade, inviting suggestions. This letter received from many persons very careful attention and the replies to it are the best sources of information as to the attitude of the American merchants towards the trade at that time.

It is significant that only one reply even mentions the subject of opium.[5] This firm wrote:

"It is most likely that the Chinese Government will urge the Commissioner to interpose the authority of his office to prevent the participation of citizens of the United States in the opium trade. But we conceive it would be extremely impolitic to assume any engagements whatever concerning this traffic that would require for their fulfillment the restraining, controlling, or influencing of our citizens in any degree. They have always been more or less engaged in the trade and probably always will be, however repugnant it unquestionably is to justice and humanity. We believe that ultimately the Emperor will find it necessary to legalize the traffic under the imposition of heavy duties."

Seven Boston firms and individual merchants united in a joint reply to Webster's request. This letter was prepared by John M. Forbes, a partner in the firm of Russell and Company who, though then a resident in the United States, had served his apprenticeship in China.[6] This communication made the following recommendations:

(1) The Mission should be accompanied by a respectable fleet, because many of the Chinese are now under the impression that the United States has only two naval vessels.

(2) No presents, *as such,* should be sent, lest the Chinese should call them tribute. But this ought not to prevent some tactful representations of friendship. "The Chinese look upon us as friends, but they have a great fear of encroachment by other foreign nations, and if we could, in a quiet way, without infringing upon the courtesies

due to Great Britain, contribute anything to the means of defense against further aggression it would open the eyes of the Emperor to the value of an alliance with us, more than the prospect of increasing their trade a hundred fold."

(3)   The Mission will find it necessary first to stop at Macao but possibly it ought to go on to Canton, or preferably to the mouth of the Pei-ho.

(4)   The Provincial authorities at Canton should be informed in advance of the coming of the Mission, and should be notified that it will proceed to the North.

(5)   Two interpreters will be necessary. Dr. Peter Parker is recommended.

(6)   The commissioner must be warned that the Chinese will be disposed to contest every point. An appeal to arms may be necessary, and it will be well, if possible, to *follow* the English in making a treaty. If the English do not go to Peking, the American minister must exercise "infinite caution" about going there. "All experience in Chinese affairs shows that no foreign nation ever yet gained any disputed point by peaceful negotiation."

The letter closes with some general advice. The signers assume that the United States is not prepared to *enforce* the reception of an envoy, or the making of a treaty. Nevertheless the opportunity is such that, although the Americans already enjoy all the privileges possessed by the English, it may be possible to secure by treaty what otherwise would be enjoyed only by the sufferance of the Chinese. However, it would be well not to become involved in any questions of diplomacy in such a way as to lose the privileges which are already enjoyed. In conclusion the merchants give the cautious advice, born of half a century of experience, "If our Envoy does not see his way to *succeed,* let him *do nothing;* let him wait the proper time to act, and if his patience fail, let him be authorized to return home, leaving some member of his mission as *Chargé* to wait an opening."

Many of the other replies to Webster's letter mentioned that a merchant should not be chosen as commissioner, because of the low esteem in which merchants were held by the Chinese. Among the grievances mentioned which the commissioner must seek to correct were the delay and method of settling claims, especially those against the insolvent hong merchants, excessive tonnage dues, the corruption of the customs house officials, and the arbitrary stopping of the entire trade.*

A memorandum note, in the archives of the State Department,[7] countersigned by President Tyler, shows the following list of furnishings with which the Mission was to be provided: a set of best charts, and if possible a globe; a pair of 6-shooting pistols, rifles, etc.; model of war-steamer; model of a steam excavator; Daguerreotype apparatus ("it can be purchased, perhaps, in France"); some approved works on fortification, gunnery, ship-building, military and naval strategy, geology, chemistry, and the "Encyclopedia Americana"; a telephone, spy-glass, barometer, and thermometer; and some useful articles made of India rubber. Against the item "a model of a locomotive steam engine, and a plan of railroad, is the pencilled notation: "Will require too much time to prepare. J. T."

INSTRUCTIONS TO CUSHING

The official instructions, prepared by Secretary of State Webster, to guide the actions and negotiations of the first

*On March 22, 1843, Levi Lincoln, collector of the port of Boston, transmitted to Daniel Webster, at the latter's request, the following list of the principal Boston and Salem houses and individuals engaged in the China trade:

William Appleton & Co.	Boston
J. L. Gardner & Co.	"
J. M. Forbes	"
Daniel C. Bacon	"
Daniel P. Parker	"
Bryant, Sturgis & Co.	"
J. J. Dixwell	"
Minot and Hooper	
F. W. Macondray	
Alfred Richardson	"
Joseph Peabody	Salem
Stephen C. Phillips	"
David A. Neal & Bros.	"
David Pingree	"
Michael Shepard & Co.	"

On March 24, 1843, J. S. Hone, assistant collector of the port of New York, transmitted the following names for New York:

N. L. & G. Griswold
Talbot, Olyphant & Co.
Howland & Aspinwall
Grinnell, Minturn & Co.
Cary & Co.
Gordon & Talbot
Boorman, Johnston & Co.
Alfred A. Low.
Goodhue & Co.

Presumably letters were addressed to all of these firms, inviting suggestions, though not all of them appear to have replied.

American commissioner constitute the first official declaration of American policy for China.[8]

The primary object of the Mission was to be "to secure the entry of American ships and cargoes into these ports [Amoy, Ningpo, Foochow and Shanghai, which had been opened to English trade by the treaty of Nanking, August 25, 1842] on terms as favorable as those which are enjoyed by English merchants." As to the manner of the negotiations the instructions were very explicit. Cushing was to use the greatest tact towards the Chinese in allaying "their repulsive feelings towards foreigners." "Your constant aim," stated the instructions, "must be to produce a full conviction in the minds of the Government and the people, that your mission is entirely pacific; that you come with no purposes of hostility or annoyance; that you are a messenger of peace, sent from the greatest Power in America to the greatest Empire in Asia, to offer respect and good will and to establish the means of friendly intercourse." In this connection the Commissioner was instructed to make very clear that the American Government, so far from supporting its citizens in smuggling of any sort, would relinquish all jurisdiction over such traders and "will not interfere to protect them from the consequences of their own illegal conduct."

Another method suggested to prove the friendly intent of the Americans, was to point out the contrasts between the United States and England.

"It cannot be wrong for you to make known, where not known, that the United States, once a country subject to England, threw off the subjection years ago, asserted its independence sword in hand, established that independence after a seven years' war, and now meets England upon equal terms upon the ocean and upon the land. The remoteness of the United States from China, and still more the fact that they have no colonial possessions in her neighborhood, will naturally lead to the indulgence of a less suspicious and more friendly feeling than may have been entertained towards England, even before the late war between England and China. It cannot be doubted that the immense power of England in India must be regarded by the Chinese Government with dissatisfaction, if not with some degree of alarm. You will take care to show strongly how free the Chinese

Government may well be from all jealousy arising from such causes towards the United States."

On the other hand Cushing was warned not to adopt any manner which could in any way be interpreted as placing him in the category of 'tribute-bearer,' where Lord Macartney, the Dutch commissioner, and Lord Amherst had been classified by the Chinese in 1793, 1795, and 1816, respectively. "You will signify to all Chinese authorities and others," read the instructions, "that it is deemed to be quite below the dignity of the Emperor of China and the President of the United States of America to be concerning themselves with such unimportant matters as presents from one to the other; that the intercourse between the heads of two such governments should be made to embrace only great political questions, the tender of mutual regard, and the establishment of useful relations."

A secondary object, quite subordinate to the first, was to reach the Emperor at Peking. The instructions to proceed to the capital of the empire were to be used as a lever for securing the primary object of the mission, rather than to be considered as constituting a primary purpose. "It is, of course, desirable that you should be able to reach Peking and the Court, and the person of the Emperor. . The purpose of seeing the Emperor must be persisted in as long as may be consistent and proper." The commissioner was accordingly instructed very carefully, in case he reached Peking, not to perform the *kotow*, on the double ground that it would compromise the independence of the United States before the Chinese, and that it would be a violation of religious principles. 'You will represent to the Chinese authorities, nevertheless, that you are directed to pay to His Majesty the Emperor, the same marks of respect and homage as are paid by your government to His Majesty the Emperor of Russia, or any other of the great Powers of the world."

In consonance with these instructions, and as still further evidence that the American Government wished to keep its hands entirely clean of the opium trade, the commissioner received (June 12, 1843) from Mr. Legare, who had succeeded Webster as acting Secretary of State, positive instructions to investigate the charge that the newly appointed consul at Canton "is likely to be associated in business with a firm avowedly engaged in the opium trade," and if the charge was proved, unless the consul would agree to resign voluntarily, to remove him immediately. No report was ever rendered by Cushing on this duty, nor was one ever officially asked for. According to all the evidence now available it would appear that the charge was entirely well founded, although it may have been true, until after the visit of Cushing, that only some of the individual partners, rather than the firm itself, were directly engaged in the trade.

In addition to his instructions Cushing carried two letters signed by President Tyler, and addressed to the Emperor of China, one, "a full power," authorizing Cushing "to sign any treaty which may be concluded" between the commissioner and the Emperor's authorized representative; the other "a letter of credence to the Emperor, to be communicated or delivered to the Sovereign in such manner as may be most convenient or agreeable to His Majesty to receive it."

Something of mystery attaches to these letters. The former, containing the "full power" is brusque, stiff and ungracious. It contains one paragraph beginning—"The Chinese love to trade with our people, and to sell them tea and silk, for which our people pay silver, and sometimes other articles"—which was certain to be regarded by the Chinese authorities as either a studied insult to the Emperor, who never demeaned himself to recognize as a consideration the profits of mere merchants, or as a colossal breach of good manners by uncouth barbarians. The other letter, briefer, is very different in tone and literary style.*

*This second letter is probably the one referred to in a communication from Cushing to the State Department (June 27, 1843) after Webster's resignation in which the commissioner encloses "a draft prepared by Mr. Webster of the President's letter to the Emperor of China. Please submit it to Mr. Upshur for the approval of the President and himself. It was Mr. Webster's plan to have it copied in an ornamental form and placed in a suitable box." •

The other letter, the one which the commissioner upon his arrival presented to show the authority vested in him to conclude a treaty, and usually ascribed to Webster, was more likely prepared by Mr. Upshur, and might have been a serious handicap to Cushing in his initial efforts to establish cordial relations with the Chinese Government. It was, in part, as follows:

"I, John Tyler, President of the United States of America—which states are: Maine, New Hampshire, Massachusetts, Rhode Island, Connecticut, Vermont, New York, New Jersey, Pennsylvania, Delaware, Maryland, Virginia, North Carolina, South Carolina, Georgia, Kentucky, Tennessee, Ohio, Louisiana, Indiana, Mississippi, Illinois, Alabama, Missouri, Arkansas, and Michigan—send you this letter of peace and friendship, signed by my own hand.

"I hope your health is good.

"Now, my words are, that the governments of two such great countries should be at peace. It is proper, and according to the will of Heaven, that they should respect each other and act wisely. I therefore send to your Court Caleb Cushing, one of the wise and learned men of this country. On his first arrival in China, he will enquire after your health. He has then strict orders to go to your great city of Pekin, and there to deliver this letter. He will have with him secretaries and interpreters.

". . . Our Minister, Caleb Cushing, is authorized to make a treaty to regulate trade. Let it be just. Let there be no unfair advantage on either side. . . . We shall not take the part of evil-doers. We shall not uphold them that break your laws. Therefore, we doubt not that you will be pleased that our messenger of peace, with this letter in his hand, shall come to Pekin, and there deliver it; that your great officers will, by your order, make a treaty with him to regulate affairs of trade—so that nothing may happen to disturb the peace between China and America. Let the treaty be signed by your own Imperial hand. It shall be signed by mine, by the authority of our great council, the Senate."

While the style and tone of this letter was hardly in keeping with the instructions as to tact and courtesy, nevertheless the veiled threat, implied in the conclusion, was fully in harmony with the policy already fixed. The last instruction to Cushing was:

"Finally, you will signify, in decided terms and a positive manner, that the Government of the United States would find it impossible to remain on terms of friendship and regard with the Emperor, if greater privileges or commercial facilities should be allowed to the subjects of any other Government than should be granted to the citizens of the United States."

CALEB CUSHING GOES TO MACAO

The China Mission as finally organized consisted of Caleb Cushing, Commissioner; Fletcher Webster, Secretary; Dr. E. K. Kane, afterwards known for his Arctic explorations, Surgeon; and a group of young men who went on their own charges, "supplying dignity and importance to the occasion," as Webster described it. The commissioner's official costume consisted of the "uniform of a major-general, with some slight additions in the way of embroideries," a showiness much deprecated by some plain Americans.[10] The Mission arrived at Macao February 24, 1844, on the *Brandywine*, and Cushing established "his miniature court in the house of a former Portuguese Governor, creating a profound sensation by the novelty and magnitude of his Mission, as well as by his attractive personal qualities." [11]

On arrival Cushing added to his staff Rev. E. C. Bridgman, D. D., and Rev. Peter Parker, M. D., who had been in China since 1830 and 1834 respectively, as joint Chinese secretaries. Later S. Wells Williams also assisted in the Chinese correspondence. This was a somewhat reassuring move, for these men had a better knowledge of the language than any other Europeans in Canton at the time, and also a better understanding of Chinese etiquette and modes of thought, and the history of preceding American relations with China. In addition to these qualifications they were well known to the Chinese. Dr. Parker had won their respect and confidence by his hospital, and Dr. Bridgman had been so honored by former Commissioner Lin as to have been invited to come to him for a special conference early in 1839 with a view to securing his advice and good offices in mitigating the acute difficulties which grew up over the surrender of the opium.

Dr. Bridgman was also made official chaplain. Cushing wrote to the New York *Commercial Advertiser:* [12]

"The newspapers will have informed you that Dr. Bridgman and Dr. Parker are joint interpreters. It ought to be understood in addition that Dr. Bridgman is chaplain of the legation in title and in fact. I have deemed it essential to have religious services performed at the residence of the legation every Lord's day and shall adhere to this practice so long as my mission lasts."

Two months after Cushing's arrival [13] an American merchant of Canton wrote:

"Your townsman, Mr. Cushing, is quietly living at Macao, preparing, as *he says,* to go to Peking. When at Macao I had the honor of seeing much of his excellency (Cushing) who has spurs on his heels, and mustachios and imperial, very flourishing! Although I like the man, I most heartily wish he were anywhere else but here and am, as well as every other American merchant here, in great fear. As Americans we are now on the very *best* terms possible with the Chinese; and as the only connection we want with China is a commercial one, I cannot see what Mr. Cushing expects to do. He *cannot* make us better off—and a very few of his important airs will make us hated by the Chinese, and then we lose all the advantages we now have over the English; and though I believe Mr. C. to be as honest as the most of politicians, yet I fear for the sake of being, as he hopes, put face to face with Taoukwang (Emperor) he will sacrifice his countrymen and the good will of the Chinese and lose all."

The question raised by the American merchant was pertinent. What could Cushing do that had not already been done? The English were disposed to treat with derision both the American and the French missions, the coming of which had already been announced. The London *Times,* in an article which was discussing the British Supplementary Treaty of 1843, said: [14]

"This treaty is looked upon in the East as the most signal triumph of the British plenipotentiary, for it renders nugatory all the attempts of the French and American diplomatic missions lately sent with such pomp to the Chinese coast. Laughter has already begun at the appearance of two ambassadors sent thither before it was known that they would be received, in order to gain a purpose which was granted before they appeared. They now have no grounds for negotiation and must return to their own country in order to be laughed at at home and abroad."

The situation was, indeed, quite unlike that in which the American merchants in Canton, immediately after six weeks imprisonment in the spring of 1839, had been led to petition Congress to send out a commissioner to effect a commercial treaty.

BIBLIOGRAPHICAL NOTES

1. The three sources of information for Edmund Roberts are: The Roberts Papers in the Department of State; the Roberts Papers in the Library of Congress (Mss. Div.); and "Embassy to the Eastern Courts of Cochin China, Siam and Muscat," by Roberts himself, and published posthumously (New York, 1837). The book is the least satisfactory of these sources because the Department of State raised objections to its publication, and to comply with its wishes as regards secrecy, particularly as to the plans for a treaty with Japan, a great deal of information was suppressed. A partial report of his first mission was printed in the Congressional Globe.
2. Batavia Consular Letters, Vol. 1, Feb. 27, 1826.
3. Paullin's "American Naval Vessels in the Orient."
4. Text of the letters which are identical to each sovereign, Robert's "Embassy, etc.," p. 204.
5. Miscellaneous Letters (Dept. of State), N. & G. Griswold to Webster, May 13, 1843.
6. *Op. cit.* Forbes to Webster, April 29, 1843; see also "Letters and Recollections of John Murray Forbes," Vol. 1, p. 115.
7. Misc. Letters (Dept. of State), April 11, 1843.
8. S. Doc. 138:28-2; Webster's Works, Vol. 6, pp. 467-9.
9. China Dispatches, Vol. 1.
10. Niles' *Register*, July 15, 1843, p. 308.
11. S. Wells Williams' "Life and Letters," p. 126.
12. Niles' *Register*, August 3, 1844, p. 363.
13. *Ibid.*, Sept. 21, 1844, p. 36.
14. *Ibid.*, Feb. 10, 1844, p. 369.

CHAPTER VIII

THE POLICY OF CALEB CUSHING

In taking up the discussion of the contribution of Caleb Cushing to the body of American policy in Asia we are again reminded of the fact that this policy at any given date might more correctly be described as the policy of Americans—a descrimination which need not be entirely limited to American foreign policies in Asia.

Before the advent of Cushing at Macao in 1844, there had been a sharply defined policy in China. It was the policy of the American residents fully approved and supported by the opinion of the merchants in the United States who were engaged in the China trade and shipping. This policy had grown up out of the economic, geographical and political necessities of the situation. The Americans had had no other choice than to seek peace and pursue it. Whether they would have adopted a different course had China been a part of the mainland of the western hemisphere is a purely speculative, though interesting, question. The success which had attended the policy adopted was, at any rate, a sufficient justification. There had been some complaints of injustice and of discrimination but they had been few and on the whole one could not claim that the secondary commercial position occupied by the Americans at Canton in 1844, or the fluctuating and uncertain growth of the trade in the preceding twenty-five years was in any way due to that policy.

In the United States during this period the fullest expression of policy towards the entire East India trade had comprised nothing more than the demand for most-favored-nation treatment. Within a decade, however, there had grown up a public sentiment against the opium trade. One

detects also in the discussions of the Anglo-Chinese War
the beginnings of a tone of resentment at Chinese arrogance.
To the growing restiveness of Americans at the exclusive
policy of the Government of China the American missionaries were making important contributions, as the pages
of the Chinese Repository clearly reveal.   China must
'bend or break,'[1] remarked the missionaries in 1840; the
missionaries had never been able really to establish themselves under the existing régime.

Daniel Webster in his instructions to Cushing may be
said to have officialized existing public sentiment.   One does
not find that in these instructions, fine as they are in diction
and spirit, Webster had made any contribution to the body
of policy.   He asked primarily for most-favored-nation
treatment in matters of trade.   To Caleb Cushing exclusively was reserved the privilege and credit of working
out a method by which the Americans, whose geographical
and political relations to China must continue to be utterly
different from those of the British, might still enjoy similar
privileges.

The Negotiations

The political situation when Cushing reached Macao,
February 24, 1844, was as follows: (1) By two treaties,
that of Nanking (1842), and that of the Bogue (1843),
England had secured a peace with China granting, in addition to $21,000,000 and the cession of Hongkong, the
opening of four additional ports, the liberty to appoint
consuls to each of them, abolition of all monopolies, a
uniform published tariff, equality between officials of corresponding rank of the two countries, and an assent in
general terms to complete extraterritoriality.   (2) By the
action of the Chinese Government, confirmed in a written
promise to Commodore Kearny, and executed by an Imperial edict, the ports had been thrown open to the trade
of all nations upon equal terms.   Moreover, the Americans
were on the full tide of their greatest prosperity, at the
beginning of the clipper ship era, highly popular by com-

parison with the English among the Chinese, and not at all eager to have conditions disturbed by the introduction of diplomatic questions which, even if settled entirely to the liking of the Americans, could not make business any better.

Nor was the American Mission welcomed by the Chinese Government. The preceding October, in obedience to instructions from Washington, Paul S. Forbes, the newly appointed consul at Canton, had both formally and informally conveyed to Kiying, the Imperial Commissioner and Governor General of Kwang-tung and Kwangsi, that the American Mission was on its way, only to be met with the reply: "Why go to Peking when the Imperial Commissioner is already at Canton, and when the Americans have already been given all the advantages in trade which have been conceded to the English?" In the formal reply to the official notification from Forbes, Kiying had stated: [2]

"The August Emperor, compassionating people from afar, certainly cannot bear that the American Minister by a circuitous route should go to Peking, wading through over-flowing difficulties. The Consul ought, therefore, to intercept and stop the American Plenipotentiary from repairing, in every respect unnecessary, to the Imperial Court."

This unwillingness and even fear on the part of the Chinese for a foreign envoy to proceed to Peking was to become the lever in the hands of Cushing, for the negotiating of the treaty. However, the concession of this point at the outset, would have embarrassed all further negotiations. Even before the arrival of the *Brandywine* at Macao a general order to the members of the mission and the officers and crew of the frigate had been issued, cautioning everyone to be most discreet in answer to any questions, and always to assert that the destination of the mission was *Peking*.

Three days after the arrival at Macao (February 27), Cushing addressed a formal letter to the acting Governor General at Canton, Kiying having found it convenient to retire to Peking, casually mentioning the fact that the

American Plenipotentiary "finds himself under the necessity of landing at Macao and remaining there a few weeks,
until the *Brandywine* shall have taken on provisions and
made other preparations to enable her to continue her
voyage to the mouth of the Pei-ho." Cushing, therefore,
availed himself of the first opportunity, in pursuance of
orders from his government, to inquire solicitously after the
health of the Emperor, and he addressed his inquiry to the
Governor because, as Cushing was careful to state, he was
'the nearest high functionary of the Chinese Government.'
The plenipotentiary intimated that an immediate answer
to his inquiry would be most acceptable.

Then followed a parley [3] which, save for the fact that it
is raised to diplomatic dignity, was otherwise not at all
dissimilar to a thousand daily passages in any bazaar in
Asia for forty centuries. This correspondence with the
acting Governor, explained Cushing, in a later dispatch to
the State Department, "not only proves to have had the
advantage of having settled many things, and thus prepared
the way for the negotiations with Kiying, but it has had
the further advantage of enabling me to say all the harsh
things which needed to be said, and to speak to the Chinese
Government with extreme plainness and frankness, in a
degree which would have been inconvenient, if not inadmissible, in immediate correspondence with Kiying."

Governor Ching allowed Cushing's letter to go un-
answered for three weeks, and then replied that it "evinces
respectful obedience, and politeness exceedingly to be
praised. The Emperor is well and enjoying a happy old
age," wrote Ching and added pointedly, "and is at peace
with all, both far and near." This touch was evidently to
show the American envoy that the government had not
overlooked the fact that the American Mission arrived in
a frigate. The Governor then took occasion to explain
to Cushing a few points in Chinese diplomatic etiquette
and law. It was not customary for envoys to proceed to
Tientsin unless they were invited. There were no linguists
there, and no commissioners empowered to receive them.

Even Sir Henry Pottinger, the English plenipotentiary, after he had signed the Treaty of Nanking, had been forced to return to Canton to negotiate the commercial agreement such as, the Governor assumed, the Americans were alone interested in. The Governor further reminded Cushing that nearly six months ago the American consul at Canton had been informed that it would be useless for the American envoy to go to Tientsin. And as for a treaty, the Governor reasserted that such an agreement was quite unnecessary. The nations were at peace, the tariff had been settled, and "already has your nation been bedewed with its advantages." The Emperor had issued orders to soothe and stop the Americans at Macao. "It is useless with lofty, polished and empty words to alter these unlimited advantages." Nevertheless, if Cushing insisted, the Governor would again memorialize the Emperor on the subject. Meanwhile, for the Americans to proceed to the North without Imperial permission would "put an end to civility."

Cushing promptly acknowledged the Governor's letter, and regretted the *impasse* to which they seemed already to come. As for himself, he was under orders to proceed to Peking. He was sorry that the Imperial Government neglected to have a commissioner waiting in the South to receive him for it was quite possible that commercial, as distinguished from political and diplomatic questions, might settled there as well as anywhere. But the most serious obstacle, in Cushing's opinion, was the fact that he was, obviously, quite unable to discuss these two questions of the right to proceed to the Pei-ho and the necessity of a treaty with any one save the Imperial Commissioner himself.

Ching replied, rather more promptly than before, that he would memorialize the Emperor, and as for himself, he could not take upon his shoulders "to commence movements which may eventuate in the loss of the invaluable blessings of peace."

Thus, in the first engagement, the American envoy had won a point; the Emperor was to be memorialized.

The correspondence, notwithstanding these obvious and acknowledged disabilities of the correspondents, continued. Ching notified Cushing (April 12) that no commissioner had yet been appointed, and that the Americans would be notified when the appointment was made. Cushing replied the next day by sending the *Brandywine* up to Whampoa, only twelve miles from Canton, "on a visit, for a few days, of courtesy and civility." The commander of the frigate carried the matter a little further by proposing a suitable exchange of salutes, and by inviting himself to visit the Governor at his yamen in the city of Canton. Ching, evidently alarmed, and yet with the customary show of Chinese official bravado, ordered the *Brandywine* to return to Macao, and remarked rather tartly, that the visit of such a formidably armed vessel was a strange exhibition of courtesy, and had a very war-like bearing.

Meanwhile Cushing continued the unofficial correspondence. He reviewed the situation and ventured to give the Governor a little instruction in the rules of international courtesy. A refusal to receive envoys is, among Western nations, considered as "an act of national insult and a just cause for war." The analogy between the course pursued with Sir Henry Pottinger and the one the Chinese were seeking to adopt with him, would hardly be complete until the Americans had fought a war with China, and had occupied one of the islands off the Chinese coast. He reminded the Governor that the season was already passing, that he had already waited a long time, that no Imperial Commissioner had even been appointed, and that he did not intend to be held at Canton until the favorable season for sailing to the North had passed with the changing of the monsoon. This drew an immediate reply from Ching that Kiying had been appointed as Imperial Commissioner and would arrive at Canton in due time.

The second engagement of mighty words, supported by the movements of the *Brandywine,* had resulted in another victory for the Americans.

Cushing pursued the advantage. He chose to feel that

he had been grossly insulted, and that the national honor of the Americans had been affected. However, Cushing "suspends all resentment" for the time being, and hoped that "suitable reparation will be made in due time." "I commit myself," he wrote solemnly, "to the integrity and honor of the Chinese Government; and if, in the sequel, I shall prove to have done this in vain, I shall then consider myself the more amply justified, in the sight of all men, for any determination which, out of regard for the honor of the United States, it may be my duty to adopt under such circumstances." The next day he notified the Governor that the *St. Louis* and *Perry* which had unfortunately been detained at the Cape of Good Hope, would soon arrive, and that the American Government had decided to enlarge the fleet in Chinese waters by the addition of the Pacific Squadron which was also soon to arrive.

The addition of the Pacific Squadron to Cushing's fleet had been suggested to the President before Cushing's departure from the United States, and Cushing had again proposed it in a dispatch to the State Department before his arrival in China. Other dispatches show that Cushing had been greatly annoyed that during these early negotiations there had not been a larger naval force at his command. It is not impossible that had the fleet been adequate and suitably provided with vessels of light draught, such as are necessary for the approach to Tientsin, he might already have sailed to the North. If so, it was a happy mischance that detained him at Macao.

Ching stated (May 4) that Kiying had already left Peking, was travelling with incredible speed, and might be expected at Canton on the fifth of June.

The interval before the arrival of Kiying was devoted to still further threats, mingled with courteous correspondence. The Imperial edict making known the appointment of Kiying mentioned the fact that the United States had never gone through the form of paying tribute to the Emperor, and made clear that Cushing had the choice between remaining at Macao and securing the desired treaty, or going to Tientsin and failing to get it. The appointment of Kiying was taken by the Americans as a favorable sign for Kiying had negotiated the English treaties, had been much in contact with the foreigners, and was greatly respected for his breadth of view, as well as for his urbanity. Therefore Cushing agreed to defer the discussion of the proposed trip to the North, and although still complaining of the inconveniences to which he had been subjected, settled down to wait for Kiying. The latter wrote to him (June 9) "In a few days we shall take each other by the hand, and converse, and rejoice together with indescribable delight." The American commissioner appeared to have won in the first skirmish of wits.

A not unimportant factor in the successful conclusion of these first stages in the negotiations had been the fact, made clear unofficially in the beginning by Dr. Peter Parker, in whom the Chinese had great confidence, and later by Cushing in the correspondence, that the American Government had no desire to dismember China or to possess any part of her territory.

The actual negotiations of the treaty with China were simple. Kiying was eager to conclude them before the arrival of the French plenipotentiary, whose approach had been announced, and the Americans had already prepared a draft of the document which they desired to have signed. Kiying arrived at the temple of the Lady of Mercy, just outside Macao, on June 17. The next few days were given to the customary visits of ceremony. Then the commissioners delegated to their subordinates the task of conferring together, and on July 3, the treaty was signed.

In submitting his *project* of the proposed treaty, Cushing had written to Kiying:

"In drawing up these minutes, I have not looked to the side of the United States alone. I felt that it would not be honorable, in dealing with your Excellency, to take a partial view of the subject. I have inserted a multitude of provisions in the interest and for the benefit of China. In a word I have sought to present this draft of a treaty which, as already intimated, shall be in all parts alike just and honorable to China and the United States."

THE IMMEDIATE APPLICATION OF THE PRINCIPLES OF THE TREATY

An incident at Canton before the arrival of Kiying had threatened to embarrass the negotiations, and the ready willingness of the Americans to respect the prejudices of the Chinese had doubtless left a favorable impression. The mission had been supplied as a part of its equipment with a flag-staff which was intended for erection over the Legation, but when Cushing established himself at Macao it was impracticable to set it up, owing to the objection of the Portuguese authorities. The flag-staff was therefore turned over to the American consul at Canton, and placed in front of the consulate. The staff was surmounted with an arrow for a weather-vane which caused great alarm to the people of the city. To its mysterious influence was ascribed the serious drought then prevailing in Canton, and some also found in the arrow a symbol of approaching war between the United States and China. At length a Chinese mob broke into the factory grounds, cut the halyards, damaged the staff and sought to remove the arrow. The Americans defended the staff and repulsed the mob with fire-arms. The next day a second mob collected. Of such incidents are wars sometimes born, but in this case the American consul agreed to remove the arrow.[4]

The episode was sufficient to illustrate the insecurity of the foreigners at Canton, however many treaties they might negotiate. Shortly after the removal of the obnoxious weather-vane a mob attacked some Americans who, in defending themselves, accidentally killed a Chinese—Hsü A-man. Governor Ching; who had himself been negligent in providing protection from the mob, demanded that the Americans surrender the murderer. The matter was referred to Cushing and Kiying. The former refused to deliver the man, ordered the calling of a jury of Americans, and the trial of the case according to American law. The jury rendered a verdict of acquittal on the ground of self-defense. Kiying accepted the settlement. Subsequently, though not as a part of the judicial action in the case, the family of Hsü A-man received some money from the Americans.[5] This incident again illustrated the danger to which the foreigners in Canton were exposed, and was the means of securing from the authorities the promise of better provision for the protection of the factories—a promise which was never fulfilled.

The Canton rabble, incited by minor officials and the literati, were in an angry mood which boded ill for the future. Kiying confessed his great difficulty in controlling the people of the city and explained to Cushing that the English had created a great deal of ill-will. "I have heard," he wrote, "that usually the citizens of Canton have respected and liked the officers and people of the United States, as they were peaceable and reasonable; that they (the Americans) would, even when there was a cause of difference, endeavor to accommodate the matter, which is very unlike the English."

Cushing seized upon the Hsü A-man affair to establish a precedent in the matter of jurisdiction over Americans accused by Chinese, and to demonstrate the principle of extraterritoriality, as it was incorporated in the new treaty. He also used it as an argument to have placed in the treaty very clear stipulations that the Chinese Government must assume the responsibility for the protection of Americans.

Before the American commissioner returned to the United States an occasion arose in which Kiying called upon the Americans for a demonstration of good faith, and received it. Before the treaty had been made two American ship-builders, Emery and Frazer, had leased some land opposite Hongkong, on the north side of the harbor, for a ship-yard. Kiying called Cushing's attention to the fact that the treaty did not provide for the leasing of land by foreigners at this place and asked for his good offices in securing the removal of the ship-yard. It was evident that the Chinese feared that this lease-hold might some day become the base for another foreign settlement. Cushing therefore, advised the Americans to relinquish their location, securing for them six months in which to find another one. To this Emery and Grazer agreed.

The primary object of the Mission had been accomplished in the signing of the treaty. The fulfillment of the secondary purpose, the visit to Peking and the delivery of the President's letter to the Emperor, greatly troubled Cushing. Shortly after the arrival of Kiying at Macao in June, Cushing had formally waived the right to go to Peking, provided the treaty was signed, but had made a reservation, viz., that if in the future any other envoy was received at Peking, the Americans should have a similar privilege. At the time he made this concession to the Chinese he supposed that he was on very safe ground for he knew that the French plenipotentiary was approaching, and he assumed that as a matter of course, France would demand the reception of its envoy at the Court. After the treaty was signed, but before the arrival of the French Mission, Cushing secured from Kiying a promise to deliver the President's letter to the Emperor, and later transferred it to the Chinese commissioner with suitable ceremony.

Greatly to Cushing's surprise the French, upon their arrival, communicated to him that they had no instructions to insist upon a visit to Peking except in extraordinary circumstances. Cushing, on the other hand, felt that his instructions to proceed to Peking were "peremptory." True the treaty had been obtained, but there seems to have been the fear in Cushing's mind that the failure to carry out the remainder of his instructions might be counted to his discredit upon his return to the United States, and he therefore made his explanations for not going to the Capital the subject of several passages in his dispatches. His principal argument was that a visit to Peking would have delayed, if not imperilled, the negotiations for the treaty, and now that the treaty had been signed, he considered that the best interests of the mission would be served by his immediate return to the United States where he could supplement by personal explanation, anything which might be lacking in his dispatches to secure the immediate ratification of the treaty. Incidentally the appropriation which had been made for the expenses of the mission was entirely exhausted. He therefore appointed Commander Foxhall A. Parker as *Chargé,* with power to attend to any diplomatic questions which might arise, while Dr. Peter Parker, the medical missionary, assumed the responsibility of acting as official interpreter without salary. Cushing embarked on the *Perry* August 24, 1844.

One other object of the mission, an object mentioned in no instructions, remained unaccomplished. Shortly after the signing of the treaty Cushing offered to Kiying some models of guns and some books on military and naval tactics, and fortifications, delicately expressing the opinion that such information might be of value to China in the future. The Chinese, however, were not ready, even after their humiliating military defeats, to concern themselves with the trappings of modern militarism, and Kiying replied politely declining the gifts, expressing the conviction that peace for China was assured, and adding: "If at a future day there be occasion to use them, then we ought to request your Honorable Nation to assist us with the strength of its arm."

Throughout the entire negotiations the relations between Cushing and Kiying bore all the outward marks of extreme cordiality and good feeling. The latter in his farewell letter to the American envoy wrote:

"I present my compliments and wishes that wherever you go happiness may attend you, and that day by day you may advance in promotion."

Imagine then the amazement of Cushing and of the other Americans as well, when a few months later a copy of Kiying's memorial report to the Emperor fell into the hands of the foreigners and, when translated, was found to contain the following:

"The original copy of the Treaty presented by the said Barbarian Envoy, contained forty-seven stipulations. Of these some were difficult of execution, others were foolish demands, whilst several of the most important points of the Treaty were omitted on the list. The sense of it was, moreover, so meanly and coarsely expressed, the words and sentences were so obscure, and there was such a variety of errors, that it was next to impossible to point them out.

"We clearly pointed out whatever was comprehensive to reason, in order to dispel their stupid ignorance, and to put a stop to (delusive) hopes, whilst expatiating with strictness upon the most binding of the statutes, while we were obliged to polish those passages which were scarcely intelligible, so as to render the sense somewhat more obvious, in order to remove all ambiguity; and only after four times altering the copies, we adopted (the paper)."

Kiying also pointed out to the Emperor that in the article in the treaty which purported to grant to the Americans the privileges of renting property in the five ports he had inserted a qualifying clause which made the renting of such property dependent upon the willingness of the neighbors to receive foreigners.

This report gives a fair intimation of what was to come in the next fifteen years when Chinese officials, sometimes friendly to foreigners and sometimes not, but always intent on retaining the favor of an ill-informed and anti-foreign Emperor, attempted to transact the international affairs of the Chinese Empire. As for the concession in the article of the treaty securing the rights of renting property, it soon became evident that Cushing, in his excess of amiability, had permitted himself to be completely hoodwinked by the wily Kiying.

The only known contemporaneous Chinese account of the negotiation of the Treaty of Wanghia is the following: [6]

"The English desired that leaders of all nations should report to them first, and then pay duties; but the French and Americans indignantly exclaimed:—'We are no dependencies of England nor have we been "treacherous and lying." ' On this, some American ship-of-war entered port, and a few mont. later, some Frenchmen too. Both of them submitted letters, begging to pay tribute, and to be allowed to express their devotion at an interview. They also requested to be allowed to leave their ships in the South, whilst the tribute-envoys and a small suite went overland to Peking; for they wished to make some confidential suggestions and to assist us."

In conducting the negotiations with the Chinese for the first American treaty, Cushing had the double advantage of the experience of the English and the good will of the Chinese. Sir Henry Pottinger had been the pioneer. His efforts had been incorporated in the Treaty of Nanking, the Treaty of the Bogue, and the Regulations for Trade which, while first promulgated by the Chinese alone, were signed by both the Chinese and the English commissioners, and incorporated as a part of the treaty agreement between the two nations. Before Cushing began the negotiations leading up to the American Treaty of Wanghia the arrangements of the English with the Chinese had been subjected to a working test in which their weakness as well as their strength had been revealed. Of even greater advantage to the American negotiations was the fact that the Chinese, while bitterly resenting the defeats they had suffered at the hands of the English, had already come to see the advantage of having the good will of other Western nations. While not fully understanding the benefits which would come to them later from having admitted into their international relationship a strong nation whose national interests in China coincided at many points with Chinese national well-being, nevertheless the Chinese were not altogether unconscious of the probable effects. This is evident from the fact that even before signing the Treaty of Nanking in 1842 they had determined to throw open the trade on equal terms to all nations.

The Chinese, notwithstanding their show of bravado at the approach of Cushing at Macao, had been cowed by their defeat. The American commissioner, had no English war preceded his efforts, might have perfected arrangements in which the position of the Americans in China would have been slightly bettered. Certainly the Americans in Canton in the summer of 1839, after Commissioner Lin had begun direct communications with the American consul, thought so. Possibly had the United States joined in a naval demonstration on the coast of China with England and France, as the memorial of the Canton merchants (May 25, 1839) to Congress had advised, some sort of diplomatic relations between China and the Western powers might have been established.* But that such sweeping concessions as the English had obtained, aside from the indemnity and the cession of Hongkong, could have been secured otherwise than as a result of military victory over the Chinese, is not to be thought of. These concessions, obtained for the English by force of arms, became freely the possession of the Americans. On the other hand, had the Americans chosen to regard the attack on the American flag-staff at Canton in June, 1844, as a cause for war, they could have doubtless, on the conclusion of war, exacted any terms they liked from the Chinese Government. It became ingloriously, yet very profitably, the rôle of the United States pacifically to follow England to China in the wake of war, and to profit greatly by the victories of British arms.

There had been, however, no alternative for the United States, save that of continuing the American trade in China without a treaty, and that would have meant trade under the ægis of England. So far as China was concerned, while Caleb Cushing won several additional concessions from China, and won them by a method hardly to be distinguished from intimidation, nevertheless the treaty with the United States was an anchor to windward for the Empire. In so far as the Chinese Government was conscious of what was being achieved, the signing of the Treaty of Wanghia may be described as a brilliant stroke of diplomacy. The subsequent history of China's international relations, with the United States eliminated, would have been quite different from what it actually was.

It ought to be added, as a preface to the comparison of the British and American treaties, that the United States had an advantage over the English in the ability of its

*The Memorial of R. B. Forbes and others, H. Doc. 40 :26-1, had expressed in conclusion, the "candid conviction that the appearance of a naval force from the United States, England and France upon the coast of China, would, without bloodshed, obtain from this Government such acknowledgments and treaties, etc."

commissioner. As a negotiator and a writer of legal documents Sir Henry Pottinger was no match for the clever
New England lawyer. In estimating the Treaty of Wanghia
an effort ought to be made to put one's self in the place of
the Chinese and seek to determine the extent in which the
document was fair and just to the Empire. Such an estimate, however, must not detract from the credit due to the
negotiator in whose hands were placed the commercial and
political interests of the United States. Caleb Cushing was
charged with making the best possible terms for his client.
That is to say, he was to make a treaty which would give
to American commercial interests in China the best possible
opportunities for the prosecution of their growing trade in
the face of British competition. No one can deny, after a
comparison of the documents, that in the Treaty of Wanghia
those interests were extremely well served.

The Superior Advantages of the Cushing Treaty

As a basis for the conduct of trade the American treaty
was greatly superior to the English agreements, made by
Sir Henry Pottinger; so superior that it became immediately
the model for the French treaty, negotiated a few weeks
later, and also for the treaty with Norway and Sweden,
signed March 29, 1847. The superior provisions of the
American treaty also immediately won the approval of the
English and were largely used by them. Indeed the Cushing
treaty became the basis of China's international relations
until it was superseded in 1858 by the treaties of Tientsin.

From the English treaties the Americans already enjoyed
the following concessions: (1) The opening of four additional ports, and the rights of residence in these ports for the
transaction of business. (2) The right of equality in consular and diplomatic intercourse. (3) A lowering of the
tonnage dues to less than one tenth of what had formerly
been paid, and a reduction of duties, confirmed by a published tariff, of from one half to seven eighths of the former
charges. (4) The abolition of all monopolies, such as the

co-hong.   (5) Sweeping concessions of extraterritorial rights. On the other hand, by means of the "most-favored-nation" clause in the Treaty of the Bogue (Article 8) the English inherited many additional advantages secured from the Treaty of Wanghia. Sir John Francis Davis, who succeeded Sir Henry Pottinger, as British Minister and Superintendent of Trade, acknowledged the following: [7]   (1) Merchant ships might remain two days at any one of the five ports without paying duties, provided they did not discharge any cargo. (2) Having paid tonnage duties ships could go to another port without having to pay such duties a second time. (3) Having landed cargo and having paid the duties, they could reship it to another port and enter it without duty by means of a customs house certificate. (4) Permission was obtained for the employment of Chinese as teachers for the foreigners and for the purchase of books. (5) It was stipulated that the treaty might be reconsidered for purposes of revision after twelve years from the date of the American treaty.

The first three of the above items obviously made for greater flexibility in the division of the foreign trade be tween the newly opened ports, especially in the early years when the trade possibilities of each port were being explored. They also opened the door part way for a coasting trade between the treaty ports in foreign vessels. The English had expected that Hongkong would serve at once as a bonded warehouse for their entire China trade, and also as a distributing point. These provisions were ingenious devices of Cushing's by which the Americans could secure advantages such as the British had expected to obtain by the cession of territory.

The permission to employ Chinese teachers and purchase Chinese books, while of general advantage to the merchants and to the foreign governments in that it made possible the development of a competent staff of interpreters and advisers, was also of peculiar advantage to the missionaries who hitherto had been able to study the Chinese language and literature only surreptitiously.

The American article providing for the revision of the treaty after twelve years, which was also incorporated into the French treaty a few weeks later, and on which the Powers rested their claims for the negotiation of new treaties in 1856, will be discussed subsequently more in detail.

EXTRATERRITORIALITY

The doctrine of extraterritoriality received amplification and greater precision of statement in the Treaty of Wanghia. Owing to Chinese reluctance to grant it, or to objections in England to the doctrine, Pottinger had not included it in either the Treaty of Nanking, or that of the Bogue. The only mention of the concession was in the Regulations of Trade, Article 13 of which read:

"Regarding the punishment of English criminals, the English Government will enact the laws necessary to attain that end and the Consul will be empowered to put them into force: and regarding the punishment of Chinese criminals, these will be tried and punished by their own laws, in the way provided for by the correspondence which took place at Nanking after the concluding of the peace."

From the phrasing of this article it is clear, even though there were no other proof, that the doctrine in substance, even though not included in the treaty, had been one of the concessions obtained by Sir Henry Pottinger as a fruit of the English victory.[8]

The correspondence referred to was never made public.*

The rights of extraterritoriality in the American treaty were defined in two articles.

"Article XXI. Subjects of China who may be guilty of any criminal act towards the citizens of the United States shall be arrested and punished by the Chinese authorities according to the laws of China; and citizens of the United States who may commit any crime

* In the final instructions issued by Lord Palmerston to Charles Elliot,[9] the concession of extraterritoriality was outlined in Art. VII of the substitute articles which were to be inserted in the proposed treaty with China in case the British representatives were unable to secure the cession to Great Britain of any islands. From the facts of the final settlement it may therefore be inferred that in 1842 the Chinese Government preferred to cede Hongkong rather than to grant extraterritoriality. It would also appear as though Lord Palmerston regarded the possession of a military and administrative base on the coast of China as, at least in part, a substitute for the concession of extraterritorial privileges.

in China shall be tried and punished only by the Consul, or other public functionary of the United States, thereto authorized, according to the laws of the United States   "

And

"Article XXV. All questions in regard to rights, whether of property or person, arising between citizens of the United States and China, shall be subject to the jurisdiction of, and regulated by the authorities of their own Government."

And this article also adds:

"And all controversies occurring in China between the citizens of the United States and the subjects of any other Government shall be regulated by the treaties existing between the United States and such Governments, respectively, without interference on the part of China."

A provision which had not been legalized before.

It is interesting to note that the extraterritorial provisions of the Treaty of Wanghia were not inserted at the demand of the American merchants. The Forbes memorial (May 25, 1839) which had outlined what seemed to the American merchants important in a possible treaty, asked for something very much less than Cushing secured. The sixth article of the memorial read:

'That until the Chinese laws are distinctly made known and recognized, the punishment for wrongs committed by foreigners upon the Chinese, or others, shall not be greater than is applicable to the like offense by the laws of the United States or England; nor shall any punishment be inflicted by the Chinese authorities upon any foreigner, until the guilt of the party shall have been fairly and clearly proven."

Cushing made the general subject and the precise stipulation of extraterritoriality in the Treaty of Wanghia the matter of a long and detailed dispatch to the Secretary of State, John C. Calhoun,[10] in which the reasons for the concession are explained in detail. The most immediate reason was that such a concession had already been made to the English. Cushing wrote:

"I found that Great Britain had stipulated for the absolute exemption of her subjects from the jurisdiction of the Empire, while the

Portuguese attained the same object through their own local jurisdiction at Macao.   And in addition to all the other considerations
affecting the question, I reflected how ignominious would be the condition of Americans in China, if subjected to local jurisdiction,
whilst the English and Portuguese among them were exempt from it."

Starting with this fact, or possibly seeking to underlay
the concession already obtained with substantial legal and
ethical principles, Cushing found them in the character of
the relations which China had sustained towards Western
nations, and in the more conspicuous incidents of the past,
particularly the Terranova case, where such a provision as
he inserted into the Treaty of Wanghia would have served
better the ends of justice.

While China could not be classified with the Mohammedan States where the doctrine of extraterritoriality had
long been applied, on the ground that China, like them, was
uncivilized, the Empire could be placed with them as a
State which did not recognize the 'law of nations.'   This
was proved, wrote Cushing, by the following facts: The
Chinese attempt to apply Chinese law to visiting foreign
war vessels; their authorities have subjected foreign consuls
to personal restraint; they disregard the flag of truce; and
they demand, at Court, the *kowtow*.   The states of Christendom, said Cushing, as distinguished from the Mohammedan and pagan states, have many of the qualities of a
confederated republic.

"How different is the condition of things out of the limits of
Christendom!   From the greater part of Asia and Africa individual
Christians are utterly excluded, either by the sanguinary barbarism of
the inhabitants, or by their phrenzied bigotry, or by the narrow-
minded policy of their governments; to their courts the ministers of
Christian governments have no means of access except by force and at
the head of fleets and armies; as between them and us, there is no
community of ideas, no common law of nations, no interchange of
good offices; and it is only during the present generation that treaties,
most of them imposed by force of arms or by terror, have begun to
bring down the great Mohammedan and Pagan Governments into a
state of inchoate peaceful association with Christendom.

"To none of the governments of this character, as it seemed to me,
was it safe to commit the lives and liberties of the citizens of the
United States."

This argument derived its most impelling force from
the Terranova case * in 1821, which had been such a trav-
esty on justice.

It would appear, however, that the significance of this
carefully drawn provision of the Cushing treaty is to be
found in Cushing's purpose in this matter, as in reexportation and the coasting trade, to secure for the Americans
guarantees of actual most-favored-nation treatment without
the acquisition of a military and naval base like Hongkong.
Extraterritoriality was in a measure, as Lord Palmerston
seems to have recognized in 1839, a substitute for the permanent occupation of territory.

The profound and brilliant legal mind of the American
commissioner found in this complex legal question of personal versus territorial jurisdiction a subject entirely to his
taste, and the result, as defined in the two articles of the
Treaty of Wanghia, was to Cushing a matter of no little
pride.

RESPONSIBILITY PLACED ON THE CHINESE

Another superiority of the American treaty which was
subsequently acknowledged and adopted by the English,
was in the locating of responsibility for the collection of
duties. Here again Cushing was applying his general policy.
The second article of the Treaty of Nanking stipulated as a
duty of the Consul "to see that the just dues and other dues
of the Chinese Government, as hereinafter provided for, are
duly discharged by Her Britannic Majesty's subjects." In
the Treaty of the Bogue England assumed additional
responsibilities to assist the Chinese Government in the
suppression of smuggling. This provision was an inherit-
ance from the days before the treaties, and even from
before the dissolution of the East India Company monopoly

* V. K. Wellington Koo, in his exposition of the Status of Aliens in China,
although examining all of the other cases of the alleged homicide by foreigners
which he finds entirely unjustifiable as a basis for the doctrine of extraterritoriality, unfortunately omits all discussion of the Terranova case, perhaps the
worst exhibition of the exercise of Chinese jurisdiction over foreigners, and
certainly the most compelling argument among Americans for the provision in
the Treaty of Wanghia.

at Canton, when the Chinese authorities were accustomed
to hold the English superintendent responsible for the conduct of his countrymen. To the Chinese, accustomed as
they were to having all merchants secured by a guarantor,
the British provisions were a satisfactory arrangement.
They might also be considered as a correlative proposition
to the doctrine of extraterritoriality, since it was over the
payment of dues and duties that the offenses of foreigners
were most likely to arise. But in practice it made the
foreign government responsible for the enforcement of the
Chinese customs laws, and it became therefore very distasteful.

"Under the Treaty of Nanking," writes a British historian, "the
British consuls were to assist the Chinese in the enforcement of the
regulations; the only result of this was to penalize British subjects
who were fined by their own consuls for offenses which other foreigners
committed with impunity." [11]

That the English were not unwilling to adopt the provisions of the American treaty with reference to smuggling
must be evident from the following letter from Sir Henry
Pottinger to Kiying, October 11, 1843, in answer to a complaint from the latter that men from an English vessel had
landed on the Chinese coast outside any treaty port and
distributed hand bills announcing that they had 'woolens,
miscellaneous articles, opium in large and small balls, etc.,'
for sale.[12]

"I have more than ten times previously explained to your Excellency and the other high Chinese officers, that the great and final
remedy for this disobedience and evil rests in the hands of the local
authorities; and I am most happy to observe that the remedy was
applied on this occasion. I allude to the people of the country being
carefully restrained from dealing or holding intercourse with the
vessels. If this rule be only rigidly enforced, the object is gained."

It is to be noted that this letter was written more than
six months before the negotiations of the Treaty of
Wanghia began, and the principle here laid down by the
British Minister is the one incorporated in the American
treaty, viz., Chinese authorities must do their own policing.

.The Treaty of Wanghia completely freed the consul from responsibility in this matter, by stipulating (Article 13) that the duties should be paid in cash, either in sycee silver, or in foreign currency. Perhaps in the long run it was better that China should not delegate, or be allowed to delegate, the responsibility which properly belonged to the Empire as a sovereign state, for the enforcement of its own laws, but the immediate effect of the provision was merely that the Government of the United States evaded responsibility for the smuggling carried on by its citizens. The Cushing treaty was, in practice, the smugglers' delight, conferring even more extended privileges in that regard than did the possession of Hongkong.

The American treaty definitely specified that communications to Peking might be made not only through the medium of the Imperial Commissioner at Canton (Article 31) but also, when necessary, through the Governor General of the Liang Kwang, or that of the Liang Kiang. This provision also was made use of by the English officials, ten years later, when the Imperial Commissioner obstinately refused to see them.

DIVERGENCE FROM BRITISH POLICY

A comparison of the American and the British treaties also shows a marked divergence of the policies between the two Western powers towards China.

Both in the text of the Treaty of Wanghia and in the annexed tariff, opium is specifically mentioned as contraband, and any opium smuggler is made liable to arrest and to the penalty of confiscation for both cargo and the vessel detected in carrying it. The text was (Article 33):

"Citizens of the United States who shall attempt to trade claudestinely with such of the ports of China as are not open to foreign commerce, or who shall trade in opium or any other contraband articles of merchandise, shall be subject to be dealt with by the Chinese Government without being entitled to any countenance or protection from that of the United States; and the United States will take measures to prevent their flag from being abused by the subjects of other nations as a cover for the violation of the laws of the Empire."

Thus, until the treaty of 1858, when this article was omitted, the name of the United States was technically clear of any complicity in the opium trade, although slight provision was ever made by the United States to prevent the abuse of the American flag either by its own citizens or those of other nations. American citizens engaged in smuggling violated the treaty, yet the United States never assumed any responsibility to prevent or punish such violations unless complaint was brought by the Chinese, and such action the Chinese were very reluctant to take. The result was that smuggling greatly increased. The only difference between the policy of the United States and that of England, in practice, was in the extent of the participation in the smuggling.

A more marked divergence of policy is to be found in the stipulations conferring on foreigners the rights of residence in treaty ports, and in the measures adopted for their protection. The Treaty of the Bogue (Article 7) provided that in the treaty ports "ground and houses . . . shall be set apart by the local officers, in communication with the consul" for the residence of foreigners. For their protection the English depended upon the naval station and garrison at Hongkong, and also upon the right secured by treaty, to station a war vessel at each port. The Treaty of Wanghia (Article 17) mentioned "churches, cemeteries and hospitals" as well as residences, and stated: "The local authorities of the two governments shall select in concert sites for the foregoing objects, having due regard for the feelings of the people in the location thereof." And Article 19 made it obligatory upon the Chinese Government to "defend them (the Americans) from all insult or injury of any sort on the part of the Chinese."

The 'setting apart' of sites for foreign settlement, as provided for in the English treaty, looked towards the establishment of 'foreign settlements' and the granting of 'concessions' which are now so numerous and which have so seriously intrenched upon the integrity of Chinese territory and the sovereignty of the nation. The presence of the war vessels looked towards the gun-boat policy, the intimidation of local officials and even the quasi-protection of smugglers. The American provision for the 'selection' of sites, and for the placing of responsibility for their protection upon the Chinese, pointed in the very opposite direction—the maintenance of the integrity of China and the support of its sovereignty. The difference was this: England was approaching China through the old world, through India and other Oriental countries, where every precedent was in favor of the policy she was laying down; the United States was approaching China as one independent nation to another, and the negotiations were in the hands of Yankees who recognized no color line and prided themselves that they yielded to no race prejudice. The provision for churches and hospitals, moreover, recalls the fact that Cushing was, at Macao, entirely in the hands of missionaries who were his only interpreters, and bears witness to the ascending missionary interest in China which in later years increased so much faster than the commercial interest.

Again, however, the theory and the practice of the Americans were not the same. Actually the Americans adopted the 'foreign settlement' plan of residence,—wherever the English established it—and probably half of the irritation growing up between the Americans and the Chinese authorities in subsequent years was over the efforts of the Americans to secure residences where 'due regard to the feelings of the people in the location thereof' gave the Chinese authorities a cover for refusing them. The lack of American war vessels in Chinese ports also permitted the growth of not a few claims, often small but exceedingly irritating, which might have been avoided had the Americans depended less upon Chinese protection and more upon show of force. Moreover in practice the Americans, unable to claim the protection of American war vessels, found their defense under the British flag.

Disregarding general principles, and viewing the treaties in the light of the actual situation which confronted the enervated and tottering Chinese dynasty in its efforts to control its foreign guests, the English treaties were, aside from the opium question, more beneficent towards China than was the Treaty of Wanghia, although the latter may have been more benevolent. Furthermore the next ten years were to show that the English Government was much better prepared than the United States to live up to the few obligations which the foreigners had assumed towards the Chinese. The United States was in the Treaty of Wanghia putting on for the first time some of the garments of imperialism, only to find that the nation itself had not at all grown up to such ample vestments.

It was a difficult road upon which the Treaty of Wanghia set the feet of the still immature and undeveloped power of the western hemisphere. Even before its boundaries had been pushed westward to the Pacific Ocean, the United States was placed in competition with older Powers, the purposes and policies of which were avowedly different from those of the United States. In this rivalry of nations new considerations of national honor and dignity must certainly prompt the United States to new policies and actions. For a comfortable relationship between merchants whose controlling purpose had been always to manage and accommodate matters to avoid disturbance of the trade, was substituted treaty obligations, violations of which became affronts to national dignity. For the newly created consular and diplomatic and judicial positions which the treaty called for, the United States had only a parochially-minded Congress to furnish the appropriations and the 'spoils system' to sup ply the officials. The appointment of faithful party politicians, usually wholly untrained in consular work and entirely inexperienced in the problems of international relations in Asia, unable, even if willing, to look forward to promotion in the same service for meritorious work, opened the doors to dangers both of omission and commission. It was a perilous path on which the United States could not long proceed successfully without altering many habits of action both at home and abroad. The policy of Caleb Cush ing was to be guide.

BIBLIOGRAPHICAL NOTES

1. Chinese Repository, May, 1840, p. 2.
2. China Dispatches. Vol. 1, Mar. 2, 1844, Cushing to Upshur.
3. The Cushing dispatches were published almost complete in S. Docs. 67 and 58:28-2, the latter containing the author's extended discussion of extraterritoriality.
4. China Dispatches, Vol. 2, May 25, 1844, Cushing to Upshur.
5. Chinese Repository, Vol. 15, June, 1846, p. 306. It has been stated, erroneously, that a payment of money entered into the settlement of the Hsü A-man affair.
6. Chinese Account of the Opium War: Pagoda Library, No. 1 (1888), E. H. Parker (translator) p. 76.
7. Davis' "China, During the War and Since the Peace," 2 vols. Vol. 2, p. 86.
8. Koo's "Status of Aliens in China," pp. 132ff.
9. Corres. Relative to Affairs in China, 1839-41; Private and Confidential, printed for the sole use of the Cabinet, Dispatch No. 1, Feb. 20, 1840, Palmerston to Elliot.
10. S. Ex. Doc. 58:28-2, Disp. No. 97.
11. A. J. Sargent's "Anglo-Chinese Commerce and Diplomacy," p. 148.
12. Accounts and Papers—China—40, 1847, Orders, Ordinances, etc., concerning China.

PART III

A PERIOD OF CONFUSION

CHAPTER IX

THE FAR EAST BECOMES A POLITICAL QUESTION

THE Treaty of Wanghia, marking the entrance of the United States into Far Eastern politics, came at the beginning of a period characterized by great confusion in Asia, Europe and America. Within a generation the Chinese Empire was to pass through the Taiping Rebellion, the greatest civil war the world has ever known. The Empire of Japan was likewise to experience a thorough, though relatively bloodless, revolution resulting in a great change of political, economic and industrial structure. Great Britain was in the struggles of educational, industrial, constitutional and fiscal reform, accompanied by the introduction of Free Trade, great increase in manufacturing, and the extension of a commercial empire; it was the age of Palmerston. On the Continent confusion was confounded in revolution and still more confounded by the entrance of Russia as a factor in the politics of both the East and the West. Europe was too engaged in domestic problems to look far beyond the borders of the continent and thus Great Britain and the United States were left almost alone to contest for the markets of the world. This contest was real but the United States was badly handicapped because, far more than its commercial rival, the United States was in confusion. The conflict between the free and the slave states, accompanied by a great westward thrust to reach and hold the Pacific Coast and to round out both northern and southern boundaries, was to issue in the American Civil War—itself the great test as to whether American republicanism would be able to endure.

American policy in Asia was fabricated in the midst of this confusion and was directly related to it. In 1840 the

American Government first faced the question of framing a policy for Asia. A preliminary sketch of the structure was finished in 1844 in the Cushing treaty with China. Within the next twenty-five years, notwithstanding the succession of changes in the administration of the Government of the United States, the break-up of political parties, and the ominous conflict of civil war, the nation had completed the drawings from the sketch which came from the hand of Caleb Cushing, and could claim a well-rounded, well-considered foreign policy for Asia which successive generations had only to apply. The creation of such a policy in such a period was a notable achievement.

THE INTERNATIONAL SITUATION

The preeminent characteristic of the period was the shortening of distances. Communications became quicker and cheaper; it was as though the globe suddenly contracted to a quarter of its former size. Clearly defined boundaries in the West, and in the East as well, became matters of supreme importance whereas they had been ignored in previous generations when time itself was the great boundary. Following rapidly upon the clipper ship with its quicker and cheaper transportation came the extended development of steam motive power, the transcontinental railway lines and the transoceanic steamers, and then with the introduction of the overland and submarine telegraph, the earth contracted again. These inventions were accompanied by the perfection of labor saving machinery and the multiplication of the uses of steam power in manufacturing. Forthwith arose the question of markets for surplus produce. Thus the entire Far Eastern question as related to the West suffered intensification and violent changes.

British foreign policy as viewed from the United States was alarming. While England was steadily consolidating her Indian Empire by the annexation of Gwalior, Sind, the Punjab, Nagpur, Berar, Hyderabad, Tanjore, the Carnatic, Oudh, Burmah and Labuan, it was confidently expected by Americans in the East that it was only a question of time when Great Britain would extend her empire beyond Hongkong to include other portions of the Chinese Empire as well as parts of the Japanese islands. England under Palmerston was apparently girding herself both industrially and politically to capture and hold the markets of Asia. To the American people, to those in the South who grew cotton, to those in the North who manufactured it, to the merchants and ship-owners who carried it to Asia and were just awaking to the boundless markets which might be open, the program of Great Britain was formidable and perilous. Perhaps these apprehensions would never have greatly influenced American foreign policy in the East, had they not been intensified by the activities of Great Britain in the western hemisphere, for after all American commercial interests there were still small. The British program in North America, however, was squarely before the entire American people. It involved questions of boundary and of strategic defense; furthermore it touched their pride. England sought to break down the Monroe Doctrine.

Twice within ten years the United States and Great Britain appeared to be moving toward war, once over the northern boundary, and again over the control of the Isthmus. Even before Caleb Cushing went to Macao the British flag had been hoisted over the Sandwich Islands and only the disavowal of the act by the British Government had averted an ominous contest. Oregon, California, Mexico, Central America, the Sandwich Islands, China, Japan—these were all for the Americans either wholly or partly problems of the Pacific, and taken collectively they created a body of public opinion in the United States which, because of the territorial and industrial questions involved, became related even to the transcending issue of slavery. American policy in Asia was a more important theme in national politics in the decade which preceded the American Civil War than it became again until the occupation of the Philippine Islands in 1898. The American people were moving westward and that portion of the world which, when

viewed from London and Paris was called the Far East, had
become to the Americans not the East at all but the
Farthest West.

A mere catalogue of the places and dates along the
Pacific seaboard would suffice to make vivid the association of American domestic problems and American foreign
policy in the Pacific and the Far East between the Anglo-
Chinese War and 1870.*

The two other foreign powers with which the United
States would have to deal in Asia were France and Russia.
Neither of these powers at first exerted themselves in any
way to attract the attention of the Americans, yet their
presence added to the complexity of the political situation,
and the manner and time of their entrance should be noted.

Immediately following the signing of the Treaty of
Wanghia, France negotiated a treaty with China which was
similar in its general outlines to the American treaty, yet
with one significant addition. This treaty, supplemented
by an imperial rescript, secured to France a somewhat vague
yet virtual protectorate over all Roman Catholic missionaries and their Chinese converts. This concession was to
become the cornerstone of French policy. France was com-

---

*1843: Lord George Paulet seizes Sandwich Islands; the United States fails
to join Great Britain and France in promise never to take possession of the
Islands.¹
   1844: Treaty of Wanghia—United States and China. With an coloniza-
tion expedition to Oregon.
   1845: Fremont exploring expedition to California. Annexation of Texas.
   1846: "Fifty-four-forty-or-fight" dispute with Great Britain terminates in
settlement of Oregon question by division of territory at 49th Parallel. American occupation of Monterey, Mexican capital of California.
   1846: Outbreak of war with Mexico. Treaty with New Granada (Colom-
bia) granting to the United States the right of communication by any form
across the Isthmus of Panama, in return for which the United States guarantees the neutrality of the route and establishes a protectorate over it in the
interest of New Granada.
   1847: Discovery of gold in California.
   1848: Treaty of peace with Mexico, placing the Rio Grande the southern
boundary of the United States. Authorization of surveys for a transcontinental
railroad and also for a transisthmian canal. Beginning of agitation for steam
navigation of the Pacific.
   1849: First American treaty with Sandwich Islands which follows immediately on French intervention at Honolulu.
   1850: Contract between Panama Railroad Company and Colombian Government, and very serious dispute with Great Britain over island of Manzanillo.
Clayton-Bulwer treaty.
   1851: Decision to make a treaty with Japan.
   1853: Gadsden Purchase.
   1854: First treaty between United States and Japan. Attempted annexation of Sandwich Islands.
   1856: Temporary recognition of Rivas-Walker government in Nicaragua.
   1867: Alaska Purchase. First proposal to open Korea. Seward favors in
certain contingencies annexation of Sandwich Islands.

mitted to the political support of Roman Catholic missions which were in turn to become the agency of French terri torial, political and economic expansion in the Far East.[2]

The Russian Emperor sent Nicholai Muravieff as Gov ernor General to the Russian possessions in eastern Siberia in 1847.[3] The steps by which this energetic official estab- lished and consolidated the Russian position in Siberia and North China—the building of Petropavlovsk on Kamchatka in 1849, the founding of Nicholaievsk at the mouth of the Amur in 1850, the expedition down the Amur in the same year, the founding of Blagoveschensk at the mouth of the Ussuri in 1858, and the treaty of Aigun of the same year in which the Russians were given the exclusive right with the Chinese to the navigation of the Amur, Sungari and Ussuri rivers—were quite unnoticed by the Americans but were not overlooked by the British who were closely watching every southward movement of Russia into Asia. By the entrance of Russia into the political and commercial arena of the Far East four foreign powers—Great Britain, the United States, France and Russia—came into direct rela- tions with each other thus making Asiatic politics often merely a phase of the politics of the western world.

MULTIPLICATION OF AMERICAN INTERESTS IN CHINA

With the tremendous expansive movement of the United States the development of American interests in China synchronized almost exactly. American ship-owners in the China trade in the fifth and sixth decades of the nineteenth century profited fabulously by the enormous freight rates at the time of the blockade of Canton at the beginning of the Anglo-Chinese War in 1840, and by the obstacles in the way of British trade at that time.[4] By the perfection of the American type of clipper ship, which appeared about 1840, they were able for a time almost to monopolize the trans- portation of tea even to England, for they could carry larger cargoes and deliver the tea in shorter time and in fresher condition than could their competitors. The rush from the

Atlantic Coast to California after the discovery of gold
created incredibly high freight and passenger rates for a
voyage which carried the ship outward more than half way
towards China.   Thus the outward voyage which under
ordinary circumstances was unremunerative because of the
lack of cargoes became even more profitable than the return
voyage.   The abolition of the British navigation laws in
1850 gave the Americans, temporarily, a still further advantage which they were well prepared to improve.   The Crimean War withdrew a large amount of European tonnage
for transport service, and again the Americans profited.

American trade at Shanghai * grew with rapidity.   This
new port was, on the one hand, nearer to the Pacific Coast
and to San Francisco, and on the other, nearer to the actual
silk-growing and tea-producing districts of China than was
the old port of Canton.   Furthermore, Shanghai, as a foreign
community, started *de novo* without the traditions which
had grown up at Canton.   The Americans were not a tradi-
tion-loving people, and especially was this true when the
backwash from San Francisco harbor began to pour its
stream of derelict Americans on to the China coast.   Yet
even among the more law-abiding residents, Canton came
to be looked upon as a pestilential spot from which it was
well, as rapidly as possible, to transfer both residence and
relations with the Chinese.   Shanghai breathed a freer air
in which life was in every way more comfortable.   For the
Americans it seemed especially desirable because it was
less overshadowed than Canton by the British settlement
of Hongkong.

The Treaty of Wanghia and the subsequent imperial
edicts of religious toleration had also opened the way for
greatly increased missionary work, and the American
Protestant Churches were the most energetic and aggressive in the extension of Protestant missions in the open
ports.   From the days of Dr. Robert Morrison down to

*So rapidly did American trade at Shanghai grow after it once started that
in the year ending September 30, 1853, although there had been 62 American
vessels as compared with 94 British vessels, the total American tonnage was
41,501 as compared with 35,610 for the British.[5]

1851 there had been a total of 150 Protestant missionaries to arrive in China. Of this number 15 had come from the Continent, 47 from England, and 88 from the United States.[6]

American interests in China, therefore, in the period after 1850 are seen to be both enlarged and multiplied over what they had been in the pre-treaty days. Down to the time of the first treaty little mattered save the preservation of undisturbed commercial relationships. Now this commerce had grown immensely and had taken very deep root in at least one other port. In addition the missionaries had come in large numbers to every open port and their advent marked the beginning in the United States of a philanthropic, and also a sentimental interest in China which operated strongly in the formation of American public opinion. Its immediate effect on the American policy in China was greatly to increase the demand for a further opening up of the country. The impatience of the missionary often exceeded that of the trader. To these two interests, one commercial and the other philanthropic, was now being added a third—a political interest.

The problems of Asia as viewed by the Western world ceased to be purely commercial; they became political. Had the Anglo-Chinese War (1839-42) been settled by a purely commercial treaty the Far Eastern question might have remained for a time a commercial one, but England planted at Hongkong an outpost of the India Empire, which had already been advancing by easy stages from Penang and Singapore. The British occupation of Hongkong compelled all other foreign nations from that time onward to deal with Asia as a political problem. It was the delusion of some American statesmen in the eighties and nineties that the United States need recognize no political problem in Asia, that American interests in the East were purely commercial, but this assumption avoided plain facts. Caleb Cushing negotiated the Treaty of Wanghia in 1844 with one eye on the political establishment of Great Britain at Hongkong. Commodore Perry in 1853-54 did not even make a commercial treaty with Japan, but he staked out a political program which failed of adoption through no timidity of its author, and notwithstanding its failure had its influence on subsequent policy. The struggle of the Americans to secure Shanghai as an international rather than a British port, at the very time Perry was in the East, was more political than commercial. The relations of the Western powers to the Taiping Rebellion, and the relations of Great Britain, France, Russia and the United States in the negotiations of the treaties of Tientsin in 1858 were very far from being purely commercial. The 'cooperative policy' and the entire course of the first ten years of American diplomatic relations with Japan were controlled by political considerations. The first American efforts to open Korea were of the same character.

The distinction between the policy of the United States and the policy of other powers in Asia in this period is not that the American policy was purely commercial while the others were political, but that the American policy, although political, followed diplomatic rather than military channels. Military proposals were not lacking from the American representatives in the East; they even issued at times from the Department of State, but with very few exceptions these proposals failed of execution and did not result in the occupation of territory. American policy was preeminently the policy of Americans. As will be elaborated in the following pages it was a composite into the making of which went a great variety of proposals, official and unofficial, some belligerent, others most pacific, but all directed towards securing for American interests in Asia a diplomatic equivalent for Hongkong and what the British possession stood for, viz., territorial occupation of Asia by Western powers.

By the Americans it was foreseen that some day their trans-Pacific commerce would be very great. This expectation reacted on American policy in the Far East in two ways. In the first place it made the Americans increasingly alert to see that no other power should take any step which would later become a handicap to American interest; that is to say, it helped to confirm an open door policy. But it did more. It raised questions of how this expected great commerce with Asia might in future years receive adequate protection. It sent the Americans into the Pacific to look for harbors, to Japan for more open ports, and to Formosa, for coal mines which were deemed a necessity for the success of steam navigation. This alertness and this search, this planning for the future, which then seemed so sure and so welcome to the cotton growers and manufacturers alike, immediately put the United States in the way of international collisions of grave import, for were not the Americans setting out upon a path already well-trodden by England? and Russia? and France? and did not the closed ports of Japan lie directly in the way?

A brief reference to details will make more intelligi ble the force of this situation as it was felt in the United States a few years after the signing of the Treaty of Wanghia.

As early as May, 1848, T. Butler King, of the Committee on Naval Affairs, introduced into the House of Representatives a report recommending steam navigation from the United States to the Sandwich Islands and China.[7] He exhibited an exhaustive analysis of the conditions of the American trade. While the United States and England were then great competitors he argued that the English imports contained one element of decay, viz., opium, and he expressed the opinion that England would in the future be very dependent upon the United States for the raw material for her cotton trade with China. The American trade, he asserted, was therefore in a far more favorable potential position. It had already been proved that the Americans could meet English competition in cheap cotton goods, and it merely remained for the American manufacturer to study more carefully and adapt his fabrics more to the wants and tastes of the Chinese people. In spite of the growing production of cotton in India, Mr. King felt assured of the American cotton market in China if only the transportation problem could be solved. He said:

"Certainty and rapidity of intercourse only are wanted to bring
these two great nations [China and the United States] nearer together,
to give them a more perfect knowledge of each other, develop their resources and build up a commerce more extensive than has probably
ever heretofore existed between two nations. The improved condition
of our relations with that country under the new treaties, and the
extension of our territorial possessions to the Pacific have placed it
in our power *ultimately* to communicate with China almost as rapidly
as we now do with Europe. To accomplish this, however, we must
extend telegraphic wires across the continent, and establish a line
of steamers from San Francisco, or Monterey, to Shanghai and
Canton."

Mr. King drew attention to the fact that a line of
steamers had already been established from New York to
Havana and Panama, and that there was already a government mail line up the California coast from the Isthmus to
the Columbia River.   Lieutenant M. F. Maury of the Naval
Observatory submitted a report which was attached to the
document showing that because of the 'great circle route'
to the East, the United States had already taken a step of
three thousand miles on its way toward China.   He pointed
out that the steamer route from Panama by way of the
'great circle' was 1200 miles shorter to China than the
route formerly taken by way of the Sandwich Islands.   New
Orleans, by this new route, was actually 3000 miles nearer
China than Panama was by way of Honolulu, and from
Monterey to Japan was not as far as from Panama to the
Sandwich Islands.

The proposed steamer line to China was not suffered to
be forgotten.   John P. Kennedy, Secretary of the Navy in
the closing days of the Pierce administration, reporting to
the Senate in response to request (February 10, 1853),[8]
urged the necessity of such a line of steamers without delay,
either by direct agency of the government, or by the encouragement of individual enterprise.   Kennedy drew attention to the need of coal which would be created if such
steamers were established.   He recommended the establishment of coal deposits on some of the islands in the Pacific,
stating that at that time the United States did not possess
a single coal depot for the supply of naval steamers in either

the Atlantic or the Pacific oceans. He proposed a plan by which he thought such depots could be supplied in the Pacific at little cost, by means of the development of an outward trade to China in tobacco and an inward trade from the Pacific islands in guano. He suggested with reference to the tobacco trade:

"The use of opium in China has been the great cause of preventing the extension of commerce into that country, while at the same time, many believe, it has almost entirely shut out the lights and advantages of Christianity. If, by any means that our government shall employ, a trade between us and China shall be opened, there is reason to suppose that our tobacco will be generally received there as a substitute for this poisonous drug. This article, now so abundantly produced in our tobacco-growing states, will then become the pioneer of our trade, and open the way for our manufactures of cotton, wool, and particularly of cutlery and other manufactures of iron—in which latter articles the trade between Great Britain and China is now very large.

"These two articles," thought Kennedy, "of *tobacco* and *guano,* would alone, without other commodities, afford the means of opening a rapid and profitable intercourse with China. The product of tobacco would be increased in a measure corresponding to the increased demand of the two hundred millions of Chinese consumers, and thus our national wealth would be greatly augmented."

The proposal for the steamship line remained in abeyance, but the Perry expedition was already on its way to secure the coal supply.

COMMISSIONERS AND CONSULS

Notwithstanding the recognition of the growing importance of American affairs in the East, they suffered neglect. That their importance was recognized may be seen in the Perry expedition; that they were neglected is proven by the records of the consulates and the legation in China. There were fits and starts; brilliant efforts and then lapses. Continuity was lacking. It would even appear as though the Americans, while well equipped to initiate things effectively in Asia, were either by temperament or by the constitutional structure of their government, incapable of seeing them through.

President Tyler had lost no time in recommending that Congress make suitable provision for the establishment of diplomatic relations with China, and for carrying out the purposes of the Treaty of Wanghia.[9] He asked for the creation of the position of permanent commissioner, the enactment of legislation for the establishment of extraterritorial authority, and the replacement of the old and objectionable merchant-consul system by an adequately manned consular establishment independent of trade. The first of these recommendations was acted on immediately although a salary was fixed at a rate too low to support the commissioner in decency; the second duty remained in abeyance until 1848 and was then delegated to wholly incompetent hands; while the merchant-consul system lingered until 1854, and then was partially replaced by consular establishments which were in a few respects better but in most respects even worse.

Early in 1845 Alexander H. Everett of Massachusetts was appointed commissioner to China at a salary of $5,000, and Dr. Peter Parker was named as secretary and interpreter. Everett was charged with 'the general superintendence of the spirit of the treaty,' and instructed to cultivate the good will of the Chinese Government and people. He was under the embarrassment, however, of being quite without authority to exercise judicial or executive functions under the extraterritorial grant.

"It cannot be pretended," read his instructions from James Buchanan, "that one of our consuls at the five ports could try and punish an American citizen for murder or any other crime. What is then to be done? Shall a citizen guilty of murder or other high crime pass unpunished? Independently of the other evil results of such an impunity, nothing would more exasperate the Chinese than to witness such a spectacle. . . . They never could be made to understand that we had not violated the treaty." [10]

The President, therefore, directed that an accused party be sent home for trial.

It speaks well for the character of the community at Canton that there were no occasions where it was necessary to fall back on this executive order. The Americans did not begin to enter and settle in numbers at the other open ports until after the consular courts had been created in 1848. The great difficulties came later when laws were ample but consuls were lacking or ineffective, and there was so little provision for the enforcement of such judgments as came from the consular courts.

The 'destitute condition of the consular establishments' was made the subject of a dispatch by Commissioner McLane in 1854. The facts reported at that time may be taken as typical of conditions for most of the period before 1860, and some of the reported deficiencies were not corrected for half a century. The consulate at Ningpo was in charge of Rev. D. B. McCartee, a medical missionary who received no salary, was allowed no funds for expenses other than stationary, had no office quarters other than the mission building, and exercised no judicial functions. A new consul had arrived a Ningpo. His salary for judicial services was one thousand dollars; for the balance of his emolument he had to depend upon consular fees which were next to nothing. He was unable to speak the language and had no allowances for an interpreter. He lived with "rigid economy" but nothing could "be more disreputable and derogatory to the dignity and honor of the country than the condition" in which he was placed. The Foochow consulate was in the hands of a merchant who had been appointed acting consul by no other authority than that of his predecessor who also had been an acting consul. The regularly appointed consul was on his way but upon arrival at his post his condition would be no less forlorn than that at Amoy. There was little or no American trade at these ports, but extraterritoriality prevailed and made them the resort of outlaws who either were American citizens or claimed their immunities. The newly appointed consul at Shanghai, whose remuneration consisted only of $1000 a year for his judicial services and his fees, was living in a seamen's boarding-house or hotel. He was without means to secure an office or a 'respectable domestic establishment and subsistence.' He was dependent upon the British consulate and upon merchants for the loan of the services of interpreters.

In contrast to this condition Mr. McLane pointed to the British establishment which consisted of a Minister with secretary and interpreter at $30,000, and five well manned consular offices at a cost of $10,000 each.[11]

The United States paid dearly in loss of prestige for these economies. The opening of the new ports and the boundless expectations for the new trade drew from the four quarters of the globe a crowd of adventurers who had no other trade or profession than to live by their wits. They were of the type which gave the reputation to the usual pioneer community of the western continent. Then came the discovery of gold in California, followed by the rush and the failure of most of the gold-seekers. Luckless adventurers drifted out to Shanghai; and the deserting sailors in San Francisco harbor were 'shanghaied' and when they reached Shanghai they promptly deserted again, scattered up and down the coast, and attempted to live as best they could off the country.

Those were wild days in the open ports—uncomfortable for all, and for the Chinese terrifying. The reports of the American consuls and the dispatches of the commissioners abound in accounts of the scandals, crimes, and atrocities of these derelicts. Commissioner Humphrey Marshall, for example, reported in 1853 as follows: [12]

"There are now in this port (Shanghai) at least one hundred and fifty sailors ashore, men of all nations, who go into the Chinese city and drink and riot and brawl, daily and nightly. They presume to defy all law, because they have tried the jail and find that they cannot be confined in it. No other punishment has been inflicted upon them yet besides confinement. They have no money from which to collect a fine. I earnestly request the President to give the authority to lease a lot of ground in this vicinity on which to erect a jail with a yard attached thereto, in which sailors may have air and exercise, and that Congress shall be urged to make an appropriation for the purpose of erecting a jail thereon. The marshal can reside in the tenement, and the fines and forfeitures will probably pay for a guard to attend the premises.

"The United States having assumed jurisdiction over their own citizens in China, are expressly bound to compel them to keep the peace, and this cannot be done as long as there is no place to confine the delinquents in, except a loathsome hole inhabited by the foulest lepers, and in itself so weak that a man of American energies can kick his way out in a few minutes."

These ruffians may have been deficient in character but they did not lack initiative. Many of them joined the military or naval service of the Taipings or of the Imperialists, defying the proclamations of the representatives of their government who ordered them to desist. Others enlisted in the opium smuggling. Some entered the coolie trade. Still others engaged in the business of 'convoying.' *

By no means all of these foreigners were Americans, but even many of those who were not found it convenient to claim citizenship in a country which was entirely without jails, without sufficient naval vessels to prevent the abuse of its flag, and possessed, at least in some cases, of indulgent consular officials who could be induced to give an approval, tacit or otherwise, to the fraudulent transfer of ship's papers, and to practices in plain violation both of the treaty and the laws of the United States. The situation was at once disgraceful to the American reputation and dangerous to the entire foreign community, for the depredations of these individuals created ill-will and wrath among the Chinese which might any day lead to the gravest consequences for all.[14]

The failure of Congress to make adequate provision for consuls and for jails was by no means the worst of the situation. Even the commissionership suffered. A brief summary of the way in which the position of commissioner was filled before 1858 will be sufficient.

Alexander H. Everett, the first commissioner, was appointed March 13, 1845, but owing to illness did not reach China until nineteen months later (October 29, 1846) and he died in China the following June. Everett was, perhaps,

*The prevalency along the coast of piracy which the Chinese Government, distracted by the Taipings and other rebels, was unable to suppress, led to the development of a system of protection for the native junks which was furnished by foreigners, unofficially, and which was paid for by the junk owners. At first the payments were made willingly, but as abuses crept in the conveying system degenerated into nothing less than blackmail and piracy.[13]

the ablest commissioner ever appointed, and the only experienced diplomat. He had served as private secretary to John Quincy Adams when the latter was Minister to Russia, had remained for a time in the diplomatic service, and had been at one time Minister at Madrid. However, he was in China too short a time to render any important service. His successor, John W. Davis, was appointed January 3, 1848, and arrived in China in August. Thus, from the time of the signing of the treaty of Wanghia until the middle of 1848—four years—there was in China a regularly appointed commissioner for only eight months. Before Everett's arrival, Commodore James Biddle, to whom Everett had delegated his powers, acted as commissioner, and after the death of Everett, Dr. Peter Parker, secretary of the legation, served as commissioner until the arrival of Davis.

John W. Davis was, by profession, a physician. He had served three terms in the House of Representatives from Indiana, and had been elected Speaker of the House in 1845. After his return from China he became governor of Oregon Territory; he was also the presiding officer of the National Democratic Convention at Baltimore in 1852. He retired from China in May, 1850, after a residence of a little less than two years. It became extremely difficult to find another to take his place. The position was offered to a lawyer from Tennessee who accepted it and then declined when he found that he would be unable to live on $2000 a year in China, as he had hoped, thus saving $4000 a year out of his salary. It was offered to another who accepted and then declined also because of the salary. To still a third it was offered only to be declined. In his annual message, December 2, 1851, President Fillmore reported: [15]

"The office of commissioner to China remains unfilled. Several persons have been appointed and the place has been offered to others, all of whom have declined its acceptance on the ground of the inadequacy of the compensation. The annual allowance by law is $6000 and there is no provision for any outfit. I earnestly recommend the consideration of this subject to Congress. China is understood to be a country in which living is very expensive, and I know no reason why the American commissioner sent thither should not be placed, in

regard to compensation, on an equal footing with ministers who represent this country at the courts of Europe."

In August, 1852, the post was offered to Humphrey Marshall of Kentucky, Congress having not heeded the President's request that the salary be increased, and Marshall accepted, reaching China in January, 1853. Meanwhile the duties of the office of commissioner had been discharged by the secretary, Dr. Parker, who had resigned his position as a missionary and was supplementing his meagre salary of $2500 by private practice as a physician.

Humphrey Marshall was a graduate of the United States Military Academy at West Point, a lawyer by profession, who had served two terms in Congress from Kentucky. After returning to the United States, he was again elected to Congress for one term. At the outbreak of the Civil War he became a Brigadier General in the Confederate service.[16] Marshall's service in China covered slightly more than a year.

Robert M. McLane, who succeeded Marshall, arrived in China in March, 1854, and left the following December. He was the son of Lewis McLane who had served as Secretary of State for a year under President Jackson and had been senator from Delaware, and United States Minister to England. The son had been a student at West Point, and was a lawyer by profession. He had served in the House of Representatives for two terms. Subsequently he held the important diplomatic posts of Minister to Mexico (1859-60) and Minister to France (1885-89).[17]

After the departure of McLane from China, Dr. Parker, as usual, became Chargé, but within a few months it became necessary for him to return to the United States for reasons of health. In his absence Commodore Joel Abbot, commanding the United States Squadron on the China station, was delegated "to meet any emergencies that may arise." [18]

In June, 1855, S. Wells Williams, an unordained missionary who had gone to China in 1834 to take charge of the printing press of the American Board of Commissioners for Foreign Missions, was notified of his appointment as

secretary and interpreter of the legation, at a salary of
$2500.* Dr. Williams had acted as interpreter for Commo-
dore Perry in the Japan expedition. A few weeks later
(September 5, 1855) Dr. Parker was appointed commissioner under the new diplomatic law of March 1, 1855, at a
salary of $15,000.† Dr. Parker reached China at the begin-
ning of the following year and served for about twenty
months, retiring by his own choice, when William B. Reed,
a Pennsylvania lawyer, was appointed to China with the
title of envoy extraordinary and minister plenipotentiary.

In the midst of these conditions of confusion—in the
United States, in England, on the Continent, and in China
—the policy of the Cushing treaty was put to its first tests.
This policy was, in a word, to occupy no portion of Asia as
a military or naval base and to depend entirely upon the
pledges of the Chinese Government. It soon developed that
American interests were to be exposed to danger at two
points; the aggressions and pretensions of other treaty
powers threatened to curtail the privileges granted to
Americans under the treaty; and, the Chinese provincial
authorities, the local gentry and rabble, sometimes supported by the Imperial Government at Peking, were unwilling in many cases to make effective the rights accorded
by treaties to which China was an unwilling party. These
tests revealed a fallacy in the Cushing policy. The policy
rested upon the false assumption that the Imperial Government was not only possessed of the utmost good will towards
the Americans, but that it was also strongly centralized and
able to enforce its commands upon the provinces; further,
that China was strong enough to resist the pressure which
the other treaty powers were able to exert by means of military force, and would protect the Americans in the enjoy-
ments of the rights which the Empire had granted.

So long as foreign powers in China were competing for

*Commodore Perry expressed a lively interest in the appointment and hoped
that Williams would accept it. "In these days it is an unheard of case; such
offices under our government being seldom given except on application, then too
frequently with little or no respect to the qualifications of the applicant. I
look upon this appointment as indicating a sort of *moral* reform at
Washington." [19]
†The following year the salary was reduced to $12,000 where it has remained
ever since.

preferred position, and so long as the Chinese of the open ports resented the presence of the foreigners, the Treaty of Wanghia was of only nominal value.

BIBLIOGRAPHICAL NOTES

1. The simplest method of following through in greater detail the policy of the United States in these particulars is tò read the historical sections under the appropriate headings to be found in the index of Moore's Digest of International Law. Copious extracts from the official documents will be found there.
2. Journal des opérations diplomatiques de la Legation française en Chine, rédigé par J. M. Callery (Macao, 1845); "Cambridge Modern History," Vol. XI, pp. 811-2.
3. Morse's "International Rel. of the Chinese Empire," Vol. 1, chap. 19.
4. Forbes' "Personal Reminiscences," p. 151.
   H. Doc. 123:33-1, p. 374; see also Morse, Vol. 1, pp. 342-3.
   Chinese Repository, Vol. 20, p. 520.
   H. Repts. 596, 30-1.
   S. Ex. Doc. 49:32-2.
   S. Ex. Doc. 58:28-2.
10. China Instructions, Vol. 1, Apr. 15, 1845 (Dept. of State). All of the instructions to Everett are printed in J. B. Moore's Works of James Buchanan, Vol 6.
11. S. Ex. Doc. 22:35-2, pp. 165-167.
12. H. Doc. 123:33-1, p. 224.
13. Morse, Vol. 1, pp. 406-8.
14. H. Doc. 123:33-1, p. 167; S. Ex. Doc. 22:35-2, pp. 422, 437, 625, 732, 823; H. Jour. 34-1, p. 1048; H. Misc. Docs. 2:35-1; H. Ex. Doc. 68:35-2.
15. Richardson's Messages, Vol. 5, p. 122.
16. Poore's "Political Register," p. 524.
17. Ibid., p. 516.
18. S. Ex. Doc. 22:35-2, p. 609.
19. S. Wells Williams' "Life and Letters," pp. 235-6.

CHAPTER X

SETTLEMENT OF THE SHANGHAI LAND QUESTION

THE British, American and French treaties with China left open for further discussion a most important principle as to the way in which the foreigners should occupy lands in the open ports. In pre-treaty days at Canton the foreigners had all lived together in the restricted area of the factories where each individual or firm, regardless of nationality, rented from the hong merchants who were the owners. The British Treaty of the Bogue (1843) provided that under the new régime in the five ports "grounds and houses . . . shall be set apart by the local officers in communication with the consul." The American treaty merely stated that the local officers of the two governments "shall select, in concert, the sites" for residences, churches, cemeteries and hospitals.

How then were the foreigners to live in the open ports? Were they to continue the practice of residing together as of old at Canton in a single international settlement set apart for their use; or, were they to scatter, each resident inde pendently, with the consent of his consul and the local Chinese official, selecting such residence as his fancy preferred; or, were the nationals of each treaty power to establish their own national settlement, thus forming in each open port a series of national concessions? When viewed in the light of subsequent history it is seen that this question involved one of the most fundamental principles in the relations of China with the treaty powers. A single international settlement in each port involved a degree of international cooperation among the treaty powers such as had no precedent. The scattering of the foreign residents among the Chinese residences was open to the gravest objections, sanitary, commercial and social. To the Chinese

194

also this was objectionable because the foreigner was exempt from Chinese laws. On the other hand the creation of separate national settlements was likely to bring the treaty powers into collision with each other and with China because of the most-favored-nation clause. In each port there was naturally a most favored site for business purposes, determined by the contour of the land and its accessibility to the best anchorage. If any single nation were to occupy this most favored site the other nations might invoke the most-favored-nation clause in their own treaties, and demand admission. The question came to an issue very soon after the opening of Shanghai to trade.

EARLY AMERICANS IN SHANGHAI

The first American resident at Shanghai was Henry G. Wolcott, representing Russell and Company. Relying on the Imperial rescript which had extended the privileges granted to the British to all foreigners he had gone to the new port even before Caleb Cushing had reached Macao to negotiate the American treaty. In the course of time Wolcott desired to lease a piece of land and went to the taotai (Prefect or Intendent of Circuit) to have the lease sanctioned.[1] This official replied that he had already entered into an agreement with the British consul, Captain G. Balfour, that all land within certain boundaries, which included the site which Wolcott desired, was to be leased only through the agency of the British consul.[2] Wolcott then addressed himself to Captain Balfour and was given permission to secure the land on conditions similar to those enjoyed by British subjects. The lease was immediately effected but complications arose. Wolcott paid a visit to the South in December, 1845, and when he returned he carried a commission granted to him by Commodore Biddle, then acting commissioner, as "acting American Consul" for Shanghai.

Wolcott immediately erected a flagstaff and proceeded to fly the American flag as suited his consular dignity. Captain Balfour formally protested to both Wolcott and the taotai, requesting the latter to prevent use of the United States flag in the British settlement. Meanwhile the British Government had extended its authority over the port to the extent of issuing certain port regulations which Wolcott was very reluctant to accept. Affairs at Shanghai had evidently reached a condition which was never contemplated in the American treaty which had been signed eighteen months before.[3]

The British claim at Shanghai had arisen in a very natural way. By Imperial rescript the taotais at the various open ports had been ordered to consult with the consuls of the treaty powers and to make the necessary arrangements by which the foreigners of all nations could establish them selves. The only consul at Shanghai was Captain Balfour, and this official naturally exercised himself to care for British interests. There is no reason to suppose that Balfour, who had come from India where all precedent was on his side, ever considered the possibility of anything but a series of national concessions at Shanghai. The taotai conferred with him and in November, 1845, issued a proclamation in which it was agreed that "the ground north of the Yang King Pang and south of the Lekea Chang (two creeks) should be rented to English merchants for erecting their buildings and residing thereon." This tract of land, lying outside the city wall and fronting on the best anchorage, was the most favorable location for foreign residence and business. The taotai further agreed in the proclamation, so it is believed, that no other than the British flag should be hoisted; "that no part of the ground should be rented to other than British subjects through and by the British consul; and, that all Chinese dwellings thereon should be as speedily as possible removed, and that no other Chinese dwellings be permitted." While the claim was established in a very natural way there is no reason to suppose that the Imperial Government had the remotest intention of granting any exclusive rights to the British at Shanghai, and the concession was certainly in conflict with the spirit and intention of the American treaty which had been signed before the taotai had issued his proclamation.

Commodore Biddle on his way to Japan in June, 1846, stopped at Shanghai and conferred with both Wolcott and Balfour. The latter explained to him that the British municipal and port regulations had been established to prevent anarchy in the new settlement, the growing trade of which required some sort of ordered government. The commodore advised Wolcott to recognize the port regulations which were obviously so necessary, but not to pull down the American flag. But Wolcott represented a Canton firm in which the old pre-treaty traditions of conciliation and com promise were very strong. He not only accepted the port regulations but also pulled down the flag.

A truce was thus established which continued until February, 1848, when the captain of the American ship *Montauk* came into collision with some additional port regulations which had been issued the preceding year. The American captain insisted upon the right to fire a morning and an evening gun. The British consul claimed that this was a violation of the regulations and called upon the taotai to forbid it. The Americans, now considerably increased in numbers over the time when Wolcott had made his surrender, replied that they did not consider themselves subject to any port regulations which had not been approved by the Government of the United States. Both the British and the Americans appealed the case to the representatives of their respective governments at Hongkong and Canton. Sir John Davis, the British minister, did not sustain the contention of the British consul. The issue was thus postponed, though only for a few months.

Shortly afterwards J. Alsop Griswold, the regularly appointed American consul, and also a member of Russell and Company, came to Shanghai and raised his flag in the Brit ish settlement, presumably at the same location where Wol cott had pulled it down two years before. The British con sul made his objections, but the flag remained.

The issue was again raised early in 1849 when the French

consul secured from the taotai an area for a French settlement between the English settlement and the city wall. In
this new area the arrangements as to leasing land were to be
similar to those in the British settlement, viz., that the person desiring to lease should first apply to the French consul.
Consul Griswold immediately protested,[4] writing to the
taotai (April 11, 1849) as follows:

"There is nothing in the said treaties which gives any foreign
representative a right to claim, or renders it incumbent on you to
grant, particular districts to one nation, excluding the people of other
countries, except by consent of the consuls to whom the grant is
made. . . . On July 14, 1846, your predecessor offered land which
includes the grant now made to the French to the United States
citizens. This tender was waived for the time being as Mr. Wolcott
considered it open for further discussion."

Griswold also pointed out to the taotai that to make such
grants to foreigners would alienate the sympathy of the
gentry for miles around. The British consul also protested
against the provision that to secure land in the French concession the subjects of other nations would have to act
through the French consul, although this provision in the
French grant had been copied from the grant made to Captain Balfour.* Thus the British and American consuls assumed a united front and both issued proclamations to their
nations informing them that the protection of the respective
flags would be given to land wherever situated.[6]

To United States Commissioner Davis at Macao, Griswold wrote:

"If we are now to admit the principles of these grants, and demand
a similar one, it could only be given in a very unfavorable position,
and the majority of our citizens who come hereafter would find it to
their interest to locate themselves near the rest of their countrymen,
and thus come within the English and French concessions, rendering
the one we may obtain of little avail, and leaving us in the power
of the Chinese and foreign representatives to restrict us to the
allotment however unsuitable it may prove for business purposes."

In this letter Griswold reviewed the history of the con
troversy and pointed out that the conditions had materially

*Morse states: "The sa i e rule 1ad been inserted in the agree 1ent for the
Englis1 settle 1 en t, but it 1ad not been acted on,"—a very inadequate state 1 ent
of w1at actually 1appened.[6]

changed. When the original grant was made to the English there were no other consuls in Shanghai. Now there were four. Captain Balfour had insisted upon exclusive jurisdiction because of the necessity of preserving order. Now the various governments were in a position to cooperate in this matter. Griswold thought that there was little to fear from the present French and English consuls, but the claims to which they held might make difficulty at some future date. He stated that he had never recognized the British claims and that he had never had any trouble in securing all the land the Americans wanted. But he thought that the time had come to protest, not only against the grants themselves, but also against the idea of putting consuls in control of them.

AMERICAN PROTESTS AGAINST EXCLUSIVE CONCESSIONS

Immediately upon the receipt of the report from Griswold, Commissioner Davis took up the matter with Sen, the Viceroy at Canton, drawing attention to the fact that the concession to France at Shanghai violated Article 17 of the Treaty of Wanghia, which provided for the residence of Americans at the five ports. Davis wrote:

"How can these immunities be enjoyed by the citizens of the United States, if all the eligible situations for the above mentioned objects have been ceded to other nations and that, too, long before they have occasion to occupy them? Disclaiming any desire to abridge the right granted by China to other nations by treaty, I must protest against this and all other acts of a subordinate officer of the Chinese Government which is intended to abrogate the rights guaranteed to American citizens by treaty, and while we look to His Imperial Majesty for the fulfillment of Treaty stipulations with us, we must regard as a nullity any act of his subordinate officers which comes in conflict with our rights under the treaty."

The Chinese High Commissioner, between two fires, agreed that the local authorities at Shanghai had no right to make such agreements but as the discussion with Davis proceeded Sen's views came to be tempered with notions of expediency. The American commissioner remained un moved, and at length Sen intimated that he could see no good reason to repudiate the conditions in which affairs had been placed by the grants to the English and the French, and he hoped that the Americans would be content to have a distinct quarter set apart for them elsewhere. Thus the matter rested for a few months, and then Davis wrote to Sen that he had decided to postpone the settlement of the concession matter until some definite case arose.*

The American consul himself soon presented an opportunity to have the case reviewed. He purchased ground inside the British concession, settled the terms with the owners of the land, and presented his conveyance for the seal of the intendant and for registration at the consulate of the United States, without in any way recognizing the right of the British consul to interfere in the transaction. His deed was examined, sealed, and registered, apparently without question; and the matter of the 'concession' to the use of the British merchants exclusively seemed to have received a practical solution, consistent with the rights and claims of the citizens of the United States. But without the knowledge of the United States consul the taotai had submitted the deeds of Mr. Griswold to the British consul for his approval.

In the spring of 1852, Mr. Roundy, an American citizen, purchased land within the British concession, and Mr. Cunningham, the vice-consul of the United States, sent in the conveyance to be examined and sealed by the taotai and returned for registration at the consulate of the United States. The official informed the vice-consul that the deed must be submitted to Her Britannic Majesty's consul, and must be registered in his office. This the vice-consul promptly and firmly refused to do; and thereupon threatened the taotai that if he did not perform his duty within forty-eight hours communications between the authorities

*This passage between Davis and Sen, in which the representative of the American Government is seen to be urging the Chinese Viceroy, with indifferent success, to enforce the rights of China under the treaty, is illustrative of the anomolous situation created by the fact that the management of the foreign affairs of the Chinese Empire were entrusted to a viceroy who was stationed at Canton. Sen was little interested in what happened at Shanghai.

of the United States and China at Shanghai would be closed. The taotai returned the deeds with the seals properly affixed (March 16).

The same day Cunningham issued a proclamation to the American residents of Shanghai drawing their attention to the fact that purchases of land within Shanghai or its neighborhood could be effected according to the terms of the treaty with the Chinese officers through the American consulate without the intervention in any manner of any other foreign consul. The right had been uniformly maintained by the United States authorities, stated the consul, and in the correspondence just closed had been fully acknowledged by the taotai.[7]

By this very energetic action the question was disposed of so far as the Chinese Government was concerned. A week later, Consul Alcock, March 23, 1852, in a private letter to Cunningham wrote very gracefully with reference to the proclamation:

"I am glad of an opportunity of saying that I by no means condemn your circular, though it must give rise to some difficulty in readjusting the terms of a joint location of foreigners recognizing no common law, authority, or jurisdiction.

"I should consider myself very unworthy of the trust confided to me as the representative of the British Government here, if I desired any exclusive advantage to the prejudice of any foreigner, and still less of an American citizen."

Nevertheless the British consul felt it to be his duty to enter an official protest to the proclamation of Cunningham in which the British claims were repudiated. This protest, with the explanatory papers was referred to the British minister at Hongkong, and by him it was referred to the Foreign Office. This question reached London for settlement at the time when the Perry expedition was on its way to Japan and American influence in the Far East was becoming a factor in international affairs. The clouds which foreshadowed the approach of the Crimean War were already gathering over Europe and the American people inclined to friendliness with Russia. Great Britain could

not well afford to add fuel to the fires which had been
kindled in Oregon and in Nicaragua a few years before
where the Americans had sometimes assumed a very belligerent attitude. How much these considerations weighed
in the decision it is impossible to say, but at any rate the
Foreign Office decided to recognize the American contention
at Shanghai.

The Municipal Code

The following May (1853), Consul Alcock advised Cunningham that "Her Majesty's Government have no desire
whatever to assert either exclusive right or jurisdiction over
the unappropriated land." Alcock thereupon submitted a
draft code of municipal regulations which, if accepted
jointly by the consuls and the taotai and then approved
by the home governments of the treaty powers, would have
the effect of converting the grant originally made to Captain Balfour into a grant for the use of all foreigners under
the joint control and supervision of the consuls and the
taotai.

This draft code was immediately submitted to U. S.
Commissioner Marshall who suggested a number of amendments which were incorporated. He objected to the provision that the British consulate site, a tract of about thirty
acres, should be exempt from taxation, and in the final
draft of the regulations it was provided that "any land hereafter acquired by the governments of France and the United
States of America" were to be exempted from the regulations, but that all such lands, the British included, would
"bear their share of the public burdens."

Marshall also objected to the provision which required
the intervention of the consul in the transfer of land from
one foreigner to another, and he found the stipulation
that a Chinese proprietor might be compelled to part with
his land at a price to be fixed by the consul and the taotai
to be 'subversive of justice.' In one other respect he proposed to curb the power of the consuls by lodging the

authority to determine the extension of roads, the building of wharves, etc., in a committee appointed by the tax-payers.

In some respects the most notable change suggested by Marshall, the more remarkable because he was a Southerner and might have been expected to possess some color prejudices, was in the provision which would have excluded the Chinese from living within the bounds of the foreign settlement. This regulation he believed to be "wholly objectionable as creating invidious distinctions against the Chinese, and exercising exactly the spirit of exclusiveness towards them which we now complain of when exercised towards ourselves. It cannot be sound policy to segregate the populations, and instead of prohibiting the settlement of Chinese among the foreigners, it should be invited. . . . Prejudices will only give way before long-continued pleasant social intercourse, and I anticipate great effect to be produced by inviting the Chinese gentlemen to live among the Americans and the English." The regulations as finally adopted did not exclude the Chinese, merely specifying very carefully the kind of houses which could be erected, with a view to safeguarding the settlement from nuisances. While the admission of the Chinese to the settlement in years to come did not always add to the comfort of the foreigners, it cannot be denied that the city thus created and governed exercised a profound influence on China, just as the American commissioner predicted.

The most significant feature of the proposed regulations was the definite and repeated acknowledgment of Chinese sovereign rights to the land. The Chinese Government was to receive a small annual tax, and deeds were to be sealed by the Chinese authorities. While the foreigners were to be permitted to form a municipal government of their own, the source of the authority by which this was to be accomplished was the Chinese Government. The rights of China as well as of the foreigners were protected.

The importance of this question to American interests on the China coast was considered by Commissioner Mar-

shall to be very great politically as well as commercially.
He pointed out to Secretary of State Marcy:

"It may be considered a matter of importance to *the government,*
as connected with the future relations of Shanghai with the Western
terminus of a Pacific railroad; *for I have no kind of a doubt that
Shanghai is destined to become the greatest city of Eastern Asia,
and most intimately of all connected with America.* These regulations will have a direct effect upon her future fortunes."

FINAL SETTLEMENT OF A VEXED QUESTION

The final settlement of the land question and the inception of a municipal government along the lines which had
been approved by the Chinese authorities and the several
governments concerned was reported to Secretary of State
Marcy by Commissioner McLane in July of the following
year.[8]

"This system," wrote McLane, "is now in full operation, and it is
respected by all. I think it has the necessary strength to command
that respect when, from any cause, it may cease to be voluntarily
rendered.

"These arrangements. are of a very comprehensive character,
securing the peace and tranquillity of the foreign settlement at
Shanghai, and the lives, property and commercial privileges of our
people; while they render it impossible for any foreign power to
obtain an undue ascendancy.

"The land regulations, signed by the ministers of the three treaty
powers, renounce the pretensions heretofore set up by Great Britain
and France to the exclusive enjoyment of certain concessions made to
them respectively by the local authorities of China, and all foreigners
under the jurisdiction of their respective consuls enjoy the same
privileges; the concurrent and joint action of the consuls and the
local authorities of China having established a fundamental basis
on which the rights and privileges of all are firmly planted."

While the Shanghai land question has been treated here
as though it were an isolated episode in the international
relations of China, the full significance of it, both as related
to the relations of China with the powers and also to the
development of American policy in the Empire can only be
appreciated when it is remembered that the final settlement
of the question was being undertaken at the time when there
were also up for discussion two other matters of the highest

importance; the question of the recognition of the Taiping rebels, and, the question of the payment of duties at Shanghai after the capture of the city by the rebels,—a situation which resulted in the establishment of the foreign inspectorate of the Chinese maritime customs.

BIBLIOGRAPHICAL NOTES

1. The most extended and coherent account of the early history of the Shanghai land question is to be found in the Marshall Correspondence. H. Doc. 123:33-1, Dispatch No. 23, July 26, 1853. Unless otherwise noted, this document is followed in the ensuing narrative. See also Historic Shanghai, by C. A. Montalto de Jesus, pp. 38-43.
2. Chinese Repository, June, 1849, p. 332.
3. China Dispatches, Vol. 4.
4. China Dispatches, Vol. 5, Davis to Secy. of State, May 21, 1849.
5. Morse, Vol. 1, p. 349.
6. Chinese Repository, June, 1849.
7. Morse, Vol. 1, p. 349.
8. McLane Correspondence, S. Ex. Doc. 22:35-2, p. 123.

CHAPTER XI

HUMPHREY MARSHALL AND THE TAIPING REBELLION

THE personal character of so much of the American policy in Asia is well illustrated in the case of Humphrey Marshall. Marshall had been chosen for the post only after it had been formally offered to three others and informally proposed to even more and by all declined. He was not admirably fitted for the duties of diplomacy; he was autocratic, dictatorial, pitifully vain, and gifted with singular capacities for controversy, yet intellectually he was an able man. In those days communication with China was so slow that the commissioner could never hope to receive precise instructions, and Marshall, because of the ignorance of Washington as to the rapid turn of events, and because the Pierce administration was just entering upon office, was left largely to his own devices. Yet it happened that his term of service coincided with what must be regarded as one of the two or three most critical years of the last century in the history of China. It fell therefore to the lot of Marshall, uninstructed, unaided, and even unappreciated, to make a most important contribution to American policy. To Marshall the United States owed the discovery of the truth that the weakness, or dissolution, of China, was a matter of national concern to the United States, and that the true policy of the American Government must be to strengthen and sustain the Chinese Government against either internal dis order or foreign aggression.

In 1853 the Cushing policy to consign American interests to the protection of China as a sovereign power was in immanent danger of shipwreck, due to the fact that the Government of China was threatened with dissolution in the Taiping Rebellion. Boldly, alone, in the face of contrary instructions and popular opinion, Marshall laid down the second plank in the platform of American policy—"the highest interests of the United States are involved in sustaining China."

The Taiping Rebellion must be reckoned as one of the most important wars of the nineteenth century when measured by the number of people whose destinies were involved, the loss of life—S. Wells Williams gave the estimate that fully 20,000,000 lives were destroyed [1]—and by the principles of action adopted by the foreign powers. The success of the Taipings would have meant the destruction of the Manchu Government and the separation of the great empire into parts. The break-up of the empire in the middle of the last century could have resulted within a few years in nothing short of the dismemberment of China by foreign powers.

GROWTH OF THE REBELLION

Like other popular revolutionary movements, the rebellion grew out of the political, economic and social conditions of the day. There was increasing corruption in and consequent increasing hatred of the Manchu Government. Its defeat in the Anglo-Chinese War had proved the Imperial power to be a hollow sham, unable to repel the foreigner, unable to stop the opium trade, impotent also to control its own soldiery. The advance of the foreign trader and missionary within the empire had been accompanied by disintegrating influences upon the old religions and customs. China was ripe for revolution, the fuel piled high awaiting only the torch in the hand of some aggressive, popular and able leader. That leader proved to be Hung-Siu-tshuen, a native of a village thirty miles from Canton, who had moved to the Province of Kwangsi to become a school teacher.

Hung-Siu-tshuen was a four-times disappointed aspirant at the triennial examinations at Canton. In 1829, at the age of sixteen, and then successively in 1833, 1837, and 1843 he had come down to the provincial city from his village where his record as a scholar had been exceptional, only to fail in the higher examinations. He was defeated, so he believed, by corrupt officials. But Hung was more than a defeated candidate; he was a pathological case such as one would not be surprised to find in India, but in stoical, common-sense China, is most unusual—a sort of Chinese Mahomet, or Mad Mullah. After his third attempt at the examinations he returned home in great depression of spirit and sank into a delirious illness which is reported to have lasted forty days. During this brief period, though never subsequently so far as is known, he became subject to cataleptic fits, and in his deliriums had visions of a more or less religious nature.[2]

While at Canton in 1837 he had purchased some tracts—"Good Words to Exhort the Age"—from Liang A-fah, their author, a colporteur of the London Missionary Society. These tracts "consisted of sixty-eight short chapters upon common topics, selected from the Bible." He took them home but when he discovered that they advocated Christianity, he put them aside as teaching a forbidden subject. Ten years later, upon the recommendation of his brother-in-law, he read them and thought that he found in their pages a clue to the meaning of the visions which had come to him in his illness. He accepted the doctrine, added to it as necessary to support his fanatical fancies, announced himself as the brother of Jesus Christ, interpreted the phrase Kingdom of God to mean China, proclaimed his mission and began to exhort people to adopt Christianity as he understood and construed it with the meagre assistance of Liang A-fah's tracts. The next year in company with some disciples, he went to the mountains of eastern Kwangsi, and two years later, having heard of the Rev. Issachar J. Roberts, an American Baptist missionary at Canton, he left disciples in charge of the preaching, and journeyed to Can ton to enroll himself as a pupil of Roberts.

Roberts [3] appears in the early records of American missionary work in Canton as an extremely aggressive, and somewhat uncouth southerner, who labored with fanatical zeal. The extent of his influence on Hung may not have been very great, for the latter remained with him only two months, not long enough to win Roberts' confidence to the point where the missionary was willing to receive him into the church, and yet Hung seems to have remembered Roberts with respect for in 1853, when the Taipings were established in Nanking, he sent for his old teacher to come to Nanking "to assist in establishing the truth." Roberts was unable to accept this invitation, perhaps because the American commissioner sternly forbade it,[4] and because of the difficulty in reaching the Taiping capital. But soon after 1860 Roberts spent fifteen months at Nanking where he lived, invested with yellow robes and a crown, in a house suitably furnished and provided by the Taiping emperor.

The course of the rebellion from the return of Hung from his visit to Roberts in 1846, can be sketched here only briefly. At first it amounted only to a religious movement, the establishment of "Associations for Worshipping God," in the villages of Kwangsi. These associations were regarded as treasonable, since only the emperor could worship God. Hung, however, proved a popular leader, drew about him some able lieutenants, and as the movement grew in popularity, and as the opposition of the government increased, it took on more and more the dimensions of a political and military as well as religious campaign. Its cardinal purpose became the expulsion of the Manchus. Its military successes were due to its able leadership, its fanatical enthusiasm, rigid discipline, and to the rottenness of Peking military affairs.

Sweeping up over the mountains north of Kwangsi into Hunan and Kiangsi, gathering the discontented and desperate as the successful armies passed by, the Taipings reached the Yangtze at the end of 1852, and, traveling down the river, captured Nanking in March, 1853. By this time Hung seems fully to have realized the strength which his religious vagaries could lend to his political ambitions, and the orders handed down to his subordinates were now issued in the form of 'revelations.' The Taipings crossed the Yangtze and marched northward towards Peking, reaching a place only twenty miles from Tientsin, and also spreading westward through the adjoining provinces. But they were soon forced to retire, not so much because of defeats suffered as because of over-extended lines, too far removed from the base which had been established on the Yangtze.

At Nanking, Hung was proclaimed by his army Emperor of the Tai (Great) Ping (Peace) Chao (Dynasty)—hence the term Taiping, which the Europeans adopted for the rebellion—and settled down to perfect his organization and court, the master of almost the entire Yangtze Valley from below Nanking westward six hundred miles to Ichang.

The Dilemma Presented to the Foreigners

The phenomenal success of the rebels, and the quasi-Christian character of the movement began to draw the attention of the world. The Roman Catholic missionaries, whose influence in France was paramount, were always opposed to the rebels because of their iconoclastic practices and their Protestant doctrines, but the Protestant mission aries, for the most part, hailed the movement with enthusi asm, believing that they saw returning to them the bread which they had for years been casting on the waters. The glowing accounts of the rebellion which reached England and America through missionary channels created a strong public sentiment in favor of the Taipings. By many they were looked upon as a rising Christian power in the pagan East destined to become the providential agency in the conversion of Asia. The movement attracted the interest, also, of the foreign governments and of the foreigners in China engaged in trade.[5]

The relation between the foreign powers and the Chinese Government was rapidly reaching a critical stage in 1853 when the Taipings were in the flood-tide of their first successes. The grievances of the foreigners were, briefly: (1) The mercantile community, especially the English, was thoroughly discontented with the commercial privileges of the treaties. Hongkong, as a commercial center, had been an indifferent success. Amoy, Foochow and Ningpo had been disappointments. There was a general feeling that nothing less than the complete opening of China to foreign trade would be satisfactory. (2) The failure to secure the legalization of the opium trade was irritating to those engaged in it, casting over them the evil reputation of smugglers although the trade was openly connived at by the Chinese officials. (3) The Chinese had been able, while keeping the letter of the treaty to render nugatory many of its provisions both as to trade and diplomatic intercourse. The city of Canton remained implacable, its gates closed, its populace sullen and insulting, its governor general who was also the viceroy delegated to conduct the foreign relations of the Empire, *incommunicado* so far as the foreign ministers were concerned. Viceroy Yeh, acting under orders from Peking as was afterwards revealed, absolutely refused to hold personal interviews with the ministers. (4) The reign of the new Emporer who had ascended the throne in 1850 was seen to be marked by a pronounced anti-foreign feeling. (5) The Chinese Government had shown a disposition to evade the settlement of claims due to infractions of the treaty and to lack of protection offered to foreigners.

Both the Americans and the English were, by 1853, agreed that the treaties of 1842-4 must be revised. Notwithstanding differences of opinion in matters of detail the foreigners were being drawn together by the obvious fact that the Chinese had no intention whatever, except under strong compulsion, of revising the treaties at all, much less of making large concessions to either the governments or the commercial interests.

To this list of general grievances were added in 1853 the disturbances of trade at Canton and Shanghai arising from the disorders of the Rebellion. The Imperial Government was showing itself to be utterly unable to maintain order, and this fact was brought home to the foreigners with peculiar force when, September 7, 1853, Shanghai itself was wrested from the imperial control by a band of rebels. For months the question had been arising whether, in the face of these facts, it would not be the part of wisdom for the foreign powers to turn to the Taipings, recognize them, give them the necessary support in return for guarantees of friendly treatment thereafter, and seize the opportunity to do away with the troublesome Manchu dynasty.

"I hope Tien-Teh" (the rebel chief), wrote a member of the house of Russell and Company at Shanghai to Humphrey Marshall March 13, 1853,[6] "will be successful and upset the present dynasty. We cannot be worse off; and he is said to be a liberal man." This expression is fairly characteristic of the prevailing public sentiment although some of the conservatives were more hesitant. The *North American Review* carried an article (July, 1854, p.199) on the rebellion in which the advantages to foreigners of a breaking up of China were pointed out in the following paragraph:

"Unwittingly to himself [Tien-Teh] perhaps, he will teach us where to introduce the wedge, where to rest the lever; and it will not be many years ere we find European influence, hitherto so powerless in the high exclusive walls of the palace of Peking, operating with wonderful force at the courts of a score of kingdoms, petty in comparison with the great aggregate of which they once formed a part, and all jealous of, if not divided against, each other."

President Pierce in his annual message December 5, 1853, appears to have had such a hope. He said·

"The condition of China at this time renders it probable that some important changes will occur in that vast Empire which will lead to a more unrestricted intercourse with it. The commissioner to that country who has been recently appointed is instructed to avail himself of all occasions to open and extend our commercial relations, not only with the Empire of China, but with other Asiatic nations."[7]

It was very generally believed that, quite aside from the fact of whether the rebellion would be a benefit, its success was assured. "I think I may safely say," wrote Marshall to the Secretary of State, April 28, 1853, "that from all I can learn the Government of China is fully employed by the rebels, and that any day may bring forth the fruits of successful revolution, in the utter overthrow of the existing dynasty."[8] Five weeks later he addressed to the Secretary of State a request for specific instructions as to the policy to be pursued in case the further success of the rebels raised the question as to whom the customs dues should be paid. This inquiry was especially pertinent in view of the fact that it was the policy of the Government of the United States to recognize *de facto* governments.[9]

Washington was entirely without information such as would enable the government to issue specific instructions to Marshall. The favorable opportunity offered by the rebellion for the foreign powers to advance their interests was pointed out to the Department of State by the British minister, and its obvious yet superficial advantages were recognized. That was the 'heydey of the filibuster' in American foreign policy, characterized by no fine moral distinctions or sense of duty towards weak yet sovereign states, but China was too far away for American filibustering. The British desired American cooperation in the Far East, but President Pierce and Secretary of State Marcy were wary. In June, 1853, Marcy wrote to Marshall that he had been apprised that Great Britain intended to avail itself of the present conditions in China to obtain 'increased facilities of intercourse,' not exclusively for its own subjects, but for all nations. It had been suggested that the Government of the United States send to its commissioner such instructions as would "empower him to take such a course in conjunction with H. M. Plenipotentiary as will be calculated to turn to the best account the opportunity offered by the present crisis to open the Chinese Empire generally to the commercial enterprise of all the civilized nations of the world."

"The end proposed commends itself to the approval of the President," wrote Marcy, who requested Marshall to do what he could in that direction, remembering that the treaty stipulations must be respected and the settled American policy of non-interference in the contests which arise between the people and their rulers must be observed. Marcy suggested that without departure from these rules of conduct it might be possible to do much in such a crises "as does or may exist in China to cause an abandonment of the

unwise restrictions imposed by China upon foreign intercourse." However, without knowing what course the British
authorities might deem it expedient to take in furtherance
of the object in view, the President "does not enjoin upon
you cooperation but only cordial relations and free conference with them." [10]

Marshall received no further instructions on the subject
but the opportunist policy of Marcy may be judged from the
instructions to McLane, the newly appointed commissioner.
McLane was vested 'with large discretionary powers' because of the disturbance of the Taiping Rebellion. If China
should be divided and several governments organized,
McLane was to present himself to each as the diplomatic
representative of the United States and make such treaties
as he thought wise.[11]

MARSHALL BECOMES SUSPICIOUS OF BRITISH DESIGNS

The policy of the British Government which had been
vaguely outlined to Marcy by the British minister in Washington assumed in China what appeared to Marshall to be
sinister aspects. On May 30 he reported to Marcy: [12]

"The British minister has been to Nanking. His interpreter has
revisited it since the departure of Sir George Bonham for Honkong.
He goes to find out 'what the rebels are about,' and his intercourse
with their camp and their princes has served to awaken in his bosom
the warmest sympathy in their cause! The long articles in the late
numbers of the *North China Herald* are attributed to Mr. Meadow's
pen. His position in the legation of Great Britain, his fluency in
speaking and writing the Chinese language, lend every opportunity
of assuming the *protectorate of the young power* to Great Britain, at
least so far as to mould its first steps to suit the policy of that government. The vigilance of England will be nothing strange to communicate to the Secretary of State. The apprehension I have is, that
Great Britain may obtain the opening of a western Chinese port
(inland) from the new Emperor at Nanking, and the right to navigate
the Yangtse Kiang closed to foreign commerce beyond the existing
port of entry. I do not doubt that with that view her war with
Burmah has been waged and her Indian Empire extended. The
portage from the Irrawaddy to the Yangtse Kiang is very short [sic].
I suggest these considerations to you frankly, because they seem to
me to point out the propriety of preparation to assume the part the

United States may find it politic to take in face of an event now so
likely as the dismemberment of the empire."

Six weeks later rumor had it that the Chinese Government had asked for assistance,* and that the Czar of Russia had already promised the necessary aid.

"Her assistance," wrote Marshall, "would probably end in passing China under a Russian protectorate, and in the extension of Russian limits to the Hoangho, or the mouth of the Yangtse; or, it may be, when circumstances and policy shall favor the scheme, in the partition of China between Great Britain and Russia. The interference of the Czar would readily suppress the rebellion, by driving the rebels from the great highways of commerce, and from the occupation of the towns on the seaboard. Whatever might be the ultimate compensation demanded by Russia for this timely service, China could not resist its collection." [14]

Marshall then went on to say, with a wisdom which stood the test of time:

"I think that almost any sacrifice should be made by the United States to keep Russia from spreading her Pacific boundary, and to avoid her coming directly to interference in Chinese domestic affairs; for China is like a lamb before the shearers, as easy a conquest as were the provinces of India. Whenever the avarice or the ambition of Russia or Great Britain shall tempt them to make the prizes, the fate of Asia will be sealed, and the future Chinese relations with the United States may be considered as closed for ages, unless *now* the United States shall foil the untoward result by adopting a sound policy."

The Commissioner adds a concluding sentence which may be taken as his summary of what he conceived to be the true American policy in the Far East.

"It is my opinion that the highest interests of the United States are involved in sustaining China—maintaining order here, and gradually engrafting on this worn-out stock the healthy principles which give life and health to governments, rather than to see China become the theatre of widespread anarchy, and ultimately the prey of European ambition."

While Marshall did not again allude to the dangers of Russian aggression, his fears possibly having been aroused

*On May 6, 1853, Commodore Perry was asked by the Shanghai officials to assist in the suppression of the rebellion. [13]

by a false rumor, he immediately began to turn his atten
tion to measures which would thwart any sinister designs
which might be entertained by England. His course was
clear. In the face of the prevailing sympathy for the Taipings, a sympathy which reached even from the United
States and which prompted severe criticism of him when his
policy became known, and in the face of contrary instruc
tions from his government, Marshall set himself to do every
thing he possibly could to support the Imperial Govern
ment. For the moment this was not much. He had quar
relled with Commodore Perry who was then wholly preoccu
pied with his expedition to Japan, and Perry had withdrawn
from all cooperation with him. The capture of Shanghai by
rebel bands on the 7th of September, however, precipitated a
situation in which Marshall proceeded to apply his policy of
upholding the Imperial authority with all the limited means
at his disposal. The action of the Britsh authorities in the
weeks immediately following the fall of the city seemed to
Marshall to confirm his fears. We are thus led to a consideration of the different policies of the American and the
English authorities after the fall of Shanghai both in the
payment of the customs dues and in the protection of the
foreign settlement.

The walled city of Shanghai came into the possession of
a band of rebels, who professed more or less close connection with the Taipings, on the 7th of September, 1853. The
customs house which was in the foreign settlement was
attacked by the rabble who took advantage of the disorder
to loot. That evening the British authorities, declaring that
a condition of anarchy existed, placed a guard over the customs house, and also at the bridges over the Yang King
Pang, the creek which flowed between the walled city and
the foreign settlement. In the placing of these guards the
Americans were not consulted.

The flight of the officers of the Imperial Customs from
their post of duty immediately created the question of
whether the foreigners ought to be expected to continue to
pay customs dues, and if they were to pay them, how and

to whom they could be paid. Upon these points there was at once a difference of opinion. Merchants argued that as the Imperial Government was no longer discharging its obligation to protect them, and was not even supplying customs officials to receive the dues, they ought to be relieved of the obligation of paying. Others, among whom Marshall was most conspicuous, argued that the foreigners were by no means relieved of such an obligation, and that if, through the failure of the Imperial Government to protect them, any foreigners suffered loss, the treaty provided that the foreigners might make claims for the losses sustained, and collect from the government. If on the other hand, the foreigners repudiated the Imperial Government by refusing to pay the duties, Marshall argued that certainly they would have no grounds for claims against the government.

The day following the fall of the city Mr. Rutherford Alcock and Mr. Edward Cunningham, the British consul and American vice consul, held a conference and agreed to issue orders to their nationals, respectively, stating that during the absence of the Imperial customs officers, they, the consuls, would collect the duties for the Imperial Government, according to the treaties. There was, however, a difference between the methods to be employed. The English consul required only that the merchants deposit at the consulate promissory notes which were to be held, pending the decision of the Foreign Office in London, as to whether the British merchants were actually to redeem the notes. It was freely predicted that the Foreign Office would decide against the Chinese Government and that the notes would be returned, as in fact they were, a year later. The Americans on the other hand were ordered to pay their duties at the consulate in specie. The American merchants, by the decree of the American consul, who was firmly supported by the American Commissioner, were thus placed under a severe handicap with reference to their British competitors. The one paid duties in notes of doubtful value; the other paid in cash. A still further element of confusion was in-jected into the situation by the fact that the merchants of nations unrepresented by consuls in Shanghai, recognized no obligations whatever to pay the duties when there were no officers to collect them. In fact the very day that Alcock and Cunningham issued their orders, the Prussian ship *Adler* departed, merely recording a simple guarantee that the duties would be paid in case they were required at some future date—very different from a promissory note, and wholly different from cash payments. Subsequently other ships of nations unrepresented by consuls departed without even a promise to pay.

The British authorities then took the position that the Imperial authorities should not be permitted to resume the collection of the customs until the Imperial authorities had retaken the walled city. However, the British authorities had also declared that the foreign settlement must remain in strict neutrality in the conflict between the rebels and the Imperialists, and that no troops, not even Imperial troops, should be permitted to enter the foreign settlement. At the same time the foreigners in the settlement were known to be not merely openly sympathizing with the rebels in the city, but also to be supplying them with ammunition. Marshall, on the other hand, recognized the establishment of a new imperial customs house although it proved to be only some old junks moored in the river below the foreign settlement.

The Americans again protested against the unequal burdens placed upon them by Marshall's decisions, but Marshall stubbornly refused to yield, asserting that the treaty was still in force, and that if they suffered losses the Chinese Government would be liable for damages.

Probably realizing that sooner or later an explanation to the State Department would be required for this ruling which was so ruinous to American merchants, Marshall made his reasons the subject of a long dispatch.[15] The American Commissioner's controlling motive was to thwart what appeared to him to be the aggressive designs of Great Britain.

"I believe that were Great Britain assured," he wrote, "that the United States would not interfere in behalf of China, she would seize and hold this city permanently, and thus command the valley of the Yangtse—the richest probably in the world. I believe she will yet do it, unless she shall be advised that such usurpation would provoke resistance on the part of the United States, to whom such a *coup d'état* would be a national calamity."

In support of this conviction Marshall submitted some facts in addition to those which have already been enumerated. The British Government, he maintained, with the cooperation of the French, were at that moment exercising the rights of sovereignty on Chinese territory, and without sufficient excuse or reason. Not only was the foreign settlement being guarded by their marines at a time when a guard seemed to him so unnecessary that he had requested no aid from the American naval force then in the harbor, but they had actually halted the Imperial commander-in-chief as he came into the settlement to pay his respects to the foreign authorities. Twice a Chinese customs boat had been driven from the anchorage in front of the foreign settlement by British men-of-war. Recently British H. M. S. *Hermes* at Amoy had 'drifted' in between the vessels of the Imperials and the rebel forces during an engagement at a time when the Imperialists seemed to be on the point of victory. He also had observed that British subjects were in communication with the rebel forces at Nanking. Recently a British subject, bearing a letter from the Taiping authorities in Nanking, when arrested by the Imperial troops as a spy and returned to the British consul for punishment, had been dismissed under the purely nominal bail of $200.

"These examples," wrote Marshall, "of incidents daily occurring in China will serve to place you in possession of the tendency of affairs in China, and to prove that, though neutrality may be the profession of Great Britain, and the aim of the Foreign Office, the practice of the public authorities among the Chinese leads to the conclusion that there is another policy in view."

Whatever may have been the truth of Marshall's allegations as to the intent of the British authorities in China in 1853, the American policy as actually applied was twofold:

immediately, to support the Imperial authority; and, to continue to recognize the sovereignty of China; and to do this for the ultimate purpose of helping China to maintain her integrity—to prevent the dismemberment which seemed so probable in event of the success of the rebellion. The practical application of Marshall's policy is to be seen in his handling of the Shanghai customs question.

SHALL SHANGHAI BECOME A FREE PORT?

The issue was this: Should the port of Shanghai during the occupation of the city by rebels and the absence of not only Imperial customs officers but also of Imperial military protection, be considered a free port? In other words was the port of Shanghai to become, at least for the time being, a port such as Hongkong had always been under the British administration? Favoring an affirmative answer to this question were the mercantile communities regardless of nationality, while the British consul, Mr. Rutherford Alcock, not caring to assume the responsibility, referred the matter to the Foreign Office, meanwhile accepting, as already described, qualified promissory notes from British merchants in payment of customs dues. This action, while not definitely declaring the port open, so far as British merchants were concerned did in effect leave the port open, and yet in such a way that the British treaties were not violated. Against this plan of an open port was the American author ity as represented in the proclamation of the consul, supported by the approval of the commissioner.*

In the face of the repeated protest of the American mer chants Marshall held his ground. Replying to a second protest of October 31, he declared: [17]

"It is my purpose to perform, punctiliously, every obligation assumed by the United States under the treaty, and to refrain from

*The full responsibility for the measures which prevented Shanghai from actually becoming a free port after the fall of the city was attributed by the leading American firms to Commissioner Marshall. In a letter of protest, signed by Smith, King & Co., Wetmore & Co., Augustine Heard & Co., Bull, Nye & Co., September 21, these merchants stated the case as follows: "We believe that, in the present lapse of legal authority, this port becomes, for the time being, a *free port;* and it certainly would be so to us now but for the presence of the officers of *our* government." [16]

embarrassing the public administration of Chinese affairs by throwing unnecessary obstacles in the way. No precedent, no example furnished by other powers, will induce me to forego the faithful and honest execution of our plain international obligations."

MARSHALL FORCES DISSOLUTION OF PROVISIONAL SYSTEM

Marshall's position, however, became increasingly difficult to maintain. The ships of non-treaty powers continued to go free. On the 4th of November, Vice-consul Cunningham at Shanghai addressed a letter to the taotai, pointing out that on a certain day two vessels had left the port, one American and one Austrian: the former paid duties according to the provisional rules, while the latter departed absolutely free. Cunningham asserted that such a situation was in violation of the most-favored-nation clause in the Treaty of Wanghia, and demanded that the Americans be placed on the same footing as the subjects of those nations whose ships were going free.

When informed of this action the American Commissioner, who was then in the South vainly seeking an interview with Viceroy Yeh, replied, intimating that as it was the duty of China to insist on her rights at Shanghai under the treaties with England and France and that if, after ample opportunity to reestablish control, China continued to concede free entry and clearance, or the payment of dues in promissory notes the redemption of which depended upon the will of the British Government, then the American Government would demand as a right under the treaty that American ships also go free. Meanwhile Viceroy Yeh seemed in no way to appreciate the battle which Marshall had undertaken at Shanghai in defense of the Imperial revenues, and Marshall became convinced that the bold policy which he had adopted in September was not bold enough. It had not brought the other foreign nations into line, and it had placed upon the American merchants an insuperable handicap. Therefore on the 4th of January, 1854, he addressed an authorization to Vice-consul Cunningham to change his policy immediately and "to clear

American ships without taking any note of the duties what
ever, without requiring any port clearance, and in all re
spect treating Shanghai *as a free port.*" In conclusion Mar
shall wrote: [18]

"I congratulate you that, by the strict pursuit of our national
duty, we are in a position, without violating a treaty stipulation or
giving just offense in any quarter, to assert all our national rights and
to maintain the commerce of the United States on the footing of the
most-favored nation, without loss from any unjust discrimination
being possible, under any regulation whatever, made or to be made
by others."

The purpose of the American Commissioner was twofold: to help the American merchants out of what was becoming an impossible situation; and to force the hand of the
British authorities, for under the new order it was the British commercial interests which were placed under a handicap; while the American ships went free, the British ships
were still required to deposit the promissory notes and it
was not yet definitely known that they would not some day
become payable. Marshall's policy was successful.

Marshall was superseded as commissioner when the
Pierce administration entered office, and he left China on
March 13, 1854, before the arrival of his successor, Robert
M. McLane. Meanwhile the confusion at Shanghai had
become very great and the British plenipotentiary, Sir John
Bowring, had had a correspondence with the secretary of the
Shanghai British Chamber of Commerce, in which was to be
observed a great change in the tone and temper of the
British authorities. McLane reported: [19]

"The undisguised hostility expressed towards the rebels is a new
feature in the intercourse which has heretofore taken place, either
between the superior and inferior British authorities themselves, or
between either of them and the Chinese authorities."

A month later McLane reported: [20] that he had been in
communication with Sir John Bowring and that the latter
had expressed the desire to see 'him personally before he
attempted to open up communications with the Chinese
Empire, and had expressed the further desire for 'hearty
cooperation' in the progress of events in China. Notwith-

standing the sympathy for the rebels which still persisted among an ill-informed public in England and America, the events in China, and a fuller knowledge of the rebel movement itself which rapidly degenerated after its establishment in Nanking, settled effectively the question of the recognition of the Taipings. Towards the Taiping Rebellion the Government of the United States pursued its settled policy of non-intervention in the affairs of other nations. In its instructions to its commissioners it followed exactly a policy of neutrality, taking the ground that China must settle her own troubles. Applying again the principle that China was a sovereign state, Secretary of State Marcy advised Dr. Parker in 1855 [21] that the Government of the United States had no right to restrain its citizens from introducing munitions of war into the five ports, even when it was known that they were intended for the rebels. On the other hand American citizens in China who did not remain neutral in the conflict, must understand that they forfeited all right to the protection of the Government of the United States and all right to claims for redress.

In addition to this both McLane and Parker in their effort to secure the appointment of commissioners to discuss supplementary articles and the revision of the treaty hinted broadly [22] that if the Imperial Government would not listen to them, they might turn to the rebels. This, however, was a mere threat and the strict neutrality declared by the American Government was in fact moderated by an increased benevolence on the part of the commissioners towards the Empire. The British policy was similar, and as for the French, their dislike of the Taipings had always been apparent.

At the beginning of the administration of President Buchanan (1857), Lord Napier, then British Minister at Washington, in the course of the conferences between the United States and China which preceded the negotiations for the revision of the treaties with China, left with Secretary of State Cass a memorandum on British policy in China in which is found an official statement of what had become the British policy with reference to the more fundamental questions of the integrity of China.

Lord Napier wrote:[23] "The dissolution of the Chinese Empire and the separation of its provinces could not fail to be accompanied by the interception of communications, the diminution of wealth, the destruction of industry, by all the calamities which check the Powers of production and consumption. Such a result would be most prejudicial to Great Britain both in reference to our exportation to China, and to our importation of tea, which is at once a source of revenue and a necessary of life."

Thus, more than three quarters of a century ago, the two great nations most interested in the trade of China, reasoning wholly from the grounds of national self-interest, reached the conclusion that the Chinese Empire ought not to be dissolved.

BIBLIOGRAPHICAL NOTES

1. Williams: "Middle Kingdom," Vol. 2, p. 624.
2. Hamberg: "The Visions of Hung-Siu-tshuen."
3. Cordier: "Histoire des Relations de la Chine," Vol. 1, p. 169; China Dispatches, Vol. 3, June 2, 1846; Vol. 5, Feb. 7, 1849 (Dept. of State).
4. Marshall Corres., pp. 183, 185; Brine's Taiping Rebellion, pp. 295-8.
5. British Parliamentary Papers, 1870, Vol. LXIX, Corres. respecting Inland Residence of English Missionaries in China, p. 10.
   Marshall Corres., p. 96.
6. Richardson's Messages, Vol. 5, p. 210.
8. Marshall Corres., p. 102.
9. Ibid., p. 168.
10. China Instructions, June, 1853 (Dept. of State).
11. McLane Instructions, S. Ex. Doc. 39:36-1.
12. Marshall Corres., pp. 168-9.
13. S. Ex. Doc. 34:33-2, Disp. No. 11, May 6, 1853.
14. Marshall Corres., p. 204.
15. Ibid., p. 290.
16. Ibid., p. 261.
17. Ibid., p. 313.
18. Ibid., pp. 366-7.
19. McLane Corres., p. 3.
20. Ibid., p. 23.
21. China Instructions, Vol. 1, Oct. 5, 1855.
22. McLane Corres., p. 145; Parker Corres., p. 945.
23. Notes from the British Legation, Vol. 34, Apr. 3, 1857 (Dept. of State).

CHAPTER XII

THE POLICY OF COMMISSIONER McLANE

THE service of Robert M. McLane as Commissioner to China was brief—only nine months long—but important. To him belongs the distinction of having devised a settlement of the vexed question of the Shanghai customs which was in line with the ideas of his predecessor whose policy he approved, and it also fell to his lot to make some new and rather startling adventures in policies of his own.

His instructions [1] which may be taken as the policy of the Pierce administration in China were specific only in the fact that they recommended cooperation with the other ✓ treaty powers. It was a timid cooperation which Marcy proposed, quite unlike the 'cooperative policy' of Seward ten years later, but it was significant as an indication of the turning tide in American foreign policy. The old aloofness, and particularly the old hatred and suspicion of Great Britain and all her works was passing. Every year the choice for the American and the British governments in the Far East between working with or against one another was presenting itself. Cooperation seemed the course of wisdom. ✓

THE INSPECTORATE OF MARITIME CUSTOMS

In the settlement of the Shanghai customs question McLane immediately assumed leadership. On February 9, 1854, the British, French and American consuls at Shanghai had united in recognizing a new Imperial customs house which was established at Soochow Creek, and the collection of dues by the Imperial authorities began forthwith. The three consuls, at the suggestion of McLane, prepared a full report * of the situation as it had developed from September 7th, for submission to their governments with a view to some final settlement.[2]

The situation at Shanghai by no means cleared up with the recognition of the reestablished customs house. The old Chinese maritime customs service was disintegrating in sheer rottenness. The city had not been retaken by the Imperial authorities, and the corruption of the officials at the customs house was such that merchants were still able to evade the payment of duties. To meet this situation the taotai notified the consuls, March 25, that by order of the governor general, the collection of Shanghai outward customs would be transferred to the interior until such time as peace was restored. To this order the foreign governments immediately objected as a violation of the treaties. R. C. Murphy, the newly arrived American consul, joined with the British and French consuls, with the full approval of McLane, in a joint communication to the taotai notifying him that they would not sanction the change in the manner of collecting the outward customs.[3] Nevertheless the customs house on Soochow Creek was abandoned by the Chinese on May 9. Shanghai became completely what it had been partially for many months—a free port. Thus the Imperial Government was entirely deprived of revenue from the port of Shanghai at a time when the empire was in the throes of rebellion, when the Imperial coffers were sadly depleted, and the dynasty was in the utmost danger of dis solution.

Meanwhile it had become clear that it was for the best interests of the foreigners, in the choice between the rebels and the Imperialists, to support and fortify the latter. The most obvious step which could be taken, in the interest of protecting the Imperial revenues, and also for the sake of

*Throughout Michie's account of the Shanghai customs question (The Eng-lishman in China), he gives Rutherford Alcock the credit for leadership among the consuls, and sees only inconsistency in the course adopted by the Americans. He states, however, that the American action in declaring for a free port forced the dissolution of the "provisional system" which had been operative so far as the Americans and English were concerned.
Morse also fails to make clear the reasons for the course adopted by the Americans.

maintaining uniformity at the five ports in the collection of customs, was to devise some plan by which the corruption in the Shanghai customs service might be eliminated, and the collection of dues restored.

On the 21st of June, in an interview with E-liang, the Viceroy and Governor General of the Liang Kiang Provinces, in which Shanghai was situated, Commissioner McLane outlined a plan by which full power "should be given to the superintendent of customs at Shanghai to enter into and conclude an arrangement with the consuls of the three treaty powers for the administration of the customs house at this port hereafter on a permanent basis." [4] It called for the reestablishment of the customs house at Soochow Creek, under the immediate direction of a board of foreign inspectors. To this plan the viceroy agreed. On the 29th of June the three consuls and the taotai at Shanghai had a conference in which the latter formally confessed his inability to secure customs house officials of sufficient probity, vigilance and knowledge of foreign languages for the effective administration of the customs. He expressed the conviction that the only solution of the problem lay in securing the services of foreigners who, having been carefully selected, should be appointed by the taotai as his representatives for the collection of the customs. It was further agreed that a suitable establishment could be effected with one or more foreigners acting under the taotai as inspectors of customs, supplemented by a staff of both foreign and Chinese subordinates. The expenses of the new system could be met out of the customs revenues. The consuls, on their part, agreed to select and nominate to the taotai, one for each consul, suitable candidates for the board of inspectors.

To safeguard the new system from the evils of the old one, these foreign inspectors were to be protected on the one hand, and the Chinese Government was to be protected on the other, by an arrangement that any charges of exaction, corruption, neglect of duty or misconduct might be made to the consuls, and trials of the accused inspector

would be held before a mixed court in the presence of the
consuls and the taotai. The inspectors would be liable to
dismissal only by this process. All subordinates would hold
office during good behavior, and subject to dismissal only
upon recommendation from the inspectors.

It was further stipulated in the agreement between the
taotai and the consuls that the records of the new customs
house would be kept in both Chinese and English, and that
an armed revenue cutter under a foreign master would be
secured.[*]

In the view of both the American State Department and
the British Foreign Office, the mode of selection of the
inspectors was objectionable in that the candidates were to
be nominated by the consuls. This, it was thought, approached too closely towards making the foreign consuls
responsible for the efficient conduct of the customs office.
In the reorganization of the foreign inspectorate under the
treaties of 1858, this provision was eliminated, and thus
China was incidentally saved, as it proved, from an invasion
by the American spoils system.

The foundations were thus laid in 1854, all the treaty
powers heartily cooperating, for the foreign inspectorate of
Chinese Maritime Customs as, with elaborations, it exists
today. Fundamentally the necessity for it grew out of the
provision of the American Treaty of Wanghia (1844) which
had thrown the entire burden for the collection of its customs from foreigners upon the Imperial Government. This
provision of the American treaty, as has been elsewhere
pointed out, had placed upon the Chinese Government the
responsibility for the existence of smuggling, and had also
placed at a disadvantage the British merchants who were
compelled to pay duties through the British consuls. The

*The credit for this plan has always been claimed for Mr. Rutherford Alcock.
On the other hand, Commissioner McLane who, unlike his predecessor, was a
very modest man, makes no special claim for credit in the matter although he
does report the fact, already noted, that he presented the plan personally to
E-liang and secured his approval. But the American merchants who protested
against the foreign inspectorate two years later stated that the system had been
established "chiefly at the suggestion and by the efforts of the Hon. Mr.
McLane." It is therefore probable that to McLane belongs the credit of having
devised the general plan and initiated it, while to Alcock, as the senior consul
in Shanghai and as obviously the best fitted to do it, fell the work of drawing
up the details of the agreement.[6]

new system, providing a way out of the difficulty for the English, was broadly in harmony with the principle of the American treaty which had come to be adopted by all treaty powers, and was effective.

So effective was it that the American merchants in Shanghai in 1856 and again in 1858, at the time of the revision of the treaties, protested against it, and petitioned for its removal, but the protests went unheeded by the American representatives who expressed the opinion that instead of removing it, the system should be extended to cover the other open ports, as well as Shanghai, an action which was taken in the revision of the treaties in 1858.[6]

The board of inspectors consisted of Thomas Francis Wade, who was loaned from the British consulate in Shanghai, Arthur Smith, nominated by the French consul, and Lewis Carr, an American. Of these three Mr. Wade alone understood Chinese, or was experienced in China, and upon him fell the duties of organizing the new service. Three years later Mr. Carr absented himself from duty for a long period. Meanwhile the American consul, Mr. Murphy, went home on leave of absence, having first secured from the taotai a promise that the latter would hold open the position for someone to be nominated by Murphy. The result was that the position remained vacant for a long time although Dr. Parker, then Commissioner, had a nominee whom he wished to place in the position. American influence in the newly developed inspectorate was, therefore, never great, the American incumbent of the board being neither useful nor ornamental. The situation was an illustration, often repeated, of how ill prepared was the United States to assume responsibilities in China, however friendly American policies and principles might be. On the resignation of Mr. Wade, Horatio N. Lay, of subsequent Lay-Osborn-Flotilla fame, was appointed, and he in turn was superseded by Robert Hart whose distinguished services for China became so well known. The Americans in China complained bitterly of the disappearance of American influence in the foreign inspectorate. The fault lay solely with the American Government which, though repeatedly importuned to provide for student interpreters and a large staff of consular officers to meet the growing opportunities and responsibilities of the United States in China, had ignored the requirements of the situation.

McLane Settles the American Claims

Having disposed of the question of the payment of customs dues, McLane turned his attention to the equally perplexing and disturbing question of the disposal of the complicated claims for duties due from Americans since the establishment of the 'provisional rules' of September 19, 1853. According to the treaty the method for settling this matter would have been for the taotai to bring a complaint in the consular court which would have come up to McLane for official review in his capacity as supreme judge, but the commissioner proposed an alternative, viz., that all the parties concerned should submit the matter to him as a 'mediator,' agreeing to abide by his decision. Both the merchants and the Chinese officials were willing to accept this alternative proposal.

While McLane had the matter under review Lord Clarendon ordered Sir John Bowring to have cancelled the promissory notes deposited by the English merchants on the ground that "the obligation on the part of British subjects to pay duties to the Chinese Government depends upon the fulfillment by the Chinese Government of its obligation to afford protection to British commerce and upon the ability of the Chinese authorities to collect the duties accruing to their Government." This order from the Foreign Office was embarrassing to Bowring who was then planning a joint expedition with McLane to the Pei-ho to secure new treaties. If the English were to cancel their notes and the Americans were to pay the duties, the English would be in an awkward position before the representatives of the Emperor, in the negotiation of a treaty. McLane recognized the difficulty of his brother plenipotentiary, and was

willing to defer his award as long as possible to enable
Bowring to bring the Foreign Office into line with the policy
which he and McLane had adopted. On the other hand,
McLane did not feel that Lord Clarendon's contention was
sound owing 'to the peculiar relations established between
the Chinese authorities and the authorities of Great Britain
and the United States' during the year of the disturbance
at Shanghai. McLane also recognized the injustice of
penalizing the American merchants for their good faith and
in the settlement he mitigated the penalty by allowing the
Chinese one third of the amount claimed, deducting a third
for losses which the Americans had suffered through the
disturbance of the trade, and a third for the increase in the
value of the specie which had occurred since the 'provisional
rules' became operative. Both merchants and taotai accepted this award.

But the question, even then, was not disposed of. About
three weeks before McLane rendered his award, Secretary
of State Marcy reached a conclusion similar to that of Lord
Clarendon's and ordered that the American notes also be
cancelled. When this order reached Dr. Parker in January,
1855, he was greatly disturbed. It did not seem to him
possible that satisfactory explanations could be made to
the Chinese for the reversal of McLane's decision. He
therefore wrote to the department explaining the situation,
and at the same time ordered Consul Murphy to return the
notes to the merchants, but to take in return the agreements
that in case the United States Government reversed its
decision, they would make payments in good faith. At the
same time he instructed Consul Murphy to explain the
matter to the taotai, and in case the latter protested the
action, to cancel the notes immediately and thus to conclude
the business. The taotai, however, was willing to wait
patiently. In due time the State Department, having
received more complete information, and having referred
the matter to Caleb Cushing, then Attorney General, decided that the award made by McLane as a mediator could
not be reversed, and the amount awarded was ordered paid.

And to the everlasting credit of the American merchants—
the same men who were then trying to have the foreign
inspectorate abolished—the money was paid without further
protest or discussion.

Treaty Revision

McLane's primary efforts in China were directed towards
securing from the Imperial Government some important
modifications of the Cushing treaty. In this as well as in the
customs matter he was following a policy which had been
initiated by his predecessor.

In July, 1853, when Marshall had been so impressed with
the danger of either Russian or British intervention, he had
outlined to Marcy a very bold policy which he had never
been able to carry out because Commodore Perry had been
unable, and also unwilling, to cooperate with him.[7] Marshall had proposed "an interference by the United States to
quiet and tranquilize China." His plan was to proceed to
Peking, convince the Emperor of the friendly purposes of
the United States and then to offer the support of the
American military and naval forces to the Imperial Government in return for certain concessions which he outlined as
follows: amnesty to all rebels who might be willing to
return to loyalty to the Manchus; freedom of religious opinion and worship; complete opening of the empire to trade;
and the establishment of diplomatic relations with treaty
powers through a department of foreign affairs.

"It would only be intervention in vindication of the
rights of the American citizens," urged Marshall, "an intervention promised in the President's inaugural address,*
wherever the citizen might of right be when the power is
involved."

*In his inaugural address, March 4, 1853, President Pierce had said: "The
rights which belong to a nation are not alone to be regarded, but those which
pertain to every citizen in his individual capacity, at home and abroad, must
be sacredly maintained. So long as he can discern every star in its place upon
that ensign, without wealth to purchase for him preferment or title to secure
for him place, it will be his privilege, and must be his acknowledged right, to
stand unabashed even in the presence of princes, with a proud consciousness
that he is himself one of a nation of sovereigns and that he cannot in legitimate
pursuit wander so far from home that the agent whom he shall leave behind
in the place which I now occupy will not see that no rude hand of power or
tyrannical passion is laid upon him with impunity." [8]

Marshall's proposal never received the approval of the Government of the United States. It is probable, however, that he would have undertaken at least that part of his program which involved going to the Pei-ho and demanding admission to the Court of Peking, had he been able to command the services of a naval vessel. Commodore Aulick, and Commodore Perry who succeeded to the command of the China Squadron shortly after Marshall's arrival in China, thwarted every effort made by Marshall to go to the Pei-ho. Perry dissented strongly from the wisdom of such an expedition, feeling that it would in all probability produce only unfriendly feelings. As for intervening on behalf of the Imperial Government against the Taipings, he was opposed to it, sympathizing rather with the rebels.[9]

Viceroy Yeh refused to meet McLane upon his arrival in China in the spring of 1854, as he had evaded a meeting with Marshall the previous year.

"The archives of our legation," wrote McLane, April 26, "present a very humiliating view of our past relations with China; the insolence of Chinese officials having rendered intercourse between the two countries most unsatisfactory. It is difficult to understand whether this be the result of an incorrigible antipathy on the part of the Chinese towards foreigners, or a refined and cunning policy, by which they maintained non-intercourse and at the same time non-resistance."[10]

Sir John Bowring immediately proposed that the two powers join in a naval demonstration against Canton for the purpose of compelling Yeh to receive them. McLane 'strenuously resisted' this proposal because the British naval forces in the Far East were then occupied with the Crimean War, and he was of the opinion that Bowring would be impotent to carry through such a policy in case of failure at Canton.

McLane abruptly terminated his correspondence with Yeh and departed for the North. At Foochow he failed to see the Governor General although the Treaty of Wanghia specified him as one of the three means of communication with Peking. At Shanghai McLane found the city under the joint protection of the English, French and American naval forces, the Imperial authority not having been restored since the fall of the city the previous year. In June he paid / a visit to the rebel capital at Nanking and became thoroughly convinced that the success of the Taipings would in no way benefit the foreign powers. On the basis of his observations he formulated a policy not very dissimilar from that of Marshall's the preceding year. He proposed to enlarge the 'protectorate character' of the existing treaty.

"Could this government be made to understand and acknowledge," wrote McLane to Marcy, June 14, 1854, "the true state of its relations with foreign nations, it would not be difficult, even at this time and in the face of the prevailing disorder, to adjust existing difficulties and greatly enlarge our commercial intercourse. To accomplish this result, whether the empire be governed in whole or in part by the ruling dynasty, or by those who are now conducting the revolutionary movement, it is necessary to enlarge the powers and duties which devolve on the United States by the terms of the treaty, both to enforce the stipulations of the same and to prevent the abuse of their flag, when used as a cover to the violation of the laws of the Chinese Empire. Without such an exercise of power on our part, it will be quite impossible to maintain the honor and integrity of our flag, or avoid those collisions which the weakness and corruption of the Chinese authorities render inevitable. As a consideration for such enlargement of the *protectorate* character of the existing treaty, the interior should be opened to us, where we would extend the moral power of our civilization, and the material power necessary to protect the lives and property of our people." [11]

A few days after writing the above letter McLane had an interview with E-liang, the Viceroy of the Liang Kiang Provinces, not far from Shanghai. In this interview E-liang complained of the conduct of the Americans in China and stated that the failure of the foreign powers to recognize the reestablished authority of the Imperial Government at Shanghai had been a great embarrassment to the government. He also complained that the foreigners had been supplying the rebels with ammunition and aiding them in other ways. McLane in turn pointed out how Marshall's policy of requiring the American merchants to continue the payment of duties at Shanghai had been an evidence of the good will of the American Government, and then proceeded to unfold his plan for some 'supplemental articles' to the Treaty of Wanghia. This *projet*, which was subsequently submitted in writing, explains very clearly what McLane meant by the enlargement of the 'protectorate character' of the existing treaty.[12]

In brief, McLane proposed that the United States would engage to exert its power to prevent the abuse of its flag, or the violation of the treaty by its citizens if, in return, the Chinese Government would enlarge the commercial privileges of the United States. McLane rested his demand that the Emperor appoint a commissioner to treat with him, not upon the revision clause of the Treaty of Wanghia, but upon the fact that 'grave cause' existed for the revision of the treaty.* The grave cause was the fact that the treaty was now in abeyance at Shanghai where the Imperial Government was unable to discharge its obligations to protect American citizens, and that the government was further unable to protect the trade of Americans at Shanghai with the interior. McLane's argument was that in as much as the Chinese could not protect the trade, the American Government should be allowed to do it. McLane then warned E-liang that if the Emperor refused to appoint a commissioner to negotiate with him the United States might feel authorized to turn to the Taipings.†

* According to the provision of Art. 34 of the Treaty of Wanghia, negotiations for the revision of the treaty might come up at the end of twelve years (i. e., in 1856). The treaty also stated: "its provisions shall not be altered without grave cause."

† McLane's proposals in detail were: 1. Americans to be admitted to any port, city or harbor on the Yangtze or its tributaries, provided that duties on imports are first paid at Shanghai, and that outward cargoes also pay duties at Shanghai.

2. For and in consideration of the rights and privileges granted to the citizens of the United States, it is further provided and stipulated that the Government of the United States shall at once take active and efficient means to enforce upon their citizens the prompt payments of the duties prescribed in the Treaty of Wanghia, and said Government of the United States further agrees to prevent, by the interposition of their own authorities, any of their citizens from abusing their flag as a cover for the violation of the laws of the Empire, or of the treaty.

But McLane did not intend to be caught in the assumption of such an obligation in any way that might in the future embarrass the trade. He therefore added: "For and in as much as this additional obligation is incurred by the Government of the United States, in consideration of the before mentioned privileges granted to their citizens, it is further provided that if similar rights and advantages should at any time be granted or conceded by China to any other nation or nations, without this formal obligation being incurred by such nation or nations, then in such case the Government of the United States shall at once be released from the obligation hereby entered into, and shall enjoy said enlarged advantages as fully and as absolutely as such other nation or nations."

3. Citizens of the United States to be allowed to go anywhere in China, to worship as they pleased, and to enjoy accommodations for houses, places of business, hospitals and churches and cemeteries, just as now at the five ports.[13]

The extraordinary proposal that the Chinese Empire be opened almost without restriction to Americans in return for the assumption of responsibility to prevent the abuse of the American flag, an obligation already assumed in the existing treaty, and for further assumption of responsibility to aid in the prevention of smuggling, an obligation which Great Britain had freely assumed in her treaties of 1842-3, was actually forwarded to Peking, although McLane was notified that it was sent only to Yeh at Canton.

In commenting on McLane's visit and demands E-liang addressed a memorial to the throne.*

"Thanks to the favor," read E-liang's report of what McLane had said, "of his Celestial Majesty, by which the five ports are open to trade, we have been enabled to steep ourselves in advantage. Of late years, however, the river communications have become impassable (owing to the rebellion) and the losses hence sustained by the merchants have determined us to request that his Majesty be entreated graciously to permit us to trade along the Yangtze River. The merchandise we bring up the river we will ourselves escort and protect. If (your excellency) will not do me the honor to make a representation for me to this effect to the throne, I shall be obliged to proceed to Tientsin.

"Your slave told him authoritatively (as his official superior) that the treaty under which the five ports were open to trade, being that to which the Imperial assent had been received with reference in the 24th year of Tau Kwang (1844), it became the duty of all alike, native and foreigner, officials and people, to observe it obediently for evermore. It was besides clearly laid down in the treaty that 'no state shall hereafter send a minister to China to raise separate (or fresh) discussions.' † The request now preferred, being at variance with the original treaty, could not well be conveyed to your Majesty."

E-liang made a fairly accurate report of McLane's other requests and then commented on his *quid pro quo* proposal as follows:

*This memorial was subsequently found in the Viceroy's yamen at Canton in January, 1858, when the British occupied the city, and was translated, along with many other similar documents, by Thomas Wade of the British Mission. It was not placed in the hands of the American Envoy, Mr. Reed, for some unexplained reason, until after he had negotiated and signed the Treaty of Tientsin. Mr. Reed stated in a speech before the Philadelphia Board of Trade, May 31, 1859, that had he known of this report when he was negotiating the Treaty of Tientsin, he might have been less good-natured in his dealings with the Chinese commissioners, and he even intimated that he might have joined with the allies, in the destruction of the Taku forts.[14]

† E-liang is quoting the clause in Art. 34 of the Treaty of Wanghia, which reads: "and no individual State of the United States can appoint or send a minister to China to call in question the provisions of the same."

"He also handed in a communication in very obscure phraseology, characters in which had been taken to signify what they did not properly mean. On the whole it differed nothing from the language he had employed except in the addition that if, on representation made to the throne, he should be honored by (your Majesty's) assent to his requests, it would behoove him, of course, to assist China in completely removing her cause of disquiet. . . .

"It is the very humble opinion of your slave, that, in as much as the American barbarians, heretofore accounted so submissive, have taken advantage of the present conjuncture to press their demands, reliance is surely not to be placed on their cooperation, though they promise it, in the restoration of order."

E-liang also observed that the French and English would probably want something if any concessions were made to the Americans.

This report of E-liang's drew from the throne an order that McLane must return to Canton, and that it would be Yeh's duty to forestall the American commissioner's malice, and to address him 'authoritatively in peremptory language.'

To the student of American policy in China the most notable feature of McLane's *projet* is the fact that, while contemplating the opening of the entire country to American trade, it departed entirely from the principles laid down in the Cushing treaty that China alone must enforce her own laws and also protect the Americans within her borders. These departures from existing American policy were entirely unauthorized, and no comment was ever made on them by Marcy.

A few weeks after the close of the correspondence with E-liang in which McLane had served notice that he would press his demands at the Pei-ho, the American commissioner received instructions from Washington to aid Sir John Bowring in the renewal of the British treaties which was due, according to the English interpretation of the American treaty, on the 29th of August of that year.*

---

*The Treaty of Nanking had been signed August 29, 1842. The Treaty of the Bogue, the following year, had contained a most-favored-nation clause. The American treaty stipulated that "inasmuch as the circumstances of the several ports of China open to foreign commerce are different, experience may show that considerable modifications are requisite in those parts which relate to commerce and navigation; in which case the two Governments will at the expiration of twelve years from the date of said convention, treat amicably concerning the same. . . ." It was on the strength of these facts that Great Britain rested the claim for a revision of the treaties—a claim which Yeh at Canton promptly rejected.

Bowring had suffered from Yeh treatment very similar to that which had been administered to Marshall and McLane, and at length formally notified Yeh that he would seek, in company with the American Minister, the revision of the treaties at the mouth of the Pei-ho.

McLane and Bowring Go to the Pei-ho

The British Minister, unlike McLane, was under very specific and well considered instructions from his government as to just what he should ask for in the treaties.*

The proposals were much more moderate, as well as more detailed, than those which McLane had presented to E-liang. Beside them the *projet* of the American Commissioner was ill-considered and rash. It is at this point that the inherent weakness of the American, as contrasted with the British, diplomatic establishment in China becomes conspicuously apparent. Bowring had been in China for many years; McLane only a few months. Lord Clarendon had been studying the relations between Great Britain and China from an exceptional point of observation for more than a score of years. President Pierce and Secretary of State Marcy had very recently come into office, and so little did they know of the actual situation in China that McLane was not only without detailed instructions covering such points as Clarendon had outlined to Bowring, but McLane's *projet* when reported to Washington, failed to draw any word of criticism or of caution. McLane enjoyed to the fullest extent the confidence of the administration and, had he not insisted on the acceptance of his resignation because of ill health, he would have been returned to China the

*These points were: 1. Access to all of China, or, failing this, free navigation of the Yangtze as far as Nangking and the opening of some more ports on the coast. 2. Legalization of the opium trade. 3. Abolishment of internal or transit dues on goods imported from foreign countries, or destined to be exported to foreign countries. 4. Provision for the effectual suppression of piracy along the coast. 5. Regulation of the emigration of Chinese laborers. 6. Permanent and honorable residence of a diplomatic representative of the British Crown at Peking; or, if this could not be obtained, then provision for habitual correspondence between the British and the Chinese authorities at the capital. 7. Provision for ready intercourse between the British representative in China and the governor of any province where the representative might be residing. 8. In the revised treaty the English version alone to be the authoritative text.

following year to take up the negotiations where he had dropped them.

On November 3 Commissioner McLane and Sir John Bowring had an interview in a tent near the Hae Kow Forts at the mouth of the Pei-ho, with Tsung Lun, an Imperial Commissioner of inferior rank. It had been intended originally that the French Minister, M. de Bourboulon, should accompany them to the Pei-ho, but an accident to the French war vessel in which he was to go made it impossible. He therefore sent Count Kleskowsky of the French legation, as his representative. The French officer was the guest of the American Commissioner on board the U. S. war steamer *Powhatan*.

In the interview of November 3, Bowring did not submit an outline of the changes in the treaty which he desired. McLane on the contrary added to his *projet* a great many details which had been omitted from the outline submitted to E-liang. The entire negotiations came to nothing. The envoys were told to go back to Canton, there to wait for an answer from the Emperor. It was already evident from the tone of Tsung Lun's comments, that the Emperor was willing to grant none of the important points proposed by McLane. The result of the expedition was that the demands of two of the treaty powers had been successfully denied by the Imperial authorities, and the meanness of their reception in the tent interview was a clear indication that the Government of China would never willingly treat with the foreign powers on terms of diplomatic equality.[15]

Tsung Lun and his associate made complete reports to the Emperor on the meeting with the foreign envoys, one of Tsung Lun's comments being: [16] "The English barbarians are .   . full of insidious schemes, uncontrollably fierce and imperious. The American nation does no more than follow their direction."

McLane returned from the Pei-ho in November in no mood for temporizing. After submitting a full report to the President he outlined the following possible courses of action: [17] (1) To adhere to the former policy of awaiting developments, preserving strict neutrality between the rebels and the Imperialists, and protecting American interests as far as possible with the United States naval forces then on the coast. (2) To aid the Imperial forces in suppressing the rebellion, or, (3) for the President to address a letter to the Emperor pointing out that China had violated her treaty with the United States, this letter to be presented at the mouth of the Pei-ho by two sloops of war and a steamer. In case the Emperor will not accede to the demand to open up friendly diplomatic intercourse with the United States to secure the settlement of these pending questions, and the revision of the treaty, then McLane proposed more vigorous action.

"I would recommend," he wrote, "that the Pei-ho and the Yangtze Kiang, as well as the River Min and the Whampoa Reach be placed under blockade by the united forces of the three treaty powers— Great Britain, France and the United States—and so held until the commercial privileges of buying from and selling to all persons in China, without limitation or restraint, is respected, and all the other treaty stipulations recognized and enforced, where the authority of the Imperial Government is paramount."

McLane felt that to pursue the first of these policies was futile, and he did not believe that the Government of the United States would favor the second. He heartily recommended the joint blockade.

To this recommendation Secretary of State Marcy replied in a letter of instructions which reached China long after McLane had left,[18] that "the President will have serious objections to uniting with Great Britain and France in what you call the aggressive policy—that is the bringing together a united naval force of the three powers in order to obtain the revision of the treaties with China, securing larger commercial privileges by intimidation, or possibly by force.   "

BIBLIOGRAPHICAL NOTES

1. S. Ex. Doc. 39:36-1.
2. McLane Corres., S. Ex. Doc. 22:35-2, May 4, '54; see also Michie's "The Englishman in China," Vol. 1, p. 149; Morse, Vol. 2, pp. 19-88.

3. McLane Corres., pp. 33-39.
4. *Ibid.*, p. 112.
5. Michie, Vol. 1, p. 152; S. Ex. Doc. 22:35-2, p. 908.
6. Sen. Ex. Doc. 22:35-2, p. 908; S. Ex. Doc 30:36-1, p. 530.
7. Marshall Corres., p. 205.
8. Richardson's Messages, Vol. 5, pp. 199-200.
9. Marshall Corres., pp. 18-24, 25, 85, 132-5, 352.
10. McLane Corres., pp. 21-2.
11. *Ibid.*, p. 54.
12. *Ibid.*, pp. 143 ff.
13. *Ibid.*, p. 147.
14. S. Ex. Doc. 30:36-1, p. 452; Reed's speech (pamphlet), p. 16.
15. For complete account of the Pei-ho expedition, see Disp. No. 20, McLane Corres., p. 285 ff.
16. S. Ex. Doc. 30:36-1, p. 478.
17. McLane Corres., pp. 287-292.
18. China Instructions, Vol. 1, Feb. 26, 1855.

CHAPTER XIII

ATTEMPTS TO OPEN JAPAN TO TRADE

WHILE the opening of Japan by Commodore Perry in 1854 came as a direct result of American trade expansion, the causes which produced it were not so simple as those which led to the Cushing Mission. In 1844 American relations with the Far East were almost exclusively with China; in 1853 they were not only with China but also with the entire North Pacific Ocean.

JAPAN AND EARLY PACIFIC TRADE

The rapid growth of the Northwest Coast fur trade had brought Japan for a few years within the interest of Americans, yet without leading to any definite results. The *Lady Washington* (Captain Kendrick) and the *Grace* (Captain Douglas) visited a southern port of Japan in 1791 in an effort to dispose of sea-otter peltries, on their way to Canton, but the Japanese had refused to trade with them. This visit and refusal made so little impression that they were almost immediately forgotten by Americans, few of whom aside from the crews of the vessels appear to have known of it.[1]

In 1807 the *Eclipse* of Boston, chartered by the Russian-American Company at Canton for Kamchatka and the Northwest Coast, and carrying several British sailors who had been induced to desert from Company ships at Whampoa, visited Nagasaki and was peacefully captured by the Japanese, supplied freely with water and permitted to depart. The *Eclipse* entered the Japanese port under the Russian flag which the Dutch superintendent advised them to haul down because the Japanese had been so enraged by the conduct of Russian officers in Sakhalen the previous year.[2] At the close of the War in 1812, the new vigor of American trade expansion is registered in the proposition made by Commodore Porter to Secretary of State Monroe to send an expedition to Japan. A frigate and two sloops of war were proposed for the enterprise but nothing was done about it.[3] Porter, during the war, had occupied Madison Island in the South Pacific, November, 1813, building a fort which he manned with four guns. A month later he was compelled to surrender to Commodore Hillyar of the British navy near Valparaiso. Porter eventually made his way back to New York where he arrived in the summer of 1815. His proposal to open Japan may be said to have marked the high tide of American interest in the Pacific until 1830.[4]

Another series of approaches to Japan were made through Batavia. In 1797 the *Eliza* (Captain Stewart) re ported as belonging to New York, and carrying the Ameri can flag, appeared at Nagasaki. Captain Stewart repre sented himself as the agent of the Dutch East India Com pany of Batavia, and in some way effected an exchange of cargo. The following year the *Eliza* returned, secured another cargo, but had the misfortune to strike a rock in Nagasaki harbor and was compelled to remain in port until the next season. In 1799 the *Eliza* sailed away with its cargo, but it did not go to Batavia. Four years later the vessel returned, still under the American flag, but from Bengal. Meanwhile both the Dutch and the Japanese had become aware that the *Eliza* was really employed by the British in an effort to create a British trade with Japan, and the vessel was refused a cargo. Captain Stewart was an Englishman and the vessel, while it may have been built in America and sold in the East, probably was entirely without legal right to fly the American flag.[5]

The first genuinely American vessel, after the *Lady Washington* and the *Grace,* to enter Japan was the *Franklin* (Captain Devereaux) of Boston, owned by the Perkinses and James Dunlap. The *Franklin* arrived at Batavia from

Boston in April, 1799, and was immediately engaged by the East India Company to take the place of the annual Dutch ship to Nagasaki, an American vessel being chosen because of its neutral character. This was the first ripple of the Napoleonic wars in Asia. Captain Devereaux was instructed to hoist the Dutch pennant "as if you were a Dutch ship" as soon as he came in sight of Japan. The instructions also contained one order which throws light on the cause of Japanese exclusiveness, harking back to history nearly two centuries old.

"All the books of the people and officers, particularly religious books, must be put in a cask and headed up [upon approaching Japan]; the officers from shore will put their seals upon the cask, and take it on shore, and on the departure of the ship, will bring it on board without having opened it."

The *Franklin* remained about four months in Nagasaki harbor, and reached Batavia again December 18, 1799.[6] In 1801 the *Margaret* (Captain Samuel Derby) of Salem, secured the contract for the East India Company voyage, and similar voyages were made in 1802, 1803, 1806, 1807 and 1809, after which the Dutch factory at Nagasaki was left without word from the outside world until near the close of the Napoleonic wars, when the British made a second unsuccessful effort to take up the trade. In view of the fact that these American vessels were compelled to hoist the Dutch flag when in Japanese waters, one wonders whether the American flag was actually shown at Nagasaki after 1791.

Edmund Roberts and Japan

The part of the program of Edmund Roberts in 1832 which included Japan has already been alluded to. From the inauguration of the Roberts Mission the idea of making a treaty with Japan appears to have grown rapidly into favor with the American Government. At the request of the Department of State John Shellaber, United States Consul at Batavia, prepared outlines of a program of treaty-making in the East which included many suggestions about Japan.[7] He advised that an attempt to make at least some sort of an agreement with the Empire would probably meet with success. Previous missions had failed, he thought, "owing to the jealous fears entertained by the Japanese Emperors that those powers would sooner or later, if any intercourse was opened, interfere with the internal affairs of the Empire, attempt to subvert its Government and probably make a conquest of the country. I allude more especially to England and Russia." Shellaber pointed out that the Americans would be free of all suspicion, and predicted that in three or four years a trade would grow up with a tonnage of 5000, amounting to $300,000. At least, thought the consul, the mission could secure in Japan a resort for American whale ships. Shellaber strongly recommended that the proposed expedition should be carried in a merchant rather than a national vessel.

A few weeks after Edmund Roberts departed from Boston in the *Peacock* a commission was issued to him (June 26, 1832) to go to Japan, but no mention was made in it of securing a treaty.[8] Four months later (October 28, 1832) Secretary of State Livingston wrote to Roberts again, stating that the government had in contemplation a separate mission to that empire, but authorizing Roberts, in case the prospects seemed favorable, "to fill out one of the letters of credence" and go to Japan. He was however cautioned to go in a merchant vessel, having the *Peacock* only as a convoy. The *Peacock* was to wait outside for a favorable development of the negotiations.[9] Roberts found it impracticable, owing to lack of funds, to carry out the suggestion of Livingston, but he reported from Batavia, June 22, 1833: [10]

"I have no doubt from information obtained from merchants of the first respectability in this place that by judicious management all the principal ports in Japan would be thrown open to the American trade. The Americans are the only people who can probably effect this. The Portuguese and Spaniards are by law of the Empire forever excluded, and the unprincipled conduct of Captain Pellew of the *Phaeton* in 1808 in the harbor of Nagasaki, has caused the Japanese

Government to reject every overture which has been made to them since that time by the British. During the last European war several American ships were chartered here for the Dutch factory at Decima, and met with no difficulty on account of the flag."

Upon Roberts' return from his first mission he made a report to Secretary of State McLane (May 12, 1834) in which he stated that the Dutch, owing to their jealousy of Americans, "whom they fear as their only rivals," had misrepresented the character of the Japanese for their own ends. He believed the Japanese to be free from every prejudice that would prevent Americans from trading with them, and suggested that the way to the trade with Korea and northern China would be open in case a treaty were made with Japan.

By means of other investigations and unknown sources the Department of State was advised that the proposed approach to Japan ought to be made in a national ship, that it should be made at some port other than Nagasaki, preferably nearer the seat of government, and that while general trade would not at first be permitted, it seemed probable that a beginning might be made. Presents to the Emperor should accompany the envoy.*

In view of the success which had attended the first Roberts mission, apparently all thought of a special mission to Japan was abandoned, and when Roberts sailed again to exchange ratifications of the treaties of Muscat and Siam, he was commissioned to resume the negotiations with Cochin China and then to proceed with all secrecy to Japan in the *Peacock*. The death of Roberts at Macao in 1836 brought this enterprise to an end.

VISIT OF THE *Morrison*, 1837

The next American effort to unlock the gates of Japan was a private one undertaken by the firm of Olyphant and Company of Canton in 1837. The Olyphant firm had come

*This information was secured in answer to a list of ten questions and was contributed by some American who had been a resident at the Dutch factory perhaps in 1807 or 1809.[11]

to occupy a unique place in the commercial life of Canton because of the refusal of the firm to deal in opium and because of the hearty support to the Protestant missionaries afforded not only by D. W. C. Olyphant the founder, but also by the younger partners. Indeed it had been in part due to Olyphant that the first American missionaries, Rev. E. C. Bridgman and Rev. Edwin Stevens, were sent to China in 1830.[12] As the Olyphant firm prospered, the support to the missionaries increased and widened. In 1835 the firm had made it possible for Medhurst and Stevens to make a voyage of missionary exploration northward along the coast in the brig *Huron*. The results of this voyage so encouraged the firm that they had the *Himmaleh* built in the United States at a cost of $20,000 and fitted out for a cruise of missionary trade and exploration in the Malay archipelago and Japan Sea. The *Himmaleh* took on Rev. Edwin Stevens of the American Board and G. Tradescant Lay, agent of the British and Foreign Bible Society and started southward. There was no opium or firearms in the cargo. The voyage proved abortive, owing in part to the death of Stevens in Singapore in January, 1837. The *Himmaleh* returned to Canton, was loaded with tea and dispatched to the United States.

The voyage of the *Morrison,* while not directly related to the previous experiments of the *Himmaleh,* is to be considered in the light of that experience. The *Morrison,* belonging to Olyphant and Company, and named after the famous missionary, arrived in China too late in the spring of 1837 to secure a return cargo. The vessel must therefore lay over a season, and C. W. King, one of the Olyphant partners, only twenty-eight years old, proposed to occupy the idle time with a voyage of exploration to Japan similar to that undertaken by the *Himmaleh* to Borneo and Celebes. There were at that time at Macao seven shipwrecked Japanese sailors, three from the Northwest coast who had reached China by way of London, and four who had been brought in from the Pacific by way of Manila. King decided not to wait for the return of the *Himmaleh* but rather to proceed at once to Japan to repatriate the Japanese, and to seize the opportunity to open up negotiations for missionary work and for trade. The *Morrison* was unarmed, and the party included S. Wells Williams, missionary printer of the American Board, Rev. Peter Parker, M. D., of the Missionary Ophthalmic Hospital at Canton, and Rev. Charles Gutzlaff who had recently entered the service of the British Government as interpreter. Gutzlaff joined the expedition at Lew Chew, Napa, to which point he was conveyed in the British sloop of war *Raleigh*.

The *Morrison* reached the Bay of Yedo in July, 1837, anchored at Uraga, and declared the purpose of the visit. It was also contemplated to offer the Japanese a teacher, i.e., a missionary, if they were willing to receive him. The authorities refused to have any dealings with the *Morrison*, ordered her away and then opened fire upon the vessel from the forts. A second effort was made at Kagoshima to open up communications with the authorities, but a second time the vessel was fired on. None of the Japanese sailors were landed.

Mr. King wrote a book—"The Claims of Japan and Malaysia upon Christendom, exhibited in notes of voyages made in 1837 from Canton in the ship *Morrison*, and the brig *Himmaleh*, under the direction of the owners"—in which he urged the American Government to take up the insult to the American flag and to demand a treaty. S. Wells Williams returned to Macao much impressed with the superior strength and culture of the Japanese, and anticipated that 'a war-like attempt upon the nation' would be attended with 'fatal influences.' He immediately undertook, with the aid of the Japanese sailors, the study of the language with a view to laying the foundations for future missionary work.[13] While the voyage of the *Morrison* had no immediate result, it may be said that from the time of its visit to Japan, the subject of opening up the country was never suffered to drop out of sight.

REVIVAL OF AMERICAN INTEREST IN JAPAN

A 'full power' to treat with the Japanese authorities was issued to Caleb Cushing, at his suggestion, August 15, 1844.[14] The Secretary of State in forwarding the letter remarked that 'little probability exists of expecting any commercial arrangement with that country.' This authority did not reach Cushing before he returned to the United States.

In less than three weeks after the publication of the Cushing correspondence on the China treaty, Zedoc Pratt, of New York, introduced a resolution in the House calling for immediate measures to effect commercial arrangements with the Empire of Japan and the Kingdom of Korea on the ground that it was important "to the general interests of the United States that a steady and persevering effort should be made for the extension of American commerce, connected as that commerce is with the agriculture and manufactures of our country." This resolution expressed the confident hope that another year would not elapse before the American people would "be able to rejoice in the knowledge that the 'star-spangled banner' is recognized as an ample passport and protection for all. . . ." The resolution, however, passed unnoticed.[15]

The whale ship *Manhattan* (Captain Mercator Cooper) of Sag Harbor, had visited the Bay of Yedo April 17, 1845, with a number of shipwrecked Japanese sailors and had been very kindly treated although not permitted to remain more than a few days. When the *Manhattan* left she carried some Japanese stowaways who had seized the opportunity thus offered to go abroad to study the western world.[16]

Alexander H. Everett, the first American Commissioner to China under the new treaty, who sailed for China early in June 1845, carried a commission to negotiate a treaty with Japan, and Commodore Biddle, who had been ordered to convey Everett to China in the U. S. S. *Columbus,* also had instructions from the Secretary of the Navy, Bancroft, permitting him to make a visit to Japan in case Everett did not decide to accompany him. The new commissioner became ill on the voyage to Rio Janeiro. He was compelled to return and did not reach China until October, 1846. Meanwhile Commodore Biddle, to whom Everett had delegated his duties, proceeded to China, exchanged ratifications of the treaty and then moved on up the coast to Shanghai where he found that Henry G. Wolcott had already begun to ship American cotton goods to Japan through the Chinese merchants.

Commodore Biddle, with the *Columbus* and the *Vincennes,* anchored in the Bay of Yedo July 20, 1846, and inquired politely whether the Government of Japan was willing to open its ports to Americans and to make a treaty. The Japanese firmly refused. The conversations were seriously handicapped by lack of suitable interpreters, and the commodore's visit was marred by an incident which otherwise might have been avoided. While Biddle was about to go on board a Japanese junk to receive the formal answer of the government, a Japanese soldier either struck or pushed him. Biddle had not been expected by the Japanese officials and there were none ready to receive him. Profuse apologies were afterwards offered and Biddle stated that he would be satisfied with whatever punishment for the soldier the Japanese law provided. The reply to Biddle's request for the opening of trade was an anonymous communication ordering him to go away and never return.[17]

The magnanimous conduct of Commodore Biddle appears to have been misinterpreted by the Japanese as weakness and lack of dignity. Accounts of the insult, magnified and misunderstood, spread not only throughout Japan, but even to the Lew Chews and the Americans were made to appear as having accepted an insult with complacency. It was believed that Biddle's visit left matters in a 'less favorable position' than before. Before the report of Biddle's visit reached Washington, a second commission had been issued to Everett to replace the one he had given to Biddle, but Everett did not live to carry out the plans of his government.[18]

From the year 1846 the subject of a treaty with Japan came more and more to engage the attention of Americans. With the increase of American shipping at Shanghai, and the increase of the whale fisheries in the North Pacific, a larger number of vessels were coming into Japanese waters. The shores of Japan were largely uncharted, and rough weather was not uncommon. There were not a few wrecks. On June 8, 1846, Senator Dix of New York presented in the Senate a memorial signed by presidents of marine insurance companies, ship-builders and steam-engine manufacturers, proposing a mission to Japan.[19]

The treatment of shipwrecked American sailors in Japan became one of the important influences which kept the subject alive. In May, 1846, the whaler *Lawrence* of Poughkeepsie (Captain Baker) was wrecked and eight of the crew reached shore. These survivors met with varied treatment, some of which was very severe. After seventeen months' imprisonment they were turned over to the Dutch factory and sent to Java on a Dutch merchantman. They had been in captivity when Commodore Biddle was anchored in the Bay of Yedo. In February, 1848, the whale ship *Lagoda* (Captain John Brown) of New Bedford struck a shoal in the Japan Sea and was wrecked. The survivors reached Matsumai and were transferred to Nagasaki where they were carefully confined. Information of their imprisonment reached United States Commissioner John W. Davis at Canton, through the Dutch consul, and Commodore David Geissinger ordered Commander James Glynn, January 31, 1849, to proceed to Nagasaki in the *Preble* to rescue them. "You will be careful," read Glynn's instructions, "not to violate the laws or customs of the country, or by any means prejudice the success of any pacific policy our government may be inclined to pursue." His conduct was to be 'conciliatory but firm.' Glynn experienced some difficulty in effecting the release of the prisoners who had been very badly treated. Had the American Government been in a mood for reprisals or war, the treatment of the *Lagoda* survivors would have afforded sufficient excuse. Early in

January, 1851, three more Americans who had found their way into Japan were repatriated through the Dutch factory.[20]

The cruel treatment to which the Americans in Japan were at times subjected is to be accounted for by the fact that the Japanese authorities, perhaps because of the increasing numbers of Americans who appeared in Japan, had come to entertain suspicions that the Americans were sending spies into the empire with sinister motives.

Other factors contributing to the creation of public opinion in regard to the opening of Japan had their origin within the United States.

China and the East generally were rapidly coming to be looked upon as the great future market for American produce, especially manufactured cottons.* [21]   The consequent new interest in Asia included Japan and Korea as well as China.   The effort of A. H. Palmer of New York, director of the American and Foreign Agency, which carried on a business as commission agents in the foreign trade, especially for steam vessels and machinery, were so extensive, so thorough, and so persistent as to warrant special notice. Palmer began a systematic study of the markets of Asia as early as 1839.   He would appear to have been father to that characteristically American method of commercial conquest by circularization.   His circulars were spread broadcast through Asia, from the shores of eastern Africa to Japan. In the five years, 1842-7, he sent no less than fourteen such communications to Nagasaki, slipping them into Japan by means of the good offices of the Dutch factory, if indeed they ever went any farther.   Palmer made a careful study of every possible market, giving especial attention to the political aspects of the questions involved and was, presumably, the best informed American on the subject in 1852.   He prepared at various times between 1846 and 1849 a number

*Unfortunately no careful study of the growth of American trade with China in this period has been made. The evidence for this statement meets one, however, throughout the British and American documents, some of which are cited subsequently.

of reports for the Department of State, one of which was addressed directly to President Polk (January 10, 1848) Palmer even prepared a plan for a mission and went so far as to submit a draft of a letter to be sent by President Taylor to the Emperor. He proposed that the Cushing treaty of 1844 should serve as a model for a treaty. Palmer was afterwards described by ex-Secretary of State Clayton as 'entitled to more credit for getting up the Japan Expedition, than any other man I know of.' [22]

Meanwhile others were approaching the problem from still another angle. The application of steam navigation to the trans-Pacific routes by American vessels met with the almost insuperable obstacle of lack of coal supplies. Steam navigation on the coast of China had been attempted with success during the Anglo-Chinese War, and had been taken up for mercantile purposes, but the coal was brought out from England and was very expensive. The voyage across the Pacific was more extended between coaling stations than any part of the voyage from England to China. The needs of American shipping companies were imperative. Japan was believed to have large supplies of coal, and her ports in the days of uncertain steam navigation were absolutely essential to the proposed line of American trans-Pacific steamers.[23]

The settlement of the Pacific Coast by Americans, and especially the discovery of gold in California yielded added argument for steam navigation of the Pacific. Then came the agitation for an Isthmian canal, the first proposal for which, apparently, was born in the brain of Captain Kendrick on the Northwest coast before 1790. As early as 1826 A. H. Palmer secured from the Republic of Central America a concession for a canal, and went to London to interest British capital in the venture.[24] In 1852 the building of the trans-Isthmian railroad and the establishment of a line of steamers up the Pacific Coast to San Francisco and the various projects for a transcontinental railroad from the Mississippi to either San Francisco or San Diego served to bring the whole question of American relations in the Pacific and in Asia more directly to the attention of Americans than ever before.

The various expansive movements, political and mili tary as well as commercial, which characterized the fifth and sixth decades of the last century of American history, all created an atmospheric condition favorable to still further adventures. The times were quite different from those when Edmund Roberts was sent out to Asia in 1832 as a ship's clerk, or even when Cushing went to Macao.

Before passing to the Perry Expedition we may appropriately review briefly the course of events in Japan in the first half of the nineteenth century.

EUROPEAN POWERS AND JAPAN

Thoughtful Japanese had been made increasingly aware, on the one hand, that the policy of exclusion was costly to Japan and on the other, that the day was rapidly approaching when the policy could not be sustained before the advance of the Western nations. To go back no further than the beginning of the nineteenth century, Japan had already felt the impact of advances from both Russia and England, and had been repeatedly warned by Holland.

Russia had made herself an uncomfortable neighbor. In 1804 Captain Krusenstern had appeared at Nagasaki to take up the negotiations which had been begun by Lieutenant Laxman in 1792. Laxman had passed a winter on the northern coast of the island of Yezo, and visited both Hakodate and Nagasaki. He had been given a paper authorizing Russian vessels to enter Nagasaki harbor. With Krusenstern came Resanoff, a special envoy, and some shipwrecked Japanese sailors who had been driven ashore on the coast of Siberia. Resanoff asked for the opening of Japan to Russian trade. The Japanese refused. In the years 1806 and 1807 Krusenstern, in retaliation for the refusal, sent two small vessels to ravage the coast of Sakhalin and Iturup. The next year a Japanese explorer went northward and ascertained for the first time, so far as the Japanese were concerned, that Sakhalen was an island rather than a peninsula of the mainland.[25] In 1811 Captain Golownin, in the sloop of war *Diana,* surveyed the Kurile Islands and was made a prisoner by the Japanese. He and several other officers were kept in Japan as prisoners for several years. Some of the Japanese improved the opportunity to learn the Russian language. In 1849 Nevelskoi, under the direction of Count Muravieff, had explored Sakhalen and established a Russian port at Dui.[26] Meanwhile the Russians had for many years maintained a diplomatic and ecclesiastical establishment in Peking and in 1850, by the convention of Kuldja, had established themselves in a more favorable position in China. Japan feared Russia.

Nor had the advances of England in Asia passed unnoticed among the Japanese. In 1808 Captain Pellew in H. M. S. *Phaeton,* which had already terrorized American shipping at Canton, sailed into Nagasaki harbor in search of Dutch merchantmen and threatened to burn the Japanese and Chinese junks if not supplied with provisions and water.[27] The supplies were forthcoming and the *Phaeton* left abruptly while the Japanese were planning a trap. The visit of Captain Pellew had revealed to the Japanese that the morale of the army was at low ebb; as a result of the humiliation administered by the British captain, several Japanese officers committed hari-kari. Five years later Sir Stamford Raffles of Singapore fame had attempted to open trade with the Japanese, but the Dutch director at Deshima * refused to recognize the English rule in Java and threatened to expose the British intrigue to the Japanese. Raffles sent Dr. Ainslie, a physician, with the expedition and he was permitted to remain, being known as an American. The attempt to open trade for British merchants came to nothing and soon afterwards Java was returned to the Netherlands. In 1818 Captain Gordon of the British navy in a trading brig of 65 tons entered the Bay of Yedo from Okhotsk. He was well treated but failed to attain his

* Deshima is a small island close to the shore in Nagasaki harbor, where the Dutch E. I. Company factory was located.

object. The outcome of the Anglo-Chinese War (1839-42)
created a profound impression in Japan. In 1845 H. M.
frigate *Samarang* visited Nagasaki, and in 1849, five weeks
after the *Preble* had left Nagasaki, the British surveying
ship *Mariner* visited both Uraga and Shimoda, making
surveys.

The French admiral Cecille appeared in Japan in 1846
shortly after Commodore Biddle left.

The Dutch trade at Deshima was not in a flourishing
condition at any time in the nineteenth century. The chief
profit was made out of the copper which was taken from
Japan to Java and there coined and circulated at a rate
above its intrinsic value. During the Napoleonic wars the
Dutch East India Company became extinct and the Dutch
Government took over the Nagasaki trade in 1817. Ten
years later the trade was turned over to a new company but
in 1829 it was returned to the government as being un-
profitable. The trade connection was retained by the
Netherlands for sentimental and political rather than for
commercial reasons. In 1844 William II of the Netherlands
addressed to the Shogun a personal letter in which he cited
the Anglo-Chinese War and stated "The future of Japan
causes us much anxiety." The king explained how the
sovereigns of Europe after the Napoleonic wars had opened
to their subjects every channel of trade with a view to the
preservation of peace. He explained how the introduction
of steam navigation had shortened distances and said that a
nation which continued to remain in seclusion could not
avoid the hostility of other nations. He feared that a disaster such as had recently come to China was threatening
the Japanese Empire. Although the Japanese had issued a
mandate in 1842 ordering kindly treatment for all foreign
vessels in distress, the Shogun replied to the king that it
would be impossible to change a policy of seclusion which
was in accord with 'ancestral law.' Japan refused to make
a treaty with the Netherlands.[28] The Dutch agents at
Deshima kept the Japanese informed as to the progress of
political events in the outside world. In 1850 they notified

the Japanese authorities that the governor general of India had secured permission to attempt to make a treaty with Japan, and when the Americans arrived in 1853 the Japanese were well informed of their approach as well as of the outcome of the recent war between the United States and Mexico.

While the official policy of the Tokugawa Government remained unaltered, Nagasaki was rapidly becoming a source of much enlightenment to the Japanese, and new educational impulses were making themselves felt. A European form of drill was adopted for the army and the Japanese were learning the art of modern ship-building. The science of western medicine was also introduced. Deshima became a window which not only disclosed a view but also let in no inconsiderable amount of light.

Meanwhile the political position of the Shogun's Government had been steadily disintegrating. Japan had never been less able to repel an attack from a foreign nation than in 1853, while the foreign nations had never been so well prepared to make one. Another situation favored the proposed American expedition to Japan: Great Britain, France and Russia were becoming occupied with the Crimean affairs leaving the Pacific for the moment more to the Americans than it had ever been before, or would be again for many decades.

In 1851, after the return of the *Preble* to the United States, interest in Japan reached a high point. Commander James Glynn, at the request of the President, submitted in writing his opinion that a commercial treaty with Japan could not be long delayed. A port in Japan was, he thought, absolutely necessary for the proposed line of trans-Pacific steamers, and he recommended that suitable efforts be made "if not peaceably, then by force." Glynn, however, counselled that the approach to Japan be made on equal terms, as to any European Power. "It may be desirable," he remarked, "on some future occasion to justify ourselves before the world in the measures used towards Japan besides mere argument or entreaty." He recommended that no complaints for past offenses should be made and that the British and Dutch governments should be conciliated.

Accepting completely this wise advice, Secretary of State Webster issued a commission to Commodore J. H. Aulick (June 10, 1851), commanding the U. S. China Squadron, to proceed to Japan for the purpose of negotiating a treaty. The commission was never executed because of the illness of Aulick and also because of charges lodged against him from which he was subsequently cleared by the Navy Department, but too late to admit him to the Japan Expedition.

BIBLIOGRAPHICAL NOTES

1. Morison: "Maritime History of Massachusetts," p. 182.
2. Archibald Campbell: "A Voyage Around the World," pp. 28-9.
3. DeBow's *Review,* Vol. 13, p. 560.
4. Capt. D. Porter: "Journal of a Cruise in the Pacific in 1812-14"; Callahan: "American Relations in the Pacific and the Far East," pp. 25-29.
5. Richard Hildreth: "Japan as It Was and Is," pp. 446-7. Hildreth cites Sir Stamford Raffles, and also a pamphlet by Hagendorp, published in Boston, 1800, to prove that the *Eliza* was an English enterprise.
6. Hist. Col. of Essex Institute, Vol. 2, pp. 287 ff., p. 166; Hildreth, p. 456.
7. Batavia Consular Letters, Vol. 1, May 30, July 1, Aug. 12, 1831.
8. Edmund Roberts Papers (Lib. of Congress).
9. S. Ex. Doc. 59:32-1, p. 63.
10. Roberts Papers (Dept. of State).
11. *Ibid.*
12. "Memoirs of Robert Morrison," Vol. 2, pp. 87, 127-8, 165, 386, 404, 458.
13. For full account of the *Morrison* visit see: "Journal of the Perry Expedition (1853-4)" in *Trans. of the Asiatic Society of Japan,* Vol. 37, Part I (1910) p. 11; Bibliography of the Voyage of the *Morrison,* in Chinese Repository, Vol. 6, (1837); "Claims of Japan and Malaysia upon Christendom," 2 vols.; and "Journal of an Expedition from Singapore to Japan," by P. Parker M. D.; Hildreth, p. 491 ff; "Life and Letters of Peter Parker," by Stevens and Marwick.
14. China Instructions, Vol. 1, Aug. 15, 1844.
15. H. Doc. 138:28-2.
16. H. Doc. 96:29-2, p. 28, gives an account of the visit of the Manhattan; see also Nitobe's Intercourse between the United States and Japan.
17. China Dispatches, Vol. 3; S. Ex. Doc. 59:32-1, pp. 64 ff.
18. S. Ex. Doc. 59:32-1, p. 69.

19. H. Doc. 96:29-2, p. 33.
20. S. Ex. Doc. 59:32-1, gives extended account of these incidents; *Preble* correspondence also published separately as H. Ex. Doc. 84:31-1.
21. See Clive Day: "Hist. of Amer. Commerce," pp. 498-514 for a convenient summary.
22. H. Doc. 96:29-2; S. Misc. Docs. 80:30-1; Natl. Intelligencer, Sept. 6, 1849; H. Misc. Docs. 10:33-2.
23. H. Rep. 569:30-1, May 4, 1848; S. Ex. Doc. 49:32-2.
24. S. Misc. Docs. 80:30-1, p. 66 ff; H. Rept. 439:31-1.
25. Stead: "Japan by the Japanese," pp. 149-50; Hildreth, pp. 446-7.
26. Stead, p. 150.
27. W. G. Aston: *Trans. of Asiatic Society of Japan,* Vol. VII, 1879.
28. D. C. Greene: *Trans. of Asiatic Society of Japan,* Vol. XXXIV, Part IV, pp. 110 ff.

CHAPTER XIV

COMMODORE PERRY'S POLICY

THE first treaty between the United States and Japan was attended by many circumstances dissimilar from those which governed the making of the Treaty of Wanghia. While Cushing was negotiating at Macao there was already a large American trade with China which must not only be protected but also left undisturbed; there was a strong and well-defined mercantile tradition as to what constituted sound policy. There were other foreign powers, particularly Great Britain and France, to be taken into consideration, the negotiator was a lawyer, and China had just emerged from disastrous war. In Japan it was different: there was no trade to protect, no traditions to be reckoned with, and no other foreign power to embarrass the proceedings; and although he was enjoined to use only peaceful methods, the negotiations were in the hands of a naval officer. There were also important differences in the temper of the American people in 1853 as compared with 1844. Within the decade the United States had pushed its way across the continent to the Pacific Coast, and by means of a successful war had extended its boundaries to the Rio Grande.

The policy of Commodore Perry for the Pacific Ocean and for Asia may properly be discussed from three points of view: the instructions from the Government of the United States which guided Perry; the negotiations of 1853 and 1854 at Yedo and the resulting treaty; and the policy of Perry himself as it appeared in his dispatches and subsequent utterances. We have again to remember that initial American policies in Japan, as in China, were largely personal. They were framed by not more than three or four people and executed by only one—Commodore Perry.

Instructions

The instructions for the Japanese Expedition underwent a distinct development before they were issued in their final form to Commodore Perry. The first set of instruc tions had been drafted by Secretary of State Webster and given to Commodore Aulick June 10, 1851.[1] They were similar in tone to, though not so complete as, those given to Caleb Cushing eight years before. Perhaps the most signifi- cant feature was the omission of all reference to the insults which had been offered to the American flag and the indig- nities and cruelties suffered by American citizens and officers in the *Morrison, Biddle, Lagoda,* and other affairs. Webster's policy was to ignore these affronts and to start anew with no thought of reparations or apologies. The Webster instructions dwelt most upon the necessity of secur- ing supplies of coal in order that steam navigation of the Pacific might be established. "We should make another appeal," wrote Webster, "to the sovereign of that country to ask him to sell to our steamers not the manufactures of his artisans, or the results of the toil of his husbandmen, but a gift of Providence deposited by the Creator of all things in the depths of the Japanese islands for the benefit of the human family." Beyond the securing of coal supplies, Aulick was authorized to secure a treaty, if possible, similar to those with Muscat, Siam and China in which protection for shipwrecked and distressed sailors would be stipulated, and 'one or more' ports opened to trade. The accompany- ing letter from President Fillmore to the Emperor of Japan, written by Webster, asked for "friendly commercial inter course and nothing more."

For the delivery of the letter and the support of the negotiations Aulick would have at his disposal on the China station a very modest fleet, the steamer *Susquehanna* and two sloops of war, the *Plymouth* and the *Saratoga.* It was not even certain that all of these could be spared from the China coast for an expedition to Japan.

The instructions issued to Perry by Acting Secretary of

State C. M. Conrad, November 5, 1852, were quite different in tone and more explicit in details.[2] Perry had accepted the appointment to the Expedition with some reluctance, and having consented to the appointment, appears to have been given a large freedom in planning the methods by which it was to be carried out. Owing to the illness of Webster, Perry was permitted to draft his own instructions which were, of course, submitted to the Department of State for revision and approval.[3] Whether any revision actually took place may best be judged by comparing the instructions as signed by Conrad with other statements of Perry in which his ideas of Far Eastern policy were unfolded. At any rate the spirit of Webster had departed from the Perry instructions.

While the objects of the expedition as stated by Webster were left practically unchanged—protection for distressed American sailors, one or more ports to be opened to trade, and the right to purchase coal—the Japanese were described as a 'weak and semi-barbarous people' whose conduct towards shipwrecked sailors had brought them into the category of those nations which "may justly be considered as the common enemy of mankind." The duty of protecting Americans who navigated those seas was one "that can no longer be deferred." "While it is true," read the instructions, "that every nation undoubtedly has the right to determine for itself the extent to which it will hold intercourse with other nations, the exercise of such a right imposes duties which cannot justly be disregarded." The disregard of the duty to care for distressed seamen was intolerable. The instructions contained a very significant paragraph in which the relations of the United States to Japan were considered in the light of the respective position of the two nations on the Pacific Ocean—the first comprehensive statement of the basis of an American policy for the Pacific. This paragraph read:

"Recent events—the navigation of the ocean by steam, the acquisition and rapid settlement by this country of a vast territory on the Pacific, the discovery of gold in that region, the rapid communication established across the Isthmus which separates the two oceans—have practically brought the countries of the east in closer proximity to our own; although the consequences of these events have scarcely begun to be felt, the intercourse between them has already greatly increased and no limits can be assigned to its future extension."

More significant than the statement of the objects to be obtained were the methods to be employed. At the time the instructions were issued it was expected that the fleet would consist of five steamers and six or more sailing vessels—by far the largest American fleet that had ever appeared in Eastern waters. This formidable fleet was to be used as a 'persuader,' to use the word of President Fillmore many years later. It was assumed that "arguments or persuasion addressed to this people, unless they are seconded by some imposing manifestation of power, will be utterly unavailing." Perry was instructed to proceed to some point on the coast of Japan with his whole force, to assure the Japanese of the friendly feelings of the United States, but to bring up the cases of the *Morrison,* the *Lagoda* and the *Lawrence,* and to explain to the authorities that the United States desired 'positive assurance' that in the future such insults and indignities would not be repeated.

These desires on the part of the United States were to be supported with explanations that in the United States religion is free and that Japan need have no fear that the American Government would, as the older European nations had done two centuries before, seek to interfere with the religion of Japan. Perry was also to disarm the fears and prejudices of the Japanese by explaining that the United States was quite separate from and very independent of Great Britain whose recent war with China had been alarming to Japan. The Japanese were to have explained to them that Japan and the United States had become neighbors across the Pacific Ocean and that the choice lay with the Japanese as to whether the two nations should be friendly neighbors. "The President desires to live in peace and friendship with the Emperor"; but "no friendship can long exist between them unless Japan should change her policy and cease to act towards the people of the United States as if they were her enemies."

If such arguments did not secure any relaxation of the policy of exclusion, or even any assurance of humane treatment for seamen, Perry was instructed to "change his tone, and to inform them in the most unequivocal terms that it is the determination of this government to insist that hereafter all citizens or vessels of the United States that may be wrecked on their coasts or driven by stress of weather into their harbors shall, so long as they are compelled to remain there, be treated with humanity; and that if any acts of cruelty should hereafter be practiced upon citizens of this country, whether by the government or the inhabitants of Japan, they will be severely chastised."

It is obvious that such instructions admitted of very wide latitude in interpretation and therefore, although Perry was "invested with large discretionary powers" he was cautioned to bear in mind that he was to avoid all provocation. The mission was to be pacific in character and was not to resort to force unless in self-defense "in the protection of the vessels and crews under his command, or to resent an act of personal violence offered to himself or to one of his officers." The President, Perry was reminded, had no power to declare war.

A new letter from President Fillmore to the Emperor, a revision of the Webster letter which had been given to Aulick, written by Edward Everett, was entrusted to Perry. It was broadly similar to yet more imperative than the Webster letter, specifying friendship, commerce, access to coal and provisions, and protection for distressed sailors as the objects. As for the last mentioned the letter stated, "we are very much in earnest about this." It was also suggested that Japan might, if not yet wholly willing to abandon the policy of exclusion, at least try the experiment of a suspension of the policy for five or ten years, making a treaty which would be terminable at the end of a given period.

The Perry Expedition, like that of Edmund Roberts, and

unlike the Cushing and the proposed Aulick missions, carried a generous supply of presents for the Emperor including a small steam engine such as had been ordered for Roberts, and suggested for Cushing.

NEGOTIATIONS AND TREATY

The Japan Expedition, greatly reduced as to size, consisting of only two steamers and two sloops of war, anchored in the Bay of Yedo off Uraga on July 8, 1853, and remained in the bay nine days.[4] Having in mind the firing on the *Morrison* in 1837, and the kidnapping of the Russian Captain Golownin in 1811, Perry ordered the decks to be cleared for action and the guns shotted as the squadron sailed up the bay.[5] The fleet was anchored with a view to possible attack and never for one moment during either the first or the second visit, were either officers or crews permitted to remove themselves so far from the vessels that they could not have been protected by the guns.

Perry adopted a policy of magnifying his own office and dignity which was fully in accord with the experience gained by Edmund Roberts, Caleb Cushing and Commodore Biddle. He permitted no friendly approaches by minor officials and surrounded himself with a majesty which the Oriental always recognizes and appreciates.

To orders to retire and go to Nagasaki the commodore was deaf; efforts to place the fleet under the guard of Japanese boats and soldiers were met by the assertion that if the Japanese authorities did not remove the guards he would remove them by force; and when the Japanese became evasive about receiving the President's letter, Perry threatened that if a suitable person was not appointed to receive the documents he would go ashore with a sufficient force and deliver them himself. While the Japanese were considering this threat Perry ordered surveying boats, well manned and armed, to begin surveys of the bay and harbor, being careful not to go outside the range of the guns. When requested to withdraw these surveying boats, Perry refused.

Indeed the *Mississippi*, the flag-ship, was sent still farther up the bay in the direction of Yedo and the surveys of the approach to the capital were extended. The commodore explained that these surveys were necessary because he intended to return in the spring with a 'larger force.' [6]

The Japanese were notified that if the President's letter to the Emperor were not duly received and replied to, he would consider his country insulted and would "not hold himself accountable for the consequences." Before such threats and intimidation the Japanese could not well do otherwise than yield, and the letter was received with suitable ceremony on shore, Perry delivering it to "the Prince of Idzu, first counsellor of the Emperor and his coadjutor, the Prince of Iwami." Perry was then ordered to depart but instead of obeying he immediately ordered the whole squadron to get under way in the direction of Yedo, and in the *Mississippi* Perry went to within seven miles of the city. Mindful of his instructions, however, Perry paused just short of the point where his movements might be regarded as provocation, and retired from Japanese waters, having notified the Japanese that he would return in the spring with a larger force to receive an answer to the President's letter and the proposals for a treaty.

Before his return Perry had established a depot with large supplies of coal at Napa,* on the island of Great Lew Chew, and had directed Commander John Kelly of the *Plymouth* to proceed to the Bonin group of islands, and formally take possession of the Baily islands in the name of the United States. This mission was accomplished October 30, 1853, the principal island being named 'Hillsborough' and the port christened 'Newport,' according to Perry's directions. That these islands had been named and claimed for Great Britain by Captain Beechy in 1827 in no way disturbed the commodore.

The report of the first visit of the American expedition to Japan, as well as the tenor of some of Perry's dispatches

---

*The spelling is varied: the Japanese now spell it Naha. The Great Lew Chew is called Okinawa (Great Napa).

had a somewhat disturbing effect in Washington where the
Pierce administration had succeeded that of Fillmore since
Perry's departure for the East. By direction of the Presi
dent, Secretary of the Navy, J. C. Dobbin, immediately
cautioned Perry again that his mission was to be one of
merely peaceful negotiation and that no violence must be
resorted to except for self-defense.[7]

The fleet, somewhat enlarged, but not so large as had
been originally planned by the Fillmore administration,
returned to the Bay of Yedo February 13, 1854. The Japanese Government had decided to meet the returning expedition with conciliation, but the policy proposed was to
prevent as far as possible the approach of the Americans in
the direction of Yedo. Perry, on the other hand, was determined to advance beyond the anchorage at Uraga where the
negotiations of the preceding summer had taken place.
When the Japanese attempted to draw him back to Kami-
kura for a conference, he asserted that he intended to go to
Yedo. A compromise was effected by which the conference
was held at Yokohama, which is less than twenty miles
from Yedo (Tokio).[8]

The reply to the President's letter contained the surprising and significant statement "for us to continue attached
to the ancient laws, seems to misunderstand the spirit of
the age." The Japanese were willing to open the port of
Nagasaki to the Americans under very stringent regulations
similar to those under which the Dutch and Chinese trade
had been conducted, and they also proposed to open a
second port to the Americans at the end of five years. They
were also prepared to give promises as to the reception of
shipwrecked sailors. However, they stipulated that whatever Americans came to Japan should be subjected to
restraints which amounted to little less than imprisonment.
Perry thereupon increased his demands: he would have
nothing to do with Nagasaki where traditions as to the
treatment of foreigners might always operate as an embarrassment to intercourse, just as similar traditions at Canton
were even then causing trouble. He asserted that he desired

a treaty similar to that existing between the United States and China and that he desired the opening of no less than three ports immediately and two more within a short time. He intimated that if Japan did not make these concessions the United States might decide to send still more ships as well as more stringent instructions. Notwithstanding the clashes of opinion the negotiations proceeded with cordiality and courtesy, and the treaty was signed March 31, 1854.

The treaty presented a singular contrast to the methods by which it had been obtained, so much of a contrast that one is justified in finding the actual American policy in the treaty and in minimizing, as so many have done, the significance of the method. Perry was so sure of the harmlessness of the treaty and even of its direct benefit to Japan that he felt able to disregard the customary methods of American diplomacy. On the other hand one cannot help but feel that in the art of negotiation the Japanese had surpassed the naval diplomat.

The Japanese had offered to open Nagasaki on terms similar to those endured by the Dutch. Perry had shown them the Cushing treaty with China and demanded three ports immediately—either Uraga in Hondo or Kagoshima in Kyushu; Matsumai in Yezo; and Napa in the Lew Chews —with the promise of two more ports at a later date. By the treaty the Americans were allowed to enter Hakodate, a smaller town but a better harbor near Matsumai, and Shimoda on the southern coast of Hondo not far from the Bay of Yedo. Shimoda was entirely without value as a port of trade and the harbor also was of less utility than was supposed by Perry. Napa was ignored in the treaty and Perry came to the conclusion before he left China that the Lew Chews were really more closely related to China than to Japan. Permanent residence for Americans at either of the two strictly Japanese ports was not contemplated in the treaty although a consul was permitted to reside at the inaccessible Shimoda. While those who temporarily visited these ports were not to be subjected to such humiliating surveillance as the Japanese had at first proposed, the trade was to be on a cash basis, specie in exchange for ship-supplies, and was to be supervised exclusively by the government officials. In fact the treaty was hardly more than a shipwreck convention, the necessities of distressed mariners being amply provided for. It bore no resemblance to and could stand no comparison with the Treaty of Wanghia.

The treaty contained, however, a most-favored-nation clause and there was one very significant omission. Perry had asked for no extraterritorial rights whatever. It has been claimed and there is no reason to question the assertion that the absence of such a provision was due to Dr. S. Wells Williams who accompanied the expedition as Chinese interpreter.[9] Williams had had an opportunity to watch the operation of extraterritoriality in China and was firmly persuaded that it was such an evil as a strong nation ought not to force upon a weak one. Perry also was familiar with the situation in China and was apparently willing to agree with Williams without question. It is in the omission of this provision in the Japanese treaty that the true character of Perry is to be read. He would bluster, threaten, even intimidate, but he would not assume the responsibility of inflicting a possible evil on the Japanese.

The treaty quite failed to grant access to the supplies of coal which had been the very first object, in the minds of many, for the expedition. Hakodate was far removed from the route of trans-Pacific travel, and even before Perry left Japan he acknowledged in a separate agreement with the Japanese that coal could not be procured at Shimoda.[10]

Having pointed out the relatively small part of Perry's original demands which had been granted, and the intentional omission of extraterritorial rights which the foreigner in China had already come to regard as too useful to be dispensed with, we must however return to the fact that the treaty had been obtained without firing a shot, and that it left no rancor. It was in fact what its language claimed— a treaty of friendship. It was far more friendly to Japan than the Cushing treaty was to China. It would not be fair, however, to award the credit for the treaty exclusively to the Americans. Perry departed in entire ignorance of the extent to which he had been aided by circumstances and influences within the Empire, and he did not live to realize the extent to which his visit had intensified the struggle already begun and not to be finished until the office of the Shogun and feudalism were both abolished.[11]

PERRY'S PROPOSALS FOR FAR EASTERN POLICY

Viewed as a step in the development of American policy in Asia the treaty of 1854, considered by itself, presents some puzzling questions. When compared with the Cushing treaty with China ten years earlier it would appear to have been a backward step, and this notwithstanding the great display of force which had attended the negotiations. If we were to limit our examination to the treaty itself, Perry would seem to have been badly outwitted by the Japanese or, at the moment when he might have gathered in the fruits of peaceful victory, to have been stricken with indecision and weakness. He had secured very little. It is not fair, however, to stop with a comparison of the treaties. The policy of Commodore Perry was much broader and far more aggressive than is indicated by the terms of the treaty. The Perry Expedition, viewed as a whole, marks something new in policy when compared with that of Caleb Cushing at Macao. Cushing had devoted himself exclusively to the protection of American mercantile interests in China; Perry felt that he was laying the foundations for an American commercial empire in Asia and on the Pacific. Indeed, Perry appears to have been the first American in official position to view not merely the commercial but also the political problems of Asia and the Pacific as a unity.

Perry looked into the future and considered American commercial interests in the Far East from the standpoint of a naval strategist. There must be an ample number of ports of refuge, trade bases, and even points from which protection might be afforded in case of war with some European power.

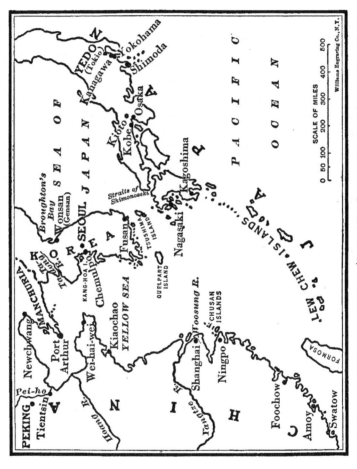

Sketch map showing geographical relation of Japan to the eastern coast line of Asia and the approaches to Chinese and Korean ports.

"It is idle to suppose," wrote Perry after his return to the United States, "that because the policy of the United States has hitherto been to avoid by all means possible any coalition, or even connection with the political acts of other nations, we can always escape from the responsibilities which our growing wealth and power must inevitably fasten upon us. The duty of protecting our vast and rapidly growing commerce will make it not only a measure of wisdom but of positive necessity, to provide timely preparation for events which must, in the ordinary course of things, transpire in the east. In the development of the future, the destinies of our nation must assume conspicuous attitudes; we cannot expect to be free from the ambitious longings of increased power, which are the natural concomitants of national success." [12]

He looked forward to the time when there would be on the Pacific and in Asia a large number of American 'settlements,' which 'would be offshoots from us rather than, strictly speaking, colonies.' These commercial settlements, as he termed them, which he thought ought not to be fortified because fortification would arouse the antagonism of European nations, would 'be vitally necessary to the continued success of our commerce in those regions.'

In one of his dispatches he went even so far as to speak of the necessity of extending the 'territorial jurisdiction' of the United States beyond the limits of the western continent. "I assume," he wrote, "the responsibility of urging the expediency of establishing a foothold in this quarter of the globe, as a measure of positive necessity to the sustainment of our maritime rights in the east." [13]

Perry designated three points where he wished to see a beginning made. They were the Bonin Islands, Great Lew Chew, and Formosa. He also intimated that the United States ought to extend its "national friendship and protection" to Siam, Cambodia, Cochin China, parts of Borneo and Sumatra, and many of the islands of the eastern archipelago.[14] No American before his time, and few after it, ever had such an extensive ambition. Herein lies the explanation of the inadequacies of the treaty with Japan. Perry believed that he was taking but the first step in a very large program which in its entirety could be realized only by degrees. A treaty of friendship with Japan was but a detail in this program.

Commodore Perry left us in no doubt as to the nature of the policy he would have liked to pursue. On the outward voyage from the United States he evolved a plan which he laid before the Secretary of the Navy in great detail.[15] He would occupy the Lew Chew Islands "for the accommodation of our ships of war and for the safe resort of merchant vessels of whatever nation." This, he thought, "would be a measure not only justified by the strictest rules of moral law, but what is also to be considered by the laws of stern necessity."

Perry was looking forward to a time when the United States would be engaged in a decisive contest with Great Britain for the control of the Pacific. He wrote·

"When we look at the possessions on the east of our great maritime rival, England, and of the constant and rapid increase of their forti fied ports, we should be admonished of the necessity of prompt measures on our part. By reference to the map of the world it will be seen that Great Britain is already in possession of the most important points in the East India and China seas, and especially with reference to the China seas. . Fortunately the Japanese and many other islands of the Pacific are still left untouched by this unconscionable government; and some of them lay in a route of a great commerce which is destined to become of great importance to the United States. No time should be lost in adopting active measures to secure a sufficient number of ports of refuge. And hence I shall look with much anxiety for the arrival of the *Powhatan* and the other vessel to be sent me."

In reply to the above described proposal Secretary of State Everett replied for the President, February 15, 1853, approving the occupation of the principal ports of the Lew Chews, which were assumed to belong to Japan, in case ports could not be obtained in Japan proper without resort to force.[16] Everett however cautioned Perry to take no supplies without paying for them and to "make no use of force, except in the last resort for defense, if attacked, and for self-preservation."

On his first visit to Japan, Perry made Great Lew Chew the rendezvous for his squadron and successfully negotiated for a coal depot at Napa which had the best harbor. During the following autumn he kept one or more of the vessels

of the fleet stationed there constantly, and just before his
return to Japan he wrote to the Secretary of the Navy
(January 25, 1854) reaffirming his intention of placing
Great Lew Chew under the American flag. He wrote:

"It is my intention, should the Japanese Government refuse to
negotiate, or to assign a port of resort for our merchant and whaling
ships, to take under surveillance of the American flag upon the
ground of reclamation for insults and injuries committed upon
American citizens, this island of Great Lew Chew, a dependency of
the empire, to be held under restraint, until the decision of my government shall be known, whether to avow or disavow my acts." [17]

To this declaration Secretary of State Dobin replied
(May 39, 1854) after consultation with President Pierce,
that the project was 'embarrassing.'

"The President," he stated, "is disinclined, without the authority
of Congress, to take and retain possession of an island in that distant
country, particularly unless more urgent and potent reasons demanded
it than now exist. If, in the future, resistance should be offered and
threatened it would be rather mortifying to surrender the island, if
once seized, and rather inconvenient and expensive to maintain a
force there to retain it." [18]

The President hoped that the contingency of occupation
would not arise. In these words of hesitation and caution
the President appears to have had in mind Perry's warning
that in case the necessary preliminary steps at the Lew
Chews were not taken immediately "the Russians, or
French, or probably the English" would anticipate the de
sign. Perry had urged that

"though it does not belong to the spirit of our institutions to extend
our dominion beyond the sea, positive necessity requires that we
should protect our commercial interests in this remote part of the
world, and in doing so, to resort to measures, however strong, to coun-
teract the schemes of powers less scrupulous than ourselves."

Perry's plans embraced also the Bonin Islands which lay
about five hundred miles south of Japan and in the direct
path of navigation between Honolulu and Shanghai. Before advancing upon Japan at all Perry personally visited
these islands and purchased for the Navy Department a
"suitable spot for the erection of offices, wharves, coal-sheds,

etc." [19] at Port Lloyd on Peel Island. Four months later, by Perry's order, Commander Kelly of the *Plymouth* took formal possession of the southern group of islands which had been named Baily's Islands by Captain Beechey of H. M. S. *Blossom,* in 1827, but which Perry rechristened Coffin Islands in honor of an American, Captain Coffin, who had visited the islands four years earlier than Beechey.[20] Perry defended this action as well as his other hostile acts on his first visit to Japan on the ground that it was necessary to work on the fears of the rulers of Japan. He did not, however, disguise his satisfaction at having secured an important port of refuge for the trans-Pacific trade about which he was so optimistic.

This unceremonious and brusque appropriation of a portion of the Bonin Islands was not permitted to pass unchallenged by Great Britain. While Perry was lying at Hongkong and gathering his forces for the second visit to Japan, Sir John Bonham, British Superintendent of Trade, was directed by Lord Clarendon to interview Perry and obtain an explanation. The approach to the subject was tactful and conciliatory as was suited to the occasion when the Crimean War was in progress and the Russian Admiral, Count Pontiatin, was in Chinese waters and very friendly with Commodore Perry. Perry set up a counter claim to the islands, resting it on the double ground that Captain Coffin had preceded Captain Beechey to the island by at least three years, and on the fact that since 1830 a group of settlers from the Sandwich Islands, in which the Americans outnumbered the British two to one, had lived at Port Lloyd.[21] Perry put forward his contention in a conciliatory spirit and suggested that Great Britain and the United States ought to cooperate rather than to oppose one another in the establishment of trans-Pacific steam navigation. Perry had in mind for the islands the creation of a free port which would be very similar, in matters of trade, to Hongkong.

In reporting Bonham's inquiry to Washington, Perry reaffirmed his general policy. He stated:

"I shall in no way allow of any infringement upon our national rights; on the contrary, I believe that this is the moment to assume a position in the east which will make the power and influence of the United States felt in such a way as to give greater importance to those rights which, among eastern nations, are generally estimated by the extent of the military force exhibited."

The conciliatory spirit in which the Japanese authorities met Perry on the occasion of his second visit to the Bay of Yedo put an entirely new face on the situation and robbed Perry of most of the reasons for his previously declared policy. The Bonin Islands were forgotten, and when Japan in 1862 proposed to assert a claim to them which antedated by centuries the claims of both Great Britain and the United States, both powers relinquished all pretensions to the islands, which were, in fact, worthless. Perry concluded a 'compact' with the king of the Lew Chews (July 11, 1854) a few months after signing the treaty with Japan, and the document was duly ratified by the Senate a few days after the ratification of the treaty with Japan.[22] This compact treated the Lew Chews as entirely independent of both Japan and China and merely secured protection of ship-wrecked sailors, and the opening of Napa as a port of supplies and trade. When, in 1872, Japan reasserted her claim to the islands the United States merely stipulated that Japan should become directly responsible to the United States for the maintenance of such rights for Americans as the islands had conceded by treaty to the United States.

When the American squadron was being dispersed after the second visit to Japan, Perry ordered two vessels to Manila and to Formosa. The object in visiting the latter point was to investigate the persistent reports that ship-wrecked American sailors were held in captivity on the islands and also to investigate the reported coal mines. No sailors were found, but coal of good quality and in abundance was discovered. No active steps were taken at the time but upon Perry's return to the United States he recommended that "the United States alone should take the initiative" in "this magnificent island."[23] We shall hear more of this project in the next chapter.

We have now before us two distinct, though not always distinctly separated, proposals for American policy in Asia. On the one hand is the policy of the Treaty of Wanghia which repudiated the idea of territorial occupation of Asiatic territory and sought to find sufficient protection for American interests in international law and treaties. On the other, we have the policy of Perry which, while no less peaceful as to ultimate purpose, was based on the assumptions that some such territorial occupation as the British had accomplished at Hongkong was essential to the protection of American interests, and that to secure concessions the Asiatic states must be intimidated. Between the two policies we find Humphrey Marshall and Robert M. McLane wavering, seeking to sustain and build up the sovereign power of China to a point where it would in fact be able to assume effectively the obligations of the Cushing treaty, and yet proposing military and naval intervention in the Taiping Rebellion for the purpose of throwing the entire Chinese Empire open to the trade of all nations. It now becomes our interesting duty to trace the fate of these two policies in the course of the next fifteen years. What attitude President Pierce and Secretary of State Marcy would have taken in the face of a violent issue requiring a definite choice between these policies it is difficult to say. It is, however, quite clear that the surrender of Japan to the peaceful demands of Commodore Perry in 1854 was a more important factor in the determination of American policy in Asia than any positive conviction enunciated by the American Government. The policy of Pierce and Marcy, while inclining towards that of Webster and Cushing, was really opportunist.

BIBLIOGRAPHICAL NOTES

1.   S. Ex. Doc. 59·32-1, p. 80.
2.   S. Ex. Doc. 34:33-2.
3.   Griffis: "Perry," p. 303.
4.   The primary sources of importance for the Perry Expedition are: the Perry Correspondence, S. Ex. Doc. 34:33-2; "Journal of the Perry Expedition (1853-4)," by S. Wells Williams, *Trans. of*

Asiatic Soc. of Japan, Vol. XXXVII, Part II, 1910; "Japan and Around the World," by J. W. Spalding; "Matthew Calbraith Perry," by Wm. Elliot Griffis; "Perry's Japan," by Francis L. Hawks; and "Narrative of the Japan Expedition," published as H. Ex. Doc. 97:33-2.

5. Spalding, p. 143.
6. S. Ex. Doc. 34:33-2, pp. 43 ff.
7. *Ibid.,* p. 57.
8. *Ibid.,* pp. 116 ff.
9. Williams' Journal, p. vii.
10. S. Ex. Doc. 34:33-2, p. 161.
11. "History of Japan from 1853 to 1869," Kinsé Shiriaku, translated by E. M. Satow; "Progress of Japan, 1853-71," by J. H. Gubbins; "Intercourse between the United States and Japan," by Inazo Nitobe; "International Position of Japan as a Great Power," by Seiji G. Hishida.
12. "Narrative of the Japan Expedition," Vol. 2, pp. 173 ff.
13. S. Ex. Doc. 34:33-2, p. 81.
14. Narrative of Jap. Exp. *op. cit.*
15. S. Ex. Doc. 34:33-2, pp. 12-4.
16. *Ibid.,* p. 15.
17. *Ibid.,* p. 109.
18. *Ibid.,* p. 112.
19. *Ibid.,* p. 39.
20. *Ibid.,* pp. 66-7; Chas. Oscar Paullin: *U. S. Naval Institute Proceedings,* 1911, p. 269-70.
21. *Ibid.,* pp. 80-86.
22. *Ibid.,* p. 174.
23. "Narrative of Japan Exped." *op. cit.*

CHAPTER XV

THE POLICY OF DR. PETER PARKER—FORMOSA

DR. PETER PARKER had arrived in China in 1834 as a medical missionary under the auspices of the American Board of Commissioners for Foreign Missions.[1] He was a native of Massachusetts, had been a student at Amherst College and had been graduated at Yale in 1831. He studied theology at Yale Divinity School and then took a course in medicine in Philadelphia. He opened the Ophthalmic Hospital at Canton the year after his arrival and thus became the founder of medical missions in China. The hospital won the support of hong merchants and foreigners alike, and Dr. Parker, who was of amiable disposition, became a very popular and trusted person. He was a member of the *Morrison* expedition to Japan, and was in Washington in 1840 when the first discussions with reference to the Anglo-Chinese War took place. He married a distant relative of Daniel Webster's while on this visit to the United States, thus forming an alliance which made his entrance into government service especially easy. He acted as one of the interpreters for Caleb Cushing in 1844, and the next year he was appointed Chinese secretary and interpreter to the newly created legation. Dr. Parker thus became the one element of continuity in the diplomatic relations of the United States with China during the many replacements and resignations of the following ten years and he was at length appointed (September, 1855) Commissioner. He was the only Commissioner or Minister ever appointed to China who could speak, read or write the Chinese language, and with two exceptions he was the only person ever appointed by way of promotion from a subordinate position in the diplomatic service in China.

Dr. Parker's service, which lasted less than two years, was characterized by three objects: the accomplishment of the revision of the Cushing treaty; the achievement of an *entente cordiale* with Great Britain and France for the pursuit of a cooperative policy; and the acquisition of the island of Formosa for the United States.

TREATY REVISION—DESTRUCTION OF BARRIER FORTS

The time for the revision of the treaty falling legally due in 1856, Dr. Parker was supplied with full powers to conduct the negotiations and was instructed to seek to obtain three concessions: (1) residence for a diplomatic officer at Peking; (2) unlimited extension of trade; (3) the removal of every restriction to personal liberty.[2] So much impressed was the American Government, in the face of the steady opposition of the Chinese to all reform and even to full compliance with the treaties, with the necessity of cooperation with the other treaty powers, that Dr. Parker was authorized to proceed to his post by way of London and Paris and to confer with Lord Clarendon and with the French Ministry of Foreign Affairs with a view to the adoption of a common policy in China. He was, however, entirely without authority to do more than have conversations. The commissioner's enthusiasm for common action may have been a little misleading to the British and the French, encouraging them to expect in the way of cooperation, very much more than the Government of the United States was prepared to give.

Of an interview with Lord Clarendon, October 26, 1855,[3] Dr. Parker reported:

"I remarked that it being the desire of the United States Government that the same concurrent policy and action which hitherto had so happily characterized the three powers in China should continue, I was solicitous to see his lordship on the subject. . . ."

In the conclusion of the interview Clarendon remarked: "I shall have great pleasure, on the opening of Parliament to speak of the *triple alliance."* Parker himself was thoroughly in favor of such a formal arrangement.

In Paris the American commissioner had a similar interview at the Ministry of Foreign Affairs, and then set out for China where he arrived in December, 1855. He was determined to take "high ground" in securing the new treaty, but Commissioner Yeh continued his insolent, unbending attitude and even refused to hold an interview with Parker The American commissioner demanded and threatened, but in vain. To Sir John Bowring and to the French represen tative Parker proposed joint energetic action but his pro gram and his methods did not commend themselves to either of these gentlemen.* Parker had apparently not made a very good impression in either London or Paris. The British, at least, had determined to proceed slowly and run no risk of a second rebuff such as had been administered to Bowring and McLane at the mouth of the Pei-ho in 1854.

Having failed to see the Viceroy at Canton Parker proceeded to Foochow where he was able to hold an interview with the Governor General, to whom he entrusted for delivery at Peking the letter from the President to the Emperor which contained the request for treaty revision. Some weeks later this letter was returned to the commissioner, the seals broken and with other marks of careless handling and of disrespect. Parker was directed to present the letter to Viceroy Yeh for transmission to Peking. The return of the letter Parker regarded as a national insult and he would have proceeded to the mouth of the Pei-ho in a war-vessel to demand explanations as well as to open treaty negotiations had not an accident to the *San Jacinto* deprived him of a means of conveyance.

In the latter part of October Admiral Seymour (British)

---

*Cordier enumerated the points in Dr. Parker's program of revision as: (1) residence of the French, British and American ministers at Peking, and the residence of Chinese ministers at Paris, London and Washington; (2) unlimited extension of trade; (3) universal liberty of opinion for the Chinese; (4) reform of the Chinese courts of justice. These were, presumably, points which Dr. Parker discussed with Count Waleski, French Minister of Foreign Affairs, when in Paris in the fall of 1855. They seem to have been discussed also with Sir John Bowring. The stipulations for the reform of the Chinese courts of justice, and for the residence of Chinese ministers in Paris, London and Washington, which were ridiculed alike by contemporaries and historians, were quite unauthorized, and in fact were never presented to the Government of China.'

had breached the walls of Canton as a result of the unwillingness of Yeh to make the required amends for an alleged
insult to the British flag in the 'Arrow Affair,' and for a few
hours had occupied the Viceroy's yamen. During the early
part of November a state of intermittent warfare was maintained. At the request of Yeh, who declared that he could
no longer protect the foreigners of neutral nations, the
Americans decided to withdraw from Canton. As Commander Foote of the American Navy was on his way up to
Canton on the 15th of November to escort the Americans
down the river, he was fired on by the Barrier Forts which,
upon the withdrawal of the British, had been reoccupied by
the Chinese. The next day Commodore James Armstrong,
commanding officer of the American naval forces on the
China station, ordered the destruction of the Barrier Forts,
and within the next two days this was accomplished. This
action was hailed with delight, not only by the Americans
but by the English as well, for it seemed to indicate that at
last the Government of the United States would be com
pelled to adopt towards China a more energetic policy. Yeh
did not fail to see the danger of the situation, and on the
5th of December rendered a complete apology.[5]

Greatly stirred by these events as well as stung by the
rebuffs of the Chinese authorities, and the recollections of
being called for more than twenty years a "foreign devil,"
Dr. Parker addressed to Marcy a comprehensive dispatch
(December 12, 1856) in which he offered the most extensive
program yet proposed for the settlement of the affairs of
the treaty powers in China. He suggested:

"Were the three representatives of England, France and America,
on presenting themselves at the Pei-ho, in case of their not being
welcomed to Peking, to say, the French flag will be hoisted in Corea,
the English again at Chusan, and the United States in Formosa, and
there remain till satisfaction for the past and a right understanding
for the future are granted; but, being granted, these possessions shall
instantly be restored, negotiation would no longer be obstructed, and
the most advantageous and desirable results to all concerned secured."

He admitted that such a novel program should be undertaken only as a 'last resort.' [6]

The events as well as the recommendations of Dr. Parker for the occupation of Chinese territory were very disquieting to President Pierce and Secretary of State Marcy. There had been reported in the London papers another incident in connection with the occupation of Canton which was equally disturbing. It was stated that the American Consul at Hongkong, James Keenan, had not only been present with the attacking British forces at Canton, but that he had actually carried the American flag over the wall into the city. No mention of this event had been made in the official reports to the Department of State. The President, while withholding severe censure from Commodore Armstrong, did regard the sending of the boat the *San Jacinto* to make soundings near the forts at a time of so much disturbance as not a 'discreet act.' "From a cursory reading of the documents which have been received," wrote Marcy to Parker,[7]

"I think he is inclined to regret that there had not been more caution on the part of our naval force in the beginning, and more forbearance in the subsequent steps. The British Government evidently has objects beyond those contemplated by the United States, and we ought not to be drawn along with it, however anxious it may be for our cooperation. The President sincerely hopes that you, as well as our naval commander, will be able to do all that is required for the defense of American citizens and the protection of their property, without being included in the British quarrel, or producing any serious disturbance in our amicable relations with China."

As for the indiscretion of Consul Keenan, provided the reports in the London papers were correct, Dr. Parker was instructed to transmit to the consul a letter removing him from office. Keenan denied Parker's authority and was never removed.

Those were the closing days of the Pierce administration and the government was disinclined to mark out a policy in China for the succeeding administration. Dr. Parker was left without further specific instructions as to treaty revision, and the rumor that he was to be superseded had already reached him. His impatient efforts "to place in the crown of the present administration the laurel of establishing the United States Legation at Peking and the material extension" of American commerce with China had come to nothing except the near approach to the gravest of entanglements in the Far East. Dr. Parker, however, found much to occupy his attention in the effort to establish an American protectorate over Formosa.

An American Protectorate for Formosa

There were three possible sources from which coal for the proposed trans-Pacific steamship line might be secured: Japan, the mainland of China, or Formosa. Of these three Formosa had, in point of time, been the first to draw the attention of the American authorities in China.

In 1847 officers of both the British and the American navy made surveys of the coal resources of Formosa. Some samples of the coal were sent to the Navy Department for analysis, and at about the same time the Peninsula and Oriental Steamship Company contracted with residents of Formosa for 7000 tons of coal at $7 a ton. Only about 300 tons were ever delivered. The Chinese Government became alarmed at the interest the foreigners were taking in the island and took possession of the mines, placing obstructions in the way of exporting coal to Hongkong.

In July, 1849, the U. S. brig *Dolphin* (Captain Ogden) made an expedition to Kilung, Formosa, for further explorations. Captain Ogden was strongly dissuaded by the magistrate from visiting the mines, and he contented himself with securing some samples for analysis. The Chinese Repository, July, 1849, in a report of this expedition stated that the coal seemed to be better than that which was brought out from Liverpool. The editor remarked:

"The existence of coal at this accessible point and the desirableness of depending less upon supplies brought from Europe, will soon induce the foreign authorities to stir in the matter."

Commodore Perry's opinion on the desirability of an American protectorate over Formosa has already been stated.

There was in Canton at that time an old friend of Parker's, Gideon Nye, Jr., whose firm had recently failed for a very large sum of money. Nye was now looking about for ways to recoup his fortunes. Formosa had been forced upon Mr. Nye's attention a few years before when the American ship *Kelpie,* carrying his brother, had sailed homeward from Canton only to be wrecked off the rocky coast of Formosa, and there had been no survivors. For years the rumor persisted in Canton and Hongkong that the survivors had been cast ashore on Formosa, and then captured and held in slavery by some savage Formosan tribe. Indeed, one of the objects of the visit of the *Dolphin* to Formosa in 1849 had been to search for the survivors of the *Kelpie.*

The visit of Commodore Perry to the island in 1854 had stimulated anew the interest of the Americans and a commercial company consisting of an American firm, Robinet (a Peruvian naval officer who had become an American citizen in a somewhat informal way) and Gideon Nye, had been formed to exploit the trade from a point called Ape's Hill. Robinet and Nye made explorations and secured a monopoly of the camphor trade, and the privilege of an establishment at Takow, in return for which the traders had agreed to pay $100 tonnage duties on each ship and to protect Takow from pirates. Improvements had been made to the extent of $45,000, and the American flag had been raised at the entrance to the harbor. More recently the natives had become dissatisfied and the traders had been obliged to "threaten them with forcible measures if they did not act faithfully." As a result of these measures the American company had become "pretty much independent of the authorities."

Nye and Robinet, realizing that it might be difficult to secure the occupation of the island by American naval forces, and that there were few precedents for what they desired, rather timidly suggested that they were perfectly willing, provided they were assured of the approval and protection of the American Government, to set up an independent government in Formosa.[8]

Parker was very hospitable to the idea. Perhaps he was the more eager because he already knew that the privilege of revising the treaty was not to be for him, and that his days in China were already numbered. Here was the oppor tunity for one grand stroke. On February 12, 1857, he wrote to the State Department, enclosing Nye's proposition:

"The subject of Formosa is becoming one of great interest to a number of our enterprising fellow-citizens, and deserves more con- sideration from the great commercial nations of the West than it has yet received; and it is much to be hoped that the Government of the United States may not *shrink* from the *action* which the interests of humanity, civilization, navigation and commerce impose upon it in relation to Tai-Wan, particularly the southeastern portion of it, at present inhabited by savages, to whose depraved cruelties we have every reason to believe many Europeans, and among them our own friends and countrymen, have fallen victims."

Parker drew attention to his dispatch of December 12, for which there had not yet been time for an answer, and solicited the earnest consideration of the President. The more Parker meditated upon the subject of Formosa, the more his imagination kindled. Ten days after sending the dispatch of February 12, becoming impatient lest delay might be fatal to the destinies of the United States in Formosa, Parker hastily summoned Commodore Armstrong from Hongkong to Macao for a conference on "this subject of great delicacy, and it may be of vast importance to the United States in particular and to the western nations generally." Parker wrote that he had reasons for feeling that if anything was to be done, it must be done quickly. The commodore came to Macao with all speed. He had a kindred spirit in the matter but had been rendered, perhaps, a little more cautious by the fact that no official approval for having destroyed the Barrier Forts three months before had as yet been received. What proposition Parker brought forward at the conference is not stated, but its nature may be inferred from the memoranda of the conference.[9]

After having read that portion of Parker's dispatch of December 12 which referred to Formosa, Armstrong agreed with Parker on the following points: (1) the measure would be justified by the acknowledged principles of international law; (2) the claims and grievances then pending with the Chinese Government amply justified reprisals; (3) Formosa was a most desirable island and would be particularly valuable to the United States; (4) but that its immediate occupation was impracticable with the present naval force, in view of the possibility that the Chinese Government might oppose it. It was admitted "that in any other country than China the measure would be regarded as a virtual dissolution of avowed amicable relations." The commodore agreed, however, that Parker had done his duty, and if the United States failed to acquire the island, the fault would not be upon the shoulders of the commissioner.

Parker followed his already numerous dispatches on Formosa with another marked 'confidential' (March 10, 1857) in which even more impatiently he urged action. He had by then forgotten entirely that part of his original proposal which concerned the immediate restoration of the island to China the moment satisfaction might be obtained. Now he wrote: [10]

"In event of the establishment of a line of steamers between California, Japan and China, this source of supply of coal will be most advantageous. That the islands may not long remain a portion of the empire is possible; and in the event of its being severed from the empire politically, as it is geographically, that the United States should possess it is obvious, particularly as respects the great principle of the balance of power."

And then the commissioner surrendered to his imagination completely.

"Great Britain has her St. Helena in the Atlantic, her Gibraltar and Malta in the Mediterranean, her Aden in the Red Sea, Mauritius, Ceylon, Penang and Singapore in the Indian Ocean, and Hongkong in the China Sea. If the United States is so disposed and can arrange for the possession of Formosa, England certainly cannot object."

As to just cause for occupying the island, Parker, smarting under twenty-five years experience of being called a "foreign devil," found ample grounds.

"If there ever was a State which has laid herself open to just reprisals it is China, 'which has refused to fulfill a perfect obligation which she has contracted' with the United States, 'and does not permit them to enjoy rights which they claim' under the solemn stipulations of treaty; and in event of her persisting in this course, it seems clear that, by the acknowledged principles of international law, the United States have the right, if they have the inclination, to take Formosa by way of reprisal 'until a satisfactory reparation should be made for injuries they have sustained.' See Wheaton's 'International Law,' p. 362."

Much reading of international law since the eye-doctor became the diplomat had made Dr. Parker a little mad. He assured the Secretary of State that he had made up his mind to exercise his 'full powers' to revise the treaty and adjust all claims and to refer the matter to Washington for approval or disavowal, but intimated that he had been unable to carry Commodore Armstrong with the logic of the case.

The weeks sped by, and yet the commissioner might expect no answer to even his first dispatch on Formosa for at least another couple of months. Meanwhile the British Admiral at Hongkong applied to Robinet (March 21) for information about Formosa, and during the conversation remarked, "This island ought not to be allowed to exist in the hands of such a people, which cannot control even the cannibals of the eastern part, who murder our wrecked seamen." Admiral Seymour then asked Robinet if he had any objection to permitting an English naval officer to come to his establishment to live a while and observe conditions. Robinet asked for time to consider the matter and quickly notified Dr. Parker.[11]

The American commissioner immediately addressed Sir John Bowring a solemn protest on behalf of the United States Government against England's taking possession of Formosa.[12]

"In event of the Island of Formosa being severed politically from the Empire of China," declared the commissioner, "I trust to be able to substantiate a priority of claim to it on the part of the United States; first by contracts already entered into with the imperial authorities of the island by citizens of the United States; and secondly by their actual settlement upon it with the consent of the

Chinese, over which the United States flag has been hoisted for more than a year. .

"I embrace this opportunity . . . to acquaint your Excellency that it is my full conviction that the Government of the United States is disposed to adopt the same policy in China as is represented by your Excellency to be that of Great Britain" (i.e., not to establish any exclusive rights or privileges).

Sir John Bowring replied immediately, disavowing any designs on Formosa and somewhat sharply making Parker a 'distinct' proposition for a more pressing task—the occupation by the combined American, French and English forces of the city of Canton. Parker was quite unable to accept such a 'distinct proposition' because he had no more authority for it than he had for the then existing American flag in Formosa. Probably Bowring knew this when he made the proposal. Parker, so intent on his project in the island, quite failed to catch the twinkle in Sir John's eye when he added to his disavowal:

"I hear for the first time, officially, that the United States flag has been hoisted for more than a year in that island. . . . I can assure your excellency I see without jealousy or annoyance the extension of American commerce in these regions, and will cordially support your excellency in the attempt to give to it the strength and security of *legality.*"

Parker, apparently wholly lacking a sense of humor, hastened to show the letter to Commodore Armstrong, and expressed great satisfaction that thus the English minister was on record in the matter. Meanwhile the commodore had been reconsidering his decisions. There were still two months before instructions could be received from Washington. Armstrong knew that he was unable to occupy the island without express orders, but he was able to think of a way out of the dilemma. He proposed to Parker that he was willing to detach an officer from the squadron to go to Formosa and make another investigation for shipwrecked sailors "with instructions to keep his headquarters and flag at the premises of our countrymen, provided such an arrangement meets with your approval and sanction." The approval and sanction were not lacking and Parker replied: [13]

"I conceive that the settlement of our countrymen at Takow will afford the best facilities for making the investigation; and the fact of this officer being there holding his headquarters and flag may have an important bearing on the future."

DISAVOWAL BY THE AMERICAN GOVERNMENT

To the later and more impetuous proposals that he be given authority to complete the acquisition of Formosa, Dr. Parker never even received an answer from the Secretary of State, but to his original proposal that the three powers join in taking temporary possession of Korea, Chusan and Formosa, he did receive the most unmistakable reply. In the closing days of the Pierce administration, Secretary of State Marcy wrote to Dr. Parker that the subject had already been submitted to the President by the French Minister and that the President did not believe

"that our relations with China warrant the 'last resort' you speak of, and if they did, the military and naval forces of the United States could only be used by the authority of Congress. The 'last resort' means war, and the executive branch of this government is not the war-making power. . . . For the protection and security of Americans in China and for the protection of their property, it may be expedient to increase our naval forces on the China station, but the President will not do it for aggressive purposes."

In less than a week the Buchanan administration came into office, William B. Reed was appointed Minister to China, and Dr. Parker immediately dropped all preparations for his expedition to Formosa. The instructions to Minister Reed are most explicit, in reply to all of Dr. Parker's proposals and to the ambitions of any Americans in China to acquire territory at the expense of the Empire.[14]

"This country, you will constantly bear in mind, is not at war with the Government of China, nor does it seek to enter into that empire for any other purpose than those of lawful commerce, and for the protection of the lives and property of its citizens. The whole nature and policy of our government must necessarily confine our action within these limits, and deprive us of all motives either for territorial aggrandizement or the acquisition of political power in that distant region. . . . You will not fail to let it be known to the Chinese authorities that we are no party to the existing hostilities, and have no intention to interfere in their political concerns, or to gain a foothold in their country. We go there to engage in trade, but under suitable guarantees for its protection. The extension of our commercial intercourse must be the work of individual enterprise, and to this element of our national character we may safely leave it."

One may close this chapter of American history with a smile, and yet one is to remember it as an illustration of the fact that, contrary to popular impression, no bacillus has ever been introduced into the blood of Americans which renders them immune to imperialistic ambitions when others have the malady and when commercial conditions favorable for the infection are present.

However, with the issuance of the instructions to Minister Reed in 1857, the policy which had been proposed by Commodore Perry came definitely to an end, never to appear again until the day more than forty years later when President McKinley cabled to the American Commissioners at Paris to demand the cession of the Philippines to the United States.

Dr. Parker's policy had not been complicated or subtle, and requires no analysis. He belonged to the Perry school of Asiatic policy.

BIBLIOGRAPHICAL NOTES

1. Stevens and Marwick: "Life and Letters of Peter Parker."
2. Parker Corres. (published with the McLane Corres. in 2 vols.), S. Ex. Doc. 22:35-2, pp. 610 ff.
3. *Ibid.*, p. 619.
4. Cordier: "L'Expedition de Chine," p. 10; Morse, Vol. 1, pp. 416-7.
5. Although the incident is fully reported in the Parker Corres., the simplest account, fairly complete, is in Morse, Vol. 1, pp. 432-3.
6. Parker Corres., p. 1083.
7. S. Ex. Doc. 30:36-1, p. 4.
8. Parker Corres., pp. 1184, 1211-5.
9. *Ibid.*, p. 1211-18.
10. *Ibid.*, p. 1208.
11. *Ibid.*, p. 1246.
12. *Ibid.*, pp. 1247-9.
13. *Ibid.*, p. 1250.
14. S. Ex. Doc. 30:36-1, p. 8.

CHAPTER XVI

THE BUCHANAN ADMINISTRATION AND THE FAR EAST

INCREASE OF AMERICAN PRESTIGE UNDER PIERCE

DURING the Pierce administration American prestige in Asia had risen rapidly to a point of determining influence. Perhaps never again in the nineteenth century did the United States possess such actual and potential influence as in 1855 and 1856. Not only had the Americans opened Japan, an accomplishment which other nations had come to regard as impossible without hostilities, but the American representatives in China had the most important achievements to their credit. The British and the French had been led to relinquish their exclusive pretensions at Shanghai, the Inspectorate of Maritime Customs under foreign direction had been set up, and the possibility of intervention in favor of the Taiping rebels had been averted. All this was fully in accord with the American policy to strengthen and support the Imperial Government of China.

Closer scrutiny, however, reveals that for these accomplishments the Pierce administration could claim little or no credit. The Japan expedition had been planned, organized and set out under Fillmore. The only changes in the original plans had been the reduction in the size of the fleet to be placed under the command of Perry. Neither Pierce nor Marcy made any positive or constructive contribution to the task of opening the ports of Japan. Marshall, who was easily the outstanding figure among the American commissioners, had been an appointee of Fillmore and had been recalled by Pierce. McLane, while in general accepting and carrying out the policy of Marshall, had made one important personal contribution—the idea of the Inspectorate of

Maritime Customs—but for this the Pierce administration could claim no credit. The step was taken by McLane uninstructed from Washington. Indeed, the American position in Asia had been magnified not at all as a result of any instructions issued from the Department of State. In part it had arisen out of the peculiarities of the European diplomatic and military situation and the Crimean War. As a powerful and successful neutral in Asia the United States not only assumed but was assigned a position of great influence.

With the return of peace to Europe Great Britain set about not merely to regain the place of preeminence which had been lost in Far Eastern affairs, but also to make another advance. These efforts coincided with the entrance of the Buchanan administration into the American Government. In the next four years we shall witness the steady retirement of American influence in Asia. The causes were not simple. Domestic problems in the United States were pressing closely upon the American people and eclipsing the former interest in the Orient. Great Britain was striving to regain her former relative place in China. And of at least equal importance was the fact that the American people and the administration did not prize or appreciate the victories which had been won in the East. Little effort was made to sustain what had already been accomplished, and the ignorance, timidity, and diplomatic ineptitude of Buchanan and Cass turned what little effort was made to the disadvantage of the United States. To this sweeping statement one exception must be made. The Townsend Harris commercial treaty with Japan in 1858 became easily the most brilliant diplomatic achievement of the United States in Asia for the entire century, a feat indeed which has never since been equalled, but one has to remember that Harris had been instructed and sent to Japan under the preceding administration, and no credit whatever for his success belongs to either Buchanan or to Cass, nor in fact to any one save Harris alone.

The study of the Buchanan-Cass policy in Asia becomes

a survey of the decay of American influence. The two questions of policy of the utmost importance were bequeathed to the administration by Pierce and Marcy: the decision as to whether the United States should enter an alliance with Great Britain and France for the settlement of the Far Eastern question; and the revision of the treaty. Without attempting to point a moral or to be wiser than those whose duty it was to solve these puzzles, let us subject these propositions to close analysis.

Ebbing Distrust of Great Britain

The history of the ebbing distrust of Great Britain and the growing desire for the adoption of a cooperative policy in China presents some interesting details. A few incidents selected from the period immediately after the ratification of the Treaty of Wanghia will illustrate the strength of the existing American sentiment against England.

Shortly after the ratifications of the Treaty of Wanghia were exchanged (December 31, 1845) by Commodore James Biddle and Kiying, the latter sent a friend to confer with the American representative about the difficulties which then existed between Kiying and Sir John Francis Davis. The English plenipotentiary had demanded of the Chinese viceroy a pledge that when the English should restore the island of Chusan and Kuling-fu, then held as security for the payment of the indemnity, the Chinese should give pledge that these islands should never be ceded to any other foreign nation. Biddle advised Kiying to resist such a demand, and seized the opportunity to point out to Kiying how much better off China would be if only she would admit resident ministers to Peking. The commodore also pressed upon the high commissioner the wisdom of having China take up the study of the modern arts of war, in order that in the future she might be able to defend herself in the conflicts which Biddle plainly foresaw.

A month later Biddle wrote to Buchanan: "The refusal (of the English) to withdraw these troops from Chusan is a clear violation of the Treaty of Nanking" (February 21, 1846).[1]

At this interview with Commodore Biddle the other chief point of irritation between the English and the Chinese was discussed—the question of the right, under the British treaty, of entrance into Canton. The British demanded that the gates of the city be opened to foreigners; the Chinese absolutely refused to yield to the demand. They based their refusal on both the hostile temper of the Canton gentry and populace and on the Chinese text of the treaty, which it had been agreed was to be equally authoritative with the English text. They explained that in the Chinese text the word used with reference to the opening of the city was not the Chinese word for 'walled city' but the word which should be translated 'port' or 'mart.' The Americans acquiesced in this explanation, and although the American consul at Canton made it the subject of a formal request, he did not press the matter.* Commodore Biddle advised Kiying's emissary that he considered that they were perfectly right in refusing to yield to Great Britain † in the matter.[2]

Four months after his arrival in China Commissioner Everett reported a conversation between Dr. Parker, secretary of the Legation, and a 'high mandarin.' [4] The latter, referring to the currently reported proposal of the English to open up relations with China through Assam, had remarked that the British seemed determined to get posses-

---

* The Chinese Repository, which was edited by Rev. E. C. Bridgman and S. Wells Williams, two of the best Chinese scholars among the foreigners, stated in a review of this question of entry into Canton (May, 1849, p. 276-9) : "It is so local (this feeling about foreigners entering Canton) that the Chinese commissioners at Nanking, having never been at Canton, seem not to have given it a thought,—at least they did not agree in plain terms that the foreigners should enter its gates, or those of any other of the five ports, and nothing in the treaty, nor in those of the Bogue, Wanghai, or Whampoa, can be construed as promising it even by implication. The idea which a native would derive from reading these four treaties is that foreigners have permission to reside *at* the five ports, in the places where trade is carried on, the term *kiang kan*, or river's mouth, referring to the location on shore where traders collect from their ships to barter and exchange their goods. Such places are not necessarily walled in, nor are they called *ching*, i.e., citadels or walled cities, and resort to the former has no reference in,—certainly does not include ingress into —the latter. The phrase is varied in the Treaty of Whampoa to *kan shî-fan ti fâng*, i.e., seaport, market places, so as to restrict the residence of French citizens where trade is carried on."

† The question of entry into Canton never became an issue between the Americans and the Chinese, notwithstanding the fact that it actually precipitated hostilities between the Chinese and the English. For a review of the long negotiations over the subject see Morse.[3]

sion of China—"not perhaps immediately but at some future
time." Everett himself was so much impressed with the
truth of this view that a month later he wrote to
Buchanan: [5]

"The conviction that the British Government is determined to
get possession of their country, which, as I mentioned in a late dispatch, was expressed to a member of this legation by one of the
leading mandarins at Canton some weeks ago, has been freely avowed,
on former occasions, to Commodore Biddle. . . . It is probably universal among the educated and well informed men of the empire."

Everett then drew on his previous experience as a diplo
mat in the courts of continental Europe, and proposed that
the United States take the lead in the formation of a com
bination of Russia, France and the United States to get
England to agree to abstain from aggressions in China. No
comment on this plan was forthcoming from Washington,
and Everett died a few months later (June 28, 1847).

Dr. Peter Parker, who became *Chargé* upon the death
of Everett was so convinced of the hostile intentions of
England in the controversy over the opening of the gates of
the city of Canton that (September 25, 1847) he addressed
a confidential dispatch to Buchanan, warning him of the
'impending crisis.' He stated that it was common remark
among the American merchants that in a little while they
would be paying duties through an English customs house
at Canton. Parker thought it likely that within another
twelve or fifteen months the British would place a minister
in Peking, and demand redress for many grievances. He
strongly urged upon the American Government the necessity of taking action at once to place an American minister
in Peking 'before the dismemberment of the empire is commenced.'

The new commissioner, John W. Davis, who arrived in
August 1848, did not share at all the suspicions of his predecessors as to the intentions of England and informed the
State Department that the English did not seem disposed
to make any trouble. The following March he reported that
some of the Americans in Canton have been urging that the

United States join with Great Britain the following month in forcing the gates of the city.[6] A year later he sent a dispatch which marked the rise, by the side of the old suspicions, of a new sentiment of cooperation between the English and the Americans. He wrote: [7]

"The English Government at Hongkong has dispatched a war steamer to the mouth of the Pei-ho with a communication from the court at London to that of this country, evidently with an intention, if possible, to open up a direct intercourse with His Imperial Majesty. Had there been a suitable American vessel of war on this station, I should have taken the responsibility of suggesting to the Commander a similar project on our part, satisfied (as I stated in a former dispatch) that until our intercourse is *directly* with the Court of this country, we must always labor under great embarrassments in all diplomatic relations and correspondence."

A few weeks later Davis returned to the United States, and Dr. Parker again became *Chargé*. The following year Dr. Parker sent a confidential dispatch to Daniel Webster, who had become for the second time Secretary of State, in which he reviewed at length the political situation both as regards England and China, and stated: [8] "To prevent the necessity of any *one* of these powers adopting coercive measures, it is proposed that joint *pacific* steps be taken by *all*." Parker then outlined a plan for the powers to proceed simultaneously to Peking, and jointly to insist upon placing representatives at the capital with access to the Imperial Court—substantially the plan which was actually adopted in 1858. He reported that Dr. John Bowring, then British consul at Canton, as well as the French and Spanish representatives, were interested in the plan. Bowring is reported by Parker to have said that if England acted it would probably be a hostile action, but if the Western powers acted conjointly the action might be peaceful. The drift of public sentiment in China may thus be clearly marked. Whereas, in 1847, the American commissioner proposed a plan to block England in any aggressions she might be considering, the new plan proposed to include England in a common program for the purpose of moderating her action. The new policy was very sound.

PROPOSALS FOR AN ALLIANCE WITH GREAT BRITAIN
AND FRANCE

The sticking-point for the Americans in the matter of
cooperation with the British or any other power in Asia,
then and always, was whether the combined power thus
obtained from cooperation would be turned at some future
time to the disadvantage of legitimate American interests.
In 1847 Great Britain had made no declaration of policy
either directly or obliquely which was to the Americans in
any way reassuring. Within the next five years the situation had materially changed. The British had at Shanghai
conceded every point for which the Americans had contended, and the British Government through its representatives in Washington had made direct overtures, accompanied
by a declaration of policy, for American cooperation. Great
Britain assured the United States that while it sought the
complete opening of China to trade, it would ask for no
exclusive advantages for itself. The reason for these overtures is obvious and was well expressed by a great British
statesman. In the great debate in the House of Commons
February, 1857, on the "*Arrow* affair" and upon the character of British policy in China, as a result of which Parliament was dissolved and Palmerston went to the country for
an approval of his policies, Disraeli remarked: [9]

"Fifty years ago Lord Hastings offered to conquer China with
20,000 men. So great a captain as the Marquess of Hastings might
have succeeded; but since the time when our Clives and Hastings
founded our Indian Empire the position of affairs in the East has
greatly changed. Great Powers have been brought into contact with
us in the East: We have the Russian Empire and the American
Republic there, and a system of political compromise has developed
itself like the balance of power in Europe; and, if you are not cautious
and careful in your conduct now in dealing with China, you will
find that you are likely not to extend commerce, but to excite the
jealousy of powerful states, and to involve yourselves in hostilities
with nations not inferior to yourselves."

That Disraeli had not misread the trend of events, and
that he had not been ill advised in thus placing in associa-

tion the two names of Russia and America in Far Eastern policy is shown by the fact that in the revision of the treaties of 1858 the American and the Russian ministers sustained to each other relations which were even more intimate than those subsisting between Lord Elgin and Baron Gros, although France and England were actually allied in China. As early as 1851 the American officials in China had been directed by the State Department to extend such assistance as was possible to Russian subjects in China and the Sandwich Islands whenever it might be necessary.[10] Russia was studiously cultivating American friendship.

Great Britain could not profitably entertain the hostility of too many Powers, and it was plain that she was in the way to acquire the active opposition of the United States to whatever she might attempt in China, at the time of the revision of the treaties when she needed cooperation. On the other hand it was equally evident to the Government of the United States that cooperation rather than irritating conflicts with Great Britain were desirable in the face of the stolid opposition of China to all friendly advance from the American representatives.

Early in 1854, Commissioner McLane noted a disposition on the part of Sir John Bowring to seek the heartiest cooperation with the United States in the revision of the treaties. Bowring did not possess the confidence of the American community in China, and McLane was cautioned by Marcy, May 8, 1854, not to rely too much upon the judgment of his British colleague.[11] McLane was, however, instructed in the same letter to cooperate, which he did in the joint expedition to the Pei-ho in November, 1854.

The visit of Dr. Peter Parker, who was a most enthusiastic advocate of cooperation, to London and Paris in the latter part of 1855, has already been referred to. The failure of this effort was due to several reasons: the British were not then ready for an active movement in China; Dr. Parker did not win the confidence of Lord Clarendon; and the Pierce administration, now drawing to a close and estranged from Great Britain by the objectionable activities of the British consuls and Sir John Crampton * in securing enlistments for the Crimean War, was hardly in a mood to cooperate with England in the Far East.

Encouraged by the visit of Dr. Parker to London the preceding year, by the cordial relations between Dr. Parker and Sir John Bowring after Dr. Parker's return to China, and then by the action of Commodore Armstrong at the Barrier Forts, Lord Clarendon felt the time opportune, at the beginning of the Buchanan administration, to sound out the American Government on the subject of an actual alliance of the three treaty powers—Great Britain, France and the United States—for a revision of the treaties. Indeed, the matter seems to have been taken up in the closing days of the preceding administration by the French Minister, for before Dr. Parker's proposal for the occupation of territory was received, President Pierce was already familiar with the plan, and had verbally expressed his disapproval.

On the 14th of March, 1857, Lord Napier, the British Minister at Washington, took up with Secretary of State Cass the request that the United States would grant that "concurrent and active cooperation which the Government of France has already accorded, and that they will authorize their naval and political authorities in China to act heartily in concert with the agents of the two allied powers." [12] At the same time the British Minister explained fully to the United States the intentions of Great Britain in China, transmitting a memorandum in which were given the instructions to Sir John Bowring for the revision of the treaties, and the instructions which had been issued to the British naval forces. The plan contemplated the complete destruction of the Barrier Forts, and, if that were not sufficient, then the blockade of the Yangtze River as far as the Grand Canal, and a further blockade of the mouth of the Pei-ho. The instructions for the revision of the treaty included: residence at Peking for diplomatic representatives of Foreign Powers; extension of commercial intercourse with

---

*The preceding summer the British minister in Washington had been given his passports by Marcy for having insisted on the right to stir up sympathy in the United States for England during the Crimean War.

the coast and into the interior; abolition of transit taxes in the interior; no exclusive privileges for Great Britain. The legalization of the opium trade was not mentioned.

The negotiations at Washington continued for a month. March 30 Lord Napier forwarded to Cass a memorandum to be placed in the hands of the President. In this document the British plan for an alliance was argued under the follow ing points:

1. China will not be able to offer greater resistance than she did in the war of 1842, for since then she has been worn down by revolution and the financial resources of the empire are exhausted. On the other hand to the strength of England is now added that of France.

2. "It is best to 'abridge' the struggle as much as possible, and not to weaken more than necessary the Imperial Government."

3. "The Allied Powers have declared their objects wsich are humane, honorable, and pregnant with future benefits. They aim at no territorial extension; their moderate and solitary demands are comprised in the establishment of diplomatic relations, the enfranchisement of the trade, and the regulation of duties, the suppression of piracy, and the toleration of the Christian religion."

As the situation then stood four Powers had recognized the intercourse with China; Great Britain and France were about to make war; Russia and the United States were neutral. The Russian Minister in Washington had expressed the opinion that Russia would not oppose the Allied Powers in China, but it was the hope of Lord Napier that the United States would not be content with a position similar to that of Russia. The relations of the United States with China, he pointed out, were quite different from the relations between Russia and China.

"No country has availed itself so extensively as the United States of the increased access first opened up by England in the year 1842, and no country has so much to gain by a perfect emancipation of the trade. The amount of business transacted by the United States with China may still be inferior to that in which Great Britain is engaged, but it increases with greater rapidity, and is now unquestionably destined to exceed that of all other nations hereafter." The United States, therefore, would find it a calamity if the ports of China were blockaded for long.

While the United States did not recognize the existence of a sufficient cause for war with China, argued Lord Napier, "there is, apparently, nothing in their political constitution, nor in the relations of domestic parties, or in the general temper of the nation, which should prevent them contributing to the success of the common cause, and the consolidation of the common good by that degree of pacific and amicable concurrence which would be embodied in the following measures:

(a) Declaration of approval of the objects of the Allied Nations;

(b) Appointment of a distinguished person as Plenipotentiary who should proceed to his destination in a vessel of war befitting the dignity of his country and his mission; the envoy to be empowered to attend the movements of the ministers of Great Britain and France, and to visit London and France to secure the most recent information about China before proceeding to his post;

(c) Increase of the American squadron in the China Seas.

"The presence of an able Plenipotentiary," continued Lord Napier, "and commander with a competent force, acting even in pacific concurrence with the agents of Great Britain and France would manifest to the Chinese that our desires are identical, though our measures may be different, and that the only course left open to them is a frank and unhesitating accession to our proposals.

"Finally, it may be remarked that if the pending differences be adjusted by the combined action of the United States with England and France, the beneficial effects of such an alliance will be felt beyond the present time, and the scene on which it is first exerted. The Chinese Government will know that it had contracted weighty engagements of future good conduct towards a confederacy prepared to enforce their rights by a harmonious cooperation, and the three Powers, fortified by the prestige of unanimity and success may then point their efforts to the improvement of their relations with Japan, which has been already partly brought within the pale of European commerce by the unaided enterprise of the United States."

To this carefully worded proposal for an alliance of the three powers for the settlement of the Far Eastern question, Cass replied, April 10, 1857:

"True wisdom . . . dictates the observance of moderation and discretion in our attempts to open China to the trade and intercourse of the world. To be safe and successful the effort must be the work of time, and of those changes which time gradually brings with it."

Cass pointed out that, under the Constitution, Congress is the war-declaring power in the United States and that a military expedition into Chinese territory could not be undertaken without the consent of the national legislature. And, moreover, the relations of the United States with China did not justify war. On the other hand, the United States would heed the request for the appointment of a new plenipotentiary, but it was clearly stated that the United States would not become a party to any treaty which might be negotiated jointly by England and France with China, and that the conventional arrangements of the United States with China would be confined solely to the two latter powers.

In May, 1857, William B. Reed was appointed envoy extraordinary and minister plenipotentiary to China and charged with the duty of revising the treaty.[13] Accompanying his instructions was the Lord Napier correspondence to which his attention was especially directed:

"There seems to be an entire unanimity of sentiment and action," wrote Cass, "between Great Britain and France, extending even to armed cooperation, and you will find from the papers annexed that the United States has been invited to join the alliance and to participate in its hostile movements. The reasons of the President for declining this participation are sufficiently stated in the communication to the British minister already referred to, together with his opinions as to the extent to which the United States may fairly cooperate with the allied powers in China."

Thus ended, so far as the United States was concerned, the first efforts on the part of another power to secure an alliance for the settlement of the Far Eastern question. Thus ended also for more than forty years any consideration of the possibilities of actual hostilities between the United States and China.

The Buchanan administration, in 1857, was faced with difficult choices in the Far East as well as at home. The President could have laid before Congress the facts that China had failed to observe the stipulations of the Treaty of Wanghia (1844). He could have pointed out that the Government of China had failed to protect the lives and property of American citizens in China and that failing in that, China had evaded payment of claims for reparation. Diplomatic correspondence had been impeded, interviews with the Imperial Commissioner at Canton, and with the Governor General at Foochow had been repelled, and a letter of President Pierce to the Emperor of China had been treated with indignity, having been returned to the commissioner without answer, and with broken seals. On the basis of these facts President Buchanan might have asked Congress to authorize a military and naval expedition to China to demand repara-

tions. Had Congress yielded to this request he might have
sought its further approval for the joint expedition with
Great Britain and France. Two American commissioners in
China had recommended such a course. Lord Napier urged
it. The American residents in China, for the most part,
would have approved. But to neither of these propositions
was it even remotely possible that Congress would have
given its assent. Public opinion would have seen in them
only a trick by which England was seeking the aid of the
United States in her efforts to secure the legalization of the
opium trade.

On the other hand, the Government of the United
States could have ignored the causes for war, which upon
examination proved to be very slight, and could have con-
tinned a policy of conciliation, waiting for time to do its
work in softening the prejudices of the Chinese and leading
them to see the advantages to them of the fullest possible
harmony and cooperation with the United States. Such a
policy, within a few years, would doubtless have met with
some success. However, one large factor in such a success
would have been the chastisement which Great Britain had
already determined to administer to China.

There had been even a third honest course open to the
United States. It could have said to Great Britain and
France that while in the approaching crisis the United
States would remain neutral, it would instruct its diplomatic
officers in China to abstain from pressing any claims on
China for the revision of the treaty, and would practically
withdraw from the open ports while the allied powers had a
free hand. This course would have been exceedingly unsatisfactory to Great Britain whose good will the United States
was then seeking to cultivate. England already felt that in
the war of 1839-42 she had really been fighting the battle of
American as well as British merchants, and that the time
had come for the United States to share some of the burdens
incident to the advantages its citizens in China enjoyed. In
the United States also there would have been an objection to
such a policy, for still in the opinion of many Great Britain

could not be trusted in China and required a great deal of watching.

The policy actually adopted represented a compromise at every point and assigned to the United States an ignominious rôle. President Buchanan rejected the proposal of war with China, but he yielded to Lord Clarendon and Lord Napier in that he agreed to dispatch to China a plenipotentiary to be present during the hostilities, with instructions to press the American claims for reparations and a revision of the treaty at any opportune time.

There is reason to believe that this decision was satisfactory to Great Britain. It involved the assent of the United States to the plan of chastisement and thus forestalled any opposition, such as Humphrey Marshall had made in 1853, to the English program of operations. While it placed upon Great Britain a burden of expense which it would have been glad to share, yet it removed from the arena a power with which England would otherwise have had to share the certain prestige of victory. In 1858 Great Britain was preparing not merely to open up China to the trade of the world, but also to 'claim her place of priority in the East,' [14] and there were few regrets that the United States was unprepared to assert a similar claim. Meanwhile an American envoy extraordinary and minister plenipotentiary was to be dispatched to the other side of the world to stand under the tree, with his basket, waiting for his associates above to shake down the fruit, and he was even instructed to offer mediation in case those in the tree became involved with the owners of the orchard. Surely a representative of the United States never played a more inglorious rôle in international affairs.

INSTRUCTIONS TO WILLIAM B. REED

As long as such a policy was to be pursued it would have been wise to select an experienced diplomat, but instead President Buchanan appointed his friend William B. Reed of Pennsylvania. Reed's diplomatic experience had been

confined to a brief period when at the age of twenty he
served as private secretary to Joel R. Poinsett, U. S. minister in Mexico (1825-7). He was a lawyer by profession and
and had been active in state politics, having been a member
of the legislature and attorney general. For the six years
previous to his departure for China he had been professor
of American history in the University of Pennsylvania.[15]
Mr. Reed's instructions from Lewis Cass were: [16]

1. Communicate freely with the British and French ministers
and make known to the Chinese that the President believes that the
objects of the Allied Powers are "just and expedient." Confine yourself to firm representations to the Chinese, bearing in mind that the
Government of the United States is not at war with China, and
leaving to the government to determine what shall be the next step in
case your representations are fruitless.

2. Have the same friendly relations with the envoy of Russia as
with those of France and England. Enlist his support for your
representations to the Chinese Government. "There is nothing in the
policy of the United States with respect to China which is not quite
consistent with the pacific relations which are understood to exist
between that empire and Russia."

3. Make clear to the Chinese authorities that the United States
seeks only the enlargement of opportunities for trade, and that it
desires neither territory nor to interfere in China's domestic affairs.

4. The United States does not seek the legalization of the opium
trade, and will not uphold its citizens in any efforts they make to
introduce the drug into the country.

5. Secure the establishment of some basis of exchange which
will provide for the recognition of the legal currency of the United
States at its true value when offered in payment for goods.

6. Secure the enforcement of the existing treaty in the matter of
the satisfaction of claims, the right of protection for the life and
property of American citizens, and obtain modifications which will
permit to Americans the right of residence in the open ports without
interference.

7. It was also intimated that Mr. Reed might assume the rôle
of mediator. "It is possible even that it [Reed's neutral position]
may be employed with advantage as a means of communication between the belligerent parties, and tend in this way to the termination
of the war."

BIBLIOGRAPHICAL NOTES

1. China Desp. Vol. 3 (Dept. of State).
2. *Ibid.*, Jan. 8, 1846.
3. Morse, Vol. 1, pp. 377-80.
4. China. Desp. Vol. 3, Feb. 28, 1847.
5. *Ibid.*, Apr. 10, 1847.

6. China Desp. Vol. 5, Mar. 26, 1849.
7. China. Desp. April 22, 1850.
8. China Desp. Vol. 6, Apr. 22, 1851.
9. Hansard, Series 3, Vol. CXLIV, Feb. 3, 1857-Mar. 21, 1857, p. 1836.
10. China Instructions, Vol. 1, June 21, 1851.
11. *Ibid.,* May 8, 1854.
12. Notes from the British Legation, Vol. 34, Napier to Cass, Mar. 14, 30, 1857 (Dept of State).
13. S. Ex. Doc. 30:36-1.
14. Walrond's Letters and Journals of James, Eighth Earl of Elgin, p. 253; see also pp. 207 and 209 for similar clues to the policy adopted by Lord Elgin in China.
15. Twentieth Century Bibliographical Dictionary of Notable Americans.
16. Reed Corres., S. Ex. Doc. 30:36-1, p. 68.

PART IV

THE COOPERATIVE POLICY

CHAPTER XVII

WILLIAM B. REED AND THE TREATY OF TIENTSIN

WILLIAM B. REED, the first American Minister Plenipotentiary to China, arrived at Hongkong in November, 1857, and six months later reached the mouth of the Pei-ho in company with Count Putiatin, Baron Gros and Lord Elgin, the Russian, French and British envoys respectively. Elgin and Gros had been instructed to demand full reparations for insults and injuries including particularly the hauling down of the British flag on the lorcha *Arrow*, a vessel which had been engaged in opium smuggling, and the murder of Abbé Chapedelaine, a French Roman Catholic missionary in Kwangsi, and also to secure a full revision of the treaties. They had been accompanied to China by formidable fleets of war vessels and transports and were fully prepared for hostilities. The American envoy was instructed to secure "modifications" of the Cushing treaty, and Putiàtin was seeking an entirely new convention which would admit Russia to the sea-borne trade of China on the same terms as those enjoyed by the other treaty powers.[1]

The events from the arrival of Reed to the beginning of negotiations at the Pei-ho must be summarized briefly. Commissioner Yeh at Canton refused to see Reed and asserted that a revision of the treaty was unnecessary. Meeting with similar treatment, Lord Elgin and Baron Gros turned matters over to the allied naval authorities and the bombardment of Canton began December 28. A week later the city was invaded and occupied. Yeh was made prisoner and subsequently transported to Calcutta where he died. The British and French troops remained in occupation of Canton while the allied envoys, preceded by Reed and

Putiatin, advanced to Shanghai. Notwithstanding some misunderstandings with Lord Elgin who from the outset assumed complete leadership of the allied expedition, Reed worked in cooperation with the allied envoys. He addressed a separate yet practically simultaneous note with the others to Peking demanding a revision of the treaties and approving the demands of the British and French. Notwithstanding this effort to cooperate, Mr. Reed was subjected to the most pusillanimous abuse by the *Times* correspondent who accompanied Lord Elgin,[2] and was made to feel that the only cooperation really desired was one in which Lord Elgin would dictate the movements and policy of the combined missions.[3] The American envoy had been assigned to an impossible rôle. At Shanghai he received additional instructions from Secretary of State Cass, again cautioning him to limit his cooperation to purely peaceful measures. The coldness of Lord Elgin and the cordiality of Count Putiatin tended more and more to separate the four envoys into pairs, and the increasing intimacy of Reed with the Russians became an additional annoyance to the British. At the Pei-ho Reed determined to adopt an independent course of action. It may be gravely questioned whether it was not a fundamental error of policy for the Americans to be pres ent at what was evidently intended to be a hostile demon stration, but being there, no other than an independent course of action was consistent with Reed's instructions, or with his self-respect.

Reed and Putiatin began negotiations with Tan, an Imperial Commissioner with limited powers, early in May. Elgin and Gros refused to meet Tan on the ground that his powers were too limited. Tan reported that the Emperor would concede the opening of seven new ports, five on the coast and two in Formosa, the absolute toleration of Christianity, a modification of the tonnage dues to the advantage of American bottoms, and an inclusive most-favored-nation clause. The opening of the rivers to trade and the right of either occasional or permanent diplomatic residence at Peking were absolutely refused.[4]

Against the advice of Lord Elgin and Baron Gros, Mr. Reed decided to continue the conferences with the Chinese officials, although it was definitely known that the refusal of the Emperor to consent to diplomatic residence at or visits to the capital, and the refusal to open up the rivers, left the allied envoys no alternative but to proceed up the river, using whatever force might be required. On the 19th of May S. Wells Williams and W. A. P. Martin were in the midst of a conference with some of the subordinate officers of the Imperial Commission where articles of the treaty were being drafted when a note from Mr. Reed warned them that the allied powers were to bombard the forts the following day. The American minister instructed them to discontinue the conference.

Promptly at ten o'clock, May 20, the allies attacked the Taku forts which offered only a feeble resistance. Having taken possession of the forts within two hours, the allied forces moved on up the river.

Mr. Reed's intention to withdraw from the scene of brief conflict was not carried out. Indeed, a large number of officers from the squadron which was compelled to lay at anchorage well off shore came inside the river to the *Antelope,* a small steamer which had been chartered at Shanghai and attached to the squadron for service in shallow water, to view the attack. Hardly was the struggle over when Dr. Williams received a note from one of the attachés of the Chinese Commission expressing the hope that the Americans would not withdraw. And the next day Count Putiatin and Mr. Reed received a formal request urging them to remain and follow the allied envoys up to Tientsin. Lord Elgin also urged that the neutral envoys continue their cooperation as far as possible. On the 29th of May Lord Elgin and Baron Gros proceeded up the river in a British vessel flying both the British and the French flags, and shortly after Count Putiatin and Mr. Reed followed in the Russian steamer *Amerika,* which flew both the Russian and the American ensigns. At Tientsin the allied plenipotentiaries took up residence in a large temple, while the neutral envoys found less commodious but more comfortable quarters together in a private residence.

This advance of the allied and neutral plenipotentiaries to a point half way between the mouth of the Pei-ho and Peking had an immediate effect on the Imperial Court. Two commissioners, Kweiliang, a cabinet minister, and Hwashana, president of the Board of Civil Office, with powers which were practically unlimited, were at once appointed to proceed to Tientsin. Lord Elgin met them for an interview on June 4th, Baron Gros the following day, and Mr. Reed on the 7th. The negotiations were carried forward with rapidity, under the steady pressure of the allied powers. The Russian treaty was signed on the 13th, the American on the 18th, the British on the 26th, and the French the next day. Before the end of the first week in July the foreigners had retired from Tientsin and returned to Shanghai.

THE TREATIES OF TIENTSIN

The negotiations of Mr. Reed when compared either with those of Caleb Cushing at Macao in 1844 or with those of Lord Elgin, were quite without distinction. The resulting treaty lacked both in detail and in thoroughness what were outstanding characteristics of the Treaty of Wanghia and also of the British treaty of Tientsin. Just as the acknowledged superiority of the Cushing treaty had made it the basis of China's foreign relations between 1844 and 1858, so the Elgin treaty became the basis of the international relations of the Chinese Empire for the future. The priority of Great Britain among the powers represented in China was established. The conspicuous mark of the Reed treaty was an exceedingly inclusive most-favored-nation provision which made the citizens of the United States the inheritors of all that had been won by allied arms, diplomacy, and a most careful study of the situation.

Mr. Reed at Tientsin had three tasks before him: the revision of the treaty; the fixing of the new tariff; and the settlement of American claims. These tasks were made the subjects of separate negotiations, and were settled in separate agreements. They therefore became the natural divisions of our study. First let us consider the more important settlements of the treaties themselves.

There had been an entire unanimity among the powers that first in importance was the establishment of diplomatic representatives of the foreign powers at Peking with the privilege of corresponding with the Imperial Government on terms of perfect equality. There was little hope of removing the causes of misunderstanding and irritation between the Imperial Government and the foreign powers so long as the diplomatic representatives of the powers were held at arm's length and treated as inferiors. The system which made the governor general of Canton the foreign minister of China seemed wholly wrong.

With the resumption of the negotiations at Tientsin, Mr. Reed assumed towards the new commissioners Kweiliang and Hwashana a more decided and positive tone, warning them that the United States which had persisted in a peaceful policy towards China would not be satisfied in the final settlement with any terms which discriminated against the Americans. The Chinese, on the other side, were convinced of the necessity of a conciliatory policy. Although still absolutely refusing to concede the right of residence in Peking, they agreed to a compromise which was written into the American treaty (Articles 4 and 5) to the effect that the highest diplomatic representative of the United States would not only have the right to correspond under seal with the Privy Council in Peking, but that whenever business required he would have the right of visit and sojourn in the capital. By the Chinese this was regarded as a great concession, and to Mr. Reed it seemed satisfactory. With him agreed Count Putiatin and Baron Gros into whose treaties, respectively, similar provisions were incorporated. These stipulations were fortified by a further agreement that if at any time another power secured the full rights of residence at Peking, the same privilege would inure to the United States.

The fundamental objection of the Chinese to admitting the foreign ministers to Peking appears to have been that it would result in a loss of prestige to the Emperor—a most serious matter at a time when the Empire was torn by ominous rebellion. Hitherto only tribute-bearing envoys had been admitted to Peking and their visits had been arranged in such a way as to indicate to the Chinese people the manifest of supremacy of their emperor over all the nations. There may also have been some fear of the English, that their entrance into Peking might result even in the overthrow of the empire itself.[5]

Lord Elgin, however, was insistent upon the stipulation for diplomatic residence at Peking, regarding it as 'far the most important matter gained by the treaty,' and even at the last moment he was prepared to insist upon it, though another show of military strength might be required to force the assent of the Emperor.[6] In the British treaty it was stipulated (Article 3) that "the Ambassador, Minister, or other Diplomatic Agent, so appointed by Her Majesty the Queen of Great Britain, may reside with his family and establishment, permanently at the capital, or may visit it occasionally, at the option of the British Government."

The other point upon which Mr. Reed at Taku had met with the firm resistance of the Imperial Government, was the free navigation of the rivers, especially the Yangtze. The demand for this concession from China had been peculiarly an American one. It had first been proposed by Humphrey Marshall in 1853, and had been in the *projet* submitted to Tsung Lun at the Pei-ho in 1854 by Robert M. McLane. Dr. Parker also had been instructed to ask for it in 1856. On the other hand, both the British and the French had been more cautious on this point. Count Walewski, Minister of Foreign Affairs, May 19, 1856, had felt that the proposed demands of Dr. Parker were probably more than the Chinese would grant and nearly a year earlier had expressed the opinion that the opening of the Yangtze even as far as Nanking might prove sufficient. In similar tone the instruction to Sir John Bowring in 1854 had only called for the opening of the Yangtze as far as Nanking.[7] Upon this question of the opening of the rivers of China to navigation by foreign vessels there was also a difference of opinion in China. S. Wells Williams wrote: [8]

"I have no doubt, the more I see the entire bearing of the demand, that the Chinese may just about as well abdicate their independence as allow the free navigation of the Yangtze River. If they could be induced to encourage their own people to buy and run foreign steamers and schooners, the desired advantages would be gained without forcing this wrong upon them. They will have to yield, I suppose, and with the liberty let go for ever the integrity of their own territory to the lust of gain and power on the part of those who ought to consider something of the results of their policy."

Mr. Rutherford Alcock, the British consul at Shanghai, in a memorandum to Lord Elgin, expressed a similar opinion: [9]

" 'The worthless character of a numerous gathering of foreigners of all nations, under no effective control, is a public calamity. They dispute the field of commerce with honester men, and convert privileges of access and trade into means of fraud and violence. In this career of license, unchecked by any fear of their own governments, and protected in a great degree by treaties, from the action of the native authorities, the Chinese are the first and greatest, but by no means the only sufferers. There is no government or nation of the great European family that does not suffer in character, and in so far as they have any interests at stake in China, in these also both immediately and prospectively. This is the danger which has long threatened the worst consequence in widespread hostility and interrupted trade.' Access to the inner waters will increase the evil to an enormous extent."

Mr. Reed came rapidly to see the force of these arguments and did not press the matter in the renewed negotiations at Tientsin. In explaining his action to Cass, after reviewing the arguments already mentioned, he added: [10]

"Besides, I could not but feel that their assertion of a right of absolute sovereignty over the rivers was one that I, least of all, had a right to question; and whilst I might wish to see them, as a matter of mere commercial interest, allow the foreigner to go and trade up their rivers at pleasure, yet they had a perfect right to refuse.

In this, as in the matter of residence at Peking, Lord Elgin was determined. Almost at the last minute before signing the British treaty the Chinese Commissioners received from Peking a refusal to grant the right of residence and the expression of a desire, on the part of the Emperor, to defer the question of the navigation of the Yangtze until the rebellion had been suppressed. Kweiliang and Hwashana feared that their own lives might be the forfeit if they were to sign away these concessions to Great Britain, and they asked Count Putiatin and Mr. Reed to take to Lord Elgin a statement of the case, and to urge him to recede from his demands.* The French treaty already drafted and approved, though not signed, had not included such an unlimited concession [11] The two neutral envoys, therefore, took the matter up with Baron Gros and he ventured to approach Lord Elgin on the subject, yet with no success. Lord Elgin himself, in a letter to his family, records his answer to Baron Gros's intervention: [12]

"I sent for the Admiral; gave him a hint that there was a great opportunity for England; that all the Powers were deserting me on a point which they had *all*, in their original applications to Peking, demanded, and which they all intended to claim if I got it; that therefore we had it in our power to claim our place of priority in the East, by obtaining this when others would not insist on it. Would he back me? . . . This was the forenoon of Saturday, 26th. The treaty was signed in the evening."

"The British treaty stipulated, Article 10, that as soon as peace had been restored in the rebellious territory, British vessels should be admitted to the Yangtze as far as Hankow, and that the port of Chingkiang, even then held by the Imperial Government, should in any event be opened at the end of a year from the signing of the treaty. The French treaty called for the opening of Nanking as soon as it should be recaptured from the rebels.[13]

Closely associated with the opening of the Yangtze was access to the interior of the Empire. In the earlier negotiations for the revision of the treaties, in 1854 and 1856, the American representatives had proposed the unlimited opening of the Empire. The objections to this

*S. Wells Williams states that the Imperial Commissioners were told that it would be worse than useless for Putiatin and Reed to interfere in their dealings with Lord Elgin.

were similar to those against the opening of the rivers to navigation, and in the American treaty of Tientsin there is no reference to it. In view of earlier American demands, Mr. Reed's comments on provisions in the British and French treaties for travel in the interior are interesting. He wrote: [14]

'This [access to the interior] is provided for in both the English and French treaties, and, of course, with its limitations, inures to us. The provision of the former treaty is very comprehensive for, with the limitation of requiring a passport, the form of which the consuls and not the Chinese are to determine, any foreigner may go anywhere in China 'for pleasure, *or for purposes of trade,* and may hire vessels for the carriage of his baggage or *merchandise.*" No routes are specified; no limit to the character or amount of merchandise which may be taken into the interior, and there is nothing to prevent a foreigner —Englishman, Frenchman, Russian, or American—from unloading his ship load of cottons or, if he happen to be unscrupulous, of opium, at Shanghai, or ——, when it shall be opened, and carrying it in one or a fleet of junks, or small craft steamers, to the frontiers of Thibet, or by the grand canal to Tientsin and Peking, or in short, any where, selling it as he goes along. But this is not all. He carries with him his 'extraterritoriality'; for the article which provides for his transit in the interior also provides for his immunity. 'If,' says the British treaty, 'he shall commit any offense against the law, he shall be handed over to the nearest consul for punishment, but he must not be subjected to ill-usage in excess of necessary restraint.' This rendered into plain language means that the foreigner who commits a rape or murder a thousand miles from the sea-board is to be gently restrained, and remitted to a consul for trial, necessarily at a remote point where testimony could hardly be obtained or relied on. These are the abuses and dangers which this new system of unlimited intercourse seems to foreshadow. . . ."

Upon the subject of extraterritoriality Mr. Reed entertained very strong convictions. He did not deny the necessity for such concessions as had been obtained by Sir Henry Pottinger in 1842 and by Caleb Cushing in 1844, but he found the American abuse of the privileges had been wholly disgraceful. He wrote: [15]

". . . no greater wrong could be done to a weak nation, no clearer violation of the letter and spirit of a treaty, than claiming exemption from the local law for our citizens who commit crime, and then failing to punish them ourselves. We extort from China 'extraterritoriality,' the amenability of guilty Americans to our law, and then we deny to our judicial officers the means of punishing them. There are consular courts in China to try American thieves and burglars and murderers, but there is not a single jail where the thief or burglar may be confined. Our consuls in this, as in many other particulars, have to appeal to the English or French liberality, and it often happens that the penitentiary accommodations of England and France are inadequate to their own necessities, and the American culprit is discharged. Hence it follows that many claim the privilege of American citizenship, in order to have the benefit of this immunity, and every vagabond Englishman, Irishman, or Scotchman, any one who, speaking our language, can make out a *prima facie* claim to citizenship, commits crime according to his inclination, secure that if he is tried in the American courts there is no power of punishment. . . .

"I consider the exaction of 'ex-territoriality' from the Chinese, so long as the United States refuse or neglect to provide the means of punishment, an opprobrium of the worst kind. It is as bad as the coolie or opium trade. Were it not that I have strong confidence that when this matter is fully understood Congress will apply the remedy, I should be ashamed to put my name to a treaty which asserts this boasted privilege of 'ex-territoriality.'"

In the revision of the articles of the treaty bearing on extraterritoriality Mr. Reed inserted an additional provision, as a protection to China, by which it became lawful for Chinese as well as American officers to arrest an American citizen, but this slight alteration in the treaty could, by itself, do little to redeem the American name from the disgrace into which it had fallen in the preceding decade.

At Taku the Chinese Commissioners had agreed to the opening of seven new ports: Tai-wan and Tam-sui in Formosa; Hai-kau on the island of Hainan; and on the mainland, Tienpeh and Swatow in Kwang-tung, Tsienchow in Fukien, and Wanchow in Chekiang.[16] At Tientsin, however, Kweiliang and Hwashana, for some unexplained reason, receded from the previous liberality and would allow Mr. Reed only two ports, the same to be chosen from those already mentioned at Taku. Accordingly, in the American treaty, the only additional ports opened were Swatow and Tai-wan. Lord Elgin, who proposed to do nothing by halves, although for some strange reason he omitted Tientsin from his list, secured the opening of no less than eleven new ports. Two of these, Tang-chow and Newchwang, afforded outlets for Shantung and Manchuria, opening up a trade along the coast northwards, fifteen hundred miles above Shanghai. Incorporated also in the British treaty were reduction of tonnage dues, and rights of exportation which, in Mr. Reed's judgment, would be likely to transfer most of the coasting trade of China from native to foreign vessels, which were already being preferred on account of their speed, safety from pirates, insurability and cheapness. Mr. Reed also believed that by these regulations the small American vessels on the coast would have an advantage over all others. In these expectations his hopes were largely realized. China was compelled to surrender not only her rights to the exclusive navigation of her rivers, but also to open her coasting trade—privileges which the United States had been accustomed to guard most jealously.

The nearest claim to distinction for the American treaty, unless it be a distinction to have abstained from demanding the above mentioned privileges of the British treaty, lay in the article granting religious toleration, which will be dealt with in a subsequent chapter.

A clause in Article 1 of the American treaty stipulated: "if any other nation should act unjustly or oppressively, the United States will exert their good offices, on being informed of the case, to bring about an amicable arrangement of the question, thus showing their friendly feelings." This became the subject of much ironical comment, which, had the clause been inserted by the Americans, would have been quite justified when one considers the circumstances under which the treaty was signed. But this clause was added to the text by one of the assistants of Kweiliang and Hwashana.[17] Such action on the part of the Chinese must not, however, be taken for more than it was worth. Although it had been a cardinal point in American policy since the days of Caleb Cushing's negotiations at Macao and before, to win just such confidence from China as this clause would seem to indicate, it actually meant in 1858 little more than that the shrewd Chinese diplomat was seeking to pay a compliment to the United States and possibly isolate them from the European powers. A few months later Mr. Williams, then acting as *Chargé,* wrote to Mr. Cass: [18]

"It is quite a mistake to suppose that the rulers of China have any *regard* for one nation more than another; that they are more friendly, for instance, towards the Americans than towards the English; they may, perhaps, *fear* the English and Russians more than they do the Americans, but they would be glad if none of them ever came near them."

It cannot be denied, however, that the American treaty of Tientsin did lay the basis for the friendship between China and the United States which grew rapidly in the next decade. Yet from the smashing blow which had been dealt to China in the British treaty of 1858 no friend could rescue her. Even had she chosen to make a friend of the United States fourteen years earlier, there was little that could have been done to save her. The Empire had brought the calamity upon itself. China has ever been the despair of her friends. This fact, however, mitigates the responsibility neither of Great Britain which had acted with so little regard for the evil consequences of such an opening up of the Empire, nor of the United States which sent an envoy to play the part of Saul holding the coats of those who committed the assault. That China in later years received benefits from the breaking down of her walls of pride and exclusion is undeniable, but it is equally undeniable that much of the evil that followed in its train might have been avoided had Lord Elgin been less possessed of the determination to chastise an ancient Empire and to establish once for all the priority of Great Britain in the Far East.

THE REVISED TARIFF—LEGALIZATION OF THE OPIUM TRADE

In the American Treaty of Tientsin it was agreed that the tariff annexed to the Treaty of Wanghia was to continue "except so far as it may be modified by treaties with other nations; it being expressly stipulated that citizens of the United States shall never pay higher duties than those paid by the most favored nation" (Article 15). In the treaty with Russia the tariff question was covered merely by the insertion of a most-favored-nation agreement. To the French treaty there had been annexed as a provisional tariff a schedule similar to the one adopted in the French Treaty of Whampoa (1844), with the understanding that it would be replaced by a new tariff to be determined subsequently at Shanghai. Lord Elgin was much more specific. In the British treaty (Article 26) it was stipulated that the Emperor was to delegate a high officer of the board of revenue to meet representatives of the British Government at Shanghai for the purpose of revising the tariff with a view to bringing it into harmony with a five per cent *ad valorem* rate.*

The British treaty also included an agreement (Article 28) for the regulation of transit dues—a vexed question which had caused a great deal of irritation to merchants of all nations, especially since the outbreak of the Taiping rebellion when local governments were greatly in need of additional revenues. Mr. Reed had felt that it was impossible to regulate the transit dues by treaty,[19] but Lord Elgin was not so easily satisfied. He secured an agreement that in no case were these dues to exceed two and one half per cent *ad valorem,* and that British merchants should have the right to pay in one sum the entire transit taxes for goods consigned inland (Article 28). To have enforced this article China would have been compelled to reorganize the entire fiscal system of the Empire. In practice the stipulation was the source of perennial irritation.

The Emperor appointed Kweiliang and Hwashana who had negotiated the treaties of Tientsin to represent China in the tariff revision conferences, but the actual work was done by secretaries and subordinates who conferred with Mr. Thomas Wade, representing Great Britain, and Dr. S. Wells Williams who, at the invitation of Lord Elgin, was delegated to represent the United States informally. Mr. H. N. Lay, formerly of the British consular service and now of the Foreign Board of Inspectorate of Customs at Shanghai, was also a member of the conference.

*The tariff of 1843, while imposing specific duties, had aimed to establish approximately a five per cent *ad valorem* rate. Since the fixing of that schedule the prices of various articles in China had, for the most part, fallen, so that in 1858 many of the specific duties were actually more than five per cent reckoned on an *ad valorem* basis.

Although Mr. Reed shifted entirely to Lord Elgin the responsibility for the revision of the tariff and for fixing the specific rates for the transit tax, and avoided becoming a party to the negotiations between Lord Elgin and the two Chinese Commissioners, he thought it well to include the tariff, when it was completed, in the form of a 'supplementary convention' which had the force of a treaty. To this proposal the Chinese assented.[20]   The general tendency of the new tariff was slightly to reduce the duties which had previously been in force, and the details are relatively unimportant.   More important than the tariff itself was the provision made for the reorganization of the Foreign Inspectorate of Chinese Customs, and the extension of the system, which had hitherto been operative only at Shanghai, to the other open ports.   Many American merchants strongly objected to the system for no very apparent reason other than that it was effective and reduced the possibilities of smuggling, but Mr. Reed, after careful investigation, gave his cordial assent to its extension.

The revised tariff was most notable in that it provided for what had so long been desired by Great Britain and by the foreigners generally in China—the legalization of the opium trade.   The part played by the American envoy in effecting this legalization requires attention.   The instructions received by Mr. Reed from Secretary of State Cass on the subject of the opium trade, while more vague were broadly similar to those which had been given to‘ Caleb Cushing by Webster.[21]

"Upon proper occasions you will make known to the Chinese officers with whom you may have communication that the Government of the United States does not seek for their citizens the legal establishment of the opium trade, nor will it uphold them in any attempt to violate the laws of China by the introduction of that article into the country."

In the first draft of the proposed treaty presented at Taku there was inserted an article 'denouncing and forbidding' the opium trade by American citizens,[22] but at Tientsin this article was withdrawn and in the treaty as signed there was no reference to opium.* Lord Elgin, although he had been definitely instructed to secure the legalization of the trade, had abstained from inserting any reference to it in the text of the treaty. Until the revision of the tariff, therefore, the status of the opium trade remained as it had been since the treaties of 1842-4. But in the revised tariff the trade in opium was legalized by the following rule:

"Opium will henceforth pay thirty taels per picul Import Duty. The importer will sell it only at the port. It will be carried into the interior by Chinese only, and only as Chinese property; the foreign trader will not be allowed to accompany it. The provisions of Article 9 of the Treaty of Tientsin, by which British subjects are authorized to proceed into the interior with passports to trade, will not extend to it, nor will those of Article 28 of the same Treaty, by which the Transit Dues are regulated. The Transit Dues on it will be arranged as the Chinese Government see fit; nor in future revisions of the Tariff is the same rule of revision to be applied to Opium as to other goods."

While Mr. Reed could not be held wholly accountable for the insertion of the above rule, he not only approved of it but even initiated the correspondence with Lord Elgin in which he recommended the legalization of the traffic, thus reversing himself and in a measure violating the instructions of his government. His reasons were that between two evils —the legalization of the trade, and the existing open defiance of the Cushing treaty in which Americans were dealing in the drug at every port and carrying it along the coast under the American flag—legalization of the trade with heavy duties and the exclusion of foreigners from the transportation and sale of the drug in the interior was preferable. It was Mr. Reed's idea that the Chinese would, under the proposed regulation, be better able than formerly to restrict the importation by fixing a high tariff and by the control of their own merchants. The American Commissioner was debating, as related to a drug, the old and also modern question of the relative merits of ineffective prohibition as compared with high license and regulation. If Mr. Reed

*In the Treaty of Wanghia trading in opium had been prohibited to American citizens, and in the annexed tariff opium had been included in the list of contraband articles.

was on the wrong side of the argument there is no reason whatever to suppose that his error was any other than that of judgment, and with him stood many foreigners of long experience in China who could be charged with no friendliness towards the opium trade. Dr. Williams in a letter to his wife said: [23]

"By this tariff you will perhaps be surprised to learn that opium is legalized and·pays thirty taels per picul as import duty. The Chinese Government has yielded in its long resistance to permitting this drug to be entered through the customs house, the opium war of 1840 ending in the Treaty of Nanking has triumphed, and the honorable English merchants and government can now exonerate themselves from the opprobrium of smuggling this article. Bad as the triumph is, I am convinced that it is the best disposition of this perplexing question; legalization is preferred to the evils attending the farce now played, and throwing ridicule on the laws against it by sending the revenue boats to the opium hulks to receive a duty or bribe from the purchaser."

Although the full correspondence of Mr. Reed with reference to the legalization of the opium trade was not only reported at the State Department but also published in 1860, the action of the American plenipotentiary seems to have aroused no general adverse comment in the United States.

SETTLEMENT OF CLAIMS

Of the two primary reasons which dispatched Mr. Reed to China in 1857, the revision of the treaty and the settlement of claims due to American citizens, the latter was the more easily to be defended, and the settlement obtained presented the brighter page in the history of the relations between the United States and China.

The first official settlement of the claims of American citizens against the Government of China was secured by Commodore Lawrence Kearny in the winter of 1842-3, and amounted to about a quarter of a million dollars.[24] These claims had arisen out of injuries suffered by Americans at the time of hostilities between the English and the Chinese in the first Anglo-Chinese War, and also from the depredations of a mob at Canton in 1842. Commodore Kearny made a peremptory demand for the payment of the losses, and the demand was complied with. There was no examination of the claims with a view to the determination of their value.

Shortly after the exchange of ratifications of the Treaty of Wanghia, a mob attacked and pillaged the house of the Rev. Issachar J. Roberts, a missionary who subsequently became associated with the Taiping rebellion. The claim presented by Roberts was regarded as excessive, and an award was made by a joint commission composed of Americans and Chinese. The Imperial High Commissioner, however, was unwilling to settle. Commissioner John W. Davis in 1848 again presented the claim to the Viceroy who again refused to pay. Davis then referred the matter to Washington with a request for instructions. The Department of State was somewhat in doubt as to the strength of the Roberts claim, and instructed Commissioner Humphrey Marshall to investigate and report as to whether it and two others were "of such a character as to warrant the official interposition of the government." [25] Marshall was of the opinion that the claim ought to be enforced, and reported that to enforce it he was prepared to blockade the port of Canton, if necessary, "in fine, to collect the money by any means short of war," [26] but nothing was done. Withholding payment for duties was strongly urged by Commissioner Robert L. McLane, as the most effective method for securing the payment of the claims which, while still not large, had greatly increased by the end of 1854.[27] In case the Chinese should attempt to retaliate by threatening to stop the trade as they had in the old pre-treaty days, he recommended that the naval forces of the United States should be used to support the action of the commissioner. This method of coercing the Chinese authorities was used in several in stances by the various consuls without authority from the commissioner. In January, 1856, the consul at Shanghai reported that he had collected a claim of $18,000 by stopping intercourse with the taotai for two weeks.[28] At about the same time the American consuls at Amoy and Shanghai threatened to use similar measures either to collect claims or to secure the attention of the Chinese authorities, but this method was promptly frowned on by the Government of the United States, and Dr. Parker was instructed to forego such belligerent methods.[29]   The consuls were reluctant to surrender such an effective weapon and the unauthorized action of the American consul at Foochow in 1857 in withholding duties.almost resulted in the declaration of Foochow as a free port.[30]   As the time for the revision of the treaty drew near, the instructions from Washington were that the settlement of claims must not be pushed to a point with the Chinese authorities which would jeopardize the revision of the treaty.

A third possible method for the settlement of claims was outlined by Dr. Peter Parker in a confidential communication to Sir John Bowring at the end of December, 1856.[31] With reference to the losses which had been suffered by the Americans in the British attack on Canton in the preceding month, Dr. Parker proposed that the British Government should assume these claims and collect them from the Government of China along with those of their own citizens. This proposal to have the British Government collect American claims was promptly repudiated by Lewis Cass, Secretary of State, in his instructions to Mr. Reed.[32]

At the time of the negotiations for the revision of the treaty Mr. Reed found the Chinese authorities at first quite unwilling to admit the validity of the claims of Americans for losses suffered during the existing war.   They implied that for these losses the English were responsible and that Great Britain rather than China ought to make the reparations.[33]   Subsequently the Chinese authorities sought to place the responsibility entirely upon the local authorities where the losses had occurred.   This was in accordance with Chinese law, or custom, for the central government did not usually assume such responsibility for local affairs.   If the local Chinese officials had done wrong, they argued, then they ought to make reparations out of the local revenues.[34] Mr. Reed yielded to Kweiliang and Hwashana on this point, and the Treaty of Tientsin was signed without any settlement of the claims.

Immediately after the signing of the treaty, however, Mr. Reed renewed the discussion. At first the commissioners were disposed to evade the matter but on the 25th day of June they entered into an agreement for settlement to "be considered as of the same force and virtue as if it was embodied in the treaty." This agreement stipulated that claims for indemnity to the amount of 600,000 taels should be liquidated by deducting one fifth of all the tonnage, import and export duties, which were paid by American ships at the three ports of Canton, Foochow and Shanghai. These deductions were to be made by the consuls and the total amount was to be reported by the American minister each year to the Chinese authorities until the entire amount of the claims had been settled.

Mr. Reed was not entirely satisfied with this settlement and therefore reopened the question a few months later at Shanghai.[35] First he asked from the American claimants for revised statements and was able to reduce the estimated damages from 600,000 to 525,000 taels. Kweiliang and Hwashana, not unwilling to do a little bargaining, then agreed that if the total amount would be reduced to 500,000 taels, they on their part would agree to the issuing of debentures, 300,000 taels for Canton, and 100,000 taels each for Foochow and Shanghai, and for the gradual payment of them out of the customs revenue from American vessels beginning with the following New Year (February 3, 1859). Mr. Reed then recommended to the President of the United States that a commission of two be appointed to examine the claims in detail and make final awards. This recommendation was accepted, approved by Congress, and the commission appointed.

One other indication of the spirit in which Mr. Reed approached the settlement of these claims is to be found in a passage in his address before the Philadelphia Board of Trade after his return to the United States. The claims, representing the bulk of the total, which arose out of the

British attack upon Canton in 1856, Mr. Reed undertook to support only with reluctance. He said: [36]

"The total amount of our pecuniary claims . . . never amounted to a million dollars, and did not at the beginning of the war amount to more than a fifth of that sum, for you will recollect the bulk of our claims are of recent occurrence, for loss of property at the factories, when the Chinese were defending their own soil, and for which they are only responsible on the un-Christian principle of English and American public. law, that the assailed party always pays the damages."

However, so eminent an authority as John W. Foster remarked, many years later, that notwithstanding the various reductions of the claims, and the close examination to which they were finally subjected, "many of those allowed were of questionable validity in international law." [37]

The claims commissioners were Charles W. Bradley, American consul at Ningpo, and Oliver E. Roberts, lately of the customs service. They began their hearings at Macao, November 10, 1859, and the report was submitted to the American minister February 27, 1860. The entire amount of the awards totalled $489,694.78, thus leaving a balance of about $220,000 which, when paid by the Chinese customs authorities, was deposited in the Oriental Bank of Hongkong.* [38]

*While the final disposition of this surplus money was not settled until 1885 when, with some further deductions for claims subsequently allowed, the surplus and accumulated interest, amounting to $453,400, was returned to China by the act of Congress, it is of interest to note various proposals which were made in the interval for the disposition of this money. When S. Wells Williams was in Washington in 1860 he submitted to the Secretary of State an outline for the utilization of it in the establishment of an American-Chinese College in China in which Chinese students should be instructed in Western learning, and in which American students could receive such instruction as would fit them for positions in the consular, diplomatic, customs and commercial life of China. Anson Burlingame supported this proposition, and it seems to have met with the approval of President Lincoln. Congress, however, took no action on it. Another proposal was that the money should be used to build American consulates and a legation in China, but this was rejected on the ground that the money really belonged to China. However, the first money paid over for the purchase of the present legation in Peking was taken from this fund, though it was afterwards returned to the fund by order of the Secretary of State. Still another proposal was that the money be held as a fund out of which any claims arising in the future might be paid. This also was discarded on the ground that the Government of China ought always to be made to feel the direct responsibility for the settlement of any claims which might arise. The most notable proposal, of course, was that involving the creation of an American-Chinese College, for in it was clearly foreshadowed the system of 'indemnity students' for which provision was made at the time of the return of the Boxer Indemnity surplus nearly 50 years later.[39] The balance of the 1858 indemnity was returned by act of Congress in 1885, two years after the return of the Japanese indemnity.

Thus was settled between the United States and China a difficult problem "without the utterance of a single harsh word."

BIBLIOGRAPHICAL NOTES

1. The important American sources for this chapter are: Reed Corres., published in full (S. Ex. Doc. No. 30:36-1); Journal of S. Wells Williams, edited by F. W. Williams (Journal of the North-China Branch of the Royal Asiatic Society, Vol. XLII, Shanghai, 1911); W. A. P. Martin: "A Cycle of Cathay"; Speech of Hon. W. B. Reed at Board of Trade, Philadelphia, May 31, 1859.
2. George Wingrove Cooke: "China," p. 380.
3. Reed. Corres., pp. 21-22.
4. *Ibid.*, p. 299.
5. Williams' Journal, p. 54.
6. Walrond: "Life and Letters of Lord Elgin," p. 253.
7. Cordier: "L'Expedition de Chine," p. 11, p. 8; Morse: Vol. 1, p. 672.
8. Williams' Journal, p. 75.
9. Cited by Sargent: Anglo-Chinese Commerce and Diplomacy, p. 102.
10. Reed Corres., p. 352.
11. Williams' Journal, p. 77.
12. Walrond, p. 253.
13. Reed Corres., p. 385.
14. *Ibid.*, p. 384.
15. *Ibid.*, p. 355.
16. *Ibid.*, p. 311.
17. Williams' Journal, p. 61; "Cycle of Cathay," p. 183.
18. Reed Corres., p. 549.
19. *Ibid.*, p. 358.
20. *Ibid.*, pp. 442, 493.
21. *Ibid.*, pp. 8-9.
22. "Cycle of Cathay," p. 184.
23. Williams' Journal, p. 96.
24. S. Doc. 139:29-1.
25. China Instructions, Vol. 1, Sept. 20, 1852 (Dept. of State); Marshall Corres., p. 223, July 30, 1853.
26. Marshall Corres., pp. 277, 283.
27. McLane Corres., p. 458.
28. Parker Corres., p. 549.
29. *Ibid.*, pp. 546, 637, 677.
30. *Ibid.*, pp. 1162, 1291, 1351, 1420; Reed Corres., pp. 34, 35, 36, 99.
31. Parker Corres., pp. 1098, 1099.
32. Reed Corres., pp. 13, 14.
33. *Ibid.*, pp. 300, 310, 316, 317.
34. *Ibid.*, pp. 371 ff.
35. *Ibid.*, pp. 520 ff.

36. Speech of William B. Reed, p. 5.
37. "American Diplomacy in the Orient," p. 244.
38. Claims Report: H. Ex. Doc. No. 29:40-3.
39. Diplomatic Corres., 1862, p. 843; 1864, p. 346; 1867, pp. 459, 507; 1868, p. 510; 1871, p. 226; 1872, p. 136; 1885, pp. 181, 182. H. Rept. 970:48-1; see also H. Rept. 113:45-3; H. Rept. 1142:46-2.

CHAPTER XVIII

WARD AND TATTNALL—EXCHANGE OF RATIFICATIONS

THE American Treaty of Tientsin was approved by the Senate and ratified by President Buchanan December 21, 1858. William B. Reed dispatched his resignation to the President even before he began the negotiations for the treaty. To John E. Ward of Georgia,[1] who had been the presiding officer at the convention which nominated Buchanan for the presidency,[2] now confirmed as Minister to China, was given the task of exchanging the ratifications. Under normal circumstances this duty would not have been difficult. The treaty and the two supplementary conventions covering the tariff and the settlement of claims had been approved by the Imperial Government before Mr. Reed left China, and was already recognized as having the force of law. To the Chinese, unaccustomed to the methods of European diplomacy, the exchange of ratifications, probably, did not seem to be a very important matter.

THE CONFLICT RENEWED

But before Mr. Ward had arrived in China the impression had become prevalent among the foreigners that China would make some effort to evade the fulfillment of the treaties, at least so far as concerned the permission for diplomatic residence in Peking. Whether this suspicion was well grounded in actual facts, or whether it grew out of the feeling, so widely prevalent, that in the affair at Taku the Imperial Government had come off too easily, and that China had not yet been sufficiently chastised, admits of dispute. It is at least clear that at the beginning of 1859

333

the foreigners, particularly the English in China, were expecting more trouble.

Mr. Ward reached Hongkong in May, 1859, and announced his arrival to Frederick W. A. Bruce, Lord Elgin's brother, now British Minister to China, and to M. de Bourboulon, the French Minister who was at Macao. Wishing, however, to avoid complications with the British Government which were threatened by the hostility of American and British sailors in the port, Mr. Ward departed almost immediately for Shanghai where the Chinese Commissioners, Kweiliang, Hwashana and Tan, who had negotiated the tariff with Lord Elgin a few months before, were staying. The American Minister addressed them a formal communication to the effect that he was in possession of the ratified copy of the Treaty of Tientsin "which he has been instructed to exchange at Peking," and that he also had a letter from the President to the Emperor which he expected to deliver to his Imperial Majesty.[3]

It did not seem to have occurred to Mr. Ward that there was nothing in the American Treaty of Tientsin which guaranteed him the right of a personal audience with the Emperor, nor did he realize, probably, that in raising such a question, he was directly stirring up a controversy—the right of audience with the Emperor—which involved the most cherished Chinese prejudices. Even in his assertion of right to exchange the ratifications of the treaty in Peking, he was on most uncertain ground. The American treaty (Article 30) merely stipulated that the ratifications should be exchanged within one year from the date of the signatures, i.e., before June 18, 1859. The place for this ceremony was not named. It is true that the treaty also provided that the American Minister could go to Peking 'whenever he has business' but this was safeguarded by the further stipulation that he should not 'request visits to the capital on trivial occasions' (Article 5).

The British treaty specified that the exchange of ratifications should take place at Peking within one year, and the provision of the French treaty was similar. But while the

American treaty was loaded down with numerous 'most favored-nation' clauses, under them it could not be held that the Americans had any rights included in the other treaties until those treaties had been ratified. Mr. Ward was there fore clearly outside his rights in his intentions to proceed to Peking to have an audience with the Emperor, and the right to exchange ratifications in Peking depended entirely upon whether such a ceremony was of sufficient importance to be dignified by such a settling. At Shanghai Ward argued this point with the Commissioners who at once appeared rather reluctant to have him proceed to the North.

The Commissioners stated that they had remained in Shanghai to complete some business with Lord Elgin, and gently urged Ward to delay a while in Shanghai. At an interview a few days later they repeated their explanations; they had promised Lord Elgin to remain in Shanghai until his return from Hongkong. He had not returned but Mr. Bruce had been appointed in Lord Elgin's stead and would be in Shanghai in a very short time. After their business with Mr. Bruce was finished they would go to Peking and there await the arrival of the allied ministers whose treaties provided that the ratifications were to be exchanged in Peking. It would be entirely agreeable to the Chinese Government to have Mr. Reed accompany the other two ministers, so that the three ratifications might be exchanged together. Although at first Mr. Ward had been reluctant to consent to such an arrangement he at length agreed, provided the commissioners would give him a statement that the validity of the treaty would in no way be affected by this delay in the exchange of the ratifications.[4]

From this point onward in the narrative not only are nearly all the facts a matter of dispute, but equally so is the interpretation of such facts as can be established. The Chinese version of the situation as it appears in the official dispatches of Mr. Ward and in the accounts of Dr. S. Wells Williams, who was present with the American Minister, vary widely from the assertions which were placed before the British Government and offered in England as the justi-

fication of the second Anglo-French War with China in
1859-60.

The Chinese explanation of the situation, which has
never been systematically set forth in histories of the
period, is as follows: When Mr. Bruce arrived at Shanghai
early in June prepared to push to Peking, the Chinese Commissioners agreed (June 6) that the ratifications should be
exchanged in Peking but they desired to have settled before
going there certain matters with reference to Canton which
still remained in the hands of the English and French.
"But as Canton is not yet restored," they remarked, "it
would seem that no time should be lost in arriving at a
satisfactory decision regarding it." On the same day, in a
separate communication, the Imperial Commissioners stated
that although ample arrangements for the reception of the
British legation at Peking would be made, the exchange of
ratifications had been assigned to them exclusively. No
one could act as their substitute. It would be impossible,
they stated courteously, for them to reach Peking for at
least two months.[5]

In his reply to these communications, Mr. Bruce immediately assumed that the Commissioners were acting in
bad faith.

"It is with regret that the undersigned finds," he stated, "at the
outset of a mission sent by her Brittanic Majesty as evidence of her
desire for peaceful relations, that he is met, not as he has a right to
expect, with a cordial and frank invitation to the capital, but with
delays and hesitations ill-calculated to cement a good understanding.
The undersigned will not, however, swerve in the least from the course
he has laid down in his letter of the 18th ultimo. He is resolved to
proceed forthwith to Peking, there to exchange the ratifications of the
treaty, and to deliver in person the letter intrusted to his charge by
his gracious sovereign to his Imperial Majesty, to whom it is addressed, nor will he quit the capital until satisfied that effect will be
given without reserve to every provision of the Treaty of Tientsin."

Mr. Bruce then notified the Commissioners that Admiral
Hope, Commander in Chief of the British naval forces, had
already started for the mouth of the Pei-ho, and warned
them that upon the Chinese Government must rest the
entire responsibility for any trouble that might arise.

The question of fact is whether the Chinese Government was actually sincere in its promise that the British and French ministers would be received in Peking according to the provisions of the treaty. The Russian minister, Nicholas Ignatieff, who could hardly be called an unbiased witness, but whose testimony in this case seems clear, stated (July 7): [6]

"   . preparations had been made here to receive, for the ratifications of the treaties of Tientsin, the plenipotentiaries of America, of France and of England. Lodgings had been arranged, by order of the Emperor, for the three embassies.

Whatever may have been the intentions of the Emperor as regards the admission to Peking, it is evident that it was not the intention of the Chinese Government that the allied envoys should proceed to the capital by way of the Taku forts and the passage to Tientsin which had been utilized by the foreigners the year before. Nor was it the disposition of the Chinese to permit the allied envoys to be accompanied to Peking by a large military force. The treaties did not specify that the route *must* be by way of Taku, and while the British treaty was silent on the subject, the American treaty clearly limited the number of those who might accompany the minister in his visits to Peking. The Chinese maintained that it had been the intention of the Imperial Government to receive the envoys at Pehtang, a place about ten miles north of Taku, on another outlet of the river. The Governor General of Chihli stated to Mr. Ward that he had received orders from Peking to receive the envoys at Pehtang and to facilitate their journey to Peking. [7]

S. Wells Williams, a careful observer, and the one among all the foreign legations most familiar with the Chinese, said: [8]

"I am convinced that the intention of the Emperor and his cabinet has been all along in favor of permitting the envoys of the three powers to go to his capital to exchange their treaties. . . ."

In reply to Mr. Bruce's communication stating that the British Admiral with his squadron had already proceeded to the Pei-ho, the Imperial Commissioners at Shanghai advised the British minister to proceed to the mouth of the Tientsin River, to "anchor his vessel of war outside the bar, and then, without much baggage, and with a moderate retinue" to proceed to the capital. Meanwhile they would notify the Peking officials of the situation, and they expressed the expectation that in view of the peaceful mission on which his excellency was bent, 'his treatment by the Government of China will not fail to be in every way most courteous.' Mr. Ward was also invited 'by the Commissioners to proceed to the mouth of the Pei-ho.

"Blood is Thicker than Water"

Upon Mr. Ward's arrival in the U. S. frigate *Powhatan* (Commodore Josiah Tattnall) June 21, he was notified by Admiral Hope that the mouth of the river had been obstructed with barriers. The British Admiral had issued an ultimatum to the authorities stating that unless they themselves removed the barriers, he would have it done, according to instructions received from the allied envoys. Mr. Ward thereupon found himself faced with a dilemma similar to that which had confronted Mr. Reed at the same place the year before and he, also, decided that he must adopt an independent course of action.[9] The American minister sought to announce to the Chinese authorities his presence and purpose. In this he was unsuccessful and the next day, June 24, in company with Commodore Tattnall, he set ou in the *Toeywan,* a small chartered steamer, for the mouth of the river with a view to passing the barrier in front of the forts. It was his intention to proceed until he was stopped, but the *Toeywan* ran aground in a falling tide. The British gun-boat *Plover* came alongside, and warned the American party that they were in danger of being fired upon. The commanding officer offered the services of the *Plover* to Commodore Tattnall, and suggested that the party transship to the gun-boat, proposing that Tattnall hoist the American flag at the *Plover's* peak. This offer was declined.

The *Plover* was unable to pull off the *Toeywan,* which was lying well inside the line of the British war vessels. A message was sent to the shore stating that the American minister was in the *Toeywan* and that he was on his way to Peking. The Chinese replied that passage by way of the river was prohibited, that there was no officer present who could receive a communication. They stated that it was rumored that the Governor General of Chihli had been instructed to meet the envoys at the north entrance to the river, some ten miles above. That evening the *Toeywan* floated and dropped down below the line of British war vessels.

During the night the British made some ineffectual efforts to blow up the barrier, and the following afternoon when the British admiral started to ascend the river with two gun-boats the forts opened fire and the battle commenced. The forts had been rebuilt and greatly strengthened since their destruction the year before by the allied forces, and the English and French, quite unprepared for so great a resistance, found the battle going against them. About five o'clock the report reached Commodore Tattnall, who with his party was witnessing the fray, that Admiral Hope had been seriously wounded. Then ensued the soon internationally famous "Blood-is-thicker-than-water" episode.

During the progress of the battle an English officer in charge of a junk loaded with British troops who had not been ordered to advance, came on board the *Toeywan* for a better view of the battle. As the struggle began to go against the allies he let it be known, although he did not directly ask for aid, that he wished to get his junk up to the line of battle but was unable to do so on account of the strength of the tide.[10] Commodore Tattnall conferred with Mr. Ward and the latter gave his unqualified approval to the suggestion that the Commodore offer the assistance of the *Toeywan* to tow up the reserves in the junks. Accordingly Tattnall transferred Mr. Ward and his suite to one of the barges still at anchor, and offered his services to the

officer of the other barges to tow them into action. The
offer was gladly accepted.

When the Commodore reached the battle, knowing that
Admiral Hope was wounded, his sense of the kinship of
Caucasian blood got the better of what little sense of neutrality had remained and, jumping into his boat, he ordered
the crew to pull him away to the *Cormorant* where he found
Admiral Hope utterly exhausted from his wound. In the
process of coming alongside the British gun-boat Tattnall's
barge was struck by a shot from the forts and the coxswain
was killed. While another barge was being found to return
the American party to the *Toeywan,* and while Commodore
Tattnall was extending his sympathy to Admiral Hope the
American sailors, by the Commodore's orders, assisted their
British companions and helped to serve the guns.* Tattnall
returned to the *Toeywan* and again towed up some barges,
and later in the evening when the British stormed the forts
the Commodore ran the *Toeywan* in towards shore and took
a number of British fugitives on board.

Three days later, "determined to leave no effort untried
to carry into effect the strongly expressed wishes of the
President" Mr. Ward sent some members of his suite in the
Toeywan to find the other entrance to the river to which he
had been already directed. Meanwhile the Chinese authori
ties on their own initiative communicated to Mr. Ward that
the way to Peking by way of Pehtang was open to him.

The British and French ministers, immediately after the
battle at Taku, broke off negotiations with the Chinese and
returned to Shanghai, strongly urging Mr. Ward to do like
wise.

THE AMERICAN MINISTER GOES TO PEKING

Mr. Ward, now relying on the provisions of the American treaty alone, announced to the Chinese that he wished

*The most reasonable explanation of this episode is to be found in the
fact that the struggle of the allied forces with the Chinese had assumed in the
eyes of both Tattnall and Ward, who were Southerners, the aspect of a conflict
of color. An eye-witness of the episode recorded in his diary that Commodore
Tattnall finally exclaimed: "Blood is thicker than water" and that he'd "be
damned if he'd stand by and see white men butchered before his eyes. No,
sir; old Tattnall isn't that kind, sir. This is the cause of humanity. Is that
boat ready? Tell the men there is no need of side-arms." [11]

to proceed to Peking upon important business, viz., the ratification of the treaty. In thus resting his case he was on solid ground, and he met with no opposition from the Imperial officers. However, his inexperience in China, coupled probably with his unwillingness to take the advice of Dr. Williams, soon placed him in difficulties which a more experienced diplomat might have avoided. The treaty provided that the Chinese authorities should arrange for the conveyance of the minister to the capital—a provision which they were glad to comply with for the manner of the first entrance of an American envoy to Peking was to them an important matter. Mr. Ward should have demanded that sedan chairs be provided for the journey, for this was the customary mode of conveyance for the highest officers of the government. Being ignorant of this fact, or not realizing its importance, he consented that the party be conveyed in carts. Thus the first American envoy and his suite to enter the Imperial capital proceeded thither in equipages similar to those in which rode the Korean and other tribute-bearing envoys in their periodical journeys to Peking, and to the inhabitants *en route,* as well as to the populace of the city, the party was represented as coming to pay tribute to the Son of Heaven.* [12]

Having reached Peking, Mr. Ward made another mistake in immediately yielding to the desires of the Chinese that the mission should not go abroad in the city until after the audience with the Emperor. Furthermore, although the American flag had been brought along, it was not permitted to be flown over the temporary legation building. Indeed the American minister and his suite were practically prisoners, denied the privilege of going out of the house, and not permitted to communicate freely with even the Russian minister. [13]

Aside from these two criticisms on points which would in prospect seem unimportant to one not familiar with

*William W. Rockhill states, although giving no authority for the assertion: "Here [Pehtang] he landed and was taken to Peking, part of the way in carts and part in boats; but over the carts and boats floated an ominous little yellow pennant with the words: 'Tribute-bearers from the United States.' " There is no question but that the mission was so represented to the Chinese people.

previous visits of embassies to Peking, Mr. Ward conducted himself with credit. The Chinese declined to discuss the matter of the exchange of ratifications until the question of the details of the audience with the Emperor had been fixed. The Imperial authorities demanded a modified *kotow* from Mr. Ward when he should be presented to his Imperial Majesty. Mr. Ward replied with firmness as well as in a characteristically Southern manner that although he was willing to 'bend the body and slightly crook the right knee,' he was accustomed to kneel only to God and woman.[14] Although the Chinese persisted, Mr. Ward remained adamant on the subject of the *kotow* and no satisfactory compromise could be reached. In the course of the prolonged discussion it became apparent that the Emperor was really more eager to see the envoy than the latter was to see his Imperial Highness.[15] At length Mr. Ward, his patience exhausted, demanded that conveyances be provided for his departure from the capital. Reluctantly the Chinese agreed, and the ratifications were exchanged at Pehtang at the conclusion of the journey to the coast.

After the exchange of ratifications the Chinese brought in an 'American prisoner' who had been captured at Taku in June.[16] This prisoner had been to the Chinese an evidence that in the battle of Taku the Americans had joined with the allies, and no doubt this conviction that the Americans had not maintained their neutrality had been a great obstacle to Mr. Ward's negotiations at Peking. But the American prisoner proved to be a Canadian who had not only asserted that he was a citizen of the United States, but had also told the Chinese that he had been one of a party of no less than two hundred Americans who had joined in the fight. The lack of truth in these assertions was satisfactorily proven to the Chinese authorities. Mr. Ward then revealed rather more kindliness of nature than the situation required by offering to take the Canadian to Shanghai and to restore him to his countrymen.

Immediately upon the conclusion of the ceremonies, the American envoy and his suite departed from Pehtang,

arriving at Shanghai August 22, 1859.   From this place Mr.
Ward reported to the Secretary of State: [17]

"The disastrous result of the battle of the Pei-ho has done much
to unsettle the condition of things in China.   The whole manner and
bearing of the Chinese population towards the foreigners have been
changed, and the people of this place have been for weeks past under
the painful apprehension of an outbreak and an attack upon the foreign settlement."

Late in 1860 Mr. Ward retired from China, hastening
home to take part in the secession.   The post of United
States Minister in China remained vacant until the appointment of Anson Burlingame the following year.

Commodore Tattnall received the approval of the Secre
tary of the Navy for his conduct at Taku .and President
Buchanan, in reporting the conclusion of the settlement
with China, complacently stated: [18]

"Our minister to China, in obedience to his instructions, has remained perfectly neutral in the war between Great Britain and
France and the Chinese Empire, although, in conjunction with the
Russian minister, he was ever ready and willing, had the opportunity
offered, to employ his good offices in restoring peace between the
parties.   It is but an act of simple justice, both to our present minister
and his predecessor, to state that they have proved fully equal to the
delicate, trying, and responsible positions in which they have on
different occasions been placed."

The story of the second Anglo-French War with China
does not require telling.   In August, 1860, the allied forces
landed at Pehtang.   Having captured the Taku forts they
advanced to Tientsin.   Rapidly the allies forced their way
towards Peking.   The Emperor fled to his hunting lodge at
Jehol.   Early in October the British and French forces
reached the capital, sacked the Summer Palace, and were
admitted without further fighting to Peking.   The Summer
Palace, already gutted of its priceless contents, was ordered
burned as a further ocular demonstration that the British
Government in Asia might not safely be trifled with.   In
the ensuing settlements, additional indemnity was agreed
to, the unreserved right of diplomatic residence in Peking
was conceded, the French secured additional concessions for
the Roman Catholic missionaries, and Tientsin was added

to the list of open ports.   Early in November the allied
troops withdrew from the city.

Beyond a doubt the great Empire of China was now
opened, for ill and for good, to the Western World.

Inasmuch as the close of the second Anglo-French War
with China, and the retirement of Ward as American minister mark the close of a period in the relations of the United
States with China, a brief summary is in order.

The war, although it had produced no effect whatever
on the great mass of the Chinese Empire, had shattered the
old system by which the Peking Government had been able
to transact the affairs of its international relations through
the southern port of Canton.   While in retirement at Jehol
the Emperor Hienfeng died (August 22, 1861).   By means
of a silent revolution within the court, Prince Kung, brother
of Hienfeng, and uncle of the boy emperor, Tungshih, became president of a newly created Board of Foreign Affairs.
Prince Kung had already come into contact with the
foreigners in the negotiations for the ratification of the
treaties in 1860 and, while by no means a liberal or enlightened statesman, he recognized the necessity of conciliating
the determined foreigners.   Associated with the prince were
Kweiliang, one of the commissioners who had met the
foreigners at Tientsin in 1858, and Wensiang, the ablest
modern Chinese statesman until the rise of Li Hung Chang.
At the same time the two dowager empresses assumed the
regency and the empress mother Yehonala, sometimes called
the Empress of the Western Palace to distinguish her from
the less able and aggressive Empress Consort who lived in
the Eastern Palace, entered upon her remarkable régime in
Chinese affairs.

For the United States also the year 1861 marks many
important changes.   Among the American merchants the
pre-treaty traditions of old Canton had entirely disappeared.
A new kind of international trade competition had arisen
in which the merchants of other nations could bring to their
help a political and military support such as the American
Government was quite unwilling to render to its nationals.

The international situation, hitherto relatively simple, with France appearing as the obliging and retiring ally of Great Britain, was changing.   Great Britain and France were falling apart as a result of Palmerston policies in Europe. Other European nations were stirring.   Russia had at length come into actual contact with the European powers in the Far East.   Within the next ten years six other nations, Germany, Portugal, Denmark, Spain, Holland and Italy, were to conclude treaties with China.   In place of the old conciliatory policies of Canton had come an intense international rivalry and trade conflict which the American Government, much against its will, had been forced to consider. The United States was not free to select and follow a policy in accord with its earlier traditions.   It must enter international politics in China or forfeit its place in the trade. In the treaty of 1858 the United States had compromised its traditional principles for the sake of holding its place in the international competition.   The treaty was not such as Mr. Reed would have liked to make.   Mr. Ward in China was like a lost soul not knowing to what world he belonged, and probably much more interested in the developments of the Secession than in the task in hand.

That American policy in China from 1854 to 1860 did not correctly express the American people becomes very evident when we compare it with the policy of the United States in Japan where the Americans, still following the cooperative policy, had none the less the acknowledged leadership.

BIBLIOGRAPHICAL NOTES

1. The Ward Correspondence is printed, in part, in S. Ex. Doc. No. 30:36-1, in the same volume with the Reed Correspondence.
2. Foster: "American Diplomacy in the Orient," p. 245.
3. Ward Corres., p. 575.
4. *Ibid.,* pp. 577-9.
5. *Ibid.,* pp. 581-5.
6. *Ibid.,* p. 611.
7. Ward Corres., p. 593.
8. Williams' Journal, p. 143
9. Ward Corres., p. 586.

10. Williams' Journal, pp. 120 ff.
11. Private papers of Rear Admiral Stephen Decatur Trenchard, U. S. Navy, ed. by Edgar Stanton Maclay: *U. S. Naval Institute Proceedings,* Vol. 40, pp. 1085 ff.
12. William W. Rockhill: "Diplomatic Missions to the Court of China": *Amer. Hist. Review,* July, 1897, p. 638.
13. Williams' Journal, pp. 169 ff.
14. Foster: "American Diplomacy in the Orient," p. 250.
15. Williams' Journal, p. 184.
16. Ward Corres., p. 598.
17. *Ibid.,* p. 618.
18. Richardson's Messages, Vol. 5, p. 643 (Annual Message, Dec. 3, 1860).

CHAPTER XIX

THE POLICY OF TOWNSEND HARRIS IN JAPAN

BEFORE considering the policy of Townsend Harris in Japan which was being written into a treaty engagement at the very time Reed was proceeding to the Pei-ho in the company of the fleets of France and England, and was being applied at the time Ward and Tattnall were participating in the attack at Taku in 1859, it will be well to review some of the fundamental differences between China and Japan as the two nations faced the future in 1858.

The Chinese Empire, notwithstanding the despotism of the Manchus, a state religion and a common classical literature was conspicuously lacking in unity. It was sprawled over half a continent, divided by great mountain ranges and deserts, without the means of rapid communication, speaking no common language, and permitting such large degree of provincial and local autonomy as greatly weakened the central authority. Japan, on the other hand, was small and compact, had relatively easy communications, a common spoken as well as written language, and while there was also a decentralized government as in China, yet the form of decentralization was feudalistic and gave to the government of the Shogun a representative character which was wholly lacking in China. The Shogun was compelled to take counsel with the feudal nobles who constituted a territorial representation in the government. The Chinese administration was in the hands of a mandarinate recruited by an impractical system of civil service: the only form of protest available for the people was either riot or rebellion. The decision of the Shogun rested more nearly than that of the Chinese Emperor on the will of the people. Japan, a compact Empire, possessed a very lively patriotism such as was impossible in decentralized China ruled by an alien dynasty. The Chinese system of government had repressed the development of political leadership, while the Japanese system had the effect of cultivating and encouraging it. In 1858 China was without competent leaders, while Japan had many of exceptional ability. To all these advantages in favor of Japan must be added the presence of a military spirit and tradition such as the needs of a small and secluded and feudalistic nation demanded, and such as China had not required and had indeed discouraged. Japan, less exposed because of her isolation and relative poverty, was vastly better prepared than China in 1858 to meet the onrush of Western aggression.

APPOINTMENT OF TOWNSEND HARRIS—INSTRUCTIONS AND
TREATY WITH SIAM

Townsend Harris [1] had been a merchant in New York City, distinguished for his public spirit and service. He had been president of the Board of Education and was "a sound, reliable and influential Democrat." Giving up his business in New York he sailed for San Francisco in May, 1849, in a vessel of which he was part owner, and later embarked upon a leisurely trading enterprise in the Pacific and Indian oceans. On Christmas, 1849, he was "at sea in the North Pacific Ocean"; 1850, at Manila; 1851, at Penang; 1852, at Singapore; 1853, at Hongkong; 1854, at Calcutta. His enterprises, while at first successful, ended in failure, and in 1853, describing himself as a resident of Hongkong, he applied for the position of American consul at either Hongkong or Canton. [2] Notwithstanding the efforts of influential friends in the United States he was assigned to the consulate at Ningpo (August 2, 1854) an unimportant and trivial post with a remuneration of $1000 for judicial services and such fees as the slight American trade at that port afforded. Harris, whose face was already turned towards home, appointed a missionary, Dr. D. C. Macgowan, as acting consul, and set out for New York. [3] Immediately upon his arrival he secured the interest of his New York friends on behalf of a possible appointment to the newly created post of consul-general in Japan. To President Pierce he wrote (August 4, 1855): "I have a perfect knowledge of the social banishment I must endure while in Japan, and the mental isolation in which I must live, and am prepared to meet it." He stated that even though he were offered the choice between the posts of commissioner to China and consul-general to Japan, he would "instantly take the latter." His efforts were successful, and within two weeks after his arrival in New York, he had received his appointment which was later confirmed by the Senate.

Harris was a man of urbanity, character and ability. While living at Hongkong he appears to have won the confidence and friendship of Sir John Bowring, and to have attracted the attention of Commodore Perry. He was also a friend of William E. Seward, then senator from New York.[4] As to convictions in Far Eastern policy Harris appears to have occupied a middle position between Perry and Parker, on the one side, and Cushing and the early Canton traders on the other. He thought, for example, the United States ought to acquire Formosa, but he would have had the acquisition made by purchase, and so recommended in a letter to Marcy.[5]

To the duties of the American representative in Japan were added those of special agent to secure a new treaty with Siam which was to be negotiated while *en route* to Shimoda. The motives of President Pierce in making the appointment were expressed by Marcy (September 12, 1855) as follows: "The President entertained the hope that by your knowledge of Eastern character and your general intelligence and experience in business you would make such an impression upon the Japanese as would in time induce them to enter into a commercial treaty with us."[6] Marcy did not outline specifically the sort of treaty which was desired but referred him to a draft of the proposed treaty with Siam, the stipulations of which would be satisfactory for a treaty with Japan—"at least for a beginning."

In addition to the written instructions Marcy appears to have given some verbal ones, including the necessity for securing extraterritoriality which had not been included in either the Roberts treaty with Siam or the Perry treaty with Japan. Marcy was somewhat apologetic about this stipulation which, he said, was necessary because the Senate would not ratify a treaty in which it was lacking.*

The Roberts treaty with Siam, while stipulating the omission of all tariff duties, had been of little value to American trade because the tonnage dues—the only charge for foreign trade, and exactly similar to those which had been included in the preceding British treaty—were so excessive as to exclude practically all foreign trade. A few years after the signing of the Roberts treaty a system of monopolies had been created in Siam which had still further retarded the trade. In 1849 Joseph Balestier,[8] consul at Singapore, had been appointed a special envoy to negotiate treaties with Siam, Cochin China, Borneo, Subi, Bally and Lambok Islands, as well as with the pepper coast of Sumatra. He was instructed to make a new treaty with Siam, correcting the tonnage dues and securing the right to appoint a consul at Bankok. Balestier's negotiations had come to nothing because of his ill temper. The Siamese had sent a message to the American Government through the missionaries and American naval officers which, after remarking that Balestier was a "person of much excitability" said:

"Should the high ministers of the United States of America appoint an officer hereafter to come here for friendly negotiations it is requested that they may appoint an efficient, prudent and well disposed person, not inclined to anger, but like Mr. Roberts."

American interests in Siam in 1855 were largely missionary, there having been American Protestant missionaries

*In a letter many years later Harris stated: "The provision of the treaty giving the right of extraterritoriality to all Americans in Japan was against my conscience. In a conversation with Governor Marcy, the Secretary of State in 1855, he strongly condemned it as an unjust interference with the municipal law of a country which no western nation would tolerate for a moment; but he said that it would be impossible to have a treaty with an Oriental nation unless it contained that provision. The examples of our treaties with Turkey, Persia, and the Barbary States gave a precedent that the Senate would not overlook." [7]

there for more than twenty years. Harris was therefore instructed to secure for them the treaty right to pursue their work unmolested, but he was cautioned that in Japan the prejudice against missionaries was so great that he would probably not be able to secure missionary liberty.

The immediate occasion of this new effort to make a treaty with Siam was the recent project of Great Britain for a new treaty. Harris was cautioned that he might expect to find the Siamese somewhat alarmed at the prospect of European aggression and he was therefore instructed to make clear the distinctions between the traditional foreign policies of the United States and Great Britain. Marcy wrote: [9]

"It is obvious . . . that you will be at no loss for argument to show the difference between the foreign policies especially of this country and Great Britain. While the latter is herself an Eastern Power and as such by the late Burmese war has since become a near neighbor to Siam, we covet no dominions in that quarter. It is undoubtedly in the interest of Siam to be liberal in her commercial policy towards the United States."

Harris proceeded to England and thence by leisurely stages to India and Ceylon and was picked up by the U. S. frigate *San Jacinto* at Penang.[10] The expedition arrived at the anchorage of the Menam River April 16, 1856. At Bankok Mr. Harry Parkes was just concluding the ratifications of the British treaty which had been negotiated by Sir John Bowring, and Harris experienced no difficulty in effecting a similar compact in which extraterritoriality was granted, the rate of import tariff fixed at 3 per cent, and export duties determined according to a schedule attached to the treaty. Revision could be effected at the end of ten years at the desire of either party. Opium was to be admitted free of all duty, but could be sold only to the "opium farmer" or his agents. The Siamese would have been very willing to go very much farther in their treaty with the United States had Harris not discouraged them. Indeed they wished an alliance, or protectorate. Harris reported: [11]

"In my confidential interviews with the ministers, they expressed both fear and hatred of England. They read in the history of Burmah the fate that probably awaits them, and which they consider only a question of time.

"They were most anxious to be taken under the protection of the United States. They plainly told me that if I would make a treaty of alliance they would give us all we could ask, even to a monopoly of the trade."

Upon leaving Siam Harris appointed as consul Rev. Stephen Mattoon, a missionary who had been there ten years. The treaty was at first an impetus to trade. Russell and Company established a branch at Bankok, and other American traders appeared, but the large extension of the open ports in China after the treaty of 1858 appears to have curtailed the development of the trade with Bankok. Russell and Company soon withdrew its representative. There was delay in securing a suitable consul for the post; Congress made no provision for a salary, and the fees were hardly sufficient to cover the necessary boat hire. American relations with Siam did not become important. However the negotiations had given Harris some practice in treaty-making and many of the provisions of the treaty between England and Siam appeared again in the first commercial treaty between the United States and Japan two years later.

ARRIVAL OF HARRIS IN JAPAN—CONVENTION OF 1857

The *San Jacinto,* after many prolonged delays due to defective machinery, arrived at Shimoda with Townsend Harris August 21, 1856. The consul general was not welcome. The Japanese officials protested that the Perry treaty did not require them to receive him; they asked him to leave; they asked him to write to his government requesting his recall, and they begged Commodore Armstrong to take him away; all in vain. After setting up a flagstaff in front of the temple which the Japanese at length placed at his disposal for a residence, and after landing the envoy with a salute of thirteen guns, yards manned, the *San Jacinto* sailed away and left him—to be unvisited by any naval vessel for fourteen months. Harris was without communications from the Department of State for eighteen months. No representative of the American Government was ever left more to his own devices.

The treaty situation at that time was as follows: [12] Admiral Sir James Sterling had concluded a convention similar to Perry's in October, 1854. It contained a most-favored-nation clause and also a stipulation for elementary extraterritoriality. This treaty was as little satisfactory to Great Britain as the Perry treaty was to Americans, and at Hongkong Sir John Bowring had told Harris that he had received a commission to proceed to Japan with a large naval force to demand and secure the complete opening of the empire to foreign trade. Bowring had given Harris permission to use this information freely in his own peaceful negotiations. However, the disturbances in China, the Indian Mutiny, and the then unformed state of British policy in China were to delay the expedition contemplated for Bowring for nearly two years.

Twenty months after the conclusion of the Perry treaty the Dutch representative, Donker Curtius, was able to effect a "preliminary Convention of Commerce," thus carrying out a project which the Netherlands had tried to accomplish in 1844. Sir John Bowring had given to Harris a copy of this convention. It marked several notable advances in concessions for foreigners. In addition to extraterritoriality, and greatly enlarged personal freedom, the island of Deshima at Nagasaki, which had served the Dutch traders at once as a prison and trading post for two centuries, was to be sold outright to the Netherlands factory, thus establishing the precedent for the sale of land to foreigners for residence and trade. The convention also mentioned the fact that the Dutch were permitted to *reside* at Nagasaki.

The Netherlands envoy secured a more elaborate commercial treaty which was signed January 30, 1856, eight months before the arrival of Harris. This treaty permitted the Dutch to bring their wives and children to the open ports, and there was a stipulation that they should be allowed "to practice their own or the Christian religion within their buildings." Import duties were fixed at 35 per cent, but the export duties were left undetermined. These agreements, consisting of a treaty, additional articles and a "supplement to additional articles," were not ratified when Harris arrived.

The Russians also had been active. Count Putiatin, who had first appeared at Nagasaki shortly after the conclusion of Perry's first visit to the Bay of Yedo, and who had vainly sought the cooperation of Perry in a joint expedition for 1854,[13] concluded a treaty of "commerce, navigation and delimitation" at Shimoda, in January, 1855. Aside from opening three ports—Nagasaki, Shimoda and Hakodate—stipulation for the residence of consuls at the two latter places, and bilateral extraterritoriality, the convention fixed the boundaries of the two nations, assigning the island of Urup to Russia, Iturup and the Kuriles to Japan, and leaving the two empires in joint occupation of Sakhalin. Russia then proceeded to further explorations of Sakhalin and discovered coal mines which led to Russian attempts to abrogate the joint possession of the island.[14] However, the ratifications of the Putiatin treaty were exchanged at Shimoda shortly after the arrival of Harris. Japan was probably even more alarmed at the advances of Russia than she was at the Anglo-French war with China.

Townsend Harris, left alone at Shimoda except for the companionship of his interpreter, C. J. Heusken, a naturalized Hollander who had been selected because Dutch was the language of diplomacy in Japan, proceeded slowly. Shimoda was wholly unsuited to either trade or diplomacy. It was the seat of a large stone quarry, but was without produce suitable for export, and was shut off from the surrounding country by almost impassable hills. The harbor was small and had been rendered nearly useless by a tidal wave which the year before had removed nearly all the "holding ground" from the bottom of the bay, and had wrecked completely the Russian corvette *Diana*. The spot had obviously been selected by the Japanese because of its inaccessibility. It was certainly not a favorable point from which to negotiate a new treaty with Yedo. Harris' first impression of the Japanese officials was unpleasant. While he became convinced that the common people were ready to welcome the foreigner, he regarded the officials as "the greatest liars on earth" and told them as much. And yet he set out to win their confidence and good will and so far succeeded as to be able to sign a convention June 17, 1857, in which the Japanese conceded directly by treaty what had by inference from the most-favored-nation clause of the Perry treaty accrued to the Americans in the British, Russian and Dutch conventions. These concessions were: the opening of Nagasaki as a port of call; the right to have a vice consul at Hakodate; extraterritoriality and the right of residence at Shimoda and Hakodate; the privilege of paying for ship's supplies in "goods" in case money were not available; and settlement of a new basis for exchange which fixed the value of the Japanese *ichibu** at 34½ cents, whereas under the Perry convention it had been valued at a dollar in silver. The convention also abrogated the agreement of the Perry treaty which had placed all trade under the im mediate supervision of the government, and greatly en larged the personal freedom of Harris by admitting that he had the right in his official capacity to travel beyond the limits of seven *ri* which had been fixed in the Perry treaty. While the new convention was not as explicit as the Dutch treaty in matters of commercial privilege and resi dence, it contained greater concessions than had been ex- pected by the American Government in 1855 when Secre- tary Marcy had issued his instructions to Harris.†

HARRIS AT YEDO

The work of Townsend Harris at Shimoda deserves a more honored place in American history than it has re- ceived. His health failed as his supplies became exhausted,

* Ichibu=one *bu;* a *bu* being a certain weight of silver or gold, not a coin.
† The treaty was duly ratified June 15, 1858, by advice of the Senate. It has been confused by at least one British historian with the amplified treaty of commerce of 1858.[16]

and his government neglected him. At length he was reduced to little more than a Japanese diet which nearly cost
him his life. He was without medical attention when it
was urgently needed, and he was "as one may say in a
prison—a large one it is true—but still a prison." Notwithstanding the handicaps laid upon him and the obvious
intentions of the authorities to thwart his purpose, we see
him entering the capital city of Yedo (November 30, 1857)
five and one-half months after signing the convention, with
the promise that he should be permitted to deliver in person the letter from President Pierce to the Shogun. It was
an extraordinary achievement in which he had surrendered
no particle of the official dignity of his position and had
won his way by argument and by absolute candor. The
contrast between Commissioner Ward's entry into Peking
and Consul-General Harris' entry into Yedo is striking. The
honor accorded to Harris was, however, a mark of the
greater political astuteness of the Japanese Government as
well as of the finer diplomatic skill of the New York merchant. Yedo had read correctly the designs of Russia, while
Peking, wholly deceived, had taken the Russian envoy to
her bosom; the mere intimation of British intentions in
Japan had been alarming, while the destruction of the Taku
forts in 1858 by the allied British and French forces had
been dismissed by the Manchu Government with fatuous
indifference.

Harris was not content at Yedo with the delivery of the
President's letter; he had come to make a commercial treaty
with the Shogun's government, and before the end of February, 1858, he had succeeded in securing the approval of
the Yedo officials to a satisfactory draft.

The arguments which Harris used are a clear revelation
of his policy.[16] Intercourse with the United States, he said,
should consist of free commerce and diplomatic representation. By means of steam navigation California was only
eighteen days removed from Japan, and by means of the
transcontinental telegraph another hour would carry a message to Washington. "To acquire possessions in Asia,"

stated Harris, remembering the failure of the American Government to act on the suggestions to acquire Formosa, and the denial of admission of the Sandwich Islands to the United States in 1854, "is prohibited by the government." Not only did the United States have no territorial ambitions, but it was even contrary to American policy to join alliances with other Western powers which had designs in Asia. He mentioned the refusal of Presidents Pierce and Buchanan to enter into an alliance with Great Britain and France in the existing war in China. He warned Japan that Great Britain had designs on Formosa, and that France wanted Korea, and expressed the opinion that if China did not now surrender to their allied arms, the two Western nations would probably divide China between them.*

'Misfortunes are now threatening Japan," stated Harris in effect, "in consequence of the state of things in England and the European states. England is not satisfied with the treaty made with Japan by Admiral Sir James Sterling. The English Government hopes to hold the same kind of intercourse with Japan as she holds with other nations, and is ready to make war on Japan, as I will now show. England greatly fears Russia will disturb her East Indian possessions. Quite lately England and France united to fight against Russia because the latter was disposed to annex other countries. England does not want Russia to hold Sakhalin and the Amur. England fears that Russia will take possession of Manchuria and China. She may then attack the possessions of England in the East Indies, and then war will break out again between England and Russia. Should Russia do as above indicated, it will become very difficult for England to defend herself, and in order to be in a position to defend herself successfully she desires to take possession of Sakhalin, Yezo and Hakodate. Should England take possession of these places, she will send a large fleet to each place and cut off communications between Petropauloski, the port of Kamtchatka and Sakhalin. England would rather have possession of Yezo than Manchuria." †

Harris explained to the Japanese that there would be a "great difference between a treaty made with a single in-

*In making these assertions Harris was doubtless correctly reflecting current opinion among the foreigners in China at the time he passed through Hongkong on his way from Bankok to Shimoda. The dispatches of Commodore Perry and the proposals of Dr. Parker for a joint naval demonstration against China for the acquisition of Formosa, reflected a similar opinion.

† This is a Japanese version of Harris's argument, and some allowances may be made for misunderstandings in the interpretation which was from English into Dutch and thence into Japanese. That Harris spoke with so much bluntness and so little qualification of statement seems unlikely, but that the Japanese had caught the main points of his argument seems very probable. Perhaps Harris spoke with the more confidence because of the very free conversations which he had had with Sir John Bowring at Hongkong in 1856.

dividual unattended, and one made with an envoy who
would bring fifty men-of-war to these shores." He warned
them against the evils of the opium trade, and recounted
what the Siamese had told him of their fears of Great
Britain. He explained to them the present condition of
India. He even offered the services of American military
and naval officers and shipyards, to help Japan strengthen
her defenses, and intimated that the United States might
be willing to accept a position as mediator in any conflicts
which Japan might have with Western powers. In con
clusion Harris argued that Japan's best safeguard against
such threatened aggressions was to abandon entirely the
policy of seclusion and admit all nations freely to her trade,
thus making the rivalries of the Western world her ally in
an effort to preserve her integrity.

Harris's representations, viewed as an expression of Far
Eastern policy, were in entire accord with what was already
traditional American policy in China. The United States
desired to see the Asiatic states sustained and made strong
to withstand by their own might the encroachments of the
European powers. Americans, argued the American representatives in China as well as in Japan, were likely to fare
better in Asia with the sovereignty and integrity of the
Asiatic states preserved, than with the territories divided
up among European governments. In short, the United
States desired for its citizens an open door to trade, and the
surest way to open this door and to keep it open, was on the
one hand to persuade the sovereign states of Asia to open
their doors, and then to strengthen these states so that they
themselves would be able to keep them open. That Harris
was correctly representing American policy in Yedo in 1858
there can be no doubt, and yet so gradual had been the ac-
cumulation of the precedents which had established this
policy, and so meagre had been the official utterances of
the American Government on the subject, that one will
search in vain in the official records for any such declarations as we have summarized above. American policy was
not a pronouncement; it was a body of precedent to which

Harris himself was in his turn making important contributions in precision of statement.

TREATY AND TARIFF OF 1858

Harris became a teacher of political economy. He proceeded to instruct the Japanese in the theories of economics —theories which he had learned in America rather than in England where the doctrine of Free Trade was more firmly established. He showed them how the revenues of the government might be met in part or even wholly by tariffs on foreign trade. He warned them against the evils of export duties, and held up the advantages of a relatively high tariff—and yet not too high. (The Dutch had already fixed the import duties at 35 per cent.) [17] When the Japanese at length agreed to make such a commercial treaty as he proposed, they entrusted to him the duty of devising the tariff, while expressing their preference for a flat $12\frac{1}{2}$ per cent rate on both exports and imports. Even $12\frac{1}{2}$ per cent seemed to Harris far too high for ship's supplies which the whaling vessels would require and which constituted at that time the only American trade in view. Harris at length induced the Japanese to agree to a 5 per cent duty on these supplies; 5 per cent on all exports; 35 per cent on imported alcoholic drinks, which he abhorred and which were not an article of American export; and 20 per cent on all other imports. This schedule was a comfortable one for Americans, reducing the import duties on the only articles which seriously interested American traders to the extent of about 85 per cent. "I have drawn regulations," reported Harris to Cass (August 7, 1858),[18] "with a view to the protection of the revenue, and the tariff is arranged with a view first to secure an income to the Japanese Government, and second to enable our whaling ships in the North Pacific Ocean to obtain their supplies on reasonable terms." It was an ingenious device: while American trade was taxed at 5 per cent it left British manufactures at 20 per cent and French wines at 35 per cent to provide the bulk

of the revenue for the Japanese Government. Needless to
say the arrangement was quite unsatisfactory to Great Britain and France. Lord Elgin [19] a few months later secured
a reduction of the tariff to .5 per cent for the bulk of British produce, and not long afterwards there were still further
reductions. Harris did not approve of this whittling down
of the Japanese revenues, and did not appear to see that the
English and French were merely applying his own
principle.[20]

The treaty of 1858 between the United States and
Japan became the basis of Japan's foreign relations until
near the close of the century, just as Cushing's treaty with
China had been the basis of China's relations with the treaty
powers until it was replaced with Lord Elgin's treaty in
1858. The Harris treaty, while including all the advantageous terms of the convention of the preceding year, went
very much farther in the direction for free diplomatic and
commercial intercourse. It consisted of thirty-four articles
and seven trade regulations, which included the tariff sched
ule. Some of the details need not be noted, but many of
the stipulations are important.

A diplomatic agent was to be permitted to reside in Yedo,
and consular agents were to reside in all the open ports.
The diplomatic representatives and the consul general were
to have the right to "travel freely" in any part of the Empire of Japan. American citizens were to reside permanently in the open ports and could "lease ground and purchase buildings thereon." Trade was to be free "without
the intervention of any Japanese officers."

It was stipulated that the President of the United
States, "at the request of the Japanese Government will
act as a friendly mediator in such matters of difference as
may arise between the Government of Japan and any European power." "There is nothing in this article," wrote
Harris in his journal,[21] "that requires a treaty stipulation,
but I inserted it to produce an impression on the government and people and it had that effect." Another article
of similar character permitted the Japanese to "purchase

or construct in the United States ships of war, steamers, merchant ships, whale ships, cannon, munitions of war, arms of all kinds," and to engage "scientific, naval and military men, artisans of all kinds, and mariners to enter its service." This article was expected to win the approval of the daimyos whose opposition to a treaty was already making itself felt at Yedo.

In drafting the treaty Harris went as far in the direction of a political alliance with Japan as he dared. While the Japanese were encouraged to look to the United States for military and naval instructors and supplies, it was agreed that Japan would open the three ports of Yokohoma, Nagasaki and Hakodate as depots of supplies for American naval vessels. Harris felt that this was a great advantage secured to his government because it would make possible the removal of the American naval depot at Hongkong. A war between Great Britain and the United States in the Far East seemed to him, as it had to Perry, a possibility. What Perry had sought to accomplish by the appropriation of naval bases at the Bonin and Lew Chew Islands, Harris felt that he had effected by pacific negotiations with the Shogun's ministers.

Americans in Japan were not only to be permitted the free exercise of their religion within their own dwellings, but were to have the right to erect suitable places of worship. Apparently as a concession to Japanese fear of missionaries this article also stipulated that neither Americans nor Japanese were to "do anything that may be calculated to excite religious animosity." The next year Harris, who had become in his lonely exile a very devout man and a great believer in Christian missions, made a strong effort to secure a concession stipulating "full toleration of religion among the Japanese themselves" but failed. However, wrote Harris, "the first blow has been struck." Even then Verbeck was on his way to Japan.

Harris at first stoutly contended for the opening of eight ports,[22] for the right of residence in Kioto which as the residence of the Mikado was considered as little less than holy ground, and for the right of unrestricted travel for all Americans of good character after a residence of one year in the open ports. He was led to abandon the second and third of these contentions when it was represented to him that they might lead to such opposition from the daimyos as would cost him the entire treaty, and he consented to a reduction of the total number of ports to six, to which was added the right of residence for all Americans in Yedo after January 1, 1862. Kanagawa, for which Yokohama was later actually substituted, and Nagasaki were to be opened July 4, 1859; Niigata, or some more suitable port on the northern coast of Hondo, January 1, 1860; and Hiogo, near Osaka, January 1, 1863.

The tariff was notable, aside from the points already mentioned, in two respects: opium was prohibited as in the Russian and Dutch treaties; and the tariff was a "conventional" one, i.e., a part of the treaty in such a way that its revision became a revision of the treaty itself. The treaty, like the British and American treaties with Siam, was subject not to termination at a definite date, but only to "revision" at the end of ten years "upon the desire of either" party, but the tariff was to be subject to revision, if the Japanese desired, five years after the opening of Kanagawa, i.e., July 4, 1864. It was farthest from Harris's intention to fasten upon Japan a 5 per cent tariff which could not be altered except with the consent of the European powers, but such was the effect of his treaty, the text of which was accepted by Lord Elgin and later envoys as the basis of the subsequent treaties with other powers.

As the treaty came from the hands of Harris in the spring of 1858 it was not only more liberal in its provisions than the Cushing treaty with China, but even more liberal than the treaties of Tientsin which had followed the occupation of Canton and the destruction of the Taku forts. The treaty was also both in intent and in the textual provisions, more just to Japan than the corresponding treaties were to China and also more expedient. Like the Perry treaty it was not a source of rancor among the Japanese.

As a means of further cementing the good relations between the two nations, it contained the provision, inserted by the Japanese, that the ratifications were to be exchanged in Washington.

Opposition to the treaty developed so fast during the negotiations, which were concluded about the end of February, that Harris was induced to consent to a delay before the final signatures were affixed in order that the Yedo officials might have time to secure the assent of the Mikado. While they had "roared with laughter" [23] a few weeks before when Harris had alluded to the supposed Japanese veneration for the Mikado, they now expressed the opinion that the Mikado's assent would add weight to the engagement and should be secured if possible. They promised Harris that the signatures would be affixed within sixty days, and told him that if the Mikado refused to confirm the agreement, they were prepared to disregard the Imperial wishes. On March 10 Harris returned to Shimoda on a Japanese Government steamer, purchased in Holland. He became very ill at Shimoda—so ill that his life was despaired of and he was attended most solicitously by the Shogun's physicians.

The Harris treaty precipitated a crisis in Japanese domestic politics.[24] The negotiation of the documents was seized upon by those daimyos who opposed the Shogun and had in mind his overthrow. The consideration of the treaty was thus not permitted to proceed on its merits alone. The Imperial Court, at first almost persuaded to give approval, was then overshadowed by the anti-Tokugawa party and the Mikado's assent was withheld. Most of the daimyos of the Empire had also opposed the proposed abrogation of the policy of seclusion.

Harris returned to Yedo in April, only to receive assurances that the treaty would be signed, but that the date of signing would be further postponed. Meanwhile the Dutch authorities, who had received a copy of the treaty, stood ready to sign one in which would be omitted the clauses and articles which were most objectionable to the Japanese.

To thwart the Dutch and to save his own treaty, Harris secured a written agreement that the Japanese would not sign any other treaty until thirty days after his was signed. Then he returned again to Shimoda.

The treaty question was abruptly taken out of domestic politics by the news of the conclusion of the treaties of Tientsin and the reported intention of Lord Elgin to proceed to Yedo immediately. On June 23 and 24, 1858, the U. S. S. *Mississippi* and *Powhatan,* respectively, arrived at Shimoda with the news. Harris seized the opportunity, returned to the Bay of Yedo with the American naval vessels, and sent a hurried call to Yedo for a conference. The Japanese were in consternation. Arriving at the conclusion which Harris had always urged, that it was safer to let the American treaty stand as a model for other treaties than to longer delay, and fortified by a written statement from Harris that he was willing to act as mediator with Great Britain and France, the compact was signed on board the *Powhatan* July 29, 1858.

The treaty did not have the approval of the Mikado, and by signing it the Shogun party had laid itself open to the most serious criticisms before the very princes and daimyos who were already seeking means whereby the Tokugawa régime in Japanese affairs might be eliminated. Harris was quite unaware of the extent of the domestic disturbance throughout the Empire to which he had been contributing.

Three other treaties followed in quick succession: with the Netherlands, August 18; with Russia, August 19; with Great Britain, August 26; and with France, October 7.

While by no means of equal importance with the diplomacy of Benjamin Franklin, there were qualities in the work of Townsend Harris at Yedo which remind one of Franklin in London and Paris. Longford, British historian, describes his service as "not exceeded by any in the entire history of the international relations of the world." [25] The further diplomatic service of Harris in Yedo will be treated in a later chapter.

THE POLICY OF TOWNSEND HARRIS IN JAPAN 365

BIBLIOGRAPHICAL NOTES

1. The primary sources for the life and diplomatic service of Townsend Harris are: Japan Despatches, Vols. 1 and 2 (Dept. of State); Griffis: "Townsend Harris", which is based on the journals of Harris and includes very generous extracts of them; a typewritten copy of a part of the Harris journal (Library of Congress); and the records of the Bureau of Appointments, Dept. of State. Very few of the Harris dispatches to the Dept. of State were ever published, but the extracts from Harris's journal, printed in Griffis's book, are in many cases practically identical with the dispatches.
2. Records of the Bureau of Appointment, Dept. of State. Griffis makes an incorrect guess as to the way in which the Harris appointment came about.
3. Ningpo Letters, Vol. 1, June 22, 1855, Macgowan to Marcy (Dept. of State).
4. Japan Instructions, Vol. 1 (Dept. of State).
5. Dip. Corres., 1862, p. 822.
6. Griffis: "Harris," pp. 15, 16.
7. E. H. House: "The Martyrdom of an Empire," *Atlantic Monthly,* Vol. XLVII, p. 622.
   Balestier Corres., S. Ex. Doc. 38:32-1.
   Japan Instructions, Vol. 1, Sept. 12, 1855.
10. W. M. Wood, U. S. Surgeon on the *San Jacinto,* wrote a book— "Fankwei"; or, "The San Jacinto in the Seas of India, China and Japan," in which eight chapters are devoted to the Harris Mission to Bankok. Japan Dispatches, Vol. 1, Nos. 5-8, contain Harris's own reports of the negotiations.
11. Japan Dispatches, Vol. 1, June 2, 1856.
12. J. H. Gubbins: "Progress of Japan," 1853-71, reprints in an appendix all of these early treaties.
13. S. Ex. Doc. No. 34:33-2.
14. Stead: "Japan by the Japanese," p. 150.
15. Sir Robert K. Douglas: "Europe and the Far East," p. 155.
16. "Foreign Relations," 1879, pp. 27 ff. These reports, while no doubt based upon inaccurate interpretation, appear to be a reliable record nowhere else obtainable of the negotiations at Yedo.
17. Gubbins: p. 257.
18. Japan Dispatches, Vol. 1, Aug. 7, 1858.
19. The Elgin negotiations are given in the British Parliamentary Papers, 1859. 2 Sess. Com. 33. Corres. rel. to the Earl of Elgin's special Mission to China and Japan, 1857-59; see also Oliphant's "Lord Elgin's Mission."
20. It is hardly fair to place the blame for reducing the tariff exclusively on Great Britain, as Payson J. Treat does in his generally admirable Early Diplomatic Relations between the United States and Japan, 1853-65, p. 117.
21. Griffis: "Harris," p. 267.

22. Harris Journal (Lib. of Cong.), Section III, p. 43.
23. *Ibid.,* p. 46.
24. The most thorough reviews, based on Japanese sources, of the domestic situation in Japan are: Treat's Early Diplomatic Relations; Gubbins: The Progress of Japan. The student is fortunate in the study of this period in that so much Japanese material has been made available in English, by both Japanese and English scholars. See Bibliography for complete list.
25. Longford: "Story of Old Japan," p. 302.

CHAPTER XX

ANSON BURLINGAME

ANSON BURLINGAME,[1] the first American Minister to reside in Peking, was about forty-one years old when he arrived in China in the latter part of 1861. By birth he belonged to pioneer American stock, his parents having moved from New England to northern New York where he was born, and then to Michigan Territory where he received his primary and academic education. But by choice Burlingame belonged to the culture and traditions of Boston; he went to Harvard for his training in law, married in Cambridge, and entered Massachusetts politics at an early age. His character and career bear witness both to the pioneering spirit of his parental heritage and the urbanity and culture of his social environment.[2]

Burlingame served three terms in Congress but in 1860, notwithstanding his anti-slavery sentiments and his support of Lincoln, he was defeated for reelection. In the House of Representatives he had served as a member of the committee on foreign affairs, where his freedom-loving nature expressed itself in an ardent championship of Kossuth and Sardinian independence. Even more characteristic of the man was his denunciation of Preston Brooks in the House of Representatives for the assault on Charles Sumner. Because of this rebuke Brooks challenged him to a duel and Burlingame promptly accepted, naming rifles as the weapons and Deer Island, near Niagara Falls, as the place. Brooks then declined to meet him. Early in 1861 President Lincoln appointed Burlingame Minister to Austria, but before he arrived at his post the Austrian Government expressed disapproval of the appointment on the ground that Burlingame had been too ardent an advocate of Kossuth.

The post at Peking was then offered to Burlingame and accepted.

Burlingame arrived in China in October, 1861, and entered upon residence in Peking in the summer of 1862. In 1865 he returned to the United States on leave, probably with the expectation of resigning his post and reentering politics, but he was persuaded to return to China. He reached Peking to begin the second part of his service in the latter part of 1866, after an absence of fifteen months, and a year later, November 21, 1867, he resigned [3] "in the interests of my country and civilization"; he had accepted the position of envoy of the Empire to all of the Western powers then having treaties with China. With two Chinese associates and a retinue of thirty people he set out for the United States.

In June, 1868, on behalf of China, he negotiated with Seward [4] eight additional articles to the Treaty of Tientsin, and then departed for London. He secured from Lord Clarendon, who had recently returned to the Foreign Office with the first Gladstone Ministry, an agreement which, while not so formal as a treaty, nevertheless fully answered his purpose. Thus strengthened by his successful negotiations with the United States and Great Britain, he moved on to the Continent visiting Paris, Berlin, and the capitals of the northern kingdoms, arriving in Petrograd early in 1870. There he contracted pneumonia and died February 23, thus terminating before the age of fifty a truly brilliant career. Some of the more conspicuous of his achievements in China and for China must be noted in detail, and in the records of these will be found the marks of his peculiar qualities of heart and mind. Burlingame was easily the most capable American diplomatic representative in China since Caleb Cushing who, though superior to him in intellect, lacked his unselfish idealism and breadth of statesmanship.

The survey of the work of Anson Burlingame falls naturally into three parts: his service in Peking; the supplementary articles to the treaty of Tientsin; and the reception of the Burlingame Mission in England and Europe, as well as its influence in China.

THE SUPPRESSION OF THE TAIPING REBELLION

Notwithstanding the continuing strength of the Taipings after the establishment of the rebel capital in Nanking in 1853—a strength which was purely relative to the utter weakness of the Imperial forces—and notwithstanding the continuance of a considerable sympathy for the rebels on the part of the Christian nations, and among foreign traders and adventurers in China who found profit in assisting and ministering to the needs of the rebels, the fate of the rebellion was sealed when Lord Elgin and Baron Gros concluded their negotiations with Prince Kung in Peking in 1860. Great Britain had decided that it was better policy to support and strengthen the dynasty than to permit the Empire to fall to pieces in rebellion. Thus the policy first advocated in theory by Humphrey Marshall for the United States became the practice of all the treaty powers, Russia included, seven years later.

For assisting the Imperial Government the United States, because of the Civil War, was quite unable, even had it been willing, to lend the aid recommended by Marshall. The American naval forces in China in 1861 were almost entirely withdrawn. The United States could do nothing except give approval to what the other powers proposed. The American share in the suppression of the Taipings, while by no means inconsiderable, was entirely unofficial and individual.

Alluring as the subject is, the part played by General Frederick T. Ward,[5] by his successor Burgevine, and by other Americans who joined the Ever-Victorious Army can hardly claim attention as important in a study of the policy of the United States in China. General Ward, who organized the force of Chinese with the assistance of a cosmopolitan corps of foreign adventurers as subordinate officers, was sponsored by Admiral Sir James Hope. and by him was introduced to Burlingame shortly after the latter's arrival in Shanghai in 1862.[6] The American minister accepted Ward because of this introduction, and because of the successes with Chinese troops which Ward had achieved, but the promotion of Ward in the Chinese service was due to his own worth and to the British Admiral's backing rather than to any assistance from American officials. Indeed the Americans,. already disgraced so often by the unrestrained license of adventurers in China, appear to have placed confidence in Ward only cautiously. In the later part of 1862 Ward was fatally wounded and the leaderless army thrown into confusion. But by that time the value of such a force was so evident that its dissolution would have been regarded by all of the foreign representatives and perhaps by the Imperial Government as a catastrophe. It had proved to be a most useful means by which the foreign governments could unofficially support the Imperial Government in its desperate struggle with the rebels, yet without raising embarrassing questions either among themselves or with the Chinese Government. Ward's force had also demonstrated a fact which must never be forgotten, namely, that the Chinese, under competent leadership, make excellent soldiers.

Meanwhile the utmost harmony existed between the representatives of the foreign powers in Peking. Upon the death of Ward it was agreed that his successor ought also, in the interests of equality of influence for the foreign powers, to be an American. The British authorities were especially willing to agree to this because at that time the offices in the Foreign Inspectorate of Customs had passed largely into British hands, and plans were already under way to create a naval flotilla for China which also would be under a British officer. Both Sir Frederick Bruce and Burlingame joined in urging the appointment to the Ever-Victorious Army of Burgevine, another American who had been an associate of Ward's and of high rank among his foreign officers. The appointment was made with disastrous results into the details of which it is not possible to go.

Burgevine was an adventurer with an exceptional imagination and perhaps cherished the idea of carving out for himself an empire in Asia.[7] His motives were suspected from the outset, and of the successes of his army Li Hung Chang, its titular head, was jealous. Burgevine lost his temper and played into the hands of Li Hung Chang. When removed from his command he deceived Burlingame and made the American minister again his advocate. For a time the Burgevine affair not only imperilled the Imperial efforts to suppress the rebels but also seriously embarrassed Mr. Burlingame's relations with the Chinese Government.[8] Had Burgevine not failed to live up to the confidence which was reposed in him, the result of the part that General Ward played in the Ever Victorious Army might have been the greatest of benefits for the improvement of the already cordial relations between Burlingame and Prince Kung. The Imperial Government, immediately after the death of Ward, heaped his memory with posthumous honors and set apart two memorial chapels to him. But the failure of Burgevine, to which was subsequently added the prolonged and irritating negotiations and representations over the Ward estate,[9] more than counteracted all the initial good so far as concerns the relations between the United States and China. To Major Gordon of the British Army was entrusted, with the approval of all, the task which fell from the hand of Ward, and the even more difficult responsibility of finally disbanding the Ever-Victorious Army before its adventurer-officers fell under the temptation to which Burgevine had succumbed and created fresh troubles for distraught China.

Burlingame's extraordinary personal magnetism as well as his evident desire to deal fairly with everyone overcame many obstacles in both his dealings with Prince Kung and with his diplomatic colleagues, and notwithstanding his mistake in supporting Burgevine, his influence in Peking increased rapidly. In the difficult matter of the disposal of the Lay-Osborn Flotilla in 1863 [10] Prince Kung sought his advice and followed it, and the confidence then acquired by the Chinese Government in his justice and sagacity contributed in large measure to his appointment as envoy to the foreign powers in 1867.

The greatest contribution of the American minister, however, to the international relations of the Chinese Empire during the period of his service, was his application of the policy of cooperation in the difficult years of 1863, 1864 and 1865.

Burlingame and Cooperation

Every American representative since the days of Humphrey Marshall had been instructed to cooperate with the other powers in every way consistent with the peaceful policy of the United States in China, and consistent with the policy of the open door of equal opportunity for all. Cooperation, however, had broken down because neither Great Britain nor France were willing to accept peaceful methods of settling disputes, because their ultimate intentions in the empire were matters of suspicion and because the American government was unwilling to incur any of the financial or political liabilities incident to cooperation. In 1863 the foreign powers had secured from China all that they desired, and the ground was therefore prepared for Burlingame. Burlingame's proposals were based upon the assumption, to which Sir Frederick Bruce heartily agreed, and to which the other ministers acceded either from convictions or because of its obvious immediate advantages, that the interests of the treaty powers in China were identical. All desired the fulfillment of treaty obligations, none of them was prepared to enforce them alone if such enforcement were to call for the last resort, and the best assurance of peaceful success was in the forgetting of rivalries and in the presentation of a united front to the Imperial Government.

One of the most important questions in which a policy of cooperation seemed necessary, was the proper interpretations of rights in the so-called concessions for the residence of foreigners. Notwithstanding the declarations at

Shanghai in 1853-1854, the tendency was for the foreigners to treat land concessions, the number of which had been greatly increased in 1858, as actual cessions of territory to which China no longer could claim the sovereign rights. In the face of all such claims Burlingame contended that "any concession of territory would be an abridgment of our treaty rights." Thus again American interests were seen to coincide with the interests of the empire itself. The territorial integrity of the Chinese Empire became a cardinal doctrine of American policy.

"I have never failed," wrote Burlingame, April 18, 1863,[11] "in my interviews [with the Chinese officials] to keep the non-concession doctrine before them, because I had been made aware in Shanghai, by conversations with the British consul, that he and the British residents supposed they had a *quasi* territorial concession at Shanghai over which they could maintain jurisdiction not only over British subjects but over Chinese. This assumption led the French to make like claims, and the result was that there was a race, apparently, between the British and French local authorities as to which could secure the most. I brought the question, in many conversations, to the attention of the British and Russian ministers, and since his arrival, to the French minister. I am happy to say that I found my views accorded with theirs, and that we are now, on this most important question, in perfect agreement; and this agreement is a guarantee of the territorial integrity of the Chinese Empire."

The policy of cooperation, under Burlingame, became very specific and practical whereas it had hitherto been theoretical and vague. Its origin, development and application may best be described in its author's own words. The basis of the policy Burlingame stated as follows:[12] ". . . if the treaty powers could agree among themselves to the neutrality of China, and together secure order in the treaty ports, and give their moral support to the party in China in favor of order, the interests of humanity would be subserved. "

"Upon my arrival at Pekin," wrote Burlingame, "I at once elaborated my views and found, upon comparing them with those held by the representatives of England and Russia, that they were in accord with theirs. After mature deliberation, we determined to consult and cooperate upon all questions. . . . Preliminary to entering into thorough cooperation, I held it to be my duty to ascertain the ulterior purposes of the treaty powers having, by position and trade, a leading place in China.

"I found Mr. Balluzec, the Russian minister, prompt to answer, in the spirit of the Russian treaty, that his government did not desire to menace at any time the territorial integrity of China, but on the contrary, wished to bring it more and more into the family of nations, subject, in its relations with foreign powers, to the obligations of international law. That he was but too happy to cooperate in a policy that would engraft western upon eastern civilization, without a disruption of the Chinese Empire.

"With Sir Frederick Bruce, the British minister, my conversations were elaborate and exhaustive. I said to him frankly, that we represented the first trading powers here, and that our interests were identical, and I was ready not only from individual desire, but because of the wishes of my government, to cooperate with him. He met me in a large and generous spirit, and said that he had ever desired to cooperate with the other treaty powers, and pointed out in dispatches to his government the evidences of such desires, and expressed his delight that the representative of the United States should hold views so coincident with his own. I said to him that while I paid full homage to the energy of his government in opening China, and for affording protection to the citizens of the United States, still I felt, looking to British antecedents, a little distrust about the future; that our trade by the way of California was increasing, and I felt anxious about its future condition. I illustrated my views of distrust by reference to the controlling influence of the British in the custom-house, and in the pretensions set up by his countrymen in the treaty ports in favor of territorial concessions. He agreed with me that the sensitiveness was natural, and replied that he would be pleased to remove every ground for it. He said that circumstances more than design had given the English the seeming control of affairs at the treaty ports; that in the first place the English trade was very large; and besides, from long connection with the East, many of his countrymen had acquired knowledge of the Chinese language, and when persons were wanted it was natural that those most qualified in that respect should be selected. He pointed out that long ago he had recommended that the custom-house should be put upon a cosmopolitan footing, and that Mr. Lay, who was at the head of it, had endeavored to carry out his views.

"I must admit that in this he was right. I was applied to by the Chinese, through their employé, Mr. Hart, then at the head of the customs, for Americans to fill places, but I could not find any who had studied Chinese. One of the first places in the Chinese service was tendered to our consul, Mr. Seward, but he could not, he thought, with justice to his own government accept it. If we had had a school for interpreters, our proper influence would have been far greater than it is now. Besides, the English have been compelled to defend the treaty ports without any assistance from us, and we have enjoyed the fruits of that protection. But in the face of these obvious facts, Sir Frederick admitted that it was not in the interest of England to hold a position which gave her special privileges, and subjected her needlessly to the criticism of the other treaty powers, and therefore he was willing to have any arrangements made by which she would not be put in a false position.

"He did not wish, as far as he was concerned, that English officers should lead against the Taipings. He prefers that the Chinese should employ for purposes of drill and discipline, men from the smaller states of Europe, and that I might rely upon it that he would do all he could to relieve England from the charge of being the 'great bully' of the East; to relieve her 'from the dilemma of being forced by local clamor to commit acts of violence which, though in accordance with past usage, and perhaps justified by our (their) former situation, do not fail to jar unpleasantly on the conscience of England and of the civilized world.' The force policy was wrong, and he was certain that his government had had enough of wars brought about through hasty action of men in the East not under the sway of large ideas. He was for a change of policy. . . .

"Upon this frank avowal of the policy of England, it would be impossible to refuse cooperation. The Russian minister and myself both concurred in the view that the position of Sir Frederick was just what we desired, and we hailed with delight its avowal. The French minister, Mr. Berthemy, agrees with us. Being a broad and experienced statesman, he at once saw the advantage that would flow from the casting down of all jealousies, and by a cooperation on every material question in China. Indeed he has realized largely the advantages of such action; the French *Chargé d'Affaires* before him, acting upon the old-school policy of antagonizing everybody, thus causing the Chinese to believe that we were divided among ourselves, for one year failed to get justice from the Chinese Government, where it was due, in a case in which we were all interested.

"The policy upon which we are agreed is briefly this: that while we claim our treaty right to buy and sell, and hire, in the treaty ports, subject, in respect to our rights of property and person, to the jurisdiction of our own governments, we will not ask for, nor take concessions of, territory in the treaty ports, or in any way interfere with the jurisdiction of the Chinese Government over its own people, nor ever menace the territorial integrity of the Chinese Empire. That we will not take part in the internal struggles in China, beyond what is necessary to maintain our treaty rights. That the latter we will unitedly sustain against all who may violate them. To this end we are now clear in the policy of defending the treaty ports against the Taipings, or rebels; but in such a way as not to make war upon that considerable body of the Chinese people, by following them into the interior of their country. In this connection, while we feel desirous, from what we know of it, to have the rebellion put down, still we have come to question the policy of lending government officers to lead the Chinese in the field, for fear of complications among ourselves, growing out of the relative number to be employed, &c. That while we wish to give our moral support to the government, at the present time the power in the country which seems disposed to maintain order and our treaty rights, we should prefer that it would organize its own people as far as possible for its own defense, taking only foreigners for instruction in the arts of peace and war, and these, as far as possible, from the smaller treaty powers.　　　＼

"To maintain the revenue laws of the government, to relieve the treaty powers from the burdens attending the suppression of piracy along the coast, the Chinese Government has been persuaded to purchase several small war steamers, and to man them temporarily with foreigners. This fleet is coming out under the command of Sherard Osborn, and is manned chiefly by English sailors, with the understanding that it is a temporary arrangement; and that, too, is to become cosmopolitan; and on the idea that we are to cooperate upon all questions in China, no special objection is made to the force by the other treaty powers. I confess that I should be pleased, were it more cosmopolitan now, but it was arranged before I came out, and before the above policy was developed and agreed upon. While Sir Frederick Bruce shall remain, or while the policy now agreed upon shall be maintained, no harm can come from it.

"That the indemnity may be collected and accounted for, and that the Chinese Government may have a fund to maintain a national force, organized upon European principles; that the local authorities may be checked in their corrupt practices, and a uniform system for the collection of the revenue maintained, it is agreed on all hands that the present foreign custom-house system is the best as yet devised, and, as it has been administered by Mr. Lay, entitled to our support. Indeed it is alone through such instrumentalities that we can hope to advance in the cause of civilization in China. As Sir Frederick states, there can be nothing more unmeaning than antagonism between the United States and Great Britain in China. I need not attempt to prove the advantages which must flow from cooperation; that we should do so all must admit. By the favored-nation clause in the treaties, no nation can gain by any sharp act of diplomacy any privilege not secured to all.

"The circumstances conspire to make this a fortunate moment in which to inaugurate the cooperative policy.

"The treaty powers are represented here by men of modern ideas; by men who, in this land, where everything is to be done, do not choose to embarrass each other by sowing distrust in the Chinese mind, but who with an open policy and common action, deepen each other's confidence and win the respect of the Chinese. That the too sanguine hopes in relation to China of our more advanced civilization may be fully realized by any action we may take, ought not to be expected. The peculiar people we are among must be remembered; how hoary is their civilization, and how proud they are, and how ignorant of us they have always been, and how little their knowledge of some of us has tended to create in their minds a desire for a change. Their government is good in theory, but not now well administered. The people are free to license, and, as in our own country, we find a portion of them in rebellion, because they have felt too little the influence of the central government.

"The trouble here now is that we are dealing with a regency which in a few years must hand over its doings to the Emperor, and those he may call around him. The regency dare not depart in the smallest particular from the old traditions, and yet these will not do for these times. They are distrustful of us, and are afraid of their censors and distant local authorities. Besides, there is a large anti-foreign party here. There are members of the foreign board who, if left to themselves, would at once place China in perfect international relations with us; but sitting with them are spies, who paralyze them in their action with us, to fall, as they frequently do, far short of their promises. In their weakness they resort to tergiversations to such an extent as to invite menace, and to cause us in our passionate modes almost to despair of holding, with dignity, any relations at all with them."

One detects in this dispatch many of the personal qualities which gave distinction to the character of its author, and especially his enthusiastic optimism. It is therefore not to be wondered at that the sober-minded and experienced Secretary of State felt that the application of such a policy was almost too much to expect. He wrote to Burlingame:[13]

"One may very reasonably fear that the beneficial policy thus agreed upon would fall into disuse if those ministers, or any of them, should at any time give place to less intelligent and able statesmen. But this consideration does not deter the President from giving it his entire approval; and he sincerely hopes that a successful trial of it, during the residence of those ministers in China, will render its continuance afterwards a cardinal fact in the policy of all the maritime powers."

Seward had indeed placed his finger on the weak spot. The policy of cooperation was purely personal, depending entirely upon the enthusiastic and sincere convictions of Bruce and Burlingame, and no sooner had these men disappeared from China than the policy began to lapse, although efforts were sometimes made to drag it out in the service of some power otherwise unable to accomplish its own peculiar purposes.

That Burlingame was not unaware of the difficulties is apparent from a subsequent letter of his to the consul general at Shanghai in which he summarized the policy as follows: [14]

"You will perceive that we are making an effort to substitute fair diplomatic action in China for force; and thus cooperation becomes the rule in carrying out these relations. It should be sincere; and to be effective requires in the first place a predisposition to get

on well with one's colleagues; and in the second, that just moderation which cannot fail to win the respect and confidence of one's
associates."

THE FIRST CHINESE MISSION—TREATY OF 1868

There were several reasons which predisposed the Im
perial Government to think well of the Burlingame Mission to the Western powers in 1867.   In addition to the
great confidence which was reposed in Burlingame was the
fact that the following year the British treaty of Tientsin
would be due for revision, and the Chinese knew that the
British merchants, never as contented as their government
with the advantages secured under that treaty, were preparing to urge upon China further demands, some of which
the Imperial authorities intended firmly to resist.   Perhaps the most important of the expected demands, in the
estimation of the Chinese, was the throwing open of China,
regardless of treaty ports, for railways and telegraphs.[15]
But there were more general reasons.   Instructed by the
experiences in 1839 and 1858, the Chinese authorities saw
clearly that any resistance to the demands of foreign powers
might lead again to invasion and war.   The more liberal
element in the Chinese Government was already having a
most difficult time in the face of the reactionary party, and
the application of further force by foreign nations would
cost the liberal party its leadership and result fatally for
the empire.

China had already assumed many obligations to the
treaty powers which the officials at Peking were not fully
able to discharge because of the large amount of autonomy
possessed by the provinces.   Peking might propose but the
provinces disposed.   Where the terms of a treaty conflicted
with the long established rights and practices of the local
authorities, it was as difficult to bring the provinces into
line as it was subsequently difficult to bring the Pacific
Coast states into harmony with the national government in
the matter of Asiatic immigration to the United States.   The
treaties of Tientsin in the duties they imposed upon China,

really called for the reorganization of the Empire itself in such grave matters as provincial autonomy, the collection of inland revenue and the disposal of military forces, but such reorganization of the Empire while the Imperial authority was so weak was utterly impossible. China was clearly not in a position with safety to itself to assume even more extensive obligations to the powers such as would be inevitable in the revision of the treaties of 1858.

Burlingame's reasons for accepting the novel post, aside from purely personal ones, are also not difficult to see. During his absence in the United States the previous year, Sir Frederick Bruce having already been transferred to Washington, the policy of cooperation among the ministers, just as Seward feared it might, had largely broken down. To resuscitate this cooperative spirit and give it guaranties for the future required something more than the personal assent of the various ministers. It must be secured by agreement with the governments they represented. On the other hand if the policy were to fail utterly it was clear to Burlingame, to Hart, to any impartial observer, that the consequences not only for China but for the entire world must eventually be most serious. The partition of the Empire following a conflict of foreign nations within the bounds of China itself seemed very possible. To contribute anything towards the avoidance of such a calamity was a motive worthy to inspire the best efforts of any man, and Burlingame was fully conscious of the vast issues which might hang on the success of his mission.

Late in February, 1868, the Burlingame Mission sailed from Shanghai for San Francisco. It met in the United States with the heartiest of receptions. The picturesque appearance of the retinue and the moving eloquence of Burlingame, who managed the tour according to the best traditions of the showman's art, captured the imagination of the American people. The people of the United States were now little interested in securing new trade concessions in China, and heartily enjoyed the diversion and entertainment which the Mission afforded. Into the details of the

tour from San Francisco eastward and the numerous receptions and dinners it is impossible to go. But the supplementary articles to the Treaty of Tientsin, usually known
as the Burlingame Treaty, signed at Washington July 28,
1868, will repay careful study as an expression of both
American opinion and American policy towards China.

Considered as a treaty, aside from the immigration stipulations, the articles are not of great importance. Their
negotiation was quite unauthorized, so far as China was
concerned. There is no reason to suppose that Prince Kung
was anything but surprised to be presented with these articles for ratification. As for the United States the articles
were unnecessary. They added little either to American
privileges or obligations. But as an expression of public
sentiment in the United States and as a solemn declaration
of official policy towards China the supplementary articles
of 1868 were, in some respects, more authoritative than
either the Cushing Treaty of 1844 or the Reed Treaty of
1858. They were entirely removed from the atmosphere of
commercial competition, they were negotiated freely and not
under compulsion, and they were written by the American
Secretary of State with the Envoy of China, as it were,
standing at his elbow, telling him what to write [16] Furthermore, the drafting of the articles had been preceded
by a period of intensive education of public opinion in which
the envoy of China had been allowed to plead his case before the American people.

There were eight articles to the agreement and for
nearly all of them there was a background of history in
Burlingame's six years of experience as American minister
in Peking.

The appointment of Chinese consuls (Article 3) in the
United States was in line with the efforts already made by
Sir Robert Hart, by Burlingame, and by Seward, to encourage the Government of China to send official representatives abroad.

Freedom from persecution because of religious beliefs
in China had been stipulated in Article 29 of the American

Treaty of Tientsin. Article 6 of the supplementary treaty extended this guarantee of tolerance to include also the Chinese in the United States. This article "recalls the great doctrine of the Constitution which gives to a man the right to hold any faith which his conscience may dictate," to use Mr. Burlingame's own explanation [17] of what therefore seems to be a quite unnecessary treaty stipulation.

Likewise the article (7) stipulating that "citizens of the United States may freely establish and maintain schools within the Empire of China at those places where foreigners are by treaty permitted to reside; and, reciprocally, Chinese subjects may enjoy the same privileges and immunities in the United States," was meaningless except as it gave the American missionary in China a little better leverage for the strengthening of his work. The missionaries had already begun to establish schools long before 1868. The remainder of this article by which access to government schools in each country should be given to students of the other, looked in the direction of a policy already urged by S. Wells Williams and Burlingame, to encourage the Chinese to take up Western education in a school to be established in China with the balance of the indemnity money. It was also in line with the fact that already Dr. W. A. P. Martin, an American missionary, was teaching in a government college in Peking where Chinese pupils were to be prepared for the customs service, and was soon to become director of the school.[18] The other articles of the treaty deal with matters of more far-reaching consequence.

The United States disclaimed and disavowed (Article 8) "any intention or right to intervene in the domestic administration of China in regard to the construction of railroads, telegraphs, or other material internal improvements." At the same time the United States engaged to nominate, if at any time they were desired, "suitable engineers to be employed by the Chinese Government." This article was, on the one hand, fully in harmony with the policy already adopted by Seward and Burlingame with reference to the efforts of an American company to secure and operate a concession for a telegraph line along the coast,[19] and on the other, looked towards the building up of a system of foreign technical advisers who should enter Chinese service as Raphael Pumpelly, an American engineer, had done in 1863.[20]   This plan was also merely an extension of the arrangement by which foreigners had taken service in the Chinese Maritime customs, and by which Anson Burlingame himself now appeared in the rôle of political adviser to the Chinese Government.   That Article 8 of the Burlingame Treaty was an expression of permanent American policy in China is amply proved by the long succession of distinguished Americans who have since appeared in the service of the Chinese Government.   The article also registered the corresponding stern disapproval by the United States of any system of commercial exploitation of the resources of China by foreigners who would depend upon the military forces of their governments to sustain and extend their privileges.

The fifth and sixth articles of the Burlingame Treaty dealing with the question of Chinese immigration to California will be considered in Chapter XXVIII.   The most significant part of the supplementary articles, however, from the viewpoint of American policy were Articles 1 and 2 in which were asserted in the most uncompromising terms that China possessed, in spite of the doctrine of extraterritoriality, and in spite of the engagement already made to the powers, full sovereign rights over her territory.   The meaning of these articles was explained by Burlingame as follows:

"In the first place, it declares the neutrality of the Chinese waters in opposition to the pretensions of the exterritoriality doctrine, that inasmuch as the persons and the property of the people of the foreign powers were under the jurisdiction of those powers, therefore it was the right of parties contending with each other to attack each other in the Chinese waters, thus making those waters the place of their conflict.   The treaty traverses all such absurd pretensions.   It strikes down the so-called concession doctrines, under which the nationals of different countries located upon spots of land in the treaty ports had come to believe that they could take jurisdiction there not only of their own nationals, not only of the person and property of their own people, but take jurisdiction of the Chinese and the people of other countries. When this question was called under discussion and referred to the home governments, not by the Chinese originally, but by those foreign nations who felt that their treaty rights were being abridged by these concession doctrines, the distant foreign countries could not stand the discussion for a moment. And I aver that every treaty power had abandoned the concession doctrines, though some of their officials at the present time in China undertake to contend for them, undertake to expel the Chinese, to attack the Chinese, to protect the Chinese, although the territory did not belong to them. China has never abandoned her eminent domain, never abandoned on that territory her jurisdiction, and I trust she never will. This treaty strikes down all the pretensions about all the concessions of territory." [21]

From such words it is clear that the intention of Mr. Burlingame in his mission to the Western powers was not merely to give his policy of cooperation among the powers in China the force of treaty engagements but also to bring the powers to the formal affirmation of the objects for which the cooperation was to be employed.[22] The policy of cooperation was a two-edged sword which might cut either way, and Burlingame was seeking a formal agreement to the principles upon which he and Sir Frederick Bruce had been in such hearty agreement in Peking a few years before but which were evidently not in accord with the ideas of the British mercantile community nor with those of the important French officials.[23] It seems equally clear that these first two articles of the Burlingame Treaty officially expressed what might already be called the traditional American policy with reference to China: the sovereignty and integrity of China must be maintained, and the door for equal opportunities in trade must be left open for the free competition of all nations with due regard for the sovereign rights of the Empire. On the other hand the articles entirely blinked the fact that the treaties of 1858 had in practice, as well as in the way in which they were negotiated, already seriously transgressed on the rights of China as a sovereign power.

Fundamentally Mr. Burlingame's object was to read China back into the family of nations from which the Empire had been read out by Caleb Cushing in 1844, when he rested his doctrine of extraterritoriality on the ground that China was a pagan state.[24]   In his address before the city council of Boston Burlingame said:

"Again this treaty recognizes China as an equal among the nations, in opposition to the old doctrine that because she was not a Christian nation, she could not be placed in the roll of nations. But I will not discuss that question. The greatest living authority upon Eastern questions is here tonight—Mr. Cushing. He has stated that position more fully than any one else, while his heart has leaned ever up to the side of the Chinese."

Mr. Burlingame's effort, however, rested upon a premise far less sound than Mr. Cushing's, for it assumed as true what was entirely contrary to fact, viz., that the Chinese Empire was a strong centralized government capable of controlling its own provinces and equally capable of dealing with the European powers on terms of military equality.

This false assumption that China was able to exercise all the functions of sovereignty has underlaid a very large part of the entire political relations of the United States with reference to China.

Before concluding a review of the Burlingame Mission in the United States one must note not merely the Burlingame Treaty but also the speeches of the man whose name it bears.   Mr. Burlingame was an orator, skilled in all the arts of a style of oratory which has now largely passed away.   His orations abounded not in logic, not in reasoned deductions from carefully ascertained and clearly described facts, but in illustrations and flights of eloquence designed not so much to induce a conclusion as to produce an impression.   While they clearly reflected his own convictions they did not always keep step with the facts as seen by more sober-minded observers.   One illustration, from his famous address at a dinner given in honor of the Mission in New York will suffice.[25]

"China, seeing another civilization approaching on every side, has her eyes open. She sees Russia on the north, Europe on the west, America on the east. She sees a cloud of sail on her coast, she sees the mighty steamers coming from everywhere—bow on. She feels the spark from the electric telegraph falling hot upon her everywhere;

she rouses herself, not in anger, but for argument. She finds that by
not being in a position to compete with other nations for so long a
time she has lost ground. She finds that she must come into relations
with this civilization that is pressing up around her, and feeling that,
she does not wait but comes out to you and extends to you her hand.
She tells you she is ready to take upon her ancient civilization the
graft of your civilization. She tells you she is ready to take back
her own inventions, with all their developments. She tells you that
she is willing to trade with you, to buy of you, to sell to you, to help
you strike off the shackles from trade. She invites your merchants,
she invites your missionaries. She tells the latter to plant the shining
cross on every hill and in every valley. For she is hospitable to fair
argument. . . .
"Let her alone; let her have her independence; let her develop
herself in her own time and in her own way. She has no hostility to
you. Let her do this and she will initiate a movement which will be
felt in every workshop of the civilized world. She says now: 'Send us
your wheat, your lumber, your coal, your silver, your goods from
everywhere—we will take as many of them as we can. We will give
you back our tea, our silk, free labor, which we have sent so largely out
into the world.'   It has overflowed upon Siam, upon the British
provinces, upon Singapore, upon Manila, upon Peru, Cuba, Australia
and California. All she asks is that you will be as kind to her nationals as she is to your nationals. She wishes simply that you will
do justice. She is willing not only to exchange goods with you, but
she is willing to exchange thoughts. She is willing to give you what
she thinks is her intellectual civilization in exchange for your material
civilization. Let her alone, and the caravans on the roads of the
north, toward Russia, will swarm in larger numbers than ever before.
Let her alone, and that silver which has been flowing for hundreds
of years into China, losing itself like the lost rivers of the West, but
which yet exists, will come out into the affairs of men. . . . The
imagination kindles at the future which may be, and which will be,
if you will be fair and just to China."

The assertion by the official spokesman of the Empire
that China invited the foreign merchants and the foreign
missionaries, and was ready for the latter to plant 'the
shining cross on every hill and in every valley' was a trav-
esty of the truth, and the statement made in the same
speech that China was willing to accept Western international law rested on little more than that Dr. W. A. P
Martin had translated Wheaton's "Elements of Inter
national Law" into Chinese, and that it was being taught
in the recently established customs college.[26]

Such assertions created wrong impressions as to the
exact condition of China and stimulated an optimism from

which there must be an inevitable reaction when the facts
were known. In China such statements filled the foreigners
with dismay.[27] Happily for the Mission when it reached
England and the Continent there were few opportunities for
speeches, and Burlingame's talents could be directed to per
sonal negotiations for which his rare political qualities
fitted him nearly as well as for speech-making.

THE BURLINGAME MISSION IN EUROPE AND CHINA

The Burlingame Treaty had the effect, most emphati-
cally, of an official approval by the American Government
on the Burlingame Mission and its objects. Far more important than as a treaty engagement, these supplementary
articles were the adroit vehicle for the pronouncement of
American policy not merely vis-à-vis China, but even more
particularly with reference to the relations of the United
States with the other foreign powers in China. This pronouncement, applied to the then immediate present, was
the official opinion of the United States as to the revision
of the British Treaty of Tientsin which was already a matter of negotiations between Sir Rutherford Alcock in Peking
and the Chinese Government. The Burlingame Treaty was
the official American declaration against the so-called "gun-
boat" policy of applying local pressure in China to secure
what between sovereign nations would ordinarily be the
subject of diplomatic action with the central government.

Fortunately for the success of the Mission in England, it
arrived in London about the time of most important
changes in the British Government. On December 4, 1868,
the first Gladstone ministry took office and Lord Clarendon
was placed in the Foreign Office. The Palmerston foreign
policy which had found its most complete expression in
China in the Anglo-French War (1857-60) was to be replaced by a policy reflecting the growing liberalism in English politics,—a policy which had been clearly foreshadowed in Peking by Sir Frederick Bruce five years earlier.

Mr. Burlingame was able to secure from Lord Claren-

don, December 28, 1868, an official declaration which was
far more practical and specific than the formal treaty stipulations of the American treaty.[28]   In a letter from Lord
Clarendon to Mr. Burlingame the former made the follow
ing statements:

1.   The Chinese Government is fully entitled to count upon the
forbearance of the foreign nations, and the British Government has
neither a desire nor intention to apply unfriendly pressure to China
to induce her government to advance more rapidly in her intercourse
with foreign nations than is consistent with safety and with due and
reasonable regard for the feelings of her subjects.
2.   On the other hand, China must observe the treaties and protect
British subjects within her empire.
3.   The British Government announces its preference rather .for
an appeal to the central government than to local authorities for the
redress of wrongs done to British subjects.   It is for the interest of
China that her central government be not only fully recognized but
also established within the empire.
4.   The British agents in China have been instructed to act in
the spirit and with the objects as explained above.

Thus armed the Burlingame Mission moved on to Paris
and the other European capitals but nowhere in Europe did
it meet with the degree of success which had been attained
in the United States and England.   France was non-com-
mittal, Bismarck was favorable, but vague; the negotiations
in St. Petersburg were left unfinished at the death of Burlingame.   This failure of the Mission in Europe—if indeed
it be just to describe as a failure an unfinished task which
was terminated by a personal fatality—may be explained
partially on grounds other than the existing political confusion on the Continent.   The truth was that while Great
Britain appeared willing to change her policy in China, yet
this change came at a time when she was already securely
established both commercially and politically in the Far
East.   The European powers, on the other hand, were being
asked, before they had secured similar power and influence
in China, to deny themselves the very methods which
Great Britain, and in some degree the United States, had
used so successfully.   The character of the reception accorded to the Burlingame Mission on the Continent clearly

foreshadowed the quarter from which the Chinese Empire might in the future expect serious dangers to both its sovereignty and its integrity.

"In one way or another, however we may disguise it," wrote Sir Rutherford Alcock,[29] "our position in China has been created by force—naked, physical force; and any intelligent policy to improve or maintain that position must still look to force in some form, latent or expressed, for the results." It was equally true that for other powers to achieve similar positions in China similar methods must be employed. To establish a solid basis for cooperation it would have been necessary for the Powers already lodged in China to surrender much that had been obtained in 1842, 1858, and 1860. Such a surrender no power was willing to make.

The success of the Burlingame Mission in the United States and England had two very definite immediate influences in China: it prevented a revision of the British treaty in a manner satisfactory to the British merchants; it also encouraged the Government of China not merely to oppose more strongly than before any increased aggressions of the foreign powers but also to stiffen their opposition to a full compliance with engagements to the powers which had already been extorted from them by the Anglo French War of the preceding decade. It encouraged them to believe that now they might indulge with more impunity the thorough-going distrust and even hatred of the foreigner which Burlingame in his fervid eloquence had perhaps never fully measured and certainly had never set forth in either the United States or England. This immediate change of front on the part of the Chinese Government was bitterly resented by most of the foreigners in China, and Burlingame, no longer able to plead his case and unable to finish in China the work which he had commenced abroad, was blamed. But in thus blaming him, might not his critics also have been bestowing upon the first Chinese Envoy to the Western powers the signal honor of having been the agent to secure for China in her otherwise impotent struggle with the Western nations a truce without which the Empire would soon have been dissolved? European colonial expansion, meeting with obstacles in the Far East, turned for a time to regions nearer home.

BIBLIOGRAPHICAL NOTES

1. The primary sources for Anson Burlingame and his work are: F. W. Williams: "Anson Burlingame and the First Chinese Mission"—a very sympathetic biography which is based on all the known sources of information; the volumes of Diplomatic Correspondence covering the period of his service in China, include practically every dispatch of any importance, as well as Seward's instructions; China Notes, Vol. 1, i.e., notes from the Chinese Legation to the Dept. of State, contain some valuable reports on the progress of the Chinese Mission in Europe.
2. Williams: "Burlingame," pp. 1 ff.
3. Dip. Corres., 1868, pp. 493-503.
4. F. W. Seward: "Reminiscences," pp. 375 ff, 378, 380-1.
5. There is no satisfactory account of Ward and Burgevine. The most complete story of their careers in China is a sketch on Ward in E. Alexander Powell's popularly written "Gentlemen Rovers." Powell uses sources of information not generally available, but does not state what they are. The general tendency of British historians, with the exception of Andrew Wilson's "The Ever-Victorious Army," is to minimize or ignore Ward and exalt Gordon. Wilson knew both Ward and Burgevine personally and is an excellent authority.
6. China Despatches, Vol. 20, Mar. 6, '62, Burlingame to Seward. (Dept. of State.)
7. Wilson: "The Ever-Victorious Army," p. 91.
8. Dip. Corres., 1863, p. 866.
9. For. Relations, 1888, pp. 199 ff; S. Ex. Doc. 48:45-2.
10. Dip. Corres., 1864, pp. 343 ff.
11. *Op. cit.,* 1864, p. 851.
12. *Ibid.,* pp. 859 ff.
13. *Ibid.,* p. 882.
14. *Op. cit.,* 1864, p. 430.
15. Cordier: "Relations de la Chine" Vol. 1, p. 285.
16. Williams: "Burlingame," p. 145.
17. *Ibid.,* p. 149.
18. Martin: "Cycle of Cathay," pp. 241, 293 ff.
19. Dip. Corres., 1867, pp. 471, 483, 509.
20. *Op. cit.,* 1864, pp. 362 ff; Pompelly: "Across America and Asia."
21. Williams: "Burlingame," pp. 148-9.
22. Notes, China, Jan. 18, 1870, Burlingame to Fish.
23. Dip. Corres., 1862, p. 838; 1863, p. 851; 1864, pp. 379, 419, 426; 1866, pp. 489, 528; 1867, pp. 429, 466; 1868, pp. 547 ff.

24. S. Ex. Doc. 58:28-2, pp. 5-14; Williams: "Burlingame," p. 149.
25. Williams: "Burlingame," pp. 138-9.
26. Martin: "Cycle of Cathay," pp. 221, 222; Dip. Corres., 1864, p. 332.
27. See Morse, Vol. 2, chap. IX, for an excellent review of the attitude of the foreigners in China towards the Mission.
28. Williams: "Burlingame": chap. "The Clarendon Letter and British Policy," pp. 161 ff; Morse, Vol. 2, pp. 197 ff; Cordier, *op. cit.*, pp. 295 ff.
29. Michie: "The Englishman in China," Vol. 2, p. 221.

CHAPTER XXI

THE UNITED STATES AND JAPAN: 1858-1869

THE phase of American relations with Japan which be gan with the signing of the treaties of 1858 came to natural end in 1869 with the beginning of the Meiji Era in Japan and the withdrawal of William E. Seward from the American Department of State. Few generalizations as to policy are possible.[1]

American interests were represented in Japan by four different men. Early in 1859, shortly after his treaty of the preceding year had been approved by the Senate, Townsend Harris was raised to the newly created post of Minister Resident. Harris presented his resignation soon after the inauguration of the Lincoln administration and was relieved by his successor, Robert H. Pruyn of Albany, in April, 1862. Pruyn, who had been prominent in New York state politics and was a friend of Seward's, served three years, after which A. L. C. Portman, Secretary of the Legation, who had been Dutch interpreter for Commodore Perry, became *Chargé d'Affaires* for one year. R. B. Van Valkenburgh, also of New York, arrived in August, 1866, and retired in November, 1869.

While such frequent changes in the service could not be otherwise than costly to American interests, and were particularly unfortunate at the time of the retirement of Pruyn, who left at a most delicate and critical stage, it may be noted that the British diplomatic service was also frequently interrupted. Rutherford Alcock,[2] after fourteen years in the British consular service in China, with the rank of consul general, was made the first British representative in Japan. He arrived in July, 1859, taking up residence in Yedo at the same time with Harris. He was absent on

leave from March, 1862, until March, 1864, having been
in the interim made a Knight Commander of the Bath.
Alcock was recalled abruptly a few months later, although
he was subsequently vindicated and promoted to Peking,
where he succeeded Sir Frederick Bruce. He was replaced
by Harry S. Parkes,[3] who also had had a long and far-
famed career in the Chinese consular service. Parkes arrived in August, 1865, thus beginning a mission in Japan
which extended over nearly twenty years. British policy,
however, was directed step by step from London, and had a
continuity and consistency which was lacking in American
policy. Before the close of the American Civil War, the
United States had yielded to England its position of priority
in Japan. Seward, distracted and preoccupied by the Civil
War, gave to American interests in Japan an astonishing
amount of attention, and yet his advice to the American
representatives was rarely helpful and of course the United
States was able to give only nominal naval support to its
ministers in Yedo. Steward's policy for Japan will be
treated in the next chapter. American policy continued
to be in Japan as it had been and was in China, the policy
of Americans more than the policy of their government.

The American Government held consistently to one
principle without compromise: the achievements of Perry
and Harris must not be lost; the Japanese must not be permitted to return to a policy of seclusion. It is in the application of this principle that we encounter difficulties in
defining policies. The Americans swung between two
courses. On the one hand it was of the utmost importance
to cooperate with the other treaty powers, particularly with
the British, French and Dutch, and on the other, it suited
the American spirit as well as the exigencies of the time,
to show towards the Japanese conciliation, moderation, and
a spirit of compromise. These two courses were often opposed to each other, for moderation was not a characteristic
of the British in Japan, and they dominated the situation.

Cooperation with the other treaty powers, even when it
required the Americans to join in a use of force such as

had never characterized the policy in China, and never again appeared in Japan, was rendered the more easy by the fact that the Japanese Empire was then passing through a momentous struggle of clan feuds and of rival rulers in which there was always one faction definitely committed to the expulsion of the foreigners and to a return to seclusion. Into the details of this most intricate and involved domestic Japanese conflict it is impossible for us to go, and yet without a knowledge of these details it is often difficult to estimate correctly the courses proposed and the actions taken by the foreigners. Briefly the situation was as follows:

Anti-foreign Agitation

The signing of the treaties (1854-8) stirred the opposition of a large section of the articulate public opinion of the Empire which was sincerely opposed to the abandonment of the policy of seclusion, and it was seized upon by powerful daimyos (feudal lords) who had no strong anti-foreign convictions but who were eager to find in the acts of the Shogun's government an object of criticism by which the Takugawa régime might be weakened and overthrown.* The anti-foreign and the anti-Shogun forces tended to coalesce into a single body demanding reform in Japanese affairs. The foreign relations of the Empire were retired to a secondary place in the public interest, and yet a by-product of the domestic struggle was a stubborn and unreasoning opposition to the foreigners, coupled with demands for their expulsion. Conciliation and isolated action were weak staffs for the foreigners to lean upon in the face of this opposition which was so blind, so indirect, and so irresponsible. A cooperative policy with force to back it up was absolutely essential and would have been necessary for the Americans had there been no Civil War to create a political reason for cultivating harmony with foreign powers.

* The Shogun (Tycoon, i.e., Great Prince) was theoretically an officer of the Imperial Court of Kioto and was appointed by the Emperor to repress disturbances and maintain order. Practically the office carried with it complete control of the Emperor whom the Shogun set up and deposed at will, and also possessed important economic and commercial privileges not equally enjoyed by the less important princes.

The course of American policy may best be reviewed, perhaps, by noting the more important steps which were taken, explaining in each case the underlying domestic situation in Japan, and then comparing the course of the Americans with that of the other foreigners.

Although the provision in the Harris Treaty stipulating that ratifications should be exchanged in Washington within one year had been inserted at the request of the Japanese, the Tycoon's officers were soon forced to seek delay for this visit to the United States.[4] Notwithstanding the representation of Lord Hotta, the Shogun's emissary to the Mikado, that the resumption of international relations might be made the first step in securing for Japan the "hegemony over all nations" which, he stated, "is doubtless in conformity with the will of Heaven,"[5] the throne withheld approval of the treaties. The Shogun was thus placed in the position of having violated a fundamental law of the Empire, and for a mission to go abroad would be to incur the death penalty. The Tycoon pleaded for delay in sending the embassy to the United States and Harris sympathetically approved, stipulating, however, that in the interim no other embassy was to depart from Japan. While the Japanese regarded all treaties in the light of "necessary evils," wrote Harris to Seward, "there is no doubt that the Japanese regard us in a more friendly light than any of the other powers with whom they have come in contact."

The embassy actually sailed February, 1860, in the U. S. S. *Powhatan,* which had been placed at its disposal by request of the Japanese. Congress appropriated $50,000 for the entertainment of the guests, who were received and feted with great ceremony. After seven weeks of amazing sight-seeing the embassy was returned directly to Japan in the U. S. S. *Niagara.*

Meanwhile affairs in Japan were becoming difficult alike for the Shogun's government and for the foreigners. Harris had even intimated to the Yedo officials that the powers might find it necessary to turn to the Mikado if the Shogun did not show a greater desire to fulfill the stipulations of the treaty. It soon became evident, however, that the Sho gun's position was not simple. He did not possess the power to enforce order or to protect the foreigners. The foreigners themselves had given great offense. The treaties had left the currency question in an unsatisfactory condition. The Japanese Government had for centuries maintained the ratio between silver and gold at about 5 to 1. The new treaties compelled the Japanese to accept foreign silver at the foreign valuation. The foreigners were not slow to see the avenue of profit thus opened to them. They could bring their foreign silver to Japan, exchange it for Japanese silver at par, and with the latter buy Japanese gold at the rate of 5 or 6 to 1, and then export the gold thus cheaply purchased to China, where it could be disposed of according to the current rates of international exchange. Nearly everyone, ministers, consuls, and naval officers, as well as merchants, joined in these speculations which began rapidly to drain the Empire of its gold. The scandal was notorious and became a subject of investigation by Parliament. Great Britain sought the cooperation of the United States in correcting the evil and Secretary of State Cass directed Harris to comply with the British request, but before the matter was adjusted much ill will had been generated.[6]

Less easily defined, yet equally productive of evil, was the personal conduct of the foreigners towards the Japanese. Most of the foreigners came to Japan from China and brought with them an impudence and arrogance which, while as irritating to Chinese as to Japanese, created more disorder in Japan because of the presence of so many skillful samurai swordsmen and retainers. The Japanese were not only inclined but were well prepared to meet insult with retaliation. Sometimes this revenge was executed directly upon the guilty party, but more often it took the form of hostility to all foreigners, and within two years after the opening of Yokohama the foreigners were actually imperilled by multitudes of assassins seeking either revenge or an opportunity to stir up trouble which might eventuate in the expulsion of the foreigners from the Empire. The Tokugawa government at Yedo, unsupported by the Kioto government, and strongly opposed in domestic affairs by many powerful princes, was quite unable to control the situation.

Early in January, 1861, Heusken, the interpreter of the American Legation, while returning home after dark, was cut down in the streets of Yedo and expired within a few hours.[7] The murder of Heusken was the seventh assassination of foreigners within eighteen months and greatly excited the foreign community. Harris, while greatly shocked, took the position that his interpreter had been foolhardy in thus exposing himself to attack in the darkness. Harris himself had been careful, even at the expense of a great deal of personal liberty, to avoid giving the sworded gentry such opportunities as they so much desired, but such a surrender of rights did not suit the dignity of many other foreigners. Rutherford Alcock,[8] with the French, Dutch and Prussian representatives retired from Yedo, as a result of the murder of the American interpreter, demanding that the government give satisfactory guarantees of security to life and property before they would return. Harris not only remained in Yedo, but even went so far as to request from his government discretionary powers to waive the right granted by treaty for foreigners to reside in Yedo after January 1, 1862.

The murder of Heusken and this request for delay in opening Yedo to residence were the first matters presented to Seward from Japan after he became Secretary of State. His attitude will be considered subsequently. Suffice it to state here that Harris's advice was accepted and reparation for the murder of Heusken was settled by the payment of $10,000 to the interpreter's mother. The contrast between the policy of Harris and that of the British representatives is illustrated not only in the withdrawal of Alcock for a time from Yedo, but also by the size of the indemnities required by the British Government for contemporaneous assassinations of British subjects. These ranged from $10,000 for wounding two members of the British Legation a few months later, to £110,000 gold for the murder of Richardson (September 14, 1862). Alcock's proposed remedy for assassination was $20,000 to $50,000 indemnity for every foreigner killed.

Harris and Alcock were irreconcilable in temperament, previous training, and in their attitude towards the Japanese. It is difficult to see how a policy of cooperation could have been carried out in Yedo had Harris remained as American minister. It also seems probable that had Harris continued in Japan, the course of American policy for the following five years would have been quite different.

One of the first requests presented to Pruyn after his arrival in 1862 was that the Japanese might exercise their treaty right to purchase three war steamers in the United States. Although the Japanese were obviously preparing not merely for possible civil war but also to defend themselves against the steadily increasing pressure of Great Britain and the other treaty powers, Pruyn approved of the request, and himself became the commercial agent for the Japanese Government in the transaction,* a highly irregular proceeding.[9]

By pressing so hard upon the Tycoon for the execution of the treaties the British Government, unknowingly, was really playing into the hands of those within the Empire who were seeking to weaken the Yedo government. The Shogun officials clearly saw the possibility of civil war early in 1863, and approached the American minister with an inquiry as to how the United States would regard such a conflict. Pruyn replied cautiously that in a conflict between supposedly anti-foreign forces and the government of the Shogun with which the treaties had been made, he believed that, if requested, all the treaty powers "would be justified" by self-defense in aiding the Shogun.[11] Further study and reflection, however, led Mr. Pruyn to modify this opinion and less than six months later (June 27, 1863), he recom-

*Gideon Welles, who subsequently became familiar with the details of the way in which this contract was executed in the United States, sharply criticized the proceedings.[10]

mended to Seward a joint naval demonstration of the treaty powers, such as Seward had proposed two years before, to compel the Mikado to ratify the treaties. Seward was willing to act on this suggestion but at that time the Lord John Russell did not favor it.

Meanwhile the Throne had issued a number of decrees ordering either the complete expulsion of the foreigners or the closing of all ports save those of Nagasaki and Hako date. Many efforts had been made to induce Pruyn to retire from Yedo and in May, 1863, the legation was burned. Six weeks later an American vessel, the *Pembroke,* was fired on in the Straits of Shimonéséki by the forces of the Prince of Choshiu and within a few days a French and a Dutch vessel also were fired on. This prince had taken literally the Mikado's orders to expel the barbarians. The Yedo officials, under orders from Kioto, formally notified the foreign representatives that the port of Yokohama was to be closed to trade. At the same time the British fleet in Japanese waters, under Admiral Kuper, now numbering ten vessels, was instructed to proceed to Kagoshima on the island of Kiushiu to demand reparations directly from the Prince of Satsuma for the murder of Richardson, who had been cut down by the express orders of one of the Satsuma daimyos. In the midst of all this confusion one fact stood out clearly: the foreigners to maintain their place in Japan must not only defend themselves but must retaliate. The Yedo government was quite powerless to control many powerful princes, or to carry out the treaties, and was apparently passing into a subordination to Kioto such as had not been known in Japan since the establishment of the Shogunate.

July, 1863, was a tumultuous month in western Japan. Commander McDougal in the U. S. S. *Wyoming,* which had fortunately appeared at Yokohama in the course of a hunt for the *Alabama,* proceeded to the Straits of Shimonéséki with the intention of capturing the offending Choshiu war vessels and presenting them to the Shogun, but when the Choshiu shore batteries opened fire upon the *Wyoming,*

McDougal engaged them in battle, and while no effort was made to capture the batteries, a war steamer and a brig were sunk.[12] A few days later the French admiral, Jaurés, landed a small force at the same spot, destroyed one of the batteries, and burned a village. Meanwhile Admiral Kuper proceeded to Kagoshima, a Satsuma city, and commenced a bombardment which resulted in the destruction of most of the city by fire. The effect of these expeditions, coupled with certain concurrent developments of domestic politics, was to reduce the opposition of the western clans to foreign intercourse and, for a time, to strengthen the Tycoon.

Acting upon emphatic and very explicit instructions from Seward, Pruyn demanded of the Yedo government the settlement of all American claims. Seward had based his instructions on the conclusion that "the Government of Japan had failed to keep its faith solemnly pledged by treaty," [13] and intimated that the United States could not maintain its dignity or self-respect if it were to permit Japan to evade the payment of the modest American claims while the other powers were making very much greater demands. Seward threatened to support the demand with an additional naval force. Pruyn asked for a total of $32,000 —$10,000 for the burning of the legation, $20,000 for assaults on Americans at Yokohama, and $2,000 for an American citizen who had been deported from the Bonin Islands by the Japanese.[14] Payment for the *Pembroke* claim, $10,000, had already been made. When the Japanese declined to meet the demands, Pruyn reminded them that the United States had never consented to the delay in the opening of Hiogo and Niigata for which discretionary powers had been given to Harris, and that if the claims were not paid, he would feel at liberty to declare that these ports were open, under the stipulations of the American treaty.

Pruyn relented slightly in the urgency of his demands which had been presented in the form of an ultimatum, but a few months later he went to Yedo in the U. S. S. *Jamestown*, landed with a guard of sixty-five sailors and marines, and secured a settlement. In this adjustment he proposed that the claims of the Americans at Yokohama should be submitted to the Emperor of Russia for arbitration, but the Japanese authorities preferred to settle them directly.

An important by-product of the conferences over the American ultimatum had been the securing of a convention by which the Japanese agreed to lower from 20 per cent to 5 per cent the import duty on machines and machinery, iron in pigs and bars, sheet iron and iron ware, tin plates, sugar, glass, clocks, watches, wines and liquors.[15] A few days later the Japanese voluntarily reduced to 6 per cent the duties on several other classes of importation.

Sir Rutherford Alcock returned to Yedo in March, 1864. His government, which had been severely criticized in Parliament for the burning of Kagoshima, had provided him with instructions of moderation. Alcock, however, became convinced that the thinly concealed object of the Japanese Government was to expel the foreigner, and he proposed to "make war for the purpose of forestalling war."[16] Thus he would prevent the closing of the port of Yokohama and at the same time he would open the Inland Sea to navigation and force the Japanese Government to change its entire policy towards the foreigners. The plan met with the approval of the other foreign representatives and was carried out in a joint naval expedition to the Straits of Shimonoséki in the latter part of August, 1864. The combined fleet consisted of nine British, four Dutch, three French and one American, vessels. The American vessel was a rented merchant steamer of light draught equipped with a few guns and sailors from the *Jamestown*, which, being a sailing vessel, was of no use to the fleet. The bombardment and assault occupied four days and as a result the Prince of Nagato agreed to the opening of the Straits, and also to pay a ransom for the city, which the allied forces had refrained from destroying.[17] The expedition had been undertaken with at least the tacit approval of the Yedo government, which had experienced the most determined opposition from this Prince.

The fleet then returned to Yokohama and the diplomatists took up the task of settlement with the government. The Yedo officials agreed (September 23) to abrogate the order closing the port of Yokohama, and also engaged to seek from the Mikado an approval of the treaties. A few days later the Tycoon agreed to assume an indemnity of $3,000,000 in six quarterly instalments to pay the expenses of the Shimoneséki expedition.[18] The method of division of the sum was left to the determination of the powers, and it was stipulated that the payment would be remitted in case the Japanese should open to trade some port in the Inland Sea.

The Shimoneséki expedition was approved by President Lincoln and Secretary Seward,[19] and although it had been undertaken in violation of instructions then on their way from Lord Russell to Alcock, its complete success was sufficient to transmute a reprimand and recall for Alcock into a promotion to Peking.[20] Viewed in the light of history, particularly Japanese domestic history, there is little to bring forward in defense of the expedition. It was certainly a marked departure from traditional American policy both in its cooperative aspects and in its confessed purpose to intervene in the domestic conflict of the Japanese Empire. It was more straightforward than Tattnall's participation in the affair at Taku in 1859, and yet it was the kind of action which both the Pierce and Buchanan administrations had declined to sanction in China. It had little to commend it but its success. The Shimoneséki expedition had broken the back of the anti-foreign movement in Japan.

CONVENTION OF 1866

Pruyn retired from Japan in April, 1865, leaving Portman as *Chargé*. A few months later Harry Parkes arrived to supersede Alcock. From the time of his arrival British influence entirely dominated the foreign relations of Japan. Parkes had entered the British service in China as a mere boy and had been reared in the traditions of the British merchants of the forties and fifties. His career had been much honored by those who advocated with Lord Pahmerston that in dealing with the Chinese people the ordinary rules of morality did not apply. Lord Elgin had commended him. By others, by most Americans probably, he was regarded as the prime evil genius in the relations between the foreigners and the Asiatics. It was Parkes' rashness which had precipitated the affair of the lorcha *Arrow* at Canton in 1856, and his services in the ensuing war had on several occasions been of an inflammatory sort. Added to his aggressiveness in every effort which looked towards the extension or protection of British trade was the fact that he had a temper which he often thought it not worth while to control.[21] The difference between Parkes in Yedo and Sir Frederick Bruce in Peking was as the difference between the poles.

Upon arrival Parkes immediately assumed the initiative and the leadership among the foreign representatives. Although he had received rather general instructions, and although Lord John Russell had always inclined towards a course of moderation, Parkes, as an American historian has aptly said, "knew what his government desired, and he proceeded to accomplish it." [22] The Shogun's government, unable to open the desired port in the Inland Sea, had elected to pay the Shimoneséki indemnity, but after the first instalment, found itself financially embarrassed and requested delay in the other payments. This request provided Parkes with the desired opportunity. He secured the assent of the other foreign representatives to a proposal which called for the transference of the negotiations from Yedo to Osaka, accompanied by a naval demonstration. This expedition, in which *Chargé* Portman represented the United States in a British war vessel, arrived at Osaka early in November, 1865.[23] Parkes' letter to the Japanese authorities, which he took the trouble to remind them was dated from the admiral's flag-ship, demanded a "prompt and satisfactory settlement." The Japanese were given the choice between punctual payment of the indemnity or the immediate opening of Hiogo and Osaka, the formal consent of the Mikado to the treaties, and "the regularization of the tariff on a basis of five per cent." In case the Japanese chose the second alternative, the treaty powers would graciously remit $2,000,000 of the indemnity. When the Japanese delayed their answer and appeared to be preparing to defy the foreign representatives, the latter sent identic notes containing a threat "to act as we may judge convenient." A Japanese minister came to the flag-ship September 24 and announced to Parkes that the Mikado had ratified the treaties, that the Shogun would consent to the revision of the tariff, but that rather than open the port before the appointed time, the government preferred to pay the full remaining indemnity. On the part of the foreigners the visit to Osaka was a brutal proceeding, the method of which the Japanese in later years found many opportunities to imitate in dealings with Korea and China.

The tariff settlement with the Japanese Government was embodied in a convention which was signed in Yedo June 25, 1866. This convention is notable in American policy for several reasons. It, and the preceding convention of 1864, which had been signed by Pruyn jointly with the British, French and Dutch representatives, are among the very few, if not the only instances in the nineteenth century in which the United States entered into a joint treaty. While it was not altogether exceptional for the United States to make similar treaties, concurrently with other powers, as in China in 1858, it marked a wide departure from traditional policy for the American Government to sign a treaty jointly with other nations. In 1857 William B. Reed had been specifically instructed not to make such a treaty. The convention was also remarkable for the fact that it stated an untruth, viz., that the foreign representatives had "received from their respective governments identical instructions for the modification of the tariff." Portman had received no such instructions. The treaty was, however, duly ratified by the American Government the following year. In the third place, the proposed "regularization" of the tariff took the form of the China treaties of 1858 in that the duties were made specific and the precise amounts estimated on *ad valorem* basis of five per cent. The tariff was not terminable at a definite date, but like both the Chinese and Japanese treaties of 1858 was merely "subject to revision" on the first day of July, 1872. The effect of this provision was to place Japan entirely within the power of the united foreign nations, or of any one of them which would not consent to revision, notwithstanding the fact that the increasing prices of many articles of trade had the effect of lowering the duty rate, estimated on an *ad valorem* basis, until in later years the duties received amounted to little more than the cost of collection. Judged by any standard of foreign policy, the convention of 1866 with Japan may be regarded as one of the most thoroughly un-American treaties ever ratified by the American Government.

The American policy of cooperation continued after the American Civil War was over, and the most urgent reasons for its practice had disappeared. Civil war broke out in Japan at the beginning of 1868 and Van Valkenburgh joined with the other foreign representatives in the approval of a joint occupation of the approaches to Yokohama by the combined naval forces.[24] The powers declared their neutrality in the domestic conflict. This had the effect of influencing the Mikado, who had taken over the powers of the Shogun at the latter's request, February 3, 1868, to seek the good will of the foreign powers. The American minister was received in audience by the Mikado at Yedo, January 3, 1869, and a month later, the Restoration having become an accomplished fact, Van Valkenburgh, in concert with the other ministers, withdrew the notice of neutrality. The American authorities then turned over to the Japanese Government a war steamer which the Shogun had previously purchased in the United States but which on its arrival at Yokohama had been retained by the American authorities in order that it might not be used by the Shogun's party to oppose the Restoration.[25]

In summary of this most complicated period we may

note two facts: just as in China at the revision of the treaties in 1858, the American Government had signally failed while sustaining a cooperative policy with the other foreign powers, to exert upon the combined action of the powers any notable influence. Cooperation had meant, after the departure of Townsend Harris, not only British leadership but, under Parkes, British dictation. On the other hand, as in China, the United States had come out of the contest with Japan with more good will from the Japanese people than was enjoyed by any other foreign power. It is doubtful whether any Japanese or any Americans in 1869 realized how the joint Convention of 1866 could be used to obstruct Japanese fiscal and industrial development. American policy was clear: the United States not only desired no exclusive advantages, but, unlike the other powers, was as thoroughly committed to supporting and sustaining Japan in its efforts to become a strong nation, just as it was committed to a similar course in China.

BIBLIOGRAPHICAL NOTES

1. The primary American sources for this period are: Japan Instructions, Vol. 1, and Japan Despatches, Vols. I-XI. (The reports for the years 1861-8 in "Diplomatic Correspondence" are very complete. Treat's "Early Diplomatic Relations between the United States and Japan, 1858-65," a most valuable intensive study, makes generous use of the papers of R. B. Pruyn which are, however, usually practically identical with the Pruyn dispatches in the Dept. of State. Treat also makes use of a large number of translations from Japanese sources some of which are unavailable in any except the best stocked American libraries. Gubbins's "Progress of Japan" presents the Japanese sources very fully. Two scholarly studies and interpretations by Japanese can be recommended—Nitobe's "Intercourse between the United States and Japan" (Johns Hopkins Univ. Studies in Hist. and Pol. Sci., extra Vol. 9, 1891), and Hishida's "International Position of Japan as a Great Power" (Columbia Univ. Studies in Hist. Economics and Public Law, Vol. 24, No. 3, 1905).
2. Alcock's "The Capital of the Tycoon, a Narrative of Three Years' Residence in Japan," 2 vols., makes a very full record of Alcock's service in Japan before 1862; see also Michie: "The Englishman in China."
3. Dickens and Lane-Poole: "Life of Sir Henry Parkes"; Sir

Ernest Satow's "A Diplomat in Japan," throws some valuable side-lights on Parkes' early career in Japan.

4. S. Ex. Doc. 25:36-1.
5. Treat: "Early Diplomatic Relations," pp. 99-100.
6. Townsend Harris' Journal, Pt. II, p. 101 (Lib. of Cong.); Japan Instructions, Vol. 1, Apr. 2, 1860, Cass to Harris; see also Satow's "A Diplomat in Japan."
7. Japan Dispatches, Vol. 5, Jan. 22, Feb. 13, '61; Dip. Corres., 1862, pp. 795 ff.
8. Alcock: "The Capital of the Tycoon," Vol. 2, chaps. 24, 25.
9. S. Ex. Doc. 33:37-3.
10. Diary of Gideon Welles, Vol. II, pp. 188-92, 561.
11. Dip. Corres., 1863, p. 982.
12. Ibid., pp. 1040 ff.
13. Ibid., p. 1057.
14. Ibid., 1864, pp. 466 ff.
15. Ibid., 1864, p. 479.
16. Parliamentary Papers, 1865, Comm. 57, pp. 18-36, cited by Treat, p. 324.
17. Dip. Corres., 1864, pp. 553 ff.
18. Ibid., p. 578.
19. Ibid. (1865), p. 229.
20. Treat: p. 373, citing British sources.
21. See Morse, Vol. 1, pp. 422 ff, for an estimate of Parkes.
22. Treat; p. 395.
23. Dip. Corres., 1865, p. 276, 1866, p. 191.
24. Japan Dispatches, Vol. 9, Apr. 3, 1868, Van Valkenburgh to Seward.
25. Dip. Corres., 1868, p. 730.

CHAPTER XXII

SEWARD'S FAR EASTERN POLICY

By 1861, by a process of negation and opportunism as well as by foresight and design, the American Government had acquired a fairly definite Far Eastern Policy. This policy had grown out of certain precedents and decisions and was incorporated in two treaties—one with China and another with Japan. The foundation of this policy was "most-favored-nation" treatment, equivalent to what is now called the "open-door" policy. Above this lay the decision, many times repeated, not to acquire any territorial possessions or protectorates in Asia or the Pacific Ocean. Deduced from the necessities of the most-favored-nation policy was the decision to "sustain China" and, by inference, to sustain Japan, thus placing the United States in opposition to any movement on the part of Western powers to injure the territorial integrity or the political sovereignty of Asiatic states. The United States desired that China and Japan become sufficiently strong to maintain their own open doors. Furthermore, the American Government had been committed by the Pierce and Buchanan administrations to cooperation with the other treaty powers in all peaceful measures to secure the execution of the treaties and the protection of foreign interests. On the other hand, the United States had declined to enter an alliance with Great Britain and France, and Mr. Reed had been instructed to avoid any joint treaty with China. Upon these foundations Seward had to build in the tempestuous years 1861-9.

Seward entered the Department of State with large and positive convictions on the nature and the future of Ameri can relations with Asia. This is evident from his previous record in the Senate. More than most men of his day his face was turned towards the West. As to the future expansion of the American people to the Pacific Coast he was firmly optimistic. He was a hearty supporter of every movement to establish American foreign trade on a firmer basis. "The nation," he said, "must command the empire of the seas, which alone is real empire." This empire, it seemed to him, must include the Pacific as well as the Atlantic. Indeed he foresaw the day when the Atlantic interests of the United States would "relatively sink in importance, while the Pacific Ocean, its shores, its islands, and the vast regions beyond" would become the "chief theatre of events in the world's great hereafter." This famous assertion, made in 1852 while the Japan Expedition was in preparation, was no isolated flight of oratory. Seward had a very definite idea as to the function of the American people in the commerce of the Pacific Ocean. Foreign trade, he thought, was to replace military conquest and to become the vehicle for a commerce of ideas. The great American contribution to the world, it seemed to him, was political theory. Just as the Atlantic states through their commercial, social and political sympathies were steadily renovating the governments and social constitutions of Europe and Africa, so "the Pacific states must necessarily perform the same sublime and beneficent functions in Asia." Seward appears to have expected that Asia thus enriched from America would repay the debt in gratitude. He said, while Perry was in the East, "Certainly no one expects the nations of Asia to be awakened by any other influence than our own from the lethargy into which they sunk nearly three thousand years ago. If they could be roused and invigorated now, would they spare their European oppressors and spite their American benefactors?"

Seward was so convinced of the value of the Pacific Coast to the United States that he would, notwithstanding his convictions on the subject of slavery, vote to receive California as a state even though it were to become slave territory. He believed in the Japan Expedition, expressing the conviction that the proper question for the Senate to ask was not why it had been sent, but why it had not been sent before. He urged the completion of surveys of the Pacific Ocean; he favored the encouragement of Chinese immigration to California; and among the projects to which he lent persistent and energetic leadership, were the construction of a transcontinental railroad and the inauguration of a line of mail steamers from San Francisco via the Sandwich Islands to Japan and China.[1] He also gave approval and support to the proposal to connect America with Asia by means of a telegraph line through Alaska, across the Aleutian Islands and down the coast of Asia to the mouth of the Amur.[2] Lincoln could not have chosen from among the conspicuous leaders of the day a secretary of state who would bring to the Far Eastern question more previous thought and conviction.

During Seward's term of service the problem of communications between Washington and the Far East, which had been almost a determining factor in the previous policies, was partially solved. The opening of the transcontinental telegraph in 1862 and the increase in the frequency of trans-Pacific travel brought Japan within a month of Washington, while a similar development of transportation and telegraphy from Hongkong to England, shortened to some degree the distance from China westward. However, during the winter months the Chinese capital was ice- and snow-bound, receiving its mail only by courier service from Shanghai. The American representatives in China, and to a less extent in Japan, must still exercise broad discretionary powers and therefore had the control of American policy largely in their own hands. As an offset to better communications came the Civil War, which so distracted the American Government as to leave little time for the consideration of Far Eastern policy. Seward, under different conditions, would probably have shown from the outset much initiative in dealing with the East, but as it was, his hands were tied. Nevertheless he found it possible in the course of eight years to bring both Alaska and Korea within the range of Far Eastern policy, and also to modify in a marked degree many of the precedents of his office. At the risk of some confusion we have already examined the contributions of Burlingame and Harris; let us now retraverse the ground and note the policies of Seward.

SEWARD, BURLINGAME AND CHINA

About Seward and China little need be said. Burlingame required few suggestions or instructions. He appeared in China in the calm which followed the storm. It was a period especially favorable for constructive work such as must follow destructive war. Notwithstanding his enthusiasm and amiability, Burlingame was a masterful personality, sure to dominate any situation. He dominated Peking while he was there, and in like measure he dominated American policy in China. Seward wisely permitted Burlingame to have his way; there were between them no conflicts, nor even differences of opinion. Even the customary long letter of instructions usually given to a new minister was omitted.[3] Seward's part in Chinese policy was limited to approval of Burlingame; the Secretary of State initiated nothing except the immigration section of the Treaty of 1868.*

Some months after Burlingame's arrival in China (March 6, 1862), Seward took occasion, while approving the minister's course in the closing contests of the Taiping Rebellion, to urge him to "consult and cooperate" with the other representatives. The instruction was hardly necessary, for the policy was already in operation and Burlingame was the sort of man who could work no other way.[4] Shortly after the close of the Civil War Seward summarized his Chinese policy (August 14, 1865) as follows:

"The Government of the United States is not disposed to be technical or exacting in its intercourse with the Chinese Government, but will deal with it in entire frankness, cordiality and friendship.

* The so-called Burlingame Treaty (1868) might more properly be called the Seward Treaty, for Seward, rather than Burlingame, appears to have especially desired it and Seward wrote it. It was really an immigration treaty to which were attached some declarations of foreign policy. As a part of Seward's policy it will be treated in Chapter XXVIII.

The United States desires neither to interfere with the distinct and ancient habits and customs of the Chinese people, nor to embarrass the members of the foreign board in their difficult and responsible task." [5]

While always insistent that American life and property must be protected, Seward was careful to avoid anything which looked towards the disregard of Chinese rights. He sustained the decision of S. Wells Williams in 1866 that the treaty of 1858 clearly prohibited the foreigners from sending steamers through the inland waterways, thus placing himself in opposition to the Shanghai merchants who were making a vigorous effort to break down the treaties.[6] He expressed himself very clearly as opposed to the abuse of the American flag, the use of which was being sold by American merchants to Chinese lorcha and junk owners.[7] When the American bark *Rover* was wrecked off the coast of Formosa in 1867, and the crew murdered by aborigines of the island, Seward ordered a thorough investigation and instructed Dr. Williams to urge the Chinese Government to occupy the ports and shores of Formosa more effectively, but at the same time he ordered it made clear to China that the United States in no case desired to "seize or hold possession" of any part of Formosa.[8] Rear Admiral Bell conducted a punitive expedition against the aborigines with the U. S. S.S. *Hartford* and *Wyoming*. With a landing party of 181 he advanced on the uncivilized people at the south end of Formosa on June 13, 1867. The savages were pursued into the hills where they frequently led the American force into ambush. The American casualties were one death and fourteen cases of sun-stroke. This expedition, an application in a measure of the "gun-boat policy" which Burlingame was so anxious to avoid, was undertaken by order of the Navy Department, yet no doubt with Seward's approval. The expedition was the precedent upon which the Japanese relied in 1874 to justify their more ambitious and inclusive attack upon the island.[9]

When Seward visited China in 1870 he took occasion to defend and justify American policy to one of his countrymen who was very critical of its weakness. Seward reviewed the difficulties of the Civil War and examined one by one the alleged deficiencies of American influence in the Empire and remarked: "I think we are obliged to conclude from all these premises that a policy of justice, moderation and friendship is the only one that we have had a choice to pursue, and that it has been as wise as it has been unavoidable." He concluded: "The United States cannot be an aggressive nation—least of all against China." [10]

COERCION IN JAPAN

Seward's policy in Japan was of a somewhat different nature. It was based on the assumption that the Japanese Government was seeking to evade the fulfillment of its obligations under the treaties, and that the foreigners were in grave danger of being expelled from some or all of the open ports. Seward was also under the impression that the domestic conflict in Japan was a clean-cut contest between the liberal forces under the leadership of the Tycoon and the reactionary and anti-foreign forces back of the Mikado. These assumptions as we have seen were quite inaccurate. The Takugawa government was evading the requirements of the treaties at least in part because it was utterly powerless to carry them out. The foreigners were probably not in such imminent danger of being expelled as they believed. The forces back of the Mikado were by no means entirely anti-foreign. In the face of what Seward believed to be the dangers of the situation his policy was aggressive and belligerent. He believed that "very large interests, not of our own country only, but of the civilized world, are involved in retaining the foothold of foreign nations already acquired in the Empire of Japan." [11]   Towards Japan Seward directed a policy far more vigorous than any preceding secretary of state had directed towards China, but at no time had China appeared to be seeking to expel the foreigners.

Immediately upon receipt of information as to the murder of Heusken, which reached Seward just at the outbreak of the Civil War, the Secretary of State initiated a proposal to the treaty powers—France, Great Britain, Russia and Prussia—for a joint naval demonstration against Japan to compel Japan to comply with the stipulations of the treaties.* [12]

This proposal, as we have seen, was quite contrary to the judgment of Townsend Harris, who even recommended that he be given discretionary powers to postpone the opening of Yedo and Osaka. Seward rather reluctantly concurred with Harris, urgently insisting, however, that there be no relaxation of the demand for the fulfillment of the treaties until the Japanese had rendered abundant satisfaction for Heusken.[14]

While Seward's energetic proposal in May, 1861, may have been a part of a larger policy by which he sought to secure the cooperation of the European powers in a joint undertaking to divert them from intervening in the domestic conflict of the United States, nevertheless Seward was not slow to return to proposals for coercive measures against Japan whenever he thought the situation required them. "You cannot too strongly advise the Government of Japan," he wrote, December 13, 1862, "that it can only have friendship or even peace with the United States by protecting the citizens and subjects of foreign powers from domestic violence." [15] Six months later (June 29, 1863) he stated:

"The United States having no grievances of their own to complain of against Japan, will not unite in hostilities against that government, but they will at the same time take care not to disapprove of or censure, without just cause, the measures of Great Britain which will result in greater security for all." [16]

A few days later he wrote that while Pruyn's whole moral influence must be exerted to preserve peace between Japan and the Western powers, the *Wyoming* would have author-

* This proposal called for the presentation of a joint note accompanied by the assembly of a combined fleet in Japanese waters. An answer to the demands was to be required after a certain period of delay. If the answer were unfavorable or evasive, Seward proposed that the diplomatic representatives be withdrawn "and such hostilities be commenced and prosecuted as the naval commanders may deem most likely to bring the Japanese to a sense of their obligations." To this proposal there were attached two qualifications: (1) that the United States would make a special demand for satisfaction for the murder of Huesken; (2) that "this convention is not to be considered as obligatory on" the United States until the sanction of Congress has been obtained to the beginning of hostilities. (May 20, 1861.) [13]

ity to "use her guns" for the protection of the Legation or of American citizens. Seward approved of the expedition of the *Wyoming* to Shimoneséki in July, 1863, and authorized Pruyn to use a firm and strong policy to induce Japan to to live up to its duties under the treaties. The joint expedition to Shimoneséki in September, 1864, met with Seward's full approval, even though it marked an absolute departure from traditional American policy in the matter of joint naval operations with other powers. He also approved, though he did not authorize, the visit of Portman to Osaka on a British war vessel in 1865 in the joint naval demonstration by which the Mikado was induced to approve the treaties, and the government made to revise and lower the tariff schedule. Indeed, one receives the impression from a review of the correspondence that with Japan Seward was disposed towards more forceful measures than the American representatives thought it wise to employ. Seward, more than any secretary of state before or since his day, was favorably disposed toward a "gun-boat policy."

How much of Seward's policy for Japan was due to the necessities of the international situation arising out of the American Civil War it is difficult to say. He was thoroughly committed to the cooperative policy, but in China the cooperation was directed towards moderation and pacific measures, while in Japan it eventuated in joint hostilities.

In his instructions to Pruyn (November 15, 1861) Seward expressed the fear that Japan, which had been "gently coerced" by the United States into friendship, might seize the present opportunity "to underrate our power" and "to disregard our rights." [17] He looked forward to the day when "our domestic differences being ended, we are able once more to demonstrate our power in the East and establish our commerce there on secure foundations." Meanwhile Pruyn was to make a brave show of confidence and power and thus seek to preserve friendly relations. The United States, declared the Secretary, sought no exclusive advantages. "Preserve friendly relations with all European powers. Leave behind you all memories of domestic or

European jealousies or antipathies." And then as the difficulties with the European powers over the Civil War increased, Seward wrote (December 19, 1861):

"I cannot too earnestly enjoin upon you the duty of cultivating the best possible understanding with these representatives [the other foreign ministers] and of doing all in your power to maintain harmony of views and policy between them and yourself." [18]

When Pruyn expressed to the ministers of the Shogun government the personal opinion that the foreign powers would be disposed to support the Shogun against the clans, Seward commented that while the United States would cooperate with the Japanese authorities to secure the fulfillment of the treaties, no inference must be drawn that the United States would separate itself from cooperation with the other treaty powers.[19] The measures to which this policy of cooperation appeared to be leading the United States in the joint Shimoneséki expedition and the joint convention which followed it, may have been a little dis quieting but nevertheless, in view of the reason for co operation, Seward wrote: "I am authorized by the President to assure you that they are fully approved."* [20]

In the revolution which accompanied the Restoration Seward advised Van Valkenburgh to adhere to the existing government, i.e., the Tycoon, so long as that government retained its power.[22] Two years later, after he had visited Japan, he stated that he had used all his influence to "prevent the late revolution" because he thought it was a "retrograde movement." "I little dreamed," he explained, "that the Mikado would excel the dethroned Tycoon in emulating Western civilization."

On the subject of religious toleration Seward entertained very decided views. When a persecution of Christians at Nagasaki broke out in 1867, he took up with other powers the question of a united appeal to Japan to repeal and abro gate the laws which prohibit Christianity. And a vear later he wrote: "Humanity indeed demands and expects a continually extending sway of the Christian religion."

*Gideon Welles expressed strong dissent from this approval.[21]

However he expected this to come by a "diffusion of knowledge and calm and persevering appeal to the reason and
consciences of men." He directed Van Valkenburgh to
warn Japan that "when one foreign Christian shall have
suffered martyrdom for his faith, Christendom will be
shocked to its center and it may demand that the policy of
forbearance and encouragement which the treaty powers
have hitherto practised in Japan shall be reversed." [23]

ALASKA AND KOREA

Seward appears not to have been conscious that the
American Civil War was to mark a new phase of American
development in which internal growth would quite eclipse
the interests of foreign trade as he had viewed them in the
fifties. He returned to his former interest in the extension
of American trade in the Pacific when the war cares were removed. He negotiated the purchase of Alaska in 1867 and
at the same time initiated a movement to secure, jointly
with France, the opening of Korea.[24]

While the motives which inspired the purchase of Alaska
have been a matter of doubt and dispute, and were carefully concealed from Stoeckl, the Russian minister, at the
time of the negotiations, it is difficult to resist the conclusion that Seward saw in Alaska and the Aleutian Islands
a way of "extending a friendly hand to Asia." [25] Indeed his
son stated definitely that the motive back of the purchase
of Alaska was the desire for "advanced naval outposts" such
as had been lacking in the north Pacific as well as in the
West Indies during the recent war.[26] The United States
took possession of the Midway Islands in August, 1867.[27]
A few months later Seward wrote to the American representative at Honolulu (September 12, 1867), "that a lawful
and peaceful annexation of the islands to the United States
with the consent of the people of the Sandwich Islands, is
deemed desirable by this government." [28] Seward had in
mind American expansion in the Pacific and shortly after
his departure from the Department of State he outlined to

the people of Oregon a program of statesmanship for the Pacific Coast which called for the United States to "own and possess" islands in the Pacific. He urged them to regard the extension of American invention and enterprise into Japan, China, Australia and India as worthy of consideration equally with international commerce between the United States and the countries of western Europe.[29]

The opening of Korea was forced upon the attention of Seward by the reported aggressions of France. In March, 1866, a number of French Roman Catholic missionaries and their converts were massacred in Korea. When rumors of the facts reached China Rear Admiral Roze, of the French squadron in the China Seas, was dispatched to Korea to make an investigation and also to conduct a preliminary survey of the coast with a view to the dispatch of a more formidable expedition later. Admiral Roze returned with the information that the *General Sherman,* an American vessel which was seeking to open up trade with the Koreans, had been burned and the crew murdered.* [30]   At about the same time an American schooner, the *Surprise,* was wrecked on the coast of Korea and the crew was treated with civility and kindness, being returned to China by way of Mukden and Newchwang.

Meanwhile the *General Sherman* affair and the French action after the murder of the missionaries was creating a great deal of uneasiness in China among the foreign representatives. M. de Bellonet, the French *Chargé,* without authorization from Paris had made an abrupt demand on the Chinese Government for satisfaction for the action of the Koreans. He addressed to Prince Kung an extraordinary note in which, reminding him that the French were a people who loved war, he calmly announced that in a few days the French military forces would "march to the

*The actual details of the *General Sherman* affair were not known for nearly twenty years. It was eventually established, however, that the *General Sherman* entered the mouth of the Ta-dong River at the time of a freshet and was stranded in the river when the water suddenly fell. The crew, which was heavily armed, misunderstood the advances of the Korean authorities, and subjected them to many indignities. Whereupon fire-rafts were set out in the river to drift down on the *General Sherman* and the crew was put to death. If the fault for the loss of the vessel and its crew was partly that of the Koreans, at least it was probably not exclusively theirs.[31]

conquest of Korea," even going so far as to state that only the Emperor of France now had the "right and power to dispose, according to his good pleasure, of the country and the vacant throne." Bellonet stated that "the prince to whom will be confided the destinies of Korea, under the protectorate of his Majesty, the Emperor (French), must become a Christian." [32] Prince Kung, probably upon the advice of Burlingame, made public the correspondence which had passed between him and the French *Chargé*, much to the latter's discomfiture. Admiral Roze followed up his preliminary survey with a strong expedition in October but was unable to accomplish anything beyond the destruction of Kang-hoa, a city on an island north of Chemulpo. The Roze expedition was looked upon by Koreans, Chinese and foreigners alike as a virtual defeat for France. It was expected that in the following spring the French would collect a more powerful expedition and make a second attack. Sir Rutherford Alcock was preparing to attend the expedition, whether invited or not, with a British naval force to look out for the British interests, and Burlingame, as alarmed as his colleagues at the disclosure of such extensive French ambitions, urged that he be instructed to join the expedition. He wrote (December 15, 1866):

"If my advice can have weight, it will be that our presence there should rather restrain than promote aggression, and serve to limit action to such satisfaction only as great and civilized nations should, under the circumstances, have from the ignorant and the weak." [33]

PROPOSED JOINT EXPEDITION TO KOREA

The interest of France in Korea was not news to the Department of State. Ten years before the French minister at Washington had solicited the cooperation of President Pierce in a plan by which France would occupy Korea as part of a joint plan to compel China to revise the treaties. In 1861 Townsend Harris had reported that there was talk, at the time the Russians occupied Tsushima, that France was contemplating with Great Britain the partition of Japan. Seward, on receipt of the reports of Bellonet's correspondence with Prince Kung and the presence of the French forces in Korea, jumped to the conclusion that the expected partition of Asia had begun. Four days after receiving the Burlingame dispatch of November 12, not knowing that the French expedition was unauthorized, Seward found an opportunity to propose to Berthemy, the French minister at Washington, that the United States and France unite in joint action to obtain from Korea satisfaction for the murders of the French and the Americans. Berthemy, ignorant of Seward's motives and knowing nothing of the Bellonet correspondence, was mystified, and yet was inclined to approve the proposal. But before Seward's proposal had reached Paris the French Government, embarrassed alike by the necessity of withdrawing the French forces from Mexico and by the reports of Admiral Roze's failure, had found it expedient to announce to the Corps Legislatif that the first reports from Korea were misleading and that actually a great victory had been achieved. M. de Bellonet, instead of being recalled in disgrace, was promoted to Stockholm, and Admiral Roze escaped reprimand. No reason now existed for a joint expedition with the American forces into Korea, so the proposal of Seward was declined graciously. By a fortuitous course of blunders and accidents the United States was thus released from obligation to carry through what could hardly have failed to be a thoroughly disagreeable program.[34]

The next year (1867) the American naval forces in the Far East made two attempts to learn the details of the fate of the *General Sherman,* but in vain. Then Seward's nephew, Consul General George F. Seward of Shanghai, sought a commission to proceed to Korea with a view to making a treaty, and the request was granted. George F. Seward was given a letter from President Johnson to the king, and was authorized to proceed to Korea, supported by a naval force, "to procure a treaty of amity and commerce as nearly similar in its provisions to those existing between the United States and Japan as may be found practicable and expedient." [35]

In the instructions to young Seward was a paragraph in which the Secretary of State, no longer embarrassed by the threatened annexation of the peninsula, resumed a policy more in accord with the general spirit of American relations in Asia. He wrote:

"The design of this government is to render your visit a generous and friendly one, reserving the question of force, if found necessary, for ultimate consideration. You will not be expected therefore either to direct the exercise or make any display of force by way of intimidation, but on the other hand you will be expected to practise discretion, prudence and patience, while firmly asserting the dignity and maintaining the demands of the United States. You will however give notice to the Korean Government, if you find it expedient, that this government cannot suffer the outrage committed in the case of the *General Sherman* to remain indefinitely without receiving proper guaranty of adequate and ample redress."

This expedition to Korea was not undertaken because when the instructions arrived in Shanghai it had been discovered that it was not likely to meet with success.

A survey of Seward's eight-year record in the Department of State leads inevitably to the conclusion that he was the greatest Secretary of State, so far as Far Eastern matters are concerned, since Daniel Webster. Indeed, we may say, at the risk of anticipating a conclusion the facts for which appear in subsequent chapters, that Seward was the only Secretary of State in the nineteenth century, until John Hay, who appears to have had a firm grip on the situation. And when compared with Hay it will be found that Seward had superior abilities to follow a policy through when beset with difficulties. In many of the stipulations of the Burlingame Treaty Americans may take honest pride, yet in this compact the immigration question was not treated with statesmanship. The most conspicuous feature of Seward's policy, aside from its aggressiveness, was his desire for cooperation with other treaty powers. Where other occupants of the office both before and after his time dodged and evaded the problem of cooperation, Seward met it boldly. For the sake of maintaining cooperation he at times sacrificed American ideals. Over against the treaty with China there stands to his credit two of the most un-American actions, one accomplished and the other proposed, in all American history. The joint Convention with Japan in 1866, and the proposed joint expedition for the coercion of Korea were not worthy, even after all possible explanations have been made and accepted, of American traditions. But in neither case was Seward acting as a free agent. He was paying the price of cooperation with states which had entirely different ideals as to the execution of their policies in Asia. To later administrations such cooperation was distasteful, and was abandoned. There is, however, this to be said, that after 1868 American interests in Asia steadily receded until three decades later when the American Government resumed the policy of cooperation. The withdrawal of the United States from cooperation was one, though not the only, cause of this retirement of American influence.

BIBLIOGRAPHICAL NOTES

1. Geo. E. Baker: "Works of William H. Seward " Vol. 1, pp. 51 ff, 236 ff, 249-50, 356; Vol. 4, p. 125, pp. 24, 25.
2. Papers Relating to the Intercontinental Telegraph; Seward to the Committee of Commerce of the Senate, Gov't. Printing Office (1864).
3. Burlingame was first appointed minister to Vienna, but was unacceptable to the Austrian Government because of his sympathies for the cause of Kossuth. While in Paris Burlingame received notice of his appointment to Pekin. This, in part, may account for Seward's failure to issue the customary instructions. China Despatches, Vol. 20, July 6, 1861, Burlingame to Seward. See F. W. Williams: "Anson Burlingame."
4. Dip. Corres., 1862, p. 839.
5. Ibid., 1865, Vol. II, p. 461, Aug. 14, 1865.
6. Ibid., 1866, p. 536.
7. Ibid., 1866, p. 536.
8. China Instructions, Vol. 1, June 20, 1867.
9. C. O. Paullin: U. S. Naval Inst. Proceedings, 1911, pp. 1139 ff.
10. William H. Seward's "Travels Around the World," p. 216.
11. Japan Instructions, Vol. 1, Dec. 19, 1861.
12. Dip. Corres., 1862, pp. 814-16, p. 547.
13. Notes to Russian Legation, Vol. VI, p. 102, May 20, 1861, Seward to Stoeckl.
14. Dip. Corres., 1862, pp. 813, 814.

15. *Ibid.*, 1862, p. 974.
16. *Ibid.*, 1863, p. 1036.
17. *Ibid.*, 1862, p. 817.
18. *Ibid.*, 1862, p. 819.
19. *Ibid.*, 1863, p. 1013.
20. *Ibid.*, 1865, p. 229.
21. Diary of Gideon Welles, Vol. 2, p. 210; Vol. 3, p. 89.
22. Dip. Corres., 1868, p. 705.
23. Japan Instructions, Vol. 1, Sept. 5, 1868; see also Oct. 7, 1867, July 14 and Oct. 5, 1868; For. Rel., 1868, p. 757.
24. See Tyler Dennett: "Seward's Far Eastern Policy," *Amer. Hist. Rev.*, Oct. 1922, pp. 45-62, for a discussion of the purchase of Alaska in the light of recently discovered evidence of a contemporaneously proposed joint expedition with the French to Korea.
25. Frank A. Golden: "Purchase of Alaska," *Amer. Hist. Rev.*, Vol. XXV, No. 3, pp. 11 ff; Speech of Chas. Sumner of Mass., on the Cession of Russian America, p. *1*.
26. F. W. Seward: Reminiscences, p. 360.
27. S. Ex. Doc. 79:40-2; S. Rept. 194:40-3; Moore's "Digest," Vol. 1, p. 555.
28. Moore's "Digest," Vol. 1, p. 484 (footnote).
29. Seward's Works, Vol. 5, pp. 577 ff.
30. Henri Cordier: "Relations de la Chine," Vol. 1, pp. 267 ff; W. E. Griffis: "Corea, the Hermit Nation," pp. 373, 482-3; Korean Repository, July, 1898; Dip. Corres., Vol. 1, pp. 414-5, 419 ff.
31. Korean Despatches, Vol. 2, Mar. 29, 1885, Foulk to Chandler (filed by date); Griffis: "Corea," p. 395 (footnote).
32. Cordier: "Relations," Vol. 1, p. 268.
33. Dip. Corres., 1867, Vol. 1, p. 426.
34. The documentary evidence of Seward's proposal for the joint expedition into Korea is a despatch of Berthemy to Marquis de Moustier, Mar. 2, 1867, in the archives of the French Embassy at Washington. See also F. F. Low to Hamilton Fish, Feb. 1, 1873, China Desp., Vol. 33, which encloses a draft of the answer which was sent to Berthemy from Paris in reply to Seward's proposal. See Tyler Dennett in *Amer. Hist. Rev.*, Oct., 1922, for a full discussion of these documents and for the details of Seward's Far Eastern policy.
35. Dispatches to Consuls, Vol. 49, p. 267; For. Rel., 1870, pp. 336-9.

PART V
THE RISE OF JAPAN

CHAPTER XXIII

FIRST STEPS IN JAPANESE EXPANSION

THE contrasts between China and Japan, always striking, were never more so than at the time of the Japanese Restoration (1867). China, spread over more than thirty degrees of longitude, including every sort of climate, soil and mineral resource, was economically self-sufficient, and believed herself to be politically independent. Japan, a small island empire of which only a little more than one-seventh was arable land, with relatively few known mineral resources, unable to procure such essential articles as sugar and cotton, frankly recognized her economic dependence and her potential political weakness. Her rocky and storm-bound coasts, a sure defense under a policy of seclusion in the days of sail-navigation were, in the new era which had been ushered in by foreigners in heavily armored, steam-propelled vessels, as much prison walls as defenses. Only the merest fringe of the Chinese Empire had been touched by the foreigner. Canton, the rocky island of Hongkong, the new city of Shanghai, Tientsin, and even Peking had at times within the past generation been occupied by foreign military forces, but these cities were only on the circumference of an immense world which comprised nearly a fourth of the population of the entire globe. Even if the foreigners had permanently held every one of these points and many more, the Chinese people would not have been greatly embarrassed commercially, industrially, or even politically. Between the mountains and the sea China had every possible resource necessary for comfort as well as for existence, and to the advance of the foreigner there was opposed a vast mass of civilized, organized, industrious humanity. In comparison with China, Japan was a prison.

Within its narrow borders the Japanese people might continue to live as they had in the past, but no longer as voluntary prisoners; they would be in the position of captives. If the foreigners were to hold her few harbors, Yokohama, Hiogo, Nagasaki, the Straits of Shimoneséki and Hakodate, which has the qualities of a Gibraltar, they could reduce the proud Japanese Empire to an industrial and political condition incomparably inferior to what was possible for any other oriental state, with the possible exception of the Malay peninsula and archipelago.

The political theories about which the two empires were organized had a common characteristic; each nation regarded its sovereign as either actually or potentially overlord of the world. In oriental political economy there were but two possible classifications of states—tribute-bearing and tribute-receiving. Both China and Japan belonged to the latter class. The Emperor of China had insisted that the European nations bring tribute and perform the kotow if they would enter his presence. Japan held its Mikado in religious reverence; he was of divine origin—a tribal god—yet possessed of discretion sufficient to prevent him from demanding in fact the obeisance of the world which was believed to be due in theory. The contrast between China and Japan at this point lay in the fact that while China's claims to over-lordship were undercut by an essentially democratic and peace-seeking domestic organization, and crumpled before the impact of the Western World, Japan's claims were supported by popular assent and religious enthusiasm and at the opening of the nation to the Western World entered a renascence of vitality.

When Lord Hotta, the Shogun's prime minister, went to Kioto in March, 1858, to seek the assent of the Mikado to the Harris treaty, he unfolded to his sovereign in an address to the throne a theory of sovereignty in which this religio political idea is defined with precision. He wrote:

"Among the rulers of the world at present, there is none so noble and illustrious as to command universal vassalage, or who can make his virtuous influence felt throughout the length and breadth of the whole world. To have such a ruler over the whole world is doubtless in conformity with the will of Heaven.

"... and in establishing relations with foreign countries, the object should always be kept in view of laying a foundation for securing the hegemony over all nations."

As a first step in the accomplishment of this purpose, after the domestic affairs of Japan had been renovated and foreign relations established, he recommended that Japan should "join hands with nations whose principles may be found identical with those of our country.

"An alliance thus formed should also be directed towards protecting harmless but powerless nations. Such a polity could be nothing else but the enforcement of the power and authority deputed (to us) by the Spirit of Heaven. Our national prestige and position thus insured, the nations of the world will come to look up to our Emperor as the Great Ruler of all the nations, and they will come to follow our policy and submit themselves to our judgment." *[1]

This same idea reappears at regular intervals in the literature of Japan throughout the remainder of the nineteenth century. There is nothing comparable to it in the utterances of contemporaneous Chinese statesmen.

THE POLITICALLY NEBULOUS EAST

With these fundamental differences between China and Japan in mind let us turn to a brief consideration of the political situation thus created.

Eastern Asia was in a politically nebulous state, which might be compared roughly to a solar system before the orbits of the planets had become fixed or the satellites properly distributed. There were certain central masses, some with greater, some with lesser degrees of specific gravity, and there were smaller organisms which swung on irregular orbits in between the larger spheres. These latter bodies, while influenced in their movements by each of the larger masses, were still not wholly assigned to any one of them.

*Prof. W. W. McLaren states: "Expansion and aggrandizement of the Empire had formed an integral part of the teaching of the loyalist schools before the Restoration. Yoshida Shoin, the Choshiu patriot, had published a book in which he had predicted, as a consequence of the restoration of the Emperor, the conquest of Formosa, the Kurile Islands, Kamchatka, Korea, and a large portion of Manchuria and Siberia." [2]

The large spheres were China, Japan, Russia in Asia and Great Britain in Asia. The potential satellites were the islands off the coast of Asia—the Kuriles, Sakhalin, Yezo, Tsushima, the Bonin Islands, the Lew Chew group, and Formosa; and the so-called tributary states surrounding China—Burmah, Annam, Tibet and Korea. Until the Europeans came with their rapid and reliable communication and attempted to apply the rules of Western international law, these regions and islands had given to the larger Asiatic states only a moderate degree of trouble; lacking the steamship and the telegraph wire both Japan and China were quite content with the political *status quo.* Now the situation was radically changed. Immediate reasons appeared for a closer organization of the politically nebulous East. We see the consolidation taking place within China and Japan; we note also a proportionate increase in the power of gravitation which these masses, with which may be included the Russian and British Empires and France, began to pull upon the intervening islands and the outlying regions. The laws of physics operated in international politics. The pull upon these semi-detached spheres was in direct ratio to the specific gravity of the neighboring masses, and in inverse ratio to the distance.

China's relation to these satellite bodies was simple. Formosa [3] was an integral part of the Chinese Empire, administered as a part of the Province of Fukien, and yet remaining largely in the possession of unconquered, unsubdued aborigines. The Lew Chew Islands [4] had their own king, who, however, received his investiture from the Chinese Emperor and paid a regular tribute to Peking through the customs officer at Foochow. Korea,[5] Burmah and Annam likewise had their own kings, but received investiture from and paid tribute to Peking. Tibet, similarly to Formosa, was an integral part of the Chinese Empire. Into the history of the origin and growth of these relationships it is not necessary to go. In the middle of the nineteenth century they were entirely voluntary and mostly ceremonial. There had been an extension of the traditional

patriarchal system on a regal scale. The dependence in so
far as it was actual was more economic than political.
China was a source upon which any economically deficient
nation might draw to supplement its resources. The trib
ute-bearing embassies were accompanied by trading expeditions. On the other hand these territories, while of no ac
tual value to China, had a potential importance in that they
would be a menace to the empire were they to fall into
unfriendly hands. Rather than call them active buffer-
states, we may describe them as comfortable cushions.
Probably none of them in the nineteenth century could or
would have gone to war to defend the Chinese Empire.
China would not have gone to war to protect them from
injury, nor did she compel Siam to continue to pay tribute
after 1834. Indeed China had not only already acquiesced
in the entrance of the British in Burmah and the French
in Annam, but had even ceded a part of one of her own
provinces, the left bank of the Amur, to Russia in 1860.

The situation with Japan was very different. To no part
of the mainland of Asia did Japan lay any claim except that
Korea, until 1832, had been accustomed to pay tribute to
Japan as well as to China.[6] The Korean tribute was partly
like that to China, ceremonial and symbolic of a trade relationship, and partly an oriental form of black-mail such as
all tribute had once been, by which Korea purchased immunity. The Lew Chew Islands paid a similar tribute
which, however, went directly to the Prince of Satsuma
rather than to the Mikado or Shogun. All of the islands
north and east of the Lew Chew group Japan claimed as a
part of the Japanese Empire. The Bonins had been discovered centuries before by a Japanese navigator. Tsushima,
lying between Japan and Korea, was purely Japanese and
under the rule of a daimio. Yezo (now called Hokkaido)
was Japanese beyond dispute, although it was sparsely settled. The Kurile Islands were claimed but not occupied.
Sakhalin also was claimed although it was not until 1808
that a Japanese navigator first sailed around the island and
discovered that it was not a peninsula of Asia.[7] Japan did

not administer Sakhalin, nor were there on the island more than a very few Japanese settlers. These islands were to the Japanese Empire what the surrounding states of her neigh bor were to China—buffers of little or no value until they were threatened by some hostile power. That these islands might be valuable as sources of raw materials did not be- come apparent to the Japanese until their potential wealth had been pointed out to them by foreigners. On the other hand, Formosa, to which the Japanese set up no sort of claim, already seemed desirable because of its supplies of tropical produce.

We have now before us a view of the stage upon which Japan was to enact the first scenes in its unfolding drama of political expansion.

The Japanese Empire Begins Consolidation

In 1861 Russia occupied the island of Tsushima, which is of great strategic value because it commands the southern entrance to the Sea of Japan. The Russians built barracks and planted seed as though they had every intention of remaining permanently. "For the last eighteen months," wrote Townsend Harris in reporting the situation, "many officials, English and French, civilians and naval men, have frequently declared that war with Japan was inevitable, and that it could only end in the partition of the country (Japan). It is said that the Russian commander justified his action by referring to these declarations, adding that he remains at Tsushima solely for the purpose of preventing its falling into the power of the English or French." [8] To this dispatch Seward replied with a confidence in his ability to influence the Far Eastern policy of Russia which now seems amazing:

"If the occupation of Tsushima is still an object of anxiety to his Majesty, the Tycoon, I will at once call the attention of the President to the matter, and with his authority, which I doubt not will be granted, I will, in the name of this government, as the friend of Japan, as well as of Russia, seek from the latter explanations which I should hope would be satisfactory to Japan."

Seward was as alert to meet any efforts looking towards the partition of Japan as Humphrey Marshall had been to prevent the partition of China.

Before Seward's offer of good offices reached Japan Admiral Sir James Hope, supported by a formidable British fleet, had ordered the Russians to leave the island and they had obeyed. Meanwhile Japan, which had other matters of dispute with Russia, had entered into friendly negotiations with her threatening neighbor through the Japanese Embassy then visiting Europe.

With Russia Japan was in the midst of prolonged negotiations over the possession of Sakhalin and the Kurile Islands. The Russians had lodged a claim for Sakhalin as early as 1804.[9] By the treaty of 1855 the boundary in the Kuriles had been fixed between Urup and Iturup but the two nations had been left in joint occupation of Sakhalin. In 1859 Count Muravieff entered Yedo accompanied by a naval force and demanded the cession of the entire island to Russia. When reminded of the treaty he declared that in making it Count Putiatin had exceeded his instructions and that the compact, notwithstanding the ratifications, was invalid. The Japanese would not yield. Three years later the two nations agreed in principle to the division of the island at the 50th parallel, but the agreement was not consummated owing to the state of Japanese domestic affairs.

In 1866 the Shogun's government sent an envoy to St. Petersburg to reach a settlement but nothing was accomplished. Four years later the newly constituted Mikado's government instituted a Board of Exploration for Sakhalin. That same year the Japanese Government sought the good offices of William H. Seward when he was passing through Japan on his tour of the world, to secure the mediation of the United States in the controversy. Seward suggested that a simple solution of the difficulty would be for Japan to buy the Russian claims to the island just as the United States had purchased Alaska.[10] The Japanese did not relish the idea of buying what they believed to be theirs by right.

The suggestion, however, was adopted, but Russia rejected the proposal. The Japanese Government made formal application through the American minister, C. E. De Long, for the good offices of the United States, and Secretary of State Fish immediately took up the matter in an informal way with the Russian Government. Russia replied both graciously and adroitly that it would not be possible to submit such a matter to mediation because a precedent would thus be established which some unfriendly European power might subsequently attempt to utilize to the disadvantage of Russia.[11]

Several attempts to fix the boundary were made in the next few years and in 1875 Admiral Enomoto signed a treaty in St. Petersburg by which Russia received the whole of Sakhalin, while certain rights in the island were secured to Japan, and Japan took most of the Kuriles. Tokio had seized a moment to settle the matter while Russia was again becoming involved in the Balkans. Japan was willing to make a concession in this settlement because by it Japan was for the first time negotiating the revision of a treaty on equal terms with a European power. This precedent Japan deemed valuable at the time when she was setting out on her long negotiations for the revision of the treaties of 1858 and 1866.[12]

Towards the end of 1861 the Japanese formally notified Townsend Harris that they intended to reoccupy the Bonin Islands which they claimed by right of discovery in the sixteenth century. They declared that the rights of Americans would not be disturbed. Seward allowed the matter to pass without comment although Commander John Kelly had formally taken possession of the Coffin group of the Bonins in 1853. Japan was forced to withdraw from the Bonins for a time during the domestic disturbances, but returned to them again. The Japanese yoke did not rest easily upon the Americans in the islands who had long been a law unto themselves and had even adopted piracy as a profession.[13] There were several protests; in 1864 Pruyn collected $1000 in settlement of a claim made by a sailor

from Perry's fleet who had been left there.[14] But in 1873
Secretary of State Fish formally ruled that inasmuch as the
possession of the islands had never been expressly sanctioned
by the American Government those citizens who had gone
there were to be regarded as having expatriated themselves.[15] Great Britain after investigation also abandoned
its claim. The Japanese came into undisputed possession of
the islands which they now regard as legally a part of the
mainland of Japan.

It was the assumption of the foreign representatives in
China in 1866 that Korea was a dependency of the Chinese
Empire.[16] Japan, while still holding to such claims on the
peninsula as had been represented by the tribute which was
paid regularly before 1832, gave tacit assent to the priority
of China in Korea. In that year Prince Kung, foreseeing
that the assertion of Chinese suzerainty over Korea at the
time of the murder of the French missionaries would lead
directly to a demand on China for reparations to be paid to
France, adopted the characteristically Chinese policy of
evading responsibility for these claims. This act of the
Chinese Government, while appearing to be the easiest way
out of a difficulty, was a repudiation by China of suzerainty
over the peninsula. The French *Chargé,* Bellonet, had
forthwith seized upon this repudiation, and proceeded
against Korea as an independent kingdom. The Chinese
Government expressed no interest in the American expeditions of the following year under Commanders Robert W
Shufeldt and John C. Febiger respectively. The contrast
between the policy of China and that of Japan at this point
is significant.

The Japanese, although in the midst of the disturbances
which preceded the Restoration, immediately expressed con
cern in both the French expeditions and the visits of the
American naval vessels. The Tycoon announced (May,
1867) to United States Minister Van Valkenburgh his intention to send an envoy to Korea because he had learned that
there was war between the French and the Koreans. He
was also much disturbed over the troubles between the

Koreans and the Americans because Korea "is a neighbor of Japan" and the "United States and Japan are friends." He extended the good offices of Japan and expressed the hope that through Japanese influence the Korean king would sue for peace, and that the flag of the United States would return to the peninsula.[17]

"This friendly proceeding is highly appreciated," replied Seward. "It is deemed proper to add that the Government of the United States will feel obliged, should no satisfactory explanation or apology be furnished by Korea, to consider how proper reparation can be obtained and honor maintained." A few months later (January 27, 1868), while he was considering the possibility of a treaty with Korea, Seward added an expression of satisfaction that "the United States may be able to avail themselves of the good offices of the proposed Japanese Legation." [18]

Meanwhile Japan experienced many difficulties in resuming intercourse with the peninsula. The Tycoon was unable to send the proposed envoy in 1867. The next year So, the daimio of Tsushima, through whose office the previous intercourse with Korea had been carried on, was ordered to send a special mission to announce the Restoration. Three years before King Chul-chong died without issue and a boy selected from another branch of the Ni family had been installed with his father, the later well known Tai-wen-Kun, as regent. The latter was anti-foreign in policy. To him is ascribed the responsibility for having caused the massacre of the French missionaries. The Tai-wen-Kun had regarded the expedition under Admiral Roze as a complete victory for Korea but it had left him greatly enraged against the Japanese because many of the troops used in the French expedition had been drawn from the French garrison at Yokohama. The regent believed that Japan should have prevented the sending of these troops, and the fact that Japan did not interfere was interpreted by him to mean that the Japanese had not only abandoned their policy of seclusion but had even gone so far as to enter into an alliance with the French. The Korean government refused to receive the Japanese mission and likewise refused to deal with two other missions dispatched in 1869.*

Thus the first overtures to Korea, with which had been coupled a demand that Korea resume the custom of paying tribute, utterly failed. In 1868 Herr von Brandt, the German representative in Tokio, whom the Japanese had invited as they did the Americans, to approach Korea through the good offices of Japan with a view to securing a treaty, was unceremoniously denied correspondence with the Korean government on the ground that he had been accompanied to Fusan by Japanese officers. To one of these Japanese commissions the Tai-wen-Kun is believed to have replied in the following bellicose manner:

"Your demand is so unreasonable that instead of Korea paying you tribute, it is for you to return the money paid by Korea. In your dispatch you have made many insinuations of your having adopted foreign customs; but we can assure you that Japan is Japan—Korea is Korea, but Korea has its own customs. Some years back we had a difference with a country called France which is, among barbarians, considered to be very powerful and very large, whilst Korea is very small—but we defeated that great country! . . . To show our honesty, when the barbarians went to your country, we immediately wrote you that we had made every preparation to help you. But when the French attacked Korea you neither sent us aid, nor any answer to our dispatch. From that day our treaty of friendship was at an end. . . .

"Not only have you broken the treaty as we have described, but you have also broken another very chief point of the treaty, in adopting the manners and customs of the Western barbarians. Our information is that you have adopted French drill—and when you want money you go to England; and if you wish to tax your own people or impose duties you take the advice from Americans. You think the Western barbarians are great people. We, Koreans, are a very small country, but yet we have the courage to put into writing to you that Western barbarians are beasts. The above is intended as a direct insult to you and your allies—the barbarians." [20]

Hanabusa, chief secretary of the Japanese Foreign Office, was sent to Korea in 1871 with two war vessels to remonstrate with the Koreans but they declined to be intimidated and the expedition accomplished nothing. The Koreans were particularly disgusted because Hanabusa had adopted

*One of these latter missions was charged with an investigation of the relations then existing between Korea and Russia. Many Japanese officials at that time were urging that Japan refuse to yield to the Russian claims for all or even any part of Sakhalin.[19]

foreign styles of clothing. Japan was now on the point of
going to war with Korea.

About this time further light on the relations between
Korea and China was being revealed through the correspondence of United States Minister F. F. Low with the
Chinese officials in Peking. In preparation of the American
expedition to Korea in 1871,* which was really the consummation of the plans made by Seward in 1868, Low
invited the good offices of China and asked the Peking
officials to transmit to Korea a letter stating the purpose of
the proposed expedition. The Chinese complied with the
request, but stated equivocally that although Korea was a
"country subordinate to China," nevertheless it was "wholly
independent in government, religion, prohibitions and laws."
Low interpreted this answer to mean that China was seeking not to make clear the relations between the two countries, but to avoid the assumption of any liability for the
loss of the General Sherman or the unrequited murder of
the French missionaries.

An answer to Mr. Low's letter to the King of Korea was
duly received in Peking before the departure of the expedition in 1871 and what purported to be a copy of it was
reluctantly transmitted to the American minister. While
in Korea Mr. Low received from the Koreans a copy of the
letter as originally addressed to the Chinese officials. When
compared with the document which the Chinese had given
to Mr. Low, it was found that the Chinese had omitted to
transcribe a part of the letter in which the King of Korea
had made the most profuse acknowledgments of vassalage
to the Emperor of China. Low reached the conclusion from
a comparison of the two documents that China was actually
very much opposed to the opening of Korea to the Western
nations. He wrote (August 3, 1871):

"That Korea acknowledges the supremacy of China in a manner
amounting almost to servility is quite apparent, and it is quite reasonable to suppose that China does and will use all the means in her
power short of provoking the hostility of western nations to maintain
and perpetuate the present status so far as the relation of the two

*The Low-Rogers Expedition is reviewed in the following chapter.

countries is concerned. So long as Korea maintains her present attitude of non-intercourse the supremacy of China will be acknowledged
and observed. This magnifies the importance of China in the estimation of her people and, in the opinion of the officials, adds to their
dignity and importance. Were Korea opened to foreign intercourse,
the bonds of vassalage which bind her to China would be weakened,
if not broken entirely, and the tribute which now comes annually
to Peking would soon be numbered among the things of the past. This
the Peking officials see clearly and hence the desire to see Korea remain as she is." [21]

JAPAN ON THE VERGE OF WAR

While affairs between Korea and Japan remained still
unsettled, the latter dispatched (April, 1871) a representative to Peking with the rank of Envoy Extraordinary and
powers to negotiate a treaty with China.[22] There were
many rumors in the foreign settlements both in Japan and
in China that the intent of this mission was to create an
offensive and defensive alliance of Japan and China which
would be directed against the foreign powers. The mission
was halted at Tientsin and a treaty was signed July 29,
1871. To the Japanese its provisions were unsatisfactory
because it did not provide for most-favored-nation treatment and because it contained only the most grudging concessions of extraterritoriality with bilateral application. In
the treaty ports Japanese merchants were to be under the
joint jurisdiction of the Japanese consul and the local
Chinese official, and in the interior under the Chinese alone.
To the foreigners there was one disquieting article in which
the rumors of the treaty ports appeared to be realized.* It
provided for a defensive alliance.

The American minister, possibly the other foreign representatives as well, felt that an alliance between China and
Japan would be "calamitous" and he exerted his influence to
have the article stricken out of the treaty. He believed that

*Article 2, according to the Chinese text, read : "The two countries having
a good understanding must naturally feel an interest in each other. If any
other country treat either with injustice, in such case each will mutually assist
the other as soon as informed of the necessity, or acting as intermediary, will
try to skillfully arrange the difficulty,—in this way the friendship will be
strengthened."

A translation of the Japanese text was more ambiguous : "China and Japan
being friendly, either shall in case of experiencing injustice or wrong from
another state, be entitled to assistance or good offices of the other." [23]

the Japanese were quite different from the Chinese and that the former represented a "power to be welcomed as an ally and to be dreaded as a foe by all civilized states should trouble occur with China, or our troubles with Korea enlarge and increase." [24] This objection to any form of alliance between the two states appears to have arisen out of the fear that in the association thus formed Japan would not only acquire the power but also the desire to adopt reactionary policies like those of China with reference to the modernizing of the empire. Secretary of State Fish, in his reply to De Long (December 30, 1872), expressed this fear.

"In any conversation you may have with a view to influencing the proceedings of the Japanese Government in its intercourse with China it is advisable to induce the Japanese to separate themselves as far as possible from the exclusive policy of the Chinese and to adopt the progressive policy of free commercial and social intercourse with the powers." * [25]

The fears of the foreigners were not very well justified by the facts of the existing situation. China had treated the Japanese mission with scant courtesy and had made few concessions. Meanwhile the Japanese were becoming convinced that the hostility of the Koreans was being inspired from Peking. A still more delicate situation was growing up over the possession of the Lew Chew Islands.

When the feudal nobles surrendered their powers to the Mikado after the Restoration, the rights of the Prince of Satsuma in the Lew Chew Islands were forthwith transferred to the Crown. The nature of these rights cannot easily be defined. Hitherto they had involved nothing more than the payment of annual tribute.† The Japanese Government now interpreted them to involve Japanese sovereignty. An order was issued (September, 1872) to the king of the Lew Chews to appear in Tokio to announce his accession to the throne and to congratulate the Japanese

---

*This reference to free social intercourse is rather amusing in view of the fact that both in China and in Japan in all social functions the foreigners had adopted the policy of rigidly excluding both Chinese and Japanese from their society[26]

†For Commodore Perry's opinion on the political status of the Lew Chews, see pp. 268, 272.[27]

upon the establishment of the new government. The kingdom of the Lew Chews was formally incorporated into the Japanese Empire, the king being reduced to the rank of Japanese prince and given a pension of 30,000 *yen*. Japan assumed the responsibilities incurred by the Lew Chewans under their treaties with the foreign powers, and the latter accepted the new status of the islands.[28] China, however, protested at what appeared to them nothing less than a high-handed piece of robbery.

In the estimation of the Chinese the Japanese added insult to injury not many months after this when the latter made a claim on China for reparations for some Lew Chew sailors who had been wrecked on the coast of Formosa and murdered by the aboriginal inhabitants. The claim was based on the ground that these sailors were subjects of Japan.

Japan thus arrived in the latter part of 1872 at a very alarming situation. Russia was clinging tenaciously to Sakhalin, Korea was insulting, China was aggrieved. There was also a most disturbed condition of domestic affairs. The ablest Japanese leaders had been dispatched on the famous Embassy to the Western powers with the hope of securing a revision of the treaties, and at home the samaurai, recently disestablished and accorded a financial settlement which proved a most unsatisfactory solace to men whose profession was arms, were in a bellicose mood which presaged either civil or foreign war. The Korean insults which had been followed by the prohibition of all trade, and the unavenged death of the Lew Chew sailors afforded an opportunity for the harassed government to divert the attention of the unhappy soldiery from a civil war which would paralyze all the recently inaugurated domestic reforms.

Minister De Long reported from Tokio in the latter part of November, 1872, that Japan was about to embark upon a most ambitious military program. The Koreans were to be punished for their persistent refusal to pay tribute as well as for the insults rendered; an expedition was to be undertaken to Formosa to punish the aborigines; and an

embassy was to be dispatched to Peking which would be
authorized to demand an audience with the Emperor and to
threaten war on China in case the audience was denied.
De Long was unable to resist the intrigues of an oriental
court and found a great deal of satisfaction in giving the
Japanese an extraordinary degree of sympathy and assistance in the execution of these rash purposes.*

In the latter part of November, 1872, C. W. Le Gendre,
United States consul at Amoy since 1862, happened to pass
through Japan on his way home on leave. He had taken a
prominent part in the American expedition to Formosa in
1868 following the wreck of the bark *Rover,* and claimed to
have a considerable amount of military experience. De
Long introduced Le Gendre to the Japanese authorities who
immediately recognized him as a valuable assistant in the
proposed negotiations with China and the expedition against
Formosa. Le Gendre advised the Japanese that the Chinese
Government did not exercise sovereignty over that portion
of Formosa where the Lew Chew sailors had been murdered.
He assured them that a small expeditionary force sent to
Formosa could easily effect a landing and that, once established, it would be very difficult to dislodge them. The
Japanese engaged Le Gendre as counsellor to the proposed
mission to Peking, agreed to make him a general in the
Japanese army in case of war with Formosa, and held out
the inducement that in case Japan were to remain permanently in Formosa, Le Gendre would be made governor of
the island. De Long felt much gratified at the arrangement
which, it seemed to him, would still farther separate Japan
from China, avert civil war in Japan, and place Formosa
and possibly Korea, under "a flag of a nation in sympathy
with the Western powers." [29] Into the details of the embassy to Peking it is not possible to go although it constitutes one of the most amusing as well as significant episodes in the history of Japanese relations with China.[30]
Soyeshima, with a diplomatic rank superior to that of any

*When the full extent of De Long's activities became known in Washington
the next year, he was immediately recalled.

diplomatic resident in Peking, with a large suite, clothed in Western dress, attended by Le Gendre as Counsellor, and accompanied by two war vessels, appeared in China in March, 1873. The ostensible purpose of the mission was to exchange ratifications of the treaty of 1871. The intent was to secure the assent of China to the annexation of the Lew Chews, to the expedition against Formosa, and also to secure from China a disclaimer of sovereignty over Korea. Li Hung Chang at Tientsin was disposed to receive the mission with contempt, and the foreign representatives at Peking were almost equally scornful. The Japanese insisted upon the most exact observance of international law, especially in the matter of diplomatic rank, thus claiming for Soyeshima as ambassador a precedence over the representatives of the foreign powers who were only ministers. Le Gendre did not prove a help to the embassy. The diplomatic negotiations, even when one accepts the Japanese account of them, could hardly be called straight-forward. The mission failed to secure Chinese assent to the annexation of the Lew Chews; but it did secure as definite a waiving of responsibility for Korea as had been given to Mr. Low in 1871, and the evasive answers of the Chinese with respect to Formosa were such as to give the Japanese at least a shadow of permission for the proposed expedition.*

Incidentally Soyeshima forced the audience question to an issue when it was hanging in suspense and while he was in Peking the entire diplomatic body was for the first time received in audience by the Emperor, Soyeshima being accorded precedence over all the other representatives.

The maturing bellicose plans of Japan now experienced an interruption from within. The Iwakura Embassy while in Europe heard of the proposed plans and were in dismay.

---

*Japan confronted China with the principle of international law that sovereignty over territory was not to be recognized where the power claiming sovereignty did not exercise the functions of government. To this claim China replied with a quotation from her classics which she understood better than international law. "Formosa is an island lying far off amidst the sea," wrote Prince Kung to the ministers of the Japanese Department of Foreign Affairs, May 14. 1874, "and we have never restrained the savages living there by any legislation, nor have we established any government over them, following in this a maxim mentioned in the *Rei Ri*: 'Do not change the usages of a people, but allow them to keep their good ones.' But the territories inhabited by these savages are truly within the jurisdiction of China." [31]

They had seen enough of European politics to realize that Asia would not be left undisturbed in the fighting of its own battles and they hastened home to plead for peace. Immediately upon their return there was a division in the cabinet between peace and war, and the issue was submitted to the Emperor. The arguments for peace were overwhelming: Japan was without an army and the only way in which one could be raised was to ask for contributions of soldiers for the ex-daimios whose return to power would be an obstruction to the newly organized government; the Empire lacked the necessary money; and then there were the Western powers to be considered. Okubo, one of the members of the Iwakura Mission, pointed out this danger, in effect, as follows:

"Of all the foreign powers Russia is the most to be feared, and her southward movement is well known; so that if Japan and Korea fight with one another, both will fall an easy prey to Russia.

"England is also a powerful nation, from whom Japan has already borrowed much money, so that if Japan and Korea fight and we cannot pay the interest in consequence of the war, she would make it a pretext for interfering in our internal affairs, thus making Japan another India." [32]

The young Emperor cast his vote for peace. This action enraged the war-seeking daimios, one of whom had been so eager for war with Korea that he had offered to go to the peninsula and expose himself to further insults and even death to provide the Japanese with a sufficient excuse for a declaration of war. But the Emperor's decision had not avoided the issue of war. If a foreign war were not to be permitted, then civil war would ensue. In the spring of 1874 Japan decided to carry out the Formosan expedition.

FORMOSA, THE LEW CHEWS AND KOREA

The Formosan Expedition was organized in April, 1874. Two Americans in addition to Le Gendre were engaged in it and an American steamer was secured as a transport. As soon as the true nature of the expedition became known the American Government requested that the Americans be detached from it, and the American steamer returned to its owners. There was much excitement along the coast of China. Le Gendre was arrested by the American consul at Amoy and sent to Shanghai. The Japanese effected a land ing early in May, and showed every intention of remaining in possession of the eastern portion of the island. In October, 1874, a Japanese envoy arrived in Peking to settle the Formosa dispute. There was a war of words and then a rupture of the negotiations. As the Japanese envoy was about to leave Peking Dr. S. Wells Williams suggested arbi tration, but the envoy stated that the matter was 'too complicated' for arbitration.[33]

But the Japanese were not to be permitted to settle the Formosan affair in their own way. Sir Thomas Wade, the British Minister, had already, so it is believed, intimated to the Japanese that Great Britain would not view the Japanese occupation of Formosa with satisfaction owing to the close trade relations of Formosa with the British merchants in China, and now he intervened and became mediator of the dispute. An agreement was signed October 31, 1874.[34]

In the treaty between China and Japan in 1874, for the settlement of the Formosan trouble, Japan cleverly inserted the following sentence: "The raw barbarians of Formosa once unlawfully inflicted injury on the people *belonging to Japan,* and the Japanese Government with the intention of making the said barbarians answer for their acts sent troops to chastize them." The treaty also stated that Japan had acted justly in the matter. Thus Japan cut the ground from under the Chinese claims of suzerainty over the Lew Chews, for the people referred to as belonging to Japan were Lew Chew sailors. The Chinese claim, in the judgment of the Japanese, no longer had a standing in international law, and when the Chinese discovered the way in which they had been outwitted, they fell back on sullen defiance. In 1879 the Lew Chew prince was still further reduced by the Japanese because his emissaries had been seeking the good offices of the American and other ministers in Tokio, with a view to having the old relationship to China restored. The

American Government had contented itself, when Japan formally annexed the islands, with the assurances that American rights would in no way be disturbed, and never interfered with the program of Japan; it regarded the controversy as purely between China, the King of the Lew Chews, and Japan.

The points of irritation between China and Japan multiplied after the Formosan affair in 1874, and when General Grant visited Peking in 1879 the two nations were on the point of war. Grant saw very clearly that the European nations might seize the opportunity to enhance their own interests. It was therefore a matter of satisfaction to General Grant when the Chinese proposed and the Japanese agreed to submit the Lew Chew question to his mediation.

After many conferences with the Chinese in Peking and a thorough review of the question in Tokio, General Grant wrote a letter, August 18, 1879, to Prince Kung which, before being sent was shown to the Emperor of Japan and received his approval.[35] In this letter Grant made the following proposals: (1) China to withdraw certain threatening and menacing dispatches which had been addressed to Japan on the subject; (2) each country to appoint a com mission, and the two commissions to confer on the subject; (3) no foreign power to be brought into the discussion, but in case the commissions could not agree they might appoint an arbitrator whose decisions should be binding on both Japan and China. General Grant then took the opportunity to point out to China the necessity for peace. His language is interesting for its earnestness and as an indication of General Grant's conclusions on the impending conflict in Asia. He wrote:

"In the vast East, embracing more than two thirds of the human population of the world there are but two nations even partially free from the domination and dictation of some one or other of the European Powers, with strength enough to maintain their independence— Japan and China are the two nations. The people of both are brave, intelligent, frugal and industrious. With a little more advancement in modern civilization, mechanics, engineering, etc., they could throw off the offensive treaties which now cripple and humiliate them, and could enter into competition for the world's commerce. . . .

"Japan is now rapidly reaching a condition of independence, and if it had now to be done over, such treaties as exist could not be forced upon her. What Japan has done, and is now doing, China has the power—and I trust the inclination—to do. I can readily conceive that there are many foreigners, particularly those interested in trade, who do not look beyond the present and who would like to have the present condition remain, only grasping more from the East, and leaving the natives of the soil merely 'hewers of wood and drawers of water' for their benefit. I have so much sympathy for the good of their children, [the foreigners] if not for them, that I hope the two countries will disappoint them."

It has been stated, and probably correctly, that General Grant went even so far as to recommend that Japan and China form an alliance against the Western powers.*

Both nations accepted Grant's proposal and the two commissions met in Peking. After three months' discussion they arrived at a settlement according to which the islands were to be divided.† However, on the day fixed for the signatures China suddenly withdrew the question from the commission and referred it to the Chinese superintendents of trade of the northern and southern districts.[38] "A glaring instance of international treachery" on the part of China, the North China *Daily News* (January 27, 1883) called it, but it was subsequently discovered that Japan, not content with the settlement of the Lew Chew question by its self, had, at the last minute, insisted upon the inclusion in the agreement of some additional provisions opening new ports and trading privileges in China to Japan.

China had been predisposed to settle the matter in 1880 because of the strained relations with Russia, although the surrender of Chinese territory to a foreign power during the minority of the emperor was a risk such as few Chinese statesmen would have dared to assume. As soon as the trouble with Russia was over, the Lew Chew question again

*The Government of the United States feared that the good offices of the United States were being accepted by the two powers under a misapprehension that General Grant in some way officially represented the United States, and instructed its representatives to make clear that he had acted in an entirely personal capacity.[36]

†It has been frequently stated [37] that General Grant himself proposed the partition of the islands between China and Japan. As a matter of fact, the most important point in the mediation by General Grant was that China and Japan should, if possible, settle their own disputes without the admission of any European into the controversy.

became the subject of great irritation. Li Hung Chang outlined China's position as follows: China would not under
any circumstances consent to the destruction of the autonomy of the islands, or the division of them between
Japan and China. He desired that the islands should be restored to their original conditions of tributary state to both
China and Japan. Failing this, he thought China would
agree to enter into treaty stipulations with Japan by which
both powers would guarantee the absolute independence of
the Lew Chews.[39]

In 1882 Li Hung Chang was not unwilling to fight Japan
for the possession of the islands and war seemed imminent.
The international situation remained the same. A war
between China and Japan would be destructive to the best
interests of both nations, and also detrimental to the inter
ests of the United States. John Russell Young, then Ameri
can minister in Peking, who as a newspaper correspondent
had accompanied General Grant around the world, and who
was also on very intimate terms with Li Hung Chang,
strongly urged the Viceroy not to enter into hostilities with
Japan. The question had passed beyond the stage where it
might be controlled by considerations of justice. China had
signed away her rights in the treaty of 1874. Japan had
formally annexed the islands and had been administering
them for several years. But more important even was the
fact that China was in no condition to enter a war. Peace
at any price was the only safe policy for the Empire.

The Lew Chew question was soon lost in the greater
problem which confronted China in the aggressions of
France upon her southern border, and the annexation of the
Lew Chews by Japan became a *fait accompli*.

Meanwhile Japan had accomplished the first step of her
program in Korea.

In September, 1875, a Japanese surveying party was
fired on while surveying the Korean coast near the mouth
of the Han River. Immediately General Kuroda and General Inouye were sent to Korea to settle the matter. At the
same time an envoy was sent to Peking. The envoy to

Peking again secured a disclaimer of any Chinese responsibility for Korea, and became convinced that China would not interfere so long as Japan did not take any Korean territory. Japan therefore decided to be content with merely opening the country, and found inspiration and suggestions for the rôle in the way Commodore Perry had opened Japan. Without bloodshed, but in the presence of an imposing naval and military force, Korea was led to make a treaty with Japan at Kang-hoa February 27, 1876.

The Treaty of Kang-hoa was Japan's entering wedge on the mainland of Asia. Its most important provision was contained in the first article: "Chosen, being an independent state, enjoys the same sovereign rights as does Nippon." [40] Thus the first step was taken; Korea was led, adroitly, to disavow Chinese suzerainty. The treaty also provided for the opening of several ports, acknowledged Japan's right to make surveys of the coast, stipulated that consular and diplomatic relations could be established and granted to Japan extraterritoriality in criminal matters. In general the treaty was unilateral, and similar to those which the foreign powers had imposed upon both China and Japan.

"The treaty of 1876," states a Japanese historian, "was the first clear announcement of Japan's foreign policy as regards Korea. The policy of annexation, though not impossible to carry out, was from the very first rejected in view of the possible conflict with China (and later with Russia also); but neither China nor any other nation was to be allowed to substantiate its claim of suzerainty over Korea on the ground of free competition." [41]

BIBLIOGRAPHICAL NOTES

1. Satah, Lord Hotta, p. 74, cited by Treat: "Early Diplomatic Relations," pp. 99-100.
2. W. W. McLaren: "Political Hist. of Japan," p. 35.
3. James W. Davidson: "The Island of Formosa" (1903), particularly chaps. 9-13.
4. Foreign Relations, 1880, pp. 194 ff, Dec. 11, 1879, Seward to Secretary of State; 1875, p. 786, Feb. 9, 1875, Bingham to Secretary of State.
5. W. W. Rockhill: "China's Intercourse with Korea from the Fifteenth Century to 1895."

6. Griffis: "Hermit Kingdom," pp. 58, 159, 372.
7. Stead: p. 150.
8. Japan Desp. Vol. 4, Oct. 7, 1861; for Seward's answer see Japan Instructions, Vol. 1, Feb. 5, 1862.
9. Stead: pp. 149 ff., give a history of the Sakhalin controversy.
10. William H. Seward's "Travels Around the World," p. 58.
11. Japan Desp. Vol. 13, Jan. 11, 1870; Japan Instr. Vol. 1, Jan. 17, 1871; Russia Instr., Nov. 11, 1870; Russia Disp., Dec. 9, 1870.
12. Stead: p. 175.
13. The Benjamin Pease, referred to in Misc. H. Doc. 31:45-2, p. 12, pp. 32, 66, 200 ff., made his headquarters in the Bonin Islands.
14. Dip. Corres., 1864, III, p. 518; Treat, *op. cit.*, pp. 309, 344.
15. For. Relations, 1874, pp. 635, 637.
16. Dip. Corres., 1867, I, pp. 419 ff.
17. Dip. Corres., 1867, II, p. 36.
18. Dip. Corres., 1868, p. 634.
19. Stead: p. 148.
20. Japan Gazette, July 18, 1872, reprinted in Japan *Weekly Mail.*
21. China Desp., Vol. 30, Aug. 3, 1871.
22. Stead: p. 154.
23. Martens' "Recueil de Traités," 61, p. 502, gives the Japanese form of this article. The treaties published by the Maritime Customs give the longer form of the article in which a definite defensive alliance is provided for. This is the first instance, of which there have been others in more recent years, where the Japanese and Chinese texts of agreements between the two nations do not agree.
24. Japan Desp., Vol. 18, July 6, 1871.
25. For. Relations, 1873, p. 567; see also Japan Instr., Vol. 1, Aug. 24, 1871.
26. See accounts of receptions to W. H. Seward in "Travels Around the World."
27. S. Ex. Doc. 34:33-2 (Perry Corres.), pp. 139, 143, 168.
28. For. Relations, 1873, pp. 553, 564.
29. Japan Desp., Vol. 21, Nov. 22, 1872.
30. While there are references to the Soyeshima Embassy in the despatches of Low to Fish (For. Relations, 1873, pp. 177, 186 *et seq.*) the most interesting account, evidently based on Japanese documentary sources or reminiscences, is found in Stead, pp. 159 ff.
31. China Desp., Vol. 36, Aug. 22, 1874, Williams to Fish.
32. Stead: p. 166.
33. China Desp., Vol. 37, Oct. 29, 1874.
34. P. P. China No. 2 (1875) Corres. resp. settlement of difficulties bet. China and Japan; Further Corres. presented Mar. 9, 1875; For. Relations, 1875, p. 221, Williams to Fish, Nov. 12, 1874.
35. China Desp., Vol. 61, Oct. 9, 1882, Young to Frelinghuysen; John Russell Young: "Men and Memories," Vol. 2, p. 294; "Around the World with General Grant," Vol. 2, pp. 410-12; 415; 543-6; 558-60 "The Loochoo Islands," by Charles S. Leavenworth, p. 159 ff., gives extracts from Li Hung Chang's Let-

ters and Despatches on the Lew Chews. These documents are not in agreement with Mr. Young's account in several details.

36. For. Relations, 1881, p. 243, Apr. 4, 1881.
37. Robert P. Porter: "Japan, the Rise of a Modern Power," p. 119; Morse: "International Relations," Vol. II, p. 322, and many others.
38. For. Relations, 1881, p. 229; see also 1873, pp. 188, 553, 564; 1879, p. 637; 1880, p. 194.
39. "Secret Memoirs of Count Tadasu Hayashi," Appendix A, pp. 316 ff.; China Desp., Vol. 58, Nov. 19, 1881.
40. Stead: p. 177, contains summary of contents with comments of Japanese historian.
41. *Ibid.*, p. 179.

CHAPTER XXIv

THE UNITED STATES AND KOREA—TREATY OF 1882

THE preceding chapter on Japanese expansion closed, not because a convenient date had been reached, but because it is now necessary to describe another line of activity before going on with the account of Japan's efforts to consolidate a satisfactory territorial position in Asia. In taking the next step in Korea, Japan was greatly aided by the desire of Western nations, particularly the United States, to see the peninsula opened to trade.

The movement to open Korea, first seriously initiated by William H. Seward in 1868 and accomplished in 1882 by Commodore R. W. Shufeldt, was by far the most important political action undertaken by the United States in Asia until the occupation of the Philippines in 1898. To disturb Korea in any way was to disturb the equilibrium of the Far East. By the treaty of 1876 in which Korea was led to disavow Chinese suzerainty, a balance had been established between China and Japan. The transcending political question for the Western nations was whether to recognize the contention thus set up by Japan that Korea was independent, or to continue to accept the evasive utterances of China as implying the existence of Chinese suzeranity.

EXPEDIENCY OF DISTURBING THE *Status Quo*

One is forced to the conclusion from a study of the declarations of both Chinese statesmen and Korean leaders of the time that there was involved for the Western nations no question of political righteousness. Notwithstanding the unconvincing nature of the disavowals of Chinese sovereignty, China in 1876 had no valid claim to Korea. Peking exercised no administrative functions and had repeatedly denied any control of Korean affairs. The Chinese had disavowed any responsibility for claims arising out of the damage to foreign life and property in the peninsula; they undertook no measures whatever to prevent shipwrecks or the recurrence of such events as the murder of the French missionaries. Even when one gives to the Chinese assertions of the subordinations of Korea to the Empire a value unmodified by the accompanying disavowals of responsibility, one is forced to the conclusion that the Chinese were pursuing merely a dog-in-the-manger policy. They did not want Korea, but they did not want Korea to come under the shadow of any other power, nor did they relish the idea of Korean independence. Likewise Japan had not the shadow of a claim to possession of Korea. Japan's claims were purely economic. In a measure Japan was dependent upon Korea for food-stuffs. To admit that the economic dependence of one nation upon another constitutes a valid claim for territorial possession by the dependent country is to admit a proposition which renders insecure the boundaries of most of the nations of the earth.

On the other hand, there was in the existing relationship between Japan and Korea a question of political expediency for the Western nations, which merited a greater degree of study than was given to it by American statesmen in their various efforts to enter into treaty relationship with the Korean people. For Korea there were four possibilities: Chinese suzerainty; Japanese suzerainty; the suzerainty of some European power such as France or of Russia; or, political independence. In framing a policy to meet such an uncertain situation the Americans could bring forward two traditional and characteristically American policies: the United States had already registered its disapproval of the advance of European powers in Asia, and was committed to a policy of recognizing and even sustaining in a feeble way the independence of the Asiastic states; and, Americans were prone to hold that every people, with the exception of the American Indians, were and by right ought to be free and independent.

Among the four possibilities enumerated above the question of the future status of Korea was purely one of expediency. The Koreans, at least their rulers, were bitterly anti-foreign. They were disposed to adhere to a blind and irrational policy of seclusion. That they did not desire to be subjected to any Western power was obvious. That they would not welcome Japanese domination was equally evident. Where they stood as between Chinese suzerainty and political independence was not clear when the Americans came to consider the question of a treaty. Obviously the United States was under no obligations to consider them independent if they did not so desire. But at this point another question intervened: which was better for American trade, Chinese suzerainty or Korean independence? Korea under the shadow of China presumably would resist rather than encourage foreign trade and domestic renovation. This consideration appears to have had influence. That a condition of technical independence, undefended and defenseless, might be worse than Chinese suzerainty, seems never to have occurred to the American Government.

There were three possible ways to approach Korea: directly, through Japan, or through China. The United States tried them all impartially, moved by a single desire to make a treaty and to open the country.

Direct negotiations were, as we have already noted, authorized by William H. Seward in 1868.[1] Had the Japanese succeeded in 1868 or 1869 in establishing friendly relations with the Koreans it is very probable that the Government of the United States would have accepted the Japanese invitation, as the German representative at Tokio did, and would have sought an entrance into Korea by means of Japanese good offices. The failure of the Japanese negotiations, however, induced the American Government to make its next effort through Peking.

The correspondence between U. S. Minister Low and the Tsung-li Yamen at Peking in 1870-1 has already been alluded to. The details of the visit of the Americans to Korea in 1871 were as follows:

The expedition under the joint direction of Mr. Low and Admiral John Rogers was designed to be carried out after the pattern of the Perry visit to Japan in 1853. It was as much of a failure as most imitations are. With a fleet of five steamships the Americans arrived off the coast on May 19, 1871, and a few days later came to anchor in the Salee River below Seoul. Communications with the shore were opened through some minor officials who visited the ship but the objects of the expedition were not revealed. Shortly afterwards a Korean fort fired on a surveying party which had proceeded up the river, and in the engagement which took place two Americans were wounded, and many Koreans were killed or wounded. Mr. Low demanded an apology which was not forthcoming. The Americans then resorted to retaliation, destroying five forts and killing or wounding 350 Koreans. Again Low demanded communications with high officials with a view to making a treaty, but now the Koreans were stubborn and refused to forward Low's letters to the King. The Americans were thus pre sented with a choice between further military measures or retirement. Not being prepared, or authorized, to under take the conquest of Korea, Rear Admiral Rogers, like his predecessor, the French Admiral Roze in 1866, decided to retire, which he did on July 3.[2]

Korea was again left in the belief that the foreigners had been compelled to retreat before her army, and the expedition was looked upon by the Chinese also as a defeat for foreigners. The outcome of the expedition was regretted by the foreign communities because it tended to lower the prestige of the foreign powers in Asia at a time when the Chinese were stiffening their opposition to the revision of the treaties. The expedition reflected no credit on the Americans.

THE UNITED STATES INCLINES TO JAPAN

The developments of the next few years materially altered the situations of both China and Japan with reference to the peninsula. Mr. Low became persuaded that the Chinese Government had been acting with duplicity, and that while professing indifference it had secretly exerted its influence to thwart the expedition. Meanwhile other factors were at work to mar the relations between the Chinese and the foreigners. While the Americans had regarded the murder of the French Catholic converts in the Tientsin massacre in 1870 as due more to the rashness and unscrupulous conduct of the French than to the savagery of the Chinese, the murder of the British envoy, Margery, on the Burmah border in 1875, had been a shock to the entire foreign body in China and a sinister reminder of the fact that China tolerated the foreigners only because their armies and navies protected them. The persecution of Christians and missionaries was increasing. Furthermore the Chinese immigration question in California was becoming acute. As an indication of the attitude of American public opinion we may cite the fact that although Congress had extended permission to the Japanese students to enter the naval academy at Annapolis, the repeated requests of the Chinese Government for a similar courtesy had been ignored.[3]

Japan, on the other hand, was steadily rising in the estimation of Americans. The first steps in the expansive movement noted in the preceding chapter had provoked admiration, although those who knew the details of the Japanese negotiations in Peking regarded them as treacherous. Meanwhile the Japanese efforts at domestic reform had won the approval of the American Government to such an extent that in 1878 Secretary of State William H. Evarts was willing to sign a revision of the treaty of 1866.

While De Long had been recalled from Tokio for his indiscretions, his contention had come to be accepted by the American Government, viz., that Japan held the key by which to unlock the East. Soyeshima in Peking in 1873 had forced the Chinese to abandon a most cherished tradition and secured for the diplomatic corps an audience with the Emperor in which no *kotow* had been exacted. Three years later Japan had succeeded in negotiating a treaty with Korea in which several ports were thrown open to Japanese trade. Although the European powers and the foreign diplomats in China were most reluctant to realize and admit it, Japan was, in the opinion of America, rapidly achieving the leadership of Eastern Asia.*

The Japanese were exerting themselves to gain this very recognition. Japanese policy was being directed towards inducing the foreign powers to deal with Korea through Japan. An article supplementary to the treaty of August 24, 1876, had stipulated that in case any foreigners were wrecked on the coast of Korea they were to be deliv ered to the Japanese authorities who would assume respon sibility for their repatriation.⁴ This article was obviously intended to transfer to Japan a relationship which had formerly existed between Korea and China. In 1866 the crew of the *Surprise* had been repatriated across the Chinese border and by the agency of Chinese officials.

The next American effort to open Korea was made by Commodore R. W. Shufeldt who had commanded the U. S. S. *Wachusetts* which visited Korea in 1866-7 to investigate the *General Sherman* affair. Shufeldt's instructions from R. W. Thompson, Secretary of the Navy, were dated October 29, 1878, and to them were added a letter from Secretary of State Evarts to Thompson, dated November 9, 1878—a little more than three months after the conclu sion of the new treaty with Japan.

Evarts expressed no great interest in the opening of Korea. So far as he knew there had been no material change in the prospects since 1871. He drew attention to the provision of the treaty of 1876 relating to the return of shipwrecked seamen by way of Japan as possibly indicating

---

* Perhaps the decisive factor in inclining American policy toward Japan, was the influence of General Grant who had, in 1879, been more favorably impressed by the Japanese. Grant's visit to the East may be reckoned as a very important date in the history of American policy in Asia.

an "intimacy between those two countries which may be taken advantage of" and stated that he would be glad to have Shufeldt investigate and report as to whether Korea would be willing to make a treaty "similar in spirit and purpose to those already in existence with other oriental countries." Thompson directed Shufeldt, in the course of a cruise in the U. S. S. *Ticonderoga* which was to include visits to unfrequented parts of Africa, Asia, and the islands of the Indian Ocean and adjacent seas, to "visit some part of Korea with the endeavor to open by peaceful measures negotiations with that government. It is believed that the attack upon the Korean forts in 1871 is susceptible of satisfactory explanation and that a moderate and conciliatory course towards the government would result in opening the ports of that country to American commerce." [5] That the American Government was aware in thus resuming the efforts to open Korea that it was taking any step of impor tance is not apparent.

In April, 1880, Commodore Shufeldt in the *Ticonderoga* reached Nagasaki. His appearance and mission took the Japanese by surprise. United States Minister John A. Bingham had been instructed to invite the Japanese Government to give to Shufeldt suitable letters of introduction to the Korean authorities. The Japanese hesitated. Foreign Minister Inouye stated that the Japanese Government was reluctant to disturb the Koreans at a time when its own relations with them were still so largely unsettled. The best that Bingham was able to secure was a letter of introduction to the Japanese consul at Fusan.

Shufeldt arrived at Fusan May 4, 1880, and immediately attempted to send a letter to the King of Korea through the Japanese consul. The consul reported that the governor of the district refused to forward the letter. Shufeldt then returned to Japan and went personally to Tokio. With no little reluctance Inouye was persuaded to send Shufeldt's letter with one of his own to the King of Korea, on the condition that Shufeldt would remain at Nagasaki for an answer. Thus the Americans were made to appear as though they were dealing with Korea through Japanese channels. This second attempt failed as dismally as the first, and in the reply of the Korean minister of ceremony there appeared the following sentence which was so lacking in truth as to raise suspicions as to its origin:

"It is well known to the world that our foreign relations are only with Japan, neighboring to us, which have been maintained since three hundred years, and that other foreign nations are not only situated far from us, but there has never been any intercourse with them." [6]

It was reasonably clear to Shufeldt that Japan was actuated by no earnest desire to have the trade of Korea thrown open to the world, and that the Japanese were manipulating the negotiations to serve their own purpose.

Shufeldt and the Good Offices of Li Hung Chang

While Shufeldt was waiting at Nagasaki for his answer from Korea his presence and purpose was made known to Li Hung Chang at Tientsin. To the Viceroy the news was, probably, somewhat alarming. China was then on the verge of war with Russia. In the prospective conflict China would be helpless as General Gordon, who was summoned to give advice because of his success in the Taiping Rebellion, bluntly advised Li Hung Chang. The presence of Shufeldt in Japan could only be interpreted as meaning that the American Government, approving the treaty of 1876 in which the Chinese suzerainty over Korea was not acknowledged, was about to throw the weight of its influence on the side of Japan in the controversy over Korea. Thus China was menaced directly by Russia and also, so it appeared, by a combination of Japan and the United States, and as a result of either of these dangers China might lose its position in the peninsula. Chinese diplomacy, however, was by no means unequal to such a situation, and Li Hung Chang lost no time in inviting Shufeldt with very flattering words to come to Tientsin. The Commodore, stung by what he believed to be Japanese duplicity, was quite willing to accept the invitation. Li assured Shufeldt that he would use his influence to secure a treaty from Korea, and then dangled before the commodore's eyes the possibility of a position in the Chinese navy. Thus the astute Viceroy scored a victory against Japan, and diverted the United States to dealing with Korea through China. As for the American Government, its purpose was merely to get results. That in some way it was being made use of first by Japan and then by China appears to have received no thoughtful consideration.

Having received from the Viceroy the assurance of his good offices, Commodore Shufeldt returned to the United States in the *Ticonderoga*. In March, 1881, Shufeldt was ordered to special duty at the U. S. Legation at Peking, under instructions from both the Secretary of the Navy and the Secretary of State. The latter requested the American minister, James B. Angell, to facilitate in any way possible the appointment of Shufeldt to the Chinese navy, and Shufeldt was instructed to follow up the promises of Li Hung Chang. Shufeldt arrived in China in June, 1881, and established himself at Tientsin.

Notwithstanding the fact that the cooperative policy which had been inaugurated under Burlingame was still supposed to be in force it was not understood among the foreign representatives that cooperation could be expected to include assistance to any one nation in securing for its nationals any of the influential positions in the Chinese service, and Shufeldt quickly fell foul of the intrigues of various powers which did not wish to see an American placed in a position of such influence. So embarrassing did the Commodore's position at Tientsin become that he finally declined to have anything more to do with the Viceroy's proposal. It is by no means sure that Li Hung Chang had ever been very much in earnest about it.

The Viceroy assured Shufeldt that he had sent a letter to Korea advising that a treaty be made, and requested that Shufeldt remain at Tientsin until a reply had been received.[7] In December, 1881, Li was willing to make the treaty. The actual negotiations took place in Tientsin in the following spring between Li Hung Chang and Shufeldt who was assisted by Chester Holcombe, then *Chargé d'Affaires* at Peking. The Viceroy's first draft is of peculiar interest because it reveals the motives of the Government of China in encouraging the treaty, and also shows the atti tude of the Chinese with reference to their own treaties with foreign powers. In the first article of the treaty Li wished to have inserted a good-offices clause similar to that in the American treaty of Tientsin, and also the phrase: "Chosen, being a dependent state of the Chinese Empire, etc." In other articles he specified: inland trade to be reserved for the Koreans; importation of opium to be prohibited; foreigners to be permitted to rent land but with the explicit understanding that the land could not be alienated from Korea; extraterritoriality to be granted 'temporarily,' but Korean officials should be permitted to arrest Koreans in the service of foreigners; no merchant consuls; missionary work to be excluded; import duties to be 10 per cent on necessities and 30 per cent on luxuries, and the export duties to be 3 per cent; the treaty to come to an end in five years; and the Chinese language to be used in official intercourse.

Shufeldt was willing to accept many of Li's propositions either as they stood or with slight modifications, but he pointed out that for the United States to sign a treaty with Korea in which the latter was stated to be a dependent state of the Chinese Empire would be equivalent to placing Korea under the joint protection of China and the United States. This was exactly what the Viceroy desired. The Commodore explained to Li that he had no authority to enter into an alliance with China, and that the presence of such a clause in the treaty would cause its rejection in the United States. The Viceroy was inclined to insist upon its inclusion and at length Shufeldt, eager to accomplish the great purpose of his life, telegraphed (April 19, 1882) to Secretary of State Frelinghuysen for instructions as to whether he should comply with the Viceroy's stipulation. No answer to this request was received. Meanwhile Shufeldt reached a compromise with the Viceroy in which he agreed to acknowledge the dependence of Korea in two ways: he would write a letter to Li officially stating that he had requested the assistance of China in making the treaty because Korea was a dependency of China; he would also transmit to the President of the United States a letter from the King of Korea in which the latter stated that the treaty had been made by consent of the Chinese Government.

The treaty as agreed upon was sent to Korea in a Chinese naval vessel and the following day Shufeldt followed in the U. S. S. *Swatara*. The compact was signed without discussion by the Korean envoys on May 22, 1882.

A letter from the King of Korea to the President of the United States was then given to Shufeldt, dated two days before the signing of the treaty, although Li had promised that it should be dated after the treaty, in which the king made the following statement:

'Chosen has been from ancient times a State tributary to China. Yet hitherto full sovereignty has been exercised by the kings of Chosen in all matters of internal administration and foreign relations. Chosen and the United States in establishing by mutual consent a treaty are dealing with each other upon a basis of equality. The King of Korea distinctly pledges his own sovereign powers for the complete enforcement in good faith of all the stipulations of the treaty in accordance with international law.

"As regards the various duties which devolve upon Chosen, as a tributary state to China, with these the United States has no concern whatever."

Li Hung Chang had failed to accomplish his purpose. Indeed at the end he had been led to approve a convention in which the Chinese claim to suzerainty was specifically ignored. The two supplementary letters which he had demanded were worthless. Li had evidently come to the conclusion that Korea could not much longer be kept in seclusion and that regardless of Chinese pretensions, it was to the advantage of both Korea and China that the first treaty be made with the United States. Had the first treaty been with France, there would probably have been a religious-toleration clause in it such as had given so much trouble to China; and had the first treaty been with England, it might have been difficult to exclude a provision for the legalization of opium. The treaty would be a model for the others, and the United States would set a liberal standard. But Li Hung Chang came bitterly to regret his mistake in permitting the Shufeldt treaty. Indeed it was one of the great mistakes of his career, largely impairing his claim as a statesman. The treaty between Japan and Korea in 1876 had been the first wedge to separate Korea from China; the Shufeldt treaty was the second wedge, and of even greater importance because by it China assented to the claim first made by Japan six years before that Korea was as independent as Japan. The Shufeldt treaty was a step towards the dismemberment of the Chinese Empire, just as surely a step in that direction as the treaties with England or France with reference to Burmah and Annam. It was an unintended blow dealt at the security of the Chinese Empire.

The United States had no direct interests to serve in making the treaty. Secretary of State James G. Blaine (November 14, 1881) in the official instructions to Shufeldt had clearly reflected the casual attitude of the American Government. He wrote·

"While no political or commercial interest renders such a treaty urgent, it is desirable that the ports of a country so near Japan and China should be opened to our trade and to the convenience of such vessels of our Navy as may be in those waters, and it is hoped that the advantages resulting from the growing and friendly relations between those great empires and the United States will have attracted the attention and awakened the interest of the Korean Government.

"If the Government of Korea (or Chosen) is willing to open its ports to our commerce as China and Japan have done, we will with pleasure establish such friendly relations, but we do not propose to use force or to entreat such action." [3]

On its surface the treaty appeared to be a highly benevolent act towards Korea for it not only opened the nation to Western civilization and trade but also, in a measure, removed it from the blight of Chinese restraint. But more closely scrutinized, and viewed in the light of history, the treaty is seen to have been the instrument which set Korea adrift on an ocean of intrigue which it was quite helpless to control.

THE PERSONAL VIEWS OF COMMODORE SHUFELDT

The treaty is another illustration of the peculiarly personal character of much of American policy in Asia. It appears to have been authorized primarily because of the ambition and importunities of Commodore Shufeldt. The ambition was entirely worthy and above reproach, but it was hardly a sufficient justification for such a project. In this connection it is of importance to note an incident in the personal relations of the Commodore and the Viceroy which also throws some light on the growing anti-Chinese sentiment in the United States.

Shufeldt returned to China in 1881 well disposed towards the Chinese for he had before him the possibility of distinguished service in building up the Chinese navy as well as the distinction of opening up Korea. At Tientsin Shufeldt was rather shabbily treated. While enduring these affronts from the Viceroy, Shufeldt wrote to Senator A. A. Sargent of California a personal letter in which he expressed his disgust with brutal frankness. Unhappily the letter was published in American papers and after Shufeldt left China was printed widely in the East. It expressed sentiments greatly at variance with the generous spirit of the treaty with Korea. The letter is to be taken rather as significant of a kind of temper and disposition towards the Chinese which had never been entirely absent from the foreign settlements in China but was rarely expressed by Americans until the Chinese immigration trouble arose. It was, however, typical of a growing sentiment in the United States which exerted an important influence in the shaping of American policy in both China and Korea.

"Six months residence in this city (Tientsin)," wrote Shufeldt, "the political center of the Chinese Government, and an intimacy rather exceptional with the ruling element, has convinced me that deceit and untruthfulness pervade all intercourse with foreigners; that an ineradicable hatred exists, and that any appeal across this barrier, either of sympathy or gratitude, is entirely idle. The only appeal or argument appreciated is *force*. . . . All sympathy will be construed into weakness, all pity into fear."

Contrasting the policies of the United States with those of Great Britain which, thought Shufeldt, was the real ruler of China, he wrote:

"The United States standing, or endeavoring to stand, upon a higher plane than that of mere physical force, pursues in China a policy of moral suasion which neither convinces nor converts the Chinaman to the doctrine of common brotherhood of men or nations for high as the heavens are above the earth, so high is his conceit; as deep as the waters of the sea is the measure of his contempt for the 'outside barbarians.' "

"Any high moral ground in the field of diplomacy—any appeal to the motives which ordinarily govern nations—indeed, any argument unaccompanied by the outward and visible sign of force, is used only for the purpose of delay, which in the end is equivalent to victory. Yet the United States has interests in China destined in the future to be greater than those of any other nation—possessing as we do the Pacific Ocean as a common highway—geographically with reference to the continent, politically with reference to each other. . . . Our policy therefore should be positive and governed, to the extent of the moral law, by American interests alone, and followed up by the argument which they understand—the argument of force, pressure, not persuasion."

Shufeldt noted with the eye of a naval man that "all martial spirit has died out" of the Chinese race, and ventured the assertion that to the American form of government the Chinese were most antagonistic. He pointed to the condition of the returned Chinese students whom, he thought, had been made the "victims of the oriental hatred of popular institutions, and the innocent cause of dislike on the part of the mandarins for everything American."

"Under these circumstances," he continued, "portrayed without prejudice, even without sentiment—I am of the earnest conviction that the policy of the United States in China, and towards the Chinese in America, should be with us as with them—*purely selfish*—coming as it ought to, under the universal law of right and justice, but by no means governed by the fallacious idea of international friendship, or even the broader ground of a common brotherhood."

It was an amazing letter, but it was far more restrained in its descriptions of the Chinese than were very many of the speeches in California and in Congress during the absorbing discussions of the Chinese exclusion question. It has been asserted that the publication of this letter, coupled with the changes in the Department of State incident to the inauguration of the Arthur administration, may account for the fact that Shufeldt was left without an answer to his telegram in which he had inquired whether the American Government would accept a treaty with Korea in which dependency upon China was expressed. It seems more likely, however, that no answer to the telegram was sent because now for the first time the Department of State was being forced to reconsider the entire question of the policy toward Korea in the light of the relations of that country to China and Japan respectively.* To the American Government this was a new and perplexing question, and before an answer was devised, Shufeldt had already signed the treaty. While the treaty was ratified, it was perhaps not exactly welcomed by Secretary of State Frelinghuysen. To the declining popularity of the Chinese in the United States, as well as to the embarrassment of the Department of State, may perhaps be assigned the reason why the letter of the King of Korea to the President, expressing dependence upon China, was promptly pigeon-holed and never officially published in any record.

BIBLIOGRAPHICAL NOTES

1. The best review of the events leading up to the opening of Korea is C. O. Paullin: "The Opening of Korea" (*Pol. Sci. Quart.*, Vol. XXV, No. 3). This article forms a chapter in Paullin's "Diplomatic Negotiations of American Naval Officers." This, however, is based on the Navy Dept. records and does not include those of the State Dept. except as the latter appear in

---

*"This telegraphic message," noted John Russell Young, who had been asked to review the Korean question and who had filed a report May 1, 1882, "read in the light of the confidential dispatch to Mr. Holcombe . . . would seem to invite the question as to whether the proposed treaty is for the benefit of China or Korea. How far should we commit ourselves to a convention which China would regard as protecting her frontiers from some dreaded ultimate danger on the part of Russia or Japan, and which Russia and Japan might deem an unwarranted interference in Asiatic affairs?" Young recommended that the question be evaded by making a purely commercial treaty. Shufeldt had, in a measure, exceeded his instructions in making so broad a treaty when he had been expected to secure little more than a shipwreck convention.⁹

Young was soon to depart for the East under appointment as minister at Peking. While passing through Tokio he learned that the treaty had actually given great offense in Japan.

the Shufeldt papers, and the Journal of the Cruise of the *Ticonderoga* (Mss.), both of which are in the Navy Dept. library. Griffis: "Hermit Empire," chaps. 44-46, 48, is also valuable.
2. Reports of the Low-Rogers Expedition, For. Relations, 1871; Nov. 22, 1870, p. 111; Apr. 3, 1871, pp. 116, 121, 124, 142; 1874, p. 254.
3. For. Relations, 1871, p. 77, Jan. 10, 1871, Low to Fish, gives a summary of conditions in China as viewed by the American minister. The empire was reported to be in a state of decline and ruin.
4. China Desp., Vol. 43, Nov. 30, 1876, Seward to Secretary of State.
5. Cruise of the *Ticonderoga* (Mss.), Navy. Dept. Archives.
6. Japan Desp., Vol. 43, Sept. 14, 1880, Bingham to Secretary of State.
7. The official reports of the Shufeldt negotiations with Li Hung Chang are in China Desp., Vols. 55, 57-59, filed according to dates: Oct. 11, 1880, Oct. 22, 1880; Dec. 19, July 1, 1881; Jan. 20, 23, Mar. 11, 28, Apr. 10, 28, May 13, 22, 24, 29, June 8, 12, 26, 1882.
8. China Instr., Vol. 3, Nov. 14, 1881.
9. China Desp., Vol. 59, May 1, 1882.

CHAPTER XXV

BEGINNING OF THE CONTEST FOR KOREA

THE signing of the Shufeldt treaty (May 22, 1882) disclosed to the world the contest which had already begun for Korea. Not only Japan and China, but every Western power interested in the Far East were involved.

JAPANESE ADVANCE

Under different conditions it might have been expected that Korea itself would cast the deciding vote as to the possession of the peninsula, but the Korean Government was utterly deficient. A change in dynasty in 1863 had brought to the throne a boy under the regency of his father who was known as the Tai-wen-Kun.[1] The regent was anti-foreign, a blind patriot, a Confucianist, usually pro-Chinese, but chiefly concerned in the retention of his personal place and clan influence. Ten years later the king attained his majority. He had married into the Min family, and thus acquired as queen a strong-minded, aggressive woman, somewhat disposed towards progress and violently opposed to the Tai-wen-Kun who was immediately retired. The treaty of 1876 had been signed with the approval of China which, in the midst of its wavering policy towards Japan was, for the moment, seeking conciliation. But the execution of the treaty met with strong opposition from the reactionary Korean party. Japan, so suave and conciliatory when dealing with the Western powers, was from the outset harsh in Korea. The reports of returning explorers, not a few of whom visited the peninsula in the next five years, are in entire agreement upon this point. Because the arrogant and ruthless character of the Japanese settlers and officials played directly into the hands of the seclusion party, Japan found it wise to proceed very cautiously in entering upon the new privileges. While a Japanese settlement was immediately developed at Fusan, where Korean trade with Japan had been transacted for centuries, it was not until 1880 that Gensan, on the eastern coast at Broughton's Bay, and In-chuin, near Chemulpo, were opened to Japanese trade and then in the face of much opposition.

The progressive element in Korea found a measure of leadership in the young king and queen, and was nourished by Japanese contacts. Two embassies were sent to Tokio where the visitors were treated to sight-seeing as the Japanese embassies of 1860 and 1872 had been treated in the United States. Just as the Americans had made efforts to stimulate progress in Japan, so Japan displayed before the astonished Koreans the advantages of Western civilization. A "Civilization Party" came into being in 1880. Thus developed a most complicated domestic conflict in Korea which somewhat resembles the pre-restoration struggles in Japan. The issue was not clear-cut between the two parties although the Tai-wen-Kun, as leader of the reactionaries, was pro-Chinese while the progressive party inclined towards the Japanese largely because Japan was at that time the only source of enlightenment. In 1881 twenty four Koreans were sent to Japan to study, but at the same time more than three times as many were sent to China for the same purpose.[2]

Japan steadily pushed its influence at Seoul and in 1882 a Japanese officer was installed as drill-master for Korean troops. Military supplies were also ordered from Japan. The intentions of the Japanese when Shufeldt arrived in Korea were unknown. As soon as it was reported in Tokio that the American envoy was about to leave Tientsin, the Japanese representative in Seoul, then in Japan, was rushed with all possible speed to Korea where he arrived the day after the appearance of Shufeldt and the Chinese fleet. Shufeldt received the impression that the Japanese would have liked to retrieve the ground lost in their blunder of two years before by manipulating the negotiations in such a way that the American treaty would have been obtained through Japanese agencies. Li Hung Chang had amply provided for such a contingency and the Japanese, who for the moment were involved in serious controversies with the Koreans, were unable to intervene.

The increase of Japanese influence, coupled with the signing of the Shufeldt treaty, provoked the reactionary forces and drew the Tai-wen-Kun again into the arena. Two months after the signing of the treaty (July 23, 1882) the ex-regent, supported by a mob, made an effort to seize the persons of the king and queen, attacked and burned the Japanese legation, and assassinated some of the more important leaders of the Civilization Party, including members of the queen's, the Min, family. The king and queen escaped, although it was at first reported that the latter had been killed, and the Japanese legation, which was a military as well as a diplomatic organization, escaped from the city, made its way to the coast, and after many adventures was picked up and taken to Japan in a British surveying vessel.

It was freely predicted in the treaty ports and also abroad that war between China and Japan was rapidly approaching.*

Undoubtedly the American Government, though unintentionally, had incurred an obligation in making a treaty with Korea. While this fact may not have been fully realized in Washington, it was evident to John Russell Young who, at the time of the disturbance in Seoul, was passing through Japan on his way to his newly appointed

*The *Spectator* (London, September 2, 1882), for example, stated: "The outbreak of hostilities between China and Japan is one of the most likely events to happen within the next few weeks." It was also remarked in this same article that in event of hostilities the United States had "always shown a greater disposition to act through Japan than through China." In a previous article (March 11) the *Spectator*, in reviewing the various steps in Japanese expansion, had characterized them as "entered without a sufficient reason and of their own accord," and described them as part of a "policy which can only be characterized as one of reckless and unscrupulous ambition." It was freely predicted that in the approaching struggle China, whose navy had been recently greatly strengthened, and then consisted of about seventy vessels, sixteen of which would compare in efficiency with those of any navy in the world, would win. China was buying her navy in England and training it under British auspices. The Chinese navy later passed under German influence.

duties as minister at Peking. Young, as already noted, had reviewed the Shufeldt despatches before leaving Washington. Better than anyone else he was able to understand their significance because he had only recently returned from the East with General Grant. Young was a devout admirer of Grant and had been fully conversant with Grant's views on the futility of war between China and Japan. In Tokio, Inouye, Japanese Minister of Foreign Affairs, had intimated to Young that Japan was disposed to feel that the Shufeldt treaty had been made in the interest of China, and that it would have the effect of disturbing the relations between Korea and Japan. In Shanghai Young learned from the Japanese consul of the events of July 23 in Seoul. From what he knew of Japanese determination to hold the place already won in Korea, the prospect for peace appeared ominous and it became necessary for him swiftly and without instructions from Washington to devise a policy. With the approval of Admiral Clitz, he despatched the U. S. S. *Monocacy* to Korea with instructions to watch the proceedings, preserve the strictest neutrality, and offer "good offices" if convenient. Commander Cotton was ordered not to join with the Japanese in any demonstration, to use his influence to dissuade the Japanese from any belligerent movement, and at the same time to make the visit of the *Monocacy* an act of courtesy to the Japanese.

While the visit of the *Monocacy* cannot be said to have been the influence which averted war, as was claimed for it, the seriousness of the situation had not been underestimated by Young. The Japanese immediately mobilized both naval and military forces and sent the Japanese minister, Hanabusa, back to Seoul with a large military escort. Meanwhile Li Hung Chang had despatched a fleet and four thousand troops "to support the government." Hanabusa reentered Seoul August 16, and two weeks later the Korean Government complied with his demands which included the promise to pay 550,000 *yen* indemnity in five yearly instalments, permission for the maintenance of Japanese troops in Seoul for the protection of the legation, a special embassy to Japan to offer apologies, and additional trade privileges for the Japanese. The Chinese envoy watched the proceedings and then retired with his troops, taking with him into exile in China the Tai-wen-Kun who had provoked the trouble. Li Hung Chang had again, just as in 1876, avoided the issue with Japan, concurring in the second advance of Japan in the peninsula.

A few weeks later the King of Korea issued a proclamation which was designed to allay the fears of the Koreans. Scholars were urging that Japan be kept at a distance, but this, urged the king, was both unwise and impossible. If Korea were to adhere to a policy of seclusion she would remain isolated, and would be deprived of all assistance. "Let there be no more talk," stated the king, "about Japanese and foreigners." [3]

CHINA AND GREAT BRITAIN AROUSED

Notwithstanding this declaration the fundamental facts of the situation remained unaltered. In September, 1882, Li Hung Chang issued some trade regulations for China and Korea which bore no evidence of having even received the approval of the King of Korea. They asserted that the peninsula was a tributary state and that the concessions granted to China were "not within the scope of the favored-nation rule existing between the several treaty powers and China." The Chinese were to be permitted to open warehouses in two suburbs of Seoul, and there was to be a uniform duty of 5 per cent on all exports and imports except red ginseng which was to pay 15 per cent. [4]

While Korean subjects in China were not to have extraterritoriality, Chinese subjects in Korea were granted greater immunities than those enjoyed by any other power. A Korean envoy was to be sent to China but he was to reside at Tientsin rather than Peking, and would have a rank equivalent only to that of consul. Li Hung Chang, to whose yamen the envoy was related, was thus elevated to a dignity equal with that of the king. Finally, the Koreans were to consent to granting a subsidy to a line of Chinese steamers between the two countries. China was thus set forth not merely as abandoning none of her former claims upon the peninsula, but as actually adopting an aggressive policy to meet the Japanese advance.

Li Hung Chang followed the proclamation of the trade regulations by placing his personal representative, Herr von Mollendorff, formerly of the German consular service, as Inspector of the Korean Customs and member of the Foreign Office.

A brief survey of the international situation thus created now becomes necessary.

China was rapidly slipping into chaotic conditions which rivalled those of the Taiping Rebellion. Domestic affairs were passing into the hands of reactionaries who were ignorant, corrupt and weak. The prevailing policy was to resist every reform and to meet every crisis with weak compromises. The management of foreign affairs was more and more being turned over to Li Hung Chang who, as Viceroy of Chili since 1871 and northern Superintendent of Trade with headquarters at Tientsin, was entrusted also with the inauguration of whatever measures were taken to renovate the defenses of the empire. Li Hung Chang was not a great statesman, except as compared with his countrymen; he was not the equal of any one of several of his Japanese contemporaries.

China was beset by hostile powers. In 1867 France had annexed three provinces of Cochin China as the first steps in a program of territorial aggression at the expense of China which was yet to be completed. Russian troops had occupied Kuldja and the province of Ili (in Chinese Turkestan) where they remained until 1881 when China regained part of the territory by the payment of an indemnity and the granting of other terms unfavorable to China. Japan had taken the Lew Chews and had shown a disposition to take Formosa. Russia as well as Japan was threatening Korea. Worst of all China was becoming the back yard of European politics. The opening of Korea disclosed the ugly outlines of European intrigue as they had not been revealed before.

Russia, although working at first quietly and secretly, was vitally interested in the future of Korea. The Trans-Siberian Railway had been projected as early as 1862, although not actually begun until 1891. Vladivostock was closed by ice from two to four months in the winter and was too far removed from the markets of Asia to be of first rate commercial importance. Korea, in the possession of a power hostile to Russia, would be not only a barrier to warm water, but also to southern markets. Whoever controlled Korea could also control the Sea of Japan and the approaches to Vladivostock. Without Korea Russia had no assurance that she could even hold what she had already obtained in Siberia, much less penetrate into Manchuria.

France, long since separated from alliance with Great Britain, was now becoming the creditor of Russia and was at the same time seeking the good will of Japan. French interests in South China as well as French interests in Russia brought France into line against China.

The opening of Korea was therefore alarming to Great Britain. The latter was primarily concerned with placing obstacles in the way of the southward movement of Russia at every point along the far-flung frontier. In this contest with Russia, China occupied the position of a gigantic barrier state between Russia and India. So long as Korea remained under the shadow of China, British interests found a measure of protection. Korea, severed from China, was all the more likely to fall into the hands of Russia. Even before Li Hung Chang had invited Shufeldt to make a treaty with Korea the Viceroy, so it is believed, had given a similar invitation to the British Minister at Peking which for some reason was declined. While Great Britain interposed no objections or obstructions to the American treaty with Korea, British interests immediately upon its signature became very active and set about to thwart the execution of the agreement in such a way as would definitely sever Korea from the Chinese Empire. Thus Great Britain became, without the formality of an alliance, the ally of China, and was ranged against not only Russia and France, but also against Japan.[5]

It had never been the intention of Li Hung Chang to relinquish Chinese claims in Korea, and when he found that the document which he and Shufeldt had drafted, instead of affording protection to Chinese interests in the peninsula actually operated to weaken them, he set about, with the advice of the British and not improbably at their instigation, to rectify his blunder.

Into this mass of conflicting interests, most of which had their roots in a century of European diplomacy and intrigue, came the United States which was not only utterly detached from the European conditions of which the Far East was coming to be but a phase, but also contemptuous of alliances and international entanglements. Where, in such slippery places as the Korean peninsula afforded, was the United States to stand? With every one of the contesting European parties the United States was on the friendliest terms, and to the proposed victims of their intrigues it was bound either by "good offices" or mediation clauses in existing treaties. Had the alignment in Korea been merely between the East and the West, the United States would not have found it difficult to choose. Traditional American policy indicated the support of the East. But the line was north and south as well as east and west. To take sides for or against either China or Japan was to depart from an historic friendship with either one or the other of the only remaining strong Eastern states. The United States had thrust itself into the situation prompted more by a spirit of adventure than led by any wise counsels of statesmanship. Once in, the American Government desired nothing but peace. The unofficial recommendations of General Grant had been taken up into the official American policy: peaceful relations between China and Japan were necessary in the interest of the building up of a strong East to meet the aggressive West,

and they were equally important for American trade interests. But American statesmanship was too unfamiliar with
the facts and too inexperienced to frame and execute a
policy which would remove the causes of war and make
peace possible.

While instructing its representatives in Tokio and
Peking to do everything possible to allay the growing irritation between the two countries, the American Government determined to adhere to the policy of regarding
Korea as a sovereign and independent state. A diplomatic
post equivalent in rank to those at Tokio and Peking was
created at Seoul and Lucius H. Foote was appointed to it
in February, 1883. Secretary of State Frelinghuysen drew
attention to the anomalous trade situation created by the
Chinese commercial regulations of the preceding year.
Under these regulations the Americans were denied the
following privileges which were permitted to the Chinese:
to reside and trade at four points in the interior; to travel
in the interior under passport; to transport native produce
from one port to another. In addition the duties were
discriminating in favor of China. "To this the United
States cannot consent," stated Frelinghuysen.[6] Minister
Foote arrived at Chemulpo May 12, 1883.

The Japanese had now become very well reconciled to
the American treaty with Korea. Foote visited Tokio on
his way through Japan and was supplied with a Japanese
interpreter who accompanied him to Seoul. The Japanese
recognized that the American policy in Korea was, in effect,
distinctly friendly to Japan. Li Hung Chang, when he
learned of the visit to Tokio and of the presence of a Japanese interpreter in the American legation at Seoul, was as
disgusted as the Japanese were pleased. The interpreter
remained only a few months.

The other foreign powers adopted towards Korea a very
different policy. While Russia remained in the background
Great Britain, Germany and France hastened to Korea after
the signing of the Shufeldt treaty. Admiral Willes concluded a treaty for Great Britain two weeks later, following

the very liberal provisions of the American treaty, but this was never ratified. In November of the following year a second treaty with less liberal provisions which were more in accord with the views of British merchants was signed by Sir Harry Parkes. A treaty with Germany was signed the same day. Great Britain then showed the trend of its policy by appointing as diplomatic representative a consul general who was made responsible to the British minister in Peking. Thus England was supporting the Chinese claim to suzerainty over Korea by making the British diplomatic establishment in the peninsula an appendage of the British Legation in China. Germany was represented by a consul who reported directly to Berlin; France by a *"Commissaire"* reporting directly to Paris; and Japan by a *Chargé,* Minister, or Ambassador Plenipotentiary, as suited the situation. In 1884 Congress reduced the post at Seoul to that of Minister Resident, equal in rank to that at Bankok. Foote thereupon resigned. The Chinese Government then requested that the American Government make the Seoul Legation an appendage of the American Legation in Peking, but the United States declined (December 5, 1885).

The policy of China was equally significant. In October, 1883, a Chinese commissioner "to manage the commerce of Korea" appeared in Seoul and without consultation with or the approval of the Korean Government posted the following astonishing notice on one of the gates of the city:

"I wish to inform the people that I have received the appointment of Commissioner for China to manage the Commerce of Korea; and also that I arrived at Chemulpo on October 14th; came to Seoul on the 16th, and opened my office on the 20th.

"Whereas Korea has been dependent upon China since the time Kuichi was appointed King of Chosen, several thousand years ago, and the people devoted themselves to the teachings of Si-Su and Rejei-Mi, and for the past two hundred years have been wonderfully obedient to our existing dynasty; and the peoples, officials and our merchants, in their intercourse with our people have acted in a laudable manner; and as at present various nations are opening commercial relations with Korea;—

"Therefore, the Chinese Government has issued trade regulations

benefiting Korea; and I hope the merchants and citizens will appreciate this fact, and obey and adhere to these regulations, that
harmonious feelings may exist between China and Korea, especially
as Korea is a dependency of China, and we wish to live in peace and
harmony. My duty is to manage the commerce which is known to
our merchants and if any questions arise, or any business needs attention of whatever import, it is your duty to appeal to me for a
proper understanding and settlement of the same.
    "Seoul, October 20, 1883.
                                                "Chin-Chu Tang."

Later the Chinese representative in Seoul was known as
a "Resident," the term being apparently borrowed from
India where the British representative in the court of a
native state is usually known as the British Resident. This
Chinese Resident, Yuan Shi Kai, was the personal representative of Li Hung Chang, acting under the immediate
direction of the Viceroy. His diplomatic status *vis-à-vis*
his European colleagues was always a delicate and irritating
point. Should he be treated as a diplomatic representative?
If so what was his relative rank in such a diplomatic corps?
This resident immediately claimed for himself a position
quite different from that of the representatives of the other
countries. He demanded and received permission to be
carried in his chair, accompanied by his attendants, through
the central gate to the palace when he came for audience
with the king, while the other representatives were compelled to leave their chairs at the gate and walk more than
half a mile to the hall of audience. His exact status and
the scope of his powers was never defined and when the
United States addressed to the Tsungli Yamen an official
inquiry about it in 1889 the Chinese officials replied with
some asperity: "It would seem to the Prince and the ministers that there is also no necessity of making inquiry
about it." [7]
Japan having won another point in the contest for
Korea in the settlement of August 30, 1882, paused and
waited for another favorable opportunity to advance. The
Yokohama Specie Bank advanced a sum of money for
founding newspapers in Korea, for training Korean soldiers,
and for other means of peaceful penetration. [8] Takezoye,

a man well learned in Chinese, was sent to Seoul as Min ister.

China, while adopting energetic measures in the pe ninsula, was not yet prepared to fight. In 1882 Li Hung Chang was requested to prepare a plan for the invasion of Japan, but he was able to persuade the Board of Military Affairs that such a step would be premature. Notwith standing the clan struggles in Japanese politics, the large national debt and the relative isolation in which Japan stood, the Viceroy was of the opinion that in case of war the Powers would be on her side.

"If Japan should discover prematurely," argued Li, "our plans to make war against her, then her government and people will be reunited, she will ally with a foreign power, and accumulate money by issuing loans, increase her army and navy, build and purchase war ships, with the result that we should be in a disadvantageous position, pregnant with danger. An ancient maxim says: 'Nothing is so dangerous as to expose one's plans before they are ripe.' It is for this reason that I recommend to your Majesty that we maintain extreme caution, carefully concealing our object whilst all the time increasing our strength." * ⁹

The King of Korea, catching a glimpse of the vistas of independence, and becoming impressed with his importance in international affairs, stood erect and turned to the Americans for help. He did not relish the idea of having three or more thousand Chinese troops quartered in Korea. Under the old relationship, whatever it may have been, not only were there no Chinese envoys and no Chinese troops in Korea, but there were no Chinese merchants ex cept at the border. The average Korean probably did not know a Chinese by sight before the Shufeldt treaty. The increase of Chinese influence in the peninsula was as much resented as the coming of the Japanese had been. The king appealed to the American Government (October, 1883) to send him an adviser for the office of foreign affairs,

*However, the evidence makes very probable the inference that Li Hung Chang did not fully appreciate the strategic value of Korea to China until after the Shufeldt treaty. He appears to have consented to the treaty of 1876 between Korea and Japan; he engineered the Shufeldt treaty; he acquiesced in the settlement with Japan in September, 1882; and he argued in the reply to the Chang Pei Lun memorial that China did not have a valid case against Japan in Korea. It appears to have been Great Britain which aroused the Viceroy to exert himself in Korea.

and asked for instructors for his army.[10]   He also placed
orders for munitions with an American firm of Yokohama.
The king even telegraphed for Commodore Shufeldt to return to Korea and enter his employ.

Shortly after the arrival of Minister Foote the Korean
Government sent an embassy to the United States. The
embassy was entertained by the American Government and
returned after a brief visit in the U. S. S. *Trenton* with
Ensign George C. Foulk of the U. S. Navy in attendance.
Foulk became Naval Attaché at the Legation and completely won the confidence of the king.[11]   When Foote returned from Seoul shortly after the *coup d'état* of 1884,
Foulk became *Chargé*.   In September, 1884, Dr. H. N.
Allen, Presbyterian medical missionary, arrived and within
a few months other missionaries followed.   The king made
an official request to the American Government for school
teachers.   American influence in Seoul was easily paramount.

The opportunity for which Japan had been waiting
came in the latter part of 1884, when China found herself
confronted with a war with France.   As soon as the hostilities had begun Takezoye waited upon the King of Korea,
painted the probable fate of China in the darkest of colors,
and offered to remit the indemnity agreed to two years
before, if the king would introduce military reforms in
Korea, with a view to the elimination of Chinese influence.
The Japanese minister promised the support of Japan if
Korea would assert her independence.   A month later he
demanded that Japanese merchants be given most-favored-
nation treatment on the basis of the Chinese trade regulations of September, 1882.   This was granted.   Still later he
pointed out the danger to Korea if Japan and China were
to fight on Korean soil, a possibility which seemed to the
Japanese minister very probable.[12]   Meanwhile a plot was
formed between Japanese officials and certain progressive
Koreans to seize the king and queen.   This plot was executed in the midst of much assassination on the night of
December 4, 1884, on the occasion of a dinner given to the

diplomatic corps to celebrate the opening of a Korean postal system. The king and queen were surrounded by the leaders of the plot and by the Japanese officials, and the following day the king issued orders creating widespread reforms, as well as declaring Korean independence of China. The next day Yuan Shi Kai with several thousand soldiers put in an appearance, recaptured the palace, and forced the Japanese—only 130 in all—to retreat to Chemulpo where they found refuge on the Japanese war vessels.

The old form of government was immediately restored under the direction of Yuan Shi Kai, and such pro-Japanese leaders as had not escaped with the Japanese were assassinated. The *coup d'état* of December 4 again brought China and Japan to the verge of war.

France had been urging Japan to declare war on China because France needed the use of Japanese ship-yards which were not available under Japan's proclamation of neutrality. Japan though willing to aid France was wary of French associations. Count Inouye proceeded to Seoul and reached an agreement with Korea (January 8, 1885) in which the latter consented to a moderate indemnity and the punishment of those guilty of the murder of a Japanese officer, and further promised to rebuild the Japanese legation and barracks for the Japanese soldiers.

Japan then despatched Count Ito to Tientsin where negotiations for a treaty with China were opened with Li Hung Chang April 3. Count Ito, according to a Japanese historian, stated his case as follows:

"The claims of China over Korea were historical only . . . The claims of Japan over Korea were economical, i.e., she did not claim any legal authority over Korea, but from her geographical position and the necessity of providing for her constantly increasing population, she was intent on utilizing Korea as the best source from which the defect in the home produce of rice was to be supplied, as well as the nearest field in which the future sons of Japan might find employment. For this purpose Japan would have Korea always independent and under no foreign influence; but within late years China was sending military and political agents to Korea, and interfering with Korean international affairs, as if she intended to make good her claim over Korea, long since become purely historical. This state of things had to be rectified, for Japan would never consent to Korea's becoming in reality a part of the Chinese Empire." [13]

Two days after the the opening of the negotiations the war between China and France was brought to a close in what amounted to at least a partial victory for China. Japan was thus left in no position to act arbitrarily at Tientsin. Count Ito had to content himself with a treaty which still fell short of a recognition of the independence of Korea, yet substantial advances were made. It was agreed that both China and Japan should have the right to send troops into Korea, upon the notification of each other, in case of emergency; the instructors of the Korean army were to be foreign drill-masters, not Chinese or Japanese; and Li Hung Chang promised to send a commission to Korea to investigate the charge that Chinese soldiers had been acting in a disorderly and brutal manner. In short, the treaty raised Japan to a position of paramount importance equal to that of China in the peninsula.

Then Russia began to show her hand. A treaty similar to those with Great Britain and Germany was signed in July, 1884. Soon there were rumors that Korea had also entered into a secret treaty by which Russia promised "to protect the integrity of Korea against all attacks by whomsoever made," in return for which Russia was to supply the instructors for the army and Korea was to "loan" Port Lazareff to Russia for a winter harbor.[14] The treaty was reported to establish complete Russian suzerainty over the peninsula. Great Britain then ordered the occupation of Port Hamilton, an island off the southern coast of Korea, and reckoned as a part of the kingdom. This was accomplished April 15, 1885.[15]

The King of Korea protested that he had no knowledge of the treaty and when Alexis de Speyer, formerly of the Russian Legation in Tokio, arrived as "Agent Provisoire" of Russia in June, 1885, the Korean Government refused to carry out the terms of the agreement on the grounds that military drill-masters had already been requested from the United States and that the treaty with Russia was unauthorized. The negotiations with Russia were found to have been the work of von Mollendorff. Probably the Viceroy had known nothing of this adventure of his autocratic representative. The latter was dismissed, the treaty went unratified, and Russia discreetly withdrew her claims.

Meanwhile the American Government delayed in securing the authorization of Congress to the loan of military instructors to Korea and it was not until April, 1888, that three officers arrived.* The Korean confidence in the United States had been greatly shaken by the delay. The United States was an uncertain friend to lean on in time of trouble.

Upon the departure of von Mollendorff, the Korean Customs, which hitherto had been managed exclusively by Korea, were unceremoniously taken under the care of Sir Robert Hart, of the Chinese Maritime Customs. Although the funds thus collected were turned over to the Korean Government, the returns were published in the Chinese Customs Reports as though Korea were a province of China. Sir Robert Hart's policy, to use his own words, was to "keep steadily in view the possibility of union between the Koreans and the Chinese Customs—such a result will be best for both Korea and China." [16] The new customs inspectorate was henceforth utilized as an agency for reclaiming the peninsula to China, and was a step in the direction of eventual annexation. Sir Robert in this instance had no difficulty in serving two masters for both the government of which he was a subject and the one of which he was an employe wanted the same thing.

The Korean Government made some feeble protests against the occupation of Port Hamilton to which were added the protests of the Chinese. Great Britain then took up negotiations with China and when China secured from Russia a distinct promise that it would not occupy any Korean territory after the evacuation of the island, the British flag was hauled down (February 27, 1887). These

*Both China and Japan had officially endorsed the Korean request for these teachers.

negotiations were conducted as though Korea were a part of the Chinese Empire.

Between Japan and the realization of her program for Korea, Great Britain as well as Russia and China were seen to stand squarely in the way. The United States stood aloof from the contest and although very kindly disposed towards Japan studied neutrality. The American policy, however, had already been to Japan as helpful as an alliance. Great Britain working in the interest of China in Korea was never able to accomplish for China as much as the United States had wrought for Japan.

KOREA, 1885-1894

Notwithstanding the fact that both the Chinese and the Japanese troops were withdrawn from the peninsula in July, 1885, the struggle between the two empires continued. Japan, now passing into the arduous labors of treaty revision, and also preoccupied with domestic reforms, was passive for several years, but China, encouraged by the support of Great Britain, became very aggressive.

The Tai-wen-Kun, after three years of comfortable exile in China, was returned to Korea with ceremonious escort. He could be counted on to oppose Japan. H. F. Merrill, an American who had served in the Chinese Customs service, replaced von Mollendorff as chief commissioner of Korean customs. Mr. Merrill was charged by Sir Robert Hart to seek the consummation of a union of the Chinese and Korean Customs.[17] At the same time Li Hung Chang, who was jealous of Hart's influence in Peking, appointed O. N. Denny, an American who had served with credit in the American consular service in China, as an adviser to the Korean Government. The Viceroy expected thus to have two representatives in Seoul—Denny and Yuan Shi Kai. These two gentlemen, however, did not get on well together. Yuan Shi Kai sought to keep Denny in a position subordinate to himself and the result of his efforts in that direction was to place Denny in opposition to Yuan and then to ally him with the cause of Korean independence. Denny resigned (April 1, 1888) after forcing an issue with Yuan Shi Kai in which Li Hung Chang sustained Yuan Shi Kai.*

In the summer of 1886 a rumor was circulated, presumably by agents of Yuan Shi Kai, and with the knowledge of Li Hung Chang, that Russia had entered into a secret treaty with Korea, the effect of which would have been to accomplish all that von Mollendorff and de Speyer had attempted the previous year, viz., to transfer to Russia the suzerainty over Korea which was claimed by China. A plot was formed by Yuan, so it is believed, to take possession of the king, queen and crown prince and deport them to China, placing the Tai-wen-Kun again in power. Thus it was hoped to accomplish the next step in the annexation of the peninsula. A forged treaty between Korea and Russia was published and circulated but the plot was detected and exposed by Denny, Merrill, the British consul general and others.[18] The scheme was reminiscent of the pro-Japanese *coup d'état* of December 4, 1884. It failed disastrously and resulted in great loss of prestige for China. At about the same time the attempt of Yuan Shi Kai to smuggle ginseng to China on Chinese war vessels was exposed.

The next year, probably as a direct result of the Chinese interference in Korean affairs, the Korean Government decided to establish regularly constituted diplomatic representation abroad. China interfered and Secretary of State Bayard telegraphed to Peking a very sharp communication expressing "surprise and regret" at the Chinese action.[19] The Korean Mission to Washington eventually effected its departure from Korea (November 13, 1887) on board the

* Morse believes that Denny "wrought much mischief," which is true if one accepts the contention that Korea should have been made into a Chinese province. Morse asserts, quoting a despatch of Rockhill, January 28, 1887, that Yuan was a progressive leader, urging Korea to adopt useful reforms. Rockhill was in Seoul for only three months, as *Chargé*, and had come from Peking where even the Americans favored the Chinese program of annexation. The consensus of opinion of the Americans in Korea for the decade, was that Yuan was actually an obstructive influence, seeking uniformly the elimination of all non-Chinese leadership in the peninsula, and opposing all reforms which would tend toward the invigoration of Korea. He opposed Dr. Allen's hospital, and even discouraged any efforts of the Americans to organize a famine relief fund.

U. S. S. *Ossipee*, thus eluding six Chinese war vessels which
had been sent to stop it.[20] Two years later when Pak Chun
Yang, the Korean minister at Washington, returned to
Korea, Yuan Shi Kai demanded that he be punished for
having acted independently of the Chinese minister in
Washington. The Korean envoy to Europe never proceeded farther than Hongkong.

At the time when Denny's controversy with Yuan Shi
Kai was agitating both Seoul and Tientsin, Li Hung Chang
asked the American Government to recall Ensign Foulk
who had been acting for the second time as *Chargé* at Seoul
since September, 1886, on the ground that Foulk as well
as Denny had been encouraging the king in independent
courses of action. This request was supported by the official
approval of the Korean Foreign Office which was completely
under the control of Yuan Shi Kai, but was somewhat
weakened by secret messages from the king imploring Foulk
to remain in Korea. At the same time the Foreign Office
issued a formal request for all foreigners to withdraw from
Seoul. Foulk was recalled, but his conduct was approved
by the Department of State and some years later, having
resigned from the United States Navy, Foulk entered the
faculty of the Doshisha, an American missionary college,
at Kioto, Japan. The request for the departure of the
foreigners from Seoul was not pressed.

China, meanwhile, set out to secure a practical monopoly of the telegraph lines. Japan had secured the rights
for a cable line from Fusan to Japan. This line was incorporated into the system of the Great Northern Telegraph
Company to which Japan had granted a monopoly of cable
lines to China. China proceeded to build a land line from
Tientsin to the border and thence to Seoul, or rather to a
suburb of Seoul. While this was in course of construction,
Japan asked for permission to build a line from Fusan to
Seoul which would thus afford Tokio also direct communication with the capital. The Korean Government refused
to grant the concession but agreed to build the line as a
Korean enterprise. This was done—but under Chinese

direction. The result of this contest was that Japan was effectually prevented from acquiring telegraph rights in the peninsula equal to those enjoyed by China.

Japan, not only preoccupied with domestic affairs and treaty revision, but also alarmed at the advance of Russia which Tokio was powerless to check, appears to have become for the time being little interested in Korean affairs.* By some this was interpreted to mean that Japan, already preparing to fight China, was not unwilling that the peninsula be annexed to China. Annexation by China would settle the question of title and leave Japan free to wrest the peninsula from her rival in a successful war.

The most sensitive feature of Japanese-Korean relations was the exportation of food-stuffs from the peninsula. Japan looked to Korea for supplies of rice and beans. In the autumn of 1889 the Korean governor of one of the eastern provinces, alleging a prospective shortage of food-stuffs, prohibited the exportation of beans or bean-cake at Wonsan (Broughton's Bay). Although the prohibition was removed in two months and Japan, at that time badly involved in domestic discord, contented itself merely with protests, two years later the controversy was revived and the Japanese minister in Seoul presented a claim for 140,000 *yen* on behalf of Japanese merchants. So much time had elapsed that investigation of the facts was difficult but the Korean Foreign Office offered 47,000 *yen* in settlement. The Japanese minister was recalled, charged with lack of energy, and was replaced by Oishi, a young Japanese politician who advanced the Japanese claim to 176,000 *yen* and presented an ultimatum (May, 1893) demanding payment within fourteen days. Japan would have been willing to accept the good offices of the American minister in Seoul, Augustine Heard, but Li Hung Chang acted quickly and met the emergency by advising Korea to settle the matter with 110,000 *yen*, an offer which was accepted by the Japa-

*"If matters in Korea come to a crisis Japanese politicians ought to make up their minds to have nothing to do with that country." Whether Korea retains its independence is a matter of "comparatively little concern to us." *Nichi Nichi Shimbun*, Mar. 7, 1887.

nese. The Koreans made the settlement reluctantly, and greatly resented the conduct of Japan. The effect was to destroy Japanese prestige which had been growing for several years during the oppressions of Yuan Shi Kai. Just as Korean sentiment had swung towards Japan after the disclosure of Yuan Shi Kai's plot in 1886, so now it turned back toward China which, whatever its intentions, knew how to temper its measures with tact.

The next autumn (1893) the Korean Government placed an embargo on the exportation of rice. There were indications that the Chinese were engaged in an effort to drive the Japanese traders from the peninsula. Korean sympathies were now running strongly against the Japanese who were acting arrogantly. The prohibition of rice exports was removed at the end of three months (February, 1894) But meanwhile the Tong-haks (Society of Eastern Learn ing) a semi-religious organization reminiscent of the Tai pings, yet conspicuously anti-Christian, and fanatically anti-foreign and anti-Japanese, began to gather force in the southern provinces, and advanced on Seoul at the end of March, 1894.* [21]

The Tong-hak movement was accompanied by the murder at Shanghai of Kim Ok-kiun, an intensely anti-Chinese and progressive Korean. Kim had been a fugitive in Japan since the *coup d'état* of December 4, 1884, and several efforts had been made, either with the approval or by the instigation of Yuan Shi Kai, to cause his assassination or bring about his extradition to Korea. Kim's murderer, a Korean, and the corpse, were returned to Korea in a Chinese war vessel. The corpse was divided into eight parts one of which was exhibited with much oriental enthusiasm in each of the eight provinces, and the murderer

---

* Morse states: ". . . such political aims as there were in the Tong-hak movement may fairly be said to have been in the interest of Japan." [22] This is true only to the extent that the movement was intensely nationalistic, and sought the elimination of all foreign influence in Korea, including the Chinese. It is true that the elimination of the Chinese was in the interest of Japan for Korea was utterly unable to maintain independence. The Tong-haks did not intend to work in the interest of Japan. Their slogan was, as Morse states, "Down with the Japanese and all foreigners." Insulting notices were even posted on the Japanese legation, and the Japanese authorities prepared to remove their women and children from Korea.

was received in Seoul with approval. The career and fate of Kim Ok-kiun from the time of the plot in 1884 until his quartered body was distributed in the provinces of Korea left the authorities of Japan, China and Korea, all, to do considerable explaining and reveals the wretched conditions which had been created in the peninsula since the first treaty in 1876. One is left with the feeling that in the approaching war there were no rights whatever except the rights of the inoffensive and oppressed Korean people, and these rights had never been an issue.

The Tong-hak movement led directly to a request from the King of Korea to Li Hung Chang for troops. Yuan Shi Kai would have preferred that the situation be made the occasion for Chinese intervention, which would have been the next logical step in Yuan's program, but the Viceroy was more cautious. The Chinese troops and war vessels were despatched from Tientsin June 6, and a notification to that effect was sent to Tokio,* in accordance with the stipulation of the treaty of 1885, but the Japanese forces were more mobile and when the Chinese arrived at Seoul they found the Japanese troops already there. Meanwhile the Tong-hak movement had been suppressed by the Korean troops. Japan then proposed to China joint action in the reformation of the Korean Government. China declined, asserting with a self-righteousness which appears amusing in the light of the history of the preceding decade, that although suzerain in the peninsula, she did not interfere in the affairs of her vassal state. Japan thereupon took the matter in her own hands, and as a first step towards the elimination of the obstructive Chinese influence, demanded that the king declare the independence of Korea. On July 27 the king, now a captive in the hands of the Japanese, complied, declared war on China, and invited the Japanese troops to expel the Chinese from his territories.

*There appears to have been no truth in the charge that China did not send this notification which the treaty required. A Japanese historian states that the notice was sent, but says that it was objectionable because it contained the statement that Korea was a protectorate and a dependency of China.[23]

BIBLIOGRAPHICAL NOTES

1. Geo. H. Jones, Korean Repository, July, 1898,—sketch of the life of the Tai-wen-Kun; see also Griffis: "Hermit Kingdom."
2. An excellent synopsis of Korean history is H. C. Allen's "A Chronological Index of Events in Korea" (Seoul, 1901). The author was closely associated with all the events after 1883, serving at various times in the employ of the Korean Government, and then as secretary, chargé, and minister for the U. S. There are some typographical errors in this index.
3. See contemporary English papers in both Japan and China.
4. Text of this treaty in Customs edition of "China Treaties and Conventions," Vol. 2, pp. 1521-7.
5. For an account of Korean history, 1882-94. in which it is assumed that China had a legal claim to suzerainty over Korea, and that it was to the interest of Korea, as well as of China and Great Britain, that the claim be sustained, see Morse, Vol. 3, chap. 1. Morse represents the prevailing British view, and more especially the ideas of Sir Robert Hart.
6. Korea Instructions, Vol. 1, May 12, 1883.
7. China Desp., Vol. 85, July 13, 1889.
8. Stead, p. 189.
9. Secret Memoirs of Count Hayashi, Appendix A, p. 318.
10. Senate Rept. 1443:48-2, Feb. 26, 1885.
11. The Papers of George C. Foulk are deposited in the New York Public Library.
12. Stead, pp. 190 ff. While Prof. Nagao Ariga, the writer of the account, does not state that Takezoye organized the coup d'état which followed, the inference that he was by no means innocently involved, as the Koreans claimed and as Foulk believed, is very reasonable.
13. Ibid., p. 197.
14. The alleged text of this treaty was published in the North China Daily News, Aug. 5, 1885. Li Hung Chang told Young that the text was substantially correct; China Desp., Vol. 76, Aug. 21, 1885.
15. China, No. 1, 1887. Port Hamilton Corres. Command Papers, 4976-5053.
16. Morse: Vol. 3, p. 13; see footnotes to following pages for Sir Robert Hart's very able defense of his objects.
17. Ibid., p. 18.
18. The facts of the plot were exposed in a pamphlet; China and Korea, by O. N. Denny, 1888.
19. For. Relations, 1888, p. 220.
20. Allen: "Chronological Index."
21. For. Relations, Vol. 2, 1894, p. 15.
22. Morse: Vol. 3, p. 20.
23. Stead: p. 203.

CHAPTER XXVI

AMERICAN GOOD OFFICES—SINO-JAPANESE WAR

THE United States was well situated to play the rôle of mediator in Asia. The American Government was far removed, by geographical position, by international policies, by commercial interests, from either the conflicts between Japan and China or the designs of other Western powers on Asiatic trade and territory. The Americans desired above all else peace in the Far East, for war meant to them a disturbance of trade. They also desired the repression of the growing European influence in those regions for the advance of Europe in Asia was a threat at the open door. This latter fact made the United States in some degree a partisan of the East against the West, and in the eyes of Europe disqualified the Americans as mediators. The powers did not desire mediation; they distrusted it. The Europeans sought not justice but privilege in Asia.

The United States was bound by treaties to extend good offices at the request of China and Korea, and to act as friendly mediator at the request of Japan. But the meaning of these pledges has been wholly misunderstood by many modern friends of the Asiatic people. "I think it proper to observe," wrote Secretary of State Fish to Minister De Long (April 28, 1871), when Japan sought the good offices of the United States in the Sakhalin dispute, that it is not supposed that the President can mediate in a controversy or dispute between Japan and other countries unless *both* parties to the controversy accept him as mediator." [1] *Both* parties, of course; or else mediation becomes nothing less than interference and intervention.

There were in the nineteenth century no disputes between either the oriental states, with trivial exceptions, or between one of them and a western nation, in which both sides honestly sought justice, or in which both parties to the controversy were prepared to submit to an examination of the facts in a court of mediation. We have now seen how Russia evaded mediation in the case of Sakhalin, and how Japan was equally reluctant to submit the Formosan question to mediation in 1874. Russia was an aggressor, Japan was equally so. Russia would not submit to mediation; Japan submitted not to mediation, but to the intervention of Great Britain. At first the Lew Chew controversy appears to be an exception to our sweeping generalization but we have seen in the end that it was not. Japan upset the decision of the conference at Peking by bringing in at the last moment some extraneous demands. Another case in point was a request for American good offices in the interval between the battle at the Taku forts (1859) and the renewal of the Anglo-French War against China in 1860. The Chinese, alarmed at their easy success at Taku where they had forced the allied fleets to withdraw, appealed to United States Minister Ward, even before the American treaty had been ratified, to mediate with the ministers of Great Britain and France. Ward invited the Chinese to renew the invitation after they had ratified the treaty upon which they were basing their appeal.[2] They were apparently ashamed to renew the request after the treatment given to the American legation in the subsequent visit to Peking, but there is no reason whatever for believing that had the request been made again the British and French representatives would have been willing to submit the facts to impartial review. The evidence in the American records leads to the conclusion that the British and French were wholly wrong, and there is nothing in their records, aside from assertions, which controverts this conclusion.

The case of the *Maria Luz* (1872) is one of the relatively trivial exceptions. A Peruvian coolie ship from China in distress was forced to put in at Yokohama. The Japanese promptly freed the coolies. Peru sought the good offices of the United States in the settlement of the consequent claim against Japan. The American Government accepted the duty with the express stipulation that it could do nothing which would imply approval of the coolie trade. At the suggestion of the United States, the claim was referred to the Emperor of Russia, who awarded the decision to Japan, May 29, 1875. The reference of this matter to Russia became especially easy because in 1864 Mr. Pruyn had agreed to submit a disputed claim of the United States against Japan, to the arbitration of the Czar. As a matter of fact the American claim had been settled without reference to St. Petersburg, but the discussion had given the United States an opportunity to show its willingness to conform its practice to its preaching.[3]

AMERICAN MEDIATION IN THE FRANCO-CHINESE WAR, 1883-1884

A more important case in which American good offices were invoked was the Franco-Chinese controversy over Annam. This is an important episode, the narration of which is also necessary in order to show more fully the nature of Chinese-American relations during the period following the Shufeldt treaty with Korea.

Soon after the French *Chargé* in Peking had announced (1866) to the astonished Yamen that his government was about to annex Korea, France would appear to have concluded to seek territorial expansion only in the south. France had made a treaty with Annam in 1862, and twelve years later concluded a second one in which France recognized the complete independence of Annam, in much the same way as Japan recognized by treaty the independence of Korea two years later. Indeed French policy in Annam afforded Japan a model for policy in Korea—a similar satellite of China. In 1874 France also actually acquired Cochin China. China protested because the treaty in effect made France, rather than China, the suzerain over Annam. The matter remained in dispute until the latter part of 1883 when Li Hung Chang signed a convention with France according to which the Chinese troops were to be withdrawn from Annam, and the two nations were jointly to guarantee the independence of this territory which for two centuries had paid tribute to Peking. There was a sudden change of government in France and the convention was repudiated at Paris. The new French cabinet proposed an expedition to China and a liberal credit was voted. Then a French officer, Riviere, was killed in an engagement with the Black Flags, an irregular company of troops which were supposed to be more or less supported by the Chinese Government. War became all but inevitable. Indeed, it seems quite plain that France was seeking to provoke war for the sake of securing more territory in the south.

China, stung by the charges of bad faith, defiant and unhumbled, still quite ignorant of the weakness of the empire, perhaps misled by encouragements from Germany and England, and quite underestimating the strength of France, was determined to yield no territory to France, and also not to yield suzerainty over Annam. At this point John Russell Young, the American minister, whose relations with Li Hung Chang were very intimate and confidential, and whose relations with Tsung-li Yamen were cordial, pleaded for peace. The question was, as he tried to explain, not whether China was in the wrong or in the right, but whether she could afford a war with a foreign power. She had relatively few troops with a modern training, and they were in the north. To transport them to Annam there was no railroad, and the Chinese Navy could not protect them by sea. France was studiously cultivating Japan with a view to securing joint action against China. Russia was an eternal menace to the Chinese northern frontier. Eng land was busy in Egypt, and presumably not unwilling that France should become involved in China. For China itself war seemed likely to end in disaster.[4]

At length the counsels of Mr. Young had their effect and he was asked to invite the good offices of the President to secure a mediation of the dispute. To this request Secretary of State Frelinghuysen replied, July 13, 1883:

"This government cannot intervene unless assured that its good offices are acceptable to both. In such case it would do all possible in the interests of peace. The United States Minister at Paris has been directed to sound French Government, and ascertain if it will admit our good offices in the sense of arbitration or settlement." [5]

The answer was not long delayed. France declined to accept the good offices of the United States. [6]

The French forthwith proceeded to declare a blockade of Tonquin and Annam, and although negotiations continued at Shanghai, the troops of the two nations came into active conflict in December, 1883. On May 11, 1884, Li Hung Chang signed with Commandant Fournier a convention which was intended by the Chinese to be the protocol to a treaty. In the Fournier Convention France waived a claim for indemnity in return for the acknowledgment of her territorial and commercial claims in Annam. There was entire disagreement between the Chinese and the French as to the interpretation of this protocol, and even as to its authorized text, and on June 23, 1884, Colonel Dugenne and twenty-two French soldiers were killed in an engagement at Baclé.*

Again China appealed to the good offices of the United States and again (July 20, 1884) Minister Young referred the matter to Washington. China wished to submit to arbitration the question as to whether she had acted in bad faith with reference to the Fournier Convention. Again France declined to admit the good offices of the United States.

China was thus brought face to face with war. The American minister renewed his efforts to find a peaceful solution, feeling that peace at any price which France might demand would be better than conflict. At length Prince Kung asked Mr. Young to go to Shanghai, see M. Patenôtre, the French representative, and obtain a settlement. China

---

*H. B. Morse, who was present at the Li Hung Chang-Fournier negotiations and saw the documents, gives personal testimony as well as other evidence to prove that the French Government was guilty of extremely bad faith in the observance of this convention. His verdict is: "It is only on the ground that an Asiatic nation has no rights which the white man is bound to respect that the course of France is to be explained." For the French statement of the case see Cordier. [7]

was even willing to agree to any indemnity which Young might recommend. The American minister referred the request to Washington for approval, but Secretary of State Frelinghuysen was wary, having already been twice repulsed by France, and withheld his approval. An August 5 Admiral Lespès attacked Keelung in Formosa. After this attack all hopes of peace vanished. The Chinese were roused. Prince Kung was retired, and with the retirement of the prince came the eclipse of Li Hung Chang, who had clearly realized the folly of resisting the French.

Early in September the China Merchants Steam Navigation Company which had been purchased a few years before from Russell and Company, was resold to the former owners, and the American flag was raised over the fleet of steamers. France, thus deprived of the opportunity of making a most profitable reprisal upon China, was now less than ever willing to accept any good offices from the United States. However, the American Government kept in very close touch with the rapidly developing situation and on several subsequent occasions was the medium of communication between Paris and Peking. Sir Robert Hart also undertook the task of mediation and after more than a year of work succeeded in bringing about the signing of a protocol, April 4, 1885.[8]

Mr. Young, although his efforts at mediation between China and France had failed, was determined to demonstrate the good faith of the United States in its advocacy of arbitration as a means of settling disputes, and was able to secure the consent of the Chinese Government to the arbitration of the 'Ashmore Fisheries Case' by the British and the Netherlands consuls at Swatow. The case involved the action of the Chinese officials in depriving Dr. W. Ashmore, an American missionary at Swatow, of a fishery which he had purchased in connection with a mission. An award of $4600 was made to Dr. Ashmore June, 1884.[9] Earlier in the same year Mr. Young had proposed that the claims of the foreigners arising out of a riot at Canton in September, 1883, be submitted to arbitration, but he was unable to secure the consent of the Chinese to such a statement of the disputed points as would have satisfied the British authorities.[10]

GOOD OFFICES OF THE UNITED STATES IN KOREA

Having in mind the foregoing review of previous American efforts to mediate the disputes of the Far East, we are in a position to return to a survey of American policy in the rapidly maturing conflict in the Korean peninsula.

Since the ratification of the Shufeldt treaty the American Government had consistently maintained a policy, sound in legality but weak in statesmanship, that it would recognize Korea as a sovereign, independent nation in all that pertained to foreign relations.* The policy would have been perfect in a perfect world, but in fact it rested upon as great a fallacy as that which had underlain the Cushing treaty with China. Korea lacked the vitality which alone makes possible the exercise of sovereignty. The Korean Government was a vine, not a very lovely one either, which trailed in the dust unless it could cling to some stronger power for support. Of independence there was nothing save a pitifully feeble cry of desire. There were many contestants for this position of supporting power in Korea, but the United States was not one of them. The Korean Government was in the position of an incompetent defective not yet committed to guardianship. The United States was her only disinterested friend—but had no intention of becoming her guardian.

When the American Government became aware that the Chinese and Japanese troops were facing each other in the peninsula the American Minister in Seoul, Mr. Sill, was instructed (June 22, 1895):

"In view of the friendly interest of the United States in the welfare of Korea and its people, you are, by direction of the President,

* "With the reserved relation of Korea to China we cannot properly interfere to raise any question unless the course of China should be such as to manifestly shift accountability as regards foreign interests and intercourse to the shoulders of China." Wharton to Heard, Aug. 25, 1890.[11]

instructed to use every possible effort for the preservation of peaceful conditions." [12]

The Koreans, caught between the mill-stones, and quite powerless to act effectively for peace, appealed to Russia, France, England, and the United States for help, and Mr. Sill, the American minister, joined with the representatives of the other powers in asking China and Japan to agree to a simultaneous withdrawal of their troops from Korean soil. Both China and Japan refused. On July 5th the Korean representative in Washington asked that the President "adjust the difficulty" arising out of the fact that the Japanese minister in Seoul had presented to the Korean King a long list of administrative reforms and was pressing that they be immediately adopted. At about the same time the Chinese Government at Peking sought the good offices of England and Russia to secure a peaceful solution. The British minister in Peking urged, through Charles Denby, Jr., American *Chargé*, that the United States take the initiative in uniting the great Powers in a joint protest at Tokio against the beginning of hostilities in Korea by Japan. On July 8 Denby wired that Li Hung Chang had officially expressed the desire that the United State take the initiative as the British minister had suggested.

It could not be argued that in the conflict now beginning for the control of the peninsula Japan was innocent of blame. The Japanese Empire, *vis à vis* Korea, was placed somewhat similarly to England and the kingdom of the Netherlands which had been created by the Congress of Vienna in 1815. The two island kingdoms could not but view with concern the nature of the control of the adjacent mainland. Great Britain was pleased to witness the creation of a Belgium; the Japanese had since 1871 been working to create on the Korean peninsula a political condition similarly favorable to their empire. Japan could not honestly assume the rôle of injured innocence. Indeed, after 1892 the attitude of Japan towards China became distinctly uncompromising and even menacing. In an address before the Diet (December, 1892) Count Aoki, Minister of Foreign

Affairs, sought to divert the attention of the Diet from troublesome criticism of domestic affairs and the failure of treaty revision. He said:

"As for the position·of the country, everybody is agreed that it is excellent. If you look at the map of the world you will see that America has her back turned to us, and that on her western coast, thousands of miles away from our shores, no good port lies open. Europe is only less distant from us for all practical purposes. But here in Asia, the case is very different. At your doors sits a nation of 2,700,000 people, ready to take your manufactures and products, and to give you its own in return. Look at the coal fields of your country in the north and in the south. Are not these landmarks set by nature to indicate the position your country ought to take?"

Thus far Aoki would appear to have been advocating merely a policy of peaceful economic penetration into the mainland of Asia, but a following paragraph practically incited an attack upon China:

"Occupying such a position and possessing such capacities, why is it that the people of Japan do not devote more thought to the foreign policy of the Empire? If you go back in your history to the Ashikaga era, you will find that the men of southern Japan whom some may perhaps call pirates, launched themselves in little boats and harried the coasts of China with its hundreds of millions of people, coming and going at will and taking and leaving at will. Surely it seems somewhat petty that the descendants of such men as those should allow their mental vista to be occupied entirely with the four ideographs *jouaku kaisei* (treaty revision). It seems to me that larger subjects invite their attention. The present, however, is not the occasion for me to dwell at length upon this phase of our foreign policy." (Reported in Japan *Daily Mail,* December 20, 1892.)

It could not have escaped the attention of the American Government that in June, 1894, Japan had reached a very ominous crisis in its domestic affairs in which a foreign war would be a very welcome diversion to the repeated interference of the Diet in the affairs of government. On June 2, 1894, the Diet had been dissolved by the Emperor for the third time since December 25, 1891. There was within the Empire a clear-cut contest between the oligarchy which had governed the country since the Restoration and a more popular form of government in which the lower house of the Diet was seeking control of the purse strings.[13] Only a foreign war, it seemed, could stop this contest, the issue of which was so greatly to be dreaded by the oligarchy.

Notwithstanding these facts the United States gave no evidence of a disposition to join with China and the European powers in opposing Japan in Korea. The treaties demanded the tender of good offices. The United States made the offer and it was rejected. The obligation under the treaties was therefore for the moment discharged. Intervention was now the only alternative, but intervention with the other foreign powers involved support of a policy which would really weaken rather than strengthen Asia.

Japan having refused to heed the protests of the United States as well as those of England and Russia, Secretary of State Gresham told the Korean envoy in Washington on July 9 that the American Government would not intervene either forcibly, or jointly, with the European powers; that it would maintain "impartial neutrality," and that it would seek to influence Japan only in a "friendly way." Mr. Gresham expressed to the Japanese minister in Washington the hope that Japan would deal "kindly and fairly with her feeble neighbor."

To China's request for intervention Gresham replied advising that China offer the whole question for friendly arbitration. He did not then believe that Japan would resort to war. China was not prepared to submit the entire question to arbitration. The fundamental point at issue was the validity of Chinese suzerainty over Korea. This pretension would have had a most doubtful status before any board of arbitration when studied in the light of the various treaties which had been made by Korea beginning with the Japanese treaty in 1876, and also when considered in the light of existing treaties between Japan and China. China by 1894 had surrendered too much and acquiesced in too much, ever to establish a position of technical suzerainty over Korea.

On October 8, the British *Chargé* approached the American Government with a proposition for joint intervention by the United States, Germany, France, Russia and Great

Britain on the basis of an indemnity to be paid by China to Japan, and the guarantee by the Powers of the independence of Korea. A month later China formally invoked the good offices of the United States, citing the treaty of 1858, and asking for joint action with the other foreign powers. Before this invitation was received, Gresham directed U. S. Minister Dun in Tokio to inquire whether good offices would be acceptable to Japan, and the same day Gresham carefully defined the position of the United States in a note which clearly explained why the American Government had been unwilling to join the European powers in intervention:

"The deplorable war between Japan and China endangers no policy of the United States in Asia. Our attitude towards the belligerents is that of an impartial and friendly neutral, desiring the welfare of both. If the struggle continues without check to Japan's military operations on land and sea, it is not improbable that other powers having interests in that quarter may demand a settlement not favorable to Japan's future security and well-being. Cherishing the most friendly sentiments of regard for Japan, the President directs that you ascertain whether the tender of his good offices in the interests of peace alike honorable to both nations would be acceptable to the Government at Tokio."

In the above friendly warning to Japan one reads between the lines that Gresham clearly understood the international situation. The proposals for intervention had been directed against Japan with a view to repressing her advancing power and influence in Asia. These proposals had not been primarily in the interests of *any* Asiatic state, but in the interests of European political and commercial ambitions in Korea. Dressed in their best clothes these proposals looked in the direction of a protectorate in Korea; viewed more cynically and critically, they looked in the direction of dismemberment not merely of Korea, but also further dismemberment of China and perhaps of Japan.

Japan, however, disregarded the admonitions of the United States, and, instead of pausing at a point where the good offices of the United States might have been valuable in saving Asia in general fro. a large increase of European influence, overreached herse f by continuing the war so

successfully begun. Japan thus invited the very intervention which Gresham expected.

From the policy of cooperation as followed by William
H. Seward and Anson Burlingame, the United States had
swung to the opposite extreme of absolute isolation. Succeeding administrations, after Seward, had no taste for active cooperation with European powers in Asia on the only
terms upon which it was offered, i.e., cooperation to repress
and weaken the Asiatic states, and there was no disposition
to knight-errantry like Burlingame's. There was at the
most only a feeble interest in Asiatic affairs. The American
Government appears to have concluded in the second Cleveland administration that if only the Monroe Doctrine could
be sustained for the entire western hemisphere, the political
conditions on the other side of the Pacific might safely be
ignored. All that can be said for this absurd assumption
is that it marked a very definite phase in the political development of the American nation.

China's position was fast becoming desperate. While
the American Government, ever since the Korean treaty of
1882, had steadily and consistently discouraged China in
the belief that in case of a crisis in Korea the United States
would support the contentions of China, Great Britain had
consistently supported China's pretensions. Now Great
Britain, aside from ineffectual efforts to draw the European
powers and the United States into a concert of intervention
to thwart Japan, did nothing. British neutrality was, in
effect, benevolent towards Japan which in an unbroken
series of victories found herself at the end of November,
1894, in possession of the seas, the peninsula, and even of
Port Arthur which practically controlled the avenues to
Peking. The American legations in Peking and Tokio, respectively, had been in charge of the Japanese and Chinese
archives since the outbreak of the war, and Japan now let
it be known that she would be willing to entertain direct
overtures from China through the Americans. On the day
after the fall of Port Arthur, November 22, Charles Denby,
American minister at Peking, was authorized by the

Tsung-li Yamen to begin negotiations through Edwin Dun, American minister at Tokio. Denby proposed peace on the following terms: the independence of Korea; and the payment by China of a reasonable indemnity. Japan replied that when peace was made she would dictate the terms as became a victor. Strategically Japan was in a position to exact any terms she might desire.

China, unable to secure any assistance from the United States and deserted by England, still clung fatuously to the belief that somewhere, somehow, help would issue out of the West. She turned again to England and she turned to Russia.* That China was not sincere in her approaches to Japan is abundantly proved by the details of the preliminary negotiations. Even while Denby, by authority of the Yamen, was negotiating through Dun in Tokio, Li Hung Chang sent Mr. G. Detring, his personal representative, to Japan as an envoy and yet without any of the powers of a plenipotentiary. The Japanese refused to receive him. A month later China sent two officials of inferior rank without suitable credentials, one of whom could not fail to be particularly objectionable to the Japanese. They were met in Japan by John W. Foster, formerly Secretary of State toward the close of the Harrison administration, and more recently legal adviser to the Chinese legation in Washington.[15] General Foster had been summoned by the Chinese Government to act as adviser in the peace negotiations. He promptly told the envoys that they were without proper credentials, and the envoys were in fact repulsed by the Japanese Government.

Japan also was not ready for peace. While the Chinese envoys were in Japan the Japanese forces were advancing on Wei-hai-wei and on January 31 this fortress was surrendered. There still remained Formosa which Japan had desired for more than twenty years and which she would

*"Negotiations were kept up between China and Japan by the American ministers until late in January, 1895. It would serve no good purpose to recount them here. The two nations mistrusted each other, and China was always trying to ascertain in advance what the demands of Japan would be.

have held in 1874 but for the intervention of Great Britain. It was not until March 20 that Li Hung Chang, equipped with full powers, met the Japanese plenipotentiaries, Count Ito and Count Mutsu, at Shimoneséki. Even then the Chinese were resting their hopes on the intervention of European powers, and it was not until May 24—more than a month after the treaty of peace between China and Japan—that the Japanese forces landed in Formosa.

Korea after the Peace of Shimoneséki

The Treaty of Shimoneséki (April 17, 1895) and the Treaty of Commerce (July 21, 1896) are important in the study of American policy in only two respects and to these we must limit our discussion. The defeat of China was the beginning of a new commercial era within that empire, the relation of which to American policy will be discussed elsewhere. The victory of Japan also carried with it the partial realization of a program of Japanese expansion which, as already noted, had been projected at least as early as the days of the Restoration. Japan came into possession of Formosa and the Pescaderoes, thus acquiring a strategic position controlling the southern avenue of approach to central China and all northern Asia. Japan also held Wei-hai-wei as well as Port Arthur and the Liaotung Peninsula which controlled the approaches to Peking. China was further compelled to recognize the full independence and autonomy of Korea, a victory for Japan which would probably have been consummated in 1885 but for the sudden ending of the Franco-Chinese War.

That Japan regarded this recognition of the independence of Korea as merely the severing of Chinese ties, and not as a satisfactory solution of the Korean question is evident from Japanese policy already inaugurated in the peninsula when the treaty of Shimoneséki was signed. While the king was practically a prisoner in his palace, the Japanese demanded a franchise for all the railroads in Korea for fifty years, all the telegraphs for twenty-five years, and all the posts for five years. They sought to eliminate the foreign advisers to the Korean Government, and they urged Korea to dispose of the Korean legation in Washington and to place Korean affairs in the United States in the hands of the Japanese legation. This program received a sudden check when Germany, Russia and France presented a joint request, amounting to a demand, that Japan recede from the Liaotung Peninsula, returning Port Arthur to China, and followed up this demand, which Japan had no choice but to agree to, by pressure to make certain the withdrawal from Wei-hai-wei, a port which Japan had agreed to hold only until the indemnity provided for in the treaty with China had been paid. Japan thus discovered, as Secretary of State Gresham had warned many months before, that she was not to be permitted to consummate her program. Meanwhile Great Britain as well as the other powers, including the United States, protested against the proposed franchises in Korea.

Japan was represented at Seoul by Viscount Miura, a military man who was fairly representative of the extreme expansionist party in Japanese politics. Meeting with resistance not only from the other treaty powers, but also from the Koreans, Miura became a party to, if not the instigator of, a plot similar to the *coup d'état* of 1884 and the abortive plans of Yuan Shi Kai two years later, to eliminate the queen and her party from Korean politics, and indeed, to demolish all opposition to Japan. This plot was accomplished October 8, 1895, in an attack on the palace and the murder of the queen followed by the burning of her body. Viscount Miura was recalled, court-martialed, and although his complicity in the crime was proven, he was acquitted on a technicality.[16] Miura had served Japan badly. When the Japanese influence at Seoul became ascendant in the summer of 1894, all foreigners who wished Korea well had been disposed to welcome the change from the reactionary régime of Yuan Shi Kai. Now the foreigners were shocked, and the Koreans also turned against Japan. Japanese influence suffered a rapid decline.

Russia, which probably would not otherwise have come forward in the peninsula until the completion of the trans-Siberian railway, now seized the opportunity and began to displace Japan, although not with the entire approval of the Koreans who wished not only to be rid of both Chinese and Japanese interference, but also to be free. The king, however, one of the most pitifully abject and unworthy sovereigns recorded in the pages of history, took refuge in the Russian legation (February 11, 1896) and Russia assumed as complete a control of Korean affairs as China and Japan, respectively, had tried and yet failed to acquire. Under Russian influence the government became more and more corrupt. By a series of agreements (Lobanoff-Yamagata, June 9, 1896, Waeber-Komura, May 14, 1897, and Rosen-Nissi, April 25, 1898) [17] Japan yielded to Russia to the extent of recognizing, for the first time, the political *status quo*, in return for which Russia granted to Japan a freedom in its commercial and industrial relations with Korea which would permit of a policy of economic penetration, and would at the same time allow Japan time enough to build the fleet and organize the army which was necessary for the conflict with Russia which was clearly in view.

This see-sawing of foreign influence in Seoul created a difficult position for the American Government. The possible pitfalls were innumerable. Both Russia and Japan made bids for American sympathy and encouraged the investment of American capital in the peninsula. Both powers were obviously seeking to commit American interests in such a way that when the crisis came the United States would turn to their respective sides. In August, 1895, Korea granted a concession to an American company for the operation of a gold-mine, and in April of the following year the contract for a railroad from Chemulpo to Seoul was awarded to Americans, with Russian approval and help. But the events of 1897 frightened American capital and the railroad contract was turned over the following year to the Japanese. Japanese capitalists then appealed to America for capital to be invested in Korea under Japanese guarantees. Concurrently the Japanese Government withdrew its protests against the annexation of Hawaii, adopted a very conciliatory policy on the immigration question, and when Philippine annexation was under discussion, expressed the hope that the Americans would retain the islands.

The Americans in Korea were less cautious than their government. When Japan promised a better government for the Koreans in 1894, they had favored the Japanese. When, after the disgraceful murder of the queen, the Russians came forward and promised to put an end to Japanese intrigues, they favored the Russians. When Russia proved to be only another wolf in the Korean fold, they fell back upon the characteristically American doctrine of Korean independence. That Korea could become actually independent only by the intervention of the American Government not merely in Korea, but also in the rapidly increasing snarl of European politics does not seem to have occurred to them.

The American Government sought to restrain its citizens, most of whom were missionaries, from contributing to the hopes of the Koreans that help must some day certainly come from the United States. But American law is deficient in its power to impose restraints on the expression of personal opinion by American citizens in foreign countries. There was, however, one thing which could be done. The American minister at Seoul, as the official representative of his government, could be restrained. Following the *emeute* of October 8, 1895, Secretary of State Gresham telegraphed to Minister Sill, "Intervention in the political concerns of Korea is not one of your functions," [18] and when the minister persistently failed to preserve the absolute neutrality which his government had assumed, he was replaced, though not until the McKinley administration had been inaugurated. Dr. H. N. Allen (July 27, 1897) was raised to the post from the position of Secretary of the Legation. The American policy was clearly defined (November 19, 1897) by Secretary of State Sherman in his instructions to Dr. Allen.

"You have been appointed to this interesting mission at a time when there is reason to believe that rival purposes and interests in the east may find in Korea a convenient ground of contention, and it behooves the United States and their representatives, as absolutely neutral parties, to say or do nothing that can in any way be construed as taking sides with or against any of the interested powers. And such particularity would not only be in itself improper but might have the undesirable and unfortunate effect of leading the Koreans themselves to regard the United States as their natural and only ally for any and all such purposes of domestic policy as Korea's rulers may adopt." [19]

The Secretary then reaffirmed the principle that the use of good offices was in no way equivalent to a promise of intervention, and was entirely dependent upon the acceptance of the good offices by both parties to the controversy.

At the end of the century the situation in Korea was as follows: The Korean Court was more corrupt than ever; while Russia still held her place nominally, Japanese influence was in the ascendancy again; and Great Britain, having deserted China, was supporting Japanese aspirations.

BIBLIOGRAPHICAL NOTES

1. Japan Instr., Vol. 1, Apr. 28, 1871, Fish to De Long.
2. Ward Corres., p. 594, Aug. 20, 1859, Ward to Cass.
3. For. Relations, 1863, II, p. 1079; 1873, I, p. 613; Payson Jackson Treat: "Japan and the United States," pp. 100, 101, 70; For. Relations, 1873, I, pp. 524-5; Moore's "Digest," II, p. 655.
4. Mr. Young refers to the conference with Li Hung Chang in "Men and Memories," Vol. 2, p. 308. See also Tyler Dennett: "American Good Offices in Asia," *Journal of International Law,* January, 1922.
5. China Instr. Vol. 3, July 13, 1883, Frelinghuysen to Young.
6. Cordier: "Relations, etc.," Vol. II, p. 399. This is the sole reference by historians to these overtures.
7. Morse: Vol. II, pp. 353-7; Cordier: Vol. II, pp. 435 ff.
8. For. Relations contain no references whatever to the Young-Li Hung Chang or the Frelinghuysen-Morton correspondence for the arbitration of the Franco-Chinese War. The Young dispatches, among the ablest papers in the archives of the Dept. of State, are as follows: China Desp., Vol. 65, Aug. 8, 1883, Aug. 16, 1883, Sept. 7, Oct. 8, 1883; Vol. 67, Dec. 24, 1883; Vol. 68, Jan. 6, 1884; Vol. 71, Aug. 21, 1864; Sept. 4, 1884; Vol. 73, Dec. 22, 1884. The details of the Hart negotiations will be found in Morse, *op. cit.,* pp. 364-7.
9. Moore's "Arbitrations," II, 1875.

10. For. Relations, 1883, p. 209; 1884, p. 46; Morse, *op. cit.*, p. 320.
11. Korean Instr., Vol. 1, Aug. 25, 1890, Wharton to Heard.
12. For. Relations, 1894, II, p. 22. The following pages in Foreign Relations bring together and give in great detail the diplomatic correspondence of the American Government in relation to the Sino-Japanese War.
13. See W. W. McLaren: "A Political History of Japan," chaps. 9, 10.
14. Charles Denby: "China and Her People," Vol. 2, p. 132.
15. John W. Foster: "Diplomatic Memories," Vol. II, chaps. 30-32. These chapters together with Denby's chap. 10 give a fairly complete account of the entire peace negotiations. The correspondence of the peace negotiations was published in the English newspapers in both Japan and China. The official documents were collected and published in pamphlet form by the Tientsin *Times*.
16. Japan *Daily Mail*, Feb. 1, 1896, gives the report of the Miura court-martial proceedings.
17. These, as well as other treaties with or concerning Korea, have been collected in a convenient booklet entitled "Korea: Treaties and Agreements," published by the Carnegie Endowment for International Peace (1921). They will also be found, of course, in the various larger collections of treaties.
18. For. Relations, 1895, p. 972, Oct. 11, 1895; see Sill's reply, p. 977.
19. Korea Instr., Vol. 1, Nov. 19, 1897, Sherman to Allen.

CHAPTER XXVII

TREATY REVISION

THE tap-root of American policy in Asia was always commercial and political most-favored-nation treatment—equality of privilege. While the other Western powers might fairly claim a similar basis for their policies, there was a difference. All treaties started with most-favored-nation treatment as a base, but the European powers and Great Britain constantly sought to whittle down to a minimum the safeguards interposed by treaties for the political and commercial independence of the Asiatic states, and to manipulate the interpretation or revision of the treaties in some way which would actually create a preferred position for the nationals of the power thus exerting itself. At this point the American Government parted company with the other treaty powers after 1866. The United States desired not merely to protect the Asiatic states in the enjoyment of the rights guaranteed by treaty, but also to remove or modify any restrictions upon their liberties which would thwart their development as strong states. The United States wanted a strong East; the other powers did not.

The United States entered the period of treaty revision with another policy not easily reconciled with the purpose to promote a strong East. Cooperation with other powers was difficult so long as that cooperation was to be manipulated for the repression of Asia. The cooperative policy, therefore, which reached its height under Seward in the Convention of 1866 and the Burlingame treaty, was abandoned. It is difficult to name an exact date when this took place. While it was nominally sustained by the Department of State until 1877 when Hamilton Fish-retired at the end of the Grant administration, actually cooperation had ceased in Japan by 1870, and in China did not survive the departure of Burlingame. The name continued in Peking throughout the century, a polite fiction, a synonym for ordinary diplomatic courtesy, but the spirit of the cooperation was well described by John Russell Young, American minister at Peking, 1882-5, who wrote:

"This policy, when studied, simply meant in practical experience that when matters went to please Great Britain there was joint action. Otherwise there would be no action until Great Britain was pleased, and as there were very few questions in which the United States were concerned, it was deemed best for the American interests that the Legation should act alone and, like its British associate, unite in "joint action" when such a course served the United States." *[1]

While the period of treaty revision did not formally start until 1868, hardly before the signatures to the treaties were dry the efforts to modify them had begun. The foreigners were bent on increasing their advantages; China and Japan were seeking to reduce them. The three main objects of attack were the five per cent tariff, extraterritoriality, and further opening of the country. To all of these provisions, in Japan as well as in China, the United States was well committed in 1858.

REVISION IN CHINA BY INTERPRETATION AND AGREEMENT

China's power of resistance reached its lowest ebb at the conclusion of the Anglo-French War in 1860, which coincided with a revival of the Taiping Rebellion. In the next forty years China lost much, both by treaty-interpretation and by new treaties, and gained nothing except as foreign powers occasionally opposed the aggressions of their own or some other's nationals. During the four years in which Sir Frederick Bruce and Anson Burlingame worked together in Peking, the efforts of the mercantile communities, notably at Shanghai, to secure loose interpretations of the

*Charles Denby, American minister at Peking from 1885 to 1898, writes of the cooperative policy as though it did not disappear until the struggle for concessions which followed the Sino-Japanese War. The erroneous nature of this assumption will appear in the following pages.[2]

treaties in favor of increased privileges for foreigners met with effective resistance. British public opinion underwent a great change in the sixties which is represented in the inauguration of the first Gladstone ministry in 1868.*

Official policies for the United States and Great Britain, respectively, are registered in the Burlingame treaty of 1868 and the Lord Clarendon letter, but after them "all regulating influences seem to have been removed," and "the utmost pretensions of the merchants, commercial, fiscal, and municipal, have in the course of time, one after another, been attained." [4] The coasting trade, contrary to the desire or intention of the Chinese Government, passed into the hands of foreigners; for many years the Americans were the chief beneficiaries. The effort to secure Chinese representation in the municipal government at Shanghai was thwarted, and while the technical sovereignty of the Empire over the city was not abolished, the power of the Imperial government to levy taxes was curtailed. Shanghai contributed nothing to the Imperial revenues except through customs. Extraterritoriality was stretched to cover law as well as jurisdiction and the foreigners even reserved for themselves the exclusive right to interpret the law under the treaties. The imperial government was prevented from fully enforcing the penalties for smuggling. Eventually the immunity from inland taxation secured under the British tariff of 1858 by the payment of an additional $2\frac{1}{2}$ per cent duty at the ports was greatly broadened to include a large amount of trade which was not only not a part of the foreign commerce of the Empire, but was not even carried on by foreigners. Thus in a measure China lost even the power to regulate internal taxation. The provision of the Burlingame treaty (Article 8) by which the United States disavowed "any intention or right to intervene in the domestic administra-

---

*"It is not too much to say that ten years later the treaty of Tientsin in its entirety would have been an impossibility; not but what the Chinese authorities could have been compelled to yield all that it contains; but that the British Government yielding to the democratic impulse that has, in the interval, passed over Europe and America, would have hesitated to impose all the conditions to which the Chinese Government then submitted." (Address of J. Barr Robertson before the North China Branch of the Royal Asiatic Society, May 16, 1870.[3])

tion of China in regard to the construction of railroads, telegraphs, or other material internal improvements," never accepted in a formal way by other powers, was of no value except to exclude Americans from privileges of interference enjoyed by their competitors. Meanwhile, because of rising prices, the five per cent duties ceased to be effectively five per cent. This also amounted to a revision in the interests of the foreigner. While the treaties of 1858 were, during the nineteenth century, never actually and formally revised, a revision by interpretation and special agreement was steadily taking place, and almost uniformly to the disadvantage of China. In 1900 the commercial and political as well as the geographical sphere in which the Empire might exercise its sovereign rights was much smaller than in 1860. As the years went on this form of revision became of less and less benefit to American interests and even became disadvantageous, but after the day of Burlingame and Seward, the American Government offered no effective opposition.[5]

Treaty revision in Japan proceeded in less subtle ways and was characterized by the very aggressive policies of the Japanese Government which forced the conflict of interests into the light of day. The steps in the revision are clearly definable. The first efforts were made immediately by the foreigners and went against Japan. They were directed first at the tariff which under Townsend Harris had been favorable to Japan as well as to the United States. In 1866 Japan was forced by a joint naval demonstration to consent to 'regularize' the various tariff reductions which had been secured by Lord Elgin, Mr. Pruyn, and by the voluntary concessions of the Japanese, in a conventional tariff of specific duties similar to those of the British tariff of Tientsin. Similarly, as in China, the rise in prices had the effect of reducing this tariff so that in another ten years the specific duties amounted to less than four per cent when calculated on an *ad valorem* basis.

After 1866 American cooperation in treaty revision ceased. From that time onward American policy is marked in five stages: Japanese efforts in 1872 to which may be joined certain decisions of the American Government in the limitation of extraterritoriality; the treaty of 1878; the Shufeldt treaty with Korea in 1882, which is an official statement of policy for that date; the treaty revision conferences, 1882-8, concluding with the unratified treaty of 1889; and the actual revision accomplished in 1894. In passing it may be noted that the history of American policy in tariff revision in Japan might, during this period, have been repeated in China had the latter government been in a position to invite it.

JAPANESE EFFORTS AT REVISION

The revision of the treaties with Japan was due in 1872. Among the foreigners there was a movement on foot to demand the unlimited opening of the country to travel, residence and trade. The Japanese, realizing the difficulties of the approaching crisis, set out to meet them just as China had done in 1868 by means of an embassy, consisting of Lord Iwakura and four "vice-ambassadors." Although American influence in Tokio had reached its lowest point since the opening of the Empire,* the United States was looked upon as friendly to Japan, and the embassy planned to visit America first, as the Burlingame mission had done, possibly with a view to securing similar official approval in the United States which might be used effectively in Europe.

While Japan gave formal notice in 1871 of its desire to revise the treaties the following year, it appears that the original intention of the Emperor had been to postpone the revision until the return of the embassy.† For some reason, perhaps because of advice received in the United States and

---

*"With the overthrow of the Tycoon American prestige in Japan went down, for with him into exile went all those others whose minds first imbibed impressions from foreign powers and wisdom from the shadow of Perry's fleet, and the wise counsels of our first minister, Mr. Harris. Since then no exhibition of our power or greatness has ever been made in these seas, whilst other nations have carefully made displays of theirs." (De Long to Fish, Jan. 19, 1871.)

†"As soon as the embassy returns home we will consider the revision of the treaties, and accomplish what we have expected and intended." (Letter of the Emperor to President Grant.)

because of the enthusiastic reception accorded to the Japanese, it was deemed wise to proceed at once to a revision of the treaty, and Ito and Okubo, two of the envoys, were sent back to Japan to secure the necessary full powers. They returned to Washington with a draft of the revision as desired by Japan. This draft contained a provision which would give to Japan tariff autonomy and probably stipulated that in return for the opening of either more ports or the interior of the Empire, the foreigners should relinquish either part or all of their extraterritorial rights.* In the midst of the negotiations which ensued the embassy withdrew the proposal, at the crafty advice, so it is said, of the German minister in Tokio, von Brandt, who advised the envoys that it was not to the advantage of Japan to negotiate separately with the different powers.[8] The American Government, it is believed, had warned Japan against making any more joint treaties, but it was always the policy of the other powers in Tokio to maintain joint action in treaty revision negotiations and usually to thwart attempts to transfer the negotiations from Japan to a foreign capital. The Japanese announced that a conference of the treaty powers soon would be called in Europe and that the negotiations would there be resumed. The embassy remained in Europe more than a year, visiting all of the capitals and studying intently every aspect of Western life, and then hurried home to avert the proposed wars in 1873 and also to report that the Western powers, by means of the treaties, had deliberately assigned Japan to an inferior political status like that of the other oriental states.† The powers were not only indisposed to make any concessions in the

---

* The writer has not seen a draft of this proposed treaty. The inferences are based on a letter from De Long to Fish (April 29, 1872) in which the former returns a draft of the treaty with comments.

† "Until the late Embassy came to Europe, no Japanese had any correct idea of the true nature or of the international bearings of the treaties which bind Japan. The higher classes had vaguely felt that the treaties were one-sided, but they did not possess sufficient knowledge of European history and law to be able to measure them with precision. It was not until the members of the Embassy reached Europe that they were able (especially during their stay in Paris) to study the question thoroughly. They then perceived that the Japan treaties are but another application of the rules and precedents which Europe has employed toward all Eastern powers since the capitulations were made with Turkey." Frederic Marshall, an attaché of the Japanese legation in Paris, to Lord Derby, May 6, 1874.[9]

revision of the treaties but were acting together to demand the unlimited opening of the Empire. There is no record of the answers prepared by the American Government to the Japanese proposals but it is probable that the United States, while refraining from demands for the unlimited opening of the Empire, would have been quite unwilling to surrender extraterritorial rights or grant tariff autonomy, although minor concessions might have been offered.

Upon the return of the Iwakura Embassy, Japan set out to devise a program for the accomplishment of treaty revision. The general principles of this program were: to establish as rapidly as possible precedents of equality in negotiations; to break down the joint action of the powers and to isolate them from each other, introducing a principle of reciprocity; and to carry on the negotiations for treaty revision away from home. The specific objects to be attained were: tariff autonomy, to which was joined the intention to raise the duties in order to increase the revenues of the government and possibly to afford protection to infant industries; recovery of control of the coasting trade; and the abolition of extraterritoriality. The method to be adopted was opportunist: not to insist upon the realization of the entire project at once, but to seize every opportunity to advance its details.

Russia and the United States provided the first opportunities. In 1875, as already noted, Russia consented to the negotiation in St. Petersburg of a revision of the boundary treaty of 1855.[10] Russia, for reasons the full force of which appear in the history of her relations with China and Korea, had never positively engaged herself to support the cooperative policy and, until the close of the Sino-Japanese War, usually preferred isolated action. The United States joined (1873) with the other treaty powers in urging Italy to refuse to ratify a treaty in which it was proposed to open the interior to Italians under Japanese jurisdiction.[11] Nevertheless that same year the American Government con sented to a Postal Convention with Japan which was nego tiated and signed in Washington (August 6, 1873). This was the first treaty with Japan in which the full equality in the negotiations was recognized.[12] This action on the part of the United States was much resented by the diplomats in Tokio. Americans were engaged to organize the Japanese postal system. The United States took other steps toward limiting the application of the principles of extraterritoriality. In the face of the pretensions of the other foreign powers that newly enacted laws were not valid for foreigners unless approved by the foreign governments—a contention which was sustained in China—the American Government ordered the Americans to conform to the hunting regulations in 1874, to the new press-laws in 1876, and to the quarantine regulations in 1878 and 1879.[13] United States Minister Bingham also assented, with the approval of the government, to the proposition that Americans, entering the interior under passport, should submit themselves to Japanese laws, it being reserved only that trial and punishment for violation of these laws must be under consular jurisdiction.[14]

POLICY OF JUDGE BINGHAM—TREATY OF 1878

Judge John A. Bingham of Ohio, American minister in Tokio from 1873 to 1885, deserves equal rank with Townsend Harris among the determined and uncompromising American friends of Japan which the last half of the nineteenth century produced in abundance. He represented not so much the American Government with which he often had differences of opinion, as the American people. He was a characteristic American of the period.*

Immediately upon his arrival in Tokio Judge Bingham set himself to secure the revision of the treaties and formal abrogation by the United States of the policy of cooperation which he detested as un-American, as inimical to Japan, and as opposed to American commercial interests. He be-

*Bingham had been long in public life before he went to Japan. He was a member of the House of Representatives almost continuously from 1855. During the Civil War he was judge advocate in the army, and took part in the trial of the Lincoln conspirators. He had been one of the managers from the House in the impeachment proceedings against President Johnson.[15]

lieved the policy of the other treaty powers was being directed to prevent Japan from becoming strong, rich or democratic, and to secure control of Japanese markets and resources. The Convention of 1866, urged Bingham, was operating in a manner detrimental to American commercial and political interests for it opened the door to excessive European importations, prevented the growth of Japanese industries, and restricted the revenues of the government. Its effect was to cause Japan to pay tribute to England at the expense of the other powers. He noted that in 1874 Japan was forced to settle the balance of trade by a payment of about $8,000,000. He pointed out that one of the causes back of the Satsuma Rebellion in 1877 was an agrarian movement arising out of the excessive land taxes which the Japanese Government, unable to increase its customs, was forced to levy. Steadily and persistently Judge Bingham denounced the existing treaties and demanded their revision, or even their abrogation.[16]

With equal vigor Bingham set himself against the co-operative policy which was being steadily invoked to sustain the political and commercial purposes of the other treaty powers. This brought him into conflict with Sir Harry Parkes who had been chiefly responsible for the Convention of 1866, and had since dominated the diplomatic corps in Tokio. It also arrayed him against the British mercantile community, and the British-owned newspapers of the open ports. Bingham was looked upon as little less than a traitor to foreign trade and the attacks upon him were vitriolic. It was a magnificent yet probably unnecessary struggle in which Japanese and American interests quickly found themselves allied. American influence in Tokio rose rapidly and Japanese opposition to the other treaty powers stiffened. The Japan *Herald* (December 12, 1873) asserted that "England should again introduce into Japan a little of the gun-boat policy." But ten years later the Japan *Weekly Mail* (January 20, 1883) mourned the fact that in Japan "British influence remains at a palpable discount" and "among all Japan's treaty friends she (the

United States) is at present the most trusted and the most consulted."

Bingham, at length supported by his government, had won his battle for Japan. Dissatisfaction with the British policy under Parkes had been making itself felt in England and a Parliamentary investigation was threatened. That year (1883) Parkes was transferred from Tokio to Peking. The greatest obstruction to treaty revision favorable to Japanese aspirations had been removed. Bingham found his own government slow to relinquish the cooperative policy although not unwilling to consider reasonable measures for treaty revision, and on at least two occasions [17] the American minister was sharply recalled to his duty of cooperation, but in the end he won a complete victory in the Department of State. In 1876 the Japanese Government, through its minister in Washington, Yoshida, approached Secretary of State Fish with a desire for a revision of "small clauses in the old treaties." [18] Yoshida pointed out that the expenses of the government had greatly increased with the coming of the foreigners and that the customs receipts had not increased proportionately. The increasing taxation laid upon the Japanese people was, he said, drying up the springs of national prosperity. The duties were now "in many cases" down to less than one per cent if calculated on an *ad valorem* basis. A return to even an effective five per cent would, for example, increase the receipts at Yokohama by at least $100,000 a year. Fish found the request "very reasonable and proper." He sympathized with the desire to increase the revenues and to "protect industries." The conversations continued for about a year.

What Japan specifically desired, stated Yoshida, was: the revision of the Convention of 1866 in separate negotiations with each power, thus breaking down the habit of joint action; the transfer of negotiations from Tokio to the foreign capitals; the recovery of control over the coasting trade which in Japan, as it had in China, was passing into the hands of foreigners; the restoration of the right of tariff autonomy, with which was joined the desire to elim-

inate conventional tariffs altogether and to increase the
duties; the introduction of a principle of reciprocity such
as would witness to the sovereign independence of the Empire. The question of extraterritoriality was for the time
being put aside. The only objection by Fish to the proposed
program was over the question of most-favored-nation treatment in case the United States were to agree to the revision
while the other powers did not. It cannot be claimed that
Fish showed as much interest in the proposed revision as did
Judge Bingham, and the negotiations remained unfinished
at the close of the Grant administration. Meanwhile Japan
was enlarging her demands.

Four months after William M. Evarts assumed his duties
of office in the Hays administration Yoshida presented
(July 27, 1877) a complete draft of the convention desired
by his government. The revision of small clauses previously proposed now appeared as a proposition for an entirely new treaty which would abrogate the Convention of
1866, and which would also carry with it the abrogation of
the treaty of 1858 in another five years. The objections of
Mr. Fish were met in the following provision:

"It is also agreed that the present convention shall take effect
when Japan shall have concluded a similar convention or conventions
either collectively or severally, with all the other parties to the
Tariff Convention of 1866, similar in effect to the present convention."

This was amended in the complete draft (Article 10) so
that to make it effective Japan would have to secure revisions not merely with the signatories of the Convention of
1866 but also with "all the other treaty powers holding
relations with Japan."

Evarts was from the outset favorably disposed toward
the treaty, the more so because of the fact that a few years
before Sir Harry Parkes, in cooperation with the German
representative, arbitrarily defined the meaning of "iron
manufactures" and Parkes had also ruled that coal should
pay an export duty only when it was taken away in sailing
vessels. These actions were taken without consultation with

either the Japanese authorities or Judge Bingham.* They were, in fact, a revision of the tariff by two treaty powers acting alone. The negotiations in Washington proceeded leisurely and in secret. After many changes in phraseology and the omission of all reference to the treaty of 1858, the treaty was signed July 25, 1878, without any consultation with the other treaty powers. The change in American policy in a decade was marked. Before signing the Burlingame treaty Seward had telegraphed the text to all the other treaty powers.[20] Now, ten years later, the American Government definitely and even secretly abrogated the cooperative policy.

The publication of the treaty was received with great displeasure alike by the American friends of Japan who objected to the reservations of Article 10, and by the foreign powers which saw not merely the advance of Japan towards the achievement of its aspirations, but also deflection from the useful cooperative policy. By Americans Evarts was accused of trickery in Article 10—a charge which was wholly groundless.[21] By Sir Julian Pauncefote, of the British Foreign Office, Evarts' independent and secret action was characterized as "contrary to all usage." [22] A combination of the European treaty powers, led by Germany and England, was immediately formed to prevent the treaty from coming into operation and this was successful, although it was known that both Italy and Russia had been favorably disposed towards revision. The rage of the British-owned journals of the treaty ports was boundless. The next year Great Britain attempted to secure an offset to the leadership of America by proposing a treaty revision conference to be held in London. Japan declined to enter it unless her right to tariff autonomy was admitted. In the tentative tariff

---

*"It appears from your dispatch, No. 276, that Great Britain and Germany changed by a protocol the terms of the Convention of 1866 in a certain particular so far as it applied to their respective countries; and in your dispatch, No. 549, you report that the British minister at Tokio has compelled the Japanese Government to adopt an apparently forced and unauthorized construction of one of the provisions of the Convention. As the Convention of 1866 was a joint convention to which the United States was a party and as other governments that participated in it have assumed to revise its provisions no objections can legitimately be urged against the United States pursuing the same course." (Evarts to Bingham, June 21, 1877.[19])

revision then being discussed the United States was to be punished for its break with the cooperative policy by having the new duty on kerosene, then the chief American import, increased from five to twenty per cent, while cottons and woolens, the chief British articles of import, were to pay only ten per cent.

The next year (1880) the United States, in return for the immigration treaty with China, negotiated at Peking a partial revision of the treaty of Tientsin in which opium was again placed on the prohibited list for American importers. This was a second though less abrupt repudiation of the cooperative policy.

THE SHUFELDT TREATY WITH JAPAN

The United States, now well embarked upon an independent course of action, turned its attention as already noted to Korea. In 1882 it was evident that even though Shufeldt were to fail a treaty with some power could not long be delayed. There had already been no less than ten efforts to open Korea.[23]

The Shufeldt treaty deserves attention in the history of treaty revision even though it was a new treaty, for it reflects the general policy of the American Government at the time, and the treaty made the following year by Sir Henry Parkes and by the German minister from Peking show with equal clearness how wide had become the gulf between American and European policies in Asia.

The only important stipulations which Li Hung Chang had failed to persuade Shufeldt to include in the Korean treaty were the acknowledgment of Chinese suzerainty, the prohibition of the importation of religious books—a provision which was aimed to prevent missionary work—and the reservation of the right to Korea to impose transit taxes. The treaty provided that while the tariff was to be issued by Korea as a sovereign power, the duties were not to exceed ten per cent on ordinary articles, or thirty per cent on luxuries. Opium was excluded, the purchase of land was not stipulated, and revision was possible in five years. A similar treaty signed by Admiral Willes for the British Government aroused great opposition from the British mercantile community.[24] The Yokohama Chamber of Commerce, representing the merchants of all nations, but chiefly composed of British subjects, even went so far as to protest officially to Judge Bingham against the restrictions to trade in the Shufeldt treaty, the ratification of which it was thought would be detrimental to the interests of the foreigners in the pending treaty revision negotiations in Japan.* British interests were also affected, as already noted, by the failure to recognize Chinese suzerainty

The Admiral Willes treaty was not ratified and the following year Sir Harry Parkes was sent to Korea to make a compact which would be satisfactory to British commercial interests. The contrasts between the compact thus negotiated and the Shufeldt treaty are marked. The right of diplomatic officers and consuls to "travel freely in any part" of the country was inserted, and the right of the Korean Government to withdraw the exequatur of consuls was omitted. Two interior points were opened to trade· British subjects were to be allowed to purchase as well as rent land; free exercise of religion was permitted; part of the yearly rental for British settlements was to be reserved as a municipal fund to be held under the joint control of the Korean and British authorities; freedom of travel for either pleasure or trade within 100 *li* of any open port was stipulated, and the tariff and trade regulations were revisable, as in Japan, only by "mutual consent." The penalty

*"Understanding that negotiation of a treaty of commerce with the Korean Government is contemplated by the Government of the United States, I am directed by the committee of the Yokohama General Chamber of Commerce to express the hope that your government will favorably consider the wish of the members of the chamber (which, you are doubtless aware, represents the general mercantile community of Yokohama and comprises firms of all nationalities) that an opportunity be afforded them of stating their views on the commercial clauses of the proposed treaty before its final ratification, and ask you to be good enough to forward this application to the proper quarter for consideration.

"It is obvious to your government, bearing in mind the negotiations now pending between the Japanese Government and the Foreign Powers for the revision of existing treaties that concessions to Korea involving restrictions on travel not hitherto in force in Japan, will undoubtedly operate prejudicially against satisfactory completion of their negotiations." (James P. Mallison to Bingham, August 23, 1882.)

for smuggling was lightened; revision of the treaty at the end of ten years was possible, again "by mutual consent"; and the Shufeldt clauses were amended as follows: the import tariff was to be conventional and specific, and was graded in four schedules of five, seven and one half, ten, and twenty per cent respectively. Cotton and woolen manufactured goods were to pay seven and one half per cent, and metals, raw cotton, thread, raw wool and yarns, constituting the bulk of the probable British importations were placed in the five per cent class. While the prohibition of opium was retained, an exception was made in favor of "medicinal opium." The coasting trade was thrown open to British subjects. In short, the new treaty was an exceedingly businesslike and thoroughgoing affair in which Korea surrendered not only what had been granted to the foreigners by treaty in both China and Japan, but also a considerable amount of what the foreigners had obtained also by the extra-treaty method of interpretation. British support to Chinese claims of suzerainty over the peninsula was purchased at the expense of Korea in a treaty which out-distanced in many particulars any treaty previously made in the interests of foreigners in the Far East. Just as the Harris treaty with Japan in 1858 and the Shufeldt treaty revealed the kind of policy the United States would like to pursue when uninfluenced by European competition, so the Parkes treaty with Korea showed the kind of policy which British and Continental commercial interests desired to follow when conditions were favorable. The effect was still further to increase American prestige in Tokio where the American policy was appreciated as much for its commercial as for its political implications.

The Unratified Treaty of 1889

The attempts at treaty revision in Japan in 1878-9 had ended in failure, but the action of the Americans had been a great encouragement. Another effort was made in 1880 in which it was proposed to deal with the treaty powers jointly, and to accomplish the recovery of both judicial and tariff autonomy by degrees, according to a graduated scale. The premature publication of a draft of this treaty by a newspaper which had received it from one of the European ministers, aroused popular opposition to such compromises and the proposal was dropped.[25]

Two years later another effort was made. Japan proposed a new tariff which would increase duties to eleven and even to twenty-six per cent. The powers replied with a counter proposal which would have yielded about $1,000,000 less revenues annually. In this draft kerosene was reduced from twenty to fifteen per cent, cotton yarn from ten to seven per cent, and opium as medicine was to be admitted at ten per cent. Looking toward the abolition of extraterritoriality the Japanese Government proposed the introduction of foreign associate judges whose services were to be continued from six to ten years. Judge Bingham sat in this conference at the request of the Japanese and with the approval of Evarts, though without the power to commit the American Government. This effort also came to nothing for a variety of reasons. The Chinese and Korean relations of Japan were becoming difficult, and great popular opposition developed in Japan when the terms of the treaty became known. The provision in regard to opium especially attracted attention because of a suspected attempt of Sir Harry Parkes some years before to introduce the opium trade in Japan.[26]

It may fairly be claimed that the next effective blow for treaty revision was struck not in Japan but in the United States. In his annual message to Congress, December 4, 1883, President Arthur took occasion to state:

"This government is disposed to consider the request of Japan to determine its own tariff duties, to provide such proper judicial tribunals as may commend themselves to the Western powers for the trial of causes to which foreigners are parties, and to assimilate the terms and duration of its treaties to those of other civilized states."[27]

This open declaration created still further discomfort in the foreign communities in Japan. It was characterized as lacking in political sagacity by the Japan *Daily Mail* (May 5, 1883) which pointed to the treaty of 1878, the Korean treaty, the return of the Shimoneséki indemnity (February 22, 1883); meanwhile the Chinese indemnity money was still withheld, and the Chinese Exclusion Act seemed to the *Daily Mail* to indicate a disposition to discriminate between China and Japan in favor of the latter which was "the smaller and in every way inferior power."

It is not possible to establish a direct connection but it seems very probable that President Arthur's declaration of December 4th had some influence on Great Britain, for seven days later Lord Granville issued a memorandum in which he expressed an hitherto unknown willingness to accept, not a restoration of autonomy, but a revision of the tariff such as had been proposed in the counter draft of 1882. Germany also assented. "Signs are not wanting," stated a writer in the London *Times*, June 9, 1884, "that the beginning of the end has come." It would, however, be unfair not to mention in this connection that for several years the tone of the British press towards treaty revision had been changing, and in 1884 Japan had some advocates in London as warm as any in the United States. Indeed, a comparison of press clippings on Japanese affairs in the British and Continental press suggests that for the past ten years Japan had been systematically carrying on a press campaign abroad to create the necessary public sentiment in support of her contentions. The beginning of 1884 may be reckoned as an important turning point in the affairs of the Far East for it marks the turn of British policy towards the conciliation of Japan. At almost any time from then until the signing of the treaties in 1894 Japan might have obtained substantial concessions from the European powers, but as the opposition began to give way Japan steadily advanced her claims and became more and more unwilling to accept compromises.

Japan received further encouragement from the United States in 1886 when (April 30), the day before another treaty revision conference opened, President Cleveland agreed to an extradition treaty with Japan, "because," as he stated later in sending the treaty to the Senate, "of the support which its conclusions would give to Japan in her efforts towards judicial autonomy and complete sovereignty." [28]

Such declarations from the United States, coupled with entire withdrawal from the cooperative policy, and the departure of Judge Bingham from Tokio in 1885 had the effect of eliminating the American Government from a position of influence in the prolonged treaty revision conferences of 1886-7. It was no longer necessary for Japan to consult and conciliate the United States and her ministers then turned their attention to the European states with a view to causing still further deflections from cooperation. It was believed that Count Ito entered into an understanding with Bismarck which, however, was quite different from that with the United States.[29] The American Government had given its support to Japan freely; Germany asked for compensation in the form of increased privileges for its nationals. The increase of German influence not merely in Tokio but even on the entire political structure of the government was marked. Neither the American nor the British ideals of democracy were consistent with the ideals cherished by Japanese leaders for their nation. Modern Germany afforded a more acceptable model. Hitherto Germany had acted in the Far East in the closest cooperation with Great Britain. The winning of Germany to the Japanese side greatly weakened the position of England, and paved the way for a better Anglo-Japanese understanding. Thus, while the Western nations were making the Far East the back yard of European politics, Japan boldly entered Europe in an effort to make the Continent the playground of Japanese statesmen only thirty years after the nation had first opened its doors to the Western world.

Into the details of the treaty revision conferences of 1884 and 1886-7 it is not necessary to go in a study of American policy. Only their abrupt termination in the summer of 1887 is important. Inouye, who had been Minister of Foreign Affairs for eight years, was on the point of concluding treaties which would have involved not merely the establishment of a judiciary of foreigners, but also the submission of Japanese laws to the approval of the treaty powers. While the proposed treaties represented an advance towards independence, they were very far removed from granting either judicial or tariff autonomy. The immediate advantage to Japan would lie in the fact that in return for a tariff which would leave British trade in nearly its old position of advantage, Great Britain was willing to yield important concessions in the matter of extraterritoriality. British and German manufactures were to be taxed, on the average about seven per cent, while American products would be taxed from twelve to fourteen per cent. Chinese sugar, China not being represented in the treaty revision conferences, was to pay twenty per cent. Great opposition to the treaties developed in Japan. Count Katsu, an influential Tokugawa leader, presented a memorandum to the Cabinet enumerating "twenty-one faults of the time" in which he severely castigated the hurried and superficial measures for westernizing the Empire which had been concomitant with the efforts to revise the treaties.[30] and General Tani, Minister of Commerce and Agriculture, who had been sent to Europe by the Emperor to study international politics, returned and entered a protest against the treaties which was emphasized by his resignation from office. The Tani memorial which, although suppressed by the government was secretly printed and circulated by the thou sands, was credited with causing the resignation of Count Inouye. This memorial throws much light on currents of Japanese thought.[31]

Viscount Tani pointed out that Japan need not be in such great haste about the revision of the treaties. While Japan was a small nation it was to be remembered that size by itself had little to do with independence. Greece, Switzerland and Belgium were independent, while India, Poland and Turkey were not. The important consideration in independence was that foreign powers have no voice in the government. The proposed treaties, therefore, marked not the independence but the dependence of Japan, for they gave to foreign powers a control over even the laws of the Empire. Tani urged the postponement of treaty revision. No nation, he thought, would be likely to send an army to Japan to compel revision, and while the international rivalries were creating so much confusion and so many jealousies, Japan was in a way to profit by waiting and by watching European politics.

"When I was abroad," wrote Tani, "I quietly observed that our government was inclined towards Germany. Science, commerce, military system and even the style of clothing, all seemed to follow Germany. . . . The object of the foreigners who cross the ocean to Japan is commerce, but if they find everything to favor Germany, and protection given only to Germans in matters of commerce in which rightfully all nations ought to be able to compete, it will only lead to our receiving the ill will of England, America, France and Russia. .

"Our condition may be compared to that of an immoral woman who endeavors to get the love of many, but at last gets a bad reputation and is rejected by all without exception. Is it not indeed shameful?

"Then what policy must we pursue?

"Cease holding the policy and principles of the past, laying aside the spirit of dependence, improve our internal government affairs, make our country secure by military preparation, not to bring disgrace upon the name and honor of our country by making an outward show only of truth, justice and authority; encourage and protect the people at home and then *wait for the time of the confusion of Europe,** which must come eventually sooner or later, and although we have no immediate concern with it ourselves we must feel it, for such an event will agitate the nations of the Orient as well, and hence, although our country is not mixed up in the matter, so far as Europe is concerned, we may then become the chief nation of the Orient.

"If, therefore, we at this time provide twenty strong warships and an army 100,000 strong we can hold the balance among the Eastern nations and show a strong front to Western countries. Then if there is war between England and Russia, Russia can control England by uniting with us, and England can crush Russia if she forms an alliance with us. In case of war between China and France, our relations towards Russia and England would be the same as already stated. Should we remain neutral the advantage to us would be great as an asylum, and for providing provisions and communications which both have such an important bearing upon success or defeat. It is therefore evident that we can seize the opportunity and obtain the balance of power in the East and thus compel others to

* Italics by T. D.

esteem and fear us. In the same way we may stand with European countries.

"Is not this a pleasant picture?"

Probably this sagacious advice of Viscount Tani, so reminiscent of Lord Hotta's memorial in 1858, was not taken very seriously by the foreign governments, although it furnishes the key to an understanding of Japanese politics both domestic and international for the next generation, but even had it been taken seriously there is nothing to indicate that the Americans would not have regarded it with complacency.

Count Okuma replaced Inouye as minister of Foreign Affairs early in 1888, and a new treaty revision program was adopted in which Japan resolved never again to enter a joint conference with the powers on the subject. The following November Japan signed a treaty with Mexico in which the national aspirations were at last realized. The treaty was uniformly bi-lateral, extraterritorial jurisdiction was eliminated, tariff autonomy was granted, and the most-favored-nation clause was so qualified that a special concession granted to one nation in a reciprocal agreement, could not be claimed by the other except in exchange for some equivalent concession. In the closing days of the Cleveland administration, Richard B. Hubbard, the American Minister in Tokio, by direction from his government, signed a somewhat similar treaty for the United States. These treaties produced the collapse of the cooperative policy. Germany signed a treaty on June 11 and Russia indicated a willingness for revision.[32]

TREATIES OF 1894

The signing of these treaties brought great confusion both to the domestic and to the international affairs of Japan. Great objection to the treaties with the United States and Germany developed in Japan because the provision for foreign judges as a temporary measure had been retained and the tariff schedule was still conventional.[33] The treaties were not regarded as any great improvement over those which had been rejected the year before. While the Cabinet was still debating the question Count Okuma was attacked by an assassin and narrowly escaped death. The Cabinet then resigned and Viscount Aoki became Minister of Foreign Affairs. Meanwhile Great Britain is believed to have secured from Germany an agreement that the treaty would not be ratified until Great Britain had taken action. This promise, whether formal or informal does not matter, had the effect of throwing the control of the situation almost entirely into the hands of Great Britain where it remained until the treaty of 1894 was actually signed. Dissatisfaction in Japan with the treaty increased and the Japanese Government asked the American Government, which had not ratified the treaty, to hold it in abeyance for the time being.

Great Britain, while still holding tenaciously to the favorable commercial privileges of the Convention of 1866, as modified by the various proposed tariff revisions in the eighties, was no longer disposed to block Japanese aspirations. Indeed England may be said to have moved measurably towards the position long held by the United States that the advance of Japan in Asia would be beneficial to Western trade. British policy tended towards conciliation and towards the admission of Japan to a place in British estimation, not equal to that of Western powers, but rather coordinate with that assigned to China. Japan, as well as China, was now seen to be essential to the British opposition to Russia. Viscount Tani's predictions were already being realized. The treaty between Great Britain and Japan was signed July 16, 1894, in London. This compact, which was to take the place of all other treaties, was a compromise. While extraterritoriality was to be abolished in five years, a partially conventional tariff was retained, and Japan did not receive the right to absolute control of her coasting trade. In return for these concessions, Japan agreed to open the Empire, with the stipulation that foreigners were not to be permitted to own land. The existing perpetual leases in the foreign settlements, however, were confirmed, thus placing upon the emancipated Empire a disfiguring mark of her former captivity. A similar yet more liberal treaty with the United States was signed in Washington, November 22, 1894.

In the long diplomatic struggle thus brought to an end we may note the following summary conclusions:

Japan had won a notable victory not merely in opening the way for the definite abrogation of extraterritoriality but also in the establishment of the beginnings of a cordial understanding with Great Britain. Japan had placed herself, potentially, above China at the very moment when China was relying on England to help her in Korea.

Great Britain, as we view the situation in the light of subsequent history, had won an even greater diplomatic victory for she had been able to transfer herself from a position of hostility to Japan to one of growing friendliness and good feeling, and this without more than a partial sacrifice of the commercial advantages of the old tariff of 1866. Japan was so filled with gratitude for the removal of British opposition that her people were inclined to overlook the fact that it was the American Government which had forced Great Britain into treaty revision. The good will which had formerly been directed towards the Americans was now turned towards the English.

The United States, having discarded all diplomacy and finesse in the abrogation of the cooperative policy and the ready concession to Japan of what were her legitimate demands, had received little material benefit. Indeed, it appears that Japan and the United States were now approaching the parting of the ways. The Japanese Government had successfully entered European politics and the United States, in the second Cleveland administration, had lapsed into almost complete political isolation. Meanwhile the question of Japanese immigration to the Pacific Coast had already appeared as a factor to disturb perfect harmony between the two powers. With the revision of the treaties and the action of the United States in the Sino-Japanese War we may say that the first chapter in the relations between Japan and the United States came to a close. There was no rupture, good feeling continued, but Japan had discovered that while it was necessary for national safety to give less and less attention to America, the other Western powers demanded a great deal of attention; if not made the friends of Japanese expansion, they would become its insuperable obstacles.

BIBLIOGRAPHICAL NOTES

1. "Men and Memories," by John Russell Young, Vol. 2, p. 322.
2. Charles Denby: "China and Her People," Vol. 2, pp. 151, 162.
3. J. Barr Robertson: "The Convention of Peking," reprinted from the North China *Herald*, June 2, 1870.
4. Morse: Vol. 2, p. 158.
5. Morse: Vol. 2, chaps. 6 and 7 give an excellent review in detail of the course of treaty revision in China.
6. Japan Disp., Vol. 17, Jan. 19, 1871, De Long to Fish.
7. Charles Lanman: "The Japanese in America" (1872) p. 37. This book by the American Secretary of the Japanese Legation in Washington gives many interesting details of the Iwakura Embassy.
8. Stead: "Japan by the Japanese," p. 156. To the student this essay by Nagao Arega, Japanese legal delegate at the first Hague Peace Conference, on Japanese diplomacy is highly recommended. It has the advantage of having been prepared by one who had access to many authentic sources of information. The sections on treaty revision are especially valuable. See also Count Aoki's review of treaty revision history before lower House of Diet Dec., 1890. Reprinted in Japan *Daily Mail* Dec. 19, 1890.
9. The Marshall letter to Lord Derby was never published.
10. Stead: p. 175.
11. For. Relations, 1874, p. 645.
12. E. H. House: "The Thraldom of Japan," *Atlantic Monthly*, Nov. 1887, pp. 731-2.
13. For. Relations, 1874, pp. 637, 645, 653, 663, 773, 779; 1878, p. 486; 1879, pp. 604 ff.; 1876, pp. 363, 367; 1878, p. 514.
14. Payson J. Treat: "Japan and the United States, 1853-1921"; pp. 119 ff. give a good review of the American policy.
15. John W. Foster: "Diplomatic Memoirs," Vol. 1, pp. 5 ff.
16. Judge Bingham arrived in Japan Sept. 25, 1873. His first dispatch urging treaty revision was dated Jan. 17, 1874. Japan Desp., Vol. 27, Jan. 17, 1874.
17. For. Relations, 1874, p. 675, Apr. 20; p. 698, Aug. 26.
18. There is a documentary record of these interesting negotiations in Notes from the Japanese Legation, Vol. 2, beginning Apr.

24, 1876, Dept. of State. See also Stead, p. 205 ff. for the statement of policy being pursued by Japan.

19. Japan Inst., Vol. 2.
20. Seward's "Travels Around the World," p. 200.
21. E. H. House: "The Martyrdom of an Empire," *Atlantic Monthly*. Jan.-June, 1881, Vol. XLVII, p. 621.
22. Moore's "Digest," Vol. 5, p. 753.
23. Allen: "Chronological Index of Korea."
24. Reports on Korea from the British Minister in Japan. Japan, 1883, (C. 3455) Japan, 1884 (C. 4044).
25. Stead: p. 206.
26. Stead: p. 207.
27. Richardson's Messages, Vol. 8, p. 175.
28. Richardson's Messages, Vol. 8, p. 402.
29. Chinese *Times* (Tientsin), Nov., 1887.
30. Stead: p. 208.
31. Stead: p. 208, refers to the "Tani Memorial," W. W. McLaren in *Transactions of the Asiatic Society of Japan,* Vol. XLII, Part I, gives what appear to be extracts from the Tani Memorial, but does not include the parts I here quote.
32. Stead: p. 211, gives a synopsis of the treaty with Germany.
33. *Ibid.*

PART VI

THE DISINTEGRATION OF THE CHINESE EMPIRE

CHAPTER XXVIII

ASIATIC IMMIGRATION AND AMERICAN FOREIGN POLICY

ASIATIC immigration in the United States viewed historically is much more than a domestic question; it has exercised a marked influence on foreign policy. We have seen in preceding chapters how in the last quarter of the nineteenth century the American Government steadily supported Japanese aspirations. We have also noted that in the conflict between China and Japan the United States, while maintaining technical neutrality, showed a tendency towards courses which were distinctly favorable to Japan. A partial explanation for this is found in a study of the Asiatic immigration question.*

The immigration problem on the Pacific Coast in the nineteenth century was compounded of three conflicts· It was economic; a struggle between working men who sought to maintain high wages and employers who desired cheap labor. It was social; a color conflict in which issues broadly similar to those of the negro question appeared in the West. It .was also political; a contest between the Democratic and Republican parties to win the support of a doubtful bloc of independent voters in the course of several hotly contested state and national elections.[1]

THE COOLIE TRAFFIC

Swift clipper ships carried across the Pacific the news of the gold-strike and of the demand at San Francisco for food-stuffs, building materials, and also for cheap labor. About the same time, in some instances even earlier, Aus-

* Another phase of the subject is discussed in Chapter XXIX, The Missionaries and American Policy in Asia.

tralia, Panama, Chili, Demarara, Cuba and other West
Indian ports began to ask for Chinese laborers. Vessels of
all nations were drawn into the transportation of laborers to
these various destinations. Competition became very keen
and abuses appeared which aroused the attention of the
civilized world. The infamous 'coolie trade' was in full
swing by 1854. This traffic, which must be distinguished
from Chinese immigration to California, employed some
American vessels.*

The evils of the coolie trade in general were as follows:
As the demand for laborers increased, artificial methods for
stimulating recruiting were employed and large numbers of
ignorant men were decoyed either to 'barracoons' at Macao
or directly to the vessels where they were detained by force
and became practically slaves. They were crowded into
ships which were sometimes not even sea-worthy, and supplied with insufficient food and water; the mortality en
route was very high, ranging in the case of vessels entering
Havana in 1857 from 9¾ per cent for American vessels to
38¼ per cent for Portuguese. At their destination the
laborers were often transferred to contractors who sold them
like slaves. They were miserably treated and subjected to
all the customary evils of the contract labor system so that
at the expiration of the term of the contract they were
unable to return to China. Although the government was
apathetic, the scandals in connection with the enlistment
of the laborers in China aroused the gentry and added to the
anti-foreign sentiment among the Chinese so that a general
uprising against foreigners was threatened at various southern ports. Great Britain took action in 1855 in the so-called
British Passengers Act which carefully regulated the trade
from Hongkong, subjecting it to close inspection and forbidding British vessels to carry contract laborers to other
than British ports. Other governments were slower to act.
The trade at the South China ports was transferred to

*At Swatow in 1855, out of a total of twelve vessels carrying 6388 coolies,
five were American; they took out 3050. The Hongkong returns for the
coolie trade for 1857 showed that out of a total of 70 vessels employed, 22
were American. In the same year 9 of the 63 vessels bringing coolies to
Havana were American.²

Macao where government officials were very indulgent, or to other ports where the control of neither the Chinese nor the treaty powers was effective, and American vessels continued to share in the opprobrious trade until 1862 when they were prohibited by act of Congress. Meanwhile the American representatives in China without the support of legislation made vain efforts to check the evils of the traffic.[3] Reputable firms withdrew entirely from the trade but individuals brought much disgrace upon the American flag and added to the anti-foreign sentiment in China.

CHINESE LABOR IN CALIFORNIA

The immigrants to California do not appear to have been, at the outset, very different in character from those to other regions. The passage to San Francisco cost about $50. This money was usually supplied by some capitalist, native or foreign. The laborer engaged himself either in China or California by contract to work for a period of years at a stipulated wage. The contracts were transferable. The Chinese usually entered into the contracts freely, no doubt, yet at their destination they did not become absolutely free laborers.[*]

In later years the management of these Chinese immigrants fell into the hands of large Chinese companies and

*Specimen of a contract: "Chin Suy to serve for ————— on whose account Bryson makes this agreement, or for any party who ————— may appoint to control his affairs, as shepherd, laborer, or in whatever capacity may be required, in the State of California, for a term of 5 years; and the said Chin Suy hereby states his readiness to obey in every respect any orders and directions which he may at any time receive either from ————— or from any party nominated by —————, or Bryson, to manage his affairs.

"And Bryson hereby agrees on the part of said ————— that Chin Suy shall receive wages at the rate of $35 per month, which shall be paid him at the close of each quarter; and that payment of wages to Chin Suy at this rate shall commence from the beginning of his service in the said state; Bryson also undertakes to provide Chin Suy with a good sleeping place and with food equal in quality to such as is ordinarily eaten by workmen in China; Chin Suy also agrees to repay by means of four equal quarterly instalments, to be deducted from his wages, the sum of $6 which has been advanced to him by Bryson, or by the party on whose account Bryson makes the agreement; and as words alone furnish no proof of the above agreement having been duly contracted, this Deed has been executed in duplicate, each of the contracting parties keeping a copy."

It will easily be seen that such a contract afforded wide latitude for abuses in the enlistment in China, on the voyage, and in California.[4] While this contract, which was used in 1852, may not be typical, it is illustrative of the method by which the trade had to be financed owing to the poverty of the laborers.

they applied a system of financing and handling of labor which, while customary and entirely acceptable in China, seemed very mysterious and un-American in California. The laborers were consigned to some Chinese company in San Francisco and upon arrival went to work, usually at some task assigned to them by the company, to pay off the debt which had been incurred for transportation. Much has been written in defense of the system to prove that these laborers were not 'coolies' such as were shipped to other countries, and that they were not slaves. One may accept this conclusion, admitting that the Chinese who came to California were superior, and were eager to come, and yet not reach the further conclusion that they were free. That some of them were free seems altogether probable, but so secretive and so impenetrable were the methods of Chinese trade relationships it was rarely possible to distinguish with certainty between the free and the contract laborer.[5]

At first the Chinese in California were welcomed by everyone, but as soon as the rush for gold subsided and ordered industrial communities developed, in which there was increasing unemployment among disappointed white gold-seekers, the Chinese, in company with all non-white laborers, became unpopular. They were the objects of attack not merely because they were cheap laborers but also because they were not Caucasians. It is estimated that about one third of the white population of California between 1850 and 1860 were from the southern states. There was also a large influx of European immigrants, mainly English and Irish. The number of Chinese on the Pacific Coast rose rapidly to about 25,000 in 1852, and 50,000 in 1867. The next year there were large importations of coolies to work on the Pacific railroads and in 1869, out of a total of 10,000 railroad laborers, nine tenths of them were Chinese. By 1875 the number of Chinese on the Pacific Coast, notwithstanding the large numbers who had returned to China, had risen to 100,000, and in 1882 there were 132,000 of whom nearly 40,000 had entered in that year.[6]

Various repressive measures were undertaken by the

Pacific Coast states to restrict this increase. The Chinese were from the outset denied citizenship, and after 1852 they were subjected to discriminating taxes. Between 1850 and 1870 one half of the total California state revenues were derived from the miners' licenses which were paid very largely by the Chinese. They were at the same time subjected to an increasing amount of abuse, injustice, intimidation and assault from the white residents, particularly in the cities where the unemployed gathered in large numbers. Without offering any justification for this treatment which was brutal and appalling, it is evident from the figures that California was actually engaged in a very elemental conflict for race supremacy. South China had a superabundant population; California was sparsely settled and yielded large returns not merely in its mines but in its agriculture to the plodding, indefatigable labor of the Oriental. If natural laws were permitted, unchecked, to assert themselves it was only a question of time when the Chinese with lower standards of living and lower wage standards, would be able to displace the whites. The condition in the southern states after the emancipation of the slaves was ever before the citizens of California, so many of whom had come from the South. On the other hand many employers, looking to the immediate returns, welcomed the cheap labor.

TREATIES OF 1868 AND 1880

William H. Seward, as was consistent with his convictions as a trade expansionist, was a cheap-labor man. So far as he had any views on the subject Anson Burlingame, coming from New England where the problem of cheap labor was being solved by European immigration, was of similar persuasion. The Burlingame treaty of 1868, which has already been discussed as to its foreign policy, was a cheap-labor treaty. Indeed the mystery of why it was thought necessary to write a treaty for the expression of what Lord Clarendon put far more tersely in a letter to Burlingame is explained when we come to study the immigration clauses of the Burlingame treaty. It would appear that Seward, who wrote the document, was as much interested in the labor problem as he was in the extension of American trade across the Pacific. At the moment he was particularly concerned about the delays in the completion of the Pacific railroad due to the inability of the contractors to secure labor. Chinese coolies offered a solution of the problem, but the supply was imperilled at two points. There was a growing hostility in California, and while the Chinese Government was apathetic, the departure of Chinese from the Empire was actually a violation of ancient Chinese law. The treaty was intended at once to regularize the Chinese immigration at its source, and to protect it in the United States.*

The text of the famous declaration (Article 5) which a subsequent American minister [8] to Peking declared to be 'buncombe' was:

"The United States of America and the Emperor of China cordially recognize the inherent and inalienable right of man to change his home and allegiance, and also the mutual advantage of the free migration and emigration of their citizens and subjects respectively from one country to the other for purposes of curiosity, of trade, or as permanent residents."

The treaty, which was bi-lateral, guaranteed to Chinese subjects "visiting or residing in the United States   . the same privileges, immunities, and exemptions in respect to travel or residence as may there be enjoyed by the citizens or subjects of the most favored nation." Nevertheless the right of naturalization was reserved; that is, it was not obligatory upon a state. The privilege of the Chinese Government to appoint consuls at American ports was stipulated. Other articles prohibited contract laborers and safeguarded the Chinese in America, as well as the Americans in China, in the exercise of religious freedom.

* "The treaty concluded with the United States recognizes broadly the right of China to the jurisdiction of its own affairs and offers substantial protection to the Chinese in California. It was this latter consideration which led to the adopting of the more solemn form of a treaty in the United States. A treaty being the supreme law of the land overrides the obnoxious local legislation against the Chinese immigrants." (Burlingame to Bismarck, written in Berlin, January 4, 1870.[7])

"If I have been rightly informed by those who ought to know, that treaty was made, not at the request of Mr. Burlingame or of the Chinese Government, but at the request of Secretary Seward." (Pres. James B. Angell, in the *Journal of Social Science*, May, 1883.)

California in 1868 was still attempting to control the Chinese immigration by means of state legislation, and the Burlingame treaty was ratified by the Senate without opposition from labor interests and to the general satisfaction of employers. But that year, a presidential year, the Democratic party in the state raised an anti-Chinese issue and elected a Democratic governor. From that time onward the immigration question became the football of politics, state and nation.[9] The number of Chinese steadily though not rapidly increased. Meanwhile various state laws directed against the Chinese were found to be unconstitutional. Oregon and Nevada became interested in the matter. The political parties in California were evenly balanced and while the Republican party, the party of Seward and Burlingame, had generally favored Chinese immigration it was now seen that to continue that support was to lose the vote in doubtful states. The Chinese question was revived again in 1876, and was fanned to a blaze in the summer of 1877 in the sand-lot meetings under the infamous appeals of Dennis Kearney. In the Constitutional Convention of 1878-9 the legislature was empowered to pass legislation prohibiting corporations from employing any Mongolian and was authorized to remove the Chinese from the state. A Republican legislature, now standing in fear of the labor vote, passed a law making it a misdemeanor for any corporation to employ a Chinese. This law was declared in a federal court to be in conflict with the Burlingame treaty.

In March, 1876, the Republican State Committee of California had passed a resolution requesting the President to enter into negotiations for a modification of the treaty of 1868, and two months later Senator A. A. Sargent introduced in Congress a bill to that effect. Instead, a Congressional investigation was ordered.[10] Owing to the illness of Senator Oliver P. Morton, chairman of the committee, and the withdrawal of members from New York and Massachusetts, the investigation was conducted before a commission made up of two Californians and one member from Tennessee. As a result of this investigation, which was devoid of all judicial character, Congress passed in 1879 the Fifteen Passenger Bill which would have limited the number of Chinese immigrants to be brought in any one vessel to fifteen. President Hayes vetoed the bill but immediately instituted a commission to proceed to China to secure either modifications of the existing treaty or a new one. The commission consisted of one Californian, John T. Swift, subsequently minister at Tokio, one southerner, W. H. Trescott of South Carolina, and President James B. Angell of the University of Michigan, who was also to be United States Minister at Peking, succeeding George F. Seward.

The commission was Republican. There was a presidential election approaching in November, 1880, and both parties had recorded themselves in their platforms as opposed to Chinese immigration. The commission arrived in China at a time when the government was particularly well disposed towards the United States because of the popularity attained by General Grant the previous year. China was greatly embarrassed by Russia over the unsettled Kuldja dispute and was contending unsuccessfully with the treaty powers for the right to increase the tariff duties. The agitation against the opium trade had been renewed and was at its point of greatest earnestness since 1838. It was a fortunate time for the Americans to bring up the immigration question. The commission asked for a revision of the treaty which would grant to the United States the right, at its discretion, not merely to regulate, limit or suspend, but also to prohibit the immigration of Chinese laborers. The Chinese Government, never greatly interested in the welfare of its subjects away from home, and for the last thirty years desperately occupied with internal questions and foreign aggressions within the empire, had never been disposed to make the treatment of Chinese abroad a subject of persistent protest, although it had not passed unnoticed. But now well informed by its diplomatic representatives in Washington of the political aspects of the trouble, and greatly encouraged by Americans who sympathized with the Chinese, the Yamen asserted itself and absolutely refused to yield the right to the American Government to prohibit the immigration. The demands of the Americans had aroused the pride of a very proud race.

The treaty which was signed November 17, 1880, was a compromise reflecting the moderating influence of President Angell, and also the fact that the presidential election, already passed, had recorded a Republican victory. To the United States was given the right to "regulate, limit or suspend" but not to prohibit the coming of Chinese laborers "whenever in the opinion of the Government of the United States, the coming of Chinese laborers to the United States, or the residence therein, affects or threatens to affect the interests of that country or of any locality within the territory thereof." Laborers already in the United States were secured in the right of most-favored-nation treatment, and "Chinese subjects, whether proceeding to the United States as teachers, students, merchants, or from curiosity" were to have equal privileges.[11] Concurrently, a treaty of commercial intercourse was negotiated in which Americans were excluded from the opium trade by a very stringent agreement. The Chinese were very much pleased with this clause "their object being, if possible," to use the words of President Angell's report, "to isolate the British Government on this question from the other Christian powers, and to compel that Government to take the odium of forcing this wicked and demoralizing traffic for the avowed purpose of financial advantage." [12] While not breaking so abruptly with the cooperative policy as in Japan, the United States thus indicated a preference for independent action in treaty revision. The commission had succeeded in handling delicate subjects successfully, and relations between the two governments remained friendly.

GROWTH OF ILL FEELING

The Pacific Coast states were not at all content with the stipulations of the treaty of 1880. They were demanding absolute exclusion. As a compromise with this extreme demand Congress passed a law, May 6, 1882, suspending the immigration of Chinese laborers for ten years, and defining the word laborer to include both skilled and unskilled workers, as well as those engaged in mining. To prevent fraud in the readmission of laborers who returned to America after a visit in China a system of customs-house registry and certificates was devised. The certificates were to be issued to all departing Chinese, with the exception of diplomatic officers.[13] The bill was passed only after President Arthur had already vetoed one providing for suspension of immigration for twenty years, but even ten years was twice as long, according to President Angell, as any period mentioned in the negotiations at Peking in 1880. The new law also prohibited any state from granting citizenship to Chinese. Two years later, just before a presidential campaign (July 5, 1884), the law was amended by making the system of identification more exact, and by the addition of a new definition of laborers which would also exclude hucksters, peddlers, or those engaged in taking, drying or otherwise preserving shell or other fish either for home consumption or for exportation. The certificates issued to returning Chinese laborers must now be viséd before departure from China by an American diplomatic or consular officer.[14] The consular service, upon which this new duty was imposed, was not strengthened to meet the responsibility, and was not prepared to comply with the law either effectively or honestly.[15] Thus in less than four years after the negotia tion of the treaty the United States, as even President Arthur stated, had clearly departed from the spirit, if not from its letter as the Chinese Government understood it.[16] The serious disturbance of friendly relations between the two governments may be said to date from this time.

The Chinese immigration question appeared as a factor in national politics at the very moment when the American Government was formulating a Korean policy. While Congress was passing the restriction law, Commodore Shufeldt was waiting at Tientsin for a reply to his telegram inquiring whether he should admit a recognition of Chinese suzerainty over Korea in the text of his proposed treaty. Another disturbing factor in the situation had been the sudden recall, the previous year, of all of the Chinese students who had been sent to America.* While it is difficult to trace with exactness the influence of the growing unpopularity and distrust of the Chinese on American policy in Korea, the fact stands out that for the next decade the Chinese were steadily losing popularity in the United States while their rivals, the Japanese, with whom the Americans had very few direct or personal contacts, were in equal measure winning confidence and approval.

The letter of Commodore Shufeldt to Senator A. A. Sargent, already alluded to, while important only because of the fact that it was written by a diplomatic officer of the government, may be cited as an indication of the growing American distrust of the Chinese.

It is not possible to show from the diplomatic records that the treatment of the Chinese in the United States caused the Chinese Government to adopt a particularly unfriendly policy towards Americans in China, although officials like Prince Kung and Li Hung Chang bitterly resented the treatment. The Chinese Government was generally anti-foreign and as between the persecution of Chinese in the United States which was remote, and the opium trade, the aggressions of France, and the general arrogance of the foreigner which was ever before the eyes of the Chinese, the Americans escaped adverse discriminatory action. It is, rather, in Washington to which the perfection of communi-

*Beginning in 1872 China had sent several companies of boys, in all more than one hundred, to be placed in American schools and colleges. The ages ranged from eight to sixteen. Various explanations—lack of funds for their support, resentment at the growing anti-Chinese feeling in America, and the growth of reactionary sentiment in China—were offered for the recall of these students. One of the students who subsequently rose to eminence in Chinese affairs, Tong Shao-yi, told the writer personally that the real cause was the fear that the boys were becoming too much Americanized. They had even petitioned their Chinese tutor for permission to cut off their queues. The tutor, himself a very conservative Chinese scholar, reported this to Peking and an order for their recall was immediately issued. The contrast thus presented between the Japanese who had gone so far as to adopt Western dress, and the Chinese who declined to permit the boys to remove their queues, is striking. There were in the United States at that time a large number of Japanese students, but they were usually of a much more mature age than the Chinese. The fundamental difficulty with the Chinese students was that they were sent away from home too young, even before they had attained a moderate mastery of their own difficult language. Whatever the cause, the withdrawal of the students made a bad impression in the United States.[17]

cations had largely transferred the direction of American policy, that we may study the influence of the anti-Chinese prejudices. Between 1885 and 1894 public opinion was being prepared for the choice between China and Japan which was presented at the outbreak of the Sino-Japanese War. During this period the Chinese representatives found abundant causes for creating many embarrassments to the Department of State. The causes were conspicuously just, but it may be questioned whether the Chinese Government would not have been more astute, in view of the graver issues in the East, in adopting a more conciliatory policy in Washington.

The inauguration of the first Cleveland administration was inauspicious for the Chinese in the United States. There had been riots at Rock Springs, Wyoming, and also at Tacoma and Seattle in which Chinese had been killed or injured. China, accustomed to prompt demands from the treaty powers for indemnity for similar events in China, now found some satisfaction in making equally prompt demands for indemnity from the American Government. President Cleveland recognized the moral obligation of the claim and made it the subject of two messages to Congress in 1886, but Congress granted it reluctantly and with poor grace after much delay. California called a state convention and addressed a memorial to Congress demanding absolute prohibition of Chinese immigration, the elimination of Chinese labor from all public works, and the boycott of all employers of Chinese labor. Then the Tsung-li Yamen proposed to Minister Denby in Peking, and Secretary of State Bayard suggested to the Chinese minister in Washington, on the same day (January 12, 1887), that a new treaty be negotiated. Bayard desired the exclusion of the Chinese laborers for thirty years; the minister declined to discuss the proposition while the claims for indemnity remained unsatisfied. However, a new treaty was signed fourteen months later (March 12, 1888), in another presidential year, which stipulated for prohibition for twenty years, and for payment of indemnity to the extent of $276,619.75. In executive session the Senate amended the treaty by the insertion of provisions which would shut out at least 20,000 Chinese who were residents of the United States but then visiting in China. On September 13, 1888, Congress enacted a law to make effective the pending treaty as soon as the treaty should be ratified.[18]

Ten days later a press report from London contained the rumor that the Chinese Government would not ratify the pending treaty. Those were the closing days of the presidential campaign in which President Cleveland was seeking reelection. In spite of the official information that China was merely reserving the treaty for further deliberation, Congress passed (October 1, 1888) the Scott Act which absolutely prohibited the return of all Chinese laborers who had gone to China for a visit,[19] even though they held certificates already issued by the customs houses. The bill was signed by President Cleveland on the ground that China had not properly cooperated with the United States in the immigration question.[20] China immediately entered a protest at the extraordinary action, and July 8, 1889, the Chinese Minister in Washington addressed an exhaustive argument to the Department of State in which he stated, tartly, that he had yet to learn that it was customary for governments to act on the strength of mere newspaper reports. "So far as the legation knows," he wrote, "the treaty is still pending, and awaiting the reply of the State Department to the amendments proposed in the legation note of September twenty-fifth last."

"I was not prepared to learn . . . that there was a way recognized in the law and practice of this country whereby your country could release itself from treaty obligations without consultation or the consent of the other party; it can hardly be contended that my government was exceeding diplomatic practice or courtesy in following the example of the Senate and proposing amendments.   "[21]

During the Harrison administration a condition amounting practically to non-intercourse existed between the Chinese legation and the Department of State. The American Government was in a position, notwithstanding its

legality as sustained by the Supreme Court, utterly inde-
fensible from the viewpoint of diplomacy. The conduct of
Lord Elgin at Tientsin and Peking, of Sir Harry Parkes in
Tokio, and of the French minister at Shanghai in 1883 was
not more brutal and bullying than that of the American
Government after 1888. The only important difference was
that the American Government had done wrongly what it
had a perfect right to do if other measures had been employed, viz., regulate its own immigration questions, while
the powers in China had done what they had no moral right
to do under any conditions. All parties had degraded the
principles of international law. It is becoming for Americans in criticizing the actions of other governments in Asia
to be humble if not charitable.*

The original restriction act of 1882, as amended two years
later, presumably did not expire until 1894 but,in 1892, with
another presidential election approaching, Congress again
took up the immigration question and enacted (May 5,
1892) the Geary law, the most stringent exclusion act yet
passed.[23] According to this law no bail was to be permitted
in *habeas corpus* proceedings, and the burden of proof that
a Chinese had the right to be in the United States was
placed upon the Chinese himself. In other words he was
presumed to be guilty of illegal residence until he could
prove himself innocent. The punishment for violation of
the law was hard labor for one year and then deportation.
Later (November 3, 1893) the definition of the word laborer
was enlarged to include certain other classes such as laun-
drymen. Under the amendment the certificate which each
laborer was required to secure as proof of his right to be in
the country must bear his photograph. In other respects
the rigor of the Geary law was somewhat modified.[24] The

---

*The resentment of the Chinese Government at the treatment of the immi-
gration question by the United States is shown in the refusal to accept Senator
Henry W. Blair of New Hampshire as minister in 1891. Blair had been so
unfortunate as to make remarks in the Senate in connection with both the
restriction act of 1882 and the acts of 1888 which rendered him *persona non
grata* to the Chinese.[22] The rejection of Blair by China accounts in part for
the fact that Charles Denby, who had been a Cleveland appointee in 1885,
continued as minister at Peking throughout the Harrison (Republican) administration. Denby was reappointed in the second Cleveland administration and
continued under McKinley until 1898.

following year (March 17, 1894) a new immigration treaty with China was signed in which the prohibition of the admission of Chinese laborers for ten years was agreed to. The exempt classes of Chinese—teachers, students, merchants, travelers and officials—were carefully defined, and transit across the country was permitted. The Chinese legally resident in the United States were guaranteed most-favored-nation treatment. The stipulation requiring regis tration was made bi-lateral, applying equally to Americans resident in China.

Clearly the American Government, after all its em barrassments in dealing with China on the immigration question, was not in any mood at the outbreak of the Sino-Japanese War to become in any marked degree a partisan of China. Scrupulous neutrality it did maintain, but the American people, who knew much by hearsay of the Chinese in America, and nothing of the Far Eastern question, were not disposed to favor an extension of Chinese influence in the Korean peninsula, or anywhere else.

The Threat of Japanese Immigration

The Japanese immigration question also exercised some influence upon American policy in Asia, though in a very different way.

Although tenaciously holding to the assertion of her rights,* the Japanese Government was very careful to avoid any clash with the American Government over the immigration question during the period of treaty revision. John T. Swift of California, who had been very active in the anti-Chinese agitation in the United States, succeeded Richard B. Hubbard of Texas as American minister at Tokio in May, 1889. Following the death of Mr. Swift at his post in March, 1891, Frank L. Coombs, also of California, was made minister for the remainder of the Harrison administration.

---

*The Japanese treaty with Peru, 1873 (Art. 7), contained a stipulation to the effect that no restriction be placed by either government on immigrant laborers in any lawful capacity and that they might go freely from one country to the other.

Thus, at the time when the Japanese immigration question was first arising, the United States was represented in Japan by men especially alert to note its possible dangers.

Swift warned his government that the treaty of 1889, negotiated by Hubbard and awaiting ratification by both governments, contained a bi-lateral immigration clause such as had already been agreed to in the Japan-Mexico treaty, which would open the United States to Japanese immigration as the Burlingame treaty had opened the country to the Chinese. For this reason the American Government was relieved of some embarrassments when Japan formally requested that the ratification of the treaty be held in abeyance. Such a provision could not have secured the approval of the Senate in 1890. Coombs, shortly after his arrival in Japan, had a conference with Viscount Enomoto who promised to bring about a satisfactory regulation of Japanese immigrants by Japan. On August 22, 1892, the Minister of Foreign Affairs issued instructions to the governor of prefectures, requiring them to discourage immigration to the United States.

"It would be needless to call your attention to the fact," he wrote, "that the most cordial and friendly relations have been happily existing between Japan and the United States; besides, our commercial interests in the United States are becoming more and more important; and these relations we cannot permit to be disturbed on account of such a minor question as labor immigration."

A month later the Minister of Foreign Affairs instructed the Japanese consul general at Honolulu to endeavor to dissuade Japanese from going to the Pacific Coast. That it was the policy of the Japanese Government to discourage undesired labor emigration was confirmed (October, 1893) by Vice Minister of Foreign Affairs Hayashi to U. S. Minister Edwin Dun.

In the treaty of 1894 between the United States and Japan the following paragraph was inserted to take care of the immigration question, as well as to safeguard Japan in her policy of withholding the right of foreigners to purchase land in Japan:

"It is, however, understood that the stipulations contained in this and the preceding article (relating to liberty of trade, residence, leasing of land, ownership of property, etc.) do not in any way effect the laws, ordinances and regulations with regard to trade, the immigration of laborers, police and public security, which are in force or which may hereafter be enacted in either of the two countries." *

Thus far the only effect of the immigration question had been to deter the United States from being the first of the great powers to ratify the revised treaty which Japan had proposed in 1888. Great Britain was awarded the credit, which more properly belonged to the United States by virtue of its consistent record on treaty revisions ever since 1878, for being the first to relieve Japan of the onerous extraterritorial stipulations.

The Japanese immigration question was, however, exerting a more positive effect on American policy in another direction. The planters of the Hawaiian Islands, gravely handicapped by lack of willing labor, had encouraged the immigration of both Chinese and Japanese coolies. The treaty of 1871 with Japan had been followed by a second convention (March 6, 1886) by which it was agreed that the Japanese Government would furnish laborers, as requested, for Hawaii, on thirty days notice. There were in 1890 slightly more than 12,000 Japanese in the Sandwich Islands, out of a total population of about 90,000. There were also 15,000 Chinese.[25] In November, 1893, at the time of the revolution in the islands, after the rejection of the American annexation treaty, the Japanese Government sent a war vessel to Honolulu to protect Japanese subjects.

After the withdrawal from the Senate of the Hawaiian annexation treaty by President Cleveland (March 9, 1893), the Japanese Government assumed a more positive tone towards the newly established Hawaiian Republic. Japan demanded that the Japanese immigrants to Hawaii be given the same rights as the native Hawaiians which included the

*"We strongly objected to this clause which America tacked on to Article 2 but our objections were of no avail. Mr. Griscom [Gresham], the American Secretary of State, absolutely refused to agree to revise the treaty at all unless the clause was admitted. We were loath to agree, but did so because the revision of the English treaty was problematical on account of the probationary clause, and it was necessary to make a start." (Secret Memoirs of Count Hayashi, p. 248.)

rights of citizenship and office-holding from which they had always been excluded.* Japan based this demand upon the most-favored-nation clause in her original treaty with Hawaii in 1873, and a treaty between Spain and Hawaii (1863) in which the Spanish had been granted the same rights and privileges as those enjoyed by the Hawaiians. The disposition of the Hawaiian Republic was to restrict all oriental immigration, but to this the Japanese Government made firm objections and in 1897 went so far as to send a war vessel to Honolulu with a demand for free immigration. Meanwhile the Republic had been unsuccessful in limiting the immigration by means of a restrictive legislation and at length arrested 1100 newly arrived Japanese with a view of deporting them.

The majority report on the joint resolution for the annexation of Hawaii presented to the House May 17, 1898, stated that this "rapid growth of Japanese element" was "a most threatening fact" in the existing Hawaiian situation for if the Japanese demands for citizenship were granted the Japanese voters (there were reported to be 24,000 Japanese in the islands at the time, 19,000 of them men) would control the government and would be able to effect a revision or abrogation of the reciprocity treaty of 1887 by which Pearl Harbor had been granted to the exclusive use of the United States as a naval base. This argument carried much weight in the debate both in the House and in the Senate. Senator George Frisbie Hoar, who only a few months later desperately opposed the annexation of the Philippines, voted for the annexation of the Hawaiian Islands and rested his argument for their acquisition in no small measure upon the menace of Japanese control of the islands. Senator Hoar stated: "They [the islands] will fall, Mr. President, if we do not prevent it, a prey to Japan, not by conquest but by immigration. This result all parties agree that we must prevent. Japan is not, according to the opponents of annexa-

*The constitution of Hawaii, promulgated July 7, 1887, had limited citizenship and office-holding to Hawaiians and to those of either American or European parentage. The Americans and Europeans were not required to forswear their original citizenship.[26]

tion of this body and of the press, to be allowed to get the Sandwich Islands either by force or by absorption. . The danger is, as I have said, that there will be an infusion of Japanese and then an attempted annexation to Japan." Senator Hoar urged that the possession of the islands must either be settled then peaceably by annexation or later by force in a conflict between America and Asia.

BIBLIOGRAPHICAL NOTES

1. The following general sources of information on Chinese immigration are recommended: J. W. Foster: "American Diplomacy in the Orient," chap. 8,—valuable because the author was intimately associated in public life and in the service of the Chinese Government with the later phases of the subject; Charles Denby: "China and Her People," Vol. 2, chap. 9—Denby was the American minister in Peking, 1885-98; Alleyne Ireland: "China and the Powers" (privately printed, 1902), chap. 3 contains concise summary; Mary Roberts Coolidge: "Chinese Immigration"—Dr. Coolidge gave to the domestic phases of the subject most exhaustive study, and yet the author was so carried away by the injustices dealt to the Chinese as to fail to present adequately the fundamental issues in the conflict of races. The bibliographical notes are exceptionally valuable. The present writer has made no very extended study of Chinese immigration as a domestic question aside from the diplomatic records of the Department of State.
2. Marshall Corres., pp. 78, 84-4, 116-7, 106; Parker Corres., pp. 632, 669; Paliamentary Papers, Accounts and Papers, 43, 1857-8, Report to the House of Commons on the Coolie traffic, ordered printed July 27, 1858, p. 78.
3. Parker Corres., p. 625; Reed Corres., pp. 67-76, 78, Reed to Cass, Jan. 13, 1858, pp. 185, 204, 489.
4. S. Doc. 99:34-1, pp. 119 ff. Parker Corres. on *Robert Browne* affair.
5 Foster, p. 282, thinks the Chinese laborers in California were "perfectly free," and cites a great many authorities. None of the similar statements on this point seems to the present writer convincing.
6. Table, Coolidge, p. 498.
7. Notes from Chinese Legation, Vol. 1, Jan. 18, 1870, Burlingame to Fish.
   Denby: Vol. 2, p. 98.
8. Coolidge is particularly valuable for tracing the various stages of the party conflict on the immigration question.
10. Foster: pp. 286 ff.; S. Rept. 689:44-2; S. Misc. Doc. 20:45-2.
11. Negotiations of the Treaty Commission, For. Relations, 1881, pp. 168-203; J. B. Angell: "Diplomatic Relations of the United

States and China," *Amer. Jour. of Social Science,* Vol. 17, pp. 24 ff.); Chester Holcombe: *The Outlook,* 1904, Apr. 23, pp. 993-4.

12. China Desp., Vol. 56 Nov. 17, 1880, Angell to Blaine. This sentence is omitted in the dispatch as printed in For. Relations, 1881.
13. St. at Large, Vol. 22, pp. 58-61.
14. St. at Large, Vol. 23, pp. 115-118.
15. Denby: Vol. 2, p. 105.
16. See Pres. Arthur's opinion, Richardson's Messages, Vol. 8, p. 236.
17. Chinese Students in U. S., For. Relations, 1872, pp. 130, 135, 138; 1873, pp. 140, 186; 1875, p. 227; 1885, p. 144.
18. Statutes at Large, Vol. 25, pp. 476-479.
19. *Ibid.,* p. 504.
20. S. Ex. Doc. 273:50-1.
21. For. Relations, 1889, p. 132.
22. Pres. Harrison's Message, Apr. 4, 1892, Rejection of Henry W. Blair; For. Relations, 1892.
23. St. at Large, Vol. 27, pp. 25-6.
24. *Ibid.,* Vol. 28, pp. 7-8.
25. S. Ex. Doc. 76:52-2, Table, p. 60.
26. *Ibid.,* p. 26.

CHAPTER XXIX

THE MISSIONARIES AND AMERICAN POLICY IN ASIA

WHILE a review of the broader aspects of the influence of the American missionaries on the social and political as well as the religious life of the Asiatic states is very alluring, we must confine ourselves rigidly to a more precise subject— the influence of the missionaries on American policy. It is discussed in the following phases: the assistance of the missionaries either as themselves official representatives of the government or to those who were officials; the status assigned to the missionaries in the various treaties or obtained by special conventions and interpretations; missionaries and American neutrality; and the protection of the missionaries by the Government of the United States.[1]

MISSIONARIES AS DIPLOMATIC AND CONSULAR OFFICERS

Notwithstanding the repeated requests of the American consuls, commissioners, and ministers from 1816, onward, their government made no provision for the training of a single interpreter for a consulate or legation until 1864.[2] Throughout the century the American officials, only a very few of whom, unless they had previously been missionaries, had any accurate knowledge of either the written or spoken language of the countries to which they were assigned, were largely dependent in China, Japan and Korea upon either native interpreters, upon foreigners of other nationalities, or upon the missionaries. There were only four salaried American interpreters connected with diplomatic and consular service in China as late as 1899, according to a report of Minister Conger. Until about 1833, when Rev. E. C. Bridgman,[3] the first American to acquire the Chinese lan-

555

guage, became available at Canton, the Americans in China depended very largely upon Rev. Robert Morrison, the British missionary employed by the East India Company, or upon his son John H. Morrison for both translation and interpreting. Bridgman, in company with Rev. David Abeel,[4] arrived in 1830. They were followed by S. Wells Williams [5] (1833), a missionary printer, and Rev. Peter Parker, M. D.[6] (1834), a missionary physician. From that time onward Bridgman, Parker or Williams actually transacted the greater part of the American official business with the representatives of the Chinese Government for nearly forty years.

In 1858 United States Minister Reed, who had come to China with scant regard for missionaries, wrote to Secretary of State Cass:

" . I am bound to say further that the studies of the missionary and those connected with the missionary cause are essential to the interests of our country. Without them as interpreters the public business could not be transacted. I could not but for them have advanced one step in the discharge of my duties here, or read, or written, or understood one word of correspondence or treaty stipulations. With them there has been no difficulty or embarrassments.

"It was the case also in 1844, when Mr. Cushing's interpreters and assistants in all their public duties were all from the same class; in 1853, with Mr. Marshall, and in 1854 with Mr. McLane, Dr. Bridgman, who was the principal assistant in all these public duties, still lives in an active exercise of his usefulness; and I am glad of the opportunity of expressing to him my thanks for the incidental assistance and constant and most valuable counsel. . . .

"There is not an American merchant in China (and I have heard of but one English) who can write or read a single sentence of Chinese." [7]

The condition described by Mr. Reed continued, and for the remainder of the century, except for the briefest intervals, there were some American missionaries employed either in important posts in the consulates or in the legation in China, and it was these men rather than their titular superiors who, in most cases, had the actual contacts with the Chinese officials. A similar condition existed in Siam as well as in Korea. Chester Holcombe, formerly a missionary and then secretary and *Chargé* in the legation at Peking, did at least half the work in the negotiation of the Shufeldt treaty with Li Hung Chang; and Dr. H. N. Allen, the first American missionary in Korea, and subsequently secretary of the Korean legation and then American minister at Seoul, carried the brunt of the diplomatic correspondence between Korea and the United States. Indeed at least one instance is known where an American minister, nameless in this record, lay hopelessly intoxicated in his legation while the missionaries not only ministered to his physical needs but even wrote the dispatches to the Department of State at a very critical moment in political affairs.

Due to the fact that the Dutch language was the *lingua franca* in Japan and that the Japanese very quickly acquired English the problem of interpretation was never so difficult in Japan as elsewhere in Asia. For this reason and also, perhaps, because the American Government was especially careful not to offend the anti-Christian prejudices of the Japanese inherited from the old Jesuit days, the missionaries never played a prominent part in the direct relations of the two governments.

The *Chinese Repository* [8] (1832-51), of which Bridgman and Williams were not merely the editors but to which they were often the chief contributors, is easily the most accurate and faithful chronicle which has come down to us of the period which it covers. Indeed, a close comparison of the *Repository* with the Treaty of Wanghia shows that Caleb Cushing in his negotiations in 1844 was very greatly indebted to Bridgman, not merely for his work as interpreter but also as adviser. Several of the articles of the treaty appear to have grown directly out of discussions which had preceded them in the *Repository*.

On Cushing's departure Dr. Parker immediately entered upon a distinguished service as unofficial and then official interpreter and secretary to the legation. This service must not be overlooked in an appraisal of his less valuable services as Commissioner (1855-7). Until 1854 the consulates at Amoy and Ningpo, when they were cared for at all, were for the most part in charge of missionaries. The remarkable services of S. Wells Williams for the government began officially in 1853-4 as interpreter in the Perry expedition, and were resumed a year later when he resigned from missionary work and became secretary and interpreter in the legation, a position which he held for twenty years, becoming during the period *chargé d'affaires* no less than seven times. After 1880 the missionary became less important as an interpreter in the legation because Li Hung Chang, with whom much of the more important business was transacted, had provided himself with interpreters, among them W. H. Pethick, drawn from the American consular service, to act as his personal interpreter. Meanwhile, however, other missionaries had been drawn into the consular service and in succeeding decades rose to positions of great responsibility either in it or in the diplomatic service.

A less direct yet even broader influence on American policy in Asia came from the books published by the missionaries. Until 1847 the American public knew about China chiefly through British writers, many of whose books were republished in the United States. In that year a New York publisher brought out the first edition of Williams' "Middle Kingdom," though not until nearly every other publisher had declined the venture and the company which undertook it was guaranteed against loss by a Canton mer chant.[9] One of the objects of this monumental work was to put an end to "that peculiar and almost indefinable im pression of ridicule" which Williams thought was being be stowed upon the Chinese "as if they were the apes of Euro peans and their social state, arts and government the bur lesque of the same things in Christendom." For the next forty years or more it is not too much to say that the books written by missionaries (including those of W. E. Griffis who, while not a missionary, occupied a similar position and view-point) were practically the only American source of any adequacy or accuracy for the formation of public opinion about China, Japan and Korea. During the greater part of the nineteenth century Americans looked upon Asia through the eyes of missionaries.

The American missionary was not merely the interpreter for his countrymen; he also played a most important rôle as the interpreter of his country to the Asiatic. Bridgman published (1838) a geographical history of the United States in the Chinese language which was twice revised (1846, 1862), and exerted an influence in predisposing the Chinese Government to friendliness towards the United States.[10] The linguistic studies of the missionaries, their dictionaries and similar works, opened up the channels of communication. While the British and Continental missionaries shared in these labors, until 1858 the Americans were the leaders. With the exception of Rev. W. A. P. Martin,[11] who entered the Chinese service in 1862 as a teacher in the Tungwen College, later becoming president of the Imperial University, and Rev. D. B. McCartee, who held important posts in the Chinese diplomatic service, American missionaries did not to a great degree become employees of the Chinese Government. But in Japan and in Korea there were notable instances where missionaries like Verbeck, Allen and Hulbert occupied official positions of influence.[12] Verbeck is credited with having proposed and stimulated the organization of the Iwakura Embassy from Japan in 1872.

The Status of Missionaries under the Treaties

The legal status of the missionaries in the various countries to which they went is not always easy to define. In China, Japan and Korea the American missionary introduced himself by subterfuge which was accompanied by the tolerance and indulgence of native officials. The first missionaries in Canton in the early part of the nineteenth century were not only without legal right to be there but were in violation of imperial regulations. They were sponsored by obliging hong merchants who represented them to be clerks attached to the mercantile houses. But in 1844, due to the gratitude of one of the subordinate Chinese commissioners whose parents had been patients of Dr. Parker,

the right to erect churches at the open ports was inserted in Article 17 of the Cushing treaty, at the suggestion of the Chinese.[13]   The treaty, however, contained no stipulation conferring upon the missionaries any liberty to seek converts.   Later, through the efforts of the French envoy, the Emperor issued a rescript granting a degree of religious toleration *[14]   This rescript referred only to the "religion of the Lord of Heaven," i.e., the Roman Catholic faith.†
Kiying, without the formality of securing a second imperial rescript, followed with an order that the Imperial proclamation should apply to Protestants as well as Catholics.

To neither Catholic nor Protestant missionaries was the rescript very satisfactory.   While it legalized their work in the open ports it shut them off from the interior of the country where the Catholic missionaries had already been at work for many years.   It was estimated by Abeel that in 1830 the Roman Catholic missionaries were employing no less than four bishops and nineteen priests—French, Portuguese, Italian and Spanish—and claimed more than 200,000 converts.   These labors were by no means confined to Macao, there being missionaries even in far-away Szechuan.   After the treaties of 1844 the missionaries, Protestant and Catholic, American and European alike, quickly spread to the newly opened ports, and notwithstanding the stipulations of

---

* "Kiying, imperial commissioner, minister of state, and governor general of Kwang-tung and Kwang-si, respectfully addresses the throne by memorial.
"On examination it appears that the religion of the Lord of Heaven is that professed by all the nations of the West; that its main object is to encourage the good and suppress the wicked; that since its introduction into China during the Ming dynasty it has never been interdicted, that subsequently, when Chinese, practising this religion, often made it a covert for wickedness, even to the seducing of wives and daughters, and to the deceitful extraction of the pupils from the eyes of the sick, government made an investigation and inflicted punishment, as is on record: and that in the reign of Kiaking special clauses were first laid down for the punishment of the guilty.   The prohibition, therefore, was directed against evil doing, under the covert of religion, and not against the religion professed by the Western foreign nations.
"Now the request of the French Ambassador, Lagrené, that those Chinese, doing well, who practise this religion, be exempt from criminality, seems feasible. It is right, therefore, to make the request, and earnestly to crave celestial favor to grant that henceforth all natives and foreigners without distinction, who learn and practise the religion of the Lord of Heaven and do not excite trouble by improper conduct, be exempted from criminality. . . . As to those of the French and other foreign nations who practise the religion, let them only be permitted to build churches at the five ports open for commercial intercourse.   They must not presume to enter the country to propagate religion. . . .
"Let it be according to the counsel (of Kiying).   This is from 'the Emperor.'"
† Subsequently the term "Religion of the Lord Jesus" was introduced into the Chinese vocabulary to designate the Protestant faith.

the rescript, frequently made tours into the surrounding country. The most awkward feature of the open violation of the laws of the empire was that regardless of whether their activities were lawful or not, the missionaries were exempted from Chinese jurisdiction by extraterritoriality. The British authorities made some efforts to restrain British and even American missionaries, but the French and the American Governments did not.[15] While no specific viola tions of the law on the part of the American missionaries were brought to the attention of the American Government in the next ten years, fully half the claims, trivial in amount yet several in number, for reparation and damages, were filed by missionaries who had proceeded to establish mission work in locations which were in violation of the Chinese interpretation of the treaty, and which had been resented in some way either by the officials, the gentry, or the rabble of the various localities. While these claims were usually settled by conciliation and compromise, they created no small amount of irritation.

The actual negotiations of the American treaty of Tien- tsin were in the hands of Dr. S. Wells Williams and Rev. W. A. P. Martin, the latter acting as interpreter of Mandarin which Williams did not at that time speak. At the preliminary negotiations at Taku, before the destruction of the forts by the British and French, Dr. Williams drew up an article stipulating full toleration for all persons profess ing Christianity, and permission for American missionaries to travel anywhere in the country, renting or buying houses or land, and living with their families. The Chinese commis sioner rejected this article as being too broad. But Count Putiatin secured an article which would permit the Russian missionaries to propagate as well as practice their faith in all open localities (*"toutes les localités ouvertes"*). This privilege was to be governed by passports to be issued by the consuls in conference with the local Chinese authorities.

At Tientsin Dr. Williams, therefore, drafted a similar article for the American treaty, but Mr. Reed objected to it because of the passport provision and also because it as-

signed to the consul and the Chinese authorities the responsibility of determining what missionaries should be worthy
to receive passes. This latter provision was then stricken
out, and the article submitted to the Chinese. They objected to it and made a proposal to limit the American mis
sionaries to the open ports, and to make their number sub
ject to the determination of the consuls alone. This was
less than had been secured in the Russian treaty which was
already signed, and was therefore very unsatisfactory to Dr.
Williams. Mr. Reed was impatient to sign the treaty the
following day, and would have omitted the article altogether
had it been necessary to secure the desired consummation of
his task. However, Dr. Williams persisted and in the morning was able to draft an article which was acceptable.[16]
It reads:

"Article 29.—The principles of the Christian religion, as professed
by the Protestant and Roman Catholic churches, are recognized as
teaching men to do good, and to do to others as they would have
others do to them. Hereafter those who quietly profess and teach
these doctrines shall not be harassed or persecuted on account of their
faith. Any person, whether citizen of the United States, or Chinese
convert, who, according to these tenets, peaceably teaches and prac-
tises the principles of Christianity shall in no case be interfered with
or molested."

It will be noted that this article omitted all definition
of locality in which the missionaries might live and work,
and that by the insertion of a provision for religious toleration within the empire into a foreign treaty, China was
actually making as much of a surrender of those sovereign
rights in domestic legislation which states usually reserve
for themselves, as in the commercial provisions of the Lord
Elgin treaty. The British treaty contained an article very
similar to that in the American treaty. The French treaty
carried provision for missionary liberty a step further by
stipulating that "an efficacious protection shall be given to
the missionaries who peaceably go into the interior. . . ."
Two years later the French Convention of Peking (October
25, 1860) added very important concessions for Roman
Catholics. China engaged to proclaim throughout the Em-

pire that people were permitted to propagate and practice the 'teachings of the Lord of Heaven,' that those who indiscriminately arrested Christians would be duly punished; and further, that all real estate formerly owned by Christians and confiscated at the time when the Catholics were expelled from the empire, would be paid for. The right to rent and purchase land and erect buildings thereon in all the prov inces was also inserted, surreptitiously, in the Chinese text of the Convention. This latter provision, although not binding upon the Chinese since the French text alone was authoritative, was later actually assented to by the Chinese Government (1865).[17]

The aggressiveness of the American missionaries in their disposition to force the opening of the empire is notable. It is entirely in accord with what had been the prevailing spirit in missionary circles from the beginning. Before 1858 the missionary suffered far more from the restriction imposed upon him than did the merchant. Consequently the missionary was the more impatient for greater liberty under treaty protection. It has already been noted that Dr. Parker, as commissioner, would have embarked upon a program looking towards the dismemberment of the empire by the appropriation of Formosa for the United States. In proposing this project he appears to have been reflecting a spirit which was at the time far more characteristic of the missionaries than of the merchants. Even the implacable Lord Elgin, fresh from his victories at Tientsin, was a little shocked at the sentiments of Dr. Bridgman, dean of the American missionaries, who appears to have been willing to go him one better.[18] The missionaries were, in 1858, greatly influenced by the Taiping Rebellion with which they for the most part greatly sympathized, and which seemed to hold out the prospect of a complete revolution. For the Manchu government the missionaries had scant respect, and the sovereignty and integrity of the Empire seemed to them much less important considerations than the opening of doors to evangelization. Theirs was not a very farsighted policy.

One may also pause at this point, which was the turning point in all missionary work, to speculate as to the impression which the American missionaries had made upon the Chinese. To the Imperial officials, wholly ignorant of the Western world, the distinction between the relation of the French Government to Roman Catholic missionaries and converts and the relation of the American Government to American missionaries could not have been very obvious. The Americans made much of the fact that in the United States there was complete separation of Church and State, and yet in China there were Bridgman, Parker and Williams negotiating the treaty of Wanghia, there was Parker entering the diplomatic service and rising to the highest rank, there were Williams and Martin at Taku and Tientsin, and at the same time there were the missionaries in frequent communication and open sympathy with the Taipings at Nanking. Not only had the Taiping-wang borrowed the color of the doctrines he was proclaiming from the missionaries, but in 1860 it was the Rev. Issachar J. Roberts, the chief rebel's old teacher, who proceeded to Nanking and, invested with yellow robes and a crown, became the erstwhile minister of foreign affairs in the rebel camp.[19] Christianity in either its Catholic or Protestant forms was a disintegrating influence in the Manchu Empire and it must have been difficult for the American missionaries to free themselves from the suspicion which was freely harbored against the French missionaries that they were in some undefined way the agents of a government which sought the disruption of China.

The American missionaries entered Japan without the protection of any express treaty stipulation for their work. The laws of Japan against the Christian religion were well known and Commodore Perry was instructed to make clear the American separation of Church and State. No mention of religion appears to have occurred in the negotiation of the treaty of 1854. But before Harris had negotiated the treaties of 1857 and 1858 the Dutch had secured toleration for the worship of "their own or the Christian religion" within their own dwellings. One of the projects nearest to the heart of Townsend Harris was to secure the opening of Japan to American missionaries and he was most careful to impress the authorities with his own personal devotion to Christian faith and practice. He had, however, at length to content himself with an article on religious freedom which merely enlarged slightly the privileges already granted to the Dutch. Americans were to be permitted the free exer cise of their religion, the erection of suitable places of wor ship, and on the other hand were not to "do anything that may be calculated to excite religious animosity." Never theless several of the American missionary societies, already informed of the possible opening for their work in Japan by S. Wells Williams and the chaplains of Perry's fleet, had undertaken to meet the situation. Rev. Guido Verbeck, born in Holland and in 1858 an applicant for American citizenship, was sent to Nagasaki by the Reformed Dutch church. Upon his arrival he found Dr. J. C. Hepburn, Presbyterian, and Rev. John Liggins and M. C. Williams, Episcopalian missionaries, had preceded him to their posts to which they had been transferred from China.[20] The existing prohibitions against aggressive evangelization were not serious handicaps for there had to be, just as previously in China, a large amount of language study before the missionaries could enter effectively upon their duties. Missionary work in Japan began, as elsewhere, with educational and medical service. Meanwhile the missionaries enjoyed merely the protection which was extended to all citizens under the treaty.

The course of American missions in Japan was in some respects quite different from that in China. Although the government was prone to look upon the Christianization of Japanese subjects as undermining loyalty to the Empire and the Mikado,* nevertheless the missionary, as a teacher of Western civilization, became more and more acceptable to

*"We . . . obtained from their high officers the distinct and positive avowal that the Mikado's government is based on the Shintoo creed, and for its per-

the Japanese, who were, unlike the Chinese, most eager to learn. As Japan entered into the long contest for treaty revision the westernization of Japan became a cult which had the support and aggressive encouragement of the highest Japanese authorities, and the missionaries greatly profited. Influential officials and Japanese students sent abroad to study became Christians and in Japan formed for the missionaries a substantial constituency such as did not exist in China at any time in the nineteenth century. Having established themselves in the treaty ports the missionaries began gradually to extend their work into the interior, using passports which granted them the right to travel for "health or scientific research." This subterfuge was winked at by the Japanese authorities until about 1888 when public opinion began to undergo a reaction against such rapid westernization of the Empire. From that time onward for a few years the authorities became more critical of the presence of missionaries in the interior, some of whom had openly established regular mission stations where they remained for long periods without other authorization than their passports.

In 1890 the anti-foreign feeling in Japan expressed itself in attacks on several missionaries, one of whom was an American. The American minister asked for a declaration of policy from the Japanese Government, and Foreign Minister, Count Aoki, stated that while the practices of the missionaries as regards travel in the interior were irregular, their privileges would not be withdrawn.[22]

In the missionary question, as well as in so many other respects, Japan became far more tactful towards the Christian nations than did China. Within a decade after the opening of Japan to trade a discovery was made that in southern Japan communities of Japanese Roman Catholic Christians, their faith and practice somewhat corrupted by their long isolation, had been able to exist during the long

petuity depends upon the maintenance of that faith at all hazards. That they foresee in the propagation of Christianity the overthrow of this faith and the consequent fall of the Mikado's dynasty. . . ." (De Long to Fish, Jan. 22, 1870.)[21]

period since the Catholics were expelled from Japan in the early part of the seventeenth century. One of the first edicts issued by the restored Mikado in 1868 renewed the prohibitions against Christianity, and forthwith the removal and banishment of the newly discovered Christians was begun. This action drew a strong and identic protest from the foreign representatives which was warmly supported by the American Government. Seward, apparently fearing that the persecution of Christians might lead to an intervention of foreign nations with direful results to the Empire, instructed Van Valkenburgh to convey to the Japanese authorities a very blunt warning. The persecution of the native Christians continued and two years later Secretary of State Fish took up with the British, French and German governments the question of joint action to restrain Japan. Lord Clarendon replied that it seemed unwise to take any action which would in any way embarrass the new sovereign in the establishment of his newly devised domestic administration, and the matter was dropped.[23]

The Japanese, however, were quick to realize in 1872 when the Iwakura Embassy reached the United States that the persecution of Christians was depriving Japan of the confidence of Christian nations which was so essential to the accomplishment of treaty revision. When Okubo and Ito were sent back to Japan for full powers and instructions for the proposed treaty with the United States they carried the message from the Embassy that Japan must abandon the program for the extirpation of Christianity.[24] Meanwhile the missionaries themselves had been winning the confidence of the authorities. Verbeck had already been called to Tokio to organize the Imperial University, and not a few of the American teachers who had been secured for the government schools were stoutly maintaining their purpose to engage in missionary work in an unofficial and personal way. The Japanese Government, at a time when Chinese authorities were seriously considering the possibility of expelling the missionaries, changed its policy and began to conciliate if not to welcome them. This contrast in policy was as profitable to Japan as it was costly to China, in the formation of public opinion. Between the American and the Japanese governments there never was any conflict or irritation on the question of missionaries or Christianity after 1870.

In Korea American missionary work started in much the same extra-legal way as in Japan and China. Catholic Christianity had been introduced into the peninsula by a Chinese priest in 1794.[25] He was put to death in 1801 but the Seminaire des Missions Étrangères of Paris took up the project and renewed the work under French priests. Some priests were decapitated in 1839. The massacre of 1866, resulting in the energetic action of M. de Bellonet and Admiral Roze, has already been referred to. France had assumed the protectorate of Roman Catholic missions and converts in the East and before 1880 had made clear that the disturbance of Christian converts was likely to be followed by demands on the part of France, not merely for large indemnities, but even for the surrender of territory. Korea was both anti-Christian and anti-foreign and China was in fear that the unauthorized projects of Bellonet might some day be renewed in more authoritative fashion. When Commodore Shufeldt arrived at Tientsin in 1881 he found that while Li Hung Chang was willing to assist in securing a treaty with Korea he was equally disposed to draft a compact in which missionary work would be prohibited. The first draft prepared by the Viceroy and submitted to Shufeldt and Holcombe contained a prohibition against the importation of religious books which was framed to accomplish this purpose. Upon the representation of Holcombe that such a stipulation would probably defeat the ratification of the treaty in the United States, the Viceroy withdrew it, leaving the treaty without any reference to religion.[26] By the treaty of 1882 the American missionary enjoyed in Korea only the rights which belonged to all American citizens.

The missionaries, long eager to enter the Hermit Kingdom, appeared at Seoul in 1883-4. Dr. H. N. Allen opened a government hospital (February, 1885) and two months later a regular Presbyterian evangelistic mission was opened by Rev. H. G. Underwood.[27] Soon after this the Methodist Episcopal church entered Korea with Rev. W. B. Scranton, M. D., and Rev. H. G. Appenzeller.[28] Another Christian influence was introduced when Korea officially requested the American Government to nominate some school teachers and Messrs. Gilmore, Bunker and Hulbert, educated in an American theological seminary, arrived in the summer of 1886. American missions, which occupied the field to a greater extent than British or Continental, not only prospered in Korea but won the confidence of the highest authorities, including the king and queen. Under the provisions of the British and German treaties, by means of the most-favored-nation clause in the American treaty, they entered the interior and established sub-stations far removed from the treaty ports. These Americans, who came in time to outnumber the mercantile representatives, became sources of a very strong unofficial American influence. Thus emerged a very difficult problem for the American Government which will be discussed in the following section.

MISSIONARIES AND NEUTRALITY

Because of the wise and conciliatory policy of Japan the missionaries within the Empire were never placed in a position which might be considered as equivalent to hostility to the existing government. In both China and Korea very different situations developed, one in connection with the Taiping Rebellion and the other in the matter of Korean independence.

The influence of the missionaries on the beginnings of the Taiping Rebellion has already been noted. The sympathy of the Protestant missionaries with the Taipings, which continued at least until 1860, has also been mentioned. When, in 1853, the American Government adopted toward the rebellion a policy of technical neutrality and non-interference, and when at the same time Marshall ignored his instructions and adopted the policy of sustaining and supporting the Imperial authority, the attitude and sympathy of the American missionaries became a great obstacle to the accomplishment of his purpose.[29]   He enjoined them to neutrality, but at least one of them defied him and visited the rebel camp at Nanking.[30]   Marshall's only recourse, for the enforcement of his injunction, was the public withdrawal of the protection of the United States from those who violated it.   He had no power to force them to desist.   At the same time the country was in great turmoil, the Imperial power was paralyzed, and the missionaries might indulge their sympathies with the utmost impunity.   Meanwhile their government in Washington, by no means as positive in its convictions as their representative in China, was disposed to look upon the revolution without disfavor.   The missionaries were in this one respect in a common class with the smugglers.   The American Government had taken the position that it was the duty of China to enforce her own laws, and so long as the Imperial Government was unable to prevent the importation of opium, or munitions for the rebels, or to prevent the communication of the missionaries with Nanking, there was nothing to be done.   No effective solution of the problem was devised and it solved itself a few years later when the missionaries, in common with other foreigners, both officials and others, came to see that their confidence in the rebels had been misplaced.

From the very beginning of diplomatic relations between the United States and Korea the American Government sought to discourage the Koreans from assuming that the American treaty implied any more than was stated, viz., that the United States recognized the independence of the kingdom.   The good offices clause was not to be interpreted as including any protectorate functions whatever.   The missionaries, however, were in a different position from the diplomatic representatives.   Very early in their work Li Hung Chang and his representative, Yuan Shi Kai, by opposing and obstructing them, forced the missionaries into opposition to the gradually unfolding purposes of China. The missionaries proceeded on the theory that the government which was most favorable to their work was the best government for the kingdom. The reduction of Korea to a province of China would mean the extension to Korea of the anti-foreign and anti-Christian influences which from the time of the Tientsin massacre were preparing the way in China for the Boxer uprising. As the Korean Government became more and more friendly towards them, the missionaries repaid the confidence with a sturdy and characteristically American support of Korean claims to *de facto* as well as *de jure* independence. This support was, in turn, a great encouragement to the Koreans. It encouraged them to oppose Yuan Shi Kai in the period preceding the Sino-Japanese War, and it was an even greater encouragement to the opposition which arose against the intrigues of Japan and Russia in the years that followed. That it misled the Korean people into the assumption that the American Government would, in some time of emergency, intervene and assume protectorate functions over the peninsula, there can be little doubt.

After the Sino-Japanese War Seoul became a center of incredible intrigue exceeding even that which preceded the war. The American missionaries openly sided with the king in his feeble efforts to preserve the independence of his kingdom. Both the Russian and the Japanese governments at different times complained at the actions of the mission aries. At length, unwillingly, and upon repeated orders from the Department of State, the American Minister sent to every American citizen in Korea the following notice which was also published in *The Independent* (Seoul, May 15, 1897):

> "Legation of the United States.
> Seoul, Korea, May 11, 1897.
>
> SIR,
>   By direction of the Secretary of State I am required to make publicly known to every citizen of the United States sojourning or being temporarily or permanently in Korea, the repeatedly expressed view of the Government of the United States that it behooves loyal

citizens of the United States in any foreign country whatsoever to observe the same scrupulous abstention from participating in the domestic concerns thereof which is internationally incumbent upon his government. They should strictly refrain from any expression of opinion or from giving advice concerning the internal management of the country, or from any intermeddling in its political questions. If they do so, it is at their own risk and peril. Neither the representative of this government in the country of their sojourn, nor the Government of the United States itself, can approve of any such action on their part, and should they disregard this advice it may perhaps not be found practicable to adequately protect them from their own consequences. Good American citizens, quitting their own land and resorting to another, can best display their devotion to the country of their allegiance and best justify a claim to its continued and efficient protection while in foreign parts, by confining themselves to their legitimate avocations, whether missionary work, or teaching in schools, or attending the sick, or other calling or business for which they resort to a foreign country,

I am Sir,

Yours respectfully,

JOHN M. B. SILL,

Minister Resident and Consul General."

PERSECUTION OF CHRISTIANS IN CHINA

The treaty of Tientsin had created an anomalous position for American missionaries in China. They were citizens of a government which had held consistently to the separation of church and state, and they were thoroughly imbued with conscientious convictions as to the rightness of this principle. Under other circumstances they probably would not have demanded preferential treatment, and yet the treaty unquestionably created them a special and preferred class with privileges not accorded to the mercantile population. Their privileges were still further defined, if not increased, by the French treaty and the Convention of 1860, the advantages of which they might claim under the most-favored-nation clause. By the Berthemy Convention (1865) all vagueness as to rights was removed when China definitely conceded the right of the French missionaries to purchase land as well as pursue their calling in every province. And yet the missionaries felt themselves to be on not very certain ground. Did they, or did they not, have all the rights of the Roman Catholic missionaries? There was not entire agreement among the succeeding American ministers and secretaries of state on this point.[31] The American Government appears to have been reluctant to recognize that the missionaries in China were a preferred class, and the missionaries themselves do not appear to have coveted the distinction, but in time all the treaty rights granted to the French missionaries and applicable to the Americans were claimed for them by their government and exercised. The missionaries established themselves in the interior, they acquired "perpetual leases" of land, and they demanded protection from the Chinese authorities. Their government collected their claims for damages and in at least one instance the American minister, with the approval of the Department of State, intervened to secure the religious toleration for native Christians which was guaranteed by treaty.[32] In 1896, following an outburst of anti-missionary and anti-foreign riots in various provinces the American Government secured a direct and explicit statement from China that the missionaries had every right which had been granted to the French.[33] In the course of years the missionary question as viewed by the American Government had come to be one of national prestige. To accept less for the Americans than was given to the French would be interpreted by the Chinese, so it was believed, as a weakness on the part of the United States which would lead to even greater troubles between the two governments.[34] The missionary question was another illustration of the fact that direct American relations with the Asiatic states were subject to the modifications of international competition.

The rights granted to the missionaries were made the basis by the merchants for a demand for further opening of the country to trade, and it seems reasonable to believe that at any time in the century at least after 1870, the Chinese Government would have at least removed all missionaries from the interior had it been free to do so.[35] The Protestant missionaries were objectionable to the local authorities, to the gentry, and to large masses of the ignorant populace because their converts rejected ancestor worship, refused to join in the expenses of idol-processions and temple repairs, and because of their generally disturbing influence on the indolent and corrupt practices of the local authori ties.[36] The Catholic missionaries were still more objection able because they claimed official rank in the hierarchy of Chinese officials, because they interfered where their con-Verts were concerned with the operations of the courts and police, and because, through the French Government, they assumed a protectorate over the Chinese converts. They were an *imperium in imperio*. Religious toleration became to the ruling classes less and less a voluntary toleration and assumed the character of still another imposition by foreign powers. Thus the missionaries came to be placed in an utterly false position such as they had escaped in Japan and Korea, and yet from which it was difficult for either them or their government to retire. Christianity was, in a measure, like opium, being imposed upon China without the consent of the people. The Chinese were free to abstain from either, but they were not free to prohibit them. No candid friend of Christianity and the missionaries can well shut his eyes to these facts.

With the details of the various riots from the massacre of Tientsin (1870) until the Boxer uprising we cannot be concerned. In general we may note that in these riots the Protestants suffered less than the Catholics, and among the former the American missions suffered least of all. This fact may be offered in testimony that the affairs of the American missions were managed with greater tact, with more concili-ation, or were less associated in the minds of the Chinese than were other missions with the suspected territorial designs of foreign governments. The American as well as the British Government consistently abstained from any cooperative action with other powers which would have tended to support the pretensions of France for the Roman Catholic missionaries and in time, i.e., in the second Cleve-land administration where the entire cooperative policy was repudiated, the United States withdrew from any cooperation whatever with other governments in the settlement of missionary troubles.

China was blindly and injudiciously contending for the integrity not merely of an empire but also of a form of social organization both of which were disintegrating before her eyes. Had China been possessed of more intelligent and skillful rulers she might have won the sympathy of the Americans in her hopeless struggle for there was a measure of justice on her side, but her leaders were utterly incompetent to meet the situation, and China lost the confidence she so sorely needed to sustain her claims to Korea and against Japan. The missionaries were contending for the establishment of religious toleration and missionary freedom without which it seemed that their work could not run its natural course. When one compares the hospitality they received from the Japanese and Korean governments which were never coerced by the foreign powers to give it, with the hostility of the Chinese who had granted freedom to missionaries in 1858 and 1860 only after they had been intimidated by the powers, one wonders whether there is not here a clear case of cause and effect. It would appear that the Christian missionary work in China did not receive a net benefit from the protection of foreign governments.

On the other hand the philanthropic and spiritual interest of an increasing number of Americans in the welfare of China, which was directly created by the missionaries, was the one constant force operating upon American public opinion in the last decades of the nineteenth century. The commercial interest of the United States in China rose and fell with the trade returns. The political interest ran parallel with the course of trade. Both declined steadily from 1860 to 1895. In general one may conclude that while the missionary contributed much to the disintegration of the Chinese Empire in the last century, and the weakness resulting from the prostration of China must by itself now be looked upon as a catastrophe, he was at the same time creating much which in more recent years has operated strongly to repair the damage which had been done.

From the history of Christian missions in China, Japan and Korea one conclusion stands out sharply: much harm and little good has come from governmental patronage and protection of missionary work; and the missionary renders the most enduring service to the people among whom he labors when he separates himself farthest from political concerns.

BIBLIOGRAPHICAL NOTES

1. The best general sources on the missionary question are: the various volumes of Foreign Relations, to consult which their index is an indispensable guide; Moore's Digest which contains important excerpts and references under appropriate headings in the sections on China, Japan and Korea, respectively; S. Wells Williams' "Life and Letters"; W. A. P. Martin's "Cycle of Cathay"; Charles Denby: "China and Her People," Vol. 1, chap. 17; Chester Holcombe: "The Real Chinese Question," chap. 6. The Missionary question in Foreign Relations is presented more completely than almost any other subject. Practically nothing of importance in the dispatches was omitted.
2. For interpreters in the consular and diplomatic service in China see H. Misc. Docs. 31:45-2, part 1, pp. 480 ff.
3. Eliza J. Gillett Bridgman: "Life and Labors of Elijah Coleman Bridgman" (New York, 1864)—a very inadequate book.
4. David Abeel: "Journal of a Residence in China" (2d Ed., N. Y., 1836).
5. S. Wells Williams' "Life and Letters"; Williams' Journal in Proceedings of the N. China Branch of the Royal Asiatic Society, and in the Japan Asiatic Society, respectively, already referred to.
6. Life, Letters and Journals of Rev. and Hon. Peter Parker, M. D.
7. Reed Corres., p. 360, June 20, 1858, Reed to Cass.
8. "Chinese Repository," Vols. 1-20, 1832-1851, Canton, Macao and Victoria. The field of the Repository, after its cessation, was occupied by the China Review and the Chinese Recorder.
9. Williams' "Life and Letters," p. 155.
10. An excellent review of the labors of the various American missionaries will be found in "Memorials of Protestant Missionaries in China" (Shanghai, 1867).
11. Martin: "Cycle of Cathay."
12. Griffis: "Verbeck of Japan"; Allen: "Chronological Index of Korea"; Homer B. Hulbert: "The Passing of Korea."
13. "Life of Peter Parker," p. 328.
14. Williams' "Middle Kingdom," Vol. 2, pp. 356 ff.; "Chinese Repository," Vol. 14, p. 195.
15. Walter Lowrie: "Memoir of the Rev. Walter M. Lowrie" (Philadelphia, 1854).

16. S. Wells Williams' Journal, p. 86.
17. Henri Cordier: "Relations," Vol. 1, chaps. 4 and 5.
18. Theodore Walrond: "Letters and Journals of James, Eighth Earl of Elgin."
19. Lindsay Brine: "The Taeping Rebellion in China," pp. 295-8.
20. Otis Cary: "A History of Christianity in Japan" (New York, 1909); W. E. Griffis: "Verbeck of Japan" (New York, 1900).
21. For. Relations, 1870, p. 461.
22. Japan Desp., Vol. 61, Jan. 2, 1890, Swift to Secy. of State.
23. For. Relations, 1868, I, pp. 749, 753, 827; 1870, pp. 455, 460, 482.
24. Stead: "Japan by the Japanese," p. 156.
25. Henri Cordier: "Relations," Vol. 1, chap. 18.
26. Holcombe, p. 163, makes a slightly different statement of the settlement of the religious question from the statement contained in the diplomatic dispatches. The writer has followed the latter. For references see chap. 24.
27. L. H. Underwood: "Underwood of Korea" (New York, 1918); "The Call of Korea," by H. G. Underwood (New York, 1908).
28. W. E. Griffis: "A Modern Pioneer in Korea" (biog. of Henry G. Appenzeller).
29. Marshall Corres., pp. 183 ff.
30. Charles Taylor, M. D.: "Five Years in China," pp. 38 ff.
31. Moore's "Digest," Vol. 5, pp. 452 ff.; see Koo: "Status of Aliens in China," chap. 16, for a digest of the policies of the various treaty powers, with special reference to Great Britain, France and Germany.
32. Moore's "Digest," Vol. 5, p. 460.
33. Ibid., p. 458; see also China Desp., Vol. 103, July 10, 1897, Denby to Secy. of State.
34. For. Relations, 1875, pp. 333, 399.
35. For Tientsin massacre and Wensiang note, see For. Rel., 1870, pp. 355 ff.; 1871, pp. 97 ff.
36. Arthur H. Smith: "China in Convulsion," Vol. 1, chaps. 3, 4, give an excellent exposition as viewed by a liberal Protestant missionary.

CHAPTER XXX

AMERICAN TRADE: 1844-1898

THE broad history of the American commerce with Asia is too large a subject to be brought within the scope of this study and yet certain phases of it cannot be neglected if one would understand the course of American policy. The very intimate relation between trade and politics in the first half of the century has already been shown. In the next fifty years both trade and politics became more complex and it is not always so easy to trace the relationship. Trade history under the treaties falls naturally into three periods, each with marked and peculiar characteristics. These periods are: 1844-58, 1859-95 and 1896-1900. The treaties of 1858 are a clear dividing line after which the trade which had hitherto been confined to China, and to five open ports, spread out to a steadily increasing number of cities in China, and also extended itself to Japan, and then to Korea. The close of the Sino-Japanese War is also a dividing line, coinciding as it does, roughly, with the new industrial and mercantile development of the United States which followed the recovery from the panic of 1893. The end of the century finds this new development in the full tide of its growth. Meanwhile the close of the war in Asia had set in motion a new commercial and political activity to which was related the McKinley-Hay policies with which our study comes to a close. A comprehensive survey of the trade history would include an examination of American relations with the Pacific Islands, and the Indian Ocean ports, but for our purposes we can afford to neglect them because they appear to have exercised practically no influence on policies. In the last quarter of the century until 1898 the attention of

Americans, in so far as it extended to Asia at all, was centered on Japan and China with occasional reference to Korea and the Hawaiian Islands.

Both American commerce and tonnage increased rapidly from 1844 to 1858. But it was also the time during which the first generation, the pioneer traders in China, disappeared. American trade was being carried on by the sons and relatives, for the most part, of the men who had founded it. The significant fact, looking towards the future, was that the third generation in these families was not remaining in the trade.* It is, probably, no injustice to those who came later, to state that the American mercantile community in the East reached its point of maximum vigor before the outbreak of the American Civil War. Dry-rot was already setting in and the domestic development of the United States was such that men of ability and character equal to that of the pioneers in Asia could now find ampler rewards at home in the fields of manufacturing, banking and transportation. The East India trade was no longer an El Dorado.

The period of 1859-95 was characterized by the decay, withdrawal or failure of all the American mercantile houses famous before the treaties of Tientsin, and by the entrance of no new merchants who rose to equal eminence. The failures of Olyphant and Company in December, 1878, and of Russell and Company in June, 1891, eliminated two of the most famous of the older American firms, and surrendered to British and German competitors a prestige and commercial leadership in China which Americans have never regained. No younger firms and no American banks had been developing to take over American interests and carry them on. The new firms which had appeared since the Civil War were, with very few notable exceptions, not well supplied with capital, and sometimes inclined to speculations and

*One may trace this fact in the history of nearly all of the American families prominently identified with the East India trade before 1850—there never were more than a score of them. In the second half of the century it is rare to find an American merchant in either China or Japan by the name of Perkins, Russell, Forbes, Cushing, Olyphant, Talbot, Griswold, Low, Wetmore or Wolcott, who was born after 1830. On the other hand these names occur with increasing frequency in the domestic commercial life of the nation.

methods which brought little credit to American trade. This was especially true in China.

In measuring the influence of trade on political policy it must also be borne in mind that the trade was never a large proportion of the total American foreign trade.[1] From 1821 to 1897 the ratio of the total value of merchandise imported into and exported from the United States in the trade with all Asia ranged from 5.90 to 6.97 per cent of the total American former trade. While it rose in an exceptional period of nine months in 1843 to nearly 14 per cent, from 1850 to 1890 it ranged either slightly above or slightly below 5 per cent. The exports from the United States were small as compared with the imports—from a third to as low as a tenth as much. The value of the trade with China dropped steadily from 1860 to 1897 from 3 to less than 2 per cent of the total American trade, and while the trade with Japan was steadily increasing from nothing, it had reached only 2 per cent of the total American foreign trade in 1897. These facts lead to the inevitable conclusion that in the four decades following the close of the American Civil War the trans-Pacific trade of the United States was of slight importance to the American people. It was the missionary and political interests of America in Asia which kept the Far Eastern problem before the American people, to even the slight degree in which it held their attention.

One finds in the relative status of the China and the Japan trade another reason why American policy steadily inclined towards Japan. While the volume of trade with China indicated a fairly steady increase after the close of the Civil War, its value showed an actual shrinkage due to the declining value of silver. The increase in volume of trade was not even sufficient to offset the decrease in values.* While the trade was valued at $22,472,605 in 1860, thirty years later it was only $19,206,680. On the other hand the trade with Japan, beginning with $193,865 in 1860, advanced to $26,335,967 in 1890, having surpassed

*The hackwan tael declined from $1.522 (January 1, 1874) to $1.01 (1893); $.849 (1894); and $.703 (1900).

VALUE IN GOLD OF MERCHANDISE IMPORTED INTO AND EXPORTED FROM THE
UNITED STATES, FISCAL YEARS 1865 TO 1904 *

YEARS	CHINESE EMPIRE [a]		HONGKONG [b]		JAPAN	
	Exports to	Imports from	Exports to	Imports from	Exports to	Imports from
	Dollars	Dollars	Dollars	Dollars	Dollars	Dollars
1865..	2,669,449	5,129,917	....	....	41,913	285,176
1866..	3,145,231	10,131,142	....	....	254,779	1,815,364
1867..	3,578,808	12,112,440	....	....	712,024	2,618,283
1868..	3,980,014	11,384,999	....	....	769,471	2,424,153
1869..	5,203,238	13,207,361	....	....	1,291,936	3,245,317
1870..	3,116,381	14,565,527	....	....	571,186	3,052,026
1871..	2,070,832	20,064,365	....	....	476,173	5,298,153
1872..	2,936,835	26,752,835	....	....	906,213	6,537,584
1873..	1,062,598	26,353,110	1,493,372	838,649	1,174,854	7,903,794
1874..	843,121	18,144,210	1,286,008	449,230	1,046,965	6,468,460
1875..	1,464,524	13,473,600	2,102,224	1,202,816	1,661,933	7,759,569
1876..	1,390,360	12,353,943	3,339,532	493,690	1,099,696	15,470,047
1877..	1,707,872	11,130,495	3,229,834	1,171,189	1,252,346	13,687,061
1878..	3,604,546	15,887,820	3,262,709	2,232,663	2,246,827	7,446,547
1879..	2,651,677	16,431,344	3,290,522	1,653,350	2,676,924	9,845,562
1880..	1,101,383	21,769,618	2,877,392	2,251,089	2,552,888	14,510,834
1881..	5,447,680	22,317,729	2,916,854	2,399,828	1,468,976	14,217,600
1882..	5,895,983	20,214,341	3,227,897	2,424,092	2,540,664	14,439,495
1883..	4,080,322	20,141,331	3,777,759	1,918,894	3,376,434	15,098,890
1884..	4,626,578	15,616,793	3,083,849	1,504,580	2,528,529	11,274,485
1885..	6,396,500	16,292,169	4,149,311	983,815	3,057,415	11,767,956
1886..	7,520,581	18,972,963	4,056,236	1,072,459	3,135,533	14,885,573
1887..	6,246,626	19,076,780	2,984,042	1,436,481	3,335,592	17,114,181
1888..	4,582,585	16,690,589	3,351,952	1,445,774	4,214,382	18,621,576
1889..	5,791,128	17,028,412	3,686,384	1,480,266	4,619,985	16,687,992
1890..	2,946,209	16,260,471	4,439,153	969,745	5,232,643	21,103,324
1891..	8,701,008	19,321,850	4,768,697	563,275	4,807,693	19,309,198
1892..	5,663,497	20,488,291	4,894,049	763,323	3,290,111	23,790,202
1893..	3,900,457	20,636,535	4,216,602	878,078	3,195,494	27,454,220
1894..	5,862,426	17,135,028	4,209,847	892,511	3,986,815	19,426,522
1895..	3,603,840	20,545,829	4,253,040	776,476	4,634,717	23,695,957
1896..	6,921,933	22,023,004	4,691,201	1,419,124	7,689,685	25,537,038
1897..	11,921,433	20,403,862	6,060,039	923,842	13,255,478	24,009,756
1898..	9,992,894	20,326,436	6,265,200	746,517	20,385,541	25,223,610
1899..	14,493,440	18,619,268	7,732,525	2,479,274	17,264,688	26,716,814
1900..	15,259,167	26,896,926	8,485,978	1,256,267	29,087,475	32,748,902
1901..	10,405,834	18,303,706	8,009,848	1,416,412	19,000,640	29,229,543
1902..	24,722,906	21,055,830	8,030,109	1,277,755	21,485,883	37,552,778
1903..	18,898,163	26,648,846	8,772,453	1,359,905	20,933,692	44,143,728
1904..	12,862,202	29,342,488	10,412,548	1,652,038	24,955,032	47,166,576

[a] From 1865 to 1872 includes Hongkong.
[b] Prior to 1873 included in "Chinese Empire."
* Adapted from *Monthly Summary of Commerce and Finance*, Sept. 1904, p. 1211.

the China trade.* After the Sino-Japanese War the entire
trade with Asia was greatly stimulated but Japan retained
the lead. In 1897 the total trade between the United States
and China was $32,328,295 while the trade with Japan had
reached $37,265,234. (See above table.) The more im-
portant factors in the increase of the Japan over the China
trade were: the purchase of an increasing proportion of tea
and silk in Japan for which China had been the sole source
before 1860; and the beginning of manufacturing in Japan
which created a market for an increasing amount of American raw cotton. The trade with Korea was trivial.† Another factor tending to promote the Japanese trade was the
entrance of Japanese commission houses into the United
States after the Centennial Exposition of 1876.

A better understanding of the trade conditions at the
beginning of the McKinley administration comes from a
review of the commercial policies of the competing nations
in the preceding generation. What were the possible methods of promoting trade and how far had the Americans
adopted those methods with success? Broadly speaking
there were, aside from the simple exchange of commodities,
the following methods: ownership of merchant fleets; placing of foreign advisers in positions of influence in the service of Asiatic states where their influence would tend to
divert purchases; securing of concessions for the operation
of telegraphs, railroads or mines; and loaning money to the
various governments.

* The statistics used for China do not include Hongkong. If the latter trade
is added, it will be found that the China trade retained first place; however,
the ratio of increase was greater for the Japan trade.
† It is difficult to appraise the exact share of the Americans in the Korean
trade which had reached a total of a little more than $9,500,000 gold in 1897.
A certain amount of American produce was brought into Korea through Japanese and Chinese sources, and the American firms in Korea dealt almost exclusively with Japanese or Chinese merchants. The Decennial Reports of the
Chinese Maritime Customs for the years 1882-91 show the Americans to have
had but 2 per cent of the import trade at Chemulpo (Jenchuan) one of the
three Korean ports of entry. The bulk of the Korean trade was divided
between the English and the Japanese with the latter steadily gaining the
ascendancy.

Decline of American Shipping

The decline of the American merchant marine which became so marked after the Civil War was somewhat re tarded in Chinese and Japanese waters by special circumstances.

The treaties of Tientsin by increasing the number of open ports and opening the Yangtze River as far as Hankow to foreign ships created a new demand for vessels which were more dependable than the native junks. The dis ordered internal conditions of China and Japan made it especially convenient not only for the foreigners but also for native merchants to entrust their cargoes to insurable vessels under foreign flags which were best able to command the respect of insurgents and most likely to have their claims paid in case of loss by capture. These conditions coincided with the improvement of steam navigation. The result was the creation immediately of a considerable fleet of relatively small steamers under foreign flags which obtained a very large share of the rapidly developing trade. The number of these vessels was swollen in China by the practice of selling to the Chinese lorcha owners the right to use a foreign flag over their vessels. This was accomplished by an ingenious transaction in which the technical ownership of the lorcha was transferred to the foreigner who in turn gave back to the Chinese a mortgage for the full value of the vessel which carried with it the right to operate the craft. The foreign flag was then hoisted as an evidence of foreign ownership but the foreigner named in the vessel's papers never appeared except in case of trouble with either the native or foreign authorities when his technical ownership was sufficient to bring any legal troubles which might arise into the extraterritorial courts. These semi-fraudulent transactions were winked at by the foreign authorities and led to great abuses for many years.[2] The lorcha *Arrow* which gave so much trouble to Viceroy Yeh at Canton in 1856 had been flying the British flag under such an arrangement. There was at least one American merchant in the two decades following the treaties of 1858 who specialized in this class of business.

The American mercantile houses had entered the coasting trade of China under the transshipment provisions of the Cushing treaty and as a part of the opium traffic, and were well prepared to enter into the new opportunities created by the treaties of 1858. Russell and Company organized the Shanghai Steam Navigation Company and within a few years had no less than sixteen steamers engaged in the coast-wise and river trade. Four of these had been built in the United States and had carried American registers. One was built in the United States and sold to a Japanese daimio who resold it to the Shanghai company. Six were built in Scotland after 1868 and brought to Shanghai under British register. Five had been built at Shanghai.[3] They were operated under the American flag under consular "sailing-letters," the flag being merely an evidence of American ownership but not, of course, of American registry. Owing to the scarcity of American seamen and masters in the Far East, and still more because Chinese or other non-American labor was cheaper it became customary to dispense almost or even entirely with American citizens in the operation of these vessels, even the master being in some cases an Englishman. The practice was at least somewhat irregular and could not stand very close scrunity according to American maritime law, but it was winked at by the Shanghai consulate and was not unknown to the Department of State. It is the presence of these vessels and the lorchas already described which partially accounts for the fact that American shipping in Chinese waters appears to have retained its place long after the American mercantile marine had begun to disappear from other foreign ports.

Another factor in keeping the American flag on the Pacific was the establishment of the Pacific Mail Steamship Company line in 1867.[4] By act of Congress (February 16, 1865) a subsidy which in the course of ten years amounted to a little more than $4,500,000 was granted in this line. In 1872 an additional vessel was authorized with an additional subsidy of $500,000 annually, but two years later it was discovered that a million dollars had been spent to secure this additional assistance from the government and in 1877 when the original grant expired all subsidy was eliminated. This line of steamers was originally intended to run by way of Honolulu to Japan and Shanghai, but the company was released from the obligation to stop at the Hawaiian Islands and was thus able to reduce the distance to be sailed by taking the great-circle route. The subsidizing of this line of steamers was often referred to in later years when the perennial question of ship-subsidies appeared, either as an argument to prove the value of them or to show their corrupting influence. Probably more important than the government aid was the rapid development of the Chinese immigration, which was extremely profitable. It is a notable fact that the Pacific Mail continued to operate its lines after the subsidy was removed, and that in later years another company, the Occidental and Oriental, put on four additional vessels. It ought also to be mentioned that these latter steamers were of British construction and ownership, being merely leased to an American company.

Neither the Japanese nor the Chinese accepted with complacency the passing of their coast-wise trade into the hands of foreigners. Japan immediately entered upon a program of nautical education and ship-building and as rapidly as possible entered both the California and the China trade, while China also displayed an unwonted degree of enterprise which resulted in the organization, under the patronage of Li Hung Chang, of the China Merchants Company, with a view to competition with the steamers under foreign flags. For the assistance of this new company a form of subsidy was devised in which the company was permitted to transport the government rice from the Yangtze and Shanghai to Tientsin at rates in excess of current freight rates. The American vessels were unable to meet this competition, accompanied as it was by the undoubted anti-foreign sentiment of Chinese merchants and government alike, and in 1877 Russell and Company sold its fleet to the China Mer-

chants.[5] During the Franco-Chinese War the entire China
Merchants fleet was resold to Russell and Company but
after the war the Chinese forced the return of the fleet by
declining to continue the rice-freights so long as the steamers remained in foreign hands. The American flag then
practically disappeared from the merchant marine in
Chinese waters. The significant facts are that this fleet had
never been under American registry and had never complied
with the American law as to American construction and operation; that at the time when the American fleet was sold
to the Chinese in 1877 a British fleet of nine steamers was
already in successful operation up the Yangtze and along the
coast; and that notwithstanding the use of the American
flag in the trans-Pacific trade, the total volume of American
trade with China does not appear to have been greatly benefited by it. The greater part of the freight from China to
America was carried in foreign vessels—after the opening of
the Suez Canal by way of the Mediterranean and across the
Atlantic. While the American fleet was of some unquestioned advantage to the American traders, the causes of the
relative unimportance of the Far Eastern trade of the
United States in the last forty years of the century lie much
deeper than in a declining merchant marine.

Foreign Advisers in China, Japan and Korea

The most remarkable instance of the use of foreign
advisers was in the Foreign Inspectorate of Chinese Maritime Customs. As already shown the Chinese Customs
came under the direction of Messrs. Wade, Lay and Hart,
respectively, not so much because British claims were being
urged, as because the Americans were simply without competent candidates. It is indeed fortunate for the Maritime
Customs that Americans did not come into control of it
for in all probability, had they done so, it would have been
made the victim of the spoils system of American politics.*

*William H. Seward, beset with office-seekers at the beginning of the Lin-
coln administration, was under the impression that he had the official right
to dictate appointments to the Chinese Maritime Customs. One of his first

The first experience of the Chinese Government with American assistants was in the employment of Ward and Burgevine in the suppression of the Taiping Rebellion. Ward rendered an honorable service, but Burgevine left a stain upon his country's reputation. The purchase of the Lay-Osborne Flotilla in England led to a new interest in coal mines, the product of which would be so much in demand for steam navigation of government vessels. Raphael Pumpelly, an American who had just completed similar geological surveys for the Japanese Government, was invited to make a report on Chinese coal resources. This might have led to an early development of Chinese mines under American supervision had not the Lay-Osborne Flotilla become such a source of embarrassment to the Tsung-li Yamen. The return of this fleet not only put an end to the interest in coal mines but also made the government wary of foreign advisers like Mr. Lay.[6]

Following the end of the Taiping Rebellion several Englishmen and Frenchmen from Ward's or Gordon's armies entered Chinese service, especially in the supervision of arsenals. No Americans were similarly employed for there were no competent candidates. The next important post in the Chinese service for which an American was a possible candidate was in connection with the Chinese navy which Li Hung Chang had begun to develop about 1880. Commodore Shufeldt thought that he was deprived of the position through the intrigues of other governments. There may have been a measure of truth in Shufeldt's suspicions, but it seems hardly probable that the man who wrote, even in confidence, the famous Sargent letter, could have rendered a very effective service to either the Chinese or his own countrymen. It cannot be denied that in the employment of foreign advisers for China the American interests were not well represented, but they would appear to have had as much representation as they deserved or as was warranted by the proportion of American to the total foreign trade of

official communications to the American representative in China was to ask him to replace an American then in the Customs service with one of Seward's political friends.

China. The failure of Russell and Company in 1891 greatly prejudiced the Chinese against Americans. The Chinese Government lost heavily in this failure and Li Hung Chang is reported to have stated shortly after the failure, which came at a time when the immigration question was producing the maximum amount of trouble, that he would never again employ an American for any purpose.

Japan turned freely to America for advice and was fortunate in securing a large number of Americans of excellent ability and character.[7]   However, the greater number of the Americans in Japanese service were employed either in the development of the school system or otherwise in positions which were only remotely related to trade. Japan turned to the United States for assistance in building her new navy after the Restoration, and even earlier had purchased several American-built naval vessels, but in such matters the Americans were at an obvious disadvantage because the American navy was itself rapidly declining, and American ship-yards had already lost their world-wide supremacy. The Japanese orders for naval vessels during the American Civil War appear to have been handled in a way which could not lead to extended future orders. Japanese interests were badly served. However the rapid increase of American trade with Japan may be somewhat attributed to the influence of American advisers as well as to the influence of the returned Japanese students, so many of whom in the seventies and eighties were being educated in the United States.

The indifference of the American Government to the desires of Korea for American advisers has already been noted, and the reason for it indicated. Korea was an impoverished country with little money to spend for any purpose and a preponderance of American influence in Korea was more embarrassing than profitable.

FOREIGN CONCESSIONS AT THE TREATY PORTS

The word concession is used loosely in two different senses meaning in the one case the foreign settlement at a treaty port, and in the other a business privilege or contract granted to foreigners by the government.

In the foreign settlements established after the treaties of Tientsin in China the Americans came out badly. While the American minister was "junketing" through Europe to the Orient and back in 1859 and 1860—the term accurately describes the conditions under which John E. Ward assumed and discharged the duties of his office—there was no one to uphold the principles of the international foreign settlement as they had been worked out at Shanghai in 1853-4. Unopposed, the British reverted to the plan which Humphrey Marshall had overthrown, and established at Hankow and Canton British settlements in which the British Government leased the land from China and then issued titles to applicants in the form of sub-leases. Thus disappeared even the safe-guard to Chinese sovereignty which had appeared in the earliest Shanghai land regulations where the title, although registered at the British consulate, was actually issued by the taotai. There was no disposition on the part of the Chinese to discriminate against the Americans and when Tientsin was opened a lease for a settlement was actually issued to the American consul, but it was never approved by his government. At the new ports the Americans were quite satisfied with their allotments of land, but the fact remains that the idea of an international settlement had been superseded by that of a series of national settlements such as the British and French had originally contemplated. The effect of this change was to place the desirable water-front or mercantile property at each newly opened treaty port under the control of some power other than China and to make the Americans tenants of some European nation. The result was that when in later years new American firms appeared in China the most desirable locations were all preempted and the Americans had to take what was left. Prospective American interests in 1858-61 suffered in this respect in China because they were indolently represented. In 1862 Burlingame found that both the French and the British residents were disposed to assume that the

leases of land in the various foreign settlements were equivalent to cession of territory. In 1862 France withdrew from
the international settlement at Shanghai. In June, 1863,
the Chinese Government formally granted permission to the
Americans to erect residences, business houses and go-downs
at Hong-kew,[8] across Soochow Creek and outside the legal
limits of the settlement, but a few months later the Americans at Hong-kew, some of whom had established themselves
there many years before without formal permission, heartily
agreed to the merging of the new area in the International
Settlement under new Land Regulations. The French, how
ever, stood aloof.

In the treaty ports in Japan, and later in Korea, different
conditions prevailed from the outset. The Japanese never
relinquished control of their ports, and although the foreign
ers virtually maintained their own municipal government
in the open ports no rights discriminating in favor of any
nation were granted. In Korea the Americans were first on
the ground, after the Japanese and obtained preferred building locations, some of which were subsequently given up
merely because there was no reason for holding them.

Telegraphs and Cables

Americans were the first to project the plan of trans-
Pacific telegraph communications. The first proposal was
for a line northward through British Columbia, thence by
way of Alaska and the Aleutian Islands, down the coast of
Siberia to the mouth of the Amur.[9] It was hoped by thus
utilizing land lines for the greater part of the way to avoid
the difficulties which were encountered with the first submarine cables. During the Civil War this project was
being urged. The necessary rights to cross British and
Russian territory were secured and Congress voted assistance. The project collapsed upon the completion and successful operation of the second Atlantic cable. In 1865
Anson Burlingame secured a verbal agreement from the
Tsung-li Yamen that China would grant permission to the

East India Telegraph Company of New York to lay cables along the coast of China as far south as Hongkong.[10] The line thus projected would be linked up to the Russian telegraph already completed to Kiatka, 800 miles from Peking, to the Russo-American line by way of Kamtchatka and Alaska, and at Hongkong to a proposed British line from India. In order to bring about an amicable adjustment of the rival claimants for this important concession it had become necessary for the Americans to agree to make the company international in character by admitting both British and French share-holders. But the East India Telegraph Company does not appear ever to have passed beyond the promotion stage. With the collapse of the Russo-American company it also disappeared. Indeed it is difficult to see how such an extensive plan could ever have been realized by Americans without generous assistance from abroad, although the Russo-American company, which was almost identical with the Western Union Telegraph company, spent $3,000,000 before abandoning the northern line.

A part of the plan thus first promoted by Americans was immediately taken up by the Danes, who occupied an especially favorable political position because they were friendly with both Russia and Great Britain. The Great Northern Telegraph Company (Danish) supported by Sir Thomas Wade at Peking secured in 1870 the privilege of laying a cable along the coast northward from Hongkong to Shanghai with the understanding that the cable ends at the various ports were to be carried to hulks moored in the ports and not to be landed. The entrance of the Danish Company marked the disappearance of American interests from the telegraph situation in China. However the Americans gave the most cordial support to the Great Northern Telegraph Company and assisted in its promotion in a multitude of ways. In 1874, when the military value of the telegraph was revealed to the Chinese at the time of the threatened Japanese attack on Formosa M. M. De Lano, the American consul at Foochow, represented the Danish interests and conducted a large part of the negotiations by which the Great Northern

Telegraph Company secured the rights not only for a cable to Formosa but also for certain land lines in Fukien.[11] At about the same time the Woosung Railway Company granted permission to the Danes to land their line at Woosung and carry it to the international settlement at Shanghai over the property recently purchased for the railway.

The Chinese, however, viewed the extension of telegraphs with timidity. Not only were there objections from the superstitious people and geomancers who urged that the wires would disturb the *fung-shui*, but the government also feared that it would be unable to protect the lines and that their injury by either thieves or the superstitious would result in the inevitable claim for damages and perhaps for further demands by the treaty powers. The Woosung-Shanghai line was ordered removed, the cable to Formosa was postponed, and the government purchased the land lines in Fukien and then destroyed them. Before 1875 the Chinese Government had adopted the policy also in operation in Japan of excluding foreigners from the ownership or control of both telegraphs and railroads. The difference between China and Japan at this point was that while the Japanese were earnestly seeking to perfect themselves in the skill necessary for the successful operation of such utilities, sending multitudes of students abroad and employing many foreign teachers at home, the Chinese Government was pursuing its customary policy of advancing to meet no problem and solving each one as much by denial and evasion as possible.

Military necessity, aided by the enlightened convictions of Li Hung Chang and a few other military officials, was nevertheless slowly crowding the Chinese Government to take action and in 1881, while retaining Chinese ownership of the lines, the Tsung-li Yamen gave to the Great Northern Telegraph Company the contract for the construction of some new land lines in the vicinity of Tientsin and Peking. The American Government viewed this advance of Danish interests without dissatisfaction, although Secretary of State Fish (March 4, 1875) had already expressed disapproval of the evident monopolistic character of the Danish intentions. But the Americans became alarmed at the advance of the Great Northern Telegraph Company when it became known that Li Hung Chang had negotiated with the company for a monopoly of the cable lines. According to the reported contract any American company would be excluded for twenty years from the right even to land a cable at a Chinese port.

The American Government protested energetically against the ratification of this contract but in vain. Prince Kung officially stated that whenever an American company might desire to lay a cable between Japan and China an arrangement would be made "which shall not disappoint the American company in the least degree."[12] This answer seemed at the time to be reasonably satisfactory but in fact it was not, for the Great Northern Telegraph Company made a secret contract with the Japanese Government which secured a monopoly of cables westward from Japan. The precise form of Prince Kung's statement leaves one wondering whether he knew of the monopoly in Japan or whether the wording of the statement had been suggested to him by those who did. At any rate the Americans were now completely excluded from carrying a trans-Pacific cable to China by way of Japan which was the natural route. More alertness in Tokio might have prevented the consummation of an arrangement so disadvantageous to Americans.*

THE FIRST RAILWAYS

Even before the Restoration was accomplished both the Japanese and the foreigners became interested in railroads in Japan. British, French and American interests were competing for privileges. While United States Minister Van Valkenburgh was absent from Yedo at the opening of Osaka in January, 1868, A. L. C. Portman, temporarily act-

---

*When in the nineties the American Government sought to promote the laying of a trans-Pacific cable, Japan was more than willing to cooperate in a Japanese-American cable, but was prevented by the Danish monopoly from granting to Americans the right to land in Japan or Formosa cables which would connect either with China or Luzon. The Americans were therefore forced to lay the trans-Pacific cable by way of Guam with extensions to Japan and China.

ing as *chargé* at Yedo, apparently without any instructions either from his superior or from Washington, and also with out any definite financial support, secured from the Yedo government (January 16, 1868) a concession for a railroad from Yokohama to Tokio to be built and owned by Americans. The contract provided that the government would have the right to purchase the road at any time at fifty per cent above its cost. The new government, however, refused to ratify the contract, and immediately adopted the policy of keeping all railroads as well as telegraph lines exclusively in Japanese ownership. Shortly afterwards H. N. Lay, of Lay-Osborne Flotilla fame, appeared in Japan as the agent of British firms which desired to build railroads. An agreement was reached as a result of which Mr. Lay proceeded to London and advertised (April 23, 1870) a loan of £100,000 to be made to Japan for the construction of a railroad. Lay stated that the receipts of the road as well as the customs of all the treaty ports would be pledged for payment. The Japanese repudiated this statement of Mr. Lay who was again betraying his inclination to misinterpret and exceed his instructions just as he had done in the purchase of the flotilla for China eight years before. The terms of the loan were changed, but British capital was secured and British engineers were engaged. The line from Yokohama to Tokio was opened in the summer of 1872, and soon construction was begun on a line from Osaka to Kioto. These two segments became part of a main trunk line from Tokio to Kobe which was rapidly pushed to completion.

The first proposal for a railway in China came from English and American merchants.[13] In 1863 the exigencies of the closing struggles with the Taipings were believed to afford a sufficient occasion for demonstrating to the Chinese the utility of steam transportation. A petition for permission to build a line from Shanghai to Soochow signed by twenty-seven foreign firms, mostly British, was presented to Li Hung Chang, who was then in general charge of the military operations, in the capacity of Imperial Commissioner and Governor of Kiangsu. Li Hung Chang with the embarrassments of the Lay-Osborne Flotilla and the defection of Burgevine fresh in his mind, replied that railways could be a benefit to China only if they were exclusively in the hands of the Chinese, and he declined even to present the petition to Peking. A few months later Sir MacDonald Stephenson came to China, at the suggestion of British merchants, and made a somewhat superficial survey of possible railway routes.

The next effort to introduce railway building into the empire was stimulated by the construction of the Yokohama-Tokio line. At the port of Shanghai there was a transportation problem somewhat like that at Tokio. The foreign shipping found it convenient to anchor in the Woosung River a dozen miles below the foreign settlement. A railroad from the anchorage to the city would serve a pur pose similar to the Yokohama-Tokio line. Oliver B. Brad ford, American vice consul at Shanghai, with the approval of George F. Seward, the consul general, and of United States Minister Low at Peking, as well as with the knowledge of the Department of State, undertook to promote the construction of a narrow gauge railroad from the anchorage at Woosung to Shanghai.[14]

Three obstacles appeared. At the request of the Chinese Government which had become alarmed at the prospective demands of foreigners for railroad privileges in the approaching revision of the treaties, Anson Burlingame had secured from the United States in the treaty of 1868 the stipulation (Article 8) that the United States "do hereby freely disclaim and disavow any intention or right to intervene in the domestic administration of China in regard to the construction of railroads, telegraphs or other material improvements." The second obstacle was that the Chinese had assumed the policy of reserving all railroad rights to themselves. Third, Bradford had no adequate financial backing. He was purely a promoter. The first obstacle was ignored, the second was met by fraud and the third, after vain attempts to interest American capital which at that time was not even equal to financing railways in America,

was overcome by admitting a preponderating British inter
est into the company.

The "Woosung Road Company" was formed by Bradford to purchase land for a "horse-road." Shortly afterwards the interests of this company were transferred to the
"Woosung Tramway Company" (in the Chinese text of the
transfer: the "Woosung Carriage-Road Company") and
land was purchased for the ostensible purpose of a carriage
road. When title to the land had been secured, grading was
begun and rails were laid with the knowledge, of course, yet
without the approval of the local Chinese officials. The
first official information received by the Chinese Government as to the true nature of the undertaking was a request
to the customs to admit duty-free the locomotive and cars
which had arrived from England. Notwithstanding the protests of the government as well as of the local Chinese land
holders the road was partially opened for traffic June 30,
1876, and continued in operation for a few weeks until at the
time of the Chefoo agreement the government secured from
Sir Thomas Wade a stipulation that China should have the
privilege of buying the line from the company which was
now a British concern. By order of Wade the operation of
trains was temporarily discontinued and when the Chinese
had completed the purchase of the line, the rails were torn
up and the entire equipment shipped to Formosa. The
immediate cause of the failure of the enterprise was the
killing of a Chinese by a train, and the opposition of the
local people, but back of this lay the belief of the Chinese
officials that if they were to permit such a high-handed
scheme to succeed a precedent would be established which
would upset entirely the Chinese policy of controlling its
own railway development.*

*"I have been to much trouble to ascertain from the Chinese officials their
reasons, etc., for their action in the premises and I submit the following, as
near their language as possible. They declare that . . . the removal of the
Woosung Railway is being carried out solely in consequence of the political
necessity of the act. That to allow it to remain where it is would utterly
stultify the action of the authorities and afford the strongest encouragement
to similar invasions of Chinese territory and of her independence as a nation.'
By a general consensus of opinion, both of the Chinese officials and Chinese
merchants, the net result of the scheme carried out by the Woosung Road Company is to brand all railway schemes (and even ordinary road-making pro-

The Woosung Railway episode has been given at some length because it serves to throw light on the contemporary conditions of American trade. American capital was not seeking an entrance into either Japan or China in this period, while British capital was eager for opportuities. The Americans who stand forth in the trade history of this period were adventurers and promoters lacking both the character and the business connections which would have been necessary to establish and carry through large under takings. They were utterly unlike the earlier Americans who by just, generous and conciliatory business methods won the confidence of Chinese merchants in the old pre treaty days at Canton. Now, while British and Continental merchants and capitalists were appearing in China with ample resources and respectable personnel, prepared to make investments, loan money, or otherwise meet the needs of the situation, the American merchants were steadily losing ground and the American consulates reeked with malodorous scandals. Americans were not prepared to do business in the East on a large scale. Both citizens and capital could find more satisfactory returns at home within the borders of the United States.

RAILWAY CONSTRUCTION IN CHINA AFTER 1885

Railway construction in China again became a mooted question in 1885, at the close of the Franco-Chinese War. In 1886 there were gathered at Tientsin and Peking the largest number of "concession-hunters" yet seen in China. A German syndicate had sent representatives who were reported to be seeking to loan to China £35,000,000 for rail-

posals) with suspicion and dislike in the eyes of the Chinese officials and the government itself, and to tend to retard for several years their introduction into the empire. This feeling has no connection with the merits of such enterprises, which the Chinese do to a considerable extent both understand and appreciate, but it is due wholly and solely to the deceit and fraud practiced at the commencement by the original promoters of the scheme." (Consul General G. Wiley Wells to Department of State, November 20, 1877.[15])

The excerpt is from a report on the moral delinquencies of the American consulate at Shanghai which resulted in an exhaustive investigation by the Department of State, a Committee of the House of Representatives, and then the proposed impeachment of George F. Seward. One of the indictments against Bradford was his connection with the railroad. Both Bradford and Seward were removed from office.

way construction. A French syndicate, encouraged by the clause in the recent French treaty of 1885 which stipulated that if China decided to build railways the French Government would give to China every facility to procure in France the personnel she might need, was established at Tientsin, in a $100,000 mansion with a liberal expense account for entertaining. Meanwhile there appeared the Kaiping Railway Company, a Chinese concern with Wu Ting Fang as director, Li Hung Chang as patron, and with construction already started on a line in the direction of the Kaiping coal mines. This company had close British affiliations. It was especially favored by the Chinese who were now clearly determined to retain control not merely of the ownership but of the construction of whatever railways might be built.

The American Government was represented by Charles Denby of Indiana who, before coming to China in 1885 as minister, had been prominently identified with railroad building in the United States. Denby was keenly and intelligently interested in the Chinese transportation problem which was in some respects so similar to that which the American people had been solving for the last quarter century. He was also convinced that the time had come when American interests in China ought to be pushed aggressively. General James H. Wilson,[16] an American engineer, arrived about the same time and no opportunity was lost to present to the Chinese the superiorities of American methods of railway construction and operation. A model of American railway track and a small train operated by clock-work was even set up within the palace grounds for the amusement of the boy Emperor and the Court. The French syndicate, however, was quick to offset this advantage by the gift of even more elaborate equipment of French design. Denby's advice was freely drawn upon, especially after he expressed his sympathy with the Chinese in their desire to retain control of their railways.*

American interests, operating through Russell and Com-

*The charter for the Kaiping Railway Company, which in 1887 became the China Railway Company, was based upon a model charter for a stock company supplied by Denby.

pany, bid for the construction of a line from Tientsin to Taku which would actually become a link in the projected Tientsin-Kaiping road, but American capitalists were unwilling to advance a loan for the work and the contract went to the Kaiping Company. At about the same time the Americans made a bid for the construction of 80 miles of road in Formosa, but were under-bid by a British company which secured the contract.

The year 1887 was one of great activity among the foreign investors. A Chinese-American bank was projected. This was supported by the so-called Philadelphia Syndicate and received the approval of Li Hung Chang. It was proposed to loan the government 80,000,000 *taels* to finance railway construction, and to organize a mint. The same interests also secured extensive concessions including the right to install telephone systems. The Yamen refused to ratify the agreement, and although efforts were made subsequently to revive the scheme nothing ever came of it. It is quite probable that it had been from the outset more a promoters' than an investors' proposition.

The French syndicate likewise failed to secure the desired concessions and was diverted to the construction of fortifications at Port Arthur. A considerable amount of American equipment was used in the Tientsin-Kaiping line which was opened in 1888, but it could not be claimed that Americans had accomplished much towards regaining the commercial position in China which they had occupied in 1860. The causes of their failure had been lack of capital and inadequate authoritative representation in China able to conclude business agreements.

The close of the Sino-Japanese War marked the beginning of an entirely new phase of China's financial relations with the West. Before 1894 the Chinese Government had been proceeding on the principle of borrowing as little as possible and retaining complete control of both mines and railroads. The policy had been successful in a purely negative way. China became debtor to foreigners to only a slight extent, but meanwhile Chinese capital had not been forthcoming to build railways. The Chinese investors distrusted Chinese stock companies and they had no relish for lending money to their government. As a matter of fact current rates of interest among the Chinese were very much higher than the rates at which money could be borrowed from abroad; it was only a question of time in 1894 when China would be forced into the foreign markets. The expenses of the war with Japan rather than the need for railways created the immediate necessity. At the close of the war China was indebted to foreign money lenders to the extent of £7,000,000 secured by the customs. It then became necessary to borrow 200,000,000 *taels* to pay the indemnity to Japan. American bankers offered to make all or part of this loan but their competitors offered more favorable terms. About £16,000,000 were supplied by Russian and French banks with interest at 4 per cent under a guaranty by the Russian Government, and an equal amount by a British-German syndicate at 5 per cent, secured by customs receipts.

China now entered upon the most discouraging and disastrous phase of her foreign relations. Having been more or less estranged from the United States by both the immigration and the Korean matters, and having been practically deserted by Great Britain in the war with Japan, the Chinese Government, led by Li Hung Chang, turned to Russia. Possibly it would be more accurate to say that Li Hung Chang had decided to enter European politics aggressively where Japan had been operating so successfully for a decade. But China, unlike Japan, was unprepared to take such a step. The Empire now had to gather the bitter harvest of a half-century of reactionary, foreign-hating policy which had been characterized by arrogance and stupidity. Even Li Hung Chang, China's most progressive and ablest leader, had never set his foot on foreign soil until he went to Shimoneséki to sign the fateful treaty with Japan. While Japan had been earnestly studying the international situation and faithfully training her leaders to cope with it, China had recalled the few students she had sent abroad and sought to turn back the hands of the clock. Now in her hour of greatest need China was helpless; rich in resources and in intellectual ability but impoverished by a corrupt and unenlightened government. By a tactful and conciliatory policy at Peking, Russia had long been preparing for this hour of opportunity. Suffice it to say, for the moment, that while it cannot be shown that in the closing years of the century American trade or American investors had actually suffered a net loss because of the disastrous treaties and agreements which China made voluntarily or otherwise with Russia, France and England, yet the presence of large European fleets and the steady pressure of the diplomatic representatives at Peking exercised a disturbing influence on the letting of such contracts for railway construction as the Americans desired. The Americans, unsupported by guarantees of their government, were at a disadvantage in bidding against Europeans who had become political agents as well as money-lenders.

Three or four American companies, one from Japan, but the others hitherto unknown in China, appeared in 1896 seeking the opportunity to build railways. A preliminary agreement was made to give the contract for a line from Hankow to Peking to one of two competing American firms but Belgians, backed by French and Russian capital, were prepared to give more favorable terms to China. The Chinese were disposed to favor the Americans and at the last minute would have given them the contract, so it is believed, but the representatives of the American banks were without authority to act quickly, if at all, and the diplomatic pressure at Peking, notwithstanding the opposition of the British, turned the contract over to the Belgian company.* The struggle for contracts had assumed a political character but the Americans retained a clear advantage over their competitors because the Chinese recognized that the United States had no territorial designs. In April, 1898, after a

---

*It has been frequently stated that this contract was lost to the Americans because the Department of State would not support the claims of the American company. This would appear to be a mistaken assumption. U. S. Minister Denby wrote, October 20, 1897: "The night before the Belgian contract for the Hankow-Paoting-fu line was let, it was offered to an American but he had no power to accept it."

great deal of manoeuvering the Chinese minister in Washington signed a contract for an American syndicate to build the Canton-Hankow line. At about the same time China expressed a willingness to give to Americans the right to build a line northward from Peking to Kalgan. With both this and the Canton-Hankow line went valuable mining privileges. When a contract was signed by which American capital would have been used to finance the Tientsin-Chinkiang line, the Germans protested, but American capital could have been admitted to a share (1898) in this line which was actually built by the British and Germans jointly, had the Americans been prepared to handle the necessary loan.

The subsequent history of the Canton-Hankow line does not come within the nineteenth century.[17] It is, however, significant for our study that the Americans delayed the beginning of operations and then allowed the control to pass contrary to the terms of the contract into Belgian hands from which it was later purchased and then resold to China. The death of Calvin Brice, the head of the syndicate formed to carry through the Canton-Hankow contract, was disastrous to the enterprise. Two conclusions of importance stand out: American capitalists, not yet seriously interested in investments in China, had actually secured more contracts than they were prepared to execute; and the loss of American prestige and influence and the lack of experience, so manifest in the business relations of the last quarter century, had now become a serious handicap to effective competition with other foreign nations.

Out of an estimated total of nearly 7500 miles of railway concessions granted before December 1, 1898 the Americans had actually accepted or secured only 300 miles. They had lost several times as much through inability to provide capital on acceptable terms.

SPHERES OF INFLUENCE

Concurrently with the struggle for contracts and concessions which followed the Sino-Japanese War, the interference of the treaty powers in the affairs of China was becoming so marked as to arouse Americans to the impending, if not present, danger. Notwithstanding the fact that in this period American capital had secured for the immediate present more than it could digest, it was felt that the future was very bright for the Americans if only the field of free competition were to remain open. In this respect the Americans of 1898 were like the China merchants in the fifties. The tide, they believed, was beginning to turn. The one unsecured essential for successful trade with China was the assurance of a field of free competition. Now the field was being threatened by a series of treaties and agreements between China and the other primary treaty powers that looked towards the closing of doors which had swung open to Americans on terms equal with those of their competitors for a hundred years. For Americans it was a day of uncertainty similar to that which preceded the treaties of Wanghia and of Tientsin. More accurately, perhaps, the Americans were face to face with the problem which Humphrey Marshall had envisaged in 1853 when he believed that foreign intervention in the Taiping Rebellion would result in the partition of China.

While it is not necessary for the purpose of this study to concern ourselves with the mass of details which attended the delimitation of spheres of influence and the execution of "non-alienation" agreements in China, it is important, as we approach the annexation of the Philippines, to have clearly in mind the extent to which the Chinese Empire in the summer of 1898 had actually been withdrawn from the field of free commercial competition.[18] France had secured from China the promise that French citizens would be preferred above those of all other nationalities in the exploitation of all mines in the three southern provinces of Yunan, Kwangsi and Kwangtung; that all railways having Pakhoi as a starting-point would be constructed by either French or Franco-Chinese companies; and that no part of the three provinces would be alienated from China or leased to any other power. France also obtained a lease for the Bay of Kwangchow-wan, the best harbor south of Hongkong. Russia had secured the right to preference in the construction of all railroads north and northeast of Peking, as well as the recognition of all Mongolia and Manchuria as a Russian sphere of influence, and had leased Port Arthur, which commanded the naval approach to Peking and North China. The Russian agreements carried administrative and military privileges which involved the actual, though not theoretical, transfer of sovereignty. Germany had secured the right to preference for capital or material needed for any purpose in Shantung, and had leased Kiaochow, the best naval base south of Port Arthur. Great Britain had secured a non-alienation agreement for the Yangtze Valley and the promise that so long as the British trade preponderated in the Empire a British subject should remain the head of the customs service. Finally Japan had secured a non-alienation agreement for the province of Fukien which carried with it the exclusion of leases to any other power.

These agreements had been accompanied by the signing of railway and mining contracts which had been secured by intimidation and had been attended by a display of naval forces in Chinese waters which revealed utter contempt for the sovereignty of the Empire. Clearly China was in danger and partition among the powers along the lines of the spheres of influence was being freely discussed. Were the dismemberment of the Empire to be accomplished, and the various regions thus marked out to fall to the exclusive con trol of the powers now claiming them, China would become a group of colonies from which the American merchant could be excluded at the will of the respective powers just at the time when, after long years of waiting, he seemed to be on the point of realizing his dreams. In fact he was already practically excluded, by agreements actually executed before the summer of 1898, from the mining and rail-

way rights in almost every valuable field. If it had been the
sincere intention of the powers to permit free competition
in their respective spheres there was obviously no reason
whatever for the existing agreements.

BIBLIOGRAPHICAL NOTES

1. Several studies of American trade with Asia were made by the
   Bureau of Statistics of the U. S. Treasury Dept. after 1898.
   The more useful of these are: "Commercial Japan in 1899";
   Monthly Summary of Commerce and Finance, July, 1899;
   "Commercial China in 1900"; *ibid.,* June, 1901; "Commercial
   Korea in 1904"; *ibid.,* Jan., 1904. See also *Monthly Summary
   of Trade and Finance,* Apr., 1898, pp. 1632-3, 1638-9; *ibid.,*
   Sept., 1904, p. 1211; Jan., 1904, p. 2330. See, "China and the
   Far East," George H. Blakeslee, editor, chaps. 2, 3, 5 and 6.
2. The use, and misuse, of the American flag in China may best
   be studied in the so-called Seward-Bradford investigation, H.
   Rept. 134:45-3, and H. Misc. Doc. 31:45-2 (Part II).
3. H. Misc. Doc. 31-45-2 (Part II), pp. 228-31.
4. Royal Meeker: "History of Shipping Subsidies" (New York,
   1905); Walter T. Dinsmore: "Shipping Subsidies" (Boston
   and New York, 1907); David A. Wells: "Our Merchant Marine" (New York, 1882); H. Rept. 1210:51-1. Meeker has a
   full bibliography. H. Rept. 1210, pp. 136 ff., gives a complete
   review of the trans-Pacific American shipping.
5. Foreign Relations, 1877, p. 88.
6. Raphael Pumpelly: "Across America and Asia" (New York,
   1870), chaps. 15-22. This book is also very valuable for the
   light it throws on the political conditions in the East in 1863.
7. Inazo Nitobe: "Intercourse between United States and Japan,"
   pp. 116 ff.; Robert E. Lewis: "The Educational Conquest of
   the Far East," especially tables, appendix, pp. 223-4.
8. H. Misc. Doc. 31:45-2 (Part II), p. 561; Historic Shanghai by
   Montalto de Jesus.
9. Papers Relating to the Intercontinental Telegraph (Govt. Printing Off., 1864); George Kennan: "Tent Life in Siberia."
10. For. Relations, 1867, Part I, pp. 452, 456, 471 ff., 484; 1866,
    Part I, p. 475; 1874, pp. 246, 323, 335; 1875, pp. 260 ff.
11. H. Misc. Doc. 31:45-2 (Part II) gives the DeLano correspondence
    very fully.
12. For. Relations, 1881, pp. 224, 275, 280; 1882, p. 115.
13. Percy Horace Kent: "Railway Enterprise in China" (London,
    1907). This is a good general survey, but for the details of
    American projects it should be supplemented by American
    sources.
14. H. Misc. Doc. 31:45-2 (Part II) gives the documentary history
    of the Woosung Railway in great detail.
15. *Ibid.,* p. 139.

16. James H. Wilson: "China: Travels in the Middle Kingdom," first edition, 1887, was the first book to be published in the United States describing the opportunities for railroad development in China. The third edition (1901) includes the author's account of the Boxer uprising; General Wilson was second in command of the American forces in China in 1900.

17. William Barclay Parsons: "An American Engineer in China" (New York, 1900). Mr. Parsons was the engineer for the Brice Syndicate for the survey of the Canton-Hankow line in 1899.

18. John V. A. MacMurray: "Treaties and Agreements with and Concerning China, 1894-1919," 2 vols. (New York, 1921). The various compacts by which China signed away so many of her sovereign liberties are given in the first volume of this invaluable collection.

CHAPTER XXXI

HAWAII AND THE PHILIPPINES

In 1898, at the end of one hundred and fourteen years of relations with the Pacific and Asia, the political aspects of the Far Eastern question were for the first time presented for the serious consideration of the American people in definite proposals for the annexation of the Hawaiian Islands and the cession of the Philippines.

There had been brief, fragmentary and partisan discussions in Congress in 1843 when the Cushing Mission was authorized, in 1852 when the Perry Expedition was on its way eastward, and for the remainder of the sixth decade of the century Congress had kept a sharp eye on the condition of affairs as is indicated by the publication during that period of the entire diplomatic correspondence with China—more than twenty-five hundred pages of documents. Indeed the first years of the Buchanan administration occupied, in relation to Far Eastern affairs, a somewhat similar position to the first years of the McKinley administration. In each case the nation, having recovered from a period of financial depression and panic, found itself with a surplus of produce for which a foreign market seemed desirable and necessary.[1] In both instances the new mercantile energy of the American people was contemporaneous with disorganization and uncertainty in the Far East to which was joined the fear that other nations might seize the opportunity to obtain preferred positions and perhaps to close the doors.* In both cases Great Britain found in the United States a sufficient encouragement to justify approaches to the American Government with a view to the achievement of a cordial under

*One does not fail to note the striking similarities of the situations in 1859 and 1897 with that at the close of the World War in 1918.

standing if not an alliance for the settlement of the Far
Eastern question.[2] Both Buchanan and Hay, who became
Secretary of State in September, 1898, were promoted to
positions of great influence in American foreign policy from
periods of acceptable diplomatic service at the Court of St.
James following crises in Anglo-American relations which
had brought the American people to the brink of war with
England. But in 1857 President Buchanan had been so sure
of the general indifference of the American people that he
had not even presented the Far Eastern question to them for
consideration, whereas forty years later McKinley had
neither the disposition nor the power to keep it from them.

The same identical questions which had been decided by
Marcy, Buchanan and Cass in the later fifties, reappeared
in the late nineties. Indeed these questions, though often
decided, had never been disposed of. Seward had faced
them; so had Fish, Frelinghuysen, Blaine, Bayard and
Gresham. They were: Should the United States establish
protectorates or acquire territory in the Pacific and the Far
East? To what extent should the United States take action
to assert and to maintain the open door in China and to
sustain its sovereignty and integrity? What were the limits
to the degree of cooperation which should be established between the United States and Great Britain in the pursuit of
a common object and policy? The broad outlines of the
American problem in Asia had not changed in forty years;
no, not in more than half a century. The task of Caleb
Cushing in 1844 had been to obtain for Americans a non-
territorial equivalent for Hongkong. He had only partially
succeeded. The task for American statesmen in the last
three years of the century was to obtain for Americans a
real equivalent, territorial or otherwise, not merely for
Hongkong but now also for Kwangchow-wan, Foochow,
Tsingtao, Wei-hai-wei and Port Arthur, spheres of influence,
and the non-alienation agreements of five powers. The reason why the task had gone so long unfinished was merely
that the American people had not cared enough about the
markets of Asia to finish it. But in March, 1897, the month

of McKinley's inauguration, American steel rails began to sell in the European markets at $18 a ton, and this was assumed to indicate that at length the American people had reached the point in their industrial development where they could no longer safely neglect the markets of the world.[3]   It was believed by McKinley, by Mark Hanna, perhaps by John Hay, and by some, though not all capitalists and "captains of industry," that the American people were now ready to resume the task for wich the policy of Daniel Webster and Caleb Cushing had proved to be so inadequate.

THE ANNEXATION OF HAWAII

The annexation of the Hawaiian Islands was the *hors d'œuvre*.   The acquisition of these islands, however, while indubitably a piece of Far Eastern policy, was equally a measure of coast defense, as is clearly revealed in the fifty-five years' history of the question.[4]

The American interest in Hawaii from 1842 onward rose and fell with the corresponding interest in the Far East.   Tyler and Webster were of the opinion (December 30, 1842) that the United States would make a "decided remonstrance" if any other power were to take possession of the islands or subvert the native government.   A few months later when Lord George Paulet seized the islands for Great Britain, Commodore Kearny, returning from his successful efforts to secure for the United States most-favored-nation treatment in China, entered a vigorous protest.   Acting Secretary of State Legaré wrote to Edward Everett in London that the American Government might feel justified in "interfering by force," and the action of Paulet was disavowed.   Otherwise it seems very probable that the Hawaiian question would have taken on something of the "fifty-four-forty-or-fight" spirit.   At that time the American interest in the islands arose out of their value to the Pacific and trans-Pacific trade, particularly to the American whalers in the North Pacific which found at Honolulu a convenient place to refit.   When the French

took possession of Honolulu in 1849, though without hauling down the Hawaiian flag, the American Government an
nounced that it could not view with indifference the passing
of the islands under the control of any other power.   Two
years later the king placed in the hands of the American
representative an unregistered deed of cession of his domains, and while the deed was never executed, Marcy
stated (December, 1853) while Perry was negotiating with
Japan, that it seemed "inevitable" that the islands would
come under the control of the United States.   Less than
four months later he authorized the American representative to sign a treaty of annexation.*   The treaty was not
ratified by the United States because of the excessive annui-
ties stipulated for the native rulers and because it provided
that the islands should be admitted into the Union as a
state.

In 1863 the rank of the American representative was
raised to that of Minister Resident.   About the time of the
purchase of Alaska and the acquisition of the Midway
Island in 1867 a new reciprocity treaty was negotiated but
it was never ratified, just as a similar reciprocity treaty of
1855 had failed.   Seward considered annexation preferable
to reciprocity if the two were in conflict.

The settlement of the Pacific Coast, the increase of
trans-Pacific commerce, and the improvement of steam
navigation now brought the Hawaiian Islands within the
purview of coast defense.   The annexation question was
revived in 1871 and Secretary of State Fish recognized the
value of Honolulu as a "resting spot in mid-ocean between
the Pacific Coast and the vast domains of Asia which are
now opening to commerce and Christian civilization."

In 1875 a convention of commercial reciprocity containing a non-alienation agreement very similar in import
to those negotiated in China in 1898-9 was effected.   The
United States was given preferred treatment not open to
other nations under the most-favored-nation clause.   In

*This authorization by Marcy was sent to Honolulu immediately after the
receipt of Perry's first dispatches in which he unfolded his plan for the extension and protection of American trade in the Pacific and the East.

1881 Blaine, while expressing the desire of the United States that the "real and substantial independence" of the islands be maintained, reasserted their strategic importance and stated that occupation by a foreign power in case of international difficulties would be a "positive threat" which could not be "lightly risked" by the United States. New factors in the situation had arisen. The Chinese immigrants, brought in to work on the sugar plantations, had increased to a point where they threatened the "substitution of Mongolian supremacy for native control," while the sugar industry under the reciprocity convention of 1875 had greatly increased the value of the islands and the wealth of the Americans. "The Hawaiian Islands," stated Blaine, "cannot be joined to the Asiatic system. If they drift from their independent station it must be toward assimilation and identification with the American system to which they belong by the operation of natural laws and must belong by the operation of political necessity."

An extension of the reciprocity treaty was negotiated in 1884 and when it reached the Senate, so important now appeared the strategic value of the islands, that an amendment to the treaty was added by which Pearl Harbor, near Honolulu, was leased to the United States as a naval base. About the time this treaty was being ratified (1887) the United States declined to enter into a convention with Great Britain and France jointly to guarantee the neutrality of the islands.

Candor must compel one to admit that the American policy in the Hawaiian Islands was showing marked parallels to the existing and later policies of China and Japan in Korea: economic penetration under the treaties of 1875 and 1887, insistence on no disturbance of the trade, and demands for preferred commercial and political treatment.

Passing over many details of the domestic political development in Honolulu we come to the peaceful revolution of 1893 which was followed by the abdication of the reactionary Queen Liliuokalani, the establishment of a provisional government with Sanford B. Dole as President, and the negotiation, concurrently, of an annexation treaty which was signed February 14, and presented to the Senate in the closing days of the Harrison administration.   The President characterized the Hawaiian monarchy as "effete," and the native government as "weak and inadequate."   The choice seemed to him to be between making a formal protectorate, which had informally existed for half a century and had come to be tacitly recognized by all powers, or annexation.   He urged the latter.

President Cleveland, scandalized at what appeared to him to have been the intervention of American citizens, if not of American officials, in the *coup d'état* of January, 1893, withdrew the treaty from the Senate and started an investigation.   The important difference between the various *coup d'états* in Korea by which the Tai-wen-Kun, the Chinese and Japanese successively sought to obtain control of the government was that at Honolulu the efforts of the Americans who were determined upon annexation were unstained by assassinations and such barbarities as the murder anᴅ burning of a queen—a very important difference.   The Cleveland investigation only served to make more certain that the Hawaiians were incapable of maintaining unaided an enlightened, just and stable government. The delay incident to the investigation proved that the newly created republic while well able to maintain itself in the face of all native dissent, was not capable of meeting the pressure of foreign powers like Japan.   One of the earliest projects of the McKinley administration was to revive the question of annexation and to negotiate a treaty to that effect (June 16, 1897).   "Annexation is not a change," stated McKinley, "it is a consummation."

SUSPICION OF JAPANESE DESIGNS IN HAWAII

The treaty met with opposition in two quarters: from certain sections of American public opinion which will be described below; and from the Japanese Government which, elated by its success in the Sino-Japanese War and enriched by the Chinese indemnity which was being devoted to naval and military purposes, was undergoing a wave of popular enthusiasm both for expansion and for the assertion of racial dignity.

The Japanese Government through United States Minister Buck at Tokio, and even more energetically through the Japanese Minister, Hoshi Toru, at Washington, entered a vigorous protest—probably the most vigorous protest that up to that time had ever been issued by Japan to another power. This protest was doubly significant because it enlarged the question which might have been supposed to concern Japan. Not only did Japan protest that the annexation of the islands would endanger the settlement of the Japanese claims over the immigration question then pending, and the general rights of Japanese in the islands under the treaties between Japan and Hawaii, but also that the annexation would "disturb the *status quo* in the Pacific." While the Japanese Government took occasion to deny that it entertained designs against the territorial integrity or the sovereignty of the islands, the fact remained that the Japanese claim for the right of citizenship in the islands was not withdrawn. Did, then, Japan have in mind a program of economic penetration similar to that which was already in operation in Korea? Such a conclusion is not absolutely necessary for it must be remembered that while Japan had succeeded in holding Formosa in 1895 the hold was not very secure, and Japan may have felt that the annexation of the Hawaiian Islands would precipitate a scramble for islands in the Pacific in the confusion of which Japan would be separated from Formosa just as she had been forced to retire from the Liaotung peninsula. The maintenance of the *status quo,* by which Japan was in possession of Formosa, the Pescaderoes, the Lew Chews, the Bonins and the Kurile islands, was an important matter to Japan.[5]

But Japan could not well afford to alienate American public opinion, nor the sympathies of the American Government which had stood Japan in such good stead for so many years. Just at the moment things were going badly with Japan in Korea. After the murder of the queen the king had taken refuge in the Russian legation, and now the political affairs of Korea were being directed from St. Petersburg. Meanwhile Japan was seeking friends for herself in the struggle for the peninsula which was merely postponed. Specifically Japan desired to induce American capital to invest in Korea under Japanese auspices with a view to ranging the United States on the Japanese side in the coming struggle. Japan quickly though informally withdrew its protest against the disturbance of the *status quo* in the Pacific and confined its later negotiations to the immigration and claims questions. It was at length agreed that the Hawaiian Republic should settle the claims for about $130,000 and Japan then adopted a conciliatory attitude on the immigration question which was at length dismissed without any specific promises having been made by the American Government. When the annexation of the islands was accomplished a stipulation was inserted that American immigration laws would be extended to the islands thus bringing the Japanese immigrants under the provision of the treaty of 1894 between Japan and the United States. To this as well as to the extension of Ameri can immigration laws to the Philippines the Japanese Gov ernment made another very sharp protest, but without effect.

While the military and economic value of the islands was sufficient to commend the annexation to many it was the Far Eastern question which at length upset the balance of opinion and hastened the incorporation of the islands. Following the declaration of a state of war with Spain (April 20, 1898) Commodore George Dewey destroyed the Spanish fleet at Manila May 1. Three days later Francis G. Newlands of Nevada introduced into the House a joint resolution to annex Hawaii to the United States. The de bate on the bill began June 11. The House approved of it by vote of 209 to 91, and the Senate passed it July 6, 42 to 21. On July 8, 1898, President McKinley gave to the joint resolution his very ready assent and the Hawaiian Islands became a part of the territory of the United States. The commission appointed by the President to make recom mendations for legislation reported (December 6, 1898). By act of Congress April 30, 1900, the "Territory of Hawaii" was created and a territorial form of government authorized.

In order that we may have clearly before us the intimate relation between events and opinions in those momentous days, and may consider together the debates on the annexation of Hawaii and the cession of the Philippines, it is well at this point to review briefly the course of the Spanish American War.

THE PHILIPPINES IN THE SPANISH-AMERICAN WAR

No relation whatever can be established between the outbreak of hostilities with Spain and the Far Eastern question except that there was a concurrence of dates in the disturbed conditions in China and the climax of the often recurring disturbances in Cuba, and that both synchronized with the expansive movement in American trade which had followed the recovery from the Panic of 1893.[6] The Sino-Japanese War had caused a very notable strength ening of Continental fleets in Chinese waters.*

Notwithstanding the warnings of naval officers fre quently offered in the last quarter of a century, the Americans were without a naval base in the Far East.† There-

*The naval forces in the Far East at the end of November, 1895, were as follows:[7]

British	— total displacement —	58,908 tons	
Russian	"	"	58,838 "
French	"	"	28,669 "
German	"	"	23,078 "
American	"	"	18,553 "

The American naval force was even weaker than the figures would indicate for it included some antiquated vessels like the Monocacy, an old side-wheeler, which upon the outbreak of the war in 1898 was stuck in the mud at Shanghai and could not be moved even to comply with the declaration of neutrality by the Chinese Government. Between 1895 and the spring of 1898 the American fleet was actually decreased, but at the battle of Manila Bay Commodore Dewey's vessels had a total displacement of about 19,000 tons.

† The Secretary of the Navy, in his annual report for 1884, about four months before the occupation of Port Hamilton by the British naval forces, recommended that "additional coaling and naval stations" be established at nine points, among which he mentioned Port Hamilton as well as Honolulu. "From which latter naval station [Port Hamilton] and the ports of Korea there

fore at the outbreak of the Spanish-American War the American fleet in the Far East was left by the declarations of neutrality of Japan, China and Great Britain, in a position which required either a retirement of the fleet to Honolulu from which a declaration of neutrality by the Hawaiian Republic might have barred it, or an attack upon Manila. The retirement of the American forces from the Far East in the spring of 1898 when the Chinese Empire was in such precarious condition would have resulted in a very great loss of American prestige and perhaps an attack upon American life and property, for the Chinese had always been quick to interpret such events as an involuntary weakening of a foreign power. American shipping, also, would have been exposed to attack from the Spanish fleet at Manila.

The attack upon Manila by the American forces was not, however, accidental or unforeseen. Commodore George Dewey was ordered to Japan (October 21, 1897) to assume command of the Far Eastern Squadron.* Ten days after the destruction of the U. S. S. *Maine* at Havana Harbor Dewey was instructed to hold himself in readiness to engage the Spanish Squadron at Manila and to conduct offensive operations against the Philippines. The intent of these orders, however, appears plainly to have been to remove the menace of the Spanish fleet rather than to acquire Manila.

The American fleet was ordered to rendezvous at Hongkong and measures were immediately taken to secure adequate supplies. Dewey was even prepared to ignore any declaration of neutrality which might be made by the Chinese Empire.[s] He was informed that Japan, which at that

should be established a regular line of steamers carrying the United States flag, connecting with the present line between San Francisco and Japan."

Dr. H. C. Allen stated that W. W. Rockhill once remarked to him that the King of Korea had at one time through Admiral Shufeldt offered Port Hamilton to the United States as a naval station. This offer was made, presumably, after the evacuation of the island by the British in 1887.

* The partisan and political influences under which the entire war with Spain was conducted are well illustrated by the fact that Dewey, in order to make sure of the assignment to the Far Eastern Squadron, felt compelled to invoke the political influences of Senator Proctor of Vermont, his native state. He took this action upon the advice of Roosevelt, then Assistant Secretary of the Navy.

time was badly frightened by the presence of such large European forces in the East, would maintain the most scrupulous neutrality—a neutrality which, nevertheless, Japan was induced to relax slightly a few months after the war broke out. Upon the announcement that a state of hostili ties existed between the United States and Spain (there was no declaration of war by either side) the British representa tives at Hongkong requested the American fleet to leave by 4 P. M., April 25. Commodore Dewey complied and with no unnecessary delay proceeded to Manila Bay. The battle of May 1st with its swift and brilliant victory left Dewey in control of the bay, with the city in his power. Owing to the lack of a sufficient landing force Dewey refrained from occupying the city which he would have been unable to police. Manila was not taken until August 13 and then after some little resistance which probably would not have been presented had the Americans been prepared on May 1st to reap the fruits of their naval victory.

Two concurrent events, significant in a study of policy, demand attention.

There had been incipient or open rebellion in the Philip pines for more than a decade. The execution by the Span ish authorities of Dr. José Rizal, the Filipino patriot, De cember 30, 1896, had produced a short-lived insurrection which was suspended early in 1897 by the arrival of Spanish reinforcements and the agreement of the rebel leaders, Andres Bonifacio and Emilio Aguinaldo, upon the payment of several hundred thousand dollars, to retire from the island. These men went to Hongkong and established a Filipino Junta with the money thus obtained and were able to continue their patriotic agitation. This Junta formally sought the intervention and protection of the United States and later proposed an alliance. The insurgents had previously sought the aid of Japan. Early in 1898 there were insurrections in both Luzon and Cebu. In April, 1898, Commodore Dewey had several conferences with the Filipino leaders at Hongkong, and in the latter part of the month E. Spencer Pratt, United States consul general at

Singapore, had an interview with Aguinaldo, recently arrived from Hongkong, and appears to have proposed to
him that he return to China, join Dewey's forces, and accompany the Americans to Manila with a view to assisting
them in the Philippines just as Gomez and Garcia had been
helping the American forces in Cuba, by promoting insurrection against the Spanish authority.   Dewey approved
of the suggestion and May 19 Aguinaldo was brought to
Manila in the U. S. dispatch boat *McColloch*, upon
Dewey's order.[9]   While Dewey was careful to make no
promises to Aguinaldo, he did give no little encouragement
and turned over to him the arsenal at Cavite and permitted
him to organize his insurgent forces within the American
lines.   Consul General Rounseville Wildman had also assisted the insurrectos to purchase arms in Hongkong.
Aguinaldo gave out the statement to the Filipinos that the
United States would assist the insurrectors.

It does not appear that Admiral Dewey or any of the
American representatives in contact with the insurgents
before the arrival of the first expeditionary forces June 30,
had any suspicion that the United States would acquire
the Philippines.   "Every American citizen who came in
contact with the Filipinos at the inception of the Spanish
War," stated General Thomas M. Anderson, who was the
first to give to Dewey the news that there was talk in the
United States of the retention of the islands, "or at any
time within a few months after hostilities began probably
told those he talked with . . . that we intended to free
them from Spanish oppression."   In other words, Consul
General Pratt, Admiral Dewey, and many more were reaffirming what had been stated hundreds of times by
American representatives in the East since the days in 1832
when Edmund Roberts made his treaties, viz., that the
United States had neither the intention nor the constitutional right to acquire colonies.   In support of this opinion
there was also the very recent declaration of President
McKinley at the outbreak of the war that the acquisition
of territory was not the purpose of the United States.

The Filipino insurgents appear, however, to have con sidered the possibility that the American Government might alter its traditional policy, and to have decided that at any rate it would be well to accept such aid as was being immediately offered and to meet future problems as they arose. Aguinaldo organized a government on June 12, proclaimed a provisional constitution June 23, and on August 6, a week before the American forces occupied Manila, issued an appeal to the nations of the world for recognition of the independence and belligerency of his government. Meanwhile the insurrectos established military control over part of Luzon.

The second significant event of this period was the action of the three European powers which only three years before had intervened to demand the recession of the Liaotung peninsula to China and subsequently forced the Empire to lease the various ports already referred to as well as to grant the spheres of influence. Germany, especially, had revealed an alarming land-hunger, and was known to be intriguing in Europe to bring about intervention in the Spanish-American war. At Hongkong Prince Henry, the Kaiser's brother, who had been dispatched to China to make sure of the lease of Kiaochow, remarked to Dewey that he did not believe that the European powers would permit the United States to retain Cuba. Shortly after May first two German cruisers appeared at Manila and other German war vessels followed. Indeed a transport with 1200 reserves was anchored in the harbor for a month. Vice Admiral von Dietrichs stated to Dewey rather sharply: "I am here by order of the Kaiser, sir," and proceeded to show a notable indifference to the blockade regulations which Dewey had established. The German force at the end of June was larger than the blockading squadron. At the same time the Germans sustained very intimate relations with the Spanish authorities within the uncaptured city, and made themselves familiar with the military situation. President McKinley is reported to have believed that war with Germany was imminent.

Meanwhile the ranking officer of the British naval vessels, Admiral Chichester, also observing the proceedings, upon orders from his government fully sustained Dewey's blockade regulations, and on August thirteenth when the American fleet proceeded to attack the city in cooperation with the American land forces, the British Admiral moved H.M.S. *Immortalité* to a point which placed it between the American fleet and the vessels of the European powers. Upon receiving notice that the city had surrendered to the Americans, the British vessel alone offered a salute to the American flag.

Peace Negotiations with Spain

The peace negotiations between the United States and Spain began July 22, with a message from the Queen to President McKinley, transmitted through Jules Cambon, the French Ambassador at Washington.[10] To the inquiry of the Queen as to the possible terms of peace the President replied, July 30, stipulating (1) the relinquishment by Spain of Cuba; (2) the cession of to the United States, and the evacuation by Spain of the islands of Porto Rico and the other islands now under sovereignty of Spain in the West Indies, and also the cession of an island in the Ladrones to be selected by the United States; (3) the right to occupy and hold "the city, bay and harbor of Manila pending the conclusion of a treaty of peace which shall determine the control, disposition, and the government of the Philippines." The question of pecuniary indemnity was reserved for subsequent discussion. The stipulation for the cession of an island in the Ladrones had reference to a cable station which, as already noted, had become necessary because of the monopoly of the Great Northern Telegraph Company in Japan and China. The carefully drawn specifications as to Manila and the Philippines indicates either that McKinley, encouraged by the decision of Congress on the Hawaiian annexation, had already determined to hold some part of the Philippines if possible, or at least that he was giving this question close consideration. It must have been quite obvious to any one familiar with the dispatches from Tokio, Seoul and Peking in the summer of 1898, that the Philippines offered a most important strategic position for the United States in case the threatened partition of China along the lines of the spheres of influence should take place. A close study of the trade conditions during the century since the American flag first appeared in Manila Bay, would have indicated that the commercial value of the islands was of very much less importance than the strategic advantages.[11]

"The terms relating to the Philippines seem," replied the Spanish Minister of State (August 7) "to our understanding, to be quite indefinite." He pointed out that the Spanish flag still waved over Manila and that the control of Spain of the archipelago was still unquestioned by any military operations. However, the protocol, signed August 12, contained the stipulation with reference to the Philippines substantially as outlined by President McKinley twelve days before.

In his instructions to the Peace Commissioners (September 16) the President revealed an expanding purpose in the Far East by ordering them to demand "the cession in full right and sovereignty of the island of Luzon, and equal port and trade rights with the Spanish in all unceded territory in the islands." McKinley elaborated his reasons for these demands:

"Without any original thought of complete or even partial acquisition, the presence and success of our arms at Manila imposes upon us obligations which we cannot disregard. The march of events rules and overrules human action. Avowing unreservedly the purpose which has animated all our efforts, and still solicitous to adhere to it, we can not be unmindful that without any desire or design on our part the war has brought us new duties and responsibilities which we must meet and discharge as becomes a great nation on whose growth and career from the beginning the Ruler of Nations has plainly written the high command and pledge of civilization."

The above paragraph was obviously a reference to the alarming international situation in the Far East. Asia was in imminent danger of a convulsion which, once started, could hardly have failed to involve the entire world. The Philippines were unlikely to remain long in the hands of Spain which, impoverished by war, was unable to defend them and badly in need of money. Either by conquest or by purchase they would very probably fall into the out-stretched hands of some waiting European power—very likely Germany—if the Americans were to stand aside.

"Incidental to our tenure of the Philippines is the commercial opportunity to which American statesmanship can not be indifferent," continued McKinley. "It is just to use every legitimate means for the enlargement of American trade; but we seek no advantages in the Orient which are not common to all. Asking only the open door for ourselves, we are ready to accord the open door to others. The commercial opportunity which is naturally and inevitably associated with this new opening depends less on large territorial possessions than upon an adequate commercial basis and upon broad and equal privileges."

This, the first use in an American document of the "open door" phrase establishes the connection between McKinley's Chinese and Philippines policies. A fortuitous concurrence of events had brought within American grasp the very expedient which Commodore Perry and Dr Peter Parker had urged in 1853 and 1857. Manila might become the equivalent for Hongkong, and the leased ports of China, for the lack of which American trade and interests in the Far East were, in the summer of 1898, in serious prospective if not present embarrassment.

Exactly forty days after signing the instructions to the Peace Commissioners who had departed immediately for Paris where the conference was held, Secretary of State Hay (October 26) still further enlarged the American demands by cabling to the Commissioners:

"The information which has come to the President since your departure convinces him that the acceptance of the cession of Luzon alone, leaving the rest of the islands subject to Spanish rule, or to be the subject of future contention, can not be justified on political, commercial, or humanitarian grounds. The cession must be of the whole of the archipelago or none. The latter is wholly inadmissible and the former must therefore be required."

The precise nature of the information which induced McKinley thus to increase his demands would appear to have been gathered from the reports of the American military and naval authorities and from the diplomatic correspondence from the various foreign capitals in both the East and the West. While Admiral Dewey had thought so little of the first German interference at Manila that at first he had not even made a report upon it, the facts were reported to Europe or London by at least one foreign consul at Manila and were known by the President. Various American military and naval officers from Manila were dispatched to Paris where they appeared before the Peace Commissioners in October and expressed themselves very frankly.* Russia was reported to be desirous of establishing at least a naval base in the islands. It was very unlikely that France, the possessions of which in South China were most immediately concerned, would let such another opportunity pass unutilized. Japan, fearful whether in another scramble for islands she might not be separated from Formosa as she had been from Port Arthur, was very desirous that the Philippines be brought under American protection, though not unwilling to effect an understanding with the United States by which the Empire could share in the possession of the islands. Great Britain was alarmed at the prospect of the increase of European influence so near Hongkong, Singapore and her South Pacific possessions. The arguments against the retention by the United States either of a mere naval base or of the island of Luzon were, from the standpoint of military and political affairs, overwhelming. The complete relinquishment or only partial possession of the islands would have promoted war rather than peace in Asia.

After many protests and with the utmost reluctance

*"Senator Frye: Q. If we should adopt your line of demarcation what do you think Spain would do with the balance of those islands?
A. Sell them to Germany.
Q. Is not Germany about as troublesome a neighbor as we could get?
A. The most so, in my opinion. I think it probable that the balance of the Spanish possessions in the Pacific not acquired by us will go to Germany. Germany has long desired to possess the Carolines, and she hoisted her flag at Yap in 1886." (Statement of Commander R. B. Bradford, U. S. N., October 14, 1898, before the United States Peace Commission at Paris.[12])

Spain, while she "relinquished" all claims to sovereignty over Cuba, "ceded" Porto Rico, Guam and the Philippines to the United States in the Treaty of Paris (December 10, 1898). It was agreed also in lieu of the assumption by the United States of the Spanish debt in Cuba or the Philippines, that Spain should receive $20,000,000 for the Philippines.

Debate on Hawaii and the Philippines

Five phases of the debates in Congress over the annexation of Hawaii and the Philippines may be distinguished. It was a partisan contest in which both the Democratic and Republican party leaders kept an eye upon the presidential campaign of 1900. There was the clear-cut legal question as to whether the American Government had the constitutional right to acquire non-contiguous territory not designed to be admitted to statehood in the Union. There was the moral question arising out of the consent-of-the-governed doctrine. There was the economic question which included on its industrial side the fear of the introduction of Asiatic cheap labor and on the commercial side the ambitions of the trade expansionists. There was, also, the question of expediency: All other phases of the subject being dismissed as settled, did political, military or commercial expediency demand annexation? It was one of the greatest debates in American congressional history.[13]

Of the partisan passages in the debate little need be said, although one would like to record them as an illustration of the futile demagogic clap-trap of the politician such as always intrudes itself in popular government.* However, neither question was decided on purely partisan lines, and in the final vote on the Treaty of Paris, while several Republicans voted against it, there were enough Democratic

*For example, in the debate on Hawaii: "But above all, William McKinley will have sore need for the three electoral votes of Hawaii in the melancholy days of November, in 1900, when he again faces at the polls the great tribune of the people, William Jennings Bryan, of Nebraska." And again: "There is a pressing necessity for two rotten borough Senators to eke out the single gold-standard majority at the other end of the capitol." These were two of the three reasons assigned by Champ Clark (Dem.) to the Republicans as being the actual motives for the annexation of Hawaii.

and Populist votes to secure the necessary two-thirds approval. At the beginning of 1899 the annexation of the Philippines had become so popular in various parts of the country that the Democratic leaders, Bryan included, deemed it unwise to oppose it. Within six months after Dewey's victory the territorial enlargement of the nation had ceased, in large measure, to be a partisan question.

The constitutional and moral aspects of the choice were discussed in able and elevated manner quite in contrast with the partisan debate. The opinion of Chief Justice Taney in the Dred Scott case was frequently alluded to.* Much was made of the fact that both in Hawaii and the Philippines whatever government might be set up after annexation had been accomplished would be without the consent of the governed, and that the transfer of the territories themselves was being advocated without any clear indication of the consent of the people. This argument, strong in fact, lost much of its force from those who while advancing it still maintained that naval bases both at Pearl Harbor and in the Philippines ought to be acquired.

The minority report on the joint resolution for the annexation of Hawaii was presented in the House by Hugh A. Dinsmore who had for two years (1887-9) been the United States Minister Resident at Seoul. Dinsmore argued that the annexation would be neither constitutional nor desirable. "If we acquire Hawaii, it is but the first step in the progress of colonial aggrandizement," stated Dinsmore. "What must we expect if we enter upon a colonial policy? Suppose we set our feet upon territory in the Orient. From that moment we become involved in every European controversy with reference to aggressions and the acquirement of territory there. No longer will our ancient peace abide with us." Much of the opposition to annexation was based on the assumption that by the continuance of a policy of territorial and political isolation it

* "There is certainly no power given by the constitution to the Federal Government to establish or maintain colonies bordering on the United States or at a distance, to be ruled and governed at its own pleasure, nor to enlarge its territorial limits in any way except by the admission of new States."

would be possible for the United States to avoid war. Senator George Frisbie Hoar (Massachusetts), although he had already set his face like flint against the acquisition of the Philippines, nevertheless saw the futility of this argument when applied to Hawaii. After a conference with President McKinley in which the latter had told him of the landing of the Japanese immigrants at Honolulu, of the evidence of their military training, of the patent determination of Japan to acquire the islands, Hoar went into the Senate and made a powerful speech in advocacy of annexation. He based his argument largely upon the conviction that the failure to annex at that time would lead to inevitable conflict with Japan at some future date. He pointed out that were a line to be drawn from the point of American territory in the Aleutian Islands nearest Asia to the southernmost point of American territory on the Pacific Coast, Hawaii would lie eastward of that line. The annexation of Hawaii was to Senator Hoar, indeed to most Americans, primarily a measure of coast defense. While Dewey's victory at Manila served to expedite the consideration of the question, it was the fear of Japanese aggression which carried the greater weight in the debate and it seems probable that this argument alone would have been sufficient to accomplish the annexation.

In the course of the Hawaiian debate practically all the partisan, constitutional, and moral grounds were traversed and in the consideration of the Philippine question no new principles were brought forward. But the facts were in some respects very different. Whatever may have been the intent of the makers of the Constitution in respect to the acquisition of non-contiguous territory for colonial purposes it is at least certain that no adequate provision had been made for specific constitutional means to meet the situation which developed at Manila after May 1st, 1898. In the first place the American fleet in Manila Bay was in actual danger. The arrival of reinforcements from Spain, the stiffening of either Spanish or Filipino opposition to Dewey's presence, or the intervention of European powers were all possible eventualities. There were the gravest military reasons for strengthening the American forces, and for the occupation of the city of Manila. Additional naval vessels were sent and by the end of July there had arrived from San Francisco an expeditionary force of nearly 11,000 although Dewey had asked for only 5000. The occupation of Manila, August 13, did not greatly alter the military situation even though an armistice had been established. Talk of European intervention still continued, the Germans extended their interest to other islands of the archipelago, and the attitude of the insurrectos was most uncertain. In all probability conflict with the Filipinos might have been avoided had the American Government possessed the power to issue immediately a statement guaranteeing ultimate autonomy to the Islands under an American or even an international protectorate. But no such power existed.

While these facts were sufficient to account for the new aspects of the case presented to Congress in December, 1898, there was another fact of greater actual potency. President McKinley and his advisers at some date which may be clearly fixed as not earlier than May 1, and not later than the end of that month, became persuaded that the retention of at least Manila would be desirable for either military or commercial reasons, or for both. The President became convinced also that the American people would support such a program. It soon became evident, however, that it would be unsafe to retain Manila without taking the entire archipelago for much the same reasons that it had been accepted as unsafe to retain Pearl Harbor without annexing all of the Hawaiian Islands. The result was that a situation was deliberately, as well as of necessity, created in the Philippines which made the debate on the approval of the Treaty of Paris somewhat different from the debate on Hawaii. When Congress met in December, and when the article of the Treaty of Paris was sent to the Senate early in January, there were already more than 15,000 American soldiers, mostly volunteers, in the Islands, and they were in danger of a Filipino uprising. This new situation abounded in opportunities to appeal to American national pride, and placed both the politician and the statesman who viewed with alarm the prospect of colonial possessions in positions where only the wisest of men ought to be.   Nothing in all previous American political expe rience afforded an adequate precedent or guide.

On December 10, 1898, the day the Treaty of Paris was signed, Senator George G. Vest (Missouri) introduced a joint resolution:

"That under the Constitution of the United States no power is given to the Federal Government to acquire territory to be held and governed permanently as colonies.

"The colonial system of European nations can not be established under our present Constitution, but all territory acquired by the Government, except such small amount as may be necessary for coaling stations, correction of boundaries, and similar governmental purposes, must be acquired and governed with the purpose of ultimately organizing such territory into States suitable for admission into the Union."

Two days later the debate began but the President did not wait for a decision.   On December 21, he instructed the War Department to extend the military government already established at Manila over the entire archipelago as rapidly as possible.   McKinley described American rights in the islands as acquired by conquest.[14]   This instruction, which was a few days later telegraphed to Manila and published, consolidated the opposition of the insurrectos to the United States, whereas the passage of the Vest resolution would probably have prevented the approaching rebellion.*

Senator Augustus O. Bacon (Georgia) introduced on January 11 a resolution which also would have prevented the impending rebellion.

"That the United States hereby disclaim any disposition or intention to. exercise sovereignty, jurisdiction or control over said islands, and assert their determination, when a stable and independent

---

*"They begged for some tangible concession from the United States Government—one which they could present to the people and which might serve to allay the excitement." (Report of meeting, January 9, 1899, of American officers appointed by Major General E. S. Otis to confer with commission representing the Aguinaldo government.) [15]

government shall have been duly erected therein entitled to recognition as such, to transfer to said government, upon terms which shall be reasonable and just, all rights secured under the cession by Spain, and to thereupon leave the government and control of the islands to their people."

The passage of this resolution would have given to the Philippines a status similar to that already accorded to Cuba. February 14th, a vote on the Bacon resolution resulted in a tie, and Vice President Hobart cast the deciding vote against it. The same day a joint resolution, previously introduced by Samuel D. McEnery (Louisiana) was passed, 26 to 22, in which it was stated that "it is the intention of the United States to establish on said islands a government suitable to the wants and conditions of the inhabitants of said islands, to prepare for them *local self-government*,* and in due time to make such disposition of said islands as will promote the interests of the citizens of the United States and the inhabitants of said islands." Permanent annexation was expressly disavowed. After so much encouragement from the opposition which was conducting an active campaign for immediate withdrawal of the American forces, the Filipinos were less than ever prepared to accept a status as a theoretically conquered people. In point of fact the American forces had not even conquered the island of Luzon. The most that can be said in extenuation is that the policy and the resolution had been adopted in great ignorance of the actual facts in the islands, and in a blissful and exalted assumption that any race ought to regard conquest by the American people as a superlative blessing.

SIGNIFICANCE OF SENATE APPROVAL OF TREATY OF PARIS

The vote on the Treaty of Paris was set for February 6. Two days before the vote the insurgents and the American military forces came into actual conflict, and some American soldiers were killed. That this fact influenced the decision of the Senate there can be little doubt.

*Italics by T. D.

The vote was 57 to 27, three Republican senators voting
with the opposition. A change of two votes would have
defeated the treaty. While there would appear to be no
foundation for the charge that the American military forces
in the Philippines had deliberately brought on the conflict
of February 4 with a view of influencing the Senate, it is
quite evident that while the treaty was under consideration,
the Administration had created a condition in the Islands
which in the end exercised a coercing influence on the
Senate. That such a policy had appeared to be necessary
at the time reveals how utterly inadequate are the provisions of the American Constitution enabling the government to initiate wise preventive measures to meet such
threatening situations as were now constantly recurring in
Asia.

"The war that followed it," wrote Senator Hoar seven years later,
"crushed the Republic that the Philippine people had set up for
themselves, deprived them of their independence, and established
there, by American power, a government in which the people have no
part, against their will. No man, I think, will seriously question
that that action was contrary to the Declaration of Independence, the
fundamental principles declared in many State constitutions, the
principles avowed by the founders of the Republic, and by our statesmen of all parties down to a time long after the death of Lincoln." [16]

Such a passage, which was and is still more or less characteristic of the opposition to the acquisition of the Islands
is worthy of note. It assumed what was not true. The
Filipinos had not set up a "republic"; the nature of the
government which they would select, or which Aguinaldo
and his advisers would have selected for them, was not clear,
and the measures which they had actually adopted by
February 1, 1899, by no means prove that they were likely
to set up democratic institutions. The rebellion arose not
in support of a republic but in opposition to the proposed
conquest by the United States.

But even were one to grant the entire truth of every
similar assertion made by Senator Hoar and so many others,
one need not reach his conclusion in the absence of any
constructive suggestion for dealing with the international

des Philippines par les états-unis," *Revue Historique,* juillet-âout, 1903, pp. 282-3, for a Continental point of view; also Baron von Eckardstein's "Ten Years at the Court of St. James 1895-1905."

7. North China *Daily News,* Nov. 29, 1895.
8. Dewey: "Autobiography," 168 ff.
9. Le Roy gives a thoroughly adequate discussion, based on Filipino as well as American documents of the relations of Pratt, Wildman and Dewey to Aguinaldo. For a much less judicial and more partisan discussion see James H. Blount: "The American Occupation of the Philippines, 1898-1912." The pamphlet literature, magazine articles, and government documents are too multitudinous to admit of inclusion here.
10. Moore's "Digest," vol. 1, pp. 520 ff. John Bassett Moore had been in the Department of State for several years, and became Secretary of the American Peace Commission at Paris.
11. For a highly enthusiastic estimate of the possibilities of American trade with Asia—really a campaign document for the Administration policy—see Frank A. Vanderlip, *Century Magazine,* August, 1898. This was partially reprinted in S. Doc. 62:55-3, Pt. I, pp. 563 ff.
12. S. Doc. 62:55-3 (Pt. I) p. 484.
13. A very adequate collection of these debates is to be found in Marion Mills Miller: "Great Debates in American History" (New York, 1913) 14 vols.—Vol. 3, chaps. 5 and 6.
14. S. Doc. 331:57-1, pp. 776-8.
15. S. Doc. 208:56-1, p. 62.
16. Hoar's "Autobiography," Vol. 2, p. 304.

ι
S
a
n
w
iı

CHAPTER XXXII

THE REASSERTION OF THE OPEN-DOOR POLICY

In the McKinley administration the most aggressive force in the relations of the Government with Asia was not the Department of State. The Philippine policy issued from the President and he entrusted its execution to the military branch of the government. The Department of State does not appear to have had much to do with it. It was carried forward by military rather than by diplomatic measures. Much subsequent trouble would probably have been avoided had it been otherwise. There are at least intimations that McKinley would have been willing to adopt in China a policy similar to that which was being applied in the Philippines. Happily the entrance of John Hay into the McKinley cabinet in the autumn of 1898 re stored the ascendancy of diplomacy over military interven tion and led to measures which not only averted the dis memberment of China but likewise rendered unnecessary a program such as McKinley might otherwise have pro- posed.* On the other hand, the determination of the Presi- dent gave to the Hay diplomacy a support without which it might have been less successful.†

*John W. Foster reports a conversation between McKinley and Hay in which the former is asserted to have expressed a willingness to share in the partition of China in case the dismemberment of the Empire were actually to take place.¹

†John Hay, U. S. Ambassador at the Court of St. James since the begin- ning of the McKinley administration, was invited to become Secretary of State, August 13, 1898, in place of R. W. Day, who had been appointed a member of the Peace Commission. Hay assumed the duties of the new office September 30. He was the most experienced diplomat appointed to this office in the nineteenth century, and one of the best informed men of his day upon European politics. In the direction of diplomatic affairs in the Far East Mr. Hay was ably assisted by W. W. Rockhill who, at that time Director of the Bureau of American Republics, had been almost continuously in the diplomatic service or the Department of State for fourteen years. Rockhill entered the diplo- matic service at his own charges at the Legation in Peking in 1884, retiring three years later. In 1887 he served for a few months as *chargé d'affaires* at Seoul at a very critical time. Subsequently he extended his knowledge of Far Eastern affairs by travels and researches, and in 1899 was exceedingly well

The Far East in 1899

The close of the Sino-Japanese War had revealed a working agreement between Russia, Germany and France. The most subtle force in this informal alliance, perhaps, was Germany, which was already seeking to divert the attention of Russia from the Near to the Far East.* Whatever the relations between Germany and Russia it is evident that the place of France in the concert was due not to any desire to assist Germany but rather to the fact that the extension of Russian military and commercial influence in the Far East promised an ever widening field for French investors. In contrast to this concert of powers we find the other three nations which were interested in China, the so-called "trading nations"—Great Britain, Japan and the United States —severally in diplomatic isolation, and yet collectively opposed to Russia, Germany and France, and thus drawn by a common interest to each other.

The diplomatic cordiality between Russia and the United States, so noticeable in China after 1850, certainly did not arise out of any spiritual kinship between the Russian and the American political theories or institutions. It was, however, profitable to both nations and was studiously cultivated by Russia. In her long struggle with England

prepared to interpret the situation in the East. It has often been said that Rockhill's position in the Bureau of American Republics was secured for him in order that the Department of State might still have the benefit of his advice on diplomatic matters in Asia. Hay regarded him as one of the two best American diplomats, the other being Henry White.[2] The extent of Hay's dependence upon Rockhill has, perhaps, not yet been fully appreciated.

*Russia was for the moment usually regarded as the leader in the concert of powers which brought about the recession of the Liaotung peninsula. There were even rumors that Li Hung Chang had been assured by Russia before the Treaty of Shimoneséki that Port Arthur would be returned to China. General Foster, who would be expected to know, denied this. Count Witte in his Memoirs states that he was the initiator of the plan and records that the decision was reached on March 30, 1895. Korff and other Russians credit Witte's statement. Cordier believes that France was the initiator, having addressed a communication to Russia on the subject April 10. The writer has heard it asserted by one who was intimately associated with the diplomatic corps at the time that it was usually accepted that the plan for intervention was first put forward by the French Legation at Peking. There is also another version of the affair which was credited by Minister Denby but which seems never to have been widely known. It was believed that throughout the negotiations at Shimoneséki Li Hung Chang was in telegraphic communication with Herr von Brandt, formerly German Minister at Peking and then attached to the German Foreign Office. It was believed that Li Hung Chang, after feigning illness for two days, signed the treaty immediately upon receipt of a telegram from von Brandt stating that the powers would come to the rescue of China. Count Hayashi believed that Germany was the initiator of the concert.[3]

she sought the United States, also opposed by England, as a friend and possible ally. So long as Great Britain was seeking to break down the Monroe Doctrine she was creat ing favorable conditions for a Russo-American understand ing. Russian friendship for the United States was always related to British policy; the sale of Alaska was a case in point. While Stoeckl made it appear that Russia was re luctant to sell, the situation was in fact quite otherwise. Russia was eager to place in the keeping of the United States a territory which Great Britain could so easily have taken from Russia in the case of a war such as seemed probable. Russia was equally glad to be free to devote her energies to Eastern Asia. Almost immediately after the sale of Alaska Russia adopted in Peking a policy which aroused the suspicion of the American representatives.*

The policy of Russia in China appears to have been always to conciliate China and win her especial good will with a view to capitalizing it subsequently as was illus trated in the relations between Russia and China after 1895. There had been many similar episodes in the preceding thirty-five years. Russia never sincerely accepted the co operative policy in China. Russian policy in Korea was equally devious. These methods and designs in the East, coinciding as they did with the reports of the Siberian exile atrocities, the new outbursts of Jewish persecutions, as well as with the new cordial understanding between the United States and Great Britain, definitely ended the traditional friendship which had led Oliver Wendell Holmes in 1871 to pen his poetic invocation: "God bless the Empire that loves the Great Union, Strength to her People! Long Life to the Czar!"

Cordial relations between Germany and the United States in China existed until 1882. Then Germany be-

---

*In a personal letter, March 13, 1873, Minister Low stated to Secretary of State Fish that he had reason to believe that Russia was not sincerely cooper ating with the other ministers in the common plan to force the audience ques tion. He believed that Russia was secretly advising the Chinese not to yield. He thought that Russia was either seeking to prevent the other powers from increasing their influence, or was hoping to provoke hostilities between China and the powers, thus creating conditions similar to 1860 which would be favorable for Russia to acquire more Chinese territory.⁴

trayed indications of an aggressive policy which raised questions as to how far the Americans ought to carry cooperation.* The advance of German influence in Japan in the next decade was accomplished at the expense of the United States and still further separated the two powers. The seizure of Kiaochow and the establishment of the German sphere of influence in Shantung brought Germany into direct conflict with fundamental American policy. At the same time the harmonious relations between Berlin and Washington were being disturbed by questions of reciprocal tariff arrangements.

There had been no kinship between the policies of France and those of the United States in China at least since 1862 when the French withdrew from the International Settlement at Shanghai. The Americans were wholly opposed to the French protectorate of the Roman Catholic missions and regarded French policy as one which tended to create general hostile feeling among the Chinese for all foreigners. American policy had, however, never taken the form of active opposition to French interests and while the United States had sought to mediate in the Franco-Chinese War (1884-5) the attitude of Frelinghuysen had been one of the most scrupulous and even timid neutrality. In 1899 the relations between the United States and France were cordial, but the American Government was as far removed from sympathy with French as with Russian or German designs in the East.

The old cordiality between Japan and the United States was cooling, but it was not cold. The United States had stood by Japan in the Sino-Japanese War, and the immigration and Hawaiian questions had only created a passing chill. The *emeute* of October 8, 1895, in Seoul, the murder of the queen and the subsequent acquittal of Miura had greatly reduced American regard for the Japanese but there

*"The government with whom we have been most in sympathy is Germany. . . ." But "in recent years Germany has shown activity in the East. Her policy has been eager, decisive, and peremptory, going so far . . . as to land troops on Chinese soil, and prevent the Chinese from carrying out their interpretation of the treaties. The advance of German influence had been marked and steady." (Young to Frelinghuysen, February 4, 1883.) Cordier relates the episode at Swatow where German marines were landed.[6]

had been little to choose between the methods of China and of Japan in Korea except that one had failed and the other had been successful. The American occupation of the Philippines was the best test of the quality of Japanese-American relations. Before 1898 the Filipino insurgents had sought aid from Japan and a small quantity of arms had been smuggled into Luzon from Japanese sources. When the insurgents turned against the United States in 1899 they again appealed to Japan for sympathy and help. Through a German firm in Japan some munitions were actually started on their way to the Philippines, but they were intercepted and there is no reason to suppose that the effort ever received any sympathy from the Japanese Government. Japan was never in a more difficult situation than in 1898 and the Japanese Government, as well as the more conservative press, expressed the earnest wish that the United States would remain in the Philippines. Among all the possible neighbors to Japan, particularly to Formosa, Japan vastly preferred the United States to any other Western power. Furthermore, the traditional American policy was as favorable to Japan in China as it had been to Japan in Korea. The closing of the doors in China before Japan had really entered them in force, or the partition of the Empire at a time when Japan was wholly unable to share in the supposed benefits, were as inimical to Japan as to the United States. The two nations were natural allies and Japan, recently so roughly treated by the concert, probably would have been not unwilling to effect a formal alliance with both Great Britain and the United States.

The relations between the United States and Great Britain in the Far East had never been actually unfriendly since 1853. They reached their maximum of cordiality in both China and Japan in 1866 and then cooled slowly until in the second Cleveland administration all semblance of cooperation disappeared. But in 1898-9 Great Britain found herself diplomatically isolated in Europe and opposed in the East by the three most powerful European powers.

She then turned again to the United States just as she had under similar conditions in 1854 at the outbreak of the Crimean War. England had always boasted that she, like the United States, desired the open door in China. The assertion was true in a measure, but with this qualification, that since 1842, while the door had been open, the vestibule, i.e., the trade routes, either by way of the Cape or by way of Gibraltar, Suez, Ceylon, Malacca, Singapore and Hongkong—the only trade routes from Europe—had been in the well fortified keeping of Great Britain. She could have effectually closed the door from Europe to Asia at any time, and no doubt would have closed it to any nation which ventured to take up arms against her, not merely in China, but anywhere else in the world. After 1895 Great Britain's strategic position in the East under went a relative diminution. Japan acquired Formosa, thus assuming potential control of the trade routes north of Hongkong. Germany obtained an equivalent to Hongkong on the Shantung peninsula which was calculated to tap the trade of North China as effectively as Hongkong had drained the trade of the South. Russia came into possession of a supposedly impregnable fortress at Port Arthur and controlled practically all the coast of Northern Asia down to Shanhaikwan where the Great Wall meets the sea. Meanwhile a new trade route in the North—the Trans-Siberian Railway—was in the course of construction. In 1899 Great Britain was in a relatively weaker position in China than she had ever been before. It is not to be won-dered at that Admiral Chichester placed the *Immortalité* between the American and the European fleets on the morning (August 13, 1898) when the Americans moved to the attack on the city of Manila. Had Russia, Germany or France, instead of the United States, been the attacking party it is difficult to see how Great Britain could have done otherwise than oppose them. And yet England, about to be engaged in South Africa, could have offered only a very uncertain resistance to any coalition of European powers.

Events thus conspired to bring the United States, Japan

and Great Britain together. Their interests in China appeared to be identical. The closing of the door was an obstacle alike to all three. As for American interests, the Spanish-American War and the Filipino insurrection had created a diplomatic situation novel in American history since the Civil War, for which the truculent, non-cooperative policy of Cleveland and Gresham was no solution.

OVERTURES FOR AN ALLIANCE

When the famous Hay notes of September 6, 1899 are isolated from the details of the international situation in which they were launched they lose much of their significance. As a definition of policy on the part of the United States we may think of them as the answer of the American Government to certain informal proposals from British sources which had invited an alliance of three or four powers for purposes very similar to those which were eventually expressed in the Anglo-Japanese alliance of 1902.

An Anglo-Japanese alliance was no new idea even in 1899. British writers had been proposing such a relationship intermittently for a quarter of a century. The steady advance of Japan had convinced many even before 1880 that the assumption of British foreign policy that Japan was a weak and negligible quantity while China was the only nation in the Far East worth cultivating, was erroneous.*

* The Japan *Daily Herald* (November 9. 1875) notes without disapproval an article in the London *Spectator* in which it was suggested that by means of an alliance with Japan England might be able to engage unemployed Japanese samurai in war against China over the murder of Margery. The *Spectator* remarked that England needed an island and an ally in the Far East. The Shanghai *Courier and Gazette* (reprinted in the Japan *Gazette*, August 5, 1876) replied that for an ally England could count on Japan, and as for an island it might be possible to secure either the Lew Chews from Japan or Quelpert from Korea. The Japan *Gazette*, February 5, 1877, reprinted from the *Pall Mall Budget* an article in which the question was raised: "Are we laying the seeds of a valuable and sincere alliance?" The German Army Gazette (alluded to in the Japan *Herald*, October 29, 1879) had advocated an offensive and defensive alliance between Germany and Japan.
Japan's unique strategic position had also not passed unnoticed by some Americans. De Long had felt that an alliance between Japan and the United States might some day be desirable. Harris appears to have been not unmindful of the advantages of such an arrangement, and General Grant may have recognized it.

The abrupt change of attitude on Japanese treaty revision in 1886 was an indication of changing British policy, but it was so little marked that until the outbreak of the war in 1894 Japan suspected that England was in secret alliance with China.[6] When it became clear that there was no such pact Japanese statesmen would appear to have begun seriously to consider the possibility of some sort of an Anglo-Japanese convention. This was fully in line with the policy which had been suggested by Lord Hotta in 1858 and by Viscount Tani in 1887. The Japanese halted between an alliance with Russia and one with England. On the whole Japan had less to forgive if she chose Russia, but she also would have more to fear.

A new impetus to the discussion was given by the visit of Lord Charles Beresford, representing the Associated Chambers of Commerce of Great Britain, to China and Japan in the winter of 1898-9. Both in China and in Japan in public addresses Lord Beresford developed at length the idea that the open door in China could not be maintained in the face of the opposition of France and Russia unless there was a combination of powers which were willing to fight to keep it open.* Beresford proposed an elaborately devised scheme for the creation of a police force in China in which Chinese troops would be directed by British, Ger-

---

*"Our policy as declared by the Cabinet, approved by the country, and I am perfectly sure by every one in this room, is what is called the 'open door.' . . . Ministers have raved with their hands over their heads, declaring that they will fight for the 'open door.' " (Speech of Beresford at annual dinner of Shanghai Branch of China Association, reported in *North China Daily News*, November 21, 1898.)

"Great Britain, as you know, has declared in the most public manner that her policy in the future with regard to the safety of her interests and trade and commerce, must be the policy of the open door, and as far as I can gather from the many kind interviews I have received in this country, the people of this great Empire are determined that the policy of the open door shall continue in China so far as they are concerned. Therefore I say that our policy and our interests for the future are identical." Beresford then proposed, as he had in China, a "commercial alliance or understanding based on the principle of the open door." But the open door would not be of very much use, he believed, unless the integrity of China was maintained. Therefore he proposed an alliance of the four trading nations—Great Britain, Japan, the United States and Germany—"with the definite understanding on the integrity of China, so that the door can be kept open." To the possible objection that Germany might not be ready to agree to the open door, Beresford pointed out that Germany had already declared Kiaochow an open port. "I am suggesting to you nothing new," remarked the speaker. The policy was supposed already to exist, but he believed that an alliance was necessary to guarantee it. (Beresford speech before the Tokio Japanese-Oriental Association, reported in the *Japan Times*, January 22, 1899.)

man, Japanese and American military instructors. The open door, he thought, would be of little use "unless the room inside is in order." The proposed police force would operate in much the same way as the Ever-Victorious Army under Ward and Gordon had aided in the suppression of the Taiping Rebellion, but Beresford's plan would have involved placing the Chinese troops under foreign control. "Why," he asked in Japan, "should not the Japanese officers try to put the Chinese army in order, on the understanding that China will keep the door open? . . . I believe I personally was the first public man in England that ventured to suggest that what would be for the interest of your country and ours would be an alliance between the Empire of the West and the Empire of the East. (*Applause.*)"

The Beresford speeches were an exercise in diplomatic kite-flying. It was officially denied in Parliament that he was speaking in any other capacity than as a representative of the Chambers of Commerce, but it is to be noted that early in 1898, before Beresford departed from England, Joseph Chamberlain and others had supported a proposal for an alliance of Great Britain with both Germany and the United States. This semi-official proposal reached the form of actual conversations with the German ambassador in London [7] and was even taken up officially with Mr. Hay.[*] Lord Beresford returned from the Far East by way of America where he made many speeches in the early part of 1899. That the Beresford proposals as outlined in China and Japan found their way to President McKinley, Secretary Hay and Mr. Rockhill, there can be little doubt.

The Beresford plan accomplished nothing except the creation of a rumor that the Department of State had made a "secret alliance with England." How utterly baseless this

[*]". . . I saw in the evening papers the news of the Anglo-German agreement to defend the integrity of China and the Open Door. This is the greatest triumph of all. Lord S. [Salisbury] proposed this to me before I left England. I could not accept it because I knew that unspeakable Senate of ours would not ratify it, and ever since I have been laboring to bring it about without any help, and succeeded as far as was possible for one power to do." (Hay to C—— S—— H——, October 29, 1900, in "Letters and Diaries of John Hay," Vol. 3, p. 199. Printed but not published, Washington, 1908.)

Hay subsequently expressed some doubt as to the sincerity of Germany in the Anglo-German convention.

rumor was ought to have been apparent when in April, 1899, Great Britain entered into a convention with Russia by which the two powers agreed to respect each other's spheres of influence in the Yangtze Valley and outside the Great Wall, respectively. This agreement was, in effect, a certificate of title granted by each to the other for special privileges in a very large part of the Chinese Empire. A similar agreement between Germany and England had been made the preceding year. Affairs in China were daily becoming more complicated and each new agreement was inimical to the United States as well as to China. It was quite true that England would have liked to save China for open trade but British diplomacy had no other resource than the alliance. British commerce was far better off with the existing low Chinese tariffs and an open door to the entire trade than it would have been with a part of China under exclusive British control and the other fragments closed to free commercial intercourse, but England apparently felt that she must fight fire with fire.* If England could not rely upon the support of the United States, and apparently she could not, she was likely to adopt a policy in China which would be as objectionable to the United States as were the policies of Russia, France and Germany. For America to ignore the British calls for help and at the same time to offer no substitute for an alliance was to drive England still farther along towards the partition of China and render more certain the dismemberment of the Empire.

The choice before the United States in 1899 was just what it had been in the fifties: cooperation with Great Britain, or independent action. To reject an alliance and offer nothing in its place was a purely negative policy which only increased the difficulties and pitted the United States against not one, but all of the other powers. It is a significant fact that the rejection of the offer of an alliance in 1857 had accomplished nothing for China and had resulted

*". . . we have hitherto, at any rate—whatever the future may have in store for us—maintained the principle of the open door in that country." (Joseph Chamberlain at the meeting of the Wolverhampton Chamber of Commerce, reported in the London *Times*, January 19, 1899.)

in the eclipse of American prestige. In the settlement at Tientsin in 1858 the United States had no influence. Otherwise the Americans might have exercised a restraint upon the dictatorial and ruthless Lord Elgin. Again, in Japan the retirement of the United States from a cordial cooperation with England had resulted in the elimination of American influence in the final treaty revision. What it had accomplished for Japan might have been obtained by other means; it had been costly to the United States. So now in 1899 the United States was in grave danger of complete elimination from influence in China. The choice was really between cooperation with such powers as had similar interests and exercising upon them as much of a restraining influence as a powerful ally always possesses, or futilely opposing the entire company of the powers.

JOHN HAY AND THE OPEN-DOOR NOTES

England wanted an alliance. It is unlikely that Japan would have hesitated to join. Probably John Hay, had he been at liberty to make a perfectly free choice, would have favored it, although the Beresford plan was in its details open to the gravest of objections.*, Beresford's plan would have driven the Chinese into the arms of Russia and provoked a war terrible to contemplate. But an alliance to protect China rather than to destroy her had much to commend it. Those who talk so glibly about the superlative advantages of independent action in American foreign relations cannot bring to the support of their arguments any large array of facts gathered from American relations with the East since 1899. It seems highly probable that an alliance of Great Britain, Japan and the United States at that time in support of a common policy in China, such as Mr. Hay could have defined and the other powers would

*"The fact is, a treaty of alliance is impossible. It could never get through the Senate. As long as I stay here no action shall be taken contrary to my conviction that the one indispensable feature of our foreign policy should be a friendly understanding with England. But an alliance must remain, in the present state of things, an unattainable dream."⁸ (Hay to Henry White, September 24, 1899.)

have accepted, would have been vastly preferable to the Anglo-Japanese alliance of 1902 which would have been rendered unnecessary.

The peculiar contribution of Hay at this critical moment was not the *invention* of the open door policy, for that was as old as our relations with China, but the directing of a diplomatic technique by which the open door could, in a measure, be guaranteed without actual resort to either force or alliances. It was not an adequate measure but it is difficult to see how any more effective measure could have been devised under the circumstances. Two factors contributing to the success of Hay's efforts were: the recent military successes of the United States and the presence in the East of a large expeditionary force with large reserves in the United States; and the natural identity of British, Japanese, and possibly German, interests in China. Although no shadow of treaty engagements existed, a certain amount of "give-and-take" had been going on between Japan, England and the United States for several months. The United States had declined to intervene in Korea after the murder of the queen, and had recalled an anti-Japanese American representative; Japan had withdrawn her protests at the annexation of Hawaii; England had stood by the United States in the Spanish-American War; and now the American Government was making the utmost effort to maintain the strictest neutrality in the Boer War in the face of no inconsiderable anti-British and pro-Boer American sentiment. The Hay-Pauncefote treaty was in process of negotiation, and England had expressed willingness to make concessions to promote the construction of an American, rather than an Anglo-American Isthmian canal. In a word, the United States was now well embarked again upon a cooperative policy like that of Seward's.

But John Hay was a very different type of man from William H. Seward, and when he turned to the Chinese question he found the model not in Seward's bellicose policy in Japan but in the more direct, straightforward, irenic and independent course of Anson Burlingame, who had set out to save China from the rapacity of the powers by agreement. On September 6, 1899, Hay instructed the American representatives in London, Berlin and St. Petersburg (Joseph H. Choate, Andrew D. White and Charlemagne Tower, respectively) to approach the governments to which they were accredited with similar though not identic propositions concerning commercial rights in China. He pointed to the various, verbal or written statements which had already been made by each power respecting freedom of trade for all nations on equal terms and asked for "formal declarations" to the following effect: [9]

"First. [That it] Will in no wise interfere with any treaty port or vested interest within any so-called 'sphere of influence' or leased territory it may have in China.

"Second. That the Chinese tariff of the time being shall apply to all merchandise landed or shipped to all such ports as are within said 'spheres of interest' (unless they be 'free ports') no matter to what nationality it may belong, and that duties so leviable shall be collected by the Chinese Government.

"Third. That it will levy no higher harbor dues on vessels of another nationality frequenting any port in such 'sphere' than shall be levied on vessels of their own nationality, and no higher railroad charges over lines built, controlled, or operated within its 'sphere' on merchandise belonging to citizens or subjects of other nationalities transported through such 'sphere' than shall be levied on similar merchandise belonging to its own nationals, transported over equal distances."

The propositions received immediate attention.* The proposals were not entirely acceptable to any of the powers addressed. Even England wished to have exceptions made to meet the peculiar conditions of her own interests. It is notable that although the notes contemplated the application of the declaration to all leased territory, Lord Salisbury excluded the newly leased area at Kowloon from his assent. Great Britain really regarded this land as for all practical purposes a part of the ceded territory of Hongkong. It had been taken in the form of a lease rather than as a cession in order that Germany, Russia and France might not have

*When the correspondence was published it was agreed to omit from it the various notes which carried the negotiations and to include only the final answers. This fact has proved misleading to many who have assumed that only Great Britain made an immediate reply.

precedent for transmuting their respective leases into actual cessions of territory. With this single, and in principle not unimportant exception, England agreed to the declaration (November 30). Germany stated (December 4) that she "would raise no objection" if the other powers agreed. France, which was approached November 22, replied December 16. Russia gave a very evasive declaration two days later. Japan and Italy, which were approached after the other powers, agreed promptly December 26 and January 7, respectively. The news of the negotiations was released to the press January 3, 1900.

WHAT WAS OBTAINED?

What had been obtained? Not so much as is popularly supposed. The United States had not secured more than already accrued to it under the "most-favored-nation" clauses in the treaties. The preferential railway and mining privileges had in no way been disturbed. Although the United States expressly stipulated that it did not recognize the spheres of influence the replies to the notes had in each case afforded an opportunity of reaffirming that there were such spheres. There remained no good harbor on the entire coast of China where the American Government could have leased a port had it so desired. On March 20, 1900, Secretary Hay announced that he regarded as "final and definitive" the declarations of the several powers that the open door would be maintained and that China would continue to collect the customs and therefore exercise the rights of sovereignty in the sphere of influence, but as a matter of fact only the partition of the Empire had been halted. The Hay notes, which are believed to have been drafted by Rockhill, were as significant in their omissions as in their contents. By their omissions they marked virtual surrenders which the American traders in the forties and fifties would probably have contemplated with little satisfaction. These notes have been popularly mislabeled. They did not secure a completely open door. But they did

avert the immediate partition of the Empire, for the Powers
assented to the recognition of the sovereign tax-collecting
rights of China.   They also averted the accomplishment
of any scheme of foreign-officered police such as Lord
Beresford had proposed.

The Hay Notes may be best appreciated when they are
regarded as a purely temporary expedient to meet a specific
situation.   As such they were a success.   As a permanent
measure they are less to be commended for they did not
secure the open door as had been hoped and they did not
avert further threatening engagements among the powers,
notably the Anglo-Japanese Alliance.   The United States
had, in fact, missed a great opportunity to serve both its
own interests and those of China, but the failure cannot be
ascribed to John Hay.

The open door policy has become so much a phrase to
conjure with in American politics that a definition of it as
it was in 1899 is in order.   Based on sixty years of history
and on the circumstances as well as the text of the notes the
definition was as follows: The United States still adhered
to the policy, to which Seward alone had made exception,
of independent rather than allied action.   This independence was not, however, to preclude cooperation.   The
American Government relinquished the right to lease a port
in China like Kiaochow or Port Arthur for all the good ports
were either leased or preempted by non-alienation agree
ments.   The United States was making no specific demand
for the open door for investments; there was not enough
American money seeking investment to make it worth while
to quarrel about the preferential rights to construct railways or operate mines which had already been given to the
other powers.   The United States merely demanded an
open door for trade in that part of China in which American
merchants were already interested, viz., the area westward
from Kwangtung on the South to Manchuria on the North.
As for Korea, the United States was not politically or commercially interested.   And as for those parts of the traditional Chinese Empire in the extreme south where France

had already carved out an empire, or along the Amur where Russia had begun the partition of China in 1860, the United States had never murmured a protest.

What the American Government would have done had the powers withheld assent from the Hay proposals is a speculative, yet interesting and important question. It seems clear that the United States would not have taken up arms either to enforce assent to the open door policy, or to prevent the partition of the Empire. On the other hand, had the dismemberment of China been started, there would have been a very strong sentiment in the United States against remaining aloof from the division of the spoils. Considering what John Hay had to work with, and what he had to work against, his must be regarded as, if not a famous victory, then at least an important diplomatic coup. The United States had not secured a great deal, as the next score of years revealed, but what it had obtained cost nothing, was accompanied by the assumption of no obligations, and was in return for no actual concessions.

BIBLIOGRAPHICAL NOTES

1. John W. Foster: "Diplomatic Memoirs," Vol. 2, p. 257.
2. William Roscoe Thayer: "Life and Letters of John Hay," Vol. 2, p. 244.
3. For the different assertions with reference to the return of Port Arthur to China, see "Memoirs of Count Witte," p. 84; S. A. Korff: "Russia's Foreign Relations during the Last Half Century," p. 57; "Recollections of a Foreign Minister" (Memoirs of Alexander Iswolsky); Chas. Louis Seeger, translator, p. 30; Cordier: "Relations, etc.," Vol. 3, p. 288; "Secret Memoirs of Count Hayashi," pp. 51 ff.
4. China Dispatches, Vol. 34, Mar. 13, 1873, Low to Fish.
5. Foreign Relations, 1883, p. 191; Cordier: "Relations," Vol. 2, pp. 577 ff.
6. Hayashi Memoirs, p. 45.
7. "Letters from the Kaiser to the Czar," p. 48.
8. Thayer: "John Hay," Vol. 2, p. 221.
9. The Hay Notes and correspondence are printed in For. Rel. 1899, pp. 128 ff. under the caption "Correspondence Concerning American Commercial Rights in China." Moore's "Digest," Vol. 5, pp. 534 ff., gives all the essential material.

CHAPTER XXXIII

THE UNITED STATES AND THE BOXER INSURRECTION

EXCLUDING all details of the Boxer affair extraneous to a study of policy, we may outline our theme in four questions: What happened? What did the American Government desire? What methods were employed? What were the successes and failures?

THE BOXER INSURRECTION

The disturbances in China which culminated in the Boxer affair had been approaching for many years. For three quarters of a century the alien Manchu dynasty had been losing the loyalty and confidence of the Chinese people. The Chinese entertained no special dislike for the Manchus as aliens or as conquerors, but the corruption and weakness of their government made them objectionable as rulers. In return for the taxes, which were steadily increasing, the government did not maintain peace within the Empire nor was it successful in protecting China from the attacks of other nations. Brigands, pirates and revolutionists continually disturbed the orderly conditions necessary for trade. The humiliating defeats at the hands of foreign powers, 1839-42, 1856-60, 1894-5, to which were added numberless other impositions and exactions by foreigners, costing the Empire large sums of money and some losses of territory, revealed the Manchus as incapable of effectively discharging the trust which had been reposed in them. After 1853 the Manchu dynasty owed its power in China not to its own vitality or the loyalty of its subjects, but rather to the fact that the foreign powers had willed that it remain. Otherwise the Manchus probably would not have survived the Taiping Rebellion.

The Chinese people do not appear to have had any conspicuous hatred of the foreigner as such. They liked the foreign trade for it was profitable. They hated the foreigner only because his presence in the Empire increased their taxes, disturbed their peace, and because his extraterritorial privileges gave to him a privileged social, religious and economic position. He was able to evade many of the onerous local taxes which fell the more heavily upon the Chinese. Roman Catholic converts, and to some slight degree Protestant converts also, passed under the protection of foreign powers. After 1860 the French missionaries went through the country and demanded the return of church property which had been sequestered more than two centuries ago and had long since passed into the possession of innocent proprietors who supposed that their titles were valid. The demands of the bishops and priests for majesterial rank was a constant irritation. The attitude of the converts was often insolent and intolerable. Likewise the opium trade, while unchallenged by the populace, aroused the resentment of the few who could justly claim public spirit and patriotism. Meanwhile the prompt and often unjust demands for reparations and for the settlement of claims, which were collected locally even though they were paid from Peking, again touched the Chinese people on their most sensitive nerve, their money, and aroused resentment. The officials and the gentry whose privileges were most threatened by the anti-Manchu movements were not slow to direct the unrest of the people against the foreigners.

In a word, both the Manchu government and the foreigners were steadily inviting and stimulating the antagonism of the Chinese. One wonders how the latter endured as much as they did.

The powers sustained the Manchu government not because they respected it, but because they did not dare to take the risk of permitting successful revolution which would have resulted either in the separation of the Empire into fragments, or the establishment of some new vigorous central authority which, while restoring order and promoting the development of the country, would likewise have been able to set up an effective opposition to the encroachment of the powers. To the latter it was most profitable to sustáin a weak government which they could intimidate and control. The policy of the foreign governments was to crowd the Chinese to a compliance with every foreign demand, but to stop just short of creating the causes for successful revolution. A weak, disintegrating China made possible the continuance of extraterritoriality, an absurdly low tariff, and an hundred kindred privileges such as the Japanese, who were eluding the grasp of the powers, were more and more able to escape. Probably the most effective ally of China was the mutual jealousies of the powers.

Had the powers realized that Japan would be victorious in the war of 1894-5 and that as a result of the Chinese defeat the Chinese people also would slip for the moment from the indirect control, presumably they would have intervened and driven the Japanese back to their island homes. What they had expected was a victory for China which would cripple Japan and restore the latter to their power. But the treaty of Shimoneséki revealed the Manchu government enfeebled beyond all hope of recovery. It also showed Japan preparing to assert herself not merely in the Korean peninsula but also elsewhere on the mainland of Asia.

The weakness of the Empire, the growing ambitions of Japan, the political rivalries of Europe and the overflowing coffers of European money-lenders, created conditions favorable for a stampede among the powers. The leasing of ports, the acquirement of spheres of influence, the non-alienation compacts followed. The Manchu government was being treated with derision by the powers, and the Chinese people saw themselves the present and future victims. They would have to pay. They were therefore ready to turn upon the Manchus not because they were Manchus but because they were collecting taxes under false pretenses.

They were rendering poor government and surrendering their domain. The Chinese were also ready to turn against the foreigners, not because they were foreigners, but because they were secondarily the disturbing influence.

Following the Sino-Japanese War the powers, had they been united in a desire to help China, might have given support to a reform movement which would have resulted in a better government and set the Chinese people on the path of advance. But the powers were utterly divided. Only the United States wanted a strong China and the United States was after all only slightly interested. The Empress Dowager therefore seized the opportunity. She, also, was not conspicuously anti-foreign, but she was shrewd enough to see that her best hope of sustaining the Manchu dynasty and her own influence was to exterminate or expel the foreigners. This program, successfully carried through, would restore the vanished prestige of her government. The powers, by their jealousy of each other and by their unvarnished greed, played directly into her hand by furnishing her each day with fresh illustrations of rapacity. The foreigners, from the Parsee opium trader up the scale to the most unselfish and untiring Christian missionary, owed their lodgment in the Empire to the "naked force" of some foreign vessel of war which had never been out of call since 1842. Between the muzzle of these guns and the people at whom they were aimed were a multitude of foreigners, many of them seekers after peace, honest and kindly in their dealings, but no amount of uprightness could conceal the guns which supported them and which were each month becoming more numerous. The people, ignorant and incredibly superstitious, were goaded to desperation. While the foreigner remained aloof, the Empress Dowager, "Old Buddha," skillfully diverted from herself and her dynasty to the foreigner the wrath which in spite of its horrible manifestations was none the less the proof of the innate vitality of the Chinese people. Thus the Manchus escaped a few years longer. The foreigners became the victims. Collectively they richly deserved their fate; but as so often happens the individuals who paid the terrible price were in equal measure innocent.

The important events of the Boxer insurrection, which have been chronicled by a multitude of writers, may be tabulated with brevity.[1] On September 22, 1898, following a "hundred days" of unintelligent and frantic reform under a rash young Emperor, the Empress Dowager resumed her place as captain of the Chinese junk of state. The following winter the Legations at Peking found it wise to bring up small companies of guards from the foreign fleets. The total number of guards that winter was 141, of which the Americans supplied 18. In the spring the guards retired and it was not thought necessary for them to return the following winter, but the rapid increase of hostility to foreigners and the murder of several of them elsewhere in North China alarmed the foreign community and May 31, 1900, a much larger force representing eight nationalities was brought up from Tientsin.* Meanwhile the Boxer bands were closing in upon Peking and were being merged in the Imperial troops. The attitude of the Chinese Government became obviously hostile and on June 10, a relief expedition from the foreign vessels of war, 475 strong, under Admiral Sir Edward H. Seymour, set out to afford the foreign community in Peking additional protection. The next day a member of the Japanese Legation was murdered and on the 14th the Legations were definitely cut off from communication with the outside world. On the 17th the forts at Taku were taken by the joint action of the foreign fleets, the Americans not participating; three days later the Imperial troops at Peking opened fire upon the Legations and the German Minister, von Ketteler, was shot in the street. The Seymour expedition had encountered resistance and had been compelled to return to Tientsin. The viceroys and governors of the Yangtze and Southern provinces held aloof from the insurrection and for the most part protected the foreigners, thus confining the conflict to the North and especially to Shantung and Chihli.

*There were 458 foreigners actually engaged as military in the siege; 56 were American.

After the capture of the Taku forts the Chinese engaged in a systematic attack upon the foreign community at Tientsin, and on July 14 the city was captured by the joint efforts of the foreign forces, the American forces participating. On July 30 the Tientsin Provisional Government, a civil organization under the direction of the military, was set up.

The Peking relief expedition did not actually start from Tientsin until August 4. It comprised about 19,000, of which 2,500 were Americans with Major General Adna R. Chaffee commanding. Germany was unrepresented in this expedition; it was composed chiefly of Russians and Japanese. There was no allied command, each nation operating independently yet with a semblance of conference between the commanding officers. The Russians betrayed a lack of good faith and revealed suspicious ulterior motives. The Legations were relieved on August 14 at the end of one of the most thrilling episodes in modern history. Although the American flag was first on the walls of the Tartar city, the British preceded the Americans into the Legation area. On August 24 Li Hung Chang and Prince Ching were formally appointed as Chinese plenipotentiaries. About two months later Count Waldersee, a German Field Marshal, with the approval of all the foreign governments, assumed the duties of Generalissimo of the foreign forces in China, and thus supplied a nominal unity to the military government, the relation of which to the diplomatic body was never very clearly defined. On December 24 the foreign representatives presented to the Chinese Government a joint note which contained their demands as a basis for peace. Two days later these demands were accepted and the negotiations for the terms of the protocol were begun. There were many delays in the perfecting of this convention, due chiefly to the inability of the powers to agree among themselves, and it was not signed until September 7, 1901.

With this rapid survey of events in mind, let us pass to a review of American policy at the end of the century.

The Desires of the American Government

When the true nature of the insurrection became known the American Government naturally shared to the fullest extent in the common desire of the powers to effect the rescue of their Legations, to make sure of reparations for the damage done and for the expense of their naval and military forces, but on the question of the correction of the conditions which had made possible the insurrection, the agreement among the powers was less marked.

The American Government had already defined the general principles of its political and commercial policy in the Hay notes, but now something more specific was required. Secretary of State Hay addressed a circular note to the powers on July 3, which became the base-line for all subsequent American policy.

"In this critical posture of affairs in China it is deemed appropriate to define the attitude of the United States as far as the present circumstances permit this to be done. We adhere to the policy initiated by us in 1857 of peace with the Chinese nation, of furtherance of lawful commerce, and of protection of lives and property of our citizens by all means guaranteed under extraterritorial treaty rights and by the law of nations. If wrong be done to our citizens we propose to hold the responsible authors to the uttermost accountability. We regard the condition at Peking as one of virtual anarchy, whereby power and responsibility are practically devolved upon the local provincial authorities. So long as they are not in overt collusion with rebellion and use their power to protect foreign life and property, we regard them as representing the Chinese people, with whom we seek to remain in peace and friendship." [2]

The reference to the policy of 1857 is illuminating, and recalls the continuity of American policy. Hay did not conceive himself to be the originator of new principles. Great Britain, France, Russia and Japan had all been at war with China; the United States, never. But the kernel of the policy in 1900 was to forestall a declaration of war and a military movement by one or more of the Powers against the Chinese Empire. "Anarchy" at Peking might be dealt with locally and was susceptible of settlement by reparations, but war against the Empire would probably involve permanent occupation or the surrender of territory. A declaration of war against China by any one of them would quite probably have been followed in a short time by hostilities between rival powers. Hay, greatly aided by the jealousies of the other powers, was entirely successful in this phase of his policy. It cannot be asserted that Hay was solely responsible for no declaration of war against China, but it seems fair to rate the circular note of July 3 as an important contribution to the peaceful solution of the Chinese problem. It was unaccompanied by any compromising acquiescence in the programs of other powers such as in 1857 had rendered the policy of Buchanan and Cass so futile and hypocritical.

Hay elaborated in a few carefully phrased sentences the general policy of the United States adding both definiteness and scope to what had been stated in the notes of the previous year:

". . .the policy of the Government of the United States is to seek a solution which may bring about permanent safety and peace to China, preserve Chinese territorial and administrative entity, protect all rights to friendly powers by treaty and international law, and safeguard for the world the principle of equal and impartial trade with all parts of the Chinese Empire."

Such phrases as "territorial and administrative entity" and "all parts of the Chinese Empire" reveal a certain vigor and precision of purpose which were lacking in the Open Door Notes. One has a feeling that since September 6, of the year previous, American policy in China had been taking shape and stiffening.

Hay's broad purpose as revealed in the course of the Protocol negotiations was substantially as follows: to maintain harmony among the Powers and by united action to secure as quickly as practical the removal of the foreign military forces from Chinese territory; to secure adequate reparations and adequate punishments for the responsible instigators of the insurrection and yet to prevent the imposition upon China of injustices which would be fruitful of new antagonisms and sow the seeds for an even more formidable popular uprising; and to secure such administrative and fiscal reforms as would make China in the future the best possible market for international trade. He viewed China as the weak link in the international political and commercial system. Enlightened self-interest dictated that the wers should unite to strengthen this link. The American policy in 1900 has since been clothed with a garb of altruism which it could not properly claim. Its motive was not conspicuously benevolent, but its object was, nevertheless, highly beneficent.

The rescue of the foreigners at Peking and the cessation of atrocities having been accomplished without a declaration of war, the next pressing questions were the punishment of the guilty and the fixing of the form and amount of reparations. Germany brought forward the proposal that the foreigners should not only designate the guilty but also become their executioners. The American Government opposed such a plan. Russia, in harmony with its established policy of conciliating China, supported the United States. In the end the views of the United States and Russia partially prevailed. The demands for capital punishment were eventually reduced from ten to four, many names were removed from the lists, and lighter forms of punishment were indicated for others. The execution of the penalties was carried out by the Chinese Government. Likewise the American Government opposed further punitive expeditions after the occupation of Peking and Tientsin. Here the policy of the United States was unsuccessful and Mr. Hay's purpose was foiled. The punitive expeditions of some of the powers, notably Germany, Russia and France, exhibited to the Chinese the worst phases of Caucasian character and made the white man in many localities of China an object of terror which still lingers.

In the determination of the amount of the indemnity the American proposals likewise failed. The Department of State reached the tentative conclusion that the most that China could pay without permanent damage to the Empire was about $150,000,000, an estimate which was subsequently increased to $200,000,000. It was believed that any larger amount "would not only entail permanent financial embarrassment on the country, but might possibly result in either international financial control, or even loss of territory." The United States was willing to accept bonds issued at par, bearing 3 per cent interest and running for thirty or forty years. The American claims were fixed at the maximum lump sum of $25,000,000. The other Powers had scant sympathy for such a proposal and the indemnity was eventually placed at $333,000,000. It would perhaps have been even larger had it not been for the opposition of the United States. The bonds were issued at par and bore 4 per cent.

Russia would have preferred that the Chinese indemnity be guaranteed by the powers rather than paid in bonds issued directly by the government. This proposal met with the immediate opposition of the powers which wished to protect China as much as possible from subsequent European interference, but Mr. Hay at length agreed that he would support the objectionable guaranty plan if measures were taken to reduce the amount of the indemnity. To this the powers would not consent. The American Government opposed the suggestion for the creation of an international fortress at Peking or elsewhere, and would not support the proposal that the powers jointly forbid the importation into China of arms, ammunition or material for their manufacture. In a word the United States opposed all measures which were calculated to weaken the resistance of China in future conflicts with encroaching powers.

Russia, which was suspected of having already entered into a secret agreement with China that she would use her influence in China's favor in return for the actual or virtual cession of Manchuria, just as in 1860 she had obtained the left bank of the Amur as a reward for her supposed influence in persuading the French and the British armies to retire from Peking, suggested that the whole question of the indemnity be referred to the Hague Tribunal. The United States supported this proposition, but the other powers would not listen to it. However, they did agree to the suggestion of Mr. Hay that the indemnity be fixed in a lump sum to be divided among the powers subsequently by mutual agreement. This arrangement protected China from the pressure of individual powers and made it impossible for any power to commute its financial claim into a demand for territory or special privilege. For the sake of further shielding the Empire from the rapacity of the powers the American Government would have liked to see the entire negotiations for the Protocol transferred from Peking to some foreign capital. This proposition received no support except from Russia which doubtless would have greatly profited from such an arrangement.

The next most important point in the negotiations was the proposal to increase the customs dues to provide more ample funds for the payment of the huge indemnity. France and Russia desired to have the tariff, which was at that time only about 3.17 per cent effective, increased to 10 per cent. Mr. Hay suggested (April 11) that there should be a thorough revision of the commercial treaties, following the signing of the Protocol, and that in return for certain long desired reforms in Chinese domestic taxation, a new tariff be made in which the duties be increased to from 5 to 15 per cent according to the character of the goods, the scale being graded according to whether the articles were necessities or luxuries.* Mr. Rockhill was very cautious in

*Paraphrase of telegram, Hay to Rockhill, April 11, 1899: ". . . the essential object of the revision of consular treaties is to favor Chinese financial stability and promote ability to buy in any market and to exchange native products, wherever produced, on equal terms with all nations. Inequalities of likin should be removed, and fixed rates for all China should be scheduled according to the importance and value of imports—some higher than now and others lower, as they can safely stand. Trade with the interior is made speculative and uncertain by the present irregular likin. Customs duties should be scheduled anew. Besides discriminating against cheaper necessaries, the present uniform rate yields inadequate revenue. Five to fifteen per cent, according to the character of the goods, would equalize trade without partiality or burden, and, as trade penetrates the interior, would yield steadily increasing revenue. Application to the whole of China of the open door is required to do this. Equal opportunity should be had by all trading nations to sell throughout the Empire. Lower duties should be attached to imports tending to develop Chinese productiveness. Agricultural implements and simpler manufacturing machinery should be especially favored."

"The Chinese can gain prosperity so as to buy what they do not produce only by developing native productions. Special trade favors to any Power on the ground of reciprocity, territories, occupation, or spheres of influence should be guarded against by stringent favored-nation clause now and for the future. It is necessary to secure increased access to interior markets. . . ." ³

committing the American Government to raising the tariff because he recognized on the part of the nations like Russia, which were least interested in the trade, a disposition to make large the indemnities and then to shift the burden of payment upon the trading nations by increasing the tariff. He also was unwilling to separate the tariff question from that of internal fiscal reform whereas the non-trading nations were not unwilling to see the continuance of the internal abuses which had always been such an embarrassment to the trader. China would, indeed, have been better off with a $150,000,000 indemnity and an only 5 per cent effective tariff than with a $333,000,000 indemnity and a 10 per cent tariff, but what was needed was a genuine fiscal reform. Mr. Rockhill specified as compensating advantages for treaty revision: abolition of likin on imports and exports, including transit pass duty; right of foreigners to reside and do business throughout the Empire; revision of inland navigation rules; creation of a mining bureau and good regulations; strict adherence to principle of equal opportunity to people of every nationality; the opening of Peking as a treaty port; and the adoption of measures for the improvement of the river approaches to Shanghai, Tientsin and Newchwang.[4]

When the stupendous indemnity had been decided upon, and when Mr. Rockhill encountered general opposition to thorough reforms Hay cabled (June 21) that the American Government was opposed to raising the revenue above 5 per cent effective.[*] At the same time he instructed Rockhill to refrain from opposing the proposition that a 10 per cent

[*]That the opposition of Mr. Hay to a 10 or even 15 per cent tariff was due to the fact that the indemnity had been raised to so high a figure and the likin was not abolished is perfectly clear from the correspondence.

John A. Kasson, special commissioner plenipotentiary, to Hay, March 2, 1901: "It would appear to be the better opinion that the duties on imports must be raised to at least 15 per cent ad valorem in lieu of the present rate. The calculations must, of course, be based upon the amount of the indemnity, now unknown. Assuming this is not to exceed $200,000,000, and further assuming that the Powers will accept the bonds of China instead of compelling her to sell these bonds to raise the indemnity money in the open market with a further loss of capital . . ."[5]

John Foord, Secretary of the American Asiatic Association, to Hay, January 25, 1901: "The American Asiatic Association, recognizing the financial necessities of the Chinese Empire, has no objection to offer to the proposed increase of duties on foreign imports. The suggestion which, according to Sir Robert Hart, was formulated last spring by the special commission appointed to consider the subject of tariff revision, is deemed a reasonable one. This was tariff be reserved for future discussion if the withdrawal of American objections would aid in bringing the Protocol negotiations to a close. Meanwhile Great Britain refused to consider a 10 per cent tariff. In the Protocol it was determined that the tariff be raised to 5 per cent effective, on the condition that all existing *ad valorem* duties be changed to specific duties, the average value of merchandise for the years 1897, 1898 and 1899 being taken as the basis of estimate. Peking was not given the status of a treaty port. The American demand for the opening of the entire Empire to trade did not commend itself to those who were most familiar with the conditions because of the extraterritorial status of foreigners. It would have been highly unjust to China to force her to admit foreigners as freely as Mr. Hay had contemplated, while they were exempt from Chinese law and so much removed from effective control by their own governments. Mr. Rockhill was, however, able to have specified in the Protocol that the river approaches to Tientsin and Shanghai be improved under a plan by which the Chinese and the foreigners jointly bore the expense. Through the jealousy and short-sightedness of the powers an opportunity. had been lost to do much towards setting China on a firm foundation which would in the end have been as profitable for the powers themselves as for the Empire. Meanwhile the United States had acquired the reputation of having opposed the increase of Chinese tariffs which is a partial and quite inaccurate statement of the facts.*

The Protocol, as signed, stipulated the following points:

to the effect that the import duty should be fixed at 10 per cent plus 5 per cent transit dues, payable simultaneously, coupled with the total abolition of all other taxes on such imports forever after and everywhere." 6

*Two other minor proposals made by the United States were lost. Mr. Hay suggested that it would be well to stipulate that in the reorganization of the Tsung-li Yamen upon which all the powers were agreed, only an official speaking some Western language be appointed to conduct the foreign relations. This proposal was unwise as Rockhill immediately pointed out, for it would have eliminated from the direction of foreign affairs all the ablest Chinese. Mr. Hay also suggested that China be made to indemnify Chinese Christians for wrongs to their persons and property. Conger, although an ardent friend of the missionaries, did not believe such a policy wise. It would have reopened the question of the French protectorate of Catholic missions in its most objectionable form. These minor proposals betray the fact that Secretary of State Hay, although directly supervising the negotiations by telegraph, actually was not at all well informed as to general conditions in China.7

(1) apology to Germany for the murder of Baron Ketteler, and the erection of a memorial to him at the place where he was shot; (2) punishment of Chinese officials responsible for the insurrection; (3) apology to Japan for the murder of Sugiyama, chancellor of the Japanese Legation; (4) suspen sion of official examinations in all cities where foreigners were attacked or murdered; (5) erection of expiatory monu ments in foreign cemeteries which had been desecrated; (6) China to forbid for two or more years the importation of arms, ammunition and materials used in their manufacture; (7) indemnity of 450,000,000 Haekwan taels and a 5 per cent effective tariff; (8) reservation of the Legation Quarter at Peking under the exclusive control of the Legations with the right to make it defensible; (9) razing of forts at Taku between Peking and the sea; (10) the occupation by the foreigners of certain points, thirteen in number including Tientsin, as a security of open communications to Peking; (11) publication of certain edicts tending to prevent renewal of Boxer propaganda; (12) China to agree to the amend- ment of commercial treaties and to the Pei-ho and Whangpu conservancy projects; (13) abolition of the Tsung-li Yamen and the creation of a Ministry of Foreign Affairs; (14) evacuation of Peking, with exception of Legation guards on September 17, 1901.

INDEPENDENT OR CONCURRENT ACTION

In the sixty years of official American relations with the Far East, the fundamental American purpose had been definite, consistent and unvarying. The United States sought the open door for American trade. But the methods employed had been subject to many changes. What the Americans asked for and what they obtained at Peking in 1900-1 is therefore of less significance than the diplomatic methods employed.

There were three possible stages of independent or iso- lated action: absolute neutrality; intervention in favor of Asia; and mediation. Likewise there were three stages of cooperation: concurrent yet separate action; joint action; and an alliance with some one or more foreign powers. Any one of these might conceivably become a means for maintaining the open door and Asiatic integrity. In the course of its diplomatic relations in Asia the United States had been forced to consider each of these methods and had employed more or less energetically every one of them except the last. In 1840, at the outbreak of the Anglo-Chinese War, some of the Americans had proposed joint naval action with England, France and Holland against China. Others suggested mediation. The United States adopted neutrality. In 1853 at the opening of Japan and during the troubles at Shanghai, the American representatives had rejected cooperation and followed an absolutely isolated course. Four years later, at the time of the revision of the Chinese treaties and of the making of the commercial treaties with Japan, the American Government, officially rejecting both isolated and joint or allied action, adopted a concurrent policy which in effect involved cooperation in all peaceful measures. During the Seward administration cooperation was the slogan. In Japan it was carried to the point of joint military action and a similar policy on an even more extended scale was contemplated in Korea. Then followed a period of non-cooperation. The opening of Korea and the revision of the Japanese treaties had been accomplished by isolated action. Both concurrent and joint action in the Sino-Japanese War had been rejected, as had also armed or allied intervention in favor of Korea. The Hay notes of 1899 may be classified in two ways. They represented isolated, diplomatic intervention in favor of China and against Europe; but they were also the expression of an underlying cooperative policy which fell only a little short of joint action with Japan and Great Britain against Russia. They were as near to an Anglo-Japanese-American alliance as the United States was able to go. Their underlying spirit was the farthest possible removed from that of Gresham in 1894.

Of these possible methods, which was the United States to choose at the outbreak of the Boxer trouble? It could not remain neutral between the East and the West, for American lives and American property had been attacked. It could not intervene against Europe—not directly. An offer of mediation would have been interpreted as an indication of American weakness and an encouragement to the Manchu government, just as the failure to support the Italian demands for a leased port in 1899 had been construed as an encouragement to China. Extreme isolated action would be futile: some form of cooperation was necessary, but an alliance was out of the question. Only concurrent or joint action was practical.

"Act independently in protection of American interests where practicable," telegraphed Hay to United States Minister E. H. Conger June 8, 1900, "and concurrently with representatives of other powers if necessity arises." [8] Two days later he amplified this with a second message: "We have no policy in China except to protect with energy American interests, and especially American citizens and the Legation. There must be nothing done which would commit us to future action inconsistent with your instructions. There must be no alliances." In the circular of July 3d to the powers Hay defined the method again: "The purpose of the President is, as it has been heretofore, to act concurrently with other powers; first, in opening up communications with Peking and rescuing the American officials, missionaries and other Americans who are in danger; secondly, in affording all possible protection everywhere in China to American life and property; thirdly, in guarding and protecting all legitimate American interests; and fourthly, in aiding to prevent a spread of the disorders to the other provinces of the Empire and a recurrence of such disasters." It will thus be seen that between June 8 and July 3 the American Government had come to see the futility of exclusively independent action, even in the protection of American interests, and was prepared for cooperation—for a larger degree of cooperation, probably, than the jealousies of the other powers made it possible to achieve. Thus while eschewing the commitments of alliances or their equivalent, in the face of a great crisis, the United States forsook the timidities of the past and announced itself as ready to lead in cooperation.

The word "concurrent" is the key to the interpretation of American policy at this time. This word had a long history. It first appeared in the discussions of the early fifties which preceded the adoption of the policy of 1857. The earlier American policy has been primarily obstructive to England. But it was seen that an independent obstructive policy might actually prove to be less obstructive to a dismemberment of China than would a cooperative policy. Concurrent action, therefore, came to mean cooperation for the purpose of restraining England and France. It utterly failed in 1858 owing to the ineptitude of the American representative, but the idea was taken up by Seward and used with some success. It succeeded in China but failed in Japan because there was lacking a man of Anson Burlingame's caliber to carry it out. The policy was sound but it required an able executive. A concurrent policy was the one to which Mr. Hay returned in the summer of 1900 and to insure its success he dispatched his trusted aid, W. W. Rockhill, as Commissioner (technically, Special Agent) to China in the latter part of July when the fate of the Legations and of Minister Conger was still in doubt. There does not appear to have been any serious differences of opinion between Conger and Rockhill, but when two men ride a horse one must ride behind and early in 1901 Mr. Conger found it desirable to ask for permission to return to the United States, leaving Mr. Rockhill as plenipotentiary to carry out the negotiations and sign the Protocol for the American Government.*

"While we maintained complete independence," stated Mr. Rockhill in making his final report, "we were able to act harmoniously in the concert of powers, the existence of which was so essential to a prompt and peaceful settlement of the situation, we retained the friendship of all the nego

---

*It is interesting to note that in the settlement of the Boxer affair the Senate had no part. Neither Rockhill's appointment as Special Agent nor the Protocol required the approval of the Senate.

tiation powers, exerted a salutary influence in the cause of moderation, humanity and justice, secured adequate reparation for wrongs done our citizens, guaranties for their future protection, and labored successfully in the interests of the world in the cause of equal and impartial trade with all parts of the Chinese Empire." [9]   Complete independence, yes; but not the sort of independence which had been maintained in Korea or the independence of President Cleveland. There was military and naval cooperation, and there was diplomatic "give and take" in which the American Govern ment most of all showed a willingness to make concessions for the sake of securing harmony of action and a real con cert of the powers.

At the signing of the Protocol the diplomatic grouping of the principal powers remained about what it had been for the preceding two years. Great Britain and Japan stood together and were separated from the United States only by the greater extent of their political and commercial interests in China. All three stood opposed to Russia which was supported consistently by France. Germany was playing a dubious game, now encouraging Russia and then making a convention with England to oppose her. Even in 1901 it probably would not have been impossible to form a convention of Great Britain, Germany, Japan and the United States to safeguard China from every assault if only the American Government could have been counted on to invest its fair share of military and naval support. The United States was in a position of potential leadership which it allowed to slip from its grasp primarily because the American people misread the events of the three preceding years. They supposed that their influence had been due to their independence and isolation, whereas it had been brought about by concurrence and cooperation. But more fundamental as a cause for the failure of the United States to grasp the opportunity to continue its beneficent work for Asia, was the fact that the American people did not prize the influence Mr. Hay and his collaborators had secured for them.[10]

BIBLIOGRAPHICAL NOTES

1. There are no books on the Boxer Insurrection or on the Protocol which can be recommended as a substitute for the official documents. Foreign Relations for 1900, and the Appendix volume for 1901 (also published as Sen. Doc. 67:57-1) containing the Rockhill Correspondence, and Notes on China, Aug., 1900,—War Dept. Document 124, Publication XXX—are the primary sources. Moore's "Digest," Vol. 5, pp. 476 ff., contains an excellent summary but does not make excerpts from correspondence not previously published. Paul H. Clements: "The Boxer Rebellion, a Political and Diplomatic Review" (Studies in History, Economics and Public Law, Columbia Univ., Vol. LXVI, No. 3) is excellent so far as it goes, but is deficient in background and not discriminating in references to earlier history. For a chronicle of events, H. B. Morse: "Intern. Rel. of the Chinese Empire," Vol. 3, is recommended. For adequate bibliography, see Clements. Stanley K. Hornbeck: "Contemporary Politics in the Far East," chap. 13, and elsewhere, is an admirable interpretation which is especially valuable for the understanding of the Protocol in the light of more recent history.
2. Rockhill Correspondence, p. 12.
3. *Ibid.*, p. 368.
4. *Ibid.*, p. 171.
5. *Ibid.*, p. 210.
6. *Ibid.*, p. 217.
7. *Ibid.*, pp. 349, 45.
8. For. Relations, 1900, p. 143.
9. Rockhill Corres., pp. 6-7.
10. Thayer's "John Hay," Vol. II, chap. XXVI, "The Boxer Ordeal and the Open Door," sheds some light on the general phases of Mr. Hay's policy, but for some reason, possibly from an excess of caution on the part of the biographer, is singularly lacking in answers to many of the important details of the negotiations; so also are the "Letters and Diaries of John Hay," 3 vols. Printed but not published, Washington, 1908.

CHAPTER XXXIV

PERSONALITIES AND PRINCIPLES

THE CONSULAR AND DIPLOMATIC SERVICE

AMERICAN relations with Asia in the nineteenth century were so largely personal and individual that the Americans who made the contacts assumed a transcending importance. At no time during the century did the Chinese or the Koreans become travelers, and while the Japanese manifested an extreme desire to go abroad and study, nevertheless for the great mass of the people what knowledge of the United States was obtained came through the American official and unofficial representatives in Japan. To the inhabitants of Eastern Asia the Government of the United States was what the American diplomatic and consular officers represented it to be. The personalities and personal character of the diplomatic and consular representatives became a legitimate object of study.

The American consular service throughout the century presents a picture over which one would wish to draw the veil. The system of merchant consuls continued in China without change until 1854 when they were replaced at the five ports by others whose only legitimate emoluments were $1000 a year for judicial services under extraterritoriality, and part or all of the fees of their office.* It was hardly a change for the better. The older merchant consuls had been of the type of the merchant prince. While it was true that they smuggled opium and manipulated the powers of their office, sometimes to the prejudice of their competitors, they did take pride in their position, and towards the

*Merchant consuls were reintroduced a few years later at unimportant points in spite of the protests of the Chinese Government.

669

Chinese they maintained the same benevolent, if patroniz-
ing, attitude which characterized their business relations.
The men who displaced them were often appointed from the
lower ranks of political "hangers-on" in the United States
and were set down in strange places where the cost of respectable living ranged upwards from three or four thousand dollars a year.   Consulates were not provided and the
allowances for rent and for clerical help were meager.   At
Canton, Shanghai and later at Yokohama they handled
large sums of money for, in addition to the fees of the office,
there was the fund for the relief of distressed seamen and
the estates of intestate deceased fellow citizens.   To the personal temptations which accompany residence in a foreign
land where public sentiment is of slight support to personal
character there was the constant temptation to peculation.
The theory of their government was to make the consular
system support itself by the fees it collected, and the prevailing theory of the occupants of office was to gather in as
much as the probably brief tenure of office would permit.
The fee system made this especially easy.[1]

We know that there were consular officers who rendered
honest and efficient service even under these adverse conditions, but it would appear, even from the printed reports of
consular inspectors, that the average grade of honesty and
efficiency was deplorably low.   In concluding his report
covering Asia and South America in 1872 Special Inspector
DeB. Randolph Keim stated:

"It will have been seen that there was not a single consulate at
which a complete set of record-books from the beginning as required
by the regulations, was to be found. . . . Almost every consulate had
some defects in its history, owing to the incompetency, low habits,
and vulgarity of some of its officers during the endless round of
evils incident to official rotation.   Abuses had been committed in the
collection of fees; in the exercise of judicial powers; in the adjustment of the business affairs of American citizens; in the settlement,
where permitted, of the estates of intestate American citizens dying
abroad; in selling the American flag; in 'running-out' * ships; in

*"Running-out" ships was a practice by which the consul connived with a
ship captain in forcing a crew shipped in an American port to desert in an
Asiatic port where a new crew of Asiatic sailors could be obtained at a very
great reduction in wages. The American sailor, forced by the abuse of the
captain to desert, lost the wages due him for the outward voyage, thus effecting
a second saving for the owners.

discharging seamen; in establishing American settlements abroad; in issuing illegal passports; in countenancing shipping-masters; in taxing Chinese emigrants. Indeed, the most important feature of my investigations was the iniquity displayed by consular officers, since the act of 1856 particularly, in defrauding the government and grasping gains from various outside sources." [2]

The best that can be said for the consular system at that time in Asia is that every instance of extreme dishonesty can be matched with one of even more extensive malfeasance from consulates in some other quarter of the globe, and one may also remember that those were the days of scandals in Washington over the payment for Alaska, the Pacific Mail Subsidy, and the Credit Mobilier. Inspector Keim expressed the opinion that the consular irregularities reached their highest point among the appointees of the Buchanan administration, but it is to be noted that at that early day many of the possible avenues of graft were still relatively unexplored and the methods of the dishonest consul underwent many refinements in the following forty years. At the end of the century the American consular establishments in Asia were still a stench which succeeding administrations had been singularly loath to correct, and the long urgent reforms did not appear until the second Roosevelt term.*

While honest American trade suffered from this procession of pilfering, low-living and inefficient officials, it was American relations with the native peoples which suffered most. The American Government had demanded the exemptions of extraterritoriality and then sent the off-scourings of the "spoils system" to become the agents of American law and justice. In the act of May 16, 1848, Congress authorized the establishment of consular courts by which the consuls were enabled to hear and determine civil cases where the debt or damage did not exceed $1000 and to try

* Third Assistant Secretary of State, Herbert H. D. Pierce, reported in 1904, after a tour of consular inspection: "Unfortunately, beset by the temptations which are rife in the East, it has sometimes happened that some of our consular officers, finding their salaries inadequate to meet the constant drain upon their resources, have yielded to this temptation and, under the cover of such protection as our unfortunate system of partial compensation by fees affords, have taken advantage of it to extort unwarranted charges for services of an unofficial character, and in other instances have employed their official positions to increase their incomes improperly, thus bringing the office into contempt." [3]

and punish criminal offenders where the fine did not exceed $100 or imprisonment for 60 days.[4] The law was to be that of the United States, supplemented by the "common law, and the law of equity and admiralty," to which might be added "decrees and regulations" having the force of law, which the minister was authorized to promulgate with the approval of such consuls as were accessible. For the more important cases, the consul was required to invite some fellow citizens to sit with him in the hearing of the case, and appeal was possible to the minister, and through him in some cases, to the United States circuit court in California. The effect of the arrangement was that the consul might combine in himself all the functions of government, legislative, judicial and executive. He was a member of the legislature, judge, jury, prosecuting attorney and police officer all in one. He was never selected for his legal training. If, in addition to all this, the consul was a dishonest man or one who nourished that contempt for the colored races which the white man often acquires when he goes to Asia, imagination fails to grasp all the possibilities which were invested in his person for the creation of ill feeling and hatred among the Orientals who were so miserable as to fall in his path. When one encounters even today the sporadic outbursts of distinctly anti-American, as well as anti-foreign feeling, in Eastern Asia, the recollection of this shameful page of past history will do much to explain and extenuate the hatred for Americans which still lingers in many an Oriental breast.

One turns with relief from the consular to the diplomatic service. From the days when John Quincy Adams in his old age was suggested as the most suitable first Commissioner to China and Edward Everett at the Court of St. James was actually appointed to the post, it was recognized by the American Government that its diplomatic representatives in the East ought to be men even above the grade of those who were sent to many European capitals. During the century, not counting those who were appointed and declined, and omitting the various *chargés d'affaires,* there were thirty-five

American diplomatic representatives in China, Japan and Korea. Peter Parker, George F. Seward, H. N. Allen, Edwin Dun and W. W. Rockhill were selected from those who had already held lower positions in the diplomatic service in the East; Alexander H. Everett had a previous and extended diplomatic career in Europe. A few typical "shirt-sleeves" diplomats like Richard B. Hubbard [5] in Tokio found their way to these high appointments, and the picture of Charles E. De Long, revolver bulging from his belt, driving ex-Secretary Seward through the streets of Tokio behind a pair of ponies and cracking his whip over the backs of scurrying pedestrians is not edifying,[6] but there were very few such ministers and at the most not more than three instances of conspicuously weak character, one of these being a dipsomaniac.[7] On the other hand Cushing, Perry, Harris, Burlingame, Young, Bingham, Denby and Rockhill represented the best of contemporary American life. Although it was customary for each new administration to make new appointments, Judge Bingham served at Tokio for thirteen years, and Colonel Denby served slightly longer at Peking and had the distinction of being in two Republican as well as in two Democratic administrations, the latter being one in which he was first appointed. In general the quality of diplomatic representation in the East rose and fell with the character of the administration and the quality of the appointees in the Department of State. On the whole the legations at Peking and Tokio compared favorably with the department to which they were responsible.

A word, in passing, ought to be added in regard to the American naval officers who also represented their government to the peoples of Eastern Asia. Usually they were an exceptionally fine set of men, sustaining a higher average, perhaps, than those of any other class. The naval officers were feared by the consuls whose delinquencies they reported, and not always welcomed by the civilian ministers who resented their frequently lordly ways, but they had a fine regard for the honor of the flag under which they served and rarely disgraced it.

The Contributors to American Policy

In bringing our study to a close it is well to repeat that American policy in Asia has been an accretion which was built up from no exclusive single source. It did not spring full-grown from the mind of any individual, nor was it care fully projected from a planning-board or group. In this respect it was utterly unlike the foreign policy of Japan, of Great Britain, and of the European powers. Contributions came from three different sources: from the American rep resentatives in Asia; from the Department of State or the administration in Washington; and, in a single instance, from Congress in response to a popular demand. We may review briefly the nature and significance of each one of these classes of contributors.

Every item in American policy in Asia as we find it at the end of the century was first the personal contribution of some individual representative of the government in Asia. To this statement there are no exceptions. It is equally notable that every item of policy was, in principle, on record before 1870. After that date came only sifting, integration, elaboration, and the application to specific situations. Throughout the century the fundamental purpose of the United States remained unaltered: the American Govern- ment demanded most-favored-nation treatment; demanded it from China, Japan and Korea, and demanded it also from Western powers which sometimes threatened to close the door of equal opportunity in regions where the American merchant was interested.

What methods should be employed to maintain the open door? Ought the United States to depend solely on treaties or ought it to acquire territory as Great Britain, Russia and France were doing? Again, ought the American Government to adopt a cooperative policy or was it wiser to keep to political isolation? The drama of the second half of the century revolves around the discussion of these differ ing methods of realizing a single purpose—most-favored nation treatment.

Caleb Cushing, in harmony with the general instructions of Daniel Webster, devised a plan by which the United States would depend solely upon the force of treaties and the strength of international law. Commodore Perry had less confidence in legal documents and earnestly recommended the acquisition of territory as a base of operations from which the door might, in case of necessity, be forced to remain open. Burlingame followed Cushing, while Parker sided with Perry, and carried forward a policy which, while rejected by his superiors, was taken up in principle by Seward. At the end of the century we find the two schools of thought both represented and merged in the McKinley administration to such a degree that we may not with certainty separate those who held one and those who advocated the other. Cushing's policy was still held to be sound in theory but in practice it had proved inadequate. Perry's method had been premature at its inception but was now found to meet the facts as they had developed and to be not exclusive of the Cushing policy. If McKinley inclined towards the school of Perry and Seward, certainly John Hay found himself more at ease with Cushing and Burlingame.

To what extent the men at the end of the century were conscious that they were following in the footsteps of predecessors we do not fully know, but in speculating upon this question we may be guided by the fact that the American Government in its foreign relations possesses a continuity which is not always appreciated by its commentators. Administrations come and go; Secretaries of State and of the Navy pass through the departments to which they are appointed, and with them come—in the past probably more than is likely in the future—new appointments to subordinate positions, but the new administrations cannot eradicate the records of the past and they ignore them at their peril. Policies as well as international law and diplomatic practice are built up layer by layer and while American foreign policies have undergone some changes and even reversals in the generations which are past, those changes were neither abrupt nor revolutionary. As concerns the Far East certain unchanging geographical, or slowly changing industrial and political facts have made a channel within the boundaries of which American policy must contain itself. It it were true that the McKinley administration adopted policies without knowing that they were returning to old ones it would also be true that two sets of men removed a generation from each other discovered the same major facts and found themselves forced to similar conclusions. That individual American representatives of the forties and fifties should have so clearly forecasted the conclusions of their successors at the end of the century, and now, is a tribute to the quality of their political sense.

Twice within the century a Secretary of State or a President picked up the Far Eastern question and set it forward with important personal contributions. That these contributions were indeed personal is only too apparent from the records. When the Senate gave its approval of the conventions of 1864 and 1866 with Japan it was still preoccupied with war-time affairs, and it is not evident that there was any intelligent appreciation of the issues involved or of Seward's way of handling them. One finds it difficult to believe that Seward would have found in Congress sufficient support for his proposed Korean policy. Seward's policies were peculiarly personal to himself and did not even have the unqualified support of his own representatives in Peking and Yedo. McKinley likewise had the advantage of a war-time Congress, and even then he had to coerce Congress to secure the approval he needed for his Philippine policy. Congress handled the Philippines more as a domestic than as a foreign question. The adroit John Hay was able to accomplish his policy in China by eliminating the Senate from its consideration and then by giving the policy an aspect of independence which concealed its true cooperative nature.

Once Congress intervened in Far Eastern affairs and seized the initiative. The Asiatic immigration policy belongs to Congress and arose directly out of the people who were being touched on the bare nerve of their industrial and social life. Congress steadily forced the hand of the Presidents and of the Secretaries of State. This policy formed the only really national item in our relations with the Far East for it was the only one which was adopted after full discussion and investigation in Congress. Unquestionably it represented the will of the people. But it is significant that the question was discussed as a purely domestic issue and was settled in utter and brutal disregard for foreign relations and existing treaties. The settlement of this question is an illustration that the American system of government presents no insuperable obstacles to the control of foreign policy by the people where the economic and social interest is sufficient, and is also a warning that other items of foreign policy are liable to initiation or revision by similar measures. That the American people are prone to resolve all questions into partisan and domestic issues and are deficient in a sense of cooperative responsibility in international affairs is evident. This fact becomes somewhat disquieting when one turns to the political situation in the Far East and notes how necessary a cooperative policy has become.

THE COOPERATIVE POLICY

When closely scrutinized it appears that the United States never during the century actually retired from the cooperative policy first timidly proposed in the fifties and then followed with so much vigor in the sixties. When the American Government withdrew from close cooperation with Great Britain, France and Russia, it had already entered, without any formality or documentary pledge, into cooperation with and support of Japan. The United States did not retire from cooperation; it merely changed partners. The corollary of the open door was the policy of promoting an Asia strong enough to be its own door-keeper. When England and France revealed a disposition to use the power of a cooperative policy to repress and weaken Asia the United States withdrew from cooperation with them and sought the accomplishment of its purpose by cooperation

with an Oriental power. Then, in the McKinley administration, when Great Britain had come to adopt the American contention that a strong Japan was advantageous to
the trading nations, the United States resumed its cooper
ative policy with England. The principles of American
policy were entirely consistent from the days of Seward
onward.

Only the cooperative policy stood the test of time. In
the necessities of the case this must have been so. An iso
lated policy committed the American Government to one of
two courses; either to retirement when American interests
were threatened, or the defense of those interests with suffi
cient force to protect them. An isolated policy in Asia tends
inevitably either to a surrender of most-favored-nation
treatment or a defiance of all comers. It is essentially belligerent. Commodore Perry was entirely consistent when, in
addition to his non-cooperative policy, he advocated the
establishment of protectorates over half a dozen pieces of
Asiatic territory. If the United States were to pit its
strength against the world in the Pacific it must fortify its
position after the most approved military manner.

That the cooperative policy suffered from mishandling
in the following forty years there can be no doubt. While
charging the other Powers with bad faith and with wresting
the power of the policy to serve purposes which were not in
the interest of all the cooperating powers, we may properly
confess the American share in the wreck of general cooperation. Seward approached dangerously close to bad faith and
he sometimes used the policy not as a statesman but as a
sharp politician. The withdrawal of the United States from,
cooperation with the European powers in Japan found an
excuse in the brutal conduct of Sir Harry Parkes, but the
withdrawal was petulant and probably unnecessary. All
that it accomplished in bringing about a change in British
policy favorable to the promotion of a strong, enlightened
and prosperous Japan, probably could have been better accomplished had the American Government continued the
cooperative policy and exercised a more diplomatic influence

upon the British Foreign Office. Judge Bingham proved himself to be a fine type of American during his long service in Tokio but he was neither a statesman nor a diplomat. The American policy in Korea also, while not properly open to the charge of having betrayed the Koreans, was certainly lacking in political sagacity and was most deficient in its contempt for general cooperation. Statesmanship was nowhere apparent.

A cooperative policy is not a trust company to which a government may consign the management of its foreign relations and then feel free to bestow its executive and diplomatic posts as badges of honor upon men who are merely loyal Republicans or sound Democrats. American interests in the Far East unquestionably suffered, but the fault was not so much in the cooperative policy as in the fact that the American representatives and the American administrations were less capable than those with which they were cooperating. Fatality to American interests always followed the appearance of an incompetent American diplomat or a provincial Secretary of State. It was true at Tientsin in 1858, in Japan after Harris left, in China after Burlingame's retirement. The wreck of the cooperative policy in the East in the nineties was due as much to American ineptitude as to European jealousies.

It was the utter wreck of the cooperative policy which made it necessary for the United States to retain the Philippines and one may at least question whether the annexation of Hawaii would have taken place had not Japan betrayed an inclination to encroach upon the islands. Only the reestablishment of cooperation between Great Britain, Japan and the United States prevented the dismemberment of the Chinese Empire. In the resumption of cooperation in 1899 the United States suffered no loss for it was ably represented.

The only unknown quantity making a cooperative policy a gamble for the United States is the quality of American representation. But the uncertainties of American politics are always a liability to be reckoned with, and as disastrous to an isolated as to a cooperative policy. The history of American policy in the nineteenth century, and there does not appear to be any different testimony from more recent history, indicates that American interests in Asia, which are best served by the open door and the development of strong Asiatic states, fare best under a cooperative policy in which the American Government is ably and energetically represented. That under such a policy the United States will attain the full measure of its desires is unlikely, but under an isolated policy it will certainly obtain even less both for itself and for Asia. The American people delight to honor Seward and Hay both of whom reached this conclusion, but perhaps even yet they have not grasped the secret of their statesmanship. The cooperative policy in Asia has not been lifted to a place in American foreign policy by the side of the Monroe Doctrine where it is above the reach of issue-hunting campaign managers.

In conclusion, we repeat that the tap-root of American policy in Asia is most-favored-nation treatment. An attitude of self-righteousness is neither becoming nor justified. American policy is not philanthropic; it is not, in its motive and history, benevolent; but it is beneficent, for the United States is so situated that American interests in Asia are best promoted by the growth of strong, prosperous and enlightened Asiatic states. Indeed it is difficult for an American to believe that the repression or weakening of any part of Asia is a benefit to any power. The United States is committed to its policy by geographical, economic and political facts, and in the same measure is also bound to a policy of cooperation with all powers which sincerely profess a similar purpose.

BIBLIOGRAPHICAL NOTES

1. The documentary and pamphlet literature on the consular system is voluminous. The student is referred to the index to Foreign Relations, and to the following documents: A Report to the Hon. George S. Boutwell, Secretary of the Treasury, upon the Consular Service of the U. S. A. by DeB. Randolph Keim (Washington, 1872); the Keim Report is also given in S. Ex.

Doc. 7:41-3; Report to the Hon. John Hay, Secretary of State, upon a tour of consular inspection in Asia, by Herbert H. D. Pierce (Washington, 1904); also H. Misc. Doc. 31:45-2 (Part 2) which contains the documentary evidence as to the conditions in the consular service of China, with special reference to Shanghai up until 1877; this document should be studied with H. Rept. 134:45-3, Investigation of Geo. F. Seward. Seward while serving as minister at Peking was charged with corruption in his previous service as Consul General at Shanghai. The Committee on Expenditures in the State Department in the House presented a bill of impeachment against Seward which was referred (June 4, 1879) to the Committee on Judiciary from which it never reappeared. The following year Seward was replaced at Peking by James B. Angell. Chester Lloyd Jones: "The Consular Service of the United States, its History and Activities" (Univ. of Pa. Series in Political Economy and Public Law, No. 18, Philadelphia, 1906) is a good general summary of the development of the entire consular system, but it contains only passing references to Asia.

2. Keim: Report, p. 183.
3. Pierce: Report, p. 15.
4. Moore's "Digest," Vol. 2, pp. 613 ff.; S. Ex. Doc. 72:31-1 (the report of John W. Davis).
5. Hubbard was so unwise as to write a book after his return from Tokio. It is a very revealing document. Richard B. Hubbard · "The United States in the Far East, or, Modern Japan and the Orient" (Richmond, Va., 1899).
   William Seward's "Travels Around the World," p. 89.
6. Foulk Papers (New York Public Library, Manuscripts Div.).

CHAPTER XXXV

NOTES ON BIBLIOGRAPHY

QUOTATION or exact citation with attached bibliographical reference where statements of fact are, or may be, matters of dispute have been uniformly utilized in this study. Other quotations have been introduced to give the reader the peculiar flavor of the sources quoted, for in the determination of policy prejudices and personal feelings were fully as influential as facts. A bibliographical list is appended which, while abbreviated in form, is sufficient for the identification of the source. In this list will be found some titles of little known contemporary sources throwing light on various phases of domestic history or on American foreign relations outside of Eastern Asia.

The attempt to supply a complete and critical bibliog raphy of the subject has been abandoned because it cannot be done satisfactorily except at great length. Such a bib liography would be most satisfactory were it the result of collaboration rather than of purely individual selection. Many general works of reference to which the student naturally turns for general information, and even many histories bearing directly upon the subject are not mentioned in the bibliographical citations. Some comments of a general nature at the end of this chapter will give the reason for this omission. The appended list, containing as it does every title cited in the text, does constitute a selected bibliography of the sources which the writer has found sufficiently accurate to justify quotation. The citation of a book for a specific reference does not however constitute an endorse ment of the book as a whole. In general books on the Orient are very uneven in quality.

The writer has had exceptional privileges of access to

the archives of the Department of State and it has seemed that the most valuable personal contribution he can make towards the critical bibliography which is so sorely needed, is in the way of comparison of these records with the printed documents and with such other manuscripts or printed sources as run parallel to the government archives. This contribution is offered in payment of the debt of gratitude due to those writers who have already pioneered in the field and have published bibliographies.

The primary documentary source for American affairs in the East Indies and Eastern Asia before 1844 are the consular letter books in the Department of State. The Canton Letters, however, begin approximately with 1800 and while the Calcutta Letters begin in 1793 they are very incomplete and the student must look elsewhere for the bulk of the material. The Miscellaneous Letters of the Department of State archives, for which there is a calendar in the Department, contain some correspondence from merchants engaged in trade and throw light on the relations of such men as Astor, Girard, and the Providence and Boston merchants to the Embargo, War of 1812, appointment of consuls, etc. The first volume of Canton Letters contains some misplaced correspondence with reference to the *Columbia* and *Lady Washington* expedition to the Northwest Coast, and a packet of letters and documents, unbound, in the State Department Library, gives further information about the Northwest Coast trade.

The most complete printed contemporary sources of in formation for the period preceding 1800 are: Shaw's Journals, published in 1847, which not only include Shaw's reports to John Jay, but also supply much additional information as to the circumstances under which the East India trade was initiated, and the manner of conducting it in the East; the O'Donnell correspondence in Diplomatic Correspondence 1783-9, Volume 3; Spark's "Life of John Ledyard"; the biographical sketches of Elias Haskett Derby and others in Hunt's "American Merchants"; the "Letters of Phineas Bond," and William Milburn's "Oriental Commerce," the editions of 1813 and 1825 being unlike and both valuable.

These printed sources are supplemented by many scattered manuscripts. The Library of Congress contains the Ingraham Journal of the Voyage of the *Hope,* a long letter from Thomas Randall to Alexander Hamilton and other less important items. The Hudson Collection in the New York Public Library contains papers relating to the building of the ship *Massachusetts* for Samuel Shaw in 1784, and the Bancroft Collection in the same library contains copies of some of the Phineas Bond letters as well as reports of other British agents which are of the utmost importance in determining the initial East India trade of Philadelphia, Baltimore, New York and the Rhode Island ports.

The documentary sources in the Massachusetts libraries are given in S. E. Morison's incomparable "Maritime History of Massachusetts" and K. S. Latourette's "Early Relations between the United States and China" gives an extensive though not complete list of contemporary sources both manuscript and printed.

The Canton Consular Letters from 1800 to 1840 were published in part in H. Doc. 119:26-1 and H. Doc. 71:26-2. While no important information bearing on the question before Congress, namely, the proposed treaty with China, was omitted from these documents the unpublished material is of the greatest historical interest, and contains many shipping reports and comments which throw much light on early American economic and industrial development. The Kearny Correspondence, published in full in S. Doc. 139:29-1, is an indispensable introduction to the Cushing negotiations, and in part supplies the deficiency due to the fact that the consular correspondence beyond 1840 was not published.

The Edmund Roberts papers are deposited in the Library of Congress. They must, however, be supplemented by the Roberts papers, unbound, in the library of the Department of State, and by the Batavia Consular Letters. The *Chinese Repository* for the period contains some important comments on the Roberts Mission. Edmund Roberts' own book is of very slight value for the historian owing to the editorial supervision it received from the Department of State.

The published consular correspondence for the period is supplemented by Paullin's "Early Voyages of American Naval Vessels in the Orient," which is based on the archives of the Navy Department, and contains full quotations and citations. Seybert, Pitkin and Milburn supply much statistical and other information, but the best sources for the conditions of American trade are found in the Parliamentary Papers. While many statements were made in the various Parliamentary investigations which tended to exaggerate the growth of American trade, these reports are, on the whole, more reliable than the incomplete figures in the Consular Letters, and are more comprehensive than those of Seybert or Pitkin.

The Caleb Cushing Correspondence is published with the omission of no important details in S. Docs. 67 and 58:28-2.

Between 1844 and 1853 very little of the diplomatic or consular correspondence was published. The *Chinese Repository* in a measure supplies this gap and is also a valuable supplement to all the published documents during the years (1832-51) of its publication. For the years 1828-61 the Hasse Index of U. S. Documents Relating to Foreign Affairs is a certain and invaluable guide which renders unnecessary the compilation of complete lists in this volume.

From 1853 to 1869 practically all of the diplomatic correspondence of the American representatives in China and Japan was published. The Department of State apparently had no compunctions about publishing material which contained or implied a criticism of other powers. The voluminous and highly entertaining as well as instructive correspondence of Humphrey Marshall for 1853 was printed almost without editing or the omission of the many confidential dispatches. This and the correspondence of his successors, McLane, Parker, Reed and Ward, more than

2500 pages in all, constitute a primary source not merely
for American but for British and French history in China.
These volumes have been uniformly ignored by the British
and French historians of the period and yet so important
is their contribution that the entire history of the period
may well be rewritten from them.   These documents, to
which may be added S. Wells Williams' Journal of the Reed
and Ward Missions, have an unique value which gives them
precedence over the British Blue Books.   The latter were
published while the British Government was being subjected to searching criticism, and they were obviously designed to justify a policy already determined upon.   The
American documents were not edited to mēet a criticism
and were designed to plead no case.   They record events,
month by month, as they occurred and are an historical
source of surpassing value.   They are the birth records of
American policy.

The Diplomatic Correspondence, begun by Seward,
when compared with the manuscript dispatches, reveals a
continuance of the policy to supply the fullest possible
information on the relations of the United States to China
and Japan.   Only a small amount of editing took place.
The China dispatches contain relatively little of importance
which was not printed.   The same may be said for Japan
with the exception that the information relative to the
convention of 1866 was very defective, and much of the
negotiation with reference to Korea, having been entirely
verbal, was omitted entirely.

The Townsend Harris correspondence was published
only in fragments but the deficiency has been largely supplied in Griffis' "Harris" which was based on Harris' Journal
and contains extensive excerpts.   The Harris Papers are
now deposited in the Library of the College of the City of
New York, and there are in addition to them some Harris
papers in the New York Public Library.   Griffis did not
have access to the latter papers but they contain nothing
which would modify greatly the facts already published.
The present writer has added in the text certain facts not

hitherto known relating to the appointment of Harris to his various posts. The Pruyn papers to which Treat had access and from which he printed many excerpts would appear to be very similar in content to the dispatches in the Department of State.

The Burlingame private papers do not appear to have been extensive and Williams' biography is complete except for certain details of the negotiations in Europe which were reported in more or less private letters to Seward and are bound up in the first volume of Notes from the Chinese Legation in the Department of State.

Some additional correspondence for the period covered by Seward's term of office appear in the documents reporting the investigations of O. B. Bradford and George F. Seward, in the document supplying information on the Ward-Hill claim against China, and in the reports relative to the return of the Chinese and Japanese indemnities.

Parts of the missing documents with reference to Seward's negotiations over Korea have been printed in the text, and more completely by the writer of this book in the *American Historical Review.*

A change of policy with reference to the publication of diplomatic correspondence by the Department of State appears after 1870. The dispatches were subjected to an increasing amount of editing. The reason may be found in the complaints of the American representatives in Peking and Tokio. The full publication of their dispatches had become a source of extreme embarrassment. The English newspapers, most of them bitterly and vituperously hostile to Americans, seized upon the volumes of Foreign Relations with avidity and published long extracts, with commentaries. For several years thereafter the ministers themselves were permitted to designate the dispatches which they were willing to have published, and then a system of editing was introduced into the State Department which was very conservative and erred only on the safe side. The effect of this system was to render the succeeding volumes of Foreign Relations of decreasing value to the student of

American policy in the East.   One is not safe in making any generalizations based on the published dispatches in Foreign Relations from 1875 to 1894.   But the relations of the American Government to the Sino-Japanese War was exhibited with no important omissions, and the Boxer correspondence is in no way misleading.

The voluminous documents relating to the Philippine question are of a different character.   They are fully and critically discussed by LeRoy.   In general we may note that they resemble in character the British Blue books on the Elgin Expedition and the Treaty of Tientsin.   They were published to justify a policy and to influence public opinion and as such must be used with the greatest caution.   They represent the first instance in the 19th century in American relations with the East where government documents were used as polemics to justify a policy already adopted.

The manuscript or printed material running parallel with the diplomatic records for the period since 1868 is scanty.   The Shufeldt papers are deposited in the Navy Department Library and the Foulk papers, containing letter-press copies of practically all his reports and diplomatic dispatches and some personal notes and correspondence (1884-7) with reference to Korean matters, are in the New York Public Library.   These two collections constitute an independent documentary record of American relations with Korea down to 1887.   They are of the utmost importance and are another block of material which materially changes a chapter of American history.   Perhaps no phase of American history has been more mishandled and more wrested to serve partisan purposes.

Other manuscript material relating to this period is known to exist but so far as the writer is aware it has not been made generally available to students.   The John Russell Young papers covering the years 1882-5, provided they are not lost, will yield a record of surpassing value for affairs in both China and Japan and also in Korea.   The Young dispatches contain the best portraiture of Li Hung Chang at that period that the writer has seen.   Likewise the Young papers will probably throw light on the international significance of the tour of General Grant in the East which, so far as American policy is concerned, marked an epoch. It is to be hoped that in time the literary records of more recent Americans, many of them still living, may find their way into libraries.

American historical literature is not rich in the biographies and published letters of American representatives in the East. Many of the Americans were not literary men and even where the records are ample it would appear that there has been a regrettable lack of interest in their publication. There are in American historical literature very few volumes comparable for historical importance and readability, with Oliphant's "Elgin Expedition," Walrond's "Letters of Lord Elgin," Michie's "Englishman in China," or Lane-Poole's "Life of Parkes." Williams' biography of Burlingame, the "Life and Letters of Williams," the Williams Journals of the Perry, Reed and Ward missions, and Foster's "Diplomatic Memoirs" only partially meet the need. The books of Young, Holcombe and Denby, while valuable, leave much to be desired. The result of this poverty of American historical literature and the general ignorance of the vast mass of government documents for the period before 1860 has been that American relations in the East have been very inadequately treated by his torians and also very badly misrepresented. One cannot refer to a single history of the period which is not exposed to the charge of grave misstatements of fact, and equally serious errors of interpretation.

Some few works by American and British writers have had such a currency and have been so widely used and generally cited as authorities that a few critical comments upon them may not be out of order.

H. B. Morse's "International Relations of the Chinese Empire," three volumes, is an invaluable chronicle of events in China. It is also an important interpretation by one who made an honest effort to be just and fair to all, and had a liberal view-point. Mr. Morse's distinguished career in the "Chinese Maritime Customs," and his close association with Sir Robert Hart gave him access to invaluable sources of information. These three volumes are an exposition of the point of view of a liberal Englishman in China. The second and third volumes reflect in a pronounced way the views of Sir Robert Hart. All the volumes have, however, two very serious deficiencies. By confining the study to China with some attention to Korea, and by excluding Japan, they present a distorted picture, for it was the policy of all the Powers to regard the Far or Extreme East as a unity. The second deficiency is due not to the limitation of the theme but to the use of sources. In the first volume, which brings the narrative down to 1860, and which covers the period in 'which American policy had its birth, Mr. Morse draws upon only seven American sources, most of which are not contemporary, and none of which are official records. The result is a volume in which the British Blue books and other British sources supply the information and control the conclusions. It is an extremely unreliable guide to the study of American policy. The two later volumes are less deficient in their use of American sources, and yet American interests are slighted and misrepresented.

The writings of S. Wells Williams demand special at tention. As a source book of Chinese history the "Middle Kingdom" still occupies a unique position. The abridgment of this monumental work by the author's son in "A History of China," shares the merits of the larger work. However, for some reason, possibly because of Dr. Williams' intimate and confidential association with the American Government for so many years, the phases of American relations with China are slighted to an extraordinary degree, and these volumes are of little value in a study of American policy. On the other hand the Williams' Journals, published in China and Japan, and little known to American readers, are of superlative importance.

John W. Foster's "American Diplomacy in the Orient" has been for nearly a score of years the only book by an American author to cover the field which the present writer has chosen. The book may not fairly be judged for what it did not purport to be. It was not based on manuscript sources, nor did it attempt a critical handling of any source. Its most important contribution was for those years in which the author was himself an actor in the events he described. Its later chapters were written with the extreme caution of a gentleman who was writing about his friends and political associates, and the entire volume reflects a complacent judgment which has had the effect of presenting American policy in Asia as a form of philanthropy. Perhaps the most serious defect of the book is its failure to bring out the importance of events before 1860. General Foster appears to have regarded the questions as they arose in the last three decades of the century as novel, whereas, in principle, they were but the recurrences of older questions in the settlement of which ample precedents had been laid down. Of more importance to the student is Foster's "Diplomatic Memoirs," the chapters of which devoted to the Sino-Japanese War and the Treaty of Shimoneséki, are a primary historical source.

There are no books on American policy in Korea which can be recommended. The information upon which they have been written has been scanty and very partisan. American policy has been misrepresented. This was not a very bright page in American history, but it is not open to the charges which have been brought against it.

The British writers, Boulger, Parker, Michie, Lane-Poole, Douglas, Alcock, and others, all have the deficiencies noted in Morse. They did not find it worth while to consult American sources of information. While not uncritical of British policy, they incline to accept the British Blue Books as the inspired word of truth, and the facts of American relations receive only passing attention and the most astonishing interpretations. They perpetuate many statements which, according to American sources of the highest historical value, would appear to be utterly untenable. Sargent's "Anglo-Chinese Commerce and Diplomacy" is of a different character, admirable and alone in its class.

In conclusion we draw attention to a group of studies by American scholars of certain limited phases of the American policy. Callahan's "American Relations in the Pacific and the Far East, 1784-1900," was the pioneer. It was written just after the occupation of the Philippines and reflects the resurgence of American imperialism of the period. It has been much criticised but it had many merits as an introduc tion to the subject. Callahan grasped the cycle of events and realized that in 1898 the United States was really re turning to a phase of policy similar to that of the fifties. This was an important contribution which not all students were ready to appropriate. Paullin's "Diplomatic Negotia-tions of American Naval Officers," and his even more valuable "Early Voyages of American Naval Vessels in the Orient" set a high standard of scholarship and remain in this field unchallenged. Their deficiency is merely in the scope, for they were based too exclusively upon the naval records. The State Department archives are necessary to complete the picture and when Paullin wrote the more re-cent ones were not available. Treat's "Diplomatic Rela-tions between the United States and Japan, 1853-65," is another scholarly study. While the present writer has not always found it possible to accept Treat's interpretations, and has rejected the valuation which he placed upon the services of one man, he has used the book with very great appreciation. Treat's more recent "Japan and the United States, 1853-1921," is of less value and the irenic nature of the lectures which it comprises would appear to have em-barrassed a perfectly impartial statement of the facts. LeRoy's intensive study of the first few years of American policy in the Philippines stands in a class by itself. It is the indispensable guide to the student. Likewise, Morison's "Maritime History of Massachusetts, 1783-1860," is an incomparable book. It has only the defect of the limita-tion of the subject. From Morison one might easily reach the conclusion that the contribution of Massachusetts to the early East India trade of the United States was greater than it actually was. Philadelphia and New York would appear from the records, incomplete though they are, to have had an importance which is not assigned to them by Morison. The most adequate single source for the entire period is the historical sections of Moore's "Digest."

Passing from the mature works of American historians we come to a group of academic studies by post graduate students. At the head of this list, in value, stands Koo's "Status of Aliens in China." Next to it is Nitobe's study which now possesses, in addition to its scholarly research, the value of a historical document for it is an interpretation by a Japanese student in an American university in the early nineties. Hinkley's "American Consular Jurisprudence in the Orient" gives a good summary of extraterritoriality; it is deficient in statements of historical fact. Latourette's "Early Relations between the United States and China," 1784-1844, is particularly valuable for its critical bibliography. Clements' "Boxer Rebellion" is good. There is a steadily increasing list of doctorate theses by Japanese and Chinese students in American universities. They are of very unequal value. Their too common defects are a neglect of original sources, and a tendency towards special pleading. Many of the Japanese students have made important contributions by supplying translations from Japanese sources not otherwise available. A few Chinese have made similar contributions, but there is a regrettable lack of Chinese source material in the output of Chinese students and an undiscriminating use of British sources which often weakens the cause so dear to their hearts. While Chinese sources may not be available to Chinese students in America, and while many of the Chinese historical records were conveniently destroyed by the vandalism of foreign invading armies at Peking in 1860 and in 1900, there is nevertheless in China a very considerable amount of historical record of the highest value which only the Chinese graduate student is competent to make use of. Hitherto China has rarely spoken for herself in the writing of history, and for this reason the Chinese story has suffered greatly in the telling. The publication of Chinese source material on the history of China's foreign relations would doubtless work havoc in all existing histories. Meanwhile the Chinese students have by no means made the most of the Chinese sources which are available in American Government documents.

It is also very regrettable that greater inducement has not been given to post-graduate historical students to edit and publish as theses the vast amount of manuscript material which lies unused and unknown in the various manuscript collections, particularly in the libraries of the northern Atlantic seaboard. Some of these manuscripts, competently edited, would be at least as good a test of scholarly ability as the theses which appear from year to year, and to the general public they would be of vastly greater value.

BIBLIOGRAPHY

MANUSCRIPTS IN UNITED STATES GOVERNMENT ARCHIVES

Department of State.
Despatches to Consuls.
Batavia Consular Letters.
Canton Consular Letters.
Honolulu Consular Letters.
Ningpo Consular Letters.
Manila Consular Letters.
Smyrna Consular Letters.
British Legation, Notes from.
China Instructions.
China Despatches.
Chinese Legation, Notes from.
Japan Instructions.
Japan Despatches.
Japanese Legation, Notes from.
Korea Instructions.
Korea Despatches.
Russia Instructions.
Russia Despatches.
Russian Legation, Notes to.
Townsend Harris Papers. Bureau of Appointments.
Capt. John Kendrick. Correspondence concerning Settlement of his Estate. Library, D. of S.
Miscellaneous Letters.
Edmund Roberts Papers.
Navy Department.
Captains' Letters.
East India Squadron Letters.
Commodore R. W. Shufeldt: "Cruise of the *Ticonderoga*."
———: Papers (deposited in Library).

OTHER MANUSCRIPTS

Bancroft Collection. America and England. New York Public Library.
Papers of Continental Congress. Library of Congress.
Philip Cuyler Letter Book. New York Public Library.
George C. Foulk Papers. New York Public Library.
Alexander Hamilton Papers. Library of Congress.
Townsend Harris Papers. College of the City of New York Library.
———. New York Public Library.
——— Journals (typewritten copy). Library of Congress.
Hudson Collection. New York Public Library.
Joseph Ingraham. "Journal of the Voyage of the *Hope*." Library of Congress.

Thomas Jefferson Papers. Library of Congress.
William Law Papers. New York Public Library.
James Madison Papers. Library of Congress.
———. New York Public Library.
Edmund Roberts Papers. Library of Congress.
Daniel Webster Papers. Library of Congress.
Oliver Wolcott and Co. Account Books. New York Historical Society.

UNITED STATES GOVERNMENT PUBLICATIONS.

Congressional Documents (given below in the order of publication).
Lowndes Report on Coinage. H. Doc. 111, 15th Cong. 2nd Sess.
Floyd Report on Oregon. H. Repts. 45, 16-2.
China Trade, Report on, Feb. 6, 1826. S. Doc. 31, 19-1.
Tea Smuggling. H. Doc. 137, 19-1.
Forbes, R. B. and Others, Memorial of. H. Doc. 40, 26-1.
Fanning, Edmund, Memorial of. H. Doc. 57, 26-1.
Canton Consular Letters. H. Doc. 119, 26-1.
Boston and Salem Merchants, Petition of. H. Doc. 170, 26-1.
China Trade, Secretary of Treas. Report on. H. Doc. 248, 26-1.
Canton Consular Letters. H. Doc. 71, 26-2.
Pres. Tyler, Message of July 1, 1842. H. Doc. 35, 27-3.
Adams, John Quincy, Report on China Mission Appropriation. H. Repts. 93, 27-3.
Cushing, Caleb, Correspondence of. S. Doc. 67, 28-2.
———. S. Doc. 58, 28-2.
Webster, Daniel, Instructions to Cushing. S. Doc. 138, 28-2.
Pratt Resolution on Treaty with Japan. H. Doc. 138, 28-2.
Kearny Correspondence. S. Doc. 139, 29-1.
Palmer, Aaron Haight, Letter to Buchanan, H. Doc. 96, 29-2.
———. Memoir Geographical, Political and Commercial on Siberia, Manchuria, and Asiatic Islands of the N. Pacific Ocean. S. Misc. Doc. 80, 30-1.
King, T. Butler, Report of Com. on Naval Affairs. H. Repts. 596, 30-1.
Davis, John W., Corres. on Consular Courts. S. Ex. Doc. 72, 31-1.
Glynn, Commander James, Correspondence of. H. Ex. Doc. 84, 31-1.
Balestier, Joseph, Correspondence of. S. Ex. Doc. 38, 32-1.
Webster, Daniel, Report on Present Relations with Japan. S. Ex. Doc. 59, 32-1.
Kennedy, John P., Report on Trans-Pacific steamers. S. Ex. Doc. 49, 32-2.
Marshall, Humphrey, Correspondence of. H. Ex. Doc. 123, 33-1.
Perry, M. C., Correspondence of. S. Ex. Doc. 34, 33-2.
Palmer, Aaron Haight, Memorial to Senate. S. Misc. Doc. 10, 33-2.
Rockhill, John A., Report on Trans-Isthmian Canal. H. Rept. 145, 33-2.
Parker, Peter, Correspondence on Coolie Trade. S. Ex. Doc. 99, 34-1.
McLane, Robert M., Correspondence of. S. Ex. Doc. 22, 35-2, 2 vols.
Parker, Peter, Correspondence of. S. Ex. Doc. 22, 35-2, 2 vols.
Consular Officers, Compensation for. H. Ex. Doc. 68, 35-2.
Reed, William B., Correspondence of. S. Ex. Doc. 30, 36-1.
Ward, John E., Correspondence of. S. Ex. Doc. 30, 36-1.
Marcy, William H., Instructions to McLane. S. Ex. Doc. 39, 36-1.
Harris, Townsend, Corres. on Japanese Mission. S. Ex. Doc. 25, 36-1.
Japan, Purchase of War Steamers in U. S. S. Ex. Doc. 33, 37-3.
Midway Islands, Occupation of. S. Ex. Doc. 79, 40-2.
Japanese Immigration to Hawaiian Islands. S. Ex. Doc. 80, 40-2.

Midway Islands, Harbor Improvement. S. Rept. 194, 40-3.
China, American Claims on. H. Ex. Doc. 29, 40-3.
Consular Service Inspection. S. Ex. Doc. 7, 41-3.
Chinese Immigration Investigation. S. Rept. 689, 44-2.
Chinese Immigration. Oliver P. Morton Opinion. S. Misc. Doc. 20 45-2.
Shanghai Consulate Investigation. H. Misc. Doc. 31, 45-2.
Seward, Geo. F., Report of Investigation. H. Rept. 134, 45-3.
Chinese Indemnity, H. Rept. 970, 48-1; see also, H. Ex. Doc. 29, 40-3;
    H. Ex. Doc. 69, 41-2; H. Rept. 113, 45-3; H. Rept. 1142, 46-2.
Korean Army, American Instructors for. S. Rept. 1443, 48-2.
China, Report on Pending Treaty, Sept. 18, 1888. S. Ex. Doc. 273, 50-1.
Merchant Marine in Foreign Trade (1890). H. Rept. 1210, 51-1.
Hawaiian Islands, Harrison Message on Annexation. S. Ex. Doc. 76, 52-2.
Philippines, McKinley Transmits Treaty of Paris to Senate. S. Doc. 62,
    55-3.
Aguinaldo, Communications with. S. Doc. 208, 56-1.
Philippine Islands, Senate Hearings. S. Doc. 331, 57-1, 3 parts.
Rockhill, W. W., Correspondence on Boxer Settlement. S. Doc. 67, 57-1.
China, U. S. Military Operations in. War Dept. Doc. 124, Pub. XXX.

(For complete list of congressional documents 1828-1861, see Adelaide
R. Hasse. Index to U. S. Docs. relating to Foreign Affairs [Washington,
1914, 3 parts]; for further details of printed diplomatic correspondence
1861-1900, see index volume to Foreign Relations.)

Other Government or Semi-official Publications.
U. S. Statutes at Large.
Diplomatic Correspondence, Sept. 19, 1783-Mar. 4, 1789.
Annals of Congress.
Intercontinental Telegraph, Seward Report to Senate (1864).
Charles Sumner, Speech on Cession of Russian America (1867).
Keim, DeB. Randolph. Report on Consular Service of U. S. (1872).
Rejection of Henry W. Blair by Chinese Government (1892).
Monthly Summary of Commerce and Finance, April, 1898.
Monthly Summary of Commerce and Finance, July, 1899.
Monthly Summary of Commerce and Finance, June, 1901.
Monthly Summary of Commerce and Finance, Jan., 1904.
Pierce, Herbert H. D. "Tour of Consular Inspection" (1904).
Moore, John Bassett. "Arbitrations" (1898).
———. "Digest of International Law" (1906).

COLLECTIONS OF TREATIES AND AGREEMENTS

"Treaties and Conventions between the United States and Other Powers
    1776-1887, with Notes" (1889).
"Treaties, Conventions, International Acts, Protocols, and Agreements
    between the United States and Other Powers 1776-1909." Compiled
    by William M. Malloy. 2 vols. S. Doc. 357, 61-2.
Rockhill, W. W. "Treaties and Conventions with or Concerning China
    and Korea, 1894-1904" (1904); Supplement (1908).
MacMurray, J. V. A. "Treaties and Agreements with and Concerning
    China, 1894-1919." 2 vols. (New York, 1921.)
"Treaties, Conventions, etc., between China and Foreign States" (Chinese
    Maritime Customs, 2d ed. Shanghai, 1917.)
"Traités et Conventions entre l'Empire du Japon et les Puissances
    Etranges" (Tokio, 1908).
Martens' "Recueil de Traités" (Deuxième Séries. Gottingue, 1876).
Korea. Treaties and Agreements (Washington, 1921.)

British Parliamentary Papers

House of Commons, 1821, Vol. 7.
House of Commons, Sessional Papers, 1830, Vols. 5-6.
Correspondence Relative to Affairs in China, 1839-41. Private and Confidential.
China. 40. 1847. Orders, Ordinances, etc. (795).
Coolie Trade and Emigration from Hongkong, 1857-8 (481).
Hansard's Debates. Series 3, Vol. CXLIV.
Lord Elgin-Yeh Correspondence. 1857-8 (2322).
Lord Elgin-Earls. of Clarendon and Malmesbury Corres. 1860 (2618).
Lord Elgin Report, 1861 (2754).
Bruce Correspondence. 1860 (2587, 2606, 2641, 2677).
Japan, Nos. 2-3, 1865 (3429, 3459).
Inland Residence of Missionaries. China. No. 9, 1870 (89).
Formosa, Settlement of Difficulty between China and Japan, 1875 (C1164, C1289).
Korea, Reports on, from British Minister in Japan. 1883 (C3455).
Korea, Treaty of, Nov. 26, 1883. 1884 (C4044).
Port Hamilton Correspondence. China, 1887 (C4991).

Books, Pamphlets, Magazines and Newspapers

(Editions noted in titles given below are those to which references are made in the foregoing pages. In many cases there are other editions.)

ABEEL, DAVID. "Journal of a Residence in China" (2d ed., New York, 1836).
ADAMS, J. Q. "Memoirs," 12 vols. (Philadelphia, 1875).
ALCOCK, RUTHERFORD. "The Capital of the Tycoon," 2 vols. (London, 1863).
ALLEN, H. N. "A Chronological Index of Events in Korean History" (Seoul, 1901).
ANGELL, JAMES B. "Diplomatic Relations of the United States and China." *American Journal of Social Science*, Vol. XVII.

BAKER, GEORGE E. "Works of William H. Seward," 5 vols. (New York and Boston, 1884).
BARRETT, WALTER CLERK. "Old Merchants of New York," 5 vols. (New York, 1885).
BENTON, T. H. "Thirty Years' View," 2 vols. (New York, 1856).
BLAKESLEE, GEORGE H. (Ed.) "China and the Far East" (New York, 1910).
BLOUNT, JAMES H. "The American Occupation of the Philippines," 1898-1912 (New York, 1912).
BRIDGMAN. ELIZA J. Gillet. "Life and Labors of Elijah Coleman Bridgman" (New York, 1864).
BRINE, LINDSAY. "The Taeping Rebellion in China" (London, 1862).
BOND, PHINEAS. Letters of. *American Historical Association Reports*, 1896, Vol. 1.

CALLAHAN, J. M. "American Relations in the Pacific and the Far East." *Johns Hopkins Studies*, Series XIX, Nos. 1-3 (1901).
CALLERY, J. M. Journal des opérations diplomatiques de la Legation française en Chine (Macao, 1845).
CAMPBELL, ARCHIBALD. "A Voyage Around the World 1806-1812." Transcribed by James Smith (Edinburgh, 1816).

Chinese Repository (Canton, Macao, Victoria, 1832-1851).
Chinese Times (Tientsin).
CLARK, ARTHUR H. "The Clipper Ship Era 1843-1869" (New York and London, 1910).
CLEMENTS, PAUL H. "The Boxer Rebellion." *Columbia University Studies in History, Economics and Public Law,* Vol. XXVI, No. 3.
"Cambridge Modern History," Vol. XI (New York, 1909).
CONANT, C. A. "The United States in the Orient" (Boston and New York, 1900).
COOKE, GEORGE WINGROVE. "China" (London and New York, 1858).
COOLIDGE, MARY ROBERTS. "Chinese Immigration" (New York, 1909).
CORDIER, HENRI. "Américanistes et Français à Canton au XVIIIe Siècle." *Journal de la Société des Américanistes de Paris* (Paris, 1898).
——. "L'Expedition de Chine 1857-1858" (Paris, 1905).
——. "Histoire des Relations de la Chine avec Les Puissances Occidentales 1860-1900," 3 vols. (Paris, 1901).

DAVIDSON, JAMES W. "The Island of Formosa" (London and New York, Yokohama, Shanghai, etc., 1903).
DAVIS, JOHN FRANCIS. "China during the War and Since the Peace," 2 vols. (London, 1852).
DAY, CLIVE. "History of American Commerce" (New York, 1920).
DeBow's Review.
DENBY, CHARLES. "China and Her People," 2 vols. (Boston, 1906).
DENNETT, TYLER. "American Good Offices in Asia." *Journal of International Law,* Vol. XVI, No. 1 (1922).
——. "Seward's Far Eastern Policy." *American Historical Review,* October, 1922.
DENNY, O. N. "China and Korea," pamphlet (Shanghai, 1888).
DEWEY, GEORGE. "Autobiography" (New York, 1913).
DICKENS, F. V. and LANE-POOLE, STANLEY. "Life of Sir Harry Parkes" (London and New York, 1894).
DINSMORE, WALTER T. "Shipping Subsidies" (Boston and New York, 1907).
Documents Relative to the Colonial History of New York (Albany, 1854).
DOUGLAS, ROBERT K. "Europe and the Far East" (Cambridge, 1904).

Essex Institute, Historical Collections of.
ECKARDSTEIN, VON, BARON. "Ten Years at the Court of St. James" (London, 1921: New York, 1922).

FANNING, EDMUND. "Voyages Round the World" (New York, 1833).
FOSTER, JOHN W. "American Diplomacy in the Orient" (Boston and New York, 1903).
FOSTER, JOHN W. "Diplomatic Memoirs," 2 vols. (Boston and New York, 1909).
FORBES, R. B. "China and the China Trade," pamphlet (Boston, 1844).
——. "Personal Reminiscences, with Recollections of China" (3d ed., Boston, 1892).

GIESECKE, A. A. "American Commercial Legislation before 1789" (New York, 1910).
GOLDEN, FRANK A. "Purchase of Alaska." *American Historical Review,* Vol. XXV, No. 3.
GRIFFIS, W. E. "Corea, the Hermit Nation" (8th ed., New York, 1907).
——. "Townsend Harris" (Boston and New York, 1895).
——. "Matthew Calbraith Perry" (Boston, 1887).
——. "Verbeck of Japan" (New York, Chicago, Toronto, 1900).

GRIFFIS, W. E. "A Modern Pioneer in Korea"—biography of Henry G. Appenzeller (New York and Chicago, 1912).
GUBBINS, J. H. "Progress of Japan 1853-71" (Oxford, 1911).

HAMBERG, THEODORE. "The Visions of Hung-Siu-tshuen, and the Origin of the Kwang-si Insurrection" (Hongkong, 1854).
HAWKS, FRANCIS L. "Narrative of the Japan Expedition," 4 vols.
———. H. Ex. Doc. 97, 33-2.
———. "Narrative of the Perry Expedition," 1 vol. (New York, 1857).
HAY, JOHN. "Addresses" (New York, 1900).
———. "Letters and Diaries." 3 vols. (Privately printed, Washington, 1908).
HAYASHI, COUNT. "Secret Memoirs" (New York, 1915).
HISHIDA, SEIJI G. "International Position of Japan as a Great Power." Columbia University Studies in History, Economics and Public Law. Vol. 24, No. 3, 1905.
HILDRETH, RICHARD. "Japan as It Was and Is" (Boston, 1855).
HINCKLEY, FRANK E. "American Consular Jurisprudence in the Orient" (Washington, 1906).
HOAR. GEORGE F. "Autobiography of Seventy Years," 2 vols. (New York, 1906).
HOLCOMBE, CHESTER. "Chinese Immigration." Outlook, April 24, 1904.
———. "The Real Chinese Question" (New York, 1900).
HOMANS, J. SMITH. "Foreign Commerce of the United States" (New York, 1857).
HORNBECK, STANLEY K. "Contemporary Politics in the Far East" (New York, 1916).
HOUSE. H. E. "The Martyrdom of Japan." Atlantic Monthly, Vol. XLVII (1881).
———. "The Thraldom of Japan." Atlantic Monthly, Vol. LX (1887).
HUBBARD, RICHARD B. "The United States in the Far East," etc. (Richmond, Va., 1899).
HUGHES, SARAH FORBES. "Letters and Recollections of John Murray Forbes," 2 vols. (Boston and New York, 1908).
HULBERT, HOMER B. "The Passing of Korea" (New York, 1906).
HUNT, FREEMAN (ed.). "Lives of American Merchants," 2 vols. (New York, 1858).
HUNTER, W. C. "The 'Fan Kwae' at Old Canton" (London, 1882).

IRELAND, ALLEYNE. "China and the Powers." (Printed privately, 1902).
ISWOLSKY, ALEXANDER. "Memoirs." Recollections of a Foreign Minister. Translated by C. L. Seeger (New York, 1921).

Japan Gazette.
Japan Daily Mail.
Japan Weekly Mail.
JOHNSON, ROSSITER. "The Twentieth Century Dictionary of Notable Americans" (Boston, 1904).
JONES, CHESTER LLOYD. "The Consular Service of the United States." University of Pennsylvania Series in Political Economy and Public Law, No. 18 (Philadelphia, 1906).

"Kaiser, Letters of the, to the Czar." Isaac Don Levine, ed. (New York, 1920).
KENNAN, GEORGE. "Tent Life in Siberia" (New York and London, 1874).
KENT, HORACE PERCY. "Railway Enterprise in China" (London, 1907).
KIMBALL, GERTRUDE SELWYN. "East India Trade of Providence 1787-1807." Brown University Historical Papers, 1-10, 1894-99.

KING, C. W. "Claims of Japan and Malaysia upon Christendom," 2 vols. (New York, 1839).

Koo, V. K. W. "The Status of Aliens in China." *Columbia University Studies in History, Economics and Public Law,* Vol. L, No. 2 (1912).

Korean Repository.

KORFF, S. A. "Russia's Foreign Relations during the Last Half Century" (New York, 1922).

LANMAN, CHARLES. "The Japanese in America" (New York, 1872).

LATOURETTE, K. C. "History of Early Relations between the United States and China 1784-1844." *Transactions of Connecticut Academy of Arts and Sciences,* Vol. 22 (New Haven, 1917).

LEAVENWORTH, C. S. "The Loochoo Islands" (Shanghai, 1905).

LEROY, JAMES A. "The Americans in the Philippines," 2 vols. (Boston and New York, 1914).

LEWIS, ROBERT E. "The Educational Conquest of the Far East" (New York and Chicago, 1903).

Littell's Living Age.

LONGFORD, J. H. "The Story of Old Japan" (New York, 1910).

"Lowrie, Walter, Memoir of" (Philadelphia, 1854).

LUBBOCK, BASIL. "The China Clippers" (2d ed., Glasgow, 1914).

MARTIN, W. A. P. "A Cycle of Cathay" (New York and Chicago, 1897).

McLAREN, W. W. "Japanese Government Documents." *Transactions of the Asiatic Society of Japan,* Vol. XLII, Part 1 (Yokohama, 1914).

———. "A Political History of Japan" (London and New York, 1916).

MEEKER, ROYAL. "History of Shipping Subsidies" (New York, 1905).

"Memorials of Protestant Missionaries in China" (Shanghai, 1867).

MICHIE, ALEXANDER. "The Englishman in China," 2 vols. (Edinburgh and London, 1900).

MILBURN, WILLIAM. "Oriental Commerce," 2 vols. (two editions, London, 1813 and 1825).

MILLER, MARION MILLS. "Great Debates in American History," 14 vols. (New York, 1913).

MONTALTO, C. A. DE JESUS. "Historic Shanghai" (Shanghai, 1909).

MOORE, J. B. "Works of James Buchanan," 12 vols. (Philadelphia, 1909).

MORISON, S. E. "Maritime History of Massachusetts" (Boston and New York, 1921).

"Morrison, Robert, Memoirs of the Life and Labors of." 2 vols. (London, 1849).

MORSE, H. B. "International Relations of the Chinese Empire," 3 vols. (London and New York; also Shanghai, Vol. 1, 1910; Vols. II and III, 1918).

Niles Register.

NITOBE, INAZO (OTA). "The Intercourse between the United States and Japan." *Johns Hopkins Studies,* Extra Vol. VIII (1891).

North American Review.

North China Daily News.

North China Herald.

OLIPHANT, LAURENCE. "Narrative of the Earl of Elgin's Mission to China and Japan" (New York, 1860).

"Opium War, Chinese Account of." Translated by E. H. Parker. Pagoda Library. No. 1 (Shanghai, 1888).

PALMER, AARON HAIGHT. "Documents and Facts Illustrating the Origin of the Mission to Japan," pamphlet (Washington, 1857).

PARKER, PETER. "Journal of an Expedition from Singapore to Japan" (London, 1838).

PARSONS, WILLIAM BARCLAY. "An American Engineer in China" (New York, 1900).

PAULLIN, C. O. "American Naval Vessels in the Orient." *United States Naval Institute Proceedings,* 1910-11.

——. "Diplomatic Negotiations of American Naval Officers" (Baltimore, 1912).

PEARCE, F. B. "Zanzibar, the Island Metropolis of Eastern Asia" (London, 1920).

PITKIN, TIMOTHY. "Statistical View of the Commerce of the United States" (Hartford, 1816; New Haven, 1835).

POORE, BEN PERLEY. "Political Register and Congressional Directory," 12 vols. (Boston, 1878).

PORTER, DAVID. "Journal of a Cruise Made to the Pacific Ocean in 1812-14" (Philadelphia, 1815).

PORTER, ROBERT P. "Japan, the Rise of a Modern Power" (Oxford, 1918).

POWELL, E. ALEXANDER. "Gentlemen Rovers" (New York, 1913).

PUMPELLY, RAPHAEL. "Across America and Asia" (New York, 1870).

QUINCY, JOSIAH. "Journals of Major Samuel Shaw" (Boston, 1847).

REED, W. B. Speech of, at Philadelphia Board of Trade, May 31, 1859, pamphlet (Philadelphia, 1859).

Richardson's Messages and Papers of the Presidents.

ROCKHILL, W. W. "China's Intercourse with Korea from the Fifteenth Century to 1895" (London, 1905).

——. "Diplomatic Missions to the Court of China." *American Historical Review,* Vol. XL, 1897.

ROBERTS, EDMUND. "Embassy to the Eastern Courts of Cochin-China, Siam and Muscat" (New York, 1837).

ROBERTSON, J. BARR. "The Convention of Peking," pamphlet (Shanghai, 1870).

SARGENT, A. J. "Anglo-Chinese Commerce and Diplomacy" (Oxford, 1907).

SATOH, HENRY. "Lord Hotta, the Pioneer Diplomat of Japan" (Tokio, 1908).

SATOW, SIR ERNEST M. "A Diplomat in Japan" (London, 1921).

—— (translator). "History of Japan from 1853 to 1869." *Kinse Shiraku* (Yokohama, 1873).

SEWARD, FREDERICK W. "Reminiscences of a War-Time Statesman" (New York, 1916).

SEWARD, W. H. "Travels Around the World," edited by Olive Risley Seward (New York, 1873).

SEYBERT, ADAM. "Statistical Annals of the United States" (Philadelphia, 1818).

SMITH, ARTHUR H. "China in Convulsion." 2 vols. (New York and Chicago, 1901).

STAUNTON, GEORGE T. "Miscellaneous Notices" (London, 1822-50).

STEAD, ALFRED (editor). "Japan by the Japanese" (London, 1904).

STERNS, WORTHY P. "Foreign Trade of the United States 1820-40." *Journal of Political Economy,* Vol. VIII, 1899-1900.

STEVENS, JOHN AUSTIN. "Progress of New York in a Century, 1776-1876" (New York, 1876).

STEVENS, G. B. and MARWICK, W. F. "Life, Letters and Journals of Peter Parker" (Boston and Chicago, 1896).
SPALDING, J. W. "Japan and Around the World" (New York, 1855).
SPARKS, JARED. "Life of John Ledyard" (Cambridge, 1828).

TAYLOR, CHARLES. "Five Years in China" (Nashville, 1860).
TAYLOR, FITCH W. "The Flag Ship," 2 vols. (New York, 1840).
THAYER, REV. THATCHER. "Sketch of the Life of D. W. C. Olyphant," pamphlet (New York, 1876).
THAYER, W. R. "Life and Letters of John Hay," 2 vols. (Boston and New York, 1914).
TOWNSEND, EBENEZER, Diary of. "Voyage of the Neptune." *Papers of the New Haven Colony Historical Society*, Vol. XIV (1888).
TREAT, PAYSON JACKSON. "Early Diplomatic Relations of the United States and Japan 1853-1865" (Baltimore, 1917).
———. "Japan and the United States" (Boston and New York, 1921).
"Trenchard, Rear Admiral Stephen Decatur, Letters of." Edited by Edgar Staunton Maclay. *United States Naval Institute Proceedings*, Vol. XL.

UNDERWOOD, H. G. "The Call of Korea" (New York, 1908).
UNDERWOOD, L. H. "Underwood of Korea" (New York, 1918).

VANDERLIP, FRANK A. "Facts about the Philippines." *Century Magazine*, August, 1898.
VIALLATE, A. "Les préliminaires de la guerre hispano-américaine et l'annexion des Philippines par les États-Unis." *Revue Historique*, Juillet-Aôut, 1903.

WALROND, THEODORE. "Letters and Journals of James, Eighth Earl of Elgin" (London, 1872).
"Welles, Gideon, Diary of," 3 vols. (Boston and New York, 1911).
WELLS, DAVID A. "Our Merchant Marine" (New York, 1882).
WILLIAMS, F. W. "Anson Burlingame and the First Chinese Mission" (New York, 1912).
———. "Journal of S. Wells Williams. Perry Expedition." *Transactions of the Asiatic Society of Japan*, Vol. XXXVII, Part 11, 1910.
———. "Journal of S. Wells Williams. Reed and Ward Missions." *Journal of the North-China Branch of the Royal Asiatic Society*, Vol. XLII, 1911.
———. "Life and Letters of Samuel Wells Williams" (New York and London, 1889).
WILLIAMS, S. WELLS. "The Middle Kingdom," 3 vols. (New York, 1883).
WILSON, ANDREW. "The Ever-Victorious Army" (London, 1868).
WILSON, JAMES H. "China: Travels in the Middle Kingdom" (1st ed. 1887; 3d ed. 1901, New York).
WOOD, W. W. "Fankwei: or, the *San Jacinto* in the Seas of India, China, and Japan" (New York, 1859).

YOUNG, JOHN RUSSELL. "Around the World with General Grant," 2 vols. (New York, 1879).
———. "Men and Memoirs." Edited by Mary D. Russell Young, 2 vols. (New York, 1901).

APPENDIX

Presidents, Secretaries of State, and Diplomatic Representatives in China, Japan, and Korea (1842-1900)

JOHN TYLER

Daniel Webster (Mass.) (Mar. 5, '41-May 8, '43).

China	Japan	Korea
Caleb Cushing,[a] (Mass.) (May 8, '43—Commissioner; also E. E. & M. P.).		

John C. Calhoun (So. Car.) (April 1, 1844-Mar. 10, 1845).

China	Japan	Korea
	Caleb Cushing[a] (Mass.) (Aug. 15, '44). Commissioner.	

JAMES K. POLK

James Buchanan (Penn.) (Mar. 11, '45-Mar. 7, '49).

China	Japan	Korea
Alexander H. Everett (Mass.) (Mar. 13, '45-June 28, '47). John W. Davis (Ind.) (Jan. 3, '48-May 25, '50).	Alexander H. Everett[a] (Mass.).	

ZACHARY TAYLOR and MILLARD FILLMORE

John M. Clayton (Del.) (Mar. 7, '49-July 22, '50).

Daniel Webster (Mass.) (July 22, '50-Oct. 24, '52).

China	Japan	Korea
Thomas A. R. Nelson (Tenn.) (Mar. 6, '51; resigned). Joseph Blunt (N. Y.) (Oct. 15, '51; declined). Humphrey Marshall (Ky.) (Aug. 4, '52-Jan. 27, '54).	John H. Aulick[a] (June 10, '51). M. C. Perry[a] (Nov. 5 '52).	

Edward Everett (Mass.) (Nov. 6, '52-Mar. 3, '53).

FRANKLIN PIERCE

William L. Marcy (N. Y.) (Mar. 7, '53-Mar. 6, '57).

China	Japan	Korea
Robert J. Walker (Miss.) (June 22, '53; declined). Robert M. McLane (Md.) (Oct. 18, '53-Dec. 12, '54). Peter Parker[a] (Mass.) (Aug. 16, '55-Aug. 25, '57).	Townsend Harris[a] (N. Y.) Conc. Gen. (Sept. 13, '56-Jan. 19, '59).	

JAMES BUCHANAN

Lewis Cass (Mich.) (Mar. 6, '57-Dec. 12, '60).

China	Japan	Korea
William B. Reed[a][b] (Pa.) (Apr. 18, '57-Dec. 8, '58). John E. Ward (Ga.) (Dec. 5, '58-Dec., '60).	Townsend Harris[d] (N. Y.) (Jan. 19, '59-Apr. 26, '62).	

ABRAHAM LINCOLN and ANDREW JOHNSON

WILLIAM H. SEWARD (N. Y.) (Mar. 6, '61-Mar. 3, '69).

China	Japan	Korea
Anson Burlingame (Mass.) (July 15, '61-Nov. 21, '67).	Robert H. Pruyn (N. Y.) (Jan. 22, '62-Oct. 25, '65).	George F. Seward [a] (N. Y.) (July 27, '68).
J. Ross Browne (Cal.) (Mar. 11, '68-July 5, '69).	Chauncey M. Depew (N. Y.) (Nov. 15, '65; declined).	
	Robert B. Van Valkenburgh (N. Y.) (Jan. 18, '66-Nov. 11, '69).	

ULYSSES S. GRANT

HAMILTON FISH (N. Y.) (Mar. 17, '69-Mar. 12, '77).

China	Japan	Korea
William A. Howard (Mich.) (Apr. 17, '69; declined).	Charles E. DeLong [b] (Nev.) (Apr. 21, '69-Oct. 7, '73).	Frederick F. Low [a] (Cal.) (1870).
Frederick F. Low (Cal.) (Dec. 21, '69-Mar. 28, '74).	John A. Bingham (Ohio) (Dec. 11, '73-July 2, '85).	
Benjamin P. Avery (Cal.) (Apr. 10, '74-Nov. 8, '75).		
George F. Seward (Cal.[?]) (Jan. 7, '76-Aug. 6, '80).		

RUTHERFORD B. HAYES

WILLIAM M. EVARTS (N. Y.) (Mar. 12, '77-Mar. 7, '81).

China	Japan	Korea
James B. Angell [a] (Mich.) (Apr. 9, '80-Oct. 4, '81).		

JAMES A. GARFIELD and CHESTER A. ARTHUR

JAMES G. BLAINE (Me.) (Mar. 7, '81-Dec. 19, '81).

China	Japan	Korea
		R. W. Shufeldt (Cal.) (Nov. 14, '81).

FREDERICK T. FRELINGHUYSEN (N. J.) (Dec. 19, '81-Mar. 6, 85).

John Russell Young (N. Y.) (Mar. 15, '82-Apr. 8, '85).		Lucius H. Foote (Cal.) (Feb. 27, '83-Jan. 19, '85).

GROVER CLEVELAND

THOMAS F. BAYARD (Del.) (Mar. 7, '85-Mar. 6, '89).

China	Japan	Korea
Charles Denby (Ind.) (May 29, '85-July 15, '98).	Richard B. Hubbard (Texas) (Apr. 2, '85-May 15, '89).	William H. Parker [c] (D. C.) (Feb. 19, '86-Oct. 29, '86).
		Hugh A. Dinsmore (Okla.) (Jan. 12, '87).

BENJAMIN HARRISON

JAMES G. BLAINE (Me.) (Mar. 7, '89-June 4, '92).

China	Japan	Korea
Henry W. Blair (N. H.) (Feb. 27, '91; unacceptable to China).	John F. Swift (Cal.) (Mar. 12, '89-Mar. 10, '91).	William O. Bradley (Ky.) (Mar. 30, '89; declined).
	Frank L. Coombs (Apr. 20, '92).	Augustine Heard (Mass.) (Jan. 30, '90-June 27, '93).

JOHN W. FOSTER (Ind.) (June 29, '92-Feb. 23, '93).

GROVER CLEVELAND

WALTER Q. GRESHAM (Ill.) (Mar 6, '93-May 28, '93).

China	*Japan*	*Korea*
	Edwin Dun (Ohio) (Apr. 4, '93-June 30, '97).	John M. B. Sill (Cal.) (Jan. 12, '94-Sept. 13, '97).

RICHARD B. OLNEY (Mass.) (June 10, '95-Mar. 5, '97).

WILLIAM McKINLEY

JOHN SHERMAN (Ohio) (Mar. 6, '97-Apr. 26, '98).

China	*Japan*	*Korea*
Edwin H. Conger (Ill.) (Jan. 19, '98-Mar. 8, 05).	Alfred E. Buck (Ga.) (Apr. 13, '97-Dec. 4, '02).	Horace N. Allen (Ohio) (July 17, '97-Dec. 10, 01).

WILLIAM R. DAY (Ohio) (Apr. 28, '98-Sept. 16, '98).

JOHN HAY (D. C.) (Sept. 30, '98-).

William W. Rockhill f (Pa.) (July 19, '98-Sept. 8, '01).

a Commissioned to make treaty.
b Post raised to Envoy Extraordinary and Minister Plenipotentiary.
c Post reduced to Minister Resident and Consul General.
d Post raised to Minister Resident.
e The dates given below the names of the diplomatic representatives indicate dates of appointment or confirmation, and of retirement or resignation.
f Special agent.

INDEX

Abbot, Com. Joel: 191
Adams, John Quincy: 89; 105; 106; lecture before Mass. Hist. Soc., 107; opium, 120; 672
Advisers, foreign: in China, 587; in Japan, 588
Africa: v; 30
Aguinaldo, Emilio: 617-8
Alaska: telegraph, 409; purchase, 416; 590; 610; 636; payment, 671
Alcock, Sir Rutherford: 201; 217ff.; 226; 228; 317; 386; "naked force," 388; 391-2; 396; policy in Japan, 400; 401; 418
Aleutian Islands: 409; 416; 590
Allen, Dr. H. N.: 478; 483; made minister, 505; 557; 569; 616
Alliance: with Great Britain, vi; 281; 298ff.; Siam, 351; 357; 361; China-Japan, 437-8; 608; overtures in 1898, 640; Beresford tour, 641-2; 664
American Policy, see United States
Amoy: 211; 327; 557
Amur River: 179; 357; 409; 429; 590; 649
Anderson, Gen. T. M.: 618
Angell, James B.: 458; on treaty of 1868, 540; treaty of 1882, 543
Anglo-Chinese War, 1839-42: American rel. to, 91ff.; cause of, 106-7; 179; 181; influence in Japan, 256; 304; 664
Anglo-French War with China: 343; 354; 386; 388; 490; 509
Anglo-Japanese alliance: 640-1; 644
Annam: 428; French relations, 491-2
Annapolis: Jap. students at naval academy, 454
Aoki, Count: address to Diet, 497; 529; missionaries, 566
Arbitration: U. S. proposed to Japan, 400; 443; 490-1; 491; 494; Sino-Jap. War, 498; Boxer Protocol discussions, 659

Archer, Samuel: 10; 18
Armstrong, Com. James: Barrier Forts, 282; Formosa, 286ff.; 300
"Arrow" affair: 282; 311; 402
Arthur, Pres. Chester A.: 464; on treaty revision, 523-4; Chinese immigration, 544
Ashmore Fisheries dispute: 494
Astor, John Jacob: 71; 78; 683
Audience question: 334; 441; 636
Aulick, Com. J. H.: commissioner to Japan, 258; 261

Bacon, Augustus O.: joint resolution, 628-9
Balestier, Joseph: 350
Balfour, Capt. G.: 195
Balluzec: Russian Minister, Peking, 374
Baltimore: 6; 26; 115; *Wabash* of, opium ship, 119-20
Bankok, see Siam
Barrier Forts: Americans attack, 282; 300
Batavia and Batavian Republic, see Java
Bayard, Thomas F.: 546; 608
Beche de mer: 34; 41
Belgium: Hankow-Peking railroad, 601-2
Benton, Senator Thos.: 112
Beresford, Lord Charles: visit to East, 641; proposes alliance, 642; 644
Berthemy, J. F. G.: 375; and Seward, 419
Betsey of N. Y.: 11
Biddle, Com. James: 190; Shanghai, 197; Japan, 249-50; and Kiying, 294
Bingham, John A.: and Shufeldt 456; on treaty revision, 515ff.; 523; retirement, 525; 673
Blaine, James G.: instructions to Shufeldt, 461; 608; Hawaii, 611
Blair, Henry W., rejection of: 548
"Blood Thicker than Water": 338ff.

709

94; opens Five Ports to all nations, 110; opium, 1817, 120-1;
189; 345; Burlingame mission,
386; policy in Korea, 460ff.
Chinese Government: Americans
apply for protection, 83-4; arrogance, 106; and treaty revision,
378-9; policy on telegraphs and
railroads, 592ff.; Woosung Railway Co., 596; turns to Russia,
600
Chinese Repository: 556; 684-5
Chinese students in U. S.: 463; 545;
600
Civil War, American: 392; 409; and
Seward's policy, 414; 416; 579;
588; 590
Claims: 169; 211; Shanghai, 1854,
230; 306; review of Am., 326ff.;
commission, 329-30; Japan, 399;
Bonin Islands, 432; Ashmore
Fisheries, 494; 651; Boxer
claims, 658-9; Ward-Hill, 687;
See also Arbitration, Good Offices,
Mediation, Indemnity
Clarendon, Lord: 230; 238; on
Bonin Islands, 275; Parker
visits, 280-1; 299; 305; 368;
Burlingame and, 386ff.; 510; 567
Clemens, Paul H.: 693
Cleveland, Pres. Grover: 524-5; 530;
Chinese immigration, 546; 547;
withdraws Hawaiian treaty,
551; 612; 640
Clippers: opium, 126-7; introduc-
tion, 179-80
Coal: 183ff.; Japan, 253; 261ff.;
269; Formosa, 276; 284ff.;
Parker to Marcy, 287; Lay-Os-
born flotilla, 587; Kaiping Com-
pany, 598
Coasting trade: China, 161; 321;
510; Japan, 514; Korea, 522;
China and Japan, 585
Cochin China, proposed treaty,
1832, 128; Roberts visit, 1832,
133; 134; 272; France annexes
471; 491-2
Co-hong, *see* Hong-merchants
Columbia, voyage of: 9; 16; 38; 683
Columbia River: 39
Commissioner, U. S.: proposed by
Tyler, 111; not merchant, 136;
See also Diplomatic service and
appendix
Commission firms: 17; 52; 60;
growth of Am. firms, 71

Communications: 176; 206; shortened, 409
See also Telegraphs, Steam Navigation, Railroads
Concessions (foreign settlements):
China, 168; 194ff.; Shanghai,
196; Burlingame doctrine, 373;
382; 589; in Japan and Korea,
590;
—(commercial): in China, 588-
90; 597-601; Korea, 504
Conger, Edwin H.: 555; 665; retires
on leave, 666
Congress: petitioned for consular
system at Canton, 76; discusses
Anglo-Chinese War, 102; 303-4;
Korea, 475; 481; Chinese immigration, 544ff.; Act of May 6,
1882, 544; Act of Sept. 13, 1888,
547; Scott Act, 547; Geary Act,
548; annexation of Hawaii, 552;
Pacific Mail subsidy, 585; trans-
Pacific Telegraph, 590; Hawaiian annexation, 614; debates
on Hawaii and Philippines, 624ff.
Congress, cruise of: 79
Connecticut: 6
Consequa: 58; petition to Pres.
Madison, 86
Consular service: 63; 75; 170;
Tyler on, 186ff.; McLane re-
port, 187; 230; courts, 319-20;
Chinese immigration, 544;
scandals, 597; general survey of,
669ff.; Keim report, 670; Pierce
report, 671; Act of May 16,
1848, 671
Cook, Capt.: 4
Coolie trade: 189; 320; *Maria Luz,*
490; 536ff.
See also Immigration
Coombs, Frank L.: 549-50
Cooperative policy: vi; at Canton,
1839, 96; rejected, 97; Canton
merchants propose, 99; Caleb
Cushing on, 104; Boston and
Salem merchants, 136; 159; 182;
211; 213; British desire, 223;
McLane instructions, 225; Bowring, 233; Shanghai, 1854, 334;
McLane's proposal for joint
blockade, 240; Parker-Claren-
don interview, 280-1; for Canton, 289; Marcy, 290; Alex. H.
Everett, 296; Buchanan-Cass,
303ff.; Reed, 312ff.; Ward,
338ff.; Burlingame and, 372ff.;

Evarts, William M.: instructions to Shufeldt, 455-6; treaty of 1878, Japan, 518-9
Ever-Victorious Army: 369-71; 642; *See also* F. T. Ward, Burgevine, Gordon
Everett, Alex. H., Com. to China, 186; sketch, 190; Japan, 249; 295
Everett, Edward: 112; 264; on Perry proposals, 273; 672
Exchange, problem of: 18ff.; bills on London, 72; basis in Japan, 355;
See also Specie
Experiment: 11
Extraterritoriality: Cushing, **vi**; Americans acknowledge Chinese jurisdiction, 84; Terranova incident, 87ff.; Canton merchants, 100; Siam, 133; Muscat, 134; Hsü A-man affair, 153; Treaty of Wanghia, 162ff.; 186; omitted, Perry treaty, 269; 319; Marcy on, Siam and Japan, 350; Siam, 351; 353; Russia-Japan, 354; 384; in Korea, 447; Korea, 470; 510; Japan, 513; 514ff.; 526; Japan treaties, 1894, 529; missionaries and, 561; and coasting trade, 583; and consuls, 669ff.; consular courts, 671;
See also Treaty revision, Treaties and Conventions

Factories, *see* Hongs
Faulkland Islands: 37
Fillmore, Pres. Millard: message, 190-1; to Emperor, Japan, 261; 263; 292-3
Fish, Hamilton: on China-Jap. alliance, 438; on mediation, 489; cooperation, 508-9; treaty revision, 517-8; missionaries, 567; on telegraph monopoly, 592-3; 608; 610
Foochow: 187, 211; McLane, 233; Parker, 281; 328
Foord, John: to Hay, 661
Foote, Com. Lucius H.: appointed to Seoul, 472; resigns, 475
Forbes, J. M.: to Webster, 135-6; 579
Forbes, Paul S.: notifies Kiying, 147
Formosa: U. S. flag over, vii; coal, 183; Perry's opinion, 272; Perry orders investigation, 276; Parker's policy of acquisition, 284ff.;

320; Townsend Harris, 349; 357; U. S. punitive exp., 411; 427; Japanese expedition, 440; 490; Sino-Jap. War, 501ff.; 591; railways, 599; 612; 638
Foster, John W.: 501; 635; books, 690
Foulk, George C. in Korea: 478; recalled from Korea, 484; papers, 688
France: expedition Korea, vi; at old Canton, 54; plenipo. at Macao, 152; 178; Shanghai, 198; Parker visits, 281; Korea, 282; 290; 296; 300; 301; 359-60; Korea, 417ff.; in E. Asia, 428; 451; Tientsin massacre, 454; 460; annexes Cochin China, 471; urges Japan to declare w. on China, 479-80; expansion, 491-2; recession of Liaotung Peninsula, 503; Tani on, 527; withdraws from intern'l settlement, Shanghai, 590; Syndicate of Tientsin, 598; Hankow-Peking railroad, 601; sphere of influence, 603-4; Sandwich Is., 612; *entente* with Ger. and Russia, 635; Franco-American relations, 637;
See also Franco-Chinese War, Anglo-French War, Treaties and Conventions
Franco-Chinese War: 478; and China-Japan treaty, 480; American good offices, 391ff.; 502; 586; 597; 637
Freight rates: 10; Hongkong-Canton, 1840, 98; 180; Chinese subsidy, 586
Frelinghuysen, F. T.: 464; instructions to Foote, 474; Franco-Chinese War, 492-4; 608; 637
French, *see* France
Fukien, Province: Japanese sphere, 604
Fur trade: price furs, 5; voyage of *Betsey,* 11; 20; 36; seal-skins, 36ff.; and opium, 118; and Japan, 242; value of: 12; 40ff.;
See also Northwest Coast, Ingraham, Columbia, Nootka Sound
Fusan: Shufeldt at, 456; Jap. settlement, 467; Japanese telegraph, 484

607-9; annexation, 609ff.; revolution, 611-2; Newlands joint resolution, 614; debates on, 624ff.; Hoar on, 626; 679

Hay, John: V; 420; 608; 622; enters cabinet, 634; Salisbury proposes alliance, 642; contribution of, 645; Hay-Pauncefote treaty, 645; open door notes, 646-7; Circular note of July 3, 1899, 656-7; Protocol negotiations, 657ff.

Hayes, Pres. Rutherford B.: Chinese immigration, 542

Heard, Augustine: 72
— —: in Korea, 485

Hepburn, Dr. J. C.: 565

Heusken, C. J.: 354; murder of, 396; Seward on, 412-3

Hienfeng, Emperor: d. 1861, 344

Higginson, James B.: U. S. consul, Calcutta, 1843, 29

Hinkley, F. E.: 693

Hiogo: 362

Hoar, George F.: on Hawaiian annex., 552; 626; Philippines, 630-1

Holcombe, Chester: assists in Korean treaty negotiations, 459; 464; 556-7

Holland: 4; 345;
See also Dutch, Treaties and Conventions

Hong-Kew: Am. settlement, 590

Hongkong: occupation predicted, 55; British occupy, 98; British expansion, 128; Am. ship-yard moved, 154; bonded warehouse, 161; 165; 181; 210; coolie trade, 536; Am. trade with, table, 581; telegraph, 591; 608; Dewey, 617

Hong-merchants: 49; 59; co-hong, opium, 117; to Wilcocks on opium, 120-1; 559

Honolulu, see Hawaiian Islands

Hope, Admiral Sir James: 336; Tattnall assists, 340; and Gen. F. T. Ward, 369-70; Tsushima, 431

Hope: 11

Hoppo: 59

Hotta, Lord: to Mikado, 394; 426-7; 528; 641

Houqua: 57; honesty, 59; sued in Phila., 85; opium, 118

House of Representatives, appropriation, China mission, 112; Burlingame in, 367
See Congress

Hubbard, Richard B.: 528; 673

Hughes, Charles E.: vi

Hung-Sin-tshuen: see Taiping Rebellion

Hunt's "Lives of Am. Merchants": 683

Ignatieff, Nicholas: 337

Immigration, Asiatic: 378; 380; Seward, 410; 454; Shufeldt-Sargent letter, 462; general survey of Am. policy, 535ff.; character of Chinese immigrants, 537-8; Treaty of 1868, 539-41; Fifteen Passengers Bill, 542; Treaty of 1882, 542-3; Act of May 6, 1882, 544; and Korean policy, 545; Scott Act, 547; Geary Act, 548; Japanese, 549ff.; Hawaiian Islands, 550-2; 585; 611; 677; Hawaiian Islands, 550-2; Gentlemen's agreement, 550; 585; 611; 677

In-chuin, see Chemulpo

Indemnity: 376; 381; Shimoneséki, 401; Korea to Japan, 469; anti-Chinese riots in U. S., 546; Boxer, 660-2;
See also Claims

India Trade: opening of, 26; special privileges, 27; extent, 28; appointment U. S. consul, 28; India-Canton trade, 29; opium, 116ff.

Ingraham, Capt. Joseph: 11; 684

Inouye: 456; and J. R. Young, 469; 479; 525

Inspectorate of Maritime Customs: 58; inauguration, 225ff.; 324; 370; efforts to make cosmopolitan, 374; British head, 604

Interpreters: at Canton, 63; Roberts mission, 133; Cushing mission, 136; 142; 161; Ningpo, 187; 230; Seoul, 474; missionaries, 555

Intervention: effect in China, 61; Marshall, 232-3

Isle de France: see Mauritius

Italy: 345; 519

Ito, Count: treaty with China, 479-80; treaty of Shimoneséki, 502ff.; 513

Irving, Washington: 40

Iturup, Island of: 354

Iwakura Embassy: 439; returns to Japan, 441-2; 559; 567